1993 United Nations List of National Parks and Protected Areas

Liste des Nations Unies des Parcs nationaux et des Aires protégées 1993

Lista de las Naciones Unidas de Parques Nacionales y Areas Protegidas 1993

IUCN – The World Conservation Union

Founded in 1948, IUCN – The World Conservation Union brings together States, government agencies and a diverse range of non-governmental organiaztions in a unique world partnership: more than 800 members in all, spread across 126 countries. The Union seeks to work with its members to achieve development that is sustainable and that provides a lasting improvement in the quality of life for people all over the world.

UICN – Union mondiale pour la nature

Fondée en 1948, l'UICN – Union mondiale pour la nature réunit des Etats, des organismes publics et un large éventail d'organisations non gouvernementales en une association mondiale unique: en tout, plus de 800 membres dans 126 pays. L'Union cherche à oeuvrer, en collaboration avec ses membres, à l'avènement d'un développement qui soit durable et améliore de manière permanente la qualité de vie de l'humanité tout entière.

UICN – Unión Mundial para la Naturaleza

Fundada en 1948, la UICN – Unión Mundial para la Naturaleza agrupa a Estados, organismos gubernamentales y una diversa gama de organizaciones no gubernamentales en una asociación mundial única en su género; cuenta en total con unos 800 miembros procedentes de 126 países. La Unión procura trabajar con sus miembros en la consecución de un tipo de desarrollo que sea sostenible, y contribuya a mejorar de forma duradera la calidad de vida de los pueblos de todo el mundo.

1993 United Nations List of National Parks and Protected Areas

Liste des Nations Unies des Parcs nationaux et des Aires protégées 1993

Lista de las Naciones Unidas de Parques Nacionales y Areas Protegidas 1993

**Prepared by the
World Conservation Monitoring Centre and the
IUCN Commission on National Parks and Protected Areas**

**Préparée par
le Centre mondial de surveillance continue de la conservation
de la nature et la Commission des parcs nationaux
et des aires protégées de l'UICN**

**Preparada por
el Centro Mundial de Monitoreo de la Conservación
y la Comisión de Parques Nacionales
y Areas Protegidas de la UICN**

**With the support of the
United Nations Environment Programme**

**Avec l'appui du
Programme des Nations Unies pour l'environnement**

**Con el apoyo del
Programa de las Naciones Unidas para el Medio Ambiente**

**IUCN/UICN
1994**

World Conservation Monitoring Centre

The World Conservation Monitoring Centre (WCMC) is a joint venture between the three partners who developed the *World Conservation Strategy* and its successor, *Caring for the Earth*: IUCN – The World Conservation Union, UNEP – United Nations Environment Programme, and WWF – World Wide Fund For Nature (formerly World Wildlife Fund). Its mission is to support conservation and sustainable development through the provision of information on the world's biological diversity.

WCMC has developed a global overview database that includes threatened plant and animal species, habitats of conservation concern, critical sites, protected areas of the world, and the utilisation and trade in wildlife species and products. Drawing on this database, WCMC provides an information service to the conservation and development communities, governments and the United Nations agencies, scientific institutions, the business and commercial sector, and the media. WCMC produces a wide variety of specialist outputs and reports based on analyses of its data. It is also actively involved in building the capabilities of other institutions, particularly in developing countries, for promoting and planning their own biological resources.

Le WCMC - Centre mondial de surveillance continue de la conservation de la nature

Le Centre mondial de surveillance continue de la conservation de la nature (WCMC) est une entreprise commune des trois partenaires de la *Stratégie mondiale de la conservation*: l'Union mondiale pour la nature (UICN), le Fonds mondial pour la nature (WWF), et le Programme des Nations Unies pour l'environnement (PNUE). Ce centre a pour mission d'appuyer la conservation et le développement durable en recueillant et en analysant les données mondiales sur la conservation, afin que les décisions concernant les ressources biologiques reposent sur les meilleures informations possibles.

Le WCMC a établi une banque de données sur la diversité biologique mondiale, qui comprend des données sur les espèces animales et végétales menacées, les biotopes préoccupants du point de vue de la conservation, les sites critiques, les aires protégées, ainsi que l'utilisation et le commerce des espèces et produits de la faune et de la flore sauvages. S'appuyant sur cette banque de données, le WCMC fournit un service d'information aux communautés de la conservation et du développement, aux gouvernements, aux institutions des Nations Unies, aux instituts scientifiques, au monde du commerce et des affaires, et aux médias. Le WCMC publie de très nombreux rapports et documents spécialisés, fondés sur l'analyse de ses données.

Centro Mundial de Monitoreo de la Conservación

El Centro Mundial de Monitoreo de la Conservación (WCMC) es una empresa conjunta entre los tres asociados que elaboraron la *Estrategia Mundial para la Conservación* y su sucesor, *Cuidar la Tierra*: la UICN – Unión Mundial para la Naturaleza –, el PNUMA – Programa de las Naciones Unidas para el Medio Ambiente –, y el WWF – Fondo Mundial para la Naturaleza (anteriormente Fondo Mundial para la Vida Silvestre). Su misión es promover la conservación y el desarrollo sustentable a través del suministro de información sobre la diversidad biológica del mundo.

El WCMC ha creado una base de datos mundial sobre especies amenazadas de animales y plantas, habitat de interés para la conservación, sitios de importancia crítica, áreas protegidas del mundo, y sobre la utilización y comercio de especies silvestres y productos derivados. Aprovechando los recursos de esta base de datos, el WCMC proporciona servicios de información a las comunidades dedicadas a la conservación y al desarrollo, los gobiernos y organismos pertenecientes a las Naciones Unidas, a las instituciones científicas, a los sectores empresarial y comercial, y a los medios de comunicación. El WCMC hace una amplia gama de contribuciones y publica informes especializados, basados en el análisis de sus datos. También participa activamente reforzando de las capacidades de otras instituciones, particularmente en los países en vía de desarrollo, con miras a la promoción y planificación de sus propios recursos biológicos.

Contents

Table des matières

Indice

1993 United Nations List of National Parks and Protected Areas

Published by:	IUCN, Gland, Switzerland and Cambridge, UK
	Prepared and published with the support of the United Nations Environment Programme and UNESCO
	A contribution to GEMS – The Global Environment Monitoring System

Copyright:	(1994) International Union for Conservation of Nature and Natural Resources
	Reproduction of this publication for educational or other non-commercial purposes is authorised without prior permission from the copyright holder.
	Reproduction for resale or other commercial purposes is prohibited without the prior written permission of the copyright holder.
Citation:	IUCN (1994). *1993 United Nations List of National Parks and Protected Areas.* Prepared by WCMC and CNPPA. IUCN, Gland, Switzerland and Cambridge, UK. xlvi + 315pp.
ISBN:	2-8317-0190-2
Printed by:	Page Brothers (Norwich) Ltd, UK
Cover design by:	IUCN Publications Services Unit
Cover photographs:	*Kilaguni Lodge, Tsavo, Kenya*: D. and I. Gordon; *Península de Paria National Park, Venezuela*: C. J. Sharpe; *Brandywine Creek State Park, USA*: Harriet Gillett; *Migrating storks, Ras Mohammed National Park, Egypt*: Mark Spalding.
Produced by:	IUCN Publications Services Unit on desktop publishing equipment purchased through a gift from Mrs Julia Ward.
Available from:	IUCN Publications Services Unit 219c Huntingdon Road, Cambridge, CB3 0DL, UK or IUCN Communications and Corporate Relations Division Rue Mauverney 28, CH-1996 Gland, Switzerland.

The designations of geographical entities in this book, and the presentation of the material, do not imply the expression of any opinion whatsoever on the part of IUCN, UNEP, UNESCO or WCMC concerning the legal status of any country, territory, or area, or of its authorities, or concerning the delimitation of its frontiers and boundaries.

The text of this book is printed on Fineblade Cartridge 90 gsm low-chlorine paper

Contents

Introduction

Protected areas make a vital contribution to the conservation of the world's natural and cultural resources. Values range from retention of representative samples of natural regions and the preservation of biological diversity, to the maintenance of environmental stability of surrounding regions. Protected areas can provide an opportunity for rural development and rational use of marginal lands, for research and monitoring, for conservation education, and for recreation and tourism. As a result, most countries have developed systems of protected areas.

However, protected area systems vary considerably from one country to another, depending on needs and priorities, and on differences in legislative, institutional and financial support. Also, the range of services and values that protected areas provide is such that some management objectives are not compatible with others. This has lead to the emergence of a wide range of protected area designations and definitions.

The aim of the *UN List* is to provide a definitive list of protected areas meeting certain criteria, which are specified below.

History of the UN List

The *United Nations List of National Parks and Equivalent Reserves* was drawn up at the request of the United Nations following a resolution adopted by the General Assembly at its Sixteenth Session in December 1962 on "Economic Development and Nature Conservation". This resolution served to endorse an earlier resolution (No. 713) of the 27th Session of the UN Economic and Social Council held in 1959, which recognized National Parks and Equivalent Reserves as an important factor in the wise use of natural resources, and led to the compilation of the first *World List of National Parks and Equivalent Reserves.*

IUCN was instrumental in the preparation of the two resolutions, and has since had primary responsibility for the compilation and maintenance of the list. The *UN List* is now prepared jointly by the IUCN Commission on National Parks and Protected Areas, and by the World Conservation Monitoring Centre. The previous edition of the *UN List* was published in 1990. Earlier editions appeared in 1961/2, 1966 (English version 1971), 1972 (addendum to the 1966/71 list), 1973, 1974, 1975, 1980, 1982 and 1985. The present title was adopted in 1982.

The IUCN Commission on National Parks and Protected Areas

IUCN's Commission on National Parks and Protected Areas (CNPPA) is the leading international scientific and technical body concerned with the selection, establishment and management of national parks and other protected areas. Its membership includes more than 500 protected areas professionals from about 120 countries. CNPPA is served by IUCN's Protected Areas Programme in order to promote the establishment of a world-wide network of effectively managed terrestrial and marine protected areas.

During preparation of this edition of the *UN List*, CNPPA has been under the chair of P.H.C (Bing) Lucas of New Zealand with Adrian Phillips of the United Kingdom as Deputy Chair. Organization of the Commission is regional, with 14 regional Vice-Chairs and two thematic Vice-Chairs (marine and mountain protected areas). There are normally two to three regional working sessions a year. Since the last *UN List* was compiled, there have been meetings in Australia, China, Sweden, Dominican Republic, Italy (for the North Africa/Middle East region), and the IV World Congress on National Parks and Protected Areas held in Venezuela also brought together over 1,800 people from all over the world.

The WCMC Protected Areas Data Unit

The Protected Areas Data Unit was established by CNPPA in 1981 to handle the increasing amount of information, and to assist the Commission in preparing publications on protected areas around the world. The unit is now a part of the World Conservation Monitoring Centre, and is based in Cambridge in the United Kingdom. One objective of WCMC's work on protected areas is to be able to provide accurate up-to-date information on individual protected areas and protected area systems of the world to those who need it, or, failing that, to identify where such information can be quickly obtained.

In order to meet this objective, WCMC collaborates with the many agencies around the world that manage protected areas, and with conservationists and scientists who work in this field. Many of the individuals involved are members of CNPPA. WCMC also has a particular responsibility for managing information on Biosphere Reserves and World Heritage Sites (accorded by the MAB Secretariat and the World Heritage Committee respectively), and collaborates with the Ramsar Convention Bureau on sites listed under the Ramsar (Wetlands) Convention.

Criteria for inclusion

There are three criteria which govern whether or not a protected area is included in the *UN List*: size, management objectives, and the authority of the management agency.

1. *Size.* Only protected areas of over 1,000 hectares are included, with the exception of offshore or oceanic islands of at least 100 hectares where the whole island is protected. One thousand hectares is equivalent to 10 square kilometres, 2,471 acres or 3.86 square miles.

2. *Management objectives.* A series of protected area management categories, defined by management objective, are identified by IUCN/CNPPA. These have been revised since the previous *UN List* was published, and definitions of each category are provided below.

   Nationally designated sites are allocated to the relevant IUCN Categories, on the basis of their legally defined management objectives, and implementation of those objectives. Where the available information suggests that management of the site is insufficient to implement nationally legislated objectives, the site may either be omitted from the list, or, where relevant, included under another category. Reasons for this might include inappropriate use, inadequate resources, severe encroachment or civil strife, and are often beyond the control of the management authority. It is anticipated that such omission or reclassification would be temporary, pending improvement in the information available, or in the actual on-site situation.

   The 1993 edition of the *UN List* includes sites in IUCN Management Categories I through V. It is intended that Category VI sites will be included in the next edition. Protected areas which are also designated Ramsar Sites, World Heritage Sites or Biosphere Reserves, are included both in the national lists and in the lists of areas of international significance.

3. *Authority of the management agency.* In the past, only those sites managed by the "highest competent authority" were included within the *UN List*, i.e those with the highest appropriate level of government. In this edition of the list, those sites managed by state authorities within the federal systems have also been included.

   The 1993 *UN List* is the fourth to be prepared jointly by WCMC and CNPPA, and, as with the previous three lists (published in 1982, 1985 and 1990), there has been a considerable expansion in the list—despite the fact that the criteria for inclusion have remained largely unchanged. While there have been some significant extensions to protected areas networks, much of the expansion of the list is due to improvements in available information, and improvements in our ability to collect and manage it. It is important to bear this in mind when using the list.

Layout of the UN List

Sites which meet the above-mentioned criteria are listed country by country (in alphabetic order of the English-language version of the country name). Within each country, sites are presented in alphabetic order by national designation (for example national parks, nature reserves, wildlife sanctuaries). Three items of information are provided about each site: its IUCN management category, its size (in hectares), and the year it was established (or significantly altered in either size or designation). For the first time, the list also includes a central latitude/longitude for each site. Further information on each of these sites is held by the World Conservation Monitoring Centre.

For practical reasons, the *1993 UN List* has been ordered according to an alphabetical listing of countries in English. French and Spanish speaking readers should consult the glossaries on pages xxvii to xlvi. These provide a translation of country names from French to English and from Spanish to English, respectively. To assist readers locate specific sections of the *UN List*, an English running head is provided. Similarly, the summary data presented at the start of each country section are entitled and annotated in English only. The equivalent terms are 'Sommaire' and 'Catégorie' in French, and 'Resumen' and 'Categoría' in Spanish.

Compilation of the UN List

WCMC and CNPPA have been collecting and managing information on protected areas for a number of years, and a large body of information is available, some of which has been published. New information is also constantly being received. In preparing the 1993 *UN List*, staff at WCMC reviewed existing material, and revised and updated lists of protected areas (which included the appropriate IUCN Management Category for each site). Draft lists for each country were sent to national management agencies, with a request that they be checked, updated, and returned. Based on the information received, WCMC staff revised this draft, following up queries with contacts in the countries concerned, or members of the CNPPA.

Copies of the revised lists were then sent to the CNPPA Regional Vice-Chairs for review, as well as to the IUCN Secretariat. The responses of national management authorities varied considerably. In total, some 455 requests were made. In the case of federal nations, for example the United States, requests were sent to individual state authorities and in instances where more than one agency is responsible for protected areas, multiple requests were sent to the same country. By October 1993, 226 responses had been received, 49% of the total. The rate of response was best in Australia with an 88% response and poorest in Francophone Africa, with only 18% response. In the event that no information was received from official sources, data were taken, where possible, from published material and other sources.

As detailed above, information for the new *UN List* was gathered from management agencies during the course of 1993. Part of this exercise included providing summary text to each agency, briefly describing the then current IUCN Management Category System, with a request that the appropriate category be applied to each site (a summary of this category system is provided at the end of this introduction). The information presented in the *1993 UN List* has been classified according to this category system which was in place at the time of data collection.

In mid-1993, a new protected areas management category system was approved by the IUCN Council, on the advice of CNPPA following review at the 1992 Forth World Congress on National Parks and Protected Areas at Caracas. This new system is introduced through the publication of the *Guidelines for Protected Area Management Categories*. The categories used in this new system are also summarised in the Annex. Subsequent editions of the *UN List* will be classified according to this new system.

Accuracy and quality of information

The global system of protected areas is changing rapidly, new areas are created, boundaries of existing areas are revised and some sites are destroyed through industrial development, shifting agriculture, natural disasters or civil strife. To state emphatically that there has been any net gain for conservation in the amount of land and water protected in the last few years is very difficult. It is not simply a question of hectares protected or of the number of areas protected, but is more a question of management effectiveness. Are the protected areas achieving the objectives for which they were established?

The quality of the information used to compile the *UN List* is very variable, and information on management effectiveness is still lacking for a number of countries. While the vast majority of the national parks which meet the relevant criteria are listed, information on the other categories of protected area is still incomplete, and much more information is necessary before we can be confident we are providing complete lists of areas in every management category. Three important sectors, forestry, private and indigenous, have not been included in the *UN List*, either because their areas do not meet the criteria or because available information is incomplete. Nevertheless, the contribution of these three sectors to conservation and sustainable development is considerable.

Managed areas in the forestry sector cover over 10% of the tropics, according to data collected by WCMC. Throughout the tropics, forestry policy is undergoing substantial change, with increased emphasis being placed on a balanced approach to sustainable production and conservation. However, there is still much to be achieved, and a need exists in many countries to properly assess the conservation value of the forest estate. Following initial review of forest reserves in tropical forest countries, carried out with the support of the UK Overseas Development Administration, WCMC is seeking to continue systematically reviewing the forest reserve systems of all countries to help assess their contribution to nature conservation objectives.

There is some debate on ethical as well as practical grounds as to what extent indigenous areas can be regarded as conservation areas. The importance of these areas for nature conservation cannot be denied, as indigenous areas collectively cover an area the size of Australia, and those correlate strongly with areas of biological richness. For example, Colombia has ceded over 25% of its territory to indigenous peoples, most of this in biologically diverse tropical forest regions. As conservationists are increasingly required to enter into dialogue with indigenous peoples over the joint conservation of cultural and biological diversity, information on indigenous areas will become more important.

Unlike the areas which fall within the other two sectors, private protected areas are not usually significant in terms of the area they cover, but they are important because of the quality of management and degree of protection afforded to them. Private areas include those areas administered by foundations and private enterprise, as well as those established and run by communities themselves. Excellent examples of private initiatives which support and complement state systems abound: The Royal Society for the Protection of Birds in the UK, The Nature Conservancy in North America, the Fundacion Moisés Bertoni in Paraguay and the Royal Society for the Conservation of Nature in Jordan. Private protected areas may increase in importance, particularly in tropical countries, where state resources are very limited.

The 1993 *UN List* undoubtedly includes mistakes and omissions, but it is hoped that these will stimulate ever more accurate information. The responsibility for errors and oversights rests with the compilers, and corrections or updates should be communicated to the:

Protected Areas Data Unit
World Conservation Monitoring Centre
219 Huntingdon Road
Cambridge CB3 0DL
United Kingdom

Telephone: (0223) 277314
Fax: (0223) 277136
e-mail: jerry.harrison@wcmc.org.uk

Acknowledgements

Compilation of the list has been carried out by many WCMC staff, including Graham Drucker, Victoria Freeman, Harriet Gillett, Donald Gordon, Michael Green, Jeremy Harrison (Head of Unit), James Paine (project coordination), Chris Sharpe, Mark Spalding and Alison Suter. Susan Hawley, Tony Rogers, Caroline Brown and Corinna Ravilious have provided tremendous support in the last stages of data entry.

Compilation has been actively supported by CNPPA, and in particular by the officers of the Commission, and Dr James Thorsell, Jeff McNeely, David Sheppard and Caroline Martinet, of the IUCN Secretariat.

The list was prepared for publication by Elaine Shaughnessy and Anne Rodford of the IUCN Publication Services Unit.

Additional financial support was provided by the United Nations Environment Programme.

Finally, many individuals in protected areas management agencies and elsewhere in each country have provided information which has been used in compiling this list. Without this input, the list could not have been completed.

1978 Protected Areas Management Categories

I. *Strict Nature Reserve/Scientific Reserve.* To protect nature and maintain natural processes in an undisturbed state in order to have ecologically representative examples of the natural environment available for scientific study, environmental monitoring, education, and for the maintenance of genetic resources in a dynamic and evolutionary state.

II. *National Park.* To protect outstanding natural and scenic areas of national or international significance for scientific, educational, and recreational use. These are relatively large natural areas not materially altered by human activity where extractive resource uses are not allowed.

III. *Natural Monument/Natural Landmark.* To protect and preserve nationally significant natural features because of their special interest or unique characteristics. These are relatively small areas focused on protection of specific features.

IV. *Managed Nature Reserve/Wildlife Sanctuary.* To assure the natural conditions necessary to protect nationally significant species, groups of species, biotic communities, or physical features of the environment where these may require specific human manipulation for their perpetuation. Controlled harvesting of some resources can be permitted.

V. *Protected Landscapes and Seascapes.* To maintain nationally significant natural landscapes which are characteristic of the harmonious interaction of man and land while providing opportunities for public enjoyment through recreation and tourism within the normal life style and economic activity of these areas. These are mixed cultural/natural landscapes of high scenic value where traditional land uses are maintained.

Liste des Nations Unies des Parcs nationaux et des Aires protégées 1993

Publiée par:	UICN, Gland, Suisse et Cambridge, Royaume-Uni.

Préparée et publiée avec la contribution du PNUE et de l'UNESCO.

Préparée dans le cadre du GEMS - Système mondial de surveillance continue de l'environnement.

Citation: UICN (1994). *Liste des Nations Unies des Parcs nationaux et des Aires protégées 1993*. Préparée par le WCMC et la CPNAP. UICN, Gland, Suisse et Cambridge, Royaume-Uni. xlvi + 315pp.

ISBN: 2-8317-0190-2

Imprimée par: Page Brothers (Norwich) Ltd, Royaume-Uni.

Couverture conçue: Service des publications de l'UICN

Photos couverture: *Kilaguni Lodge, Tsavo, Kenya*: D. et I. Gordon; *Parc national de la Péninsule de Paria, Venezuela*: C. J. Sharpe; *Parc d'Etat de Brandywine Creek, Etats-Unis d'Amérique*: Harriet Gillet; *cigognes migratrices, Parc national de Ras Mohammed, Egypte*: Mark Spalding.

Mise en page: Service des publications de l'UICN, Cambridge, Royaume-Uni. Publication de l'UICN assistée par ordinateur et rendue possible grâce à un don de Madame Julia Ward.

Disponible auprès: du Service des publications de l'UICN
219c Huntingdon Road, Cambridge, CB3 0DL, Royaume-Uni ou
de la Division de la Communication et des Relations publiques
Rue Mauverney 28, CH-1196 Gland, Suisse

La terminologie géographique employée dans cet ouvrage, de même que sa présentation, ne sont en aucune manière l'expression d'une opinion quelconque de la part de l'UICN, du PNUE, de l'UNESCO ou du WCMC en ce qui concerne le statut juridique ou l'autorité de quelque Etat, territoire ou région que ce soit ou en ce qui concerne la délimitation de leurs frontières.

Cet ouvrage est imprimé sur papier Fineblade Cartridge faiblement chloré (90 g/m^2)

Table des matières

Introduction

Les aires protégées apportent une contribution vitale à la conservation des ressources naturelles et culturelles de la planète. Elles ont aussi bien pour fonction de préserver des échantillons représentatifs de régions naturelles et la diversité biologique que de maintenir la stabilité écologique des régions qui les entourent. Elles sont un moteur pour le développement rural et l'utilisation rationnelle des terres marginales, la recherche et la surveillance continue, l'éducation à la conservation, les loisirs et le tourisme. Pour toutes ces raisons, la plupart des pays se sont dotés d'un réseau d'aires protégées.

Toutefois, les réseaux d'aires protégées varient énormément d'un pays à l'autre, selon les besoins et les priorités, selon les différences entre les moyens législatifs, institutionnels et financiers disponibles. En outre, la gamme des services et valeurs des aires protégées est telle que certains objectifs de gestion sont incompatibles avec d'autres. Une multitude de termes et définitions sont donc appliqués aux aires protégées.

La *Liste des Nations Unies* a pour objectif de donner une liste définitive d'aires protégées répondant à certains critères qui sont spécifiés ci-après.

Histoire de la Liste des Nations Unies

La *Liste des Nations Unies des parcs nationaux et réserves analogues* a été établie selon le voeu des Nations Unies et dans l'esprit d'une résolution sur le "développement économique et la conservation de la nature", adoptée par l'Assemblée générale à sa 16e Session, en décembre 1962. Cette résolution entérinait une résolution précédente (No 713) de la 27e Session du Conseil économique et social, tenue en 1959. Cette dernière résolution reconnaissait que les parcs nationaux et réserves analogues sont un instrument important de l'utilisation rationnelle des ressources naturelles et a débouché sur l'établissement de la première *Liste mondiale des parcs nationaux et réserves analogues.*

L'UICN a joué un rôle central dans la préparation des deux résolutions et, depuis lors, est responsable de la compilation et de la mise à jour de la Liste. La *Liste des Nations Unies* est aujourd'hui compilée par la Commission des parcs nationaux et des aires protégées de l'UICN et le Centre mondial de surveillance continue de la conservation de la nature (WCMC). La version précédente de la *Liste des Nations Unies* a été publiée en 1990. De plus anciennes versions datent de 1961/1962, 1966 (version anglaise 1971), 1972 (ajout à la Liste de 1966/1971), 1973, 1974, 1975, 1980, 1982 et 1985. Le titre actuel a été adopté en 1982.

La Commission des parcs nationaux et des aires protégées de l'UICN

La Commission des parcs nationaux et des aires protégées de l'UICN (CPNAP) est le principal organe international, scientifique et technique s'intéressant au choix, à la création et à l'aménagement des parcs nationaux et des aires protégées en général. Elle compte parmi ses membres plus de 500 spécialistes des parcs nationaux et autres aires protégées, de quelque 120 pays. La CPNAP est appuyée par le Programme pour les aires protégées de l'UICN et s'attache à encourager la mise en place et la gestion efficace d'un réseau mondial d'aires protégées terrestres et marines.

Durant la préparation de la présente édition de la *Liste des Nations Unies,* la CPNAP était placée sous la présidence de P.H.C. (Bing) Lucas, de la Nouvelle-Zélande, et sous la vice-présidence d'Adrian Phillips, du Royaume-Uni. La Commission est organisée sur une base régionale. Elle compte 14 vice-présidents régionaux et 2 vice-présidents thématiques (aires protégées marines et montagnardes). Elle tient normalement deux ou trois réunions de travail par an. Depuis la compilation de la dernière *Liste des Nations Unies*, des réunions ont eu lieu en Australie, en Chine, en Suède, en République dominicaine, en Italie (pour la région Afrique du Nord/Moyen-Orient), et le IVe Congrès mondial des parcs nationaux et des aires protégées, tenu au Venezuela, a également rassemblé plus de 1800 personnes du monde entier.

L'Unité de données sur les aires protégées du WCMC

L'Unité de données sur les aires protégées a été créée par la CPNAP en 1981, chargée de traiter la quantité croissante de données et d'aider la Commission à préparer des publications sur les aires protégées du monde entier. L'Unité est maintenant intégrée au Centre mondial de surveillance continue de la conservation de la nature et basée à Cambridge, au Royaume-Uni. Les travaux du WCMC concernant les aires protégées visent à fournir des informations précises et à jour sur chaque aire protégée, chaque réseau d'aires protégées, à ceux qui en ont besoin ou, à défaut, de trouver où obtenir rapidement cette information.

Afin d'atteindre cet objectif, le WCMC collabore avec les nombreux organismes qui, dans le monde entier, sont chargés de gérer les aires protégées ainsi qu'avec des spécialistes de la conservation et des scientifiques actifs dans ce domaine. La plupart des personnes concernées sont membres de la CPNAP. Le WCMC est également chargé de gérer l'information sur les réserves de la biosphère et les biens du patrimoine mondial (responsabilités qui lui sont confiées respectivement par le Secrétariat du MAB et le Comité du patrimoine mondial) ainsi que, en collaboration avec le Bureau de la Convention de Ramsar, sur les sites de la Liste de ladite Convention (zones humides).

Critères d'inscription sur la Liste

Trois critères gouvernent l'inscription d'une aire protégée sur la *Liste des Nations Unies:* ses dimensions, les objectifs de gestion et l'autorité de l'organe de gestion.

1. *Les dimensions*: seules sont incluses les aires protégées de plus de 1000 hectares, à l'exception d'îles océaniques qui couvrent au moins 100 hectares, si elles sont entièrement protégées. Mille hectares équivalent à 10 kilomètres carrés.

2. *Les objectifs de gestion*: une série de catégories de gestion pour les aires protégées, définies en fonction de l'objectif de gestion, a été établie par la CPNAP/UICN. Les catégories ont été révisées depuis la publication de la dernière *Liste des Nations Unies,* et les définitions en question sont données ci-après.

   Les sites désignés au plan national sont classés dans les catégories appropriées de l'UICN, en fonction de leurs objectifs de gestion définis juridiquement et de la façon dont ces objectifs sont mis en oeuvre. Lorsqu'il est apparent, à travers l'information disponible, qu'un site n'est pas géré de façon à appliquer les objectifs fixés par la législation nationale, ce site peut être omis de la Liste ou, le cas échéant, inclus dans une autre catégorie. Cela peut se produire dans le cas d'utilisation inappropriée du site, de ressources inadéquates, d'empiétement grave ou de guerre civile, événements sur lesquels l'organe de gestion n'a souvent aucune prise. Il est entendu que l'omission ou le reclassement sont temporaires, en attendant de meilleures informations ou une amélioration de la situation sur le terrain.

   L'édition 1993 de la *Liste des Nations Unies* inclut les sites des catégories de gestion UICN de I à V. Il est prévu d'ajouter une catégorie VI dans la prochaine édition. Les aires protégées qui sont également des sites Ramsar, des biens du patrimoine mondial ou des réserves de la biosphère figurent à la fois dans les listes nationales et dans les listes d'aires d'importance internationale.

3. *Autorité de l'organe de gestion*: jusqu'à maintenant, seuls étaient inclus dans la *Liste des Nations Unies* les sites gérés par la "plus haute autorité compétente", c'est-à-dire le plus haut organe gouvernemental approprié. La présente édition de la Liste inclut également les sites qui, dans les systèmes fédéraux, sont gérés par des autorités d'Etat.

   La *Liste des Nations Unies 1993* est la quatrième que préparent de concert le WCMC et la CPNAP et, comme dans le cas des trois précédentes (publiées en 1982, 1985 et 1990), cette Liste a été considérablement élargie, bien que les critères d'inscription soient restés largement inchangés. Les réseaux d'aires protégées ont connu une forte expansion mais, en fait, celle de la Liste est due, en grande partie, à l'amélioration des informations disponibles et à une meilleure capacité mise en place pour les recueillir et les gérer. Il importe d'avoir cela présent à l'esprit pour bien utiliser la Liste.

Présentation de la Liste des Nations Unies

Les sites qui satisfont aux critères susmentionnés sont classés pays par pays (dans l'ordre alphabétique du nom anglais du pays). Pour chaque pays, les sites figurent par ordre alphabétique, selon l'appellation nationale (par exemple parcs nationaux, réserves naturelles, sanctuaires de faune sauvage). Pour chaque site, trois éléments d'information sont fournis: la catégorie de gestion selon l'UICN, les dimensions (en hectares) et l'année de création (ou de modification importante des dimensions ou de l'appellation). C'est la première fois que la Liste indique également la latitude/longitude du centre de chaque site. Le WCMC détient de plus amples informations sur tous les sites.

Pour des raisons d'ordre pratique, la *Liste des Nations Unies 1993* classe les pays dans l'ordre alphabétique anglais. Les lecteurs francophones et hispanophones trouveront, dans les lexiques des pages xxvii à xlvi, les noms des pays traduits de français en anglais et d'espagnol en anglais. Pour aider les lecteurs à localiser des sections spécifiques de la Liste, un titre courant générique est fourni en anglais. De même, les données résumées figurant au début de chaque entrée de pays comportent un titre et des annotations en anglais uniquement. Les termes équivalents sont "Sommaire" et "Catégorie" en français et "Resumen" et "Categoría" en espagnol.

Compilation de la Liste des Nations Unies

Le WCMC et la CPNAP rassemblent et traitent des informations sur les aires protégées depuis plusieurs années. Ils disposent donc d'un vaste capital de données dont certaines ont été publiées. Ils reçoivent, en permanence, de nouvelles informations. Pour préparer la *Liste des Nations Unies 1993*, le personnel du WCMC a examiné le matériel existant, révisé et mis à jour des listes d'aires protégées (qui comprenaient la catégorie de gestion UICN appropriée pour chaque site). Des projets de listes de chaque pays ont été envoyés aux organes de gestion nationaux, qui les ont vérifiés et mis à jour. Avec l'information reçue en retour, le WCMC a révisé les projets, résolvant les questions pendantes avec ses contacts dans les pays concernés ou avec les membres de la CPNAP.

Des projets de listes ont été envoyés pour examen aux vice-présidents régionaux de la CPNAP ainsi qu'au secrétariat de l'UICN. Les réponses des organes de gestion nationaux ont été très variées. Au total, environ 455 projets de listes ont été envoyés. Dans le cas des Etats fédéraux, par exemple les Etats-Unis d'Amérique, ces projets ont été envoyés aux autorités d'Etat et, lorsqu'il y avait plus d'un organe responsable des aires protégées, plusieurs copies ont été envoyées dans le même pays. En octobre 1993, 226 réponses avaient été reçues, soit 49% du total. Le meilleur taux de réponse a été enregistré en Australie et le plus faible en Afrique francophone. Pour les pays n'ayant pas envoyé d'information de sources officielles, les données ont, dans la mesure du possible, été puisées dans des publications et autres sources d'information.

Comme cela est précisé ailleurs, les informations destinées à la nouvelle *Liste des Nations Unies* ont été obtenues, en 1993, auprès des organes de gestion. Pour les aider, un texte résumé avait été fourni à chaque organe de gestion, décrivant brièvement le Système de classement alors appliqué par l'UICN, en leur demandant de classer chaque site dans la catégorie appropriée (un résumé de ce système de classement figure à la fin de la présente introduction). Les informations présentées dans la *Liste des Nations Unies 1993* ont donc été classées selon le système en vigueur au moment où les données ont été recueillies.

Au milieu de 1993, un nouveau système de classement a été approuvé par le Conseil de l'UICN, en consultation avec la CPNAP, à l'issue d'un examen effectué par le IVe Congrès mondial des parcs nationaux et des aires protégées, tenu à Caracas en 1992. Ce nouveau système est introduit par la publication des *Lignes directrices pour les catégories de gestion des aires protégées*. Les catégories utilisées dans ce nouveau système sont également résumées en Annexe. Les futures éditions de la *Liste des Nations Unies* seront classées selon ce nouveau système.

Exactitude et qualité de l'information

Le réseau mondial des aires protégées évolue rapidement: on crée de nouvelles aires, on modifie les limites de celles qui existent tandis que d'autres sont détruites par le développement industriel, l'agriculture itinérante, les catastrophes naturelles ou les conflits civils. Dire franchement que la conservation a fait des progrès ces dernières années, du point de vue de l'augmentation de la superficie terrestre ou aquatique protégée, serait très difficile. Il ne s'agit pas simplement d'hectares protégés ou du nombre d'aires protégées mais plutôt de l'efficacité de la gestion. Les aires protégées remplissent-elles les objectifs qui ont présidé à leur création?

La qualité de l'information qui sert de base à la compilation de la *Liste des Nations Unies* est très variable et l'information sur l'efficacité de la gestion fait encore défaut pour un certain nombre de pays. Alors que la vaste majorité des parcs nationaux remplissant les critères appropriés figure sur la Liste, l'information sur les autres catégories d'aires protégées est encore incomplète et il faudra rassembler encore beaucoup de données avant d'avoir la certitude que les listes sont complètes pour chaque catégorie.

Trois secteurs importants, forestier, privé et autochtone, n'ont pas été inclus dans la *Liste des Nations Unies*, soit parce que leurs superficies ne répondaient pas aux critères, soit parce que les informations disponibles étaient incomplètes. La contribution de ces trois secteurs à la conservation et au développement durable n'en est pas moins considérable.

Selon des données recueillies par le WCMC, les aires gérées du secteur forestier couvrent plus de 10% de la superficie des tropiques. La politique forestière de l'ensemble de cette région est en pleine mutation et s'oriente de plus en plus vers une conception intégrée de la production durable et de la conservation. Il reste cependant encore beaucoup à faire et, dans de nombreux pays, il n'existe aucune estimation précise de la valeur du domaine forestier pour la conservation. Le WCMC, en se fondant sur une première étude des réserves forestières des pays forestiers tropicaux, réalisée avec l'appui de la Overseas Development Administration du Royaume-Uni, s'attache à poursuivre l'examen systématique des réseaux de réserves forestières de tous les pays, afin de les aider à évaluer leur contribution aux objectifs de la conservation de la nature.

La mesure dans laquelle les aires autochtones peuvent être considérées comme des aires de conservation fait l'objet d'une certaine controverse, du point de vue tant éthique que pratique. On ne saurait cependant nier l'importance de ces aires pour la conservation de la nature, étant donné que leur superficie totale équivaut à celle de l'Australie, et qu'elles sont en étroite corrélation avec des zones d'une richesse biologique considérable. Par exemple, la Colombie a cédé aux populations autochtones plus de 25% de son territoire, dont l'essentiel se trouve dans des régions de forêts tropicales caractérisées par une très grande diversité biologique. Plus les défenseurs de la conservation de la nature dialogueront avec les populations autochtones sur la conservation conjointe de la diversité culturelle et biologique, plus il y aura d'information sur les aires autochtones.

Contrairement aux aires des deux autres secteurs, l'importance des aires protégées du secteur privé n'est généralement pas liée à leur superficie, mais à la qualité de leur gestion et au degré de protection dont elles bénéficient. Ces aires privées incluent celles qui sont administrées par des fondations et des entreprises privées, et celles qui ont été établies et sont gérées par les communautés elles-mêmes. Parmi les exemples d'initiatives privées venant appuyer et compléter les systèmes réseaux nationaux, on peut citer: The Royal Society for the Protection of Birds (Royaume-Uni), The Nature Conservancy (Amérique du Nord), la Fundación Moisés Bertoni (Paraguay) et la Royal Society for the Conservation of Nature (Jordanie). L'importance des aires protégées privées est vouée à augmenter, surtout dans les pays tropicaux, où les ressources de l'Etat sont très limitées.

Il va de soi qu'il reste sans doute des erreurs ou des omissions dans la *Liste des Nations Unies 1993*. Nous espérons néanmoins que ces erreurs et omissions nous permettront de recevoir des informations encore plus précises. Les compilateurs assument l'entière responsabilité de ces erreurs ou omissions et toute correction ou mise à jour devrait leur être communiquée à l'adresse suivante:

> Protected Areas Data Unit
> World Conservation Monitoring Centre
> 219 Huntingdon Road, Cambridge CB3 0DL
> Angleterre
>
> Téléphone: (0223) 277314
> Télécopieur: (0223) 277136
> Courrier électronique: jerry.harrison@wcmc.org.uk

Remerciements

La Liste a été compilée par l'ensemble du personnel du WCMC, y compris Graham Drucker, Victoria Freeman, Harriet Gillett, Donald Gordon, Michael Green, Jeremy Harrison (chef de l'Unité), James Paine (coordonnateur de projet), Chris Sharpe, Mark Spalding et Alison Suter. Susan Hawley, Tony Rogers, Caroline Brown et Corinna Ravilious ont été d'une aide très précieuse pour terminer la saisie des données.

La compilation a été activement soutenue par la CPNAP et, en particulier, par les cadres de la Commission, ainsi que par James Thorsell, Jeff McNeely, David Sheppard et Caroline Martinet, du secrétariat de l'UICN.

La Liste a été préparée pour la publication par Elaine Shaughnessy et Anne Rodford du Service des publications de l'UICN.

Un soutien financier complémentaire a été fourni par le Programme des Nations Unies pour l'environnement.

Enfin, de nombreuses personnes, notamment des organes de gestion des aires protégées de chaque pays, ont fourni des informations utilisées pour compiler cette Liste. Sans elles, la Liste n'aurait pu être terminée.

Catégories de gestion des aires protégées de l'UICN (1978)

I.   *Réserve naturelle intégrale/Réserve scientifique.* Protéger la nature et maintenir les processus naturels dans un état non perturbé afin de disposer d'exemples représentatifs du milieu naturel pour les études scientifiques, la surveillance continue de l'environnement, l'éducation et pour le maintien des ressources génétiques dans un état dynamique et évolutif.

II. *Parc national.* Protéger des régions naturelles et des paysages exceptionnels, d'importance nationale ou internationale, à des fins scientifiques, éducatives et récréatives. Ce sont des aires naturelles relativement vastes, non altérées par les activités de l'homme, où l'exploitation extractive des ressources n'est pas autorisée.

III. *Monument naturel/Elément naturel marquant.* Protéger et préserver des éléments naturels d'importance nationale en raison de leur intérêt particulier ou de leurs caractéristiques uniques. Ce sont des régions relativement petites où la protection est axée sur des éléments spécifiques.

IV. *Réserve naturelle dirigée/Sanctuaire de faune.* Garantir le maintien des conditions naturelles nécessaires pour protéger des espèces, groupes d'espèces, communautés biologiques ou traits physiques d'importance nationale lorsque leur perpétuation peut nécessiter une intervention spécifique de l'homme. Un prélèvement contrôlé de certaines ressources peut être autorisé.

V.   *Paysages terrestres et marins protégés.* Maintenir des paysages naturels d'importance nationale, caractéristiques de l'interaction harmonieuse entre l'homme et la terre, tout en donnant au public la possibilité de jouir, par des activités de loisirs et de tourisme, du mode de vie normal et de l'activité économique de ces régions. Ce sont des paysages mixtes, naturels et culturels ayant une valeur esthétique élevée où les modes traditionnels d'utilisation des sols sont maintenus.

Lista de las Naciones Unidas de Parques Nacionales y Areas Protegidas 1993

Publicado por: UICN, Gland, Suiza y Cambridge, Reino Unido.

Preparado y publicado con el apoyo del PNUMA y de la UNESCO .

Una contribución para el SIMUVIMA—Sistema Mundial de Vigilancia del Medio Ambiente

Citación: UICN (1994). *Lista de las Naciones Unidas de Parques Nacionales y Areas Protegidas 1993*. Preparada por el WCMC y la CPNAP.UICN, Gland, Suiza y Cambridge, Reino Unido. xlvi + 315pp.

ISBN: 2-8317-0190-2

Impreso en: Page Brothers (Norwich) Ltd., Reino Unido

Diseño de portada: Servicio de Publicaciones de UICN

Fotos de portada: *Kilaguni Lodge, Tsavo, Kenia*: D. y I. Gordon; *Parque Nacional Península de Paria, Venezuela*: C. J. Sharpe; *Brandywine Creek State Park, Estados Unidos*: Harriet Gillett; *Cigueñas migrando, Ras Mohammed National Park, Egipto*: Mark Spalding.

Producido por: Servicio de Publicaciones de la UICN, Cambridge, Reino Unido, con equipo de publicación comprado mediante una donación de la Sra Julia Ward

Disponible en: Servicio de Publicaciones de la UICN
219c Huntingdon Road, CambridgeCB3 0DL, Reino Unido o
División de Comunicaciones y Relaciones con Empresas UICN
Rue Mauverney 28, CH-1196 Gland, Suiza

La designación de entidadesgeográficas en este libro y la presentación del material no implica la expresión de ninguna opinión por parte de la UICN, el PNUMA, la UNESCO o el WCMC con relación al status legal de ningún país, territorio o área, o sus autoridades, ni con relación a la delimitación de sus fronteras y límites geográficos.

El texto de este libro fue impreso en papel Fineblade Cartridge 90 gsm con bajo contenido de cloro

Indice

Introducción

Las áreas protegidas aportan una contribución vital a la conservación de los recursos naturales y culturales del mundo. Sus funciones varían desde la preservación de ejemplos representativos de regiones naturales y de la diversidad biológica, hasta el mantenimiento de la estabilidad ecológica de las zonas que las rodean. Las áreas protegidas pueden consistuir una oportunidad para el desarrollo rural y la utilización de tierras marginales a nivel regional, para la investigación y el monitoreo, para la educación en materia de conservación, y para la recreación y el turismo. Por todas estas razones, la mayoría de países ha establecido sistemas de áreas protegidas.

Sin embargo, los sistemas de áreas protegidas varían enormemente de un país a otro, en función de las necesidades y prioridades, y según el nivel de apoyo legislativo, institucional y financiero que reciben. Asimismo, la gama de servicios y valores de las áreas protegidas es tal, que ciertos objetivos de manejo son incompatibles con otros. Ello ha conducido a aplicar a las áreas protegidas toda una serie de designaciones y definiciones.

La finalidad de la *Lista de las Naciones Unidas* es obtener un listado definitivo de las áreas protegidas que cumplan con determinados criterios, los cuales se presentan más adelante.

Historia de la Lista de las Naciones Unidas

La *Lista de las Naciones Unidas de Parques Nacionales y Reservas Equivalentes* se elaboró atendiendo la solicitud de las Naciones Unidas siguiendo una Resolución sobre "Desarrollo Económico y Conservación de la Naturaleza", adoptada por la Asamblea General en su 16ava Sesión, celebrada en Diciembre de 1962. Esta Resolución sirvió para apoyar una resolución anterior (No. 713) de la 27ava Sesión del Consejo Económico y Social de las Naciones Unidas, celebrada en 1959; esta resolución reconocía la importancia de los parques nacionales y las reservas equivalentes como instrumento para la utilización racional de los recursos naturales, y condujo a la elaboración de la primera *Lista Mundial de Parques Nacionales y Reservas Equivalentes*.

La UICN desempeñó un papel crucial en la preparación de las dos Resoluciones, y desde entonces ha sido la principal responsable de la compilación y actualización de la Lista. Actualmente la Comisión de Parques Nacionales y Areas Protegidas de la UICN junto con el Centro Mundial de Monitoreo de la Conservación, se encarga de preparar la *Lista de las Naciones Unidas*. La edición anterior de la *Lista de las Naciones Unidas* fue publicada en 1990. Previamente se publicaron otras versiones en 1961/1962, 1966 (versión inglesa, 1971), 1972 (adenda a la Lista de 1966/1971), 1973, 1974, 1975, 1980, 1982 y 1985. El título actual se adoptó en 1982.

La Comisión de Parques Nacionales y Areas Protegidas de la UICN

La Comisión de Parques Nacionales y Areas Protegidas (CPNAP) de la UICN es el principal órgano internacional de carácter científico y técnico encargado de la selección, del establecimiento y del manejo de parques nacionales y otras áreas protegidas. Entre sus miembros figuran más de 500 especialistas en áreas protegidas, procedentes de unos 120 países. La CPNAP cuenta con los servicios del Programa de Areas Protegidas de la UICN, con miras a promover el establecimiento y la gestión eficaz de una red mundial de áreas terrestres y marinas protegidas.

Durante la elaboración de la presente edición de la *Lista de las Naciones Unidas*, la CPNAP estuvo presidida por el Sr. P.H.C. (Bing) Lucas de Nueva Zelandia, y el Sr. Adrian Phillips del Reino Unido actuó como

Presidente Adjunto. La Comisión está organizada sobre una base regional, y cuenta con 14 vicepresidentes regionales y dos vicepresidentes de programas temáticos (áreas protegidas, marinas y de montaña). Por lo general se celebran dos o tres reuniones regionales al año. Desde que se compiló la ultima *Lista de las Naciones Unidas,* se han celebrado reuniones en Australia, China, Suecia, República Dominicana, Italia (para la región de Africa del Norte/Medio Oriente), y ha tenido lugar en Venezuela el IV Congreso Mundial de Parques Nacionales y Areas Protegidas, al que asistieron más de 1.800 participantes procedentes de todo el mundo.

Unidad de Datos sobre Areas Protegidas del WCMC

La Unidad de Datos sobre Areas Protegidas fue creada por la CPNAP en 1981, con el fin de procesar el creciente volumen de información disponible y ayudar a la Comisión a preparar publicaciones sobre las áreas protegidas en todo el mundo. Actualmente la Unidad forma parte del Centro Mundial de Monitoreo de la Conservación, con base en Cambridge, Reino Unido. Uno de los objetivos de la labor del WCMC en materia de áreas protegidas es proporcionar información actualizada y precisa sobre áreas protegidas individuales y sobre los sistemas de áreas protegidas del mundo a todos los que la necesiten o, si no se dispone de ella, averiguar dónde puede obtenerse rápidamente.

Con el fin de lograr este objetivo, el WCMC colabora con los numerosos organismos de todo el mundo que se dedican a la gestión de las áreas protegidas, así como con los especialistas en conservación y los científicos activos en esta esfera. Muchas de las personas interesadas son miembros de la CPNAP. El WCMC también tiene una responsabilidad especial en cuanto al procesamiento de la información sobre Reservas de la Biosfera y Sitios del Patrimonio Mundial (responsabilidad que le ha sido asignada por la Secretaría del MAB y el Comité del Patrimonio Mundial, respectivamente), y colabora con la Mesa Directiva de la Convención de Ramsar (de Humedales) en relación con los sitios enumerados en dicha Convención.

Criterios para la inclusión

Hay tres criterios en función de los cuales se determina la inclusión de un área protegida en la *Lista de las Naciones Unidas*: su tamaño, los objetivos de manejo y la autoridad del organismo de gestión.

1. *Tamaño.* Sólo se incluyen áreas de más de mil hectáreas, con excepción de las islas extracosteras u oceánicas de por lo menos 100 hectáreas, en cuyo caso se confiere protección a la totalidad de la isla. Mil hectáreas equivalen a 10 km^2, 2.471 acres o 3,86 millas cuadradas.

2. *Objetivos de manejo.* La UICN/CPNAP ha identificado una serie de categorías de manejo de áreas protegidas, definidas en función del objetivo de las actividades de manejo. Estas categorías se han revisado después de que se publicó la última *Lista de las Naciones Unidas,* y más adelante se presentan las definiciones correspondientes a cada una de ellas.

   Los sitios designados a nivel nacional se clasifican en las Categorías pertinentes de la UICN, en función de sus objetivos de manejo definidos jurídicamente y de la manera como se tratan de alcanzar esos objetivos. Cuando la información disponible indica que el manejo del sitio no basta para realizar los objetivos fijados por la legislación nacional, el sitio se puede suprimir de la Lista o, cuando proceda, se puede incluir en otra categoría. Entre las razones para adoptar esta decisión se tiene una utilización inadecuada, insuficiencia de recursos, invasión grave o conflicto civil, factores que a menudo están fuera del control del órgano de gestión. Queda entendido que dicha supresión o reclasificación puede ser temporal, en espera de recibir información más detallada o de se mejore la situación en el terreno.

   La edición de 1993 de la *Lista de las Naciones Unidas* incluye los sitios que figuran en las Categorías de Manejo I a V de la UICN. Se pretende incluir en la próxima edición los sitios de la Categoría VI. Las áreas protegidas que son igualmente Sitios de Ramsar, Sitios del Patrimonio Mundial o Reservas de la Biosfera, figuran tanto en las listas nacionales como en las listas de áreas de importancia internacional.

3. *Autoridad del organismo de gestión.* En el pasado sólo se incluían en la *Lista de las Naciones Unidas* los sitios administrados por la "más alta autoridad competente", esto es, el máximo órgano gubernamental competente. En esta versión también se han incluido en la Lista los sitios de cuya administración se encargan autoridades estatales en el marco de sistemas federales.

La *Lista de las Naciones Unidas* de 1993 es la cuarta que preparan conjuntamente el WCMC y la CPNAP y, como en el caso de las tres listas precedentes (publicadas en 1982, 1985 y 1990), ésta se ha ampliado notablemente, aunque los criterios de inscripción hayan permanecido en su mayor parte inalterados. Aunque las redes de áreas protegidas se han extendido considerablemente, la ampliación de la Lista obedece en gran parte a la mejora de la información disponible, y a nuestra mayor capacidad para compilar y procesar los datos. Al utilizar la Lista es importante tener en cuenta este aspecto.

Formato de la Lista de las Naciones Unidas

Los sitios que satisfacen los criterios antes mencionados se clasifican país por país (siguiendo el orden alfabético del nombre del país en inglés). Para cada país, los sitios figuran en orden alfabético según la designación nacional (por ejemplo, parques nacionales, reservas naturales, santuarios de vida silvestre). Para cada sitio se proporciona tres tipos de información: su categoría de manejo según la UICN, su dimensión (en hectáreas) y el año de creación (o de modificación importante en tamaño o designación). En esta lista también se proporciona por primera vez una latitud/longitud central para cada sitio. El Centro Mundial de Monitoreo de la Conservación posee información más detallada sobre cada uno de estos sitios.

Por razones prácticas, la *Lista de las Naciones Unidas* de 1993 se ha ordenado siguiendo el listado de los países en inglés, por orden alfabético. Los lectores de lengua francesa y española deberán consultar los glosarios que figuran en las páginas xxvii a xlvi; éstos contienen una traducción de los nombres de los países del francés al inglés y del español al inglés, respectivamente. Para ayudar a los lectores a ubicar secciones específicas de la Lista, se proprociona una secuencia de encabezamientos en inglés. Análogamente, los datos resumidos que figuran al comienzo de cada sección nacional se titulan y anotan en inglés únicamente. Los términos equivalentes son "Sommaire" y "Catégorie" en francés, y "Resumen" y "Categoría" en español.

Compilación de la Lista de las Naciones Unidas

El WCMC y la CPNAP vienen compilando y procesando información sobre áreas protegidas desde hace varios años, y actualmente se cuenta con una cantidad importante de información, parte de la cual ha sido publicada. El Centro y la Comisión reciben constantemente nuevas informaciones. Al preparar la *Lista de las Naciones Unidas* de 1993, el personal del WCMC analizó el material existente y revisó y actualizó las listas de áreas protegidas (que incluyen la correspondiente Categoría de Manejo de la UICN para cada sitio). Los borradores de las listas de cada país se enviaron a los órganos nacionales encargados de la gestión, junto con una petición para que fueran verificados, actualizados y devueltos. Sobre la base de la información recibida, el personal del WCMC revisó esas listas preliminares, resolviendo las cuestiones pendientes a través de sus contactos en los países interesados o con los miembros de la CPNAP.

Se envió copia de las listas revisadas, tanto a los Vicepresidentes Regionales de la CPNAP, como a la Secretería de la UICN para sus comentarios. Las respuestas de los órganos nacionales de gestión fueron muy variadas. Se formularon en total unas 455 peticiones. En el caso de las naciones federales, como los Estados Unidos, las peticiones se enviaron a las diferentes autoridades estatales, y en los casos en los cuales las responsabilidad de las áreas protegidas corresponde a más de un organismo, se enviaron múltiples peticiones al mismo país. En Octubre de 1993 se habían recibido 226 respuestas, es decir el 49% del total de peticiones. El mayor número de respuestas provino de Australia con un 88% de respuesta y el menor de Africa francóparlante con sólo el 18% de respuesta. Cuando no se recibió información de fuentes oficiales, los datos se extrajeron, siempre fue posible, de materiales publicados y de otras fuentes.

Como se indica en otra sección del presente documento, durante 1993 se compiló información de los organismos encargados de la gestión para elaborar la nueva Lista de las Naciones Unidas. Como parte de ese ejercicio, se proporcionó a cada uno de esos organismos un texto con una descripción sucinta del actual Sistema de Categorías de Manejo de la UICN, junto con la petición de que se aplicase a cada sitio la categoría pertinente (al final de esta introducción se presenta un resumen de ese sistema de categorias). La información contenida en la Lista de las Naciones Unidas ha sido clasificada con base en ese sistema de categorías, que ya se había establecido en el momento de compilar los datos.

A mediados de 1993 el Consejo de la UICN, atendiendo el concepto de la CPNAP tras un análisis efectuado en el IV Congreso Mundial de Parques Nacionales y Areas Protegidas, aprobó un nuevo sistema de categorías de manejo de áreas protegidas. Este sistema se introduce a través de la publicación de las *Directrices sobre las Categorias de Manejo de Areas Protegidas*. Las categorías utilizadas en este nuevo sistema también se reumen en el Anexo. Las ediciones ulteriores de la Lista de las Naciones Unidas se clasificarán de conformidad con este nuevo sistema.

Exactitud y calidad de la información

El sistema mundial de áreas protegidas está evolucionando rápidamente: se crean nuevas áreas, se modifican las fronteras de las existentes, y algunos sitios son destruidos por el desarrollo industrial, la agricultura itinerante, los desastres naturales o las guerras civiles. Sería muy difícil asegurar firmemente que en los últimos años la conservación ha hecho progresos netos en lo que respecta a la superficie de tierras o aguas protegidas. No se trata simplemente de las hectáreas protegidas o del número de áreas protegidas, sino más bien de la eficacia de las actividades de manejo. ¿Están alcanzando las áreas protegidas los objetivos para los cuales se crearon?

La calidad de la información utilizada para compilar la *Lista de las Naciones Unidas* es muy variable, y aún se carece de información sobre la eficacia de la gestión en varios países. Aunque en la Lista figura la gran mayoría de los parques nacionales que satisfacen los criterios pertinentes, la información sobre las otras categorías de áreas protegidas sigue siendo incompleta, y habrá que obtener muchos más datos para tener la certeza de que las listas estan completas para cada categoría de manejo. En la *Lista de las Naciones Unidas* no se han incluido las áreas de tres importantes sectores, a saber, el forestal, el privado y las reservas indígenas ya sea porque las áreas correspondientes no satisfacen los criterios, o bien porque la información disponible es incompleta. No obstante, la contribución de estos tres sectores a la conservación y al desarrollo sustentable es considerable.

De conformidad con los datos compilados por el WCMC, las áreas manejadas en el sector forestal cubren más del 10% de las regiones tropicales. En todas estas regiones tropicales la política forestal se está modificando radicalmente, y se está haciendo cada vez mayor hincapié en un enfoque equilibrado para la producción y conservación sustentables. Sin embargo, aún queda mucho por hacer, y es necesario que muchos países evalúen debidamente el valor de sus bosques desde el punto de vista de la conservación. Tras un análisis inicial de las reservas forestales de los países que poseen bosques tropicales, llevada a cabo con el apoyo de la Administración para el Desarrollo de Ultramar (Overseas Development Administration) del Reino Unido, el WCMC sigue trabajando con miras al análisis sistemático de los sistemas de reservas forestales de todos los países, con el fin de ayudar a evaluar su contribución a los objetivos de conservación de la naturaleza.

Por razones éticas y prácticas, existe cierta divergencia de opiniones, respecto de la medida en la cual las reservas indígenas pueden ser consideradas como áreas de conservación. La importancia que revisten estas áreas para la conservación de la naturaleza es incuestionable, dado que las reservas indígenas cubren en conjunto una superficie del tamaño de Australia, y en general corresponden marcadamente a regiones de gran riqueza biológica. Colombia, por ejemplo, ha cedido más del 25% de su territorio a las poblaciones autóctonas, y la mayoría de esas tierras se encuentran en regiones de bosques tropicales con gran diversidad biológica. Dado que cada vez es más necesario que los encargados de la conservación entablen un diálogo con las poblaciones autóctonas , con miras a la conservación conjunta de la diversidad cultural y biológica, la información sobre las reservas indígenas es cada vez más importante.

A diferencia de las áreas que caen dentro del ámbito de los otros dos sectores mencionados, normalmente las áreas protegidas del sector privado no son significativas en cuanto a la superficie que cubren, pero son importantes a causa de la calidad del manejo y del grado de protección que se les confiere. Las áreas privadas comprenden zonas administradas por fundaciones y empresas privadas, así como las establecidas y manejadas por las propias comunidades. Hay numerosos ejemplos notables de iniciativas privadas que sirven de apoyo y complemento a los sistemas estatales: The Royal Society for the Protection of Birds en el Reino Unido, The Nature Conservancy en América del Norte, la Fundación Moisés Bertone en Paraguay y la Royal Society for the Conservation of Nature en Jordania. La importancia de las áreas protegidas de propiedad privada puede ir en aumento, especialmente en los países tropicales, en los cuales los recursos estatales son muy limitados.

Sin duda alguna la *Lista de las Naciones Unidas* de 1993 incluye errores y omisiones, pero se espera que éstos sirvan para estimular el envío de informaciones más precisas. Los editores asumen la responsabilidad de esos errores y omisiones, y ruegan que cualquier corrección o actualización se comunique a:

Protected Areas Data Unit
World Conservation Monitoring Centre
219 Huntingdon Road
Cambridge CB3 ODL
Reino Unido

Teléfono: (0223) 277314
Fax: (0223) 277136

Correo electrónico: jerry.harrison@wcmc.org.uk

Agradecimientos

La Lista ha sido compilada por numerosos miembros del personal del WCMC, incluyendo a Graham Drucker, Victoria Freeman, Harriet Gillett, Donald Gordon, Michael Green, Jeremy Harrison (Presidente de la Unidad), James Paine (coordinación del proyecto), Chris Sharpe, Mark Spalding y Alison Suter. Susan Hawley, Tony Rogers, Caroline Brown y Corinna Ravilious han contribuido enormemente en las últimas etapas de la introducción de datos.

En la preparación se ha contando con el apoyo activo de la CPNAP, y en particular de los altos funcionarios de la Comisión y del Dr. James Thorsell, Jeff McNeely, David Sheppard y Caroline Martinet, de la Secretaría de la UICN.

La lista ha sido preparada para su publicación por Elaine Shaughnessy y Anne Rodford, de la Unidad de Servicios de Publicación de la UICN.

El Programa de las Naciones Unidas para el Medio Ambiente aportó apoyo financiero adicional.

Por último, numerosos particulares de los organismos encargados de la gestión de las áreas protegidas en cada país y de otras fuentes, han proporcionado información utilizada para la elaboración de la Lista y sin la cual ésta no habría podido terminarse.

Categorías de Manejo de Areas Protegidas de 1978

I. *Reserva Natural Estricta/Reserva Científica.* Su fin es proteger la naturaleza y mantener inalterados los procesos naturales, con el objeto de contar con ejemplos ecológicamente representativos del medio ambiente natural, para fines científicos, de monitoreo ambiental, de educación y de mantenimiento de los recursos genéticos en un estado dinámico y evolutivo.

II. *Parque Nacional.* Su fin es proteger áreas naturales y escénicas sobresalientes de importancia nacional o internacional para usos científicos, educativos y recreativos. Son áreas relativamente grandes que no han sido sustancialmente alteradas por la actividad humana, y donde no se permite la utilización de recursos naturales con fines extractivos.

III. *Monumento Natural.* Su fin es preservar y proteger elementos naturales específicos de relevancia nacional, debido a sus características únicas o su interés especial. Estas áreas son relativamente pequeñas y están enfocadas a la protección de rasgos naturales específicos.

IV. *Reserva Natural Manejada/Santuario de Vida Silvestre.* Su fin es garantizar las condiciones naturales necesarias para proteger especies de relevancia nacional, grupos de especies, comunidades bióticas o características físicas del medio ambiente cuando estos requieran de manipulación artificial humana para su perpetuación. El aprovechamiento controlado de algunos de sus recursos naturales puede permitirse.

V. *Paisajes Terrestres o Marinos Protegidos.* Su fin es mantener paisajes de relevancia nacional, que sean característicos de una interacción armónica entre el hombre y la tierra a la vez que proveer oportunidades de goce público a través de la recreación y del turismo, dentro del contexto del estilo de vida local y de las actividades económicas propias del sitio. Son áreas que contienen un mosaico de paisajes naturales y culturales de gran calidad escénica y donde se mantienen los usos tradicionales del suelo.

Lexique français/anglais

français	anglais
Afghanistan	Afghanistan
Afrique du Sud	South Africa
Albanie	Albania
Algérie	Algeria
Allemagne	Germany, Federal Republic of
Andorre	Andorra
Angola	Angola
Anguilla	Anguilla
Antarctique	Antarctic Treaty Territory
Antigua-et-Barbuda	Antigua and Barbuda
Antilles néerlandaises	Netherlands Antilles
Arabie saoudite	Saudi Arabia
Argentine	Argentina
Arménie	Armenia
Aruba (Pays-Bas)	Aruba (Netherlands)
Australie	Australia
Autriche	Austria
Azerbaïdjan	Azerbaijan
Açores (Portugal)	Azores (Portugal)
Bahamas	Bahamas
Bahreïn	Bahrain
Bangladesh	Bangladesh
Barbade	Barbados
Bélarus	Belarus
Belgique	Belgium
Belize	Belize
Bénin	Benin
Bermudes	Bermuda
Bhoutan	Bhutan
Bolivie	Bolivia
Bosnie-Herzégovine	Bosnia and Herzegovina
Botswana	Botswana
Bouvet, Ile (Norvège)	Bouvet Island (Norway)
Brunéi Darussalam	Brunei Darussalam
Brésil	Brazil
Bulgarie	Bulgaria
Burkina Faso	Burkina Faso
Burundi	Burundi
Cambodge	Cambodia
Cameroun	Cameroon
Canada	Canada
Cap-Vert	Cape Verde
Caïmanes, Iles (Royaume-Uni)	Cayman Islands (United Kingdom)
Chili	Chile
Chine	China
Chypre	Cyprus
Cocos (Keeling), Iles des (Australie)	Cocos (Keeling) Islands (Australia)
Colombie	Colombia
Comores	Comoros
Congo	Congo

Cook, Iles (Nouvelle Zélande)	Cook Islands (New Zealand)
Costa Rica	Costa Rica
Côte d'Ivoire	Côte d'Ivoire
Croatie	Croatia
Cuba	Cuba
Danemark	Denmark
Djibouti	Djibouti
Dominique	Dominica
Egypte	Egypt
El Salvador	El Salvador
Emirats arabes unis	United Arab Emirates
Equateur	Ecuador
Erythrée	Eritrea
Espagne	Spain
Estonie	Estonia
Etats-Unis d'Amérique	United States of America
Ethiopie	Ethiopia
Fidji	Fiji
Finlande	Finland
France	France
Fédération de Russie	Russian Federation
Féroé, Iles (Danemark)	Faroe Islands (Denmark)
Gabon	Gabon
Gambie	Gambia
Ghana	Ghana
Gibraltar (Royaume Uni)	Gibraltar (United Kingdom)
Grèce	Greece
Grenade	Grenada
Groenland (Danemark)	Greenland (Denmark)
Guadeloupe (France)	Guadeloupe (France)
Guam	Guam
Guatemala	Guatemala
Guinée-Bissau	Guinea-Bissau
Guinée	Guinea
Guinée équatoriale	Equatorial Guinea
Guyana	Guyana
Guyane (France)	French Guiana (France)
Géorgie	Georgia
Géorgie du Sud/les îles Sandwich du Sud (Royaume-Uni)	South Georgia/South Sandwich (United Kingdom)
Haïti	Haiti
Heard et Mc Donald, Iles (Australie)	Heard and McDonald Islands (Australia)
Honduras	Honduras
Hong-Kong (Royaume-Uni)	Hong Kong (United Kingdom)
Hongrie	Hungary
Iles anglo-normandes (Royaume-Uni)	Channel Islands (United Kingdom)
Iles Falkland (Malouines) (Royaume-Uni)	Falkland Islands (United Kingdom)
Iles mineures éloignées des États-Unis (États-Unis)	United States Minor Outlying Islands (United States)
Ile Montserrat	Montserrat
Ile Pitcairn (Royaume-Uni)	Pitcairn Island (United Kingdom)
Iles Turques et Caïques	Turks and Caicos Islands
Iles vierges (britanniques) (Royaume-Uni)	Virgin Islands (British)
Iles vierges (américaines) (États-Unis)	Virgin Islands (United States)
Iles Wallis et Futuna	Wallis and Futuna (France)
Inde	India
Indonésie	Indonesia
Iran, Répubique islamique d'	Iran, Islamic Republic of
Iraq	Iraq
Irlande	Ireland
Islande	Iceland

Israël	Israel
Italie	Italy
Jamahiriya arabe libyenne	Libyan Arab Jamahiriya
Jamaïque	Jamaica
Japon	Japan
Jordanie	Jordan
Kazakhstan	Kazakhstan
Kenya	Kenya
Kirghizistan	Kyrgyzstan
Kiribati	Kiribati
Koweït	Kuwait
Lesotho	Lesotho
Lettonie	Latvia
Liban	Lebanon
Libéria	Liberia
Liechtenstein	Liechtenstein
Lituanie	Lithuania
Luxembourg	Luxembourg
Macao (Portugal)	Macau (Portugal)
Macédoine (ex-République yougoslave de)	Macedonia (former Yugoslav Republic of)
Madagascar	Madagascar
Madère (Portugal)	Madeira (Portugal)
Malaisie	Malaysia
Malawi	Malawi
Maldives	Maldives
Mali	Mali
Malte	Malta
Mariannes du Nord, Iles	Northern Mariana Islands
Maroc	Morocco
Marshall, Iles	Marshall Islands
Martinique (France)	Martinique (France)
Maurice	Mauritius
Mauritanie	Mauritania
Mayotte (France)	Mayotte (France)
Mexique	Mexico
Micronésie, Etats fédérés de	Micronesia, Federated States of
Monaco	Monaco
Mongolie	Mongolia
Montserrat (Royaume-Uni)	Montserrat (United Kingdom)
Mozambique	Mozambique
Myanmar	Myanmar
Namibie	Namibia
Nauru	Nauru
Nepal	Napal
Nicaragua	Nicaragua
Niger	Niger
Nigéria	Nigeria
Nioué (Nouvelle-Zélande)	Niue (New Zealand)
Norfolk, Ile (Australie)	Norfolk Island (Australia)
Norvège	Norway
Nouvelle-Calédonie (France)	New Caledonia (France)
Nouvelle-Zélande	New Zealand
Népal	Nepal
Océan Indien, Territoire britannique de l'(Royaume-Uni)	British Indian Ocean Territory (United Kingdom)
Oman	Oman
Ouganda	Uganda
Ouzbékistan	Uzbekistan
Pakistan	Pakistan
Palau	Palau
Panama	Panama

Papouasie-Nouvelle-Guinée	Papua New Guinea
Paraguay	Paraguay
Pays-Bas	Netherlands
Pérou	Peru
Philippines	Philippines
Pitcairn (Royaume Uni)	Pitcairn (United Kingdom)
Pologne	Poland
Polynésie française (France)	French Polynesia (France)
Porto Rico	Puerto Rico
Portugal	Portugal
Qatar	Qatar
République populaire démocratique de Corée	Korea, Democratic People's Republic of
République arabe syrienne	Syrian Arab Republic
République centrafricaine	Central African Republic
République de Corée	Korea, Republic of
République de Moldova	Moldova, Republic of
République dominicaine	Dominican Republic
République démocratique populaire lao	Lao People's Democratic Republic
République tchèque	Czech Republic
République-Unie de Tanzanie	Tanzania, United Republic of
Réunion (France)	Réunion (France)
Roumanie	Romania
Royaume-Uni	United Kingdom
Rwanda	Rwanda
Sahara occidental	Western Sahara
Saint-Kitts-et-Nevis	Saint Kitts and Nevis
Saint-Marin	San Marino
Saint-Pierre et Miquelon (France)	St. Pierre and Miquelon
Saint-Siège	Vatican City State (Holy See)
Saint-Vincent-et-les-Grenadines	Saint Vincent and the Grenadines
Sainte-Hélène (Royaume-Uni)	St. Helena (United Kingdom)
Sainte-Lucie	Saint Lucia
Salomon, Iles	Solomon Islands
Samoa	Western Samoa
Samoa américaines (États-Unis)	American Samoa (United States)
Sao Tomé-et-Principe	Sao Tome and Principe
Seychelles	Seychelles
Sierra Leone	Sierra Leone
Singapour	Singapore
Slovaquie	Slovakia
Slovénie	Slovenia
Somalie	Somalia
Soudan	Sudan
Sri Lanka	Sri Lanka
Suisse	Switzerland
Suriname	Suriname
Suède	Sweden
Svalbard et île Jan Mayen (Norvège)	Svalbard and Jan Mayen Islands (Norway)
Swaziland	Swaziland
Sénégal	Senegal
Tadjikistan	Tajikistan
Taiwan (Province chinoise de)	Taiwan, Province of China
Tchad	Chad
Tchécoslovaquie	Czechoslovakia
Terres australes françaises (France)	French Southern Territories (France)
Thaïlande	Thailand
Togo	Togo
Tokélaou	Tokelau
Tonga	Tonga
Trinité-et-Tobago	Trinidad and Tobago
Tunisie	Tunisia

Turkménistan	Turkmenistan
Turquie	Turkey
Tuvalu (Nouvelle-Zélande)	Tuvalu (New Zealand)
Ukraine	Ukraine
Uruguay	Uruguay
Vanuatu	Vanuatu
Venezuela	Venezuela
Viet Nam	Viet Nam
Yougoslavie	Yugoslavia
Yémen	Yemen
Zambie	Zambia
Zaïre	Zaire
Zimbabwe	Zimbabwe

———————————

Glosario Inglés-Español

Español	Inglés
Afganistán	Afghanistan
Albania	Albania
Alemania	Germany, Federal Republic of
Andorra	Andorra
Angola	Angola
Antigua y Barbuda	Antigua and Barbuda
Arabia Saudita	Saudi Arabia
Argelia	Algeria
Argentina	Argentina
Armenia	Armenia
Aruba (Países Bajos)	Aruba (Netherlands)
Australia	Australia
Austria	Austria
Azerbaiyán	Azerbaijan
Bahamas	Bahamas
Bahrein	Bahrain
Bangladesh	Bangladesh
Barbados	Barbados
Belarús	Belarus
Belice	Belize
Benin	Benin
Bhután	Bhutan
Bolivia	Bolivia
Bosnia y Herzegovina	Bosnia and Herzegovina
Botswana	Botswana
Brasil	Brazil
Brunei Darussalam	Brunei Darussalam
Bulgaria	Bulgaria
Burkina Faso	Burkina Faso
Burundi	Burundi
Bélgica	Belgium
Cabo Verde	Cape Verde
Camboya	Cambodia
Camerún	Cameroon
Canadá	Canada
Colombia	Colombia
Comoras	Comoros
Congo	Congo
Costa Rica	Costa Rica
Croacia	Croatia
Cuba	Cuba
Côte d'Ivoire	Côte d'Ivoire
Chad	Chad
Chile	Chile
China	China
Chipre	Cyprus
Dinamarca	Denmark
Djibouti	Djibouti
Dominica	Dominica
Ecuador	Ecuador

Egipto	Egypt
Eritrea	Eritrea
El Salvador	El Salvador
Emiratos Arabes Unidos	United Arab Emirates
Eslovaquia	Slovakia
Eslovenia	Slovenia
España	Spain
Estados Unidos de América	United States
Estonia	Estonia
Etiopía	Ethiopia
Federación de Rusia	Russian Federation
Fiji	Fiji
Filipinas	Philippines
Finlandia	Finland
Francia	France
Gabón	Gabon
Gambia	Gambia
Georgia	Georgia
Georgia del Sur/Las Islas Sandwich del Sur (Reino Unido)	South Georgia/South Sandwich Islands (United Kingdom)
Ghana	Ghana
Granada	Grenada
Grecia	Greece
Groenlandia (Dinamarca)	Greenland (Denmark)
Guam (Estados Unidos)	Guam (United States)
Guatemala	Guatemala
Guinea	Guinea
Guinea Ecuatorial	Equatorial Guinea
Guinea-Bissau	Guinea-Bissau
Guyana	Guyana
Haití	Haiti
Honduras	Honduras
Hong Kong (Reino Unido)	Hong Kong (United Kingdom)
Hungría	Hungary
India	India
Indonesia	Indonesia
Iraq	Iraq
Irlanda	Ireland
Irán, República Islámica del	Iran, Islamic Republic of
Islandia	Iceland
Islas Cook (Nueva Zelandia)	Cook Islands (New Zealand)
Islas Faroe (Dinamarca)	Faroe Islands (Denmark)
Islas Heard y McDonald (Australia)	Heard and McDonald Islands (Australia)
Territorio Británico del Océano Indico (Reino Unido)	British Indian Ocean Territory (United Kingdom)
Islas Jan Mayen y Svalbard (Noruega)	Svalbard and Jan Mayen Islands (Norway)
Islas Malvinas (Reino Unido)	Falkland Islands (United Kingdom)
Islas de la Mancha (Reino Unido)	Channel Islands (United Kingdom)
Islas Marshall	Marshall Islands
Isla Norfolk (Australia)	Norfolk Island (Australia)
Isla Pitcairn (Reino Unido)	Pitcairn Island (United Kingdom)
Islas Salomón	Solomon Islands
Islas Turks y Caicos	Turks and Caicos
Israel	Israel
Italia	Italy
Jamahiriya Arabe Libia	Libyan Arab Jamahiriya
Jamaica	Jamaica
Japón	Japan
Jordania	Jordan
Kazajstán	Kazakhstan
Kenia	Kenya

Kirguistán	Kyrgyzstan
Kiribati	Kiribati
Kuwait	Kuwait
Lesotho	Lesotho
Letonia	Latvia
Liberia	Liberia
Liechtenstein	Liechtenstein
Lituania	Lithuania
Luxemburgo	Luxembourg
Líbano	Lebanon
Macedonia	Macedonia
Madagascar	Madagascar
Malasia	Malaysia
Malawi	Malawi
Maldivas	Maldives
Malí	Mali
Malta	Malta
Marruecos	Morocco
Martinica (Francia)	Martinique (France)
Mauricio	Mauritius
Mauritania	Mauritania
Micronesia, Estados Federados de	Micronesia, Federated States of
Mongolia	Mongolia
Mozambique	Mozambique
Myanmar	Myanmar
México	Mexico
Mónaco	Monaco
Namibia	Namibia
Nauru	Nauru
Nepal	Nepal
Nicaragua	Nicaragua
Niger	Niger
Nigeria	Nigeria
Noruega	Norway
Nueva Zelandia	New Zealand
Níger	Niger
Niue (Nueva Zelandia)	Niue (New Zealand)
Omán	Oman
Pakistán	Pakistan
Panamá	Panama
Papua Nueva Guinea	Papua New Guinea
Paraguay	Paraguay
Países Bajos	Netherlands
Perú	Peru
Polonia	Poland
Portugal	Portugal
Qatar	Qatar
Reino Unido	United Kingdom
República Arabe Siria	Syrian Arab Republic
República Centroafricana	Central African Republic
República Checa	Czech Republic
República Democrática Popular Lao	Lao People's Democratic Republic
República Dominicana	Dominican Republic
República Popular Democrática de Corea	Korea, Democratic People's Republic of
República Unida de Tanzanía	Tanzania, United Republic of
República de Corea	Korea, Republic of
República de Moldova	Moldova
Republic of Reunión (Francia)e	Réunion (France)
Rumania	Romania
Rwanda	Rwanda
Samoa Americana (Estados Unidos)	American Samoa (United States)

Samoa Occidental	Western Samoa
Santa Helena	Saint Helena
Santa Kitts y Nevis	Saint Kitts and Nevis
San Marino	San Marino
Santa Helena (Reino Unido)	Saint Helena (United Kingdom)
San Vicente y las Granadinas	Saint Vincent and the Grenadines
Santa Lucía	Saint Lucia
Santa Sede	Vatican City State (Holy See)
Santa Tomé y Príncipe	Sao Tome and Principe
Senegal	Senegal
Seychelles	Seychelles
Sierra Leona	Sierra Leone
Singapur	Singapore
Somalia	Somalia
Sri Lanka	Sri Lanka
Sudáfrica	South Africa
Sudán	Sudan
Suecia	Sweden
Suiza	Switzerland
Suriname	Suriname
Swazilandia	Swaziland
Tailandia	Thailand
Tayikistán	Tajikistan
Territorios Franceses del Sur (Francia)	French Southern Territories (France)
Togo	Togo
Tokelau (Nueva Zelandia)	Tokelau (New Zealand)
Tonga	Tonga
Trinidad y Tobago	Trinidad and Tobago
Túnez	Tunisia
Turkmenistán	Turkmenistan
Turquía	Turkey
Tuvalu	Tuvalu
Ucrania	Ukraine
Uganda	Uganda
Uruguay	Uruguay
Uzbekistán	Uzbekistan
Vanuatu	Vanuatu
Venezuela	Venezuela
Viet Nam	Viet Nam
Yemen	Yemen
Yugoslavia	Yugoslavia
Zaire	Zaire
Zambia	Zambia
Zimbabwe	Zimbabwe

1993 United Nations List of National Parks and Protected Areas

Liste des Nations Unies des Parcs nationaux et des Aires protégées 1993

Lista de las Naciones Unidas de Parques Nacionales y Areas Protegidas 1993

1993 United Nations List of National Parks and Protected Areas

Liste des Nations Unies des Parcs nationaux et des Aires protégées 1993

Lista de las Naciones Unidas de Parques Nacionales y Areas Protegidas 1993

Legal Designation /Désignation juridique/ Designación Legal Name of Area/Nom de l'aire/ Nombre de Unidad	IUCN Category Catégorie UICN Categoría de la UICN	Latitude/longitude Latitude/longitude Latitud/longitud	Area (ha) Superficie (ha) Superficie(ha)	Year Année Año

AFGHANISTAN/AFGANISTAN

	Summary		
Category I	0	0	
Category II	1	41,000	
Category III	0	0	
Category IV	5	177,438	
Category V	0	0	
Total	**6**	**218,438**	

National Park

Band-e Amir	II	34°50'N/67°13'E	41,000	1973

Waterfowl Sanctuary

Ab-i-Estada	IV	32°30'N/67°50'E	27,000	1977
Dashte-Nawar	IV	33°50'N/67°45'E	7,500	1977
Hamun-i-Puzak	IV	31°30'N/61°45'E	35,000	1973

Wildlife Reserve

Ajar Valley	IV	36°40'N/67°37'E	40,000	1978
Pamir-i-Buzurg	IV	37°10'N/73°00'E	67,938	1978

ALBANIA/ALBANIE

	Summary		
Category I	0	0	
Category II	6	9,600	
Category III	0	0	
Category IV	5	24,400	
Category V	0	0	
Total	**11**	**34,000**	

National Park

Bredhi Drenoves	II	40°34'N/20°50'E	1,400	1966
Dajti	II	41°21'N/19°55'E	2,100	1966
Divjaka	II	41°00'N/19°29'E	1,200	1966

Llogaraja	II	40°13'N/19°35'E	1,000	1966
Lura	II	41°46'N/20°12'E	1,300	1966
Thethi	II	42°25'N/19°46'E	2,600	1966

Nature Reserve

Canganj	IV	40°41'N/20°54'E	2,800	1969
Fushe-Kuqe Negel-Patok	IV	41°38'N/19°36'E	1,200	1962
Karaburun-Llogara	IV	40°19'N/19°25'E	17,000	1968
Kune-Vain	IV	41°45'N/19°36'E	2,100	1969
Kuturman	IV	41°12'N/20°15'E	1,300	1977

ALGERIA/ALGERIE/ARGELIA

	Summary	
Category I	4	36,800
Category II	8	11,764,543
Category III	0	0
Category IV	6	41,507
Category V	1	76,438
Total	**19**	**11,919,288**

Hunting Reserve

Djelfa	IV	34°40'N/3°15'E	20,000	1974
Lac Tonga	IV	36°53'N/8°31'E	2,392	1983
Mascara	IV	35°31'N/0°11'W	6,000	1985
Moulay Ismail	IV	?/?	1,000	?
Tlemcen	IV	34°52'N/1°15'E	10,000	1983

National Park

Ahaggar	II	23°00'N/5°00'E	4,500,000	1987
Belezma	II	35°34'N/6°16'E	11,250	1985
Chrea	II	36°21'N/2°45'E	26,587	1983
Djurdjura	II	36°26'N/4°06'E	18,500	1983
El Kala	V	36°54'N/8°27'E	76,438	1983
Gouraya	II	36°47'N/5°06'E	2,086	1983
Tassili N'Ajjer	II	24°55'N/8°40'E	7,200,000	1972
Taza	II	36°36'N/5°30'E	3,720	1985
Theniet el Had	II	35°40'N/1°50'E	2,400	1983

National Reserve

Akfadou	IV	36°41'N/4°27'E	2,115	?
Babor	I	36°30'N/5°30'E	2,300	1985
Beni-Salah	I	36°30'N/7°45'E	2,000	1985
La Macta	I	35°45'N/0°05'W	20,000	1985
Mergueb	I	35°26'N/4°20'E	12,500	1985

ANDORRA/ANDORRE

No Areas Listed

ANGOLA

	Summary	
Category I	0	0
Category II	1	790,000
Category III	0	0
Category IV	3	891,200
Category V	2	960,000
Total	**6**	**2,641,200**

Integral Nature Reserve

| Ilheu dos Passaros | IV | 8°56'S/13°08'E | 200 | 1973 |
| Luando | IV | 11°05'S/17°20'E | 828,000 | 1955 |

National Park

Bikuar	II	15°16'S/14°47'E	790,000	1964
Kangandala	IV	9°50'S/16°43'E	63,000	1970
Kisama	V	9°46'S/13°38'E	950,000	1957

Regional Nature Park

Chimalavera	V	13°28'S/12°29'E	10,000	1974

ANTARCTIC TREATY TERRITORY/ TERRITOIRE DU TRAITE DE L'ANTARCTIQUE/ TERRITORIO DEL TRATADO DE ANTARTIDA

Summary		
Category I	19	242,535
Category II	0	0
Category III	0	0
Category IV	0	0
Category V	0	0
Total	**19**	**242,535**

Site of Special Scientific Interest

Ablation Point - Ganymede Heights, Alexander Is.	I	70°49'S/68°25'W	18,000	1990
Ardley Island	I	62°13'S/58°54'W	300	?
Barwick Valley	I	77°19'S/161°00'E	29,120	1975
Byers Peninsula	I	62°38'S/61°05'W	6,000	1975
Cierva Point	I	64°10'S/60°57'W	850	1985
East Dallman Bay	I	64°00'S/62°50'W	60,000	1991
Harmony Point	I	62°18'S/59°14'W	1,300	1985
Marine Plain, Mule Peninsula	I	68°38'S/78°08'E	2,340	1987
North-west White Island	I	78°10'S/167°25'E	1,350	1985
Western Bransfield Strait	I	63°20'S/61°45'W	103,000	1991
Western Shore, Admiralty Bay	I	62°12'S/58°28'W	12,000	1979

Specially Protected Area

Ardery and Odbert Island	I	66°22'S/110°31'E	220	1966
Beaufort Island	I	76°58'S/167°03'E	1,865	1966
Dion Islands	I	67°52'S/68°43'W	100	1966
Lagotellerie Island	I	67°53'S/67°24'W	130	1985
Litchfield Island	I	66°16'S/64°06'W	250	1975
Moe Island	I	60°45'S/45°41'W	100	1966
North Coronation Island	I	60°34'S/45°35'W	5,000	1985
Southern Powell & adjacent islands	I	60°45'S/45°02'W	610	1966

ANTIGUA AND BARBUDA/ANTIGUA-ET-BARBUDA/ANTIGUA Y BARBUDA

Summary		
Category I	0	0
Category II	2	6,128
Category III	0	0
Category IV	0	0
Category V	0	0
Total	**2**	**6,128**

Marine National Park

Salt Fish Tail Reef (Diamond Reef)	II	17°11'N/61°51'W	2,000	1973

National Park

Nelson's Dockyard	II	17°00'N/61°46'W	4,128	1984

ARGENTINA/ARGENTINE

Summary		
Category I	32	1,330,184
Category II	32	1,675,539
Category III	2	19,500
Category IV	18	1,327,691
Category V	2	20,140
Total	**86**	**4,373,054**

Biosphere Reserve				
San Guillermo	IV	29°02'S/69°24'W	860,000	1972
Ecological Reserve				
Ñacuñan	I	34°02'S/67°52'W	12,880	1961
Faunal Nature Reserve				
Laguna la Felipa	IV	33°10'S/63°43'W	1,307	1986
Faunal Reserve				
Laguna de Llancanelo	I	35°36'S/69°06'W	40,000	1980
Flora and Fauna Reserve				
Telteca	IV	32°21'S/68°10'W	20,400	1986
Fundación Elsa Shaw de Pearson Reserve				
El Destino	I	35°01'S/57°38'W	1,500	?
Integral Nature Reserve				
Bahía San Blas - Isla Gama	I	40°26'S/62°11'W	7,386	1987
Integral Nature Reserve with Restricted Access				
Isla Botija	I	33°58'S/58°45'W	730	1958
Rincón de Ajo	IV	36°19'S/56°58'W	2,311	1988
Managed Nature Reserve				
Potrero 7-B	IV	29°19'S/60°15'W	2,010	1992
National Monument				
Bosques Petrificados	III	47°39'S/68°13'W	3,500	1954
National Park				
Baritú	II	22°37'S/64°37'W	14,279	1974
Calilegua	II	23°41'S/64°46'W	24,000	1980
Chaco	II	26°55'S/59°46'W	7,100	1954
El Palmar	II	31°54'S/58°15'W	4,627	1966
El Rey	II	24°43'S/64°37'W	14,279	1948
Iguazú	II	25°39'S/54°23'W	5,200	1934
La Azotea (Predelta)	II	32°08'S/60°36'W	2,458	1991
Lago Puelo	II	42°11'S/71°42'W	11,700	1971
Laguna Blanca	II	39°00'S/70°25'W	6,672	1940
Lanín	II	39°56'S/71°28'W	142,600	1937
Lihué Calel	II	37°57'S/65°39'W	4,850	1977
Los Alerces	II	42°55'S/71°52'W	45,466	1937
Los Arrayanes	II	40°56'S/71°37'W	1,840	1974
Los Glaciares	II	49°58'S/73°08'W	161,790	1937
Nahuel Huapi	II	41°03'S/71°35'W	372,130	1934
Perito Moreno	II	47°48'S/72°14'W	6,700	1937
Río Pilcomayo	II	25°02'S/58°12'W	28,000	1951
Sierra de Las Quijadas	II	32°29'S/67°02'W	150,000	1991
Tierra del Fuego	II	54°30'S/68°30'W	34,500	1960
Natural Forest Reserve				
Chancani	IV	31°23'S/65°27'W	3,884	1986

Natural Water Reserve				
La Quebrada	IV	31°04'S/64°19'W	4,200	1987
Nature Monument				
Laguna de los Pozuelos	III	22°28'S/66°02'W	16,000	1979
Nature Park				
La Florida	V	27°09'S/65°51'W	9,892	1936
Nature Reserve				
Pichi Mahuida	IV	38°46'S/64°36'W	4,119	1974
Private Reserve				
Cañadón del Duraznillo	IV	?/?	1,740	1990
El Bagual	I	?/?	3,000	1986
El Bagual	IV	?/?	3,000	1986
Private Wildlife Refuge				
Aguaray-Mi	I	26°01'S/54°22'W	4,050	1988
Bouvier	I	25°27'S/57°35'W	5,000	1990
Dicky	IV	53°19'S/68°23'W	1,900	1991
Provincial Faunal Reserve				
Complejo Islote Lobos	IV	41°39'S/64°55'W	800	1977
Provincial Nature Park				
Chancani	II	31°20'S/65°27'W	1,035	1986
Provincial Nature Reserve				
Ischigualasto	II	30°05'S/67°54'W	62,916	1971
Provincial Park				
Aconcagua	II	32°26'S/70°01'W	70,000	1983
Copahue	II	37°54'S/71°00'W	28,300	1962
El Tromen	II	36°58'S/69°59'W	24,000	1971
Ernesto Tornquist	II	38°03'S/62°02'W	6,090	1958
Fuerte Esperanza	I	25°07'S/61°51'W	11,619	?
Guasamayo	II	30°33'S/66°33'W	9,000	1963
Pampa del Indio	II	26°13'S/60°00'W	8,633	1957
Potrero de Yala	II	24°04'S/65°27'W	4,200	1952
Talampaya	II	29°46'S/67°54'W	215,000	1975
Urugua-I	II	25°58'S/54°06'W	84,000	1988
Volcán Tupungato	II	33°21'S/69°43'W	110,000	1985
Provincial Park and Forest Reserve				
Pereyra Iraola	V	34°51'S/58°13'W	10,248	1949
Provincial Reserve				
Cabo Vírgenes	IV	52°20'S/68°21'W	1,230	1986
Strict Nature Reserve				
Baritú	I	22°37'S/64°37'W	54,000	1974
Bosques Petrificados	I	47°52'S/68°00'W	6,500	1954
Calilegua	I	23°41'S/64°46'W	52,000	1980
Chaco	I	26°40'S/59°48'W	7,900	1954
El Palmar	I	31°54'S/58°15'W	3,873	1966
El Rey	I	24°38'S/64°37'W	29,883	1948
Iguazú	I	25°39'S/54°23'W	44,000	1934
Lago Puelo	I	42°11'S/71°42'W	12,000	1971
Laguna Blanca	I	39°00'S/70°25'W	1,541	1940
Lanín	I	39°56'S/71°28'W	60,500	1937
Lihué Calel	I	37°57'S/65°33'W	5,050	1977
Los Alerces	I	42°55'S/71°52'W	147,678	1937
Los Glaciares	I	49°58'S/73°08'W	377,510	1937

Nahuel Huapi	I	41°03'S/71°35'W	103,500	1934
Otamendi	I	34°12'S/58°55'W	2,632	1990
Perito Moreno	I	47°48'S/72°14'W	78,800	1937
Río Pilcomayo	I	25°02'S/58°12'W	19,000	1951
Tierra del Fuego	I	54°30'S/68°30'W	28,500	1960

Total Provincial Reserve

El Payén	I	36°30'S/69°13'W	192,996	1982

Touristic Nature Reserve

Punta Delgada	IV	42°46'S/63°38'W	2,829	1969
Punta León	I	43°04'S/64°29'W	1,000	1985
Punta Loma	IV	42°49'S/64°53'W	1,707	1967

University Park

Sierra de San Javier	II	26°43'S/65°22'W	14,174	1973

Vicuña Reserve

Laguna Brava	IV	28°20'S/69°04'W	405,000	1980

Wildlife Refuge

Las Dos Hermanas	IV	33°01'S/62°04'W	1,055	1989
Monte de las Barrancas	I	30°01'S/64°54'W	7,656	1988
San Juan Poriahu	IV	27°45'S/57°16'W	10,199	1989
San Juan Poriahu	I	27°45'S/57°16'W	4,000	1989

Wildlife Reserve

Campos del Tuyú	I	36°19'S/56°49'W	3,500	1978

ARMENIA/ARMENIE

Summary		
Category I	3	63,900
Category II	1	150,000
Category III	0	0
Category IV	0	0
Category V	0	0
Total	**4**	**213,900**

National Park

Sevan	II	40°20'N/45°25'E	150,000	1978

Zapovednik

Dilizhanskiy	I	39°17'N/45°02'E	24,200	1958
Khosrovskiy	I	40°03'N/44°49'E	29,700	1958
Shikaokhskiy	I	32°58'N/46°26'E	10,000	1975

AUSTRALIA/AUSTRALIE

Summary		
Category I	80	3,816,022
Category II	415	27,849,176
Category III	71	262,416
Category IV	294	13,344,479
Category V	32	48,273,364
Total	**892**	**93,545,457**

Commonwealth

Marine National Nature Reserve

Ashmore Reef	I	12°15'S/123°05'E	58,412	1983
Coringa-Herald	I	16°58'S/149°55'E	885,724	1982
Elizabeth and Middleton Reefs	I	29°42'S/159°02'E	188,000	1987

Lihou Reef	I	17°25'S/151°44'E	843,691	1982
Mermaid Reef	I	17°07'S/119°37'E	53,984	1991

Marine Park

Great Barrier Reef	V	17°30'S/147°00'E	34,380,000	1979
Ningaloo	V	22°37'S/113°32'E	194,257	1987

National Park

Christmas Island	II	10°35'S/105°29'E	8,952	1980
Kakadu	II	12°09'S/132°32'E	2,027,710	1979
Uluru (Ayers Rock-Mount Olga)	II	25°20'S/131°00'E	132,566	1977

Nature Reserve

Jervis Bay	II	35°09'S/150°40'E	4,139	1971

Other area

Territory of Heard Island and MacDonald Island	I	53°00'S/74°00'E	1,138,260	1987

Australian Capital Territory

Reserved Area

Bullen Nature Reserve	II	35°23'S/148°59'E	3,570	1991
Gigerline Nature Reserve	II	35°23'S/149°06'E	1,550	1991
Lanyon Landscape Conservation Reserve	V	35°30'S/149°03'E	1,300	1985
Namadgi National Park	II	35°40'S/148°57'E	105,000	1984
Tidbinbilla Nature Reserve	II	35°29'S/148°54'E	5,450	1991

Cocos (Keeling) Islands

No Areas Listed

New South Wales

Aboriginal Area

Pindera Downs	V	?/?	11,433	1986

Flora Reserve

Gilgai	II	30°30'S/149°20'E	2,400	1980
Moira Lakes	IV	35°56'S/144°56'E	1,435	1986
Nunnock Swamp	I	37°43'S/149°26'E	1,820	1985
Scrubby Mountain	IV	32°14'S/146°20'E	1,718	1992
The Castles	II	30°59'S/152°19'E	2,360	1988
Toolum Scrub	IV	28°28'S/152°27'E	1,665	1937
Waihou	IV	30°03'S/153°01'E	1,800	1985

Historic Site

Mount Grenfell	V	31°18'S/145°18'E	1,357	1979

Marine Reserve

Solitary Islands	IV	30°00'S/153°19'E	95,000	1991

National Park

Bald Rock	II	28°51'S/152°03'E	5,451	1971
Barrington Tops	II	32°03'S/151°30'E	39,121	1969
Ben Boyd	II	37°10'S/149°00'E	9,455	1971
Blue Mountains	II	33°37'S/150°25'E	247,021	1959
Boonoo Boonoo	II	28°50'S/152°10'E	2,692	1982
Booti Booti	II	32°17'S/152°31'E	1,488	1992
Border Ranges	II	28°20'S/153°05'E	31,508	1979
Bouddi	II	33°30'S/151°25'E	1,167	1935
Bournda	II	36°48'S/149°52'E	2,344	1992
Brisbane Water	II	33°27'S/151°18'E	11,372	1959
Broadwater	II	29°04'S/153°25'E	3,737	1974
Budawang	II	35°30'S/149°00'E	16,102	1977
Budderoo	II	34°39'S/150°42'E	5,746	1986
Bundjalung	II	29°20'S/153°20'E	17,679	1980

Cathedral Rock	II	30°25'S/152°15'E	6,529	1978
Cocoparra	II	34°08'S/146°14'E	8,358	1969
Conimbla	II	33°46'S/148°28'E	7,590	1980
Crowdy Bay	II	31°50'S/152°40'E	8,005	1972
Deua	II	35°55'S/149°45'E	81,763	1979
Dharug	II	33°22'S/151°05'E	14,834	1967
Dorrigo	II	30°23'S/152°45'E	7,885	1927
Garigal	II	33°42'S/151°15'E	1,978	1991
Gibraltar Range	II	29°30'S/152°17'E	17,273	1963
Goulburn River	II	32°15'S/149°00'E	69,312	1983
Guy Fawkes River	II	30°02'S/152°18'E	35,630	1970
Hat Head	II	31°04'S/153°01'E	6,445	1972
Heathcote	II	34°06'S/150°58'E	2,251	1963
Kanangra-Boyd	II	33°00'S/150°05'E	68,276	1969
Kingchega	II	32°30'S/142°20'E	44,182	1967
Kings Plains	II	26°34'S/151°20'E	3,713	1988
Kosciusko	II	35°00'S/148°20'E	646,911	1944
Ku-Ring-Gai Chase	II	33°37'S/151°12'E	14,797	1894
Macquarie Pass	II	34°34'S/150°39'E	1,064	1969
Mallee Cliffs	II	34°12'S/142°28'E	57,969	1977
Marramarra	II	33°32'S/151°04'E	11,759	1979
Mimosa Rocks	II	36°35'S/150°04'E	5,179	1973
Mootwingee	II	31°10'S/142°30'E	68,912	1967
Morton	II	34°14'S/150°12'E	162,386	1938
Mount Imlay	II	37°10'S/149°45'E	3,808	1972
Mount Kaputar	II	30°16'S/150°10'E	36,817	1925
Mount Warning	II	28°24'S/153°16'E	2,380	1966
Mungo	II	33°44'S/143°02'E	27,847	1979
Murramarang	II	35°38'S/150°19'E	1,609	1973
Myall Lakes	II	32°26'S/152°22'E	31,501	1972
Nalbaugh	II	37°05'S/149°25'E	4,106	1972
Nangar	II	34°10'S/150°25'E	3,492	1982
New England	II	30°30'S/152°30'E	29,985	1935
Nightcap	II	28°33'S/153°20'E	4,945	1983
Nungatta	II	37°13'S/149°22'E	6,100	1973
Nymboida	II	29°41'S/152°33'E	18,998	1980
Oxley Wild Rivers	II	31°06'S/151°54'E	90,216	1986
Royal	II	34°08'S/151°03'E	15,069	1879
Sturt	II	29°13'S/141°58'E	310,634	1972
Tarlo River	II	34°13'S/150°33'E	6,759	1982
Wadbilliga	II	36°30'S/149°45'E	77,465	1982
Wallaga Lake	II	36°23'S/149°00'E	1,237	1972
Warrabah	II	30°32'S/150°56'E	3,471	1984
Warrumbungle	II	31°14'S/149°01'E	20,914	1953
Washpool	II	29°22'S/152°20'E	27,715	1983
Weddin Mountains	II	33°00'S/147°00'E	8,361	1971
Werrikimbe	II	31°12'S/152°13'E	35,178	1975
Willandra	II	33°30'S/145°30'E	19,386	1972
Woko	II	31°45'S/151°45'E	8,285	1982
Yengo	II	32°00'S/150°55'E	139,861	1988
Yuraygir	II	29°54'S/153°15'E	18,285	1975

Nature Reserve

Avisford	I	32°39'S/149°31'E	2,437	1985
Banyabba	I	29°25'S/152°56'E	12,560	1969
Barren Grounds	I	34°41'S/150°43'E	2,024	1956
Bimberi	I	35°35'S/148°45'E	7,100	1985
Binnaway	I	31°30'S/149°29'E	3,699	1976
Burrinjuck	I	35°58'S/148°36'E	1,300	1984
Camerons Gorge	I	31°54'S/150°59'E	1,280	1987
Cocoparra	I	34°01'S/146°11'E	4,647	1969
Coolbaggie	I	31°59'S/148°41'E	1,793	1963

Copperhannia	I	33°51'S/149°13'E	3,494	1972
Coturaundee	I	30°57'S/142°40'E	6,688	1979
Curumbenya	I	33°02'S/148°25'E	9,380	1964
Dananbilla	I	34°12'S/148°30'E	1,855	1983
Egan Peakes	I	37°01'S/149°41'E	2,145	1972
Georges Creek	I	30°42'S/152°12'E	1,190	1967
Guy Fawkes River	I	30°21'S/152°16'E	1,534	1970
Ingalba	I	34°30'S/147°23'E	4,012	1970
Ironbark	I	30°20'S/149°54'E	1,604	1985
Kajuligah	I	32°41'S/144°40'E	13,660	1979
Kemendok	I	34°32'S/142°24'E	1,043	1988
Kooragang	I	32°52'S/151°47'E	2,926	1983
Lake Innes	I	31°30'S/152°51'E	3,509	1984
Limeburners Creek	I	31°23'S/152°53'E	9,083	1971
Limpinwood	I	28°19'S/153°10'E	2,647	1963
Macquarie Marshes	I	31°26'S/152°55'E	18,013	1971
Mann River	I	29°45'S/152°03'E	5,640	1985
Manobalai	I	32°13'S/150°36'E	3,733	1967
Mount Hyland	I	30°10'S/152°26'E	1,636	1984
Mount Neville	I	29°11'S/152°48'E	2,666	1987
Mount Seaview	I	31°23'S/152°12'E	1,704	1965
Mundoonen	I	34°50'S/149°03'E	1,374	1970
Munghorn Gap	I	32°25'S/149°47'E	5,935	1961
Muogamarra	I	33°35'S/151°11'E	2,274	1954
Nadgee	I	37°19'S/149°56'E	17,116	1957
Narran Lake	I	29°45'S/147°25'E	4,527	1988
Nearie Lake	I	33°25'S/141°52'E	4,347	1973
Nocoleche	I	29°55'S/144°10'E	74,000	1979
Nombinnie	I	32°00'S/145°00'E	70,000	1988
Pantoneys Crown	I	33°09'S/150°04'E	3,230	1977
Pilliga	I	30°54'S/149°30'E	71,510	1968
Razorback	I	34°06'S/149°16'E	2,595	1988
Round Hill	I	33°03'S/146°12'E	13,630	1960
Scabby Range	I	35°46'S/148°52'E	3,449	1982
Severn River	I	29°25'S/151°21'E	1,947	1968
Sherwood	I	29°59'S/153°01'E	2,444	1966
The Basin	I	30°10'S/151°16'E	2,318	1964
Tinderry	I	35°42'S/149°16'E	11,559	1981
Tollingo	I	32°42'S/146°48'E	3,232	1988
Ulandra	I	34°50'S/147°56'E	3,931	1981
Wallabadah	I	31°37'S/150°59'E	1,132	1973
Watsons Creek	I	30°48'S/151°02'E	1,260	1980
Winburndale	I	33°18'S/149°46'E	9,396	1967
Wingen Maid	I	31°53'S/150°50'E	1,077	1974
Woggoon	I	32°49'S/146°56'E	6,565	1974
Yanga	I	34°41'S/143°48'E	1,773	1972
Yathong	I	32°36'S/145°24'E	107,241	1971

Permanent Park Preserve

Lord Howe Island	II	31°35'S/159°10'E	1,175	1982

State Recreation Area

Bungonia	II	34°50'S/150°01'E	3,836	1974
Illawarra Escarpment	II	34°26'S/150°48'E	1,266	1980
Munmorah	II	33°11'S/151°09'E	1,220	1977
Parr	II	33°20'S/150°45'E	38,000	1988
Yerranderie	II	34°07'S/150°17'E	12,192	1991

Northern Territory

Aboriginal land managed as National Parks

Barranyi (North Island)	II	15°35'S/136°52'E	5,421	1991
Gurig	II	11°22'S/132°15'E	220,700	1981
Nitmiluk (Katherine Gorge)	II	14°08'S/132°31'E	100,002	1989

Conservation Reserve

Cape Hotham	IV	12°15'S/131°19'E	12,900	1978
Connells Lagoon	IV	18°47'S/136°33'E	25,890	1984
Devils Marbles	III	20°34'S/134°18'E	1,802	1961
Fogg Dam	IV	12°35'S/131°18'E	1,569	1982
Mac Clark (Acacia peuce)	IV	25°06'S/135°31'E	3,042	1982
Rainbow Valley	IV	24°20'S/133°33'E	2,483	1990
Tnorla (Gosse Bluff)	IV	23°51'S/132°19'E	4,759	1969

Historical Reserve

Alice Springs Telegraph Station	V	23°41'S/133°53'E	2,004	1963
Arltunga	V	23°27'S/134°43'E	5,498	1978
Tennant Creek Telegraph Station	V	19°36'S/133°16'E	1,797	1986

Management Agreement Area

Junction Reserve	IV	18°00'S/133°54'E	19,930	?

Marine Park

Cobourg	II	11°22'S/132°15'E	229,000	1983

National Park

Elsey	II	14°58'S/133°11'E	13,840	1990
Finke Gorge	II	24°10'S/132°49'E	45,843	1967
Gregory	II	16°22'S/130°28'E	978,100	1990
Katherine Gorge (CLC)	II	14°06'S/132°28'E	80,350	1963
Keep River	II	15°48'S/129°10'E	56,889	1981
Litchfield	II	13°17'S/130°53'E	146,118	1986
Watarrka (Kings Canyon)	II	24°16'S/131°40'E	71,720	1989
West MacDonnell	II	23°38'S/131°41'E	205,756	1992

Nature Park

Cutta Cutta Caves	V	14°34'S/132°27'E	1,499	1979
Douglas Hot Springs	V	13°46'S/131°27'E	3,107	1969
Howard Springs	V	12°27'S/131°03'E	1,009	1957
Ruby Gap	V	23°29'S/135°01'E	9,257	1984
Trephina Gorge	V	23°31'S/134°23'E	1,771	1966

Queensland

Environmental Park

Goneaway	II	23°48'S/142°12'E	24,800	1974
Lake Broadwater	II	27°21'S/151°06'E	1,220	1981
Mount Archer	II	23°20'S/150°30'E	2,270	1987
Mount Zamia	II	24°06'S/148°03'E	1,140	1978
Townsville Town Common	IV	19°12'S/146°45'E	2,920	1980
Wilandspey	II	21°44'S/146°32'E	5,200	1977

Faunal Refuge

Taunton	IV	23°20'S/149°13'E	5,346	1980

Fish Habitat Reserve

Admiralty Island	IV	16°59'S/145°47'E	1,900	1989
Beelbi	IV	25°14'S/152°39'E	1,250	1986
Bowling Green Bay	IV	19°20'S/147°15'E	68,600	1989
Broad Sound	IV	22°20'S/149°50'E	165,000	1986
Burrum-Iris	IV	25°15'S/152°33'E	2,200	1986
Bustard	IV	24°04'S/151°44'E	4,550	1983
Cape Palmerston	IV	21°32'S/149°25'E	12,000	1986
Colosseum	IV	24°02'S/151°27'E	5,370	1983
Corio Bay	IV	22°57'S/150°45'E	4,090	1983
Deception Bay	IV	27°10'S/153°02'E	1,500	1983
Eight-Mile Creek	IV	16°47'S/138°30'E	5,690	1990
Escape River	IV	10°56'S/142°36'E	25,800	1983

Hays Inlet	IV	27°16'S/153°3'E	1,250	1983
Hinchinbrook	IV	18°20'S/146°10'E	13,200	1983
Innes	IV	24°04'S/151°33'E	4,650	1983
Jumpinpin-Broadwater	IV	27°49'S/153°24'E	6,671	1983
Kauri Creek	IV	25°49'S/153°01'E	6,500	1983
Maaroom	IV	25°32'S/152°56'E	23,000	1983
Moreton Banks	IV	27°20'S/153°24'E	4,460	1983
Morning Inlet-Bynoe River	IV	17°38'S/140°28'E	18,336	1990
Myora Extension	IV	27°26'S/153°23'E	6,470	1992
Nassau River	IV	15°56'S/141°23'E	4,970	1990
Noosa River	IV	26°18'S/153°00'E	2,300	1983
Peel Island	IV	27°30'S/153°21'E	1,180	1983
Princess Charlotte Bay	IV	14°24'S/143°47'E	20,035	1983
Pumicestone Passage	IV	26°57'S/153°04'E	2,670	1983
Repulse	IV	20°40'S/148°50'E	71,000	1986
Repulse Bay	IV	20°18'S/148°33'E	4,000	1983
Rodds Harbour	IV	24°03'S/151°39'E	6,830	1983
Sand Bay	IV	20°58'S/149°03'E	11,500	1986
Silver Plains	IV	13°42'S/143°32'E	7,900	1983
Staaten-Gilbert	IV	16°29'S/141°18'E	10,175	1990
Susan River	IV	25°25'S/152°53'E	4,900	1986
Temple Bay	IV	12°16'S/143°05'E	4,300	1983
Tin Can Inlet	IV	25°56'S/153°02'E	1,110	1983
West Hill	IV	21°50'S/149°27'E	5,500	1986
Weyba	IV	26°25'S/153°04'E	1,250	1983

Marine Park

Cairns	V	16°30'S/145°30'E	429,000	1989
Hervey Bay	V	24°55'S/153°00'E	255,000	1989
Mackay-Capricorn	V	22°00'S/150°30'E	2,598,000	1988
Pumicestone Passage	V	26°58'S/153°07'E	630,000	1986
Townsville-Whitsunday	V	19°20'S/147°15'E	520,500	1987
Woongarra	V	24°50'S/157°27'E	12,000	1991

National Park

Archer Bend	II	13°43'S/141°59'E	166,000	1977
Barron Gorge	II	16°52'S/145°39'E	2,784	1940
Blackdown Tableland	II	23°43'S/149°05'E	23,800	1980
Blackwood	II	21°28'S/146°43'E	1,648	1991
Bladensburg	II	22°31'S/143°05'E	33,700	1984
Bowling Green Bay	II	19°28'S/147°14'E	55,400	1977
Bulleringa	II	17°40'S/144°00'E	54,400	1992
Bunya Mountains	II	26°50'S/151°33'E	11,700	1908
Burrum River	II	25°13'S/152°35'E	2,010	1960
Byfield	II	22°53'S/150°46'E	8,450	1988
Camooweal Caves	II	20°20'S/138°20'E	13,800	1988
Cania Gorge	II	24°43'S/150°59'E	3,000	1977
Cape Melville	II	14°34'S/144°40'E	36,000	1973
Cape Palmerston	II	21°36'S/149°25'E	7,160	1976
Cape Tribulation	II	16°17'S/145°27'E	16,965	1964
Cape Upstart	II	19°44'S/147°48'E	5,640	1969
Carnarvon	II	24°59'S/148°00'E	251,000	1932
Castle Tower	II	24°12'S/151°22'E	4,980	1961
Cedar Bay	II	15°48'S/145°20'E	5,650	1977
Chesterton Range	II	26°12'S/147°24'E	16,100	1992
Conondale	II	26°42'S/152°39'E	1,740	1977
Conway	II	20°22'S/148°51'E	23,800	1938
Cooloola	II	26°05'S/153°00'E	54,700	1975
Currawinya	II	28°45'S/144°30'E	148,000	1991
Curtis Island	II	23°32'S/151°14'E	1,550	1992
Deepwater	II	24°19'S/151°56'E	4,090	1988
Dipperu	II	21°56'S/148°43'E	11,100	1969
Dryander (Mainland Islands)	II	20°05'S/148°33'E	13,400	1938

Dunk Island	III	17°57'S/146°10'E	730	1937
Edmund Kennedy	II	18°09'S/145°59'E	6,200	1977
Ella Bay	II	17°25'S/146°03'E	3,430	1952
Endeavour River	II	15°27'S/145°13'E	1,840	1975
Epping Forest	I	22°21'S/146°42'E	3,160	1971
Eubenangee Swamp	II	17°25'S/145°58'E	1,550	1968
Eungella	II	20°55'S/148°33'E	50,800	1936
Eurimbula	II	24°14'S/151°37'E	7,830	1977
Flinders Group	II	14°10'S/144°15'E	2,960	1939
Forty Mile Scrub	II	18°05'S/144°52'E	6,180	1970
Girraween	II	28°51'S/151°58'E	11,399	1932
Graham Range	II	17°16'S/145°59'E	2,930	1980
Great Basalt Wall	II	19°50'S/145°30'E	30,500	1987
Great Sandy	II	24°59'S/153°17'E	74,900	1971
Hann Tableland	II	?/?	4,839	1989
Haslewood Island	II	20°17'S/149°05'E	1,210	1940
Hell Hole Gorge	II	25°30'S/144°22'E	12,700	1992
Hinchinbrook Channel	II	18°28'S/146°09'E	5,573	1968
Hinchinbrook Island	II	18°22'S/146°15'E	39,900	1932
Hook Island	II	20°06'S/148°55'E	5,180	1971
Hull River	II	17°57'S/146°01'E	1,470	1968
Idalia	II	25°00'S/144°45'E	144,000	1990
Iron Range	II	12°44'S/143°16'E	34,600	1977
Isla Gorge	II	25°09'S/149°55'E	7,830	1964
Jardine River	II	11°15'S/142°37'E	237,000	1977
Kinkuna	II	25°02'S/152°28'E	13,300	1991
Kroombit Tops	II	24°23'S/151°02'E	2,360	1974
Lake Bindegolly	II	28°00'S/144°12'E	11,930	1991
Lake Nuga Nuga	II	24°58'S/148°40'E	2,550	1991
Lakefield	II	14°57'S/144°04'E	537,000	1979
Lamington	II	28°17'S/153°04'E	20,500	1915
Lawn Hill	II	18°45'S/138°27'E	262,000	1984
Lindeman and Little Lindeman Island	III	20°27'S/149°03'E	605	1941
Littabella	II	24°36'S/152°04'E	2,420	1980
Lizard Island	III	14°40'S/145°28'E	990	1939
Magnetic Island	II	19°08'S/146°50'E	2,790	1954
Maiala	II	27°19'S/152°46'E	1,140	1940
Main Range	II	28°16'S/152°32'E	11,500	1965
Mariala	II	26°00'S/145°00'E	27,300	1992
Mazeppa	II	22°14'S/147°18'E	4,130	1972
Minerva Hills	II	?/?	1,650	1992
Mitchell Alice Rivers	II	15°30'S/142°05'E	37,100	1977
Moreton Island	II	27°19'S/153°25'E	16,800	1966
Mount Aberdeen	II	20°00'S/147°55'E	1,667	1952
Mount Barney	II	28°14'S/152°38'E	11,900	1947
Mount Chinghee	III	28°18'S/152°56'E	1,110	1975
Mount Mandurana	III	21°04'S/149°01'E	1,830	1949
Mount Mistake	II	27°53'S/152°20'E	5,850	1967
Mount Spec/Crystal Creek	II	18°58'S/146°14'E	10,600	1952
Mount Walsh	II	25°36'S/152°03'E	5,170	1947
Narrien Range	II	22°54'S/146°58'E	4,020	1991
Noosa/Lake Weyba	II	26°23'S/153°07'E	1,580	1939
Orpheus Island	III	18°37'S/146°30'E	1,300	1960
Palmgrove	II	24°58'S/149°23'E	25,600	1991
Porcupine Gorge	II	20°26'S/144°27'E	4,100	1970
Possession Island	III	10°43'S/142°24'E	510	1977
Precipice (Nathan Gorge)	II	25°19'S/150°05'E	9,050	1989
Pumicestone	II	26°58'S/153°05'E	2,350	1988
Rodds Peninsula	II	24°02'S/151°41'E	4,150	1990
Rokeby	II	13°40'S/142°55'E	291,000	1981
Royal Arch Caves	II	17°12'S/144°30'E	1,514	1940
Rundle Range	II	23°39'S/150°59'E	2,170	1990
Scawfell	II	20°52'S/149°37'E	1,090	1938

Shaw Island	II	20°29'S/149°05'E	1,660	1936
Simpson Desert	II	25°36'S/138°16'E	1,012,000	1967
Snake Range	II	24°03'S/147°36'E	1,210	1972
South Island	II	21°45'S/150°20'E	1,620	1941
Southwood	II	27°50'S/150°07'E	7,120	1970
Staaten River	II	16°37'S/142°51'E	470,000	1977
Starcke	II	14°56'S/145°03'E	7,960	1977
Sundown	II	28°53'S/151°37'E	11,200	1977
Thistlebank	II	22°07'S/145°12'E	5,890	1991
Thrushton	II	27°44'S/141°40'E	25,652	1990
West Hill Island	III	21°50'S/149°29'E	398	1938
White Mountains	II	20°30'S/144°55'E	52,100	1990
Whitsunday Island	II	20°16'S/148°59'E	10,900	1944
Wild Duck Island	III	22°01'S/149°51'E	207	1980
Wondul Range	II	?/?	3,555	1992
Woodgate	II	25°09'S/152°35'E	5,490	1974
Woody and Little Woody Island	III	25°18'S/152°58'E	660	1960

Scientific Area

No 33 (Hurdle Gully Scrub)	I	24°54'S/151°00'E	1,674	1982
No 39 (North Bargoo Creek)	I	16°13'S/145°02'E	1,000	1986
No 40 (West Spencer Creek)	I	16°17'S/145°01'E	3,700	1986
No 46 (Platypus Creek)	I	16°28'S/145°15'E	1,200	1987

Scientific Purpose Reserve

Taunton	I	23°30'S/149°13'E	11,626	1979

Wetland Reserve

Bohle River	IV	19°12'S/146°42'E	1,130	1983
Bribie Island	IV	27°02'S/153°07'E	2,405	1983
Burrum-Toogoom	IV	25°15'S/152°40'E	2,300	1986
Carmilla	IV	21°56'S/149°28'E	1,750	1986
Cattle Creek	IV	18°52'S/146°15'E	1,900	1983
Fraser Island	IV	25°27'S/153°09'E	18,000	1983
Halifax	IV	18°34'S/146°19'E	3,290	1983
Kolan River	IV	24°41'S/152°51'E	1,400	1983
Marion	IV	21°45'S/149°26'E	2,100	1986
Midge	IV	20°44'S/148°47'E	8,000	1986
Rocky Dam	IV	21°30'S/149°18'E	3,300	1986
Trinity Inlet	IV	16°59'S/145°47'E	1,200	1989
Wild Cattle	IV	23°59'S/151°24'E	1,140	1983

South Australia

Aquatic Reserve

American River	IV	35°49'S/137°47'E	1,525	1971
Barker Inlet-St Kilda	IV	34°47'S/138°32'E	2,055	1973
Blanche Harbour-Douglas Bank	IV	32°45'S/137°48'E	3,160	1980
Seal Beach-Bales Bay	IV	36°01'S/137°17'E	1,140	1971
West Island	IV	35°37'S/138°35'E	150	1971
Whyalla-Cowleds Landing	IV	33°06'S/137°33'E	3,230	1980
Yatala Harbour	IV	32°45'S/137°55'E	1,426	1980

Conservation Park

Bakara	II	?/?	1,022	1986
Barwell	II	33°31'S/135°34'E	4,561	1988
Bascombe Well	II	33°40'S/135°29'E	32,200	1970
Big Heath	II	37°07'S/140°34'E	2,351	1964
Billiatt	II	35°01'S/140°24'E	59,148	1940
Brookfield	II	34°22'S/139°30'E	6,333	1978
Calpatanna Waterhole	II	33°00'S/134°21'E	3,630	1974
Cape Gantheaume	II	36°02'S/137°28'E	24,316	1971
Carcuma	II	35°38'S/140°05'E	2,881	1969
Clinton	II	34°08'S/138°06'E	2,129	1970

Cocata	II	33°18'S/135°12'E	6,876	1988
Danggali	II	33°24'S/140°45'E	253,660	1976
Deep Creek	II	35°38'S/138°15'E	4,184	1971
Dudley	II	35°49'S/137°52'E	1,122	1970
Elliot Price	II	28°44'S/137°19'E	64,570	1967
Fairview	II	36°50'S/140°25'E	1,398	1960
Franklin Harbor	II	33°45'S/136°56'E	1,334	1976
Gum Lagoon	II	36°17'S/140°01'E	6,589	1970
Hambidge	II	33°27'S/135°56'E	37,992	1941
Hincks	II	33°56'S/136°01'E	66,285	1941
Isles of St Francis	II	32°34'S/133°19'E	1,320	1967
Karte	II	35°07'S/140°43'E	3,565	1969
Kellidie Bay	II	34°37'S/135°31'E	1,780	1954
Kelly Hill	II	36°01'S/136°55'E	7,374	1971
Kulliparu	II	33°06'S/134°55'E	13,536	1985
Lake Gilles	II	32°58'S/136°45'E	45,114	1971
Lathami	II	?/?	1,190	1987
Little Dip	II	37°15'S/139°48'E	1,977	1975
Martin Washpool	II	36°10'S/139°43'E	1,883	1969
Messent	II	36°04'S/139°46'E	12,246	1964
Mount Boothby	II	35°51'S/139°47'E	4,045	1967
Mount Rescue	II	35°51'S/140°21'E	28,385	1953
Mount Scott	II	36°50'S/140°04'E	1,238	1972
Mount Shaugh	II	35°50'S/140°57'E	3,460	1971
Munyaroo	II	33°22'S/137°20'E	12,385	1977
Ngarkat	II	35°47'S/140°36'E	207,941	1979
Nuyts Archipelago	II	32°26'S/133°36'E	5,420	1967
Pandappa	II	33°12'S/139°08'E	1,057	1973
Peebinga	II	34°59'S/140°49'E	3,371	1940
Pinkawillinie	II	33°09'S/136°06'E	127,164	1970
Pooginook	II	34°07'S/140°06'E	2,852	1970
Pureba	II	?/?	144,470	1990
Scorpion Springs	II	35°31'S/140°54'E	30,366	1970
Simpson Desert	II	26°14'S/137°52'E	692,680	1967
Sir Joseph Banks Group	II	34°36'S/136°16'E	2,033	1967
Swan Reach	II	34°36'S/139°30'E	2,016	1970
Telowie Gorge	II	33°02'S/138°08'E	1,946	1970
The Dutchmans Stern	II	32°19'S/137°57'E	3,532	1987
Unnamed	II	28°26'S/129°29'E	2,132,600	1970
Venus Bay	II	33°13'S/134°37'E	1,460	1976
Verran Tanks	II	?/?	1,181	1983
Warrenben	II	35°08'S/137°03'E	4,061	1969
Western River	II	35°42'S/136°55'E	2,364	1971
Whyalla	II	32°57'S/137°32'E	1,011	1971
Winninowie	II	?/?	4,318	1990
Yeldalknie	II	33°39'S/136°34'E	3,273	1989
Yumbarra	II	31°42'S/133°26'E	327,589	1968

Game Reserve

Bool Lagoon	IV	37°07'S/140°42'E	2,690	1967
Coorong	IV	36°07'S/139°36'E	6,841	1968
Loch Luna	IV	?/?	1,905	1985
Moorook	IV	34°15'S/140°22'E	1,236	1976

National Park

Canunda	II	37°42'S/140°26'E	9,385	1959
Coffin Bay	II	34°36'S/135°20'E	30,380	1982
Coorong	II	36°01'S/139°32'E	39,904	1966
Flinders Chase	II	35°55'S/136°43'E	73,841	1919
Flinders Ranges	II	31°22'S/138°40'E	94,908	1945
Gammon Ranges	II	30°29'S/139°10'E	128,228	1970
Innes	II	35°12'S/136°50'E	9,141	1970
Lake Eyre	II	28°30'S/137°30'E	1,356,000	1985

Lincoln	II	34°57'S/136°01'E	29,060	1941
Mount Remarkable	II	32°50'S/138°10'E	8,649	1952
Murray River	II	34°24'S/140°32'E	13,287	1991
Nullarbor	II	31°28'S/130°31'E	593,000	1979
Witjira	II	26°20'S/135°25'E	776,900	1985

Native Forest Reserve

Mount Crawford Forest Reserve (n=5)	IV	?/?	2,184	?
Mount Gambier Forest Reserve (n=9)	IV	?/?	3,305	?
Mt Burr Forest Reserve (n=16)	IV	37°43'S/140°33'E	2,658	?
Murtho	IV	34°05'S/140°46'E	1,910	?

Recreation Park

Onkaparinga River	V	35°10'S/138°33'E	1,671	1985
Para Wirra	V	34°41'S/138°49'E	1,409	1962

Regional Reserve

Innamincka	V	27°30'S/140°30'E	1,381,995	1988
Nullarbor	V	?/?	2,280,000	1989
Simpson Desert	V	26°30'S/137°45'E	2,964,200	1988
Yellabinna	V	?/?	2,522,700	1990

Tasmania

Conservation Area

Adamsfield	IV	42°44'S/146°20'E	5,400	1990
Central Plateau	IV	41°50'S/146°30'E	89,200	1990
Derwent River Wildlife Sanctuary	IV	42°44'S/147°11'E	1,568	1941
Egg Islands	IV	43°04'S/147°01'E	128	1975
Logan Lagoon	IV	40°11'S/148°19'E	2,256	1968
South Port Lagoon Wildlife Sanctuary	IV	43°29'S/146°58'E	3,556	1976
Tamar River	IV	41°20'S/147°02'E	4,600	1978

Forest Reserve

Abel Tasman	II	43°06'S/147°57'E	3,700	1992
Liffey	II	41°42'S/146°44'E	1,055	1980
Meander	II	41°43'S/146°31'E	1,660	1980
Mt Maurice	II	41°18'S/147°34'E	3,700	1979
Mt Victoria	II	41°20'S/147°51'E	3,200	1983

Game Reserve

Bruny Island Neck	IV	43°15'S/147°24'E	1,450	1979
Farm Cove	IV	42°21'S/145°31'E	1,720	1990
Moulting Lagoon	IV	42°03'S/148°11'E	4,760	1988
New Year Island	IV	39°40'S/143°49'E	112	1981
North East Island	IV	39°47'S/147°49'E	2,405	1991

Historic Site

Macquarie Harbour	V	42°22'S/145°33'E	15,300	1990

National Park

Asbestos Range	II	41°08'S/146°39'E	4,349	1976
Ben Lomond	II	41°34'S/147°41'E	16,527	1947
Cradle Mountain-Lake St Clair	II	41°52'S/145°59'E	161,108	1922
Douglas-Apsley	II	41°46'S/148°13'E	16,080	1989
Freycinet	II	42°13'S/148°19'E	11,930	1916
Hartz Mountains	II	43°14'S/146°45'E	7,140	1939
Maria Island	II	42°39'S/148°06'E	11,550	1972
Mount Field	II	42°40'S/146°35'E	16,265	1916
Mount William	II	40°56'S/148°15'E	13,899	1973
Rocky Cape	II	40°44'S/145°35'E	3,064	1967
Southwest	II	43°32'S/146°22'E	608,298	1951
Strzelecki	II	40°14'S/148°06'E	4,215	1967
Walls of Jerusalem	II	41°48'S/146°19'E	51,800	1981

Nature Reserve

Betsey Island	IV	43°03'S/147°29'E	181	1981
Big Green Island	IV	40°11'S/147°59'E	270	1983
Chappell Islands	IV	40°19'S/147°53'E	1,350	1975
East Kangaroo Island	IV	40°11'S/147°54'E	200	1984
Lavinia	IV	39°42'S/144°04'E	6,800	1975
Lime Bay	IV	42°58'S/147°42'E	1,310	1976
Macquarie Island	IV	54°37'S/158°54'E	12,785	1972
Three Hummock Island	IV	40°26'S/144°54'E	7,284	1977
Wingaroo	IV	39°51'S/147°57'E	9,144	1991

State Reserve

Alum Cliffs	III	41°31'S/146°27'E	1,540	1979
Cape Pillar	II	43°11'S/147°57'E	3,200	1974
Cape Raoul	II	43°13'S/147°47'E	2,089	1978
Labillardiere	II	43°27'S/147°09'E	2,332	1975
Pieman River	II	41°39'S/145°03'E	3,314	1936

Victoria

Coastal Park

Discovery Bay	III	38°10'S/141°15'E	8,590	1979
Gippsland Lakes	III	37°59'S/147°41'E	17,200	1979

Flora and Fauna Reserve

Annuello	III	?/?	35,030	?
Barrabool	III	?/?	1,050	1989
Bull Beef Creek	III	?/?	1,490	1986
Carpendeit	III	?/?	1,242	1982
Deep Lead	III	?/?	1,120	1987
Inverleigh Common	III	?/?	1,051	1983
Jan Juc(1)	III	?/?	1,105	1992
Jilpanger	III	?/?	8,980	1989
Lake Timboram	III	?/?	2,060	1989
Landsborough	III	?/?	1,880	?
Moomowroong (Crinoline Ck)	III	?/?	1,550	?
Mount Bolangum	III	?/?	2,930	?
Mount Ida	III	?/?	1,050	1989
Mount Wombat-Garden Range	III	?/?	1,400	1988
Mullungdung	III	?/?	1,700	1989
Providence Ponds	III	?/?	1,650	?
Stradbroke (1)	III	?/?	2,200	1989
Sweetwater Creek	III	?/?	1,240	1988
Timberoo	III	?/?	1,240	1986
Towan Plains	III	?/?	1,086	?
Wilkin	III	?/?	3,600	?
Wychitella	III	36°20'S/143°40'E	2,690	1985
Yarrangook	III	?/?	1,525	1989
Yarrara (1)	III	?/?	2,200	?

Historic Park

Beechworth	III	36°30'S/146°45'E	1,130	1980

Marine and Coastal Park

Corner Inlet	V	38°47'S/146°18'E	18,000	1986
Nooramunga	V	38°40'S/146°42'E	15,000	1986
Shallow Inlet	V	38°49'S/146°09'E	2,000	1986

Marine Park

Wilsons Promontory	V	39°00'S/146°22'E	7,000	1986

Marine Reserve

Harold Holt - Swan Bay	V	38°14'S/144°40'E	2,300	1979
Wilsons Promontory	V	39°00'S/146°22'E	3,000	1986

National Park

Alfred	II	37°33'S/149°22'E	3,050	1925
Alpine	IV	37°00'S/147°00'E	642,080	1989
Baw Baw	II	37°52'S/146°21'E	13,300	1979
Brisbane Ranges	II	37°51'S/144°11'E	7,517	1973
Burrowa-Pine Mountain	II	36°06'S/147°44'E	18,400	1978
Coopracambra	II	37°19'S/149°23'E	38,800	1988
Croajingolong	II	37°44'S/149°04'E	87,500	1979
Dandenong Ranges	II	37°55'S/145°22'E	1,920	1987
Errinundra	II	37°21'S/148°55'E	25,600	1988
Fraser	II	37°10'S/145°50'E	3,750	1957
Grampians	II	37°14'S/142°25'E	167,000	1984
Hattah-Kulkyne	II	34°39'S/142°22'E	48,000	1960
Kinglake	II	37°30'S/145°20'E	11,430	1926
Lind	II	37°35'S/148°58'E	1,365	1925
Little Desert	II	36°25'S/141°45'E	132,000	1968
Lower Glenelg	II	38°03'S/141°17'E	27,300	1969
Mitchell River	II	37°45'S/147°25'E	11,900	1986
Mount Buffalo	II	36°43'S/146°47'E	31,000	1898
Mount Eccles	II	38°04'S/141°55'E	5,470	1960
Mount Richmond	II	38°16'S/141°25'E	1,733	1960
Murray-Sunset	II	34°45'S/141°30'E	633,000	1991
Otway	II	38°45'S/143°14'E	12,750	1981
Point Nepean	II	38°28'S/144°55'E	2,450	1988
Port Campbell	II	38°39'S/143°05'E	1,750	1964
Snowy River	II	35°50'S/148°20'E	98,700	1979
Tarra-Bulga	II	38°35'S/146°40'E	1,522	1986
The Lakes	II	37°59'S/147°40'E	2,390	1927
Wilsons Promontory	II	39°00'S/146°22'E	49,000	1898
Wyperfeld	II	?/?	356,800	1909

Other area

Wabba Wilderness Park	II	36°20'S/147°40'E	20,100	1992
Wychitella Flora Fauna Reserve	III	36°20'S/143°40'E	3,780	1985

Park

Chiltern	III	36°10'S/146°39'E	4,300	1980
Gembrook	III	38°00'S/145°05'E	2,650	1992
Lake Albacutya	III	35°44'S/141°58'E	8,300	1980
Lysterfield Lake	III	37°57'S/145°18'E	1,151	1981
Murray-Kulkyne	III	34°38'S/142°27'E	3,530	1980
Reef Hills	III	36°58'S/145°58'E	2,040	1986
Tyers	III	38°07'S/146°24'E	1,810	1986

Reference Area

Benedore River	I	?/?	1,200	?
Bungil	I	?/?	1,750	?
Burbibyong Creek	I	?/?	1,300	?
Burnside	I	?/?	1,190	?
Disappointment	I	?/?	1,195	?
Dry Forest Creek	I	?/?	1,390	?
Roseneath	I	?/?	2,172	?
Sunset	I	?/?	8,400	?
Telopea Downs	I	?/?	2,500	?
Walsh Creek	I	?/?	1,050	?

State Park

Angahook-Lorne	II	38°50'S/143°58'E	21,000	1987
Barmah	III	35°55'S/145°00'E	7,900	1987
Black Range	II	37°05'S/142°05'E	11,700	1988
Bunyip	II	38°00'S/145°40'E	13,900	1992
Carlisle	II	38°40'S/143°30'E	5,600	1988
Cathedral Range	II	37°23'S/145°45'E	3,577	1979

Dergholm	II	37°20'S/141°18'E	10,400	1992
Eildon SP	II	37°16'S/146°04'E	24,000	1980
French Island	II	38°25'S/145°20'E	8,300	1988
Holey Plains	II	38°13'S/146°56'E	10,576	1978
Kamarooka	II	36°20'S/144°20'E	6,900	1986
Kara Kara	II	36°55'S/143°22'E	3,840	1986
Kooyoora	II	36°40'S/143°40'E	3,593	1985
Langi Ghiran	II	?/?	2,695	1987
Lerderderg	II	37°30'S/144°30'E	14,100	1988
Moondarra	II	38°03'S/146°19'E	6,292	1986
Mount Arapiles Tooan	II	36°50'S/141°45'E	5,060	1987
Mount Buangor	II	37°18'S/143°15'E	2,400	1989
Mount Lawson	II	36°05'S/147°30'E	13,150	1988
Mount Napier	II	36°58'S/141°45'E	2,800	1987
Mount Samaria	II	36°52'S/146°04'E	7,600	1979
Mount Worth	III	38°17'S/145°59'E	1,040	1978
Paddys Ranges	II	37°05'S/143°12'E	1,670	1989
Terrick Terrick	III	35°55'S/143°55'E	2,493	1988
Warby Range	II	36°22'S/146°13'E	6,880	1978
Whipstick	II	36°40'S/144°25'E	2,300	1986

Wilderness Park

Avon	II	37°45'S/146°55'E	39,650	1987
Big Desert	II	35°35'S/141°08'E	113,500	1979
Wabba	II	36°20'S/147°40'E	20,100	1992

Wildlife Reserve

Blond Bay	III	38°00'S/147°33'E	1,898	1986
Bronzewing	III	34°15'S/142°20'E	11,200	?
Clydebank Morass	III	38°03'S/147°15'E	1,180	1977
Dowd Morass	III	38°09'S/147°12'E	1,516	1961
Ewing Morass	III	37°48'S/148°17'E	7,300	?
Jack Smith Lake	III	38°30'S/147°00'E	2,730	1988
Kings Billabong	III	?/?	2,140	?
Koorangie (The Marshes)	III	35°37'S/143°41'E	1,725	1976
Lake Coleman	III	38°10'S/147°19'E	2,000	1987
Lake Connewarre	III	38°14'S/144°28'E	3,114	1982
Lake Curlip	III	37°45'S/148°34'E	1,061	1981
Lake Murdeduke	III	38°10'S/143°43'E	1,500	1982
Lake Timboram	III	35°19'S/143°03'E	2,060	1989
Lake Tyrrell	III	?/?	15,000	?
Red Bluff(1)	III	35°51'S/141°01'E	8,800	1983
Reedy Lake	III	36°43'S/145°06'E	1,400	?
Tooloy-Lake Mundi	III	37°28'S/141°02'E	4,012	1979
Wandown	III	34°48'S/142°59'E	1,590	1980
Wathe	III	35°32'S/142°26'E	5,875	1965
Western Port	III	38°14'S/145°20'E	1,650	1979

Western Australia

Conservation Park

26666	II	?/?	9,328	1992
39819	II	?/?	1,755	1993
39820	II	?/?	3,028	1993
39822	II	?/?	2,593	1993
39823	II	?/?	2,582	1993
39824	II	?/?	5,798	1993
41850	II	?/?	1,209	1992
41864	II	?/?	5,998	1992
42165	II	?/?	10,359	1992
42196	II	?/?	1,466	1992

Conservation/Recreation Reserve

No 17715	II	?/?	1,370	1922

No 22519	II	?/?	1,688	1977
No 27216	II	?/?	1,576	1965
No 36907	II	?/?	1,050	1987
No 36909	II	?/?	2,144	1987
No 39821	II	?/?	29,331	1987
No 39826 (Mondanocks)	II	?/?	15,418	1987
No 39827 (Lane Pool)	II	?/?	12,359	1987
No 39898	II	?/?	110,602	1987
Marine Nature Reserve				
Hamelin Pool	IV	?/?	132,000	1990
Marine Park				
Marmion	IV	31°49'S/115°42'E	9,500	1987
Ningaloo (State Waters)	IV	22°37'S/113°32'E	225,003	1987
Rowley Shoals	IV	?/?	23,250	1990
Shark Bay	IV	?/?	748,735	1990
Shoalwater Islands	IV	?/?	6,545	1990
National Park				
Alexander Morrison	II	30°04'S/115°36'E	8,501	1969
Avon Valley	II	31°37'S/116°13'E	4,366	1970
Badgingarra	II	30°27'S/115°25'E	13,121	1973
Beedelup	II	?/?	1,530	1901
Boorabbin	III	31°13'S/120°10'E	26,000	1977
Cape Arid	II	33°40'S/123°24'E	279,415	1954
Cape Le Grand	II	33°55'S/122°19'E	31,578	1948
Cape Range	II	22°09'S/113°55'E	50,581	1964
Collier Range	II	24°41'S/119°09'E	277,841	1978
D'Entrecasteaux	II	34°41'S/115°58'E	58,109	1963
Drovers Cave	II	30°14'S/115°05'E	2,681	1972
Drysdale River	II	15°04'S/126°43'E	435,906	1974
Eucla	II	31°41'S/128°58'E	3,342	1948
Fitzgerald River	II	?/?	329,039	1973
Francois Peron	II	?/?	52,529	1993
Frank Hann	II	33°01'S/119°59'E	61,420	1963
Geikie Gorge	II	18°05'S/125°45'E	3,136	1967
Goongarrie	II	29°58'S/121°34'E	60,356	1978
Hassell	II	34°41'S/118°20'E	1,265	1963
Hidden Valley	II	15°46'S/128°47'E	2,068	?
John Forrest	II	31°53'S/116°05'E	2,676	1900
Kalbarri	II	27°44'S/114°23'E	186,050	1963
Karijini	II	22°41'S/118°15'E	606,597	1969
Kennedy Range	II	?/?	141,660	1993
Leeuwin-Naturaliste	II	34°07'S/115°04'E	18,966	1902
Lesueur	II	?/?	26,987	1992
Millstream-Chichester	II	21°25'S/117°20'E	199,736	1956
Moore River	II	31°06'S/115°40'E	17,543	1967
Mt Agustus	II	?/?	9,169	1989
Mt Frankland	II	34°45'S/116°43'E	30,830	1988
Nambung	II	30°36'S/115°09'E	18,319	1967
Neerabup	II	31°41'S/115°44'E	1,069	1965
Peak Charles	II	32°55'S/121°06'E	39,959	1979
Porongurup	II	34°41'S/117°53'E	2,511	1925
Purnululu (Bungle Bungle)	II	?/?	208,723	1987
Rudall River	II	22°31'S/122°35'E	1,569,459	1977
Scott	II	34°16'S/115°15'E	3,273	1959
Serpentine	II	32°22'S/116°01'E	4,363	1968
Shannon	II	34°40'S/116°23'E	52,598	1988
Stirling Range	II	34°17'S/117°42'E	115,661	1913
Stokes	II	33°51'S/121°04'E	9,743	1974
Tathra	II	29°48'S/115°31'E	4,322	1969

Torndirrup	II	35°06'S/117°54'E	3,936	1955
Tuart Forest	II	?/?	1,785	1967
Walpole-Nornalup	II	35°01'S/116°56'E	15,861	1972
Walyunga	II	31°44'S/116°04'E	1,812	1985
Warren	II	?/?	2,982	1901
Watheroo	II	30°14'S/115°52'E	44,474	1955
Waychinicup	II	?/?	3,983	1990
West Cape Howe	II	?/?	3,517	1962
William Bay	II	35°01'S/117°15'E	1,739	1909
Windjana Gorge	II	17°25'S/124°59'E	2,134	1971
Wolf Creek Crater	II	19°11'S/127°47'E	1,460	1968
Yalgorup	II	32°53'S/115°41'E	12,888	1909
Yanchep	II	?/?	2,842	1905

Nature Reserve

No 02179 (Duladgin)	IV	?/?	1,305	1969
No 04990 (Austin Bay)	IV	?/?	1,659	1970
No 07634 (Clear Muddy Lakes)	IV	?/?	1,926	1981
No 09550 (Taarblin Lake)	IV	?/?	1,013	1963
No 11648 (Barrow Island)	IV	?/?	23,483	1985
No 14275	IV	?/?	1,486	0
No 14429	IV	?/?	6,637	1979
No 16000	IV	31°22'S/118°48'E	1,341	1979
No 16305	IV	?/?	1,235	1978
No 18583	IV	31°22'S/118°43'E	1,156	1978
No 18739 (Mill Brook)	IV	?/?	1,484	1977
No 19210	IV	?/?	5,262	1983
No 19881	IV	34°53'S/116°59'E	1,128	1928
No 20218 (Kathleen)	IV	?/?	1,191	1979
No 20262 (Jilbadji Rock)	IV	?/?	1,019	1970
No 20338 (North Karlgarin)	IV	?/?	5,186	1970
No 20339 (Roe)	IV	?/?	1,246	1978
No 20610 (Boyagin)	IV	?/?	4,845	1991
No 21253 (Lake Gounter)	IV	?/?	3,327	1974
No 22519 (Kondinin Lake)	IV	?/?	1,688	?
No 22796 (Recherche Archipelago)	IV	?/?	6,495	1948
No 22921 (Durokopping)	IV	?/?	1,030	1971
No 23756 (Kooljerrenup)	IV	?/?	1,019	1973
No 23825 (Mullet Lake)	IV	?/?	1,917	1970
No 24049 (Jilbadji)	IV	?/?	208,866	1977
No 24486	IV	?/?	12,617	1956
No 24496	IV	?/?	69,161	1956
No 24589 (Corneecup)	IV	?/?	1,952	1975
No 24618 (Capamauro)	IV	?/?	4,686	1971
No 24789 (Lake Campion)	IV	?/?	10,752	1979
No 24869 (Bernier Dorre Islands)	IV	?/?	9,720	1957
No 25062	IV	?/?	1,149	1980
No 25113 (Lake Magenta)	IV	?/?	107,615	1958
No 25134 (Coblinine)	IV	?/?	1,178	1958
No 25136 (Coblinine)	IV	?/?	1,845	1958
No 25210 (Pinjarrega)	IV	?/?	18,221	1974
No 25506 (Quindinup)	IV	?/?	2,653	1985
No 25555 (Tutanning)	IV	?/?	2,206	1970
No 25681 (Bendering)	IV	?/?	1,602	?
No 25711 (Tarin Rock)	IV	?/?	2,011	1969
No 25798 (Unicup)	IV	?/?	3,290	1960
No 26160 (Jebarjup)	IV	?/?	1,016	1962
No 26161 (Camel Lake)	IV	?/?	3,215	1962
No 26259 (Carlyarn)	IV	?/?	2,723	1974
No 26385 (North Sister)	IV	?/?	1,008	1962
No 26442 (Yarra Yarra)	IV	29°36'S/115°46'E	1,400	1980
No 26663 (Burma Road)	IV	?/?	6,890	1980

No 26664 (Dumbleyung Lake)	IV	?/?	3,959	1963
No 26688 (South Stirling)	IV	?/?	1,710	1974
No 26692 (Kondinin Salt Marsh)	IV	?/?	1,915	1974
No 26763 (South Buniche)	IV	?/?	1,298	1970
No 26789 (Arthur River)	IV	?/?	1,069	1963
No 26792	IV	33°59'S/118°39'E	1,039	1978
No 26793 (Corackerup)	IV	?/?	4,334	1970
No 26808 (Barlee Range)	IV	?/?	104,544	1963
No 26837 (Buntine)	IV	?/?	1,919	1963
No 26885	IV	33°49'S/121°26'E	5,200	1963
No 27164 (Prince Regent)	IV	?/?	634,952	1964
No 27283 (Goodlands)	IV	?/?	1,349	1965
No 27386	IV	33°27'S/122°02'E	1,417	1988
No 27388	IV	33°33'S/122°12'E	4,467	1983
No 27487	IV	?/?	1,468	1965
No 27632 (Nuytsland)	IV	?/?	625,344	1965
No 27768	IV	33°16'S/121°48'E	1,106	1979
No 27837 (Lake Hurlstone)	IV	?/?	2,154	1973
No 27872 (Boothendarra)	IV	?/?	2,075	1976
No 27886 (South Eneabba)	IV	?/?	1,140	1972
No 27888	IV	33°48'S/121°20'E	4,341	1965
No 27927 (Lake Hurstone)	IV	?/?	2,388	1969
No 27928 (Lake Varley)	IV	?/?	2,096	1970
No 27956 (Two Peoples Bay)	IV	?/?	4,745	1966
No 27985	IV	?/?	6,066	1970
No 28088 (Yenyening Lakes)	IV	?/?	2,435	1973
No 28323	IV	31°47'S/119°08'E	1,180	1991
No 28324 (Cairlocup)	IV	?/?	1,577	1966
No 28395 (Chinocup)	IV	?/?	19,825	1979
No 28558 (Namming)	IV	?/?	5,432	1967
No 28940	IV	31°36'S/118°46'E	4,377	1968
No 29012	IV	?/?	1,404	1983
No 29018 (Silver Wattle Hill)	IV	?/?	1,660	1968
No 29019 (Breakaway Ridge)	IV	?/?	3,323	1968
No 29020	IV	?/?	1,528	1968
No 29023 (Lakeland)	IV	?/?	1,529	1968
No 29024 (Lakeland)	IV	?/?	1,579	1968
No 29027	IV	32°33'S/119°17'E	1,252	1980
No 29073	IV	?/?	4,835	1968
No 29128 (Basil Road)	IV	?/?	1,162	1978
No 29184	IV	33°18'S/120°04'E	1,309	1979
No 29231 (East Yuna)	IV	?/?	1,467	1970
No 29617 (Rock View)	IV	?/?	1,733	1969
No 29806 (Wotto)	IV	?/?	2,892	1977
No 29810 (Lake Liddelow)	IV	?/?	1,133	1969
No 29857 (North Tarin Rock)	IV	?/?	1,416	1969
No 29860 (Pallarup)	IV	?/?	4,191	1969
No 29920	IV	?/?	1,036	1969
No 29983 (Point Coulomb)	IV	?/?	28,676	1969
No 30191 (Moondyne)	IV	?/?	1,991	1970
No 30305 (Welsh)	IV	?/?	1,717	1970
No 30463 (Bakers Junction)	IV	?/?	1,090	1977
No 30490 (Great Victoria Desert)	IV	?/?	2,495,777	1970
No 30491 (Queen Victoria Spring)	IV	?/?	272,598	1970
No 30583	IV	33°20'S/121°00'E	5,418	1985
No 30626 (Gingilup Swamps)	IV	?/?	4,323	1970
No 30897 (Wanjarri)	IV	?/?	53,248	1971
No 31030 (South Eneabba)	IV	?/?	6,776	1971
No 31128 (Kundip)	IV	?/?	2,170	1980
No 31424	IV	33°30'S/119°43'E	2,936	1972
No 31429 (Mungaroona Range)	IV	?/?	105,842	1972

No 31675 (Wanagarren)	IV	?/?	11,069	1972
No 31742	IV	?/?	1,179	1973
No 31754 (Cheadanup)	IV	?/?	6,813	1973
No 31781 (Nilgen)	IV	?/?	5,507	1973
No 31799	IV	?/?	3,618	1973
No 31880 (Lake Muir)	IV	?/?	11,310	1978
No 31913 (Haddleton)	IV	?/?	1,161	?
No 31967	IV	?/?	78,842	1973
No 32129	IV	?/?	1,752	1973
No 32130	IV	?/?	2,481	1973
No 32131	IV	?/?	1,058	1973
No 32339 (Lake Shaster)	IV	?/?	10,505	1973
No 32549 (Harris)	IV	?/?	3,610	1980
No 32776	IV	?/?	4,732	1974
No 32777	IV	?/?	8,551	1974
No 32779	IV	?/?	1,046	1974
No 32780	IV	?/?	1,485	1974
No 32783	IV	?/?	7,082	1974
No 32784	IV	?/?	1,709	1974
No 32864	IV	30°29'S/118°38'E	1,437	1983
No 32995	IV	?/?	1,886	1974
No 33113	IV	?/?	8,860	1975
No 33300 (Kambalda)	IV	?/?	3,683	1975
No 33466	IV	?/?	5,131	1975
No 33475	IV	?/?	3,600	1975
No 33842 (Quarram	IV	?/?	3,825	1976
No 34442 (Dobaderry)	IV	?/?	1,896	1978
No 34522 (Lake Ace)	IV	?/?	2,392	1977
No 34604 (Mungilli Calypan)	IV	?/?	3,636	1977
No 34605 (Plumridge Lakes)	IV	?/?	308,990	1977
No 34606 (Gibson Desert)	IV	?/?	1,859,286	1977
No 34720 (Neale Junction)	IV	?/?	723,073	1977
No 34771 (Zuytdorp)	IV	?/?	58,850	?
No 34776	IV	?/?	2,249	1977
No 34944 (Dolphin Island)	IV	?/?	3,203	1977
No 35168 (Sheepwash Creek)	IV	?/?	1,111	1978
No 35659	IV	33°15'S/121°05'E	1,009	1990
No 35752 (Walyahmoning)	IV	?/?	20,925	1979
No 35918	IV	?/?	14,182	1979
No 36003	IV	32°14'S/119°01'E	1,113	1979
No 36028 (Mt Manypeaks)	IV	?/?	1,330	1979
No 36053	IV	30°26'S/115°06'E	10,841	1979
No 36128 (Dragon Rocks)	IV	?/?	32,219	1979
No 36203 (Yardonogo)	IV	29°24'S/115°05'E	6,612	1979
No 36208 (Mt Manning)	IV	?/?	153,293	1979
No 36271 (Yeo Lake)	IV	?/?	321,946	1979
No 36388 (Wandana)	IV	?/?	54,821	1979
No 36419 (Stockyard Gully)	IV	?/?	1,406	1979
No 36445 (Dunn Rock)	IV	?/?	27,349	1980
No 36526 (Lake Cronin)	IV	?/?	1,016	1980
No 36907	IV	?/?	1,050	?
No 36909	IV	?/?	2,144	?
No 36913	IV	20°25'S/116°51'E	3,402	1980
No 36915	IV	20°29'S/116°35'E	4,435	1980
No 36918	IV	30°51'S/119°22'E	13,750	1980
No 36936 (Karroun Hill)	IV	29°59'S/118°12'E	309,678	1983
No 36957	IV	?/?	780,883	1981
No 37034 (Jouerdine)	IV	?/?	1,117	1981
No 37083 (Wilson)	IV	29°33'S/115°26'E	1,099	1983
No 37306 (Dobaderry)	IV	?/?	1,307	1981
No 38450	IV	32°54'S/119°37'E	1,009	1983
No 38545	IV	?/?	1,671	1983

No 39422	IV	?/?	40,105	1986
No 39744	IV	?/?	2,683	1989
No 40156	IV	?/?	7,584	1987
No 40161	IV	?/?	1,170	1987
No 40628	IV	?/?	405,424	1988
No 40916	IV	?/?	1,012	1989
No 41010	IV	?/?	2,430	1989
No 41805	IV	?/?	9,250	1991
No 41830	IV	?/?	4,722	1991
No 41831	IV	?/?	74,935	1991
No 41885	IV	?/?	2,626	1991
No 41933	IV	?/?	8,815	1991
No 41934	IV	?/?	6,738	1991
No 41936	IV	?/?	32,798	1991
No 41938	IV	?/?	3,210	1991
No 41986	IV	?/?	2,369	1992
No 42155	IV	?/?	36,111	1992

AUSTRIA/AUTRICHE

Summary		
Category I	0	0
Category II	1	76,000
Category III	0	0
Category IV	47	372,046
Category V	122	1,633,284
Total	**170**	**2,005,475**

Landscape Protected Area

Aeusseres Poellatal	V	47°02'N/13°31'E	1,730	1973
Ammering, Stubalpe	V	47°04'N/14°50'E	22,000	1981
Baerenkopf	V	?/?	1,300	1989
Berg - und Hugelland Westlich von Graz	V	47°03'N/15°22'E	5,792	1981
Bernstein-Lockenhaus-Rechnitz	V	47°23'N/16°22'E	25,883	1972
Bisamberg und seine Umgebung	V	48°12'N/16°26'E	2,000	1979
Bundschuhtal-Lungauer Nockgebiet	V	46°59'N/13°46'E	2,250	1980
Dachstein, Salzkammergut	V	47°34'N/13°53'E	54,000	1981
Dobersberg	V	48°13'N/16°28'E	1,600	1979
Dobratsch (Villacher Alpe)	V	46°34'N/13°43'E	3,904	1970
Doebling	V	?/?	1,205	1990
Donau-March-Thaya-Auen	V	48°11'N/16°55'E	20,500	1982
Ennstaler und Eisenerzer Alpen	V	47°35'N/14°36'E	64,300	1981
Enzesfeld-Lindabrunn-Hernstein	V	47°56'N/16°04'E	7,000	1979
Falkenstein	V	48°46'N/16°32'E	3,458	1981
Felbertal, Ammertaleroed, Dorferoed	V	47°12'N/12°31'E	9,500	1980
Forstheide	V	48°04'N/14°49'E	1,250	1983
Friesingwand Talenge St.Peter-Freienstei	V	47°24'N/15°03'E	1,060	1981
Gamsstein-Voralpe	V	47°45'N/14°48'E	4,845	1987
Gasteiner Tal	V	47°03'N/13°08'E	13,860	1980
Geras und seine Umgebung	V	48°48'N/15°40'E	3,250	1979
Gleichenberger Kogel, Kapfenstein, Stradner Kogel	V	46°52'N/15°56'E	5,280	1981
Goell-, Hagen, Hochkoenigsgebirge, Steinernes Meer	V	47°27'N/13°04'E	3,700	1980
Grebenzen, Furtnerteich	V	?/?	6,600	1981
Grossfragant	V	46°56'N/13°00'E	1,115	1973
Hefferthorn-Fellhorn-Sonnenberg	V	?/?	6,800	1983
Herberstein-Klamm, Freienberger-Klamm	V	47°13'N/15°47'E	2,160	1981
Hochalpe	V	47°19'N/15°13'E	7,140	1981
Hochschwab Staritzen	V	47°34'N/15°09'E	37,080	1981
Hohe Wand-Duerre Wand	V	47°50'N/16°03'E	12,800	1979
Huegelland noerdlich und oestlich von Graz	V	47°06'N/15°30'E	11,670	1981

Huettschlager Talschluesse	V	47°07'N/13°16'E	6,350	1980
Johannisbachklamm	V	47°47'N/16°00'E	2,000	1979
Kamptal	V	48°35'N/15°29'E	35,000	1979
Keutschacher See-Tal	V	?/?	2,532	1970
Koenisgleiten-Salzachursprung-Nadernachtal	V	47°17'N/12°07'E	3,600	1980
Koralpe	V	46°47'N/15°02'E	3,200	1981
Lantschfeldtal, Oberes Zederhaustal, Oberes Murtal	V	47°09'N/13°24'E	25,400	1989
Leiser Berge	V	48°35'N/16°22'E	7,000	1979
Mariazell, Seeberg	V	47°43'N/15°21'E	23,460	1981
Martinswand-Solstein-Reither Spitze	V	?/?	4,773	1989
Millstaetter See-Sued	V	46°45'N/13°33'E	1,984	1970
Mittleres Ennstal	V	47°33'N/14°15'E	5,120	1981
Murauen Graz - Werndorf	V	46°57'N/15°30'E	1,480	1981
Murauen im Leibnitzer Feld	V	46°47'N/15°35'E	1,380	1981
Murauen Mureck-Radkersberg-Kloech	V	46°43'N/15°57'E	11,280	1981
Niedere Tauern	V	47°13'N/13°44'E	20,000	1986
Noesslachjoch-Obernberger See-Tribulaune	V	?/?	9,200	1984
Nordkette	V	?/?	1,846	1989
Oberes Ennstal	V	47°25'N/13°54'E	7,400	1981
Oberes Pulkautal	V	48°43'N/15°49'E	3,500	1979
Obertauern	V	47°15'N/13°31'E	3,714	1980
Oetscher-Duerrenstein	V	47°51'N/15°08'E	80,000	1979
Pack-Reinischkogel-Rosenkogel	V	46°54'N/15°06'E	23,480	1981
Palten-und Liesingtal	V	47°29'N/14°30'E	3,930	1981
Peggauer Wand	V	47°12'N/15°22'E	1,140	1981
Plesch, Walzkogel, Pfaffenkogel	V	47°08'N/15°15'E	6,500	1981
Pleschaitz-Puxberg	V	47°08'N/14°20'E	2,400	1981
Poellauer Tal	V	47°19'N/15°49'E	12,100	1979
Postalm	V	47°39'N/13°27'E	1,405	1980
Priedroef	V	?/?	1,650	1986
Rax-Schneeberg	V	47°46'N/15°48'E	71,500	1979
Reiting, Eisenerzer Reichenstein	V	47°27'N/14°54'E	10,280	1981
Rosaliengebirge (Forchtenstein, Rosalia)	V	?/?	3,838	1968
Rottenmanner-Triebener Tauern Seckauer Alpen	V	47°23'N/14°32'E	53,260	1981
Salzberg-Sued	V	47°46'N/13°05'E	1,248	1981
Sausal	V	46°47'N/15°28'E	6,200	1981
Schafberg, Salzkammergutseen	V	47°46'N/13°26'E	5,769	1981
Schladminger Tauern	V	47°18'N/13°53'E	58,480	1981
Schlossberg bei Leutschach	V	46°37'N/15°30'E	2,120	1981
Schoeckl, Weizklamm, Hochlantsch	V	47°17'N/15°32'E	30,660	1981
Schoenberg, Gfoeller Riegel	V	47°14'N/14°25'E	1,680	1981
Serles-Habicht-Zuckerhutl	V	?/?	18,000	1984
Sierningtal	V	47°45'N/15°58'E	3,100	1979
Soboth, Radlpass	V	46°40'N/15°09'E	10,660	1981
Spertental-Rettenstein	V	?/?	4,100	1984
Strudengau u. Umgeburg	V	48°12'N/15°00'E	12,600	1979
Stuhleck-Pretul	V	47°34'N/15°46'E	9,180	1981
Suedburgenlaendisches Huegel-und Terrassenland	V	47°07'N/16°25'E	14,272	1974
Tennengebirge	V	47°28'N/13°16'E	2,500	1986
Thayatal	V	48°51'N/15°35'E	1,700	1979
Thayatal	V	?/?	1,200	1979
Trumer Seen	V	?/?	6,700	1986
Turracherhohe, Eisenhut, Frauenalpe	V	46°59'N/13°58'E	26,620	1981
Untersberg	V	47°44'N/13°00'E	4,242	1981
Veitsch-Schneealpe-Rax	V	47°41'N/15°33'E	23,560	1981
Vorberg	V	?/?	2,450	1989
Wachau und Umgebung	V	48°20'N/15°26'E	46,300	1979
Waldbach, Vorau, Hochwechsel	V	47°28'N/15°52'E	20,120	1981
Waldheimat	V	47°29'N/15°38'E	5,640	1981
Waller oder Seekirchrer See	V	47°55'N/13°12'E	1,412	1980

Warscheneck-Gruppe	V	47°35'N/14°11'E	13,880	1981
Weissbacher-Gemeinschaftsalmen	V	?/?	1,150	1989
Weissensee	V	46°41'N/13°19'E	7,648	1970
Wienerwald	V	48°09'N/16°05'E	105,000	1979
Wildegg-Speikkogel	V	47°14'N/15°02'E	9,000	1981
Wildgerlostal, Krimmler Achental, Oberes.	V	47°14'N/12°10'E	5,000	1981
Woelzer Tauern	V	47°19'N/14°14'E	22,880	1981
Wollanig-Oswaldiberg	V	46°38'N/13°47'E	1,120	1970
Zirbitzkogel	V	47°03'N/14°35'E	9,200	1981

National Park

Hohe Tauern (Kaerten)	V	47°05'N/12°46'E	37,263	1986
Hohe Tauern (Salzburg)	V	47°05'N/12°46'E	80,514	1984
Hohe Tauern (Tirol)	V	?/?	60,996	1992
Neusiedler See	II	47°49'N/16°47'E	76,000	1993
Nockberge	V	46°52'N/13°43'E	18,410	1986

Nature Park

Eichenhain	V	48°18'N/16°14'E	3,500	1983
Eisenwurzen	V	47°45'N/14°48'E	4,845	1987
Foehrenberge	V	48°05'N/16°12'E	6,600	1979
Grebenzen, Furtnerteich	V	47°03'N/14°22'E	6,600	1982
Hohe Wand	V	47°50'N/16°02'E	2,000	1979
Jauerling-Wachau	V	48°19'N/15°21'E	3,600	1983
Kamptal-Schoenberg	V	48°32'N/15°41'E	1,515	1986
Leiserberge	V	48°35'N/16°21'E	4,500	1979
Oetscher-Tormaeuern	V	47°55'N/15°16'E	9,000	1979
Poellauer Tal	V	47°19'N/15°49'E	12,100	1982
Sierningtal	V	?/?	1,600	1979

Nature Reserve

Altausseer See	V	47°39'N/13°50'E	1,050	1991
Arnspitze	IV	47°23'N/11°13'E	12,500	1942
Bazora	IV	47°11'N/9°38'E	1,096	1962
Bodensee-Sattenbachtal	IV	47°18'N/13°50'E	1,400	1982
Dachsteingebiet	V	?/?	20,000	1964
Eisenerzer Reichenstein-Krumpensee	IV	47°29'N/14°57'E	1,000	1973
Gadental	IV	?/?	1,336	1987
Gesause und anschliessendes Ennstal	IV	47°33'N/14°37'E	13,700	1958
Grundlsee mit Toplitzee, Kammersee und Teile.	IV	47°39'N/14°01'E	9,700	1959
Gurkursprung	IV	46°53'N/13°55'E	1,497	1981
Hochifen, Gottesackerwaende	IV	47°21'N/10°08'E	2,956	1964
Hohe Kugel, Hoher Freschen, Mellental	IV	47°18'N/9°46'E	7,500	1979
Huhe Kugel	IV	?/?	1,050	1973
Inneres Poellatal	IV	47°02'N/13°27'E	3,200	1973
Kaisergebirge	V	47°34'N/12°20'E	10,200	1963
Kalkhochalpen	IV	47°27'N/13°01'E	24,066	1983
Karwendel	IV	?/?	54,325	1989
Klafferkessel	IV	47°21'N/13°51'E	1,200	1980
Krakau-Schoeder	IV	?/?	6,245	1987
Lainzer Tiergarten	V	?/?	2,450	1941
Lobau	IV	?/?	2,619	1978
Loser-Braeuning-Zinken	IV	?/?	1,750	1974
Muttersberg	IV	47°12'N/9°54'E	1,146	1959
Nasskoehr	IV	47°43'N/15°33'E	1,000	1971
Nenzinger Himmel	IV	47°06'N/9°40'E	1,051	1958
Neusiedlersee	V	47°49'N/16°47'E	49,606	1980
Niedere	IV	?/?	1,283	1974
Nordwestlicher Teil der Gemeinde Ramsau am Dachste	IV	?/?	1,288	1972
Obertauern	IV	?/?	1,500	1986
Patscherkofel	IV	47°13'N/11°29'E	1,200	1947
Rheindelta	IV	47°29'N/9°42'E	1,972	1993

Riesachtal	IV	?/?	1,337	1991
Rosanin	IV	46°56'N/13°47'E	1,100	1983
Seekar, Barental	IV	46°47'N/15°00'E	1,100	1981
Sengsengebierge	IV	47°47'N/14°19'E	3,400	1976
Sonntag	IV	47°17'N/10°00'E	6,313	1968
Steirische Nockberge	IV	?/?	2,074	1988
Tennengebirge	IV	47°31'N/13°16'E	4,400	1981
Tiefenwald-Staffl	IV	47°16'N/9°54'E	1,156	1974
Untere Marchauen	IV	48°20'N/16°52'E	1,166	1978
Vadans-Tschagguns	IV	47°02'N/9°49'E	4,062	1963
Valsertal	V	47°03'N/11°38'E	3,300	1941
Villacher Alpe (Dobratsch)	IV	46°34'N/13°39'E	1,902	1967
Vilsalpsee	V	47°28'N/10°31'E	1,510	1957
Wildalpenar Salzatal	IV	47°40'N/15°02'E	51,460	1958
Wolayersee und Umgebung	IV	46°37'N/12°51'E	1,939	1983
Zirbitzkogel	IV	?/?	2,314	1966

Rest Area/Ruhegebiet

Achental West	IV	?/?	3,812	1989
Eppzirl	IV	?/?	3,341	1989
Kalkkoegel	IV	?/?	7,770	1983
Muttekopf	IV	?/?	3,800	1991
Otztaler Alpen	IV	?/?	39,600	1981
Stubaier Alpen	IV	?/?	35,220	1983
Zillertaler Hauptkamm	IV	?/?	37,200	1991

AZERBAIJAN/AZERBAÏDJAN/AZERBAIYAN

Summary		
Category I	12	190,860
Category II	0	0
Category III	0	0
Category IV	0	0
Category V	0	0
Total	**12**	**190,860**

Zapovednik

Ak-Gel'skiy	I	40°00'N/47°40'E	4,400	1978
Alty-Agachskiy	I	?/?	4,400	1990
Geigel'skiy	I	39°36'N/46°24'E	7,100	1965
Girkanskiy	I	39°21'N/48°45'E	2,900	1969
Ilisuinsky	I	?/?	9,300	1987
Ismaillinskiy	I	39°08'N/48°11'E	5,800	1981
Karayazskiy	I	38°40'N/45°21'E	4,900	1978
Kyzylagachskiy	I	38°53'N/49°00'E	88,360	1929
Pirkulinskiy	I	39°12'N/48°36'E	1,500	1968
Shirvanskiy	I	38°34'N/49°10'E	25,800	1969
Turianchaiskiy	I	39°12'N/47°23'E	12,600	1958
Zakatal'skiy	I	40°13'N/46°36'E	23,800	1929

BAHAMAS

Summary		
Category I	1	1,813
Category II	4	121,576
Category III	0	0
Category IV	5	975
Category V	0	0
Total	**10**	**124,364**

Managed Nature Reserve

Union Creek	I	21°08'N/73°35'W	1,813	1965

National Park

Conception Island	II	23°50'N/75°07'W	809	1973
Exuma Land and Sea Park	II	24°31'N/76°39'W	45,584	1958
Inagua	II	21°05'N/73°24'W	74,333	1965
Pelican Cays Land and Sea Park	II	26°24'N/77°00'W	850	1981

Wild Bird Reserve

Big Darby Island	IV	23°50'N/76°12'W	202	1951
Grassy Creek Cays and Rocks	IV	23°50'N/77°25'W	172	1954
Little Derby Island	IV	23°50'N/76°11'W	136	1951
Little San Salvador (Little Island)	IV	24°35'N/75°56'W	182	1961
Paradise Island	IV	25°05'N/77°19'W	283	1956

BAHRAIN/BAHREIN

No Areas Listed

BANGLADESH

Summary		
Category I	0	0
Category II	0	0
Category III	0	0
Category IV	6	83,332
Category V	2	13,458
Total	**8**	**96,790**

National Park

Bhawal	V	24°01'N/90°20'E	5,022	1982
Madhupur	V	24°45'N/90°05'E	8,436	1982

Wildlife Sanctuary

Chunati	IV	21°40'N/92°07'E	7,764	1986
Pablakhali	IV	23°08'N/92°16'E	42,087	1983
Rema-Kalenga	IV	24°05'N/91°37'E	1,095	1981
Sundarbans East	IV	21°53'N/89°47'E	5,439	1977
Sundarbans South	IV	21°50'N/89°24'E	17,878	1977
Sundarbans West	IV	21°44'N/89°15'E	9,069	1977

BARBADOS/BARBADE

No Areas Listed

BELARUS

Summary		
Category I	1	63,458
Category II	1	81,023
Category III	0	0
Category IV	0	0
Category V	8	98,007
Total	**10**	**242,488**

National Park

Belovezhskaya Pushcha	V	52°41'N/24°35'E	87,607	1939

Zakaznik

Dolgoe	V	?/?	3,300	1979

Godubpe Ozera	V	?/?	1,500	1972
Krivoe	V	?/?	1,200	1979
Mezhozernyy	V	?/?	1,000	1970
Moznrskie Ovragi	V	?/?	1,100	1986
Richi	V	?/?	1,300	1979
Svitazyanskiy	V	?/?	1,000	1970

Zapovednik

Berezinskiy	II	54°38'N/28°21'E	81,023	1925
Prypyatskiy	I	51°59'N/28°00'E	63,458	1969

BELGIUM/BELGIQUE/BELGICA

Summary		
Category I	0	0
Category II	0	0
Category III	0	0
Category IV	1	3,988
Category V	2	73,150
Total	**3**	**77,138**

Nature Park

Burdinale and Mehaigne Valleys	V	50°32'N/5°10'E	5,300	1991
Hautes Fagnes-Eifel	V	50°29'N/6°10'E	67,850	1985

State Nature Reserve

Hautes Fagnes	IV	50°26'N/6°10'E	3,988	1957

BELIZE/BELICE

Summary		
Category I	3	44,401
Category II	4	115,565
Category III	0	0
Category IV	7	163,155
Category V	0	0
Total	**14**	**323,121**

Archaelogical Reserve

Caracol	IV	16°45'N/89°00'W	20,000	?

Marine Nature Reserve

Hol Chan	II	17°52'N/88°00'W	411	1987

National Monument

Half Moon Caye	II	17°13'N/87°31'W	3,925	1982

National Park

Aguas Turbias	II	?/?	3,622	1992
Chiquibul	II	16°45'N/89°00'W	107,607	1991

Nature Reserve

Bladen Branch	I	16°30'N/88°58'W	39,256	1990
Burdon Canal	I	15°28'N/88°15'W	2,416	1992
Paynes Creek	IV	?/?	11,331	1992
Río Grande	IV	16°20'N/89°58'W	2,340	1968
Sarstoon/Temash	IV	?/?	16,592	1992
Society Hall	I	?/?	2,729	1986

Private Reserve

Shipstern	IV	?/?	9,022	1987

Wildlife Sanctuary

Cockscomb Basin	IV	16°47'N/88°29'W	102,400	1986
Crooked Tree	IV	17°46'N/88°33'W	1,470	1984

BENIN

Summary		
Category I	0	0
Category II	2	777,500
Category III	0	0
Category IV	0	0
Category V	0	0
Total	**2**	**777,500**

National Park

Boucle de la Pendjari	II	11°14'N/1°32'E	275,500	1961
W du Benin	II	11°55'N/2°45'E	502,000	1954

BHUTAN/BHOUTAN

Summary		
Category I	1	64,400
Category II	4	660,600
Category III	0	0
Category IV	4	241,100
Category V	0	0
Total	**9**	**966,100**

National Park

Black Mountain	II	27°20N/30°18'E	130,000	1993
Jigme Dorji	II	27°56'N/83°35'E	390,000	1993
Royal Manas	II	26°52'N/90°56'E	65,800	1988
Thrumsing La	II	27°19'N/90°49'E	74,800	1993

Strict Nature Reserve

Torsa	I	27°19'N/89°4'E	64,400	1993

Wildlife Sanctuary

Khaling/Neoli	IV	26°53'N/30°02'E	27,300	1993
Kulong Chu	IV	27°55'N/91°20'E	125,000	1993
Phibsoo	IV	26°38'N/91°58'E	27,800	1993
Sakteng	IV	27°20'N/91°58'E	61,000	1993

BOLIVIA/BOLIVIE

Summary		
Category I	1	135,000
Category II	7	3,638,520
Category III	0	0
Category IV	16	5,446,199
Category V	1	13,300
Total	**25**	**9,233,019**

Biological Station

Beni	I	14°49'S/66°30'W	135,000	1982

National Park

Amboró	II	17°45'S/63°52'W	180,000	1973
Carrasco Ichilo	II	17°16'S/64°24'W	1,300,000	1988
Isiboro Sécure	II	16°11'S/66°02'W	1,100,000	1965
Llica	II	19°49'S/68°11'W	97,500	1991
Noel Kempff Mercado	II	14°17'S/60°35'W	914,000	1979

Sajama	II	18°09'S/68°59'W	29,940	1939
Santa Cruz la Vieja	II	17°59'S/60°42'W	17,080	1989

Regional Park

Lomas Arena	V	17°51'S/63°03'W	13,300	1989

Wildlife Refuge

El Dorado	IV	13°07'S/67°20'W	180,000	1988
Estancias Elsner Espíritu	IV	14°15'S/66°47'W	70,000	1978
Estancias Elsner San Rafael	IV	15°32'S/64°47'W	20,000	1978
Huancaroma	IV	17°35'S/67°08'W	11,000	1975

Reserve

Altamachi Vicuña	IV	?/?	100,000	1977
Huancaroma Vicuña	IV	17°40'S/67°10'W	140,429	1975

National Reserve

Cordillera de Sama	IV	?/?	108,500	1991
Eduardo Avaroa	IV	22°31'S/67°26'W	714,000	1973
Incacasani-Altamachi	IV	?/?	23,000	1991
Lagunas del Beni y Pando	IV	?/?	275,000	1961
Manuripi Heath	IV	11°39'S/67°31'W	1,884,000	1973
Noel Kempff Mercado	IV	?/?	21,900	1988
Ríos Blanco y Negro	IV	14°29'S/62°49'W	1,400,000	1990
Tariquia	IV	21°58'S/64°24'W	246,870	1989
Ulla Ulla	IV	14°58'S/69°11'W	250,000	1972

Sanctuary

Cavernas El Repechón	IV	17°00'S/65°29'W	1,500	1986

BOSNIA AND HERZEGOVINA/
BOSNIE-HERZEGOVINE/
BOSNIA Y HERZEGOVINA

Summary		
Category I	0	0
Category II	1	17,250
Category III	0	0
Category IV	1	1,434
Category V	3	6,375
Total	**5**	**25,059**

National Park

Kozara	V	45°01'N/16°59'E	3,375	1967
Sutjeska	II	43°20'N/18°45'E	17,250	1965

Nature Reserve

Prasuma perucica	IV	43°30'N/18°50'E	1,434	1954

Regional Nature Park

Jahorina	V	?/?	2,000	1954
Trebeno	V	?/?	1,000	1954

BOTSWANA

Summary		
Category I	0	0
Category II	5	9,731,450
Category III	0	0
Category IV	4	931,830
Category V	0	0
Total	**9**	**10,663,280**

Game Reserve

Central Kalahari	II	22°04'S/24°11'E	5,180,000	1961
Khutse	IV	23°26'S/24°20'E	260,000	1971
Mabuasehube	IV	24°35'S/21°56'E	166,500	1971
Moremi	IV	19°20'S/23°11'E	496,830	1965

National Park

Chobe	II	18°02'S/24°20'E	1,057,000	1968
Gemsbok	II	25°10'S/20°47'E	2,766,500	1971
Makgadikgadi	II	20°32'S/24°46'E	487,710	1992
Nxai Pan	II	19°52'S/24°49'E	240,240	1971

Sanctuary

Maun	IV	20°00'S/23°25'E	8,500	1975

BRAZIL/BRESIL/BRASIL

Summary		
Category I	53	3,940,314
Category II	97	16,483,686
Category III	0	0
Category IV	49	4,453,098
Category V	74	7,312,739
Total	**273**	**32,189,837**

Acre

Federal Ecological Station

Rio Acre	IV	10°55'S/70°15'W	77,500	1981

National Park

Serra do Divisor	II	7°36'S/73°33'W	605,000	1989

Alagoas

Federal Biological Reserve

Pedra Talhada	I	9°40'S/37°57'W	4,469	1989

Federal Ecological Station

Foz do Sao Francisco/Praia do Peba	IV	10°21'S/36°28'W	5,322	1981

Federal Environment Protection Area

Piaçabuçu	V	10°03'S/36°10'W	5,500	1983

State Environment Protection Area

Marituba do Peixe	V	10°17'S/36°25'W	8,600	1988
Santa Rita	V	9°37'S/35°50'W	8,800	1984

Amapá

Federal Biological Reserve

Lago Piratuba	I	1°38'N/50°05'W	357,000	1980

Federal Ecological Station

Ilha Maracá-Jipioca	IV	2°02'N/50°29'W	72,000	1981

National Park

Cabo Orange	II	3°58'N/51°22'W	619,000	1980

State Environment Protection Area

Curiaú	V	0°10'N/51°05'W	23,000	1990

Amazonas

Federal Area of Outstanding Ecological Interest

Javari-Buriti	V	3°11'S/67°50'W	15,000	1985

Projeto Dinamica de Fragmentos Florestais	V	2°24'S/59°52'W	3,288	1985
Federal Biological Reserve				
Abufari	I	5°12'S/63°03'W	288,000	1982
Uatuma	I	1°15'S/60°13'W	560,000	1990
Federal Ecological Reserve				
Juami-Japurá	V	1°58'S/67°54'W	273,283	1983
Jutaí-Solimoes	I	3°11'S/67°37'W	288,187	1983
Federal Ecological Station				
Anavilhanas	IV	2°36'S/60°50'W	330,018	1981
Juami-Japurá	IV	2°26'S/68°31'W	572,650	1985
National Park				
Jaú	II	2°13'S/62°43'W	2,272,000	1980
Pico da Neblina	II	0°20'N/66°02'W	2,200,000	1979
State Biological Reserve				
Morro dos Seis Lagos	I	00°22'N/66°45'W	36,900	1982
State Ecological Station				
Mamirauá	IV	2°13'S/65°49'W	1,124,000	1990
State Environment Protection Area				
Caverna do Moroaga	V	1°57'S/59°56'W	278,500	1990
Lago Ayapua	V	4°30'S/62°21'W	610,000	1990
Nhamundá	V	2°21'S/56°43'W	195,900	1990
State Park				
Nhamundá	II	2°12'S/56°58'W	28,370	1989
Serra do Araçá	II	1°34'N/63°29'W	1,818,700	1990

Bahia

Ecological Station				
Pau-Brasil	I	?/?	1,145	1969
Federal Biological Reserve				
Una	I	15°17'S/39°08'W	11,400	1980
Federal Ecological Reserve				
Raso da Catarina	I	9°35'S/38°35'W	200,000	1983
Municipal Park				
Lagoas e Dunas do Abaeté	II	?/?	1,470	1977
Metropolitan Park				
Sitio Histórico Municipal de Pirajá	II	?/?	1,550	1978
National Park				
Chapada Diamantina	II	12°31'S/41°44'W	152,000	1985
Grande Sertao Veredas	II	?/?	84,000	1989
Marinho dos Abrolhos	II	17°53'S/38°56'W	91,300	1983
Monte Pascoal	II	16°54'S/39°16'W	22,500	1961
State Environment Protection Area				
Abaeté	V	?/?	1,800	1987
Bacia Hidrográfica do Joanes	V	?/?	5,022	1991
Gruta dos Brejoes/Vereda do Romao Gramacho	V	?/?	11,900	1985
Guaibim	V	?/?	2,000	1992
Islas de Tinharé e Boipeba	V	?/?	34,000	1992
Litoral Norte da Bahia	V	?/?	142,000	1992
Mangue Seco	V	?/?	3,395	1991

State Park

Ilha de Itaparica	II	?/?	2,180	1978
Morro do Chapéu	II	?/?	6,000	1973
Rio Capivara	II	?/?	1,100	1975

Ceará

Federal Ecological Station

Aiuaba	IV	5°29'S/40°51'W	12,000	1978

Federal Environment Protection Area

Jericoacoara	V	2°49'S/040°30'W	5,480	1984

State Environment Protection Area

Serra de Baturité	V	4°17'S/38°58'W	32,690	1990

Distrito Federal

Federal Environment Protection Area

Bacia do Descoberto	V	15°42'S/48°10'W	39,100	1983
Bacia do Rio Sao Bartolomeu	V	15°47'S/47°41'W	84,100	1983

National Park

Brasilia	II	15°40'S/48°00'W	28,000	1961

State Area of Outstanding Ecological Interest

Córregos Taquara e Capetinga	IV	15°58'S/47°57'W	1,660	1985

State Ecological Station

Aguas Emendadas	I	15°34'S/46°36'W	10,547	1968
Jardim Botânico	I	15°54'S/47°51'W	3,991	1992

State Environment Protection Area

Bacias do Gama e Cabeça do Veado	V	15°54'S/47°54'W	25,000	1986
Cafuringa	V	15°37'S/48°00'W	30,000	1988
Lago Paranoá	V	15°47'S/47°50'W	16,000	1989

Espírito Santo

Federal Biological Reserve

Augusto Ruschi (Nova Lombardia)	I	19°51'S/40°32'W	4,000	1982
Corrego do Veado	I	18°21'S/40°09'W	2,392	1982
Corrego Grande	I	18°15'S/39°47'W	1,504	1989
Sooretama	I	18°59'S/40°05'W	24,000	1982

National Park

Caparao	II	20°28'S/41°48'W	26,000	1961

State Biological Reserve

Duas Bocas	IV	20°17'S/40°30'W	2,910	1965
Mestre Alvaro	I	20°10'S/40°18'W	3,470	1976
Pedra Azul	I	20°27'S/41°00'W	1,240	1960

State Park

Itaunas	IV	18°23'S/39°45'W	3,150	1992
Setiba	IV	20°33'S/40°24'W	1,500	1990

Goiás

Federal Ecological Station

Coco-Javaes	IV	10°08'S/49°34'W	37,000	1981

National Park

Araguaia	II	10°45'S/50°10'W	562,312	1959
Chapada dos Veadeiros	II	14°01'S/47°41'W	60,000	1961

Emas (GO-MT)	II	18°02'S/52°50'W	131,868	1961
State Biological Reserve				
Parauna	I	?/?	3,490	1979
State Park				
Serra Caldas Novas	II	?/?	12,315	1970
Terra Ronca	II	?/?	14,493	?

Maranhão

Federal Ecological Station				
Piria-Gurupi	I	3°38'S/46°37'W	341,650	1988
Federal Environment Protection Area				
Serra da Tabatinga	V	?/?	61,000	1990
National Park				
Lencois Maranhenses	II	2°32'S/43°08'W	155,000	1981
State Park				
Bacanga	II	?/?	3,075	1980
Mirador	II	?/?	385,000	1980

Mato Grosso

Federal Biological Reserve				
Caracara	I	17°39'S/57°32'W	61,126	1971
Federal Ecological Station				
Ique	IV	12°13'S/59°24'W	200,000	1981
Ique Juruena	IV	?/?	160,000	?
Ique-Aripuana	IV	11°56'S/59°17'W	226,000	?
Serra das Araras	IV	15°53'S/57°19'W	115,000	1982
Taiama	IV	16°50'S/57°31'W	12,000	1981
National Park				
Chapada dos Guimaraes	II	16°40'S/54°21'W	33,000	1989
Pantanal Matogrossense	II	17°40'S/57°28'W	135,000	1981
Xingu	II	11°20'S/53°05'W	2,200,000	1961
State Ecological Reserve				
Culuene	IV	?/?	3,000	1989
State Park				
Aguas Quentes	II	15°53'S/55°32'W	1,487	1978

Mato Grosso do Sul

No Areas Listed

Minas Gerais

Federal Ecological Station				
Ilhas das Marias	IV	?/?	1,000	1980
Pirapitinga	IV	18°11'S/45°16'W	1,090	1987
Federal Environment Protection Area				
Carstre do Lagoa Santa	V	20°54'S/42°30'W	35,600	1990
Cavernas do Peruacu	V	15°15'S/43°13'W	150,000	1989
Morro da Pedreira	V	20°42'S/42°58'W	66,200	1990
Serra da Mantiqueira	V	?/?	402,517	1985
Municipal Biological Reserve				
Santa Clara	I	?/?	1,452	?
National Park				
Serra da Canastra	II	20°06'S/46°36'W	71,525	1972

Serra do Cipo	II	19°53'S/43°51'W	33,800	1984
State Biological Reserve				
Acaua	I	?/?	5,195	1974
Colonia 31 de Março	I	?/?	5,033	1974
Mata Acaua	I	?/?	5,000	1974
State Ecological Station				
Papagaio	V	?/?	26,788	1990
State Environment Protection Area				
Cachoeira Andorinhas	V	20°21'S/43°30'W	18,700	1989
State Forest Park				
Rio Doce	II	19°37'S/42°40'W	35,973	1944
State Park				
Ibitipoca	II	?/?	1,488	1973
Itacolomi	II	20°26'S/43°27'W	7,542	1967
Jaiba	II	?/?	6,358	1973
Serra do Brigadeiro	II	21°17'S/42°30'W	32,500	1988
Sumidouro	II	?/?	1,300	1980

Pará

Federal Biological Reserve				
Rio Trombetas	I	0°59'S/56°41'W	385,000	1979
Tapirape	I	5°50'S/50°40'W	103,000	1989
Federal Ecological Station				
Jari	IV	0°42'S/52°48'W	227,126	1982
Federal Environment Protection Area				
Igarape Gelado	V	6°00'S/50°30'W	21,600	1989
National Park				
Amazonia	II	4°30'S/56°43'W	994,000	1974
State Environment Protection Area				
Algodoal	V	0°45'S/47°50'W	2,367	1990

Paraíba

Federal Area of Outstanding Ecological Interest				
Manguezais da Foz do Rio Mamanguape	IV	6°56'S/35°06'W	5,721	1985
Federal Biological Reserve				
Guaribas	I	7°10'S/35°06'W	4,321	1990
State Ecological Reserve				
Rio Vermelho	I	6°47'S/35°06'W	1,500	1992

Paraná

Federal Ecological Station				
Guaraqueçaba	IV	25°13'S/48°35'W	13,638	1982
Federal Environment Protection Area				
Guaraqueçaba	V	25°06'S/48°32'W	291,500	1985
National Park				
Iguaçu	II	25°23'S/54°07'W	170,000	1939
Superagui	II	25°06'S/48°18'W	21,000	1989
Special Area of Touristic Interest				
Marumbi	V	?/?	66,732	1992

State Ecological Station

Ilha do Mel	IV	?/?	2,240	1982

State Environment Protection Area

Escarpa Devoniana	V	?/?	392,363	1992
Guaraqueçaba	V	?/?	192,595	1992
Guaratuba	V	?/?	199,596	1992
Passaúna	V	?/?	36,020	1991
Serra da Esperança	V	?/?	87,750	1992

State Park

Agudo da Cotia	II	20°16'S/048°49'W	1,009	1990
Caxambu	II	24°32'S/49°55'W	1,040	1979
Diamante do Norte	II	22°40'S/051°29'W	1,427	?
Graciosa	II	25°23'S/048°55'W	1,189	1990
Lauráceas	II	25°19'S/48°35'W	23,863	1989
Pico do Marumbi	II	25°27'S/048°55'W	1,957	1990
Quartelá	II	?/?	4,389	1992
Vila Velha	II	25°17'S/50°02'W	3,245	1953

Pernambuco

Federal Biological Reserve

Serra Negra	I	9°48'S/38°07'W	1,100	1982

Federal Environment Protection Area

Fernando de Noronha	V	3°41'S/33°02'W	1,692	1986

National Park

Marinho Fernando de Noronha	II	3°45'S/33°00'W	11,270	1988

State Ecological Reserve

Sistema Gurjaú	I	?/?	1,362	1987

State Environment Protection Area

Canal de Santa Cruz	V	?/?	5,292	1986
Rio Formoso	V	?/?	2,724	1986
Rio Itapessoca	V	?/?	3,998	1986
Rio Timbo	V	?/?	1,397	1986
Rios Goiana/Megao	V	?/?	4,776	1986
Rios Jaboatao/Pirapama	V	?/?	1,285	1986
Rios Serinhaem/Maracaipe	V	?/?	3,335	1986

Piaui

Federal Ecological Station

Urucui-Una	IV	9°44'S/45°07'W	135,000	1981

National Park

Serra da Capivara	II	9°32'S/42°41'W	97,933	1979
Sete Cidades	II	4°18'S/41°42'W	6,221	1961

State Environment Protection Area

Serra das Mangabeiras	V	?/?	96,743	1983

Rio de Janeiro

Federal Biological Reserve

Poco das Antas	I	22°39'S/42°06'W	5,000	1974
Tingua	I	22°30'S/43°11'W	26,000	1989

Federal Ecological Station

Pirai	IV	22°51'S/43°27'W	4,000	1982
Tamoios	IV	22°55'S/44°16'W	4,070	1990

Federal Environment Protection Area

Cairucu	V	22°48'S/43°59'W	33,800	1983
Guapi-Mirim	V	22°56'S/42°02'W	14,340	1984
Petropolis	V	22°30'S/43°00'W	44,000	1982

National Park

Itatiaia	II	22°23'S/44°27'W	30,000	1937
Serra dos Oragos	II	22°25'S/42°53'W	11,000	1939
Tijuca	II	22°53'S/43°12'W	3,200	1961

State Biological Reserve

Araras	I	22°27'S/43°15'W	2,068	1972
Jacaranda	I	?/?	2,700	1985
Massambara	I	?/?	1,680	1986
Praia do Sul	I	23°10'S/44°17'W	3,600	1981

State Ecological Station

Paraiso	IV	?/?	4,920	1987

State Environment Protection Area

Floresta do Jacaranda	V	?/?	2,700	1983
Mangaratiba	V	?/?	22,936	1987

State Park

Desengano	V	21°52'S/41°48'W	22,500	1983
Ilha Grande	II	23°10'S/44°14'W	15,000	1978
Pedra Branca	II	22°59'S/43°28'W	12,500	1974

Rio Grande do Norte

Federal Biological Reserve

Atol das Rocas	I	3°33'S/33°36'W	36,249	1979

Federal Ecological Station

Serido	IV	6°42'S/36°51'W	1,116	1982

State Ecological Park

Cabugi	V	?/?	2,164	?

State Environment Protection Area

Piquiri-Una	V	?/?	96,743	1983

State Park

Dunas de Natal	II	?/?	1,172	1977

Rio Grande do Sul

Area of Special Historic and Touristic Interest

Ferrabraz	II	29°36'S/50°57'W	1,000	1987

Federal Ecological Station

Taim	IV	31°14'S/52°46'W	33,995	1986

Federal Environment Protection Area

Ibirapuita	V	?/?	318,000	1992

Municipal Biological Reserve

Banhado Grande	I	29°57'S/51°00'W	7,340	1981

Municipal Park

Saint-Hilaire	II	?/?	1,180	1947

National Park

Aparados da Serra	II	29°16'S/50°25'W	10,250	1959
Lagoa do Peixe	II	31°21'S/51°12'W	34,357	1986
Serra Geral	II	29°00'S/50°00'W	17,300	1992

State Biological Reserve

Ilha da Polvora e das Pombas	I	29°30'S/51°15'W	17,245	1976
Mato Grande	I	32°15'S/52°40'W	5,161	1975
Sao Donato	I	29°00'S/56°30'W	4,392	1975
Serra Geral	I	29°34'S/50°14'W	1,700	1982

State Park

Camaqua	II	31°15'S/51°45'W	7,992	1975
Delta do Jacui	II	29°30'S/51°15'W	4,322	1976
Espigao Alto	II	30°36'S/51°29'W	1,319	1949
Itapuâ	II	30°22'S/51°02'W	5,533	1957
Nonoai	II	27°22'S/53°30'W	17,498	1949
Podocarpus	II	30°30'S/52°30'W	3,645	1975
Rondinha	II	27°50'S/52°00'W	1,000	1982
Tainhas	II	29°10'S/50°20'W	4,924	1975
Torres (Guarita)	II	25°22'S/49°40'W	1,540	1953
Turvo	II	27°10'S/53°30'W	17,491	1947

Rondônia

Federal Biological Reserve

Guaporé	I	12°30'S/62°48'W	600,000	1982
Jaru	I	9°52'S/61°40'W	268,150	1979

Federal Ecological Station

Cunia	IV	8°16'S/63°21'W	104,000	1982

Municipal Park

Ouro Preto	II	10°43'S/62°15'W	222,082	1986

National Park

Pacaas Novos	II	11°13'S/63°28'W	764,801	1979

State Biological Reserve

Rio Ouro Preto	I	10°54'S/64°39'W	46,438	1990
Tracadal	I	11°23'S/64°50'W	22,540	1990

State Ecological Station

Samuel	I	8°59'S/63°13'W	20,865	1990
Serra dos Tres Irmaos	I	9°12'S/64°47'W	99,813	1990

State Park

Candeias	II	8°53'S/63°36'W	8,985	1990
Corumbiara	II	13°12'S/6138'W	586,031	1990
Guajara-Mirim	II	10°34'S/64°19'W	258,813	1990
Rio Cautario	II	11°41'S/64°09'W	121,167	1990
Serra dos Parecis	II	12°25'S/61°46'W	38,950	1990
Serra dos Reis	II	12°12'S/62°55'W	100,948	1990

Roraima

Federal Ecological Station

Caracarai	IV	2°44'N/61°34'W	394,560	1982
Maracá	IV	3°25'N/61°40'W	101,312	1981
Niquia	IV	2°29'N/61°18'W	286,600	1985

National Park

Monte Roraima	II	5°09'N/60°18'W	116,000	1989

Santa Catarina

Federal Biological Reserve

Marinha do Arvoredo	I	?/?	17,600	1990

Federal Ecological Station

Babitonga	IV	25°59'S/48°49'W	7,833	1987
Carijós	IV	27°21'S/48°31'W	11,295	1987

Municipal Park				
Lagoa do Peri	II	?/?	2,030	1981
National Park				
Sao Joaquim	II	28°08'S/49°33'W	49,300	1961
State Biological Reserve				
Aguaí	I	28°33'S/49°38'W	7,672	1983
Canela Preta	I	27°16'S/49°08'W	18,445	1980
Sassafraz	I	?/?	5,416	1977
State Ecological Station				
Bracinho	IV	?/?	4,606	1984
State Park				
Serra do Tabuleiro	II	28°08'S/48°50'W	87,405	1975
Serra Furada	II	26°09'S/49°24'W	1,329	1980

São Paulo

Faunal Reserve				
Secundario Perimetro de Sao Roque	IV	23°56'S/47°18'W	23,900	1978
Federal Ecological Station				
Jureia	IV	24°27'S/47°17'W	24,065	1986
Tupinambas	IV	23°45'S/46°08'W	4,628	1987
Federal Environment Protection Area				
Cananeia - Iguape e Peruibe	V	24°54'S/47°38'W	202,832	1984
National Park				
Serra da Bocaina	II	23°01'S/44°41'W	100,000	1971
State Ecological Station				
Angatuba	IV	?/?	1,394	1985
Caetetus	IV	22°25'S/49°42'W	2,188	1987
Chauas	IV	?/?	2,700	1987
Itirapina	IV	?/?	2,300	1984
Jatai	IV	?/?	4,532	1982
Jureia-Itatins	IV	?/?	80,000	1987
Santa Barbara	IV	?/?	2,712	1984
Xitue	IV	24°19'S/48°23'W	3,095	1987
State Environment Protection Area				
Bacia dos Rios Piracicaba e Juqueri - Mirim	V	?/?	390,000	1987
Cabreuva	V	?/?	26,100	1984
Cajamar	V	?/?	13,400	1987
Campos do Jordao	V	?/?	26,900	1984
Corumbatai-Botucatu-Tejupa	V	?/?	641,000	1984
Ibitinga	V	?/?	64,900	1987
Ilha Comprida	V	?/?	19,375	1987
Jundiai	V	?/?	43,200	1984
Serra do Mar	V	?/?	548,100	1984
Silveiras	V	?/?	42,700	1984
Tiete	V	?/?	45,100	1983
Varzea do Alto Tiete	V	?/?	8,500	1987
State Park				
Alto Ribeira	II	24°29'S/48°35'W	37,712	1958
Campos do Jordao	II	22°35'S/45°29'W	8,286	1941
Cantareira	II	?/?	7,000	?
Carlos Botelho	II	24°10'S/48°00'W	37,797	1982
Ilha Anchieta	II	22°34'S/45°03'W	828	1977
Ilha Bela	II	23°51'S/45°14'W	27,025	1958
Ilha do Cardoso	II	25°10'S/47°59'W	22,500	1962
Jacupiranga	II	24°53'S/48°22'W	150,000	1969

Morro do Diabo	II	22°34'S/52°16'W	34,441	1986
Serra do Mar	II	23°44'S/46°01'W	314,800	1969
Vascununca	II	21°35'S/47°57'W	1,484	1970

Sergipe

Federal Biological Reserve

Santa Izabel	I	11°11'S/37°17'W	2,766	1988

Federal Ecological Station

Serra de Itabaiana	IV	11°00'S/37°24'W	1,752	1987

State Environment Protection Area

Litoral Sul	V	11°20'S/37°28'W	440,500	1993
Morro do Urubu	V	11°15'S/37°20'W	213,872	1993
Platô de Neópolis	V	11°45'S/37°45'W	2,149	1993

Tocantins

No Areas Listed

BRUNEI DARUSSALAM

Summary		
Category I	9	66,274
Category II	1	48,859
Category III	0	0
Category IV	0	0
Category V	0	0
Total	**10**	**115,133**

Forest Reserve

Batu Apoi (Conservation) Extension	I	4°30'N/115°06'E	2,644	1987
Belait Peat Swamp (Conservation)	I	4°33'N/114°19'E	1,492	1982
Belait Peat Swamp (Ulu Mendaram Conservation)	I	4°16'N/114°23'E	6,170	1982
Bukit Biang (Conservation)	I	4°41'N/115°05'E	2,730	1987
Labi Hills (Bukit Teraja Protection)	I	4°18'N/114°27'E	6,825	1947
Labi Hills (Sungai Ingei Conservation)	I	4°10'N/114°45'E	18,491	1947
Ladan Hills (Bentuan Catchment Protection)	I	4°38'N/114°46'E	2,932	1950
Ladan Hills (Bukit Bedwan Protection)	I	4°28'N/114°48'E	7,633	1950
Ladan Hills (Productive Production)	I	4°30'N/114°47'E	17,357	1950

National Park

Ulu Temburong	II	4°30'N/115°11'E	48,859	1991

BULGARIA/BULGARIE

Summary		
Category I	26	61,824
Category II	3	221,253
Category III	2	4,424
Category IV	13	50,748
Category V	2	31,641
Total	**46**	**369,890**

National Monument

Melnishki Piramidi	III	41°32'N/23°26'E	1,165	1960

National Park

Balkan Central	II	42°41'N/24°44'E	73,262	1991
Choumensko plato	IV	43°17'N/26°51'E	3,930	1980
Pirin	II	41°47'N/23°28'E	40,067	1963
Rila	II	42°09'N/23°32'E	107,924	1992
Roussenski Lom	III	43°40'N/26°05'E	3,259	1970

Sinite kamani	IV	42°45'N/26°20'E	6,685	1981
Vitocha	IV	42°33'N/23°15'E	26,607	1934
Vratchanski balkan	V	43°10'N/23°28'E	30,130	1988
Zlatni pyassatsi	IV	43°20'N/28°02'E	1,320	1943

Protected Landscape

Embouchure de la Veleka	V	42°03'N/27°16'E	1,511	1992

Reserve

Alibotouche	I	41°26'N/23°41'E	1,628	1951
Atanasovsko ezero	IV	42°33'N/27°32'E	1,650	1980
Baiuvi doupki-Djindjiritsa	I	41°49'N/23°21'E	2,873	1934
Beglika	I	41°57'N/24°01'E	1,463	1960
Beli Lom	IV	43°39'N/26°18'E	1,051	1980
Bistrichko branichte	I	42°32'N/23°18'E	1,062	1935
Boatine	I	42°46'N/24°13'E	1,597	1948
Central Rila	I	42°09'N/23°32'E	12,394	1992
Djendema	I	42°40'N/24°53'E	4,220	1953
Doupkata	I	41°47'N/24°16'E	1,211	1956
Fôret du Monastère de Rila	I	42°09'N/23°21'E	3,677	1986
Ibar	I	42°12'N/23°42'E	2,249	1985
Kamenchtitsa	I	42°40'N/25°21'E	1,018	1984
Kamtchia	IV	43°02'N/27°51'E	1,445	1951
Kongoura	I	41°22'N/23°14'E	1,312	1988
Koupena	I	41°58'N/24°18'E	1,761	1961
Mantaritza	I	41°58'N/24°02'E	1,069	1968
Oreliak	IV	41°35'N/23°38'E	1,228	1985
Ouzounboudjak	I	41°57'N/27°54'E	2,575	1956
Parangalitsa	I	42°01'N/23°24'E	1,508	1933
Peechti skali	I	42°43'N/24°58'E	1,465	1979
Persin (îles de)	IV	43°40'N/25°17'E	1,715	1981
Ropotamo	I	42°19'N/27°46'E	1,001	1992
Severen Djendem	I	42°44'N/24°51'E	1,610	1983
Sokolna	I	42°40'N/25°03'E	1,250	1979
Srebarna	IV	44°09'N/27°06'E	1,143	1948
Stara reka	I	42°39'N/24°44'E	1,975	1981
Steneto	I	42°42'N/24°38'E	3,579	1980
Tchervenata stena	I	41°53'N/24°49'E	3,029	1962
Tchouprene	I	43°26'N/22°36'E	1,440	1974
Tissata (Tissova Bartchina)	IV	41°46'N/23°11'E	1,452	1949
Tissovitsa	IV	42°06'N/27°46'E	1,251	1990
Tsaritchina	I	42°45'N/24°20'E	3,419	1949
Veleka	IV	42°03'N/27°36'E	1,271	1989
Vratchanski karst	I	43°13'N/23°30'E	1,439	1983

BURKINA FASO

Summary		
Category I	0	0
Category II	3	489,300
Category III	0	0
Category IV	9	2,172,600
Category V	0	0
Total	**12**	**2,661,900**

Classified Forest

Mare aux Hippototames	IV	11°38'N/4°08'W	19,200	1937

National Park

Deux Bales	II	11°40'N/2°41'W	56,600	1967
Kabore-Tambi	II	11°30'N/1°20'W	242,700	1976
W du Burkina Faso	II	12°00'N/2°00'E	190,000	1954

Partial Faunal Reserve

Arly	IV	11°30'N/1°30'E	130,000	1954
Kourtiagou	IV	11°37'N/2°02'E	51,000	1957
Pama	IV	11°30'N/0°45'E	74,700	1955
Sahel	IV	14°30'N/1°00'W	1,600,000	1970

Total Faunal Reserve

Arly	IV	11°30'N/1°30'E	76,000	1954
Bontioli	IV	10°40'N/3°00'W	12,700	1957
Madjoari	IV	?/?	17,000	1955
Singou	IV	11°55'N/1°00'E	192,000	1955

BURUNDI

Summary		
Category I	0	0
Category II	0	0
Category III	0	0
Category IV	0	0
Category V	3	88,865
Total	**3**	**88,865**

National Park

Kibira	V	3°00'S/29°22'E	40,000	1933
Rusizi	V	3°15'S/29°15'E	5,235	1974
Ruvubu	V	3°00'S/30°23'E	43,630	1980

CAMBODIA/CAMBODGE/CAMBOYA

No Areas Listed

CAMEROON/CAMEROUN/CAMERUN

Summary		
Category I	0	0
Category II	7	1,031,800
Category III	0	0
Category IV	7	1,018,625
Category V	0	0
Total	**14**	**2,050,425**

Faunal Reserve

Campo	IV	2°30'N/10°04'E	300,000	1932
Dja	IV	3°06'N/13°00'E	526,000	1950
Douala-Edea	IV	3°32'N/10°12'E	160,000	1932
Kimbi	IV	6°30'N/10°30'E	5,625	1964
Lac Ossa	IV	?/?	4,000	1968
Nanga-Eboke	IV	?/?	16,000	?
Santchou	IV	?/?	7,000	1933

National Park

Benoué	II	8°25'N/13°48'E	180,000	1968
Bouba Ndjidah	II	8°40'N/14°40'E	220,000	1968
Faro	II	8°10'N/12°39'E	330,000	1980
Kalamaloue	II	12°08'N/14°53'E	4,500	1972
Korup	II	5°10'N/9°18'E	125,900	1986
Mozogo-Gokoro	II	10°53'N/13°46'E	1,400	1968
Waza	II	11°15'N/14°44'E	170,000	1968

CANADA

	Summary	
Category I	100	1,481,114
Category II	251	32,940,384
Category III	2	2,693
Category IV	176	38,676,635
Category V	111	9,444,666
Total	**640**	**82,545,492**

Alberta

Ecological Reserve

Athabasca Dunes	I	58°10'N/110°50'W	3,770	1987
Goose Mountain	I	54°45'N/115°58'W	1,247	1987
Hand Hills	I	51°24'N/112°17'W	2,229	1988
Kennedy Coulee	I	49°00'N/110°43'W	1,068	1987
Kootenay Plains	I	52°03'N/116°25'W	3,204	1987
Plateau Mountain	I	50°12'N/114°31'W	2,323	1991
Rumsey	I	51°55'N/112°45'W	3,432	1990
Silver Valley	I	56°12'N/119°35'W	1,805	1987
Upper Bob Creek	I	49°58'N/114°15'W	2,601	1989
Wainwright Dunes	I	52°35'N/110°37'W	2,821	1988

Game Bird Sanctuary

Birch Lake	IV	53°19'N/111°35'W	3,015	1974
Lac La Biche	IV	54°49'N/112°10'W	22,561	1947
Many Island Lake	IV	50°08'N/110°03'W	4,791	1974
Ministik Lake	IV	53°21'N/113°01'W	6,623	1974
Miquelon Lake	IV	53°15'N/112°53'W	11,331	1974
Pakowki Lake	IV	49°20'N/110°55'W	12,536	1974

Migratory Bird Sanctuary

Richardson Lake	IV	58°24'N/111°04'W	12,725	1953
Saskatoon Lake	IV	55°13'N/119°05'W	1,140	1948

National Park

Banff	II	51°32'N/116°07'W	664,080	1885
Elk Island	II	53°34'N/112°52'W	19,430	1913
Jasper	II	52°50'N/117°58'W	1,087,800	1907
Waterton Lakes	II	49°04'N/113°55'W	50,500	1895
Wood Buffalo	II	58°30'N/115°00'W	4,480,700	1922

National Wildlife Area

Middle Sand Hills	IV	?/?	42,000	?

Natural Area

Beehive	IV	50°04'N/114°38'W	5,662	1987
Kootenay Plains	IV	52°06'N/116°24'W	3,378	1978
Milk River	IV	49°03'N/110°41'W	5,490	1987
Pine Sands	IV	54°58'N/112°52'W	1,350	1987
Redwater	IV	53°57'N/113°06'W	1,811	1971
Spruce Island Lake	IV	54°29'N/113°47'W	6,480	1992
White Earth Valley	IV	54°04'N/112°14'W	2,055	1990

Provincial Park

Bow Valley	II	51°04'N/115°04'W	1,261	1959
Carson Pegasus	II	54°18'N/115°39'W	1,210	1982
Crimson Lake	II	52°28'N/115°02'W	3,209	1955
Cross Lake	II	54°39'N/113°47'W	2,076	1955
Cypress Hills	II	49°38'N/110°12'W	20,451	1951
Dinosaur	II	50°47'N/111°30'W	6,622	1955

Dry Island Buffalo Jump	II	51°57'N/112°57'W	1,180	1970
Fish Creek	II	50°55'N/114°02'W	1,159	1975
Hilliard's Bay	II	55°30'N/116°00'W	2,329	1978
Kananaskis	II	50°39'N/115°08'W	50,308	1977
Lakeland	II	?/?	14,701	1992
Lesser Slave Lake	II	55°26'N/114°49'W	7,557	1966
Notikewin	II	57°14'N/117°07'W	9,697	1979
Peter Lougheed	II	50°40'N/115°10'W	50,142	1977
Whitney Lake	II	53°51'N/110°32'W	1,489	1982
William A. Switzer	II	53°30'N/117°48'W	2,686	1958
Winagami	II	55°37'N/116°39'W	1,211	1956
Writing-on-stone	II	49°05'N/111°38'W	1,722	1957
Young's Point	II	55°08'N/117°35'W	1,090	1971

Recreation Area

Cooking Lake Blackfoot	II	?/?	9,701	?
Lakeland	II	?/?	44,330	1992

Wilderness Area

Ghost River	I	51°22'N/115°25'W	15,317	1967
Siffeur	I	52°54'N/116°23'W	41,215	1965
White Goat	I	52°13'N/116°50'W	44,457	1965

Wilderness Park

Willmore	II	53°45'N/119°30'W	459,671	1959

Wildlife Sanctuary

Camp 1	IV	?/?	10,639	1990
Sheep River	IV	50°44'N/113°51'W	8,466	1974

British Columbia

Ecological Reserve

Byers/Conroy/Harvey/Sinnett Islands	I	52°30'N/129°18'W	12,205	1981
Checleset Bay	I	50°04'N/127°37'W	34,650	1981
Dewdney and Glide Islands	I	52°58'N/129°35'W	3,845	1971
East Redonda Island	I	50°22'N/124°19'W	6,212	1971
Gamble Creek	I	54°12'N/130°01'W	1,026	1991
Gingietl Creek	I	55°12'N/129°16'W	2,873	1985
Gladys Lake	I	57°33'N/128°50'W	48,560	1975
Goosegrass Creek	I	52°00'N/118°15'W	2,185	1974
Ilgachuz Range	I	52°47'N/125°17'W	2,914	1975
Kingfisher Creek	I	50°48'N/118°47'W	1,441	1973
Lasquet Island	I	49°28'N/124°17'W	201	1971
Mount Griffin	I	50°53'N/118°33'W	1,376	1972
Murtle Lake Nature Conservancy	I	50°00'N/119°00'W	212,742	1968
Narcosli Lake	I	52°57'N/124°06'W	1,098	1973
Ningunsaw River	I	56°54'N/130°07'W	2,046	1975
Robson Bight	I	50°30'N/126°34'W	1,753	1982
Saturna Island	I	48°47'N/123°09'W	131	1971
Sikanni Chief	I	57°17'N/124°07'W	2,401	1973
Smith River	I	59°41'N/126°30'W	1,326	1977
V.J. Krajina	I	53°35'N/132°00'W	9,834	1973

Migratory Bird Sanctuary

Victoria Harbour	IV	48°25'N/123°20'W	1,700	1923

National Park

Glacier	II	51°16'N/117°31'W	134,930	1886
Kootenay	II	50°57'N/116°02'W	140,600	1920
Mount Revelstoke	II	51°05'N/118°02'W	25,970	1914
Yoho	II	51°23'N/116°31'W	131,300	1886

National Park Reserve

Pacific Rim	II	49°04'N/125°45'W	50,000	1970
South Moresby	II	52°04'N/131°12'W	147,000	1988

National Wildlife Area

Columbia	I	50°45'N/116°15'W	1,001	1978

Provincial Park

Atlin	II	59°13'N/133°54'W	232,695	1973
Birkenhead Lake	II	50°32'N/122°42'W	3,642	1963
Bowron Lake	II	53°10'N/121°05'W	123,117	1961
Boya Lake	II	59°23'N/129°05'W	4,597	1965
Broughton Archipelago Marine	II	50°42'N/126°41'W	11,679	1992
Cape Scott	II	50°44'N/128°20'W	15,070	1973
Carmanah Pacific	II	48°39'N/124°40'W	3,592	1991
Carp Lake	II	54°45'N/123°22'W	19,344	1973
Cathedral	II	49°04'N/120°11'W	33,272	1968
Champion Lakes	II	49°11'N/117°37'W	1,424	1955
Cypress	II	49°27'N/123°12'W	3,012	1975
Darke Lake	II	49°44'N/119°52'W	1,470	1943
Desolation Sound Marine	II	50°12'N/124°44'W	8,256	1973
E.C. Manning	II	49°06'N/120°48'W	65,884	1941
Elk Falls	II	50°03'N/125°19'W	1,087	1940
Elk Lakes Cla	II	50°32'N/115°07'W	5,625	1973
Eneas Lakes	II	49°45'N/119°56'W	1,036	1968
Eskers	II	53°50'N/123°14'W	1,603	1987
Garibaldi	II	50°00'N/122°45'W	194,654	1927
Golden Ears	II	49°37'N/122°30'W	55,596	1927
Gwillim Lake	II	55°21'N/121°17'W	9,199	1971
Hamber	II	52°22'N/117°52'W	24,518	1941
Helliwell	II	49°31'N/124°35'W	2,872	1966
International Ridge	II	49°02'N/121°58'W	1,905	1969
Kinaskan Lake	II	57°35'N/130°15'W	1,800	1987
Kokanee Glacier	II	49°57'N/117°10'W	25,832	1922
Kwadacha Wilderness	II	57°48'N/125°07'W	114,444	1973
Mitlenatch Island	II	49°57'N/125°00'W	155	1961
Monashee	II	50°31'N/118°15'W	7,514	1962
Monkman	II	54°36'N/121°11'W	40,170	1981
Mount Assiniboine	II	50°50'N/115°35'W	39,052	1922
Mount Edziza	II	57°35'N/130°40'W	228,702	1972
Mount Judge Howay	II	49°30'N/122°18'W	6,180	1967
Mount Robson	II	52°48'N/118°40'W	219,534	1913
Mount Seymour	II	49°23'N/122°55'W	3,508	1936
Mount Terry Fox	II	52°57'N/119°15'W	1,930	1982
Muncho Lake	II	59°10'N/126°01'W	88,416	1957
Naikoon	II	53°53'N/130°55'W	72,641	1973
Newcastle Island	II	49°11'N/123°56'W	336	1961
Nisga'a Memorial Lava Bed	II	55°06'N/128°54'W	11,243	1992
Okanagan Mountain	II	49°43'N/119°38'W	10,650	1973
Penrose Island Marine	II	51°28'N/127°44'W	2,013	1992
Sasquatch	II	49°21'N/121°42'W	1,217	1968
Schoen Lake	II	50°10'N/126°15'W	8,170	1977
Silver Star Cla	II	50°22'N/119°04'W	6,092	1940
Spatsizi Plateau Wilderness	II	58°00'N/129°00'W	608,225	1975
St. Mary's Alpine	II	49°52'N/116°20'W	9,146	1973
Stagleap	II	49°03'N/117°03'W	1,133	1964
Stone Mountain	II	58°35'N/124°45'W	25,691	1957
Strathcona	II	49°40'N/125°40'W	219,304	1911
Strathcona-Westmin	II	49°40'N/125°40'W	3,328	1987
Tatlatui	II	56°58'N/127°23'W	105,829	1973
Tatshenshini-Alsek Wilderness	II	?/?	958,000	?
Top Of The World	II	49°51'N/115°24'W	8,791	1973

Tweedsmuir	II	53°06'N/126°00'W	960,918	1938
Valhalla	II	49°52'N/117°34'W	49,800	1983
Wells Gray	II	52°25'N/121°00'W	515,785	1939
White Pelican	II	52°17'N/123°02'W	1,247	1971
Whiteswan Lake	II	50°09'N/115°30'W	1,994	1978

Recreation Area

Akamina-Kishinena	II	49°03'N/114°16'W	10,915	1986
Atlin	II	59°12'N/134°16'W	38,445	1973
Babine Mountains	II	54°55'N/126°53'W	32,400	1984
Brooks Peninsula	II	50°10'N/127°45'W	28,780	1986
Bugaboo Alpine	II	50°48'N/115°52'W	24,912	1969
Cascade	II	49°10'N/120°52'W	16,680	1987
Coquihalla Summit	II	49°30'N/121°05'W	5,750	1987
Elk Lakes	II	49°18'N/115°07'W	11,620	1986
Fiordland	II	52°54'N/128°07'W	91,000	1987
Gitnadoix River	II	54°19'N/129°12'W	58,000	1986
Hakai	II	51°43'N/128°04'W	122,998	1987
Joffre Lakes	II	50°20'N/122°30'W	1,460	1988
Kakwa	II	54°01'N/120°10'W	127,690	1987
Kokanee Glacier	II	49°47'N/117°10'W	6,305	1987
Kwadacha	II	57°52'N/125°00'W	44,031	1987
Lake Lovely Water	II	49°45'N/123°15'W	1,300	1988
Mount Edziza	II	57°45'N/130°50'W	4,000	1972
Nancy Green	II	49°07'N/117°51'W	4,937	1969
Nisga'a Memorial Lava Bed	II	55°10'N/128°50'W	6,440	1992
Skagit Valley	II	49°07'N/121°10'W	32,508	1973
Stikine River	II	56°39'N/131°50'W	217,000	1987
Tweedsmuir	II	53°06'N/125°53'W	33,328	1987
Wells Gray	II	52°30'N/120°00'W	13,963	1985
Wokkpash	II	58°27'N/124°51'W	37,800	1986

Regional District Park

East Sooke	V	48°22'N/123°41'W	1,422	1970

Wilderness Area

Height-Of-The-Rockies	II	50°28'N/115°24'W	68,000	1987
Lower Stein	II	50°28'N/121°50'W	33,000	1987
Swan Lake	II	59°30'N/135°00'W	19,000	1991
Upper Stein	II	50°20'N/121°50'W	10,000	1987

Wilderness Conservancy

Purcell	II	50°08'N/116°30'W	131,500	1974

Wildlife Management Area

Creston Valley	IV	49°14'N/116°52'W	6,900	1969
Dewdrop-Roseau Creek	IV	50°47'N/120°55'W	4,240	1987
Junction	IV	55°45'N/122°38'W	5,300	1987
Pitt-Addington Marsh	IV	49°15'N/122°38'W	4,058	1987
Upper Cariboo River	IV	52°52'N/121°10'W	3,090	1987

Manitoba

Ecological Reserve

Baralzon Lake	I	59°55'N/98°00'W	39,000	1989
Long Point	I	52°59'N/98°45'W	1,600	1987
Reindeer Island	I	52°25'N/98°00'W	14,200	1976

National Park

Riding Mountain	II	50°44'N/99°47'W	297,590	1929

Provincial Park

Asessipi	V	50°59'N/101°20'W	2,460	1964

Atikaki Wilderness	II	51°36'N/95°39'W	466,841	1985
Birds Hill	II	50°01'N/96°53'W	3,521	1964
Clearwater Lake	II	54°05'N/101°05'W	59,570	1962
Duck Mountain	II	51°40'N/100°55'W	127,400	1961
Elk Island	II	50°45'N/96°32'W	1,000	1974
Grass River	II	50°40'N/100°50'W	228,960	1962
Grindstone	V	51°20'N/96°41'W	25,841	1969
Hecla	V	51°20'N/96°40'W	86,309	1969
Nopiming	V	50°44'N/95°26'W	143,740	1976
Paint Lake	II	55°29'N/97°57'W	22,660	1971
Spruce Woods	V	49°43'N/99°05'W	24,860	1964
Turtle Mountain	II	49°03'N/100°15'W	18,910	1961
Whiteshell	V	50°00'N/95°30'W	273,400	1961

Wildlife Management Area

Alonsa	V	50°57'N/99°14'W	10,559	1974
Assiniboine Corridor	V	49°53'N/97°07'W	2,207	1984
Basket Lake	V	51°49'N/99°03'W	7,190	1974
Broad Valley	V	50°58'N/97°42'W	3,692	1969
Cape Churchill	IV	58°46'N/93°12'W	13,707,210	1978
Cape Tatnam	V	57°16'N/91°00'W	522,267	1973
Catfish Creek	V	50°30'N/96°30'W	6,281	?
Cayer	V	51°25'N/99°15'W	1,522	?
Clematis	V	50°37'N/97°33'W	6,828	1969
Dog Lake	V	51°03'N/98°33'W	32,389	1972
Grahamdale	V	51°26'N/98°23'W	1,489	1974
Gypsumville	V	51°49'N/98°37'W	2,465	1969
Hilbre	V	51°31'N/98°42'W	3,527	1969
Inwood	V	50°27'N/97°30'W	2,719	1969
Lake Francis	V	50°18'N/97°58'W	6,416	1990
Langruth	V	50°27'N/98°45'W	1,781	1965
Lauder Sandhills	V	49°29'N/100°40'W	3,011	1971
Lee Lake	V	51°10'N/97°19'W	6,966	1969
Little Birch	V	51°09'N/98°13'W	22,802	1969
Lundar	V	50°44'N/97°50'W	1,101	1969
Mantagao Lake	V	51°22'N/97°56'W	50,339	1968
Marshy Point	V	50°34'N/98°07'W	1,490	1984
Moose Creek	V	49°30'N/97°00'W	78,917	?
Narcisse	V	50°43'N/97°35'W	13,781	1969
Oak Hammock Marsh	V	50°12'N/97°08'W	3,488	1974
Pembina Valley	V	49°00'N/98°12'W	1,910	1976
Peonan Point	V	51°34'N/98°56'W	2,339	1969
Point River	V	52°48'N/100°49'W	3,370	1984
Portage Sandhills	V	49°03'N/98°15'W	1,328	1984
Proulx Lake	V	51°45'N/99°13'W	3,302	1974
Proven Lake	V	50°33'N/99°59'W	1,908	1984
Rembrandt	V	50°48'N/97°08'W	1,360	1974
Sandridge	V	50°36'N/97°29'W	1,879	1969
Saskeram	V	53°50'N/101°30'W	96,648	1963
Sharpewood	V	50°51'N/97°50'W	2,266	1969
Sleeve Lake	V	51°00'N/97°57'W	14,964	1969
Souris River Bend	V	49°40'N/99°34'W	2,073	1968
Steeprock	V	52°47'N/101°01'W	1,890	1966
Washow Bay	V	51°20'N/97°05'W	1,392	?
Watson P. Davidson	V	49°15'N/96°30'W	5,827	1961
Westlake	V	51°15'N/99°20'W	5,739	1984
Whitewater Lake	V	49°14'N/100°19'W	8,977	1974

New Brunswick

Heritage River

St Croix Waterway	V	?/?	3,652	?

National Historic Park

Beaubear's Island	V	46°58'N/65°34'W	179	1975

National Park

Fundy	II	45°39'N/65°04'W	20,590	1948
Kouchibouguac	II	46°45'N/64°54'W	23,880	1979

National Wildlife Area

Portage Island	IV	47°10'N/65°02'W	439	1979
Portobello Creek	IV	45°55'N/60°20'W	2,097	1988
Tintamarre	IV	45°58'N/64°16'W	1,990	1978

Nature Park

Roosevelt International	V	?/?	1,052	1962

Nature Reserve

Grand Manan	IV	44°39'N/66°47'W	250	1931

Provincial Park

Mount Carleton Resource	II	47°23'N/66°53'W	17,427	1970
Sugar Loaf	II	45°59'N/66°48'W	1,150	1971

Wildlife Management Area

Bantalor	IV	46°15'N/66°20'W	15,287	1930
Becaguimec	IV	46°13'N/67°21'W	11,142	1929
Big Tracadie River	IV	47°34'N/65°22'W	3,915	1937
Burpee	IV	46°00'N/66°20'W	18,177	1934
Canaan River	IV	46°12'N/65°17'W	22,543	1921
Kedgwick	IV	47°50'N/67°35'W	82,914	1923
King's Landing	IV	45°53'N/66°58'W	53,238	1980
Lepreau River	IV	45°18'N/66°33'W	24,356	1927
Plaster Rock-renous	IV	46°52'N/66°45'W	84,175	1939

Wildlife Protection Area

University Of New Brunswick Refuge	IV	45°55'N/66°42'W	1,518	1949
Utopia Refuge	IV	45°09'N/66°44'W	3,109	1940

Newfoundland

Ecological Reserve

Cape St Mary's Seabird	I	46°50'N/54°11'W	1,210	1983
Gannet Islands	I	54°50'N/56°33'W	202	1983
Hare Bay Islands	I	51°14'N/55°54'W	442	1983
King George VI Provisional	I	48°10'N/57°54'W	1,900	1984
Watt's Point Provisional	I	51°28'N/56°15'W	3,090	1990
West Brook Provisional	I	49°22'N/56°17'W	1,074	1990
Witless Bay (sbs)	I	47°14'N/52°48'W	140	1983

National Park

Gros Morne	II	49°38'N/57°43'W	194,250	1973
Terra Nova	II	48°31'N/53°56'W	39,990	1957

Provincial Park

Barachois Pond	II	48°07'N/52°48'W	3,497	1961
Butter Pot	II	47°24'N/53°03'W	2,833	1964
Chance Cove	II	47°41'N/53°50'W	2,068	1974
La Manche	II	47°10'N/52°54'W	1,394	1966
Squires Memorial	II	49°21'N/57°13'W	1,574	1959
Stag Lake	II	48°50'N/58°03'W	1,278	1979

Wilderness Area

Avalon	II	47°04'N/53°13'W	107,000	1986
Bay Du Nord	II	47°40'N/55°30'W	289,500	1990

Northwest Territories

Migratory Bird Sanctuary

Akimiski Island	IV	53°02'N/81°15'W	336,700	1941
Anderson River Delta	IV	69°42'N/129°00'W	108,300	1961
Banks Island No.1	IV	72°40'N/123°30'W	2,051,800	1961
Banks Island No.2	IV	74°00'N/1145'W	14,200	1961
Bylot Island	IV	73°13'N/78°39'W	1,087,810	1965
Cape Dorset	IV	64°15'N/76°00'W	25,900	1958
Dewey Soper	IV	66°10'N/73°30'W	815,900	1957
East Bay	IV	64°00'N/82°00'W	116,600	1959
Harry Gibbons	IV	63°45'N/85°40'W	148,900	1959
Kendall Island	IV	69°25'N/135°30'W	60,600	1961
McConnell River	IV	60°40'N/94°20'W	32,900	1960
Prince Leopold Island	IV	?/?	30,305	1991
Queen Maude Gulf	IV	67°00'N/100°30'W	6,278,200	1961
Seymour Island	IV	76°48'N/101°16'W	800	1954

National Park Reserve

Auyuittuq	II	67°15'N/66°00'W	2,147,110	1976
Nahanni	II	61°35'N/125°53'W	476,560	1976
Northern Ellesmere Island	II	81°50'N/70°25'W	3,950,000	1982

National Wildlife Area

Polar Bear Pass	I	75°43'N/98°40'W	81,000	1982

Territorial Park

Blackstone	II	61°05'N/122°55'W	1,430	1982
Reid Lake	II	62°28'N/113°23'W	1,085	1975

Wildlife Sanctuary

Bowman Bay	IV	65°30'N/73°40'W	107,900	1957
Thelon	IV	63°30'N/103°00'W	2,396,000	1927
Twin Islands	IV	53°18'N/80°00'W	142,500	1939

Nova Scotia

Game Sanctuary

Chignieto	IV	45°33'N/64°30'W	22,099	1937
Liscomb	IV	45°14'N/62°28'W	45,327	1928
Waverley	IV	44°47'N/63°36'W	5,698	1926

Migratory Bird Sanctuary

Sable River	IV	43°56'N/60°00'W	2,350	1977

National Park

Cape Breton Highlands	II	46°44'N/60°30'W	95,050	1936
Kejimkujik	II	44°20'N/65°20'W	40,370	1974

National Wildlife Area

Boot Island	IV	45°08'N/64°16'W	144	1979
Chignecto River	IV	45°47'N/64°15'W	1,020	1980

Provincial Park

Dollar Lake	II	44°56'N/63°20'W	1,193	1981

Wildlife Management Area

Eastern Shore Islands	IV	44°51'N/62°15'W	11,767	1976
Musquodoboit Harbour Outer River Estuary	IV	44°44'N/63°07'W	1,200	1987
Scatarie Island	IV	46°00'N/59°44'W	1,555	1976
South Bight-Minas River Basin	IV	45°09'N/64°19'W	26,800	1987
Tobeatic	IV	44°12'N/65°22'W	49,213	1968

Ontario

Conservation Authority Area

Authority Forest	V	44°18'N/78°19'W	1,094	?
Belwood Lake (No. 43)	V	43°26'N/80°20'W	1,348	?
Conestogo Lake (No. 40)	V	43°42'N/80°44'W	2,348	?
Depot Lakes (No. 132)	V	44°32'N/76°43'W	1,000	?
Fanshawe (No. 21)	V	43°04'N/81°11'W	1,200	?
Greenock Swamp	V	44°09'N/81°22'W	7,300	?
Guelph Lake (No. 38)	V	43°36'N/80°15'W	1,607	?
Luther Marsh (No. 44)	V	43°57'N/80°26'W	4,800	?
Wildwood (No. 22)	V	43°15'N/81°06'W	1,255	?

Crown Game Preserve

Brigden	IV	42°49'N/82°17'W	2,613	?
Chapleau	IV	48°00'N/83°30'W	811,054	?
Dumfries	IV	43°17'N/80°23'W	1,000	?
Geikie Island	IV	50°00'N/88°35'W	5,527	?
Himsworth	IV	46°10'N/79°25'W	2,659	?
Nipissing	IV	46°35'N/79°40'W	62,454	?
Shirley Bay	IV	45°22'N/75°54'W	1,849	?
Yarmouth	IV	42°43'N/81°09'W	1,318	?

Migratory Bird Sanctuary

Fielding	IV	46°27'N/81°04'W	1,300	1952
Hanna Bay	IV	51°20'N/79°38'W	29,800	1939
Moose River	IV	51°20'N/80°25'W	1,450	1958
Upper Canada	IV	44°57'N/75°03'W	2,660	1961

National Capital Commission Area

Carlsbad Springs	V	45°22'N/75°28'W	1,655	?
Mer Bleue	V	45°24'N/75°30'W	1,086	?
The Greenbelt	V	45°20'N/75°48'W	11,824	?

National Park

Bruce Peninsula	II	45°16'N/81°40'W	26,630	1987
Georgian Bay Islands	II	44°55'N/79°55'W	2,530	1929
Point Pelee	II	41°58'N/82°32'W	1,550	1918
Pukaskwa	II	48°20'N/85°55'W	187,780	1978

National Wildlife Area

Long Point	IV	42°37'N/80°15'W	3,250	1980

Nature Reserve

Agassiz Peatlands	I	48°50'N/94°30'W	2,315	1985
Black Duck River	I	54°44'N/82°25'W	100,000	1970
Brent Crater	I	46°04'N/78°29'W	1,390	1893
Brule Harbour	I	47°49'N/84°55'W	1,274	1950
Cape Chaillon	I	47°44'N/84°57'W	1,948	1950
Centennial Lake	I	45°13'N/76°53'W	3,830	1989
Coldspring Lake Watershed	I	45°51'N/78°48'W	5,396	1893
Gina Lake	I	48°19'N/85°05'W	1,323	1967
Greenleaf Creek Watershed	I	45°52'N/77°58'W	3,730	1893
Hailstorm Creek	I	45°42'N/78°29'W	1,092	1893
Johnston Herb	I	45°06'N/81°31'W	2,008	1989
Knife Creek	I	48°19'N/85°05'W	1,495	1967
Lower Agawa River	I	47°22'N/84°35'W	2,393	1950
Lower Sand River	I	47°42'N/84°47'W	1,150	1950
Minnitaki Kames	I	49°54'N/91°50'W	4,340	1989
Nadine Lake Hardwoods	I	45°57'N/78°44'W	1,105	1893
Nr Zone-1	I	44°30'N/80°03'W	1,000	1959
O'Conner	I	47°35'N/84°45'W	1,565	1950
Pantagruel Creek	I	49°47'N/89°26'W	2,200	1989

Petawawa Rapids	I	46°03'N/77°50'W	1,411	1893
Pigeon River Clay Plain	I	48°01'N/89°55'W	2,870	1989
Round Lake	I	45°30'N/80°05'W	4,620	1989
Site 416	I	54°47'N/82°22'W	9,300	1984
Site 421	I	54°42'N/83°25'W	9,300	1984
Tarn Lake	I	45°48'N/77°42'W	1,004	1893
Treeby Lake	I	47°52'N/84°49'W	1,005	1950
Trout Lake	I	51°10'N/93°25'W	7,850	1988
Wachi Creek	I	55°14'N/84°34'W	50,000	1984
Windigo Bay	I	50°10'N/88°47'W	8,300	1989
Wood Creek	I	55°41'N/86°02'W	50,000	1984

Provincial Park

Abitibi-de-troyes	II	48°47'N/80°30'W	11,068	1985
Algonquin	IV	45°45'N/78°25'W	765,345	1893
Aubrey Falls	II	46°58'N/83°10'W	4,860	1985
Awenda	II	44°50'N/79°59'W	2,917	1975
Bigwind Lake	II	45°05'N/79°01'W	1,970	1985
Bon Echo	II	44°55'N/77°16'W	6,644	1971
Butler Lake Nature Reserve	I	49°42'N/92°43'W	3,400	1985
Cabot Head Nature Reserve	I	45°14'N/81°29'W	4,514	1985
Carillon	II	45°33'N/74°26'W	1,417	1966
Castle Creek Nature Reserve	I	48°12'N/90°04'W	1,075	1985
Chapleau-Nemegosenda River	II	48°16'N/83°10'W	8,165	1973
Cranberry Lake Nature Reserve	I	48°52'N/94°21'W	2,800	1985
Dana-Jowsey Lakes	V	?/?	2,538	1989
Esker Lakes	II	48°20'N/79°53'W	3,237	1957
Fathom Five	II	45°16'N/81°43'W	9,976	1972
Fawn River	V	?/?	12,140	1989
French River	V	?/?	51,120	1989
Fushimi Lake	II	49°49'N/83°54'W	5,294	1979
Greenwater	II	49°13'N/81°17'W	5,350	1957
Grundy Lake	II	45°57'N/80°32'W	2,554	1959
Halfway Lake	II	46°55'N/81°39'W	4,730	1980
Ivanhoe Lake	II	48°09'N/82°32'W	1,589	1957
Kabitotikwia River Nature Reserve	I	49°42'N/89°05'W	1,965	1985
Kashabowie	II	48°41'N/90°21'W	2,055	1985
Kawartha Highlands	IV	?/?	1,800	1989
Kesagami Wilderness	II	50°25'N/80°10'W	55,977	1983
Kettle Lakes	II	48°34'N/80°52'W	1,261	1957
Killarney Wilderness	II	46°08'N/81°25'W	48,500	1964
Killbear	II	45°21'N/80°11'W	1,756	1971
Kopka River	V	?/?	16,200	1989
La Cloche	II	46°07'N/82°02'W	7,448	1985
La Verendrye River	V	?/?	18,335	1989
Lady Evelyn Smoothwater	II	47°23'N/80°30'W	72,400	1983
Lake Nipigon	II	49°29'N/88°07'W	1,458	1960
Lake Of The Woods	II	49°06'N/94°33'W	12,900	1967
Lake Superior	IV	47°35'N/84°45'W	155,659	1950
Larder River	II	47°56'N/79°39'W	2,500	1985
Little Abitibi	IV	?/?	20,000	1985
Little Current River	V	?/?	9,930	1989
Livingstone Point Nature Reserve	I	49°55'N/88°11'W	1,800	1985
Lola Lake Nature Reserve	I	49°48'N/92°33'W	6,572	1985
Lower Madawaska River	V	?/?	1,200	1989
MacGregor Point	II	4424'N/81°29'W	1,204	1975
Makobe-grays River	II	4737'N/80°24'W	1,427	1985
Matawin River Nature Reserve	I	4824'N/90°10'W	2,615	1985
Mattawa River	II	4618'N/79°05'W	3,258	1970
Michipicoten Island	II	4745'N/85°45'W	36,740	1985
Missinaibi	II	4825'N/83°34'W	44,061	1970
Mississagi	II	4635'N/82°42'W	2,883	1973

Mississagi Delta Nature Reserve	I	46°11'N/83°04'W	2,395	1985
Mississagi River	II	47°16'N/82°17'W	19,814	1974
Murphy's Point	II	44°47'N/76°13'W	1,240	1967
Nagagami Lake Nature Reserve	I	49°26'N/84°58'W	1,650	1985
Nagagamisis	II	49°27'N/84°42'W	8,131	1957
Neys	II	48°45'N/86°35'W	3,445	1965
Niagara Escarpment	V	44°09'N/80°21'W	1,900	1985
Obabika River	V	?/?	17,000	1989
Obatanga	II	48°20'N/85°05'W	9,409	1967
Ojibway	II	50°00'N/92°08'W	2,630	1963
Opasquia Wilderness	II	53°33'N/93°05'W	473,000	1983
Otoskwin-Attawapiskat River	V	?/?	82,569	1989
Petroglyphs	II	44°37'N/78°03'W	1,555	1976
Pipestone River	V	?/?	97,375	1989
Polar Bear	II	54°15'N/82°30'W	2,408,700	1970
Quetico	II	48°30'N/91°30'W	475,819	1950
Quetico Wilderness	II	48°30'N/91°30'W	475,819	1950
Rene Brunelle	II	49°28'N/82°09'W	2,964	1957
Restoule	II	46°04'N/79°47'W	1,200	1963
Rondeau	II	42°17'N/81°51'W	3,254	1894
Sable Islands Nature Reserve	I	48°54'N/94°38'W	1,980	1985
Samuel De Champlain	II	46°18'N/78°52'W	2,550	1967
Sandbanks	II	43°55'N/77°16'W	1,509	1970
Sandbar Lake	II	49°28'N/91°34'W	5,083	1970
Sedgman Lake Nature Reserve	I	50°39'N/87°41'W	5,710	1985
Severn River	V	?/?	82,960	1989
Sibley	II	48°26'N/88°47'W	24,435	1950
Silent Lake	II	44°55'N/78°04'W	1,450	1977
Silver Falls	II	48°41'N/89°36'W	3,261	1985
Slate Islands	II	48°20'N/87°00'W	6,570	1985
Solace	V	?/?	5,943	1989
South Bay	II	46°08'N/79°36'W	1,525	1985
Steel River	V	?/?	11,240	1989
Sturgeon River	V	?/?	3,350	1989
The Pinery	II	43°15'N/81°51'W	2,533	1957
The Shoals	II	47°54'N/83°50'W	10,644	1970
Turtle River	V	?/?	40,052	1989
Upper Madawaska River	V	?/?	1,085	1989
Wabakimi Wilderness	II	50°35'N/89°35'W	155,000	1983
Wakami Lake	II	47°29'N/82°15'W	8,806	1973
Wanapitei	II	46°48'N/80°45'W	2,700	1985
Wasaga Beach	II	44°30'N/80°03'W	1,545	1959
West Bay Nature Reserve	I	49°54'N/88°56'W	1,120	1985
White Lake	II	48°42'N/85°40'W	1,726	1963
Winisk River	II	53°00'N/86°25'W	173,530	1969
Winnange Lake	II	49°47'N/93°41'W	4,745	1985
Woodland Caribou Wilderness	II	51°00'N/94°45'W	450,000	1983

Wilderness Area

Cape Henrietta-Marie	I	55°07'N/82°37'W	58,320	1970

Wildlife Area

Camden Lake	IV	44°25'N/76°52'W	1,052	?
Hullett	IV	43°30'N/81°25'W	2,100	?
Luther Marsh	IV	43°57'N/80°26'W	5,666	?
Mountain	IV	45°02'N/75°30'W	1,457	?
Point Petre	IV	43°52'N/77°09'W	1,276	?
St. Edmunds	IV	45°12'N/81°35'W	6,799	?

Prince Edward Island

National Park

Prince Edward Island	II	46°31'N/63°28'W	2,590	1937

Wildlife Management Area

Malpeque Bay River Wetlands	IV	46°32'N/63°47'W	24,440	1988

Québec

Ecological Reserve

Ile Brion	I	47°40'N/61°30'W	650	1987
J.-Clovis-Laflamme	I	48°20'N/72°33'W	1,015	1991
Judith-De Brésoles	I	47°36'N/72°18'W	1,120	1992
Lac-Malakisis	I	46°42'N/78°39'W	1,965	1978
Louis-Babel	I	51°27'N/68°41'W	23,540	1991
Rolland-Germain	I	46°39'N/76°05'W	1,370	1991
Tantaré	I	47°04'N/71°32'W	1,450	1978

Forest Education Centre

Laurentides	IV	46°03'N/74°28'W	1,732	1980
Macpès	IV	48°17'N/68°30'W	1,950	1982
Outaouais	IV	45°44'N/75°16'W	1,975	1982
Pallisades	IV	47°53'N/69°59'W	2,656	1972
Parke	IV	47°33'N/69°29'W	3,424	1974

Forest Station

Duchesnay	IV	?/?	9,000	1982

Forest Training and Research Centre

Comeau	IV	49°13'N/68°26'W	3,190	1991
Harricana	IV	48°46'N/77°49'W	2,128	1992
Macpès	IV	48°18'N/68°32'W	2,576	1989
Mailhot	IV	47°27'N/72°42'W	1,686	1991
Mont-Saint-Hilaire	IV	45°33'N/73°10'W	1,100	1958
Montmorency	IV	47°16'N/71°10'W	6,665	1987
Mousseau	IV	46°35'N/74°56'W	3,465	1990
Sicotte	IV	46°36'N/75°48'W	1,281	1990
Simoncouche	IV	48°12'N/71°14'W	2,730	1990
Vallée-de-la-Matapédia	IV	48°22'N/67°01'W	1,118	1989

Migratory Bird Sanctuary

Baie des Loups	IV	50°02'N/60°03'W	4,000	1925
Boatswain Bay	IV	51°50'N/78°55'W	17,700	1941
Ile à la Brume	IV	50°01'N/60°11'W	4,450	1925
Ile aux Basques	IV	48°07'N/69°14'W	1,000	1927
Ile Bonaventure et Rocher de Percé	IV	48°32'N/64°13'W	1,340	1919
Iles de la Paix	IV	45°21'N/73°50'W	1,100	1972
Iles Saint-Marie	IV	50°04'N/59°48'W	4,500	1925
Nicolet	IV	46°13'N/72°38'W	2,850	1986
Saint-Augustin	IV	51°13'N/58°39'W	5,300	1925
Watshishou	IV	50°11'N/63°05'W	11,200	1925

National Capital Commission Area

Parc de la Gatineau	II	45°34'N/75°57'W	34,400	1937

National Park

Forillon	II	48°50'N/64°25'W	24,040	1974
La Mauricie	II	46°45'N/73°00'W	54,390	1977
Archipel Mingan	II	50°13'N/63°37'W	15,070	1984

National Wildlife Area

Réserve de Cap Tourmente	IV	47°04'N/70°46'W	2,398	1978
Lac St-Francois	IV	45°02'N/74°27'W	1,347	1978

Nature Park

Forêt-Ouareau	V	46°15'N/74°09'W	14,100	?
Hautes-Gorges-de-la-Rivière-Malbaie	V	47°56'N/70°27'W	23,300	?
Massif-de-la-Petite-Rivière-Saint-François	V	47°18'N/70°34'W	4,400	?
Mont-Sainte-Anne	V	47°05'N/70°56'W	7,700	1968

Provincial Park

Aiguebelle	II	48°30'N/78°45'W	24,170	1985
Bic	II	48°22'N/68°43'W	3,320	1984
Frontenac	II	45°50'N/71°10'W	15,530	1987
Gaspésie	II	48°56'N/66°00'W	80,200	1981
Grands Jardins	II	47°40'N/70°50'W	31,000	1981
Jacques Cartier	II	47°20'N/71°15'W	67,060	1981
Mont-Orford	II	45°25'N/72°15'W	5,837	1980
Mont-Tremblant	II	46°30'N/74°30'W	149,000	1981
Oka	II	45°30'N/73°58'W	2,370	1963
Pointe-taillon	II	48°42'N/72°00'W	9,220	1985
Saguenay	II	48°20'N/70°18'W	28,360	1983
Yamaska	II	46°06'N/72°56'W	1,290	1983

Wildlife Sanctuary

Aiguebelle	IV	48°30'N/78°45'W	3,950	1945
Ashuapmushuan	IV	49°10'N/73°46'W	448,700	1946
Assinica	IV	50°30'N/75°16'W	888,500	1961
Baie Trinité	V	49°25'N/67°18'W	35,600	1974
Baldwin	IV	48°41'N/66°01'W	22,900	1974
Cap-chat	IV	49°05'N/66°35'W	12,100	1964
Chics-chocs	IV	49°05'N/65°50'W	112,600	1949
Duchenier	IV	48°10'N/68°40'W	27,000	1977
Duchesnay	V	46°54'N/71°38'W	8,800	1972
Dunière	IV	48°45'N/66°41'W	55,300	1972
Eastmain	V	45°18'N/72°19'W	434,400	1976
Fort George	V	54°15'N/78°00'W	1,816,600	1976
Fort Rupert	V	51°30'N/78°45'W	1,124,000	1976
Frontenac	IV	45°50'N/71°10'W	11,900	1978
Grande-Ile	IV	46°07'N/73°01'W	1,025	1992
Ile Bonaventure	V	48°30'N/64°10'W	400	1971
Ile D'anticosti	IV	49°48'N/64°20'W	30,300	1974
Iles aux Grues, Dune, L'oignon, P.cochon	V	47°04'N/70°33'W	2,500	1977
Intowin	V	56°15'N/67°00'W	8,800	1976
Kipawa	V	47°00'N/78°50'W	463,600	1950
La Verendrye	IV	48°00'N/76°00'W	1,361,000	1939
Lacs Albanel, Mistassini & Waconichi	IV	50°00'N/75°00'W	1,640,000	1953
Laurentides	IV	47°00'N/72°00'W	793,400	1895
Mastigouche	IV	46°33'N/73°41'W	157,400	1971
Matane	IV	48°44'N/66°55'W	128,400	1962
Mistassini	V	51°30'N/73°15'W	1,787,000	1953
Nemiscau	V	51°25'N/76°40'W	233,800	1976
Nouveau Comptoir	V	53°00'N/78°00'W	752,100	1976
Papineau Labelle	IV	45°55'N/75°25'W	166,700	1971
Parke	V	47°37'N/69°32'W	12,000	1961
Petite Nation	V	45°35'N/75°06'W	25,000	1934
Plaisance	IV	45°37'N/75°07'W	2,600	1978
Pointe-taillon	V	48°46'N/72°03'W	7,500	1965
Port Daniel	IV	48°17'N/64°55'W	5,700	1953
Portneuf	IV	46°42'N/71°53'W	77,400	1968
Poste de la Baleine	V	55°17'N/77°45'W	535,400	1976
Rimouski	IV	48°03'N/68°15'W	73,500	1958
Rivière Cascapedia	IV	48°09'N/65°51'W	2,000	1982
Rivière Matamec	V	50°17'N/65°58'W	103,600	1970
Rivière Matane	IV	48°45'N/67°00'W	1,400	1972
Rivière Matapedia	IV	48°11'N/67°09'W	1,000	1974
Rivière Petite Cascapedia	IV	48°11'N/65°50'W	1,700	1945
Rivière Port-Daniel	IV	48°18'N/64°55'W	3,600	1948
Rouge-Mattawin	IV	46°40'N/74°32'W	139,400	1935
Saint-Maurice	IV	47°05'N/73°15'W	78,200	1963
Sept Iles-port Cartier	IV	50°30'N/67°12'W	642,300	1965
Waswanipi	IV	51°00'N/76°30'W	847,000	1976

Saskatchewan

Game Preserve

Berube Lake	IV	53°29'N/106°57'W	1,554	1953
Candle Lake	IV	54°09'N/105°34'W	82,100	1985
Crystal Beach Lake	IV	51°41'N/107°34'W	7,770	1946
Dafocal	IV	51°46'N/104°31'W	1,295	1951
McLaren Lake	IV	50°18'N/109°54'W	1,036	1953
Melville	IV	50°57'N/102°51'W	1,295	1939
Outlook	IV	51°35'N/107°05'W	3,108	1953
Scentgrass Lake	IV	52°57'N/108°09'W	1,360	1948
Squaw Rapids	IV	53°40'N/103°22'W	3,040	1985
Wascana	IV	50°25'N/104°34'W	1,165	1941
Willow Bunch	IV	49°28'N/105°35'W	1,036	1956
Wood Moutain	IV	49°18'N/106°16'W	3,885	1949

Migratory Bird Sanctuary

Basin and Middle Lake	IV	52°33'N/105°10'W	8,702	1925
Duncairn Reservoir	IV	52°02'N/108°06'W	1,546	1948
Last Mountain Lake	IV	51°22'N/105°12'W	4,740	1887
Lenore Lake	IV	52°30'N/105°00'W	8,830	1925
Murray Lake	IV	53°03'N/108°17'W	1,165	1948
Old Wives Lake	IV	50°06'N/106°00'W	26,060	1925
Opuntia Lake	IV	51°48'N/108°35'W	1,395	1952
Redberry Lake	IV	52°42'N/107°10'W	6,395	1925

National Park

Prince Albert	II	53°57'N/106°22'W	387,464	1927

National Park Reserve

Grasslands	II	49°14'N/107°43'W	90,000	1988

National Wildlife Area

Last Mountain Lake Coop	IV	51°22'N/105°12'W	15,602	1989
Prairie	IV	51°50'N/107°15'W	2,949	1977
Stalwart	IV	51°15'N/105°25'W	1,525	1969

Protected Area

Brocklebank Hill	II	52°38'N/101°47'W	1,295	1992
Waskwei River	III	53°34'N/101°46'W	1,093	1964

Provincial Park

Athabasca Sand Dunes Wilderness	I	59°03'N/108°40'W	192,500	1992
Buffalo Pound	V	50°35'N/105°25'W	1,927	1963
Candle Lake	V	53°47'N/105°19'W	7,874	1986
Clearwater River Wilderness	I	56°42'N/109°59'W	224,035	1986
Cypress Hills	II	49°45'N/109°40'W	18,351	1931
Danielson	V	51°16'N/106°50'W	2,153	1971
Douglas	II	51°03'N/106°28'W	6,144	1973
Duck Mountain	II	51°45'N/101°50'W	26,159	1931
Good Spirit Lake	II	51°35'N/102°55'W	1,971	1931
Green-Water Lake	II	52°30'N/103°35'W	20,720	1932
Lac La Ronge	II	55°25'N/104°40'W	336,197	1939
Makwa Lake	II	54°02'N/109°14'W	2,558	1986
Meadow Lake	II	54°25'N/109°00'W	165,893	1959
Moose Mountain	II	49°55'N/102°30'W	40,060	1931
Narrow Hills	II	53°58'N/104°30'W	53,613	1931
Saskatchewan Landing	II	50°38'N/107°59'W	5,597	1973
Wildcat Hill Wilderness	I	53°15'N/102°30'W	21,772	1992

Recreation Site

Anglin Lake	V	53°43'N/105°56'W	1,360	1976
Big Buffalo Beach	V	55°52'N/108°37'W	3,650	1986

Bronson Forest	V	53°50'N/109°32'W	14,500	1974
Jan Lake	V	54°53'N/102°48'W	2,070	1976
Nisbet Trails	V	53°14'N/105°45'W	1,730	1986
Whiteswan Lake (Whelan Bay)	V	54°02'N/105°07'W	1,834	1984
Woody River	V	52°08'N/101°35'W	2,200	1986

Wildlife Refuge

Nisku	IV	50°55'N/106°10'W	1,709	1970

Yukon Territory

Ecological Reserve

Coal River Hot Springs	III	69°05'N/139°30'W	1,600	1991

National Park Reserve

Kluane	II	60°30'N/140°00'W	2,201,500	1976
Northern Yukon	II	69°05'N/139°30'W	1,016,840	1984

Territorial Park

Herschel Island	I	69°36'N/139°20'W	11,400	1989

Wildlife Sanctuary

Kluane	IV	61°45'N/140°50'W	422,220	1943
MacArthur	IV	63°08'N/135°38'W	169,600	1958

CAPE VERDE/CAP-VERT/CABO VERDE

No Areas Listed

CENTRAL AFRICAN REPUBLIC/ REPUBLIQUE CENTRAFRICAINE/ REPÚBLICA CENTROAFRICANA

Summary		
Category I	1	86,000
Category II	4	3,102,000
Category III	0	0
Category IV	8	2,918,000
Category V	0	0
Total	**13**	**6,106,000**

Faunal Reserve

Aouk-Aoukale	IV	9°41'N/21°22'E	330,000	1939
Gribingui-Bamingui	IV	7°35'N/19°38'E	438,000	1940
Koukourou-Bamingui	IV	7°35'N/19°38'E	110,000	1940
Nana-Barya	IV	7°40'N/17°30'E	230,000	1960
Ouandjia-Vakaga	IV	9°02'N/22°15'E	130,000	1925
Yata-Ngaya	IV	9°12'N/23°14'E	420,000	1960
Zemongo	IV	6°49'N/25°20'E	1,010,000	1925

National Park

André Felix	II	9°21'N/23°17'E	170,000	1960
Bamingui-Bangoran	II	7°35'N/19°38'E	1,070,000	1933
Dzanga-Ndoki	II	?/?	122,000	1990
Manovo-Gounda-Saint Floris	II	8°55'N/21°25'E	1,740,000	1933

Private Reserve

Parc présidentiel Avakaba	IV	8°40'N/20°40'E	250,000	1980

Strict Nature Reserve

Vassako-Bolo	I	7°35'N/19°38'E	86,000	1960

CHAD/TCHAD

Summary		
Category I	0	0
Category II	2	414,000
Category III	0	0
Category IV	7	11,080,000
Category V	0	0
Total	**9**	**11,494,000**

Faunal Reserve

Abou Telfane	IV	11°56'N/18°51'E	110,000	1955
Bahr Salamat	IV	10°33'N/19°26'E	2,060,000	1964
Binder-Léré	IV	9°40'N/14°28'E	135,000	1974
Fada Archei	IV	16°55'N/21°21'E	211,000	1967
Mandelia	IV	11°32'N/15°08'E	138,000	1969
Ouadi Rimé-Ouadi Achim	IV	15°41'N/19°40'E	8,000,000	1969
Siniaka-Minia	IV	10°26'N/18°02'E	426,000	1965

National Park

Manda	II	9°23'N/17°59'E	114,000	1969
Zakouma	II	10°50'N/19°40'E	300,000	1963

CHILE/CHILI

Summary		
Category I	0	0
Category II	30	8,361,367
Category III	2	13,606
Category IV	34	5,350,152
Category V	0	0
Total	**66**	**13,725,125**

Nature Monument

Alerce Costero	III	40°10'S/73°30'W	2,308	1964
Salar de Surire	III	18°52'S/69°05'W	11,298	1983

National Park

Alberto de Agostini	II	54°55'S/70°30'W	1,460,000	1965
Alerce Andino	II	41°50'S/72°35'W	39,255	1982
Archipiélago de Juan Fernández	II	33°40'S/79°47'W	9,109	1935
Bernardo O'Higgins	II	50°00'S/74°00'W	3,525,901	1969
Bosque Fray Jorge	II	30°34'S/71°40'W	9,959	1941
Cabo de Hornos	II	55°45'S/67°20'W	63,093	1945
Chiloé	II	42°30'S/74°05'W	43,057	1982
Conguillío	II	38°40'S/71°42'W	60,832	1950
El Morado	II	33°48'S/70°00'W	3,000	1974
Hornopirén	II	41°50'S/72°20'W	48,232	1988
Huerquehue	II	39°10'S/71°40'W	12,500	1967
Isla Guamblin	II	44°50'S/75°05'W	10,625	1967
Isla Magdalena	II	44°45'S/73°05'W	157,640	1983
La Campana	II	32°55'S/71°05'W	8,000	1967
Laguna del Laja	II	37°25'S/71°20'W	11,600	1958
Laguna San Rafael	II	46°39'S/74°32'W	1,742,000	1959
Las Palmas de Cocalán	II	34°15'S/71°12'W	3,709	1972
Lauca	II	18°11'S/69°13'W	137,883	1970
Nahuelbuta	II	37°45'S/73°00'W	6,832	1939
Pali-Aike	II	52°06'S/69°40'W	3,000	1970
Pan de Azúcar	II	26°00'S/70°40'W	43,754	1986
Puyehue	II	40°40'S/72°10'W	107,000	1941
Queulat	II	44°20'S/72°30'W	154,093	1983
Rapa Nui	II	27°10'S/109°26'W	6,666	1935

Río Simpson	II	45°30'S/72°25'W	40,790	1967
Tolhuaca	II	38°18'S/71°45'W	6,374	1935
Torres del Paine	II	50°41'S/73°56'W	184,414	1959
Vicente Pérez Rosales	II	41°10'S/72°15'W	226,305	1926
Villarrica	II	39°30'S/71°45'W	61,000	1940
Volcán Isluga	II	19°10'S/68°50'W	174,744	1967

National Reserve

Alacalufes	IV	52°00'S/74°00'W	2,313,875	1969
Alto Bío-Bío	IV	38°35'S/70°58'W	35,000	1912
Cerro Castillo	IV	46°00'S/72°00'W	179,550	1970
China Muerta	IV	38°48'S/71°30'W	9,887	1968
Coihaique	IV	45°30'S/72°05'W	2,150	1948
Isla Mocha	IV	38°20'S/73°54'W	2,368	1988
Katalalixar	IV	48°00'S/75°00'W	674,500	1983
La Chimba	IV	23°30'S/73°20'W	2,583	1988
Lago Carlota	IV	44°30'S/71°30'W	27,110	1965
Lago Cochrane	IV	47°12'S/72°30'W	8,361	1967
Lago General Carrera	IV	46°40'S/72°10'W	178,400	1974
Lago Jeinimeni	IV	46°48'S/72°00'W	38,700	1967
Lago Las Torres	IV	44°48'S/72°12'W	16,516	1969
Lago Palena	IV	43°55'S/71°55'W	41,356	1965
Lago Peñuelas	IV	33°10'S/71°33'W	9,094	1952
Lago Rosselot	IV	44°05'S/72°20'W	12,725	1968
Laguna Parrillar	IV	53°20'S/71°15'W	18,814	1977
Las Chinchillas	IV	31°30'S/71°06'W	4,229	1983
Las Guaitecas	IV	45°00'S/74°00'W	1,097,975	1938
Las Vicuñas	IV	48°30'S/69°08'W	209,131	1983
Llanquihue	IV	41°25'S/72°25'W	33,972	1912
Los Flamencos	IV	23°00'S/68°00'W	73,987	1990
Magallanes	IV	53°10'S/71°00'W	13,500	1932
Malalcahuello	IV	38°20'S/71°35'W	17,530	1931
Malleco	IV	38°12'S/71°50'W	17,371	1907
Nalcas	IV	38°12'S/71°35'W	13,775	1967
Pampa del Tamarugal	IV	20°30'S/69°45'W	100,650	1988
Ralco	IV	37°48'S/71°30'W	12,421	1972
Río Blanco	IV	32°55'S/70°30'W	10,175	1932
Río Clarillo	IV	33°40'S/70°30'W	10,185	1982
Río de Los Cipreses	IV	34°30'S/70°25'W	38,582	1986
Valdivia	IV	40°00'S/73°25'W	9,727	1929
Villarrica	IV	39°12'S/71°30'W	60,005	1912
Ñuble	IV	37°05'S/71°15'W	55,948	1978

CHINA/CHINE

Summary		
Category I	3	98,425
Category II	0	0
Category III	1	30,000
Category IV	421	55,590,538
Category V	38	2,347,600
Total	**463**	**58,066,563**

Anhui

Nature Reserve

Guniuxiang	IV	30°03'N/117°28'E	6,433	1982
Huangfu Mountain	IV	32°21'N/117°01'E	3,587	1982
Huangzangyu	IV	34°10'N/117°05'E	2,333	1980
Mazongling	IV	?/?	3,490	1980
Qingliangfeng	IV	30°10'N/118°44'E	3,000	1986
Qingliangfeng 2	IV	29°59'N/118°39'E	1,038	1979
Shengjin Lake	IV	?/?	33,333	1986

Tian Tang Zhai	IV	?/?	1,330	1990
Yangtze Alligator	IV	30°55'N/118°53'E	1,500	1977

Scenic Area

Huangshan	V	30°40'N/118°09'E	15,400	1982
Langya Mountain	V	?/?	11,500	1987

Beijing

Nature Reserve

Baihua Mountain	IV	?/?	1,700	1985
Song Mountain	IV	?/?	6,667	1985

Fujian

Nature Reserve

Daiyun Mountain	IV	?/?	9,731	1985
Jiangshi	IV	?/?	1,187	1986
Mandarin Duck	IV	?/?	1,039	1984
Meihua Mountain	IV	?/?	22,133	1985
Wuyi Mountains	IV	27°45'N/117°38'E	56,527	1977
Xinkou	IV	26°07'N/117°24'E	1,126	1964

Scenic Area

Gulangyu Island	V	?/?	23,000	?
Qingyuanshan	V	?/?	5,000	1987
Tailaoshan	V	?/?	6,000	1987

Gansu

Nature Reserve

Annanba	IV	39°22'N/94°06'E	390,000	1982
Anxi Gobi Desert Meadow	IV	40°40'N/96°10'E	340,000	1985
Baishu River	I	32°39'N/104°29'E	95,292	1963
Changling Mountain	IV	37°56'N/102°02'E	3,670	1980
Dongda Mountain	IV	39°05'N/100°30'E	4,921	1980
Gahai	IV	34°29'N/103°26'E	3,500	1982
Great Suhai Lake	IV	39°57'N/93°44'E	3,500	1982
Guozhagou	IV	34°48'N/102°29'E	2,509	1982
Hei River	IV	34°21'N/106°19'E	4,200	1982
Jian Shan	IV	?/?	4,000	1990
Kontong Mountain	IV	35°24'N/106°40'E	1,089	1982
Liangucheng	IV	39°04'N/103°53'E	14,000	1982
Lianhua Mountain	IV	35°17'N/102°46'E	6,855	1982
Maicaogou	IV	35°02'N/106°13'E	3,567	1982
Shoulu Mountain	IV	37°08'N/104°29'E	11,060	1980
Tou'ersantan	IV	37°21'N/104°35'E	31,937	1982
Xinglong Mountain	IV	35°44'N/103°49'E	2,219	1982
Yanchiwan	IV	39°23'N/94°41'E	424,800	1982

Guangdong (Hainan Island)

Nature Reserve

Algae	IV	?/?	4,400	1983
Bawangling	IV	19°20'N/109°10'E	2,000	1980
Changhang Bawanglin	I	?/?	2,000	1980
Coral Reef	IV	?/?	32,400	1986
Datian	IV	19°02'N/108°49'E	2,500	1976
Da Zhou Dao Hai Yang Sheng Tai	IV	?/?	7,000	1990
Diaoluo Mountain	IV	?/?	4,002	1984
Dongzhaigang	IV	20°00'N/1103°5'E	2,601	1980
Fanjia	IV	?/?	5,336	1984
Fuwan Reservoir	IV	?/?	3,333	1975
Ganshiling	IV	18°23'N/109°40'E	2,000	1985
Huishan	IV	19°04'N/110°08'E	5,336	1984

Jianfengling	IV	?/?	1,600	1960
Jianling Managed	IV	18°53'N/110°14'E	2,600	1984
Jiaxi	IV	18°53'N/109°10'E	8,671	1982
Jiaxin Managed	IV	18°38'N/110°09'E	2,667	1984
Lingaojiao	IV	?/?	3,467	1986
Liulianling	IV	19°02'N/110°26'E	2,200	1981
Nanlin Managed	IV	18°45'N/110°04'E	4,400	1984
Nanxi	IV	?/?	15,341	1983
Piyelingshui	IV	?/?	1,380	1986
Qinglangang	IV	19°32'N/110°49'E	2,000	1982
Qizhi Ridge	IV	?/?	3,000	1983
San Ya Shan Hu Jiao	IV	?/?	5,500	1990
Shangxi Managed	IV	18°47'N/110°11'E	2,134	1984
Shan Kou Hong Shu Lin	IV	?/?	3,710	1990
Shellfish	IV	?/?	4,400	1983
Stellate-Hair Vatica Forest	IV	?/?	1,666	1980
Tongghu Ridge	IV	19°44'N/110°56'E	1,333	1986
Wencheng Mangrove Forest	IV	?/?	2,000	1981
Wuzhi Mountain	IV	18°55'N/109°46'E	18,664	1985

Guangdong

Nature Reserve

Babao Mountain	IV	?/?	3,200	1984
Bai Yong	IV	?/?	3,700	1990
Baishuiling	IV	18°39'N/109°51'E	4,000	1984
Chebaling	IV	?/?	7,545	1982
Chengjia	IV	?/?	7,867	1983
Dadong Mountain	IV	?/?	8,000	1985
Dan Gan Dao	IV	?/?	1,000	1990
Dapingdong	IV	?/?	2,667	1983
Dinghu Mountain	IV	?/?	1,140	1956
Guanyin Mountain	IV	?/?	3,000	1985
Gutian	IV	?/?	4,300	1984
Heishiding	IV	?/?	4,000	1979
Luofu Mountain	IV	?/?	2,400	1985
Mangrove Forest	IV	?/?	3,733	1982
Nankun Mountain	IV	?/?	2,000	1984
Qingpilin	IV	?/?	1,066	1980
Qingxidong	IV	24°50'N/113°40'E	3,133	1976
Shang Chuan Dao	IV	?/?	1,300	1990
Shao Guan Hua Nan Hu (South China)	IV	?/?	100,000	1990
Xisha	IV	?/?	330	1980
Yun Bing Shan	IV	?/?	2,000	1990
Zhan Jiang Hong Shu Lin (Mangrove)	IV	?/?	4,500	1990
Zhaoqing Dinghushan	I	?/?	1,133	1956

Scenic Area

Danxia Mountain	V	?/?	18,000	?
Xiqiao Mountain	V	?/?	1,400	?

Guangxi

Nature Reserve

Baidong River	IV	?/?	36,000	1982
Buliu River	IV	?/?	45,300	1982
Chengbi River	IV	?/?	16,200	1980
Chongzuo	IV	?/?	35,000	1981
Chuandong River	IV	?/?	11,600	1982
Chunxiu	IV	?/?	5,000	1982
Conserving Water Hsienmu Forest	IV	?/?	10,600	1982
Dahong River	IV	?/?	18,100	1982
Daming Mountain	IV	23°17'N/108°22'E	58,200	1980

Daping Mountain	IV	?/?	20,400	1982
Dawangling	IV	?/?	19,200	1980
Daxin	IV	?/?	29,900	1980
Dayao Mountain	IV	?/?	13,500	1982
Dehou	IV	?/?	12,200	1980
Dengbi River	IV	?/?	59,300	1982
Dizhou	IV	?/?	6,000	1982
Dugong	IV	?/?	200,000	1986
Fusui	IV	?/?	10,000	1981
Gulong Mountain	IV	?/?	20,400	1982
Gupo Mountain	IV	?/?	7,100	1982
Haiyang Mountain	IV	?/?	106,700	1982
Heqiao Ridge	IV	?/?	67,000	1982
Huagong	IV	?/?	15,700	1982
Huaping	IV	25°43'N/109°50'E	17,400	1961
Huashuichong	IV	24°23'N/111°54'E	12,000	1982
Jinxiu	IV	?/?	185,000	1982
Jinzhong Mountain	IV	?/?	22,100	1982
Jiuwan Mountain	IV	?/?	44,400	1982
Laoshan	IV	?/?	14,500	1982
Longgang	IV	22°24'N/106°59'E	8,000	1979
Longrui	IV	22°06'N/107°13'E	2,100	1980
Maojie Birds	IV	?/?	8,800	1982
Miao'er Mountain	IV	25°43'N/110°29'E	45,100	1976
Nalin	IV	?/?	6,100	1982
Nazuo	IV	?/?	41,600	1982
Nongxin	IV	?/?	10,500	1980
Qinglong Mountain	IV	?/?	15,100	1982
Qingshitan	IV	?/?	35,500	1982
Sanpihu	IV	?/?	4,200	1982
Shangyue Camellia	IV	?/?	2,600	1986
Shiwandashan	IV	21°51'N/107°52'E	26,700	1980
Shoucheng	IV	?/?	65,000	1982
Taiping Mountain	IV	?/?	17,800	1982
Wufubaoding	IV	?/?	6,400	1982
Xialei	IV	?/?	7,900	1982
Xiling	IV	?/?	14,600	1982
Yinding Mountain	IV	?/?	21,000	1982
Yinzhwaoshan	IV	?/?	1,900	1982
Yuanbao Mountain	IV	?/?	8,100	1982
Yueyu	IV	?/?	2,300	1982

Scenic Area

Guiping West Hill	V	?/?	200,000	?
Huashan	V	?/?	280,000	?

Guizhou

Nature Reserve

Caohai	IV	?/?	5,334	1985
Cathay Silver Fir	IV	?/?	4,600	1984
Chi Shui Yuan Sheng Lin	IV	?/?	40,000	1990
Hongfeng Lake	IV	?/?	11,000	1981
Jiulongkou	IV	?/?	1,333	1985
Leigong Mountain	IV	?/?	47,300	1982
Mount Fanjing	IV	?/?	41,902	1978
Precious Birds	IV	?/?	1,870	1983

Scenic Area

Huangguoshu Waterfalls	V	26°13'N/105°38'E	11,500	1980
Lake Hongfeng	V	?/?	5,700	1987
Longgong Palace	V	?/?	2,400	1987
Wuyang River	V	?/?	40,000	1987
Zhijin Cavern	V	?/?	45,000	1987

Hebei

Nature Reserve

Chang Li Gold Coast	III	?/?	30,000	1990
Lesser Wutai Mountain	IV	?/?	22,000	1983
Wuling Mountain	IV	?/?	14,580	1983

Scenic Area

Cangyanshan	V	?/?	18,000	?
Yiesanpuo	V	?/?	46,000	?

Heilongjiang

Nature Reserve

Agate	IV	?/?	1,352	1987
Dahei Mountain	IV	?/?	2,100	1986
Dapingtai	IV	?/?	25,000	1985
Fenglin	IV	48°05'N/129°07'E	18,400	1958
Five Joined Lakes	IV	48°45'N/126°12'E	70,000	1980
Heilonggong	IV	45°31'N/127°51'E	3,600	1982
Hong River	IV	47°50'N/133°40'E	16,333	1984
Huma River	IV	?/?	30,000	1982
Huzhong	IV	?/?	194,000	1983
Jingpo Lake	IV	43°50'N/128°54'E	120,000	1980
Kuerbin	IV	?/?	250,000	1985
Liangshui	IV	?/?	6,394	1980
Mudan Peak	IV	44°25'N/129°47'E	40,000	1981
North-east Black Bee	IV	?/?	270,000	1980
Peony Peak	IV	?/?	40,000	1980
Qixinglazi	IV	46°34'N/131°02'E	33,000	1980
Shatian Garania	IV	?/?	13,333	1986
Songfeng Mountain	IV	45°30'N/127°30'E	1,465	1984
Xingkai Lake	IV	?/?	16,537	1986
Xunbiela River	IV	?/?	14,000	1982
Yueya Lake	IV	?/?	5,133	1986
Zhalong	IV	47°15'N/124°15'E	210,000	1979

Henan

Nature Reserve

Bai Song Ling	IV	?/?	3,000	1990
Baotianman (Henan)	IV	33°29'N/111°57'E	3,333	1982
Baotianman (Neixiang)	IV	33°15'N/111°55'E	4,200	1980
Dongzhai	IV	?/?	9,333	1982
Giant Salamander (Lushi)	IV	?/?	65,000	1982
Hua Guo Shan	IV	?/?	4,200	1991
Jigong Mountain	IV	?/?	3,000	1982
Jingangtai	IV	?/?	4,200	1982
Laojieling	IV	?/?	15,333	1982
Laojun Mountain (Henan)	IV	?/?	2,000	1982
Lesser Qinling Mountain	IV	?/?	4,000	1982
Liankang Mountain	IV	?/?	2,000	1982
Longchiman	IV	?/?	7,502	1982
Rhesus Macaque	IV	?/?	10,667	1982
Shiren Mountain	IV	?/?	1,333	1982
Taibaiding	IV	?/?	3,533	1982
Taihang	IV	?/?	2,000	1982
Xiaoqin Ridge	IV	?/?	4,000	1982

Hubei

Nature Reserve

Huping Mountain	IV	30°03'N/110°44'E	13,333	1982

Jiugong	IV	29°28'N/114°38'E	3,995	1983
Qing Long Shan	IV	?/?	1,920	1990
Qi Zi Mei Shan	IV	?/?	1,760	1990
Shennongja	IV	31°29'N/110°35'E	77,333	1978
Wild Winterswect	IV	?/?	2,800	1985
Wu Dang Shan	IV	?/?	29,090	1990
Wu Dao Xia	IV	?/?	1,670	1990
Xiao River	IV	30°01'N/109°30'E	60,000	1981
Xingdou	IV	30°03'N/109°07'E	2,880	1981

Scenic Area

Dahong Mountain	V	?/?	33,000	1987

Hunan

Nature Reserve

Badagong Mountain	IV	?/?	20,000	1982
Bamian Mountain	IV	260°0'N/113°45'E	20,000	1982
Damiaokou	IV	?/?	11,333	1982
Dawie Mountain	IV	?/?	6,300	1982
Dayuanyuankou	IV	24°59'N/111°06'E	9,866	1982
Dong-tin Lake	IV	?/?	184,300	?
Gaozeyuan	IV	?/?	8,000	1982
Huangsang	IV	26°24'N/110°06'E	15,700	1982
Jou-li Mountain	IV	?/?	5,700	1982
Jun Mountain	IV	29°23'N/113°20'E	84,000	1982
Mang Mountain	IV	24°58'N/112°50'E	6,667	1982
Mu Ping Hu	IV	?/?	27,000	1991
Nanyue	IV	27°17'N/112°45'E	13,333	1982
Qianjiadong	IV	25°30'N/111°37'E	5,300	1982
Shunhuang Mountain (Dong'an)	IV	26°27'N/111°12'E	10,000	1982
Shunhuang Mountain (Xinling)	IV	?/?	3,000	1982
Suoxiyu	IV	29°22'N/110°40'E	5,333	1982
Taoyuandong	IV	26°15'N/113°45'E	10,000	1982
Tianzi Mountain	IV	?/?	3,340	1982
Xiaoxi	IV	28°53'N/109°51'E	10,000	1982
Yangming Mountain	IV	26°02'N/111°50'E	2,800	1982
Yun Mountain	IV	26°38'N/110°45'E	3,333	1982
Zhang-jia-jic State Forest	IV	?/?	5,000	?
Ziyunwanfeng Mountain	IV	26°25'N/110°39'E	22,840	1982

Scenic Area

Wulingyuan	V	29°20'N/110°32'E	26,400	1988

Jiangsu

Nature Reserve

Chaihe Reservoir	IV	?/?	30,300	1987
Nanusilia	IV	?/?	4,000	1986
Suzihe	IV	?/?	360,000	1987
Yancheng	IV	33°31'N/120°11'E	40,000	1983

Scenic Area

Yuntaishan Mountain	V	?/?	18,000	1984

Jiangxi

Nature Reserve

Guan Mountain	IV	28°39'N/114°36'E	6,467	1976
Jinggang Mountains	IV	26°35'N/114°14'E	15,873	1981
Jiulian Mountain	IV	24°35'N/114°28'E	4,067	1976
Lu Mountain	IV	29°36'N/115°59'E	30,493	1981
Poyang Lake	IV	?/?	22,400	1984
River Mussel	IV	?/?	22,833	1980

Taohongling	IV	29°53'N/116°41'E	4,500	1981
Wuyi Mountain	IV	27°17'N/117°01'E	5,333	1981
Xiazhuang	IV	?/?	2,000	1984
Yan Mountain	IV	?/?	5,333	1977

Scenic Area

Longhu Mountain	V	?/?	20,000	1985
Sanqing Mountain	V	?/?	22,000	1985

Jilin

Nature Reserve

Chagan Lake	IV	?/?	48,000	1986
Changbai Mountains	IV	42°04'N/127°58'E	190,582	1961
Songhua Lake	IV	43°20'N/127°04'E	354,098	1982
Xianghai	IV	44°33'N/123°02'E	105,467	1981
Yaojingzi Praire	IV	?/?	23,800	1986
Yitong Volcanic Complex	IV	?/?	64,100	1984
Zuojia	IV	43°33'N/126°46'E	6,008	1982

Scenic Area

Badabu - Jingyue Pool	V	?/?	15,100	?
Songhua Lake	V	?/?	70,000	?

Liaoning

Nature Reserve

Baishilazi	IV	?/?	6,667	1981
Bali Indian Azalea	IV	?/?	12,000	1984
Fenghuang Mountain	IV	?/?	2,600	1981
Glabrous Leaf Epaulette Tree Forest	IV	?/?	2,580	1985
Gushan	IV	?/?	7,000	1987
Haitang Mountain	IV	?/?	3,156	1986
Huakun-Sunjiagou	IV	?/?	3,333	1981
Hunhe	IV	?/?	23,000	1986
Immortal's Cave	IV	?/?	1,733	1981
Laohu Cave	IV	?/?	11,000	1986
Laotudingzi	IV	?/?	6,000	1981
Liupaoshougou	IV	?/?	2,000	1981
Lu Shun Kou	IV	?/?	2,740	1990
Mongolian Scotch Pine Seed Stand	IV	?/?	1,314	1981
Nanliuzhangzi	IV	?/?	1,333	1984
Nianzigou	IV	?/?	1,133	1984
Old Baldy Summit	IV	?/?	5,930	1981
Phoenix Mountain	IV	?/?	3,900	1981
Pi Mountain	IV	?/?	3,333	1981
Qianshan	IV	?/?	4,500	1985
Shaguogou	IV	?/?	1,200	1984
Shajintai Praire	IV	?/?	12,900	1986
Shuangtaizi Estuary	IV	?/?	7,000	1985
Snake Island and Laotieshan	IV	38°51'N/121°26'E	190,000	1980
Tanghe	IV	?/?	42,000	1986
Xipin	IV	?/?	1,466	1984
Yiwulu Mountain	IV	41°37'N/121°40'E	14,000	1981

Scenic Area

Dalian Beach-Lushunkou	V	?/?	10,500	?
Jinshitan	V	?/?	11,000	?
Xincheng	V	?/?	4,200	?
Yalujiang	V	?/?	40,000	?

Nei Monggol

Nature Reserve

Aibugai River	IV	?/?	1,000	1984

Bamao River	IV	?/?	31,000	1984
Bayanaobao	IV	43°16'N/117°29'E	6,737	1980
Dalai Lake	IV	?/?	400,000	1986
Daqinggou	IV	42°45'N/122°11'E	8,183	1980
Hanma	IV	?/?	135,187	?
Helam Mountain	IV	?/?	10,350	1980
Maoienaobao Wetland Birds	IV	?/?	134,000	1985
Nudeng	IV	40°32'N/108°12'E	28,040	1983
Nuomin Virgin Forest	IV	?/?	149,770	?
Xilin Gol Prairie	IV	?/?	1,078,600	1985

Ningxia

Nature Reserve

Helan Mountains	IV	?/?	61,000	1982
Liupan Mountain	IV	?/?	7,000	1982
Luo Mountain	IV	?/?	8,900	1982
Qingtongxia	IV	?/?	3,333	1984
Shapotou	IV	?/?	12,000	1983
Yunwu Mountain	IV	?/?	1,300	1982

Qinghai

Nature Reserve

Bird Island (Niao Dao)	IV	37°00'N/99°41'E	53,550	1975
Longbao	IV	33°19'N/96°42'E	10,000	1984
Mengda	IV	36°06'N/102°03'E	9,544	1980
Qinghaihu Waterfowl Island	IV	36°59'N/99°51'E	7,850	1975

Shaanxi

Nature Reserve

Crested Ibis	IV	?/?	5,000	1983
Foping	IV	33°38'N/107°49'E	35,000	1978
Golden Monkey	IV	?/?	54,700	1980
Sanmenxia Waterfowl	IV	?/?	39,000	1980
Savin Juniper	IV	38°55'N/110°55'E	7,666	1976
Stiff-leaf Juniper	IV	39°15'N/111°03'E	6,354	1961
Taibai Mountains	IV	33°59'N/107°37'E	54,103	1965
Zhashui Takin	IV	?/?	1,600	1980

Shandong

Nature Reserve

Ai Mountain	IV	?/?	5,333	1984
Bao Du Gu	IV	?/?	1,000	1991
Cha Mountain	IV	?/?	2,667	1984
Changdao	IV	38°08'N/120°46'E	5,250	1986
Dagu River	IV	?/?	463,100	1984
Dujia Mountain	IV	?/?	6,667	1984
Fu Mountain	IV	?/?	60,700	1984
Huanglei River	IV	?/?	65,200	1984
Huangshui River	IV	?/?	98,300	1984
Jia River	IV	?/?	200,000	1984
Longshan	IV	?/?	6,667	1984
Muzhu River	IV	?/?	127,800	1984
Nansi Hu	IV	34°53'N/116°58'E	126,600	1982
Qingdao Bird	IV	?/?	1,065,400	1982
Rizhao	IV	35°20'N/119°30'E	40,000	1982
Rushan River	IV	?/?	95,400	1984
Tanyang	IV	?/?	10,000	1984
Wang River	IV	?/?	7,600	1984
Weide Mountain	IV	?/?	6,667	1984
Weihai	IV	?/?	39,800	1984
Wulong River	IV	?/?	265,200	1984

Ya Mountain	IV	?/?	6,667	1984
Yi Mountain	IV	?/?	3,200	1982
Yuan Mountain	IV	?/?	1,000	1985
Zhaohu Mountain	IV	?/?	6,667	1984
Zhifu	IV	?/?	22,750	1984

Shanxi

Nature Reserve

Li Mountain	IV	35°34'N/112°04'E	24,800	1983
Luya Mountain	IV	38°43'N/111°56'E	21,453	1980
Mang River	IV	35°19'N/112°27'E	5,600	1983
Pangquangou	IV	37°51'N/111°32'E	10,446	1980
Wutai Mountain	IV	?/?	3,333	1986

Scenic Area

| Yellow River Hukou Waterfalls | V | ?/? | 10,000 | ? |

Sichuan

Nature Reserve

Baihe	IV	33°25'N/104°05'E	20,000	1963
Dafengding Panda	IV	?/?	30,000	1978
Fengtongzai	IV	30°40'N/102°54'E	40,000	1978
Gar Qu	IV	33°18'N/103°29'E	20,000	1963
Huanglongsi	IV	32°32'N/103°50'E	40,000	1983
Jinyun Mountain	IV	29°49'N/106°26'E	1,400	1979
Jiuzhaigou	IV	33°10'N/103°55'E	60,000	1978
Laba River	IV	30°22'N/102°28'E	12,000	1963
Mabian Dafengding	IV	28°32'N/103°16'E	30,000	1978
Meigudafengding	IV	28°44'N/103°09'E	16,000	1978
Tangjia River	IV	32°29'N/104°45'E	28,000	1978
Tiebu	IV	33°58'N/102°25'E	23,000	1965
Wanglang	IV	32°42'N/103°56'E	27,700	1963
Wolong	IV	31°08'N/103°07'E	200,000	1975
Xiaozhaizigou	IV	32°06'N/103°54'E	6,700	1979

Scenic Area

Bamboo Forest	V	?/?	12,000	1986
Gongya Mountain	V	?/?	1,000,000	1986
Huanglong	V	32°46'N/103°53'E	70,000	1982
Jinfo Mountain	V	?/?	26,000	1986
Juizhaigou Valley	V	33°07'N/103°55'E	72,000	1982

Xinjiang Uygur Zizhiqu

Nature Reserve

A Er Jin Shan (Arjin Mountains)	IV	36°59'N/89°15'E	4,512,000	1985
A Er Jin Shan Ye Luo (Arjin)	IV	36°30'N/88°00'E	15,125	1986
Bayanbulak	IV	40°33'N/83°18'E	100,000	1980
Bulgan River	IV	46°10'N/90°45'E	5,000	1980
Bunge Ash	IV	?/?	1,400	1983
Chinese Walnut	IV	44°07'N/80°54'E	1,180	1983
Fuhai Jengsetas	IV	44°27'N/88°31'E	9,767	1986
Ganjia Lake	IV	43°43'N/82°42'E	1,042,000	1983
Hanas	IV	48°52'N/87°30'E	250,000	1980
Huocheng	IV	41°52'N/86°01'E	35,000	1983
Kalamaili Mountain	IV	45°29'N/89°15'E	1,700,000	1982
Lake of Heaven	IV	44°30'N/86°08'E	38,069	1980
Mount Tomur	IV	41°45'N/80°08'E	100,000	1980
Naz-Quelute	IV	44°29'N/80°39'E	16,400	1986
Qitai	IV	44°03'N/89°33'E	12,333	1986
Schrenk Spruce	IV	43°08'N/82°14'E	28,000	1983
Tacheng	IV	47°00'N/83°17'E	1,500	1980

Tarim	IV	41°31'N/86°23'E	387,900	1980
Taxkorgan	IV	36°42'N/76°08'E	1,500,000	1984
Tianchi	IV	43°45'N/88°00'E	38,063	1980
Urumqi Geological	IV	43°51'N/88°27'E	200,000	1986

Xizang Zizhiqu

Nature Reserve

Gang	IV	30°38'N/95°33'E	4,600	1985
Jiangcun	IV	?/?	34,060	1985
Jiang Tang	IV	?/?	24,000,000	1990
Mang Kang	IV	?/?	6,000	1990
Medog	IV	29°50'N/94°25'E	62,620	1985
Qomolangma	IV	28°35'N/86°16'E	3,500,000	1989
Riwoqi (Lei Wu Qi)	IV	?/?	20,000	1990
Shen Zha	IV	?/?	3,000,000	1990
Zayu	IV	29°28'N/95°41'E	101,400	1985
Zham	IV	?/?	6,852	1985

Yunnan

Nature Reserve

Ailao Mountain	IV	24°26'N/101°09'E	50,360	1986
Baima Mountain	IV	28°01'N/99°09'E	180,000	1983
Bitahai	IV	27°59'N/99°57'E	14,133	1984
Cangshan Erhai	IV	25°58'N/100°26'E	70,000	1981
Dawei Mountain	IV	22°48'N/103°41'E	10,533	1982
Daxue Mountain	IV	24°08'N/99°33'E	15,787	1986
Erhai Lake	IV	25°39'N/100°15'E	24,976	?
Fenshuiling	IV	22°44'N/103°21'E	10,760	1986
Gaoligong Mountain	IV	25°45'N/98°44'E	123,333	1983
Haba Mountain	IV	27°24'N/100°09'E	21,907	1984
Haiziping	IV	27°32'N/104°24'E	2,780	1984
Heaven Lake	IV	25°19'N/99°24'E	6,667	1983
Huanglian Mountain	IV	22°53'N/102°17'E	13,835	1983
Jiache	IV	25°54'N/103°20'E	8,287	1984
Jizu Mountain	IV	23°05'N/102°25'E	2,000	1983
Kunming	IV	23°53'N/102°19'E	143,000	1981
Laiyang River	IV	22°34'N/101°15'E	7,000	1986
Laojun Mountain (Yunnan)	IV	22°58'N/104°30'E	4,507	1986
Lugu Lake	IV	27°44'N/100°47'E	8,127	1986
Mengla	IV	?/?	100,000	1958
Mengluen	IV	?/?	9,000	1958
Mengyang	IV	?/?	90,000	1958
Nangun River	IV	23°15'N/99°02'E	7,000	1980
Napahai	IV	27°54'N/99°37'E	2,067	1984
Nu River	IV	27°52'N/98°30'E	375,433	1986
Shibalianshan	IV	25°30'N/104°16'E	1,213	?
Songhuaba	IV	24°06'N/101°41'E	60,000	1981
Stone Grove	IV	26°12'N/101°28'E	9,000	1981
Tianchi (Yunlong)	IV	26°02'N/99°11'E	7,000	1983
Tongbiguan	IV	24°36'N/97°37'E	34,160	1986
Weiyuan River	IV	23°07'N/100°24'E	7,780	1983
Wuliang Mountain	IV	24°27'N/100°45'E	23,353	1986
Xiaomengyang	IV	?/?	86,666	1958
Xiaoqiaogou	IV	23°20'N/104°42'E	1,894	1986
Xishuangbanna	IV	21°47'N/100°59'E	207,000	1958
Yaoshan	IV	27°13'N/102°03'E	10,213	1984
Yulong Mountain	IV	27°11'N/100°09'E	26,000	1984

Scenic Area

Dianchi Lake	V	?/?	30,000	?
Lijiang Yulong Mountain Landscape	V	?/?	77,000	?
Lunan Scenic Area of the Stone Forest	V	24°48'N/103°20'E	35,000	1982

Zhejiang

Nature Reserve

Baishanzu	IV	?/?	1,333	1985
Fengyang Mountain	IV	28°25'N/119°05'E	4,667	1975
Gutian Mountain	IV	29°20'N/118°14'E	1,333	1962
Jiulong Mountain	IV	28°21'N/118°52'E	2,000	1983
Longwang Mountain	IV	?/?	1,200	1985
Nan Ji Lei Dao	IV	?/?	16,200	1992
Nanjilie Islands	IV	?/?	1,600	1986
Pu Tuo Shan	IV	?/?	1,130	1990
West Tianmu Mountain	IV	30°21'N/119°22'E	1,000	1962
Yan Dang Shan	IV	?/?	1,000	1990

Scenic Area

Chengsi Islands	V	?/?	6,000	1985
Tiantaishan Mountain	V	?/?	10,500	1985

COLOMBIA/COLOMBIE

Summary		
Category I	5	45,365
Category II	33	7,020,690
Category III	2	1,947,000
Category IV	1	2,045
Category V	38	342,911
Total	**79**	**9,358,011**

Fauna and Flora Sanctuary

Ciénaga Grande de Santa Marta	I	10°52'N/74°23'W	23,000	1977
Galeras	I	1°12'N/77°22'W	7,615	1985
Iguaque	I	5°38'N/73°27'W	6,750	1977
Los Colorados	I	9°55'N/75°08'W	1,000	1977
Los Flamencos	I	11°23'N/73°08'W	7,000	1977

Natural National Park

Amacayacu	II	3°25'S/70°12'W	293,000	1975
Cahuinarí	II	1°24'S/71°07'W	575,500	1987
Catatumbo-Bari	II	9°00'N/73°10'W	158,125	1989
Chingaza	II	4°33'N/73°45'W	50,374	1977
Chiribiquete	II	0°42'N/72°46'W	1,280,000	1989
Corales del Rosario	II	10°09'N/75°45'W	19,506	1977
Cordillera de los Picachos	II	2°47'N/74°35'W	439,000	1977
Cueva de los Guácharos	II	1°35'N/76°02'W	9,000	1960
El Cocuy	II	6°34'S/72°20'W	306,000	1977
El Tuparro	II	5°17'N/68°31'W	548,000	1970
Farallones de Cali	II	3°13'N/76°46'W	150,000	1968
Isla de Salamanca	II	11°02'N/74°40'W	21,000	1969
Isla Gorgona	II	25°58'N/78°11'W	49,200	1984
La Paya	II	0°10'N/75°09'W	422,000	1984
Las Hermosas	II	3°45'N/75°55'W	125,000	1977
Las Orquídeas	II	6°35'N/76°15'W	32,000	1974
Los Katíos	II	7°48'N/77°08'W	72,000	1973
Los Nevados	II	4°47'N/75°23'W	38,000	1959
Macuira	II	12°09'N/71°20'W	25,000	1977
Munchique	II	2°42'N/77°00'W	44,000	1977
Nevado del Huila	II	3°04'N/75°57'W	158,000	1977
Paramillo	II	7°34'N/76°07'W	460,000	1977
Pisba	II	5°53'N/72°32'W	45,000	1977
Puracé	II	2°09'N/76°32'W	83,000	1968
Sanquianga	II	2°33'N/78°22'W	80,000	1977

Sierra de la Macarena	II	2°37'N/73°34'W	630,000	1948
Sierra Nevada de Santa Marta	II	11°18'N/74°10'W	383,000	1959
Sumapaz	II	3°53'N/74°08'W	154,000	1977
Tamá	II	7°15'N/72°13'W	48,000	1977
Tatamá	II	?/?	51,900	1987
Tayrona	II	11°20'N/74°02'W	15,000	1964
Tinigua	II	2°28'N/74°06'W	201,785	1989
Utría	II	6°00'N/77°17'W	54,300	1987

Natural National Reserve

Nukak	III	1°53'N/71°31'W	855,000	1989
Puinawai	III	2°15'N/64°11'W	1,092,000	1989

Natural Reserve

Laguna de Sonso	IV	?/?	2,045	1979

Protection Forest Reserve

Bosque Oriental de Bogotá	V	?/?	17,625	1976
Caños La Esperanza, Negro y la Lindosa	V	?/?	5,600	1982
Cerro Quinini	V	?/?	1,800	1987
Cuchilla Peñas Blancas	V	?/?	1,630	1983
Cuchilla Sucuncuca	V	?/?	1,710	1989
Embalse El Peñol-Río Guatapé	V	?/?	13,100	1985
Escarpas Occidental y Malpaso	V	?/?	3,160	1982
Frontera Colombo-Panameña	V	?/?	62,375	1977
Lago Sochagota	V	?/?	8,150	1986
Laguna La Cocha y Cerro de Patascoy	V	?/?	8,500	1973
Predio La Bolsa	V	?/?	2,700	1990
Predio La Planada	V	?/?	1,667	1984
Predio Río Sucio	V	?/?	1,360	1987
Páramo de Chingaza	V	?/?	20,000	1971
Páramo de Sumapaz	V	?/?	30,000	1971
Páramo El Atravesado	V	?/?	3,044	1971
Páramo Urrao	V	?/?	4,000	1975
Quebrada La Tablona #1	V	?/?	1,420	1981
Quebrada La Tablona #2	V	?/?	2,700	1991
Quebrada Mutatá	V	?/?	1,500	1985
Quebrada Piedras Blancas	V	?/?	11,825	1970
Río Algodonal	V	?/?	8,200	1984
Río Blanco-Olivares	V	?/?	4,900	1989
Río Cravo Sur	V	?/?	5,000	1985
Río Las Ceibas	V	?/?	6,370	1983
Río León	V	?/?	29,000	1971
Río Mocoa	V	?/?	34,500	1984
Río Nembí	V	?/?	5,800	1984
Río San Francisco	V	?/?	2,880	1981
Río Satocá	V	?/?	4,200	1989
Río Tame	V	?/?	1,900	1985
Río Tejo	V	?/?	2,500	1984
Ríos Blanco y Negro	V	?/?	11,925	1982
Ríos Chorreras-Concepción	V	?/?	4,450	1991
Ríos Escalerete-San Cipriano	V	?/?	5,400	1982
Serranía de Coraza y Montes de María	V	?/?	6,370	1983
Sierra El Peligro	V	?/?	1,650	1988
Zona Musinga-Carauta	V	?/?	4,000	1975

COMOROS/COMORES/COMORAS

No Areas Listed

CONGO

	Summary	
Category I	0	0
Category II	1	126,600
Category III	0	0
Category IV	9	1,050,794
Category V	0	0
Total	**10**	**1,177,394**

Faunal Reserve

Conkouati	IV	4°00'S/11°20'W	144,294	1980
Lefini	IV	3°00'S/15°32'E	630,000	1951
Lekoli-Pandaka	IV	0°38'N/14°52'E	68,200	1955
Mont Fouari	IV	2°47'S/11°20'E	15,600	1958
Nyanga Nord	IV	2°45'S/11°45'E	7,700	1958
Tsoulou	IV	3°35'S/12°30'E	30,000	1963

Hunting Reserve

M'boko	IV	0°38'N/14°52'E	90,000	1955
Mont Mavoumbou	IV	2°55'S/11°26'E	42,000	1955
Nyanga Sud	IV	2°55'S/11°21'E	23,000	1958

National Park

Odzala	II	0°50'N/14°53'E	126,600	1940

COSTA RICA

	Summary	
Category I	4	15,169
Category II	13	488,337
Category III	0	0
Category IV	9	129,387
Category V	3	5,671
Total	**29**	**638,564**

Biological Reserve

Cabo Blanco	I	9°34'N/85°08'W	1,172	1963
Carara	I	9°45'N/84°38'W	4,700	1978
Hitoy-Cerere	I	9°35'N/83°05'W	9,154	1978
Isla del Caño	IV	8°42'N/83°53'W	200	1978
Islas Guayabo y Negritos	I	9°52'N/84°52'W	143	1973
Lomas Barbudal	IV	10°27'N/85°20'W	2,279	1986

National Park

Arenal	II	10°31'N/84°50'W	2,000	1991
Ballena Marino	IV	10°08'N/83°43'W	4,200	1990
Barra Honda	V	10°10'N/85°23'W	2,295	1974
Braulio Carrillo	II	10°10'N/84°00'W	45,899	1978
Cahuita	V	9°44'N/82°47'W	1,067	1970
Chirripó	II	9°29'N/83°27'W	50,150	1975
Corcovado	II	8°30'N/83°35'W	54,539	1975
Guanacaste	II	10°57'N/85°32'W	32,512	1991
Isla del Coco	II	5°32'N/87°04'W	2,400	1978
Juan Castro Blanco	II	?/?	14,258	1992
La Amistad (Talamanca)	II	9°11'N/82°54'W	193,929	1982
Palo Verde	II	10°25'N/84°22'W	16,804	1982
Santa Rosa	II	10°50'N/85°39'W	37,217	1971
Tapantí	IV	?/?	6,080	1992
Tortuguero	II	10°27'N/83°29'W	18,946	1975

Volcán Irazú	V	9°58'N/83°50'W	2,309	1955
Volcán Poás	II	10°12'N/84°14'W	5,600	1971
Volcán Rincón de la Vieja	II	10°35'N/85°30'W	14,083	1973

Wildlife Refuge

Barra del Colorado	IV	10°45'N/83°43'W	92,000	1985
Caño Negro	IV	10°55'N/84°45'W	9,969	1983
Gandoca y Manzanillo	IV	?/?	9,449	1985
Golfito	IV	?/?	2,810	1985
Peñas Blancas	IV	?/?	2,400	1992

CÔTE D'IVOIRE

Summary		
Category I	2	128,000
Category II	8	1,762,500
Category III	0	0
Category IV	2	102,350
Category V	0	0
Total	**12**	**1,992,850**

Botanical Reserve

Divo	IV	5°53'N/5°15'W	7,350	1975

Fauna and Flora Reserve

Haut Bandama	I	8°27'N/5°29'W	123,000	1973

National Park

Azagny	II	5°13'N/4°53'W	19,000	1981
Banco	II	5°19'N/4°02'W	3,000	1953
Comoé	II	8°35'N/3°33'W	1,150,000	1968
Iles Ehotile	II	5°10'N/3°14'W	10,500	1974
Marahoue	II	7°35'N/5°59'W	101,000	1968
Mont Peko	II	7°01'N/7°16'W	34,000	1968
Mont Sangbe	II	8°15'N/7°20'W	95,000	1976
Taï	II	5°45'N/7°00'W	350,000	1973

Partial Faunal Reserve

N'Zo	IV	6°08'N/7°15'W	95,000	1972

Strict Nature Reserve

Mont Nimba	I	7°18'N/10°35'W	5,000	1944

CROATIA/CROATIE/CROACIA

Summary		
Category I	4	19,784
Category II	5	46,331
Category III	1	1,100
Category IV	5	15,418
Category V	14	302,711
Total	**29**	**385,344**

Forest Park

Kotar-Stari Gaj	IV	45°20'N/16°20'E	5,218	1975

Landscape Park

Zvecevo na papuku	V	45°20'N/17°40'E	2,586	1966

National Park

Briuni	V	44°55'N/13°45'E	4,660	1983

Kornati	II	43°50'N/15°20'E	22,400	1980
Krka	II	43°53'N/15°59'E	14,200	1985
Mljet	II	42°47'N/17°22'E	3,100	1960
Paklenica	II	44°20'N/15°30'E	3,617	1949
Plitvicka jezera	V	44°53'N/15°37'E	19,172	1949
Risnjak	II	45°26'N/14°38'E	3,014	1953

Nature Park

Biokovo	V	43°21'N/17°03'E	19,550	1981
Kopacki Rit	V	45°36'N/18°54'E	17,200	1967
Lonjsko polje	V	45°30'N/17°00'E	50,650	1990
Medvednica	V	45°53'N/15°58'E	22,826	1981
Telascica	V	43°52'N/15°12'E	6,706	1988
Velebit	V	44°30'N/15°30'E	150,000	1981

Nature Reserve

Bijele i Samarske Stijene	I	45°15'N/15°10'E	1,175	1985
Hajducki i Rozanski Kukovi	I	?/?	1,220	1969
Malostonski Zaljev	I	42°49'N/17°27'E	10,389	1983
Neretva Delta	IV	42°57'N/17°34'E	1,200	?

Protected Landscape

Bijeli Potoci-Kamensko	V	44°40'N/15°50'E	1,057	1972
Cetina-kanjon	III	43°30'N/16°40'E	1,100	1963
Kalnik	V	46°10'N/16°30'E	4,200	1985
Prolosko blato	V	43°30'N/17°10'E	1,024	1971
Rovinj-otoci i priobalno podruscje	V	45°05'N/13°45'E	1,200	1968
Vidora gora	V	43°20'N/16°40'E	1,880	1970

Special Reserve

Glavina-Mala Luka	IV	45°00'N/14°48'E	1,000	1969
Kopacki Rit	I	45°36'N/18°54'E	7,000	1976
Otok Krk Rta Glavine do Uvale Mala Luka	IV	?/?	1,000	1969
Prvic	IV	44°55'N/14°52'E	7,000	1972

CUBA

Summary		
Category I	9	39,978
Category II	9	116,942
Category III	0	0
Category IV	15	163,161
Category V	20	572,676
Total	**53**	**892,757**

Ecological Reserve

Los Indios	IV	?/?	3,250	?
Punta Negra - Punta Quemados	IV	?/?	3,972	?

Faunal Refuge

Alto de Iberia	I	20°31'N/74°40'W	5,673	1987
Cayo Cantiles	I	21°37'N/81°55'W	3,800	1986
Cayos de Ana María	IV	?/?	6,900	?
Delta del Cauto	IV	?/?	60,000	?
Hatibonico	IV	?/?	5,220	1980
Las Salinas	IV	22°09'N/81°18'W	31,800	1936
Ojito de Agua	IV	?/?	3,739	1987
Río Máximo	IV	?/?	10,000	?
Santo Tomás	IV	22°26'N/81°31'W	14,800	1936

Integral Management Area

Guanaroca	V	?/?	2,690	?
La Isleta - Nuevas Grandes	V	?/?	13,000	?
Subarchipiélago de Jardines de la Reina	V	?/?	30,580	?
Subarchipiélago de los Canarreos	V	?/?	33,110	?
Subarchipiélago de Sabana - Camaguey	V	?/?	178,908	?

Managed Floristic Reserve

Arenas Blancas	IV	20°31'N/74°50'W	1,500	?
Cayo Caguanes/Cayos de Piedra	IV	22°25'N/79°09'W	1,500	1966
Cerro Galano	IV	20°43'N/76°02'W	2,770	?
El Toldo	IV	20°31'N/74°50'W	5,638	1987
Monte Ramonal	IV	?/?	2,572	?
Parnaso - Los Montes	IV	?/?	9,500	?

Marine National Park

Bahía del Naranjo	II	?/?	6,800	?
Cayo Caguama	II	?/?	1,200	?

National Park

Desembarco del Granma	II	?/?	25,764	1980
Gran Piedra	II	?/?	3,354	1980
La Bayamesa	II	20°00'N/76°30'W	16,500	1980
Pico Cristal	II	?/?	15,000	1930
Punta Francés - Punta Pederales	II	?/?	17,424	1985
Turquino	II	?/?	17,464	1959
Vinales	II	?/?	13,436	?

Natural Touristic Area

Cayo Algodón Grande	V	?/?	3,600	?
Cayo Coco/Cayo Guillermo	V	22°29'N/78°29'W	32,000	1986
Cayo Gruz	V	?/?	1,400	?
Cayo Guajaba	V	?/?	9,168	?
Cayo Largo - Cayo Rosario	V	21°38'N/81°28'W	18,610	1986
Cayo Paredón Grande	V	?/?	3,500	?
Cayo Sabinal	V	?/?	33,500	?
Cayo Santa María	V	?/?	6,250	?
Covarrubias	V	?/?	10,200	?
Playa Cajuajo - Boca del Yumurí	V	?/?	5,500	?
Playa Santa Lucía	V	?/?	1,100	?
Punta del Este	V	?/?	5,300	?

Nature Park

Cayo Romano	V	22°00'N/77°45'W	92,000	1986
Sur Isla de la Juventud	V	?/?	80,000	1992
Topes de Collantes	V	?/?	12,260	?

Nature Reserve

Cabo Corrientes	I	21°48'N/84°27'W	1,578	1963
Cupeyal del Norte	I	20°30'N/75°02'W	10,260	1980
El Veral	I	21°58'N/84°35'W	7,535	1963
Imias	I	?/?	2,600	?
Jaguani	I	20°26'N/74°45'W	4,932	1963
Loma de la Mensura	I	?/?	2,400	?
Tacre	I	?/?	1,200	?

CYPRUS/CHYPRE/CHIPRE

	Summary	
Category I	0	0
Category II	1	9,337
Category III	0	0
Category IV	3	66,000
Category V	0	0
Total	**4**	**75,337**

Game Reserve

Limassol Lake (Akrotiri)	IV	34°37'N/32°57'E	2,000	1963
Listovounos Rotary Wildlife Friendship Park	IV	33°10'N/34°30'E	2,950	1951
Paphos	IV	35°05'N/32°40'E	61,050	1961

State Forest

Troodos (Paphos) State Forest	II	34°55'N/32°52'E	9,337	1992

CZECH REPUBLIC/
REPUBLIQUE TCHEQUE/
REPUBLICA CHECA

	Summary	
Category I	4	12,876
Category II	2	74,820
Category III	0	0
Category IV	4	6,361
Category V	24	972,751
Total	**34**	**1,066,808**

National Nature Reserve

Adrspassko Teplicke skaly	IV	50°35'N/16°07'E	1,772	1933
Karlstejn	IV	49°57'N/14°09'E	1,547	1955
Kokorinsky dul	I	50°27'N/14°36'E	2,097	1953
Modravske slati	I	?/?	3,615	1989
Prameny labe	I	50°46'N/15°32'E	2,884	1980
Prameny upy	I	50°44'N/15°41'E	4,280	1980
Stara Reka	IV	49°01'N/14°50'E	1,197	1956
Vltavsky Luh	IV	?/?	1,845	1989

National Park

Krkonose	V	50°43'N/15°40'E	36,300	1963
Podyji	II	48°51'N/15°57'E	6,300	1991
Sumava	II	49°00'N/13°50'E	68,520	1991

Protected Landscape Area

Beskydy	V	49°26'N/18°20'E	117,319	1973
Bile Karpaty	V	48°57'N/17°45'E	71,291	1980
Blanik	V	49°39'N/14°52'E	4,057	1981
Blansky les	V	?/?	21,235	1989
Broumovsko	V	?/?	41,000	1991
Cesky kras	V	49°57'N/14°11'E	12,458	1972
Cesky raj	V	50°32'N/15°09'E	8,646	1955
Jeseniky	V	50°06'N/17°16'E	73,689	1969
Jizerske hory	V	50°50'N/15°15'E	35,002	1967
Kokorinsko	V	50°29'N/14°33'E	26,726	1976
Krivoklatsko	V	50°00'N/13°52'E	63,346	1978
Labske Piskovce	V	50°51'N/14°19'E	32,474	1972
Litovelske pomoravi	V	?/?	9,600	1990
Moravsky kras	V	?/?	8,545	1956

Orlicke hory	V	50°15'N/16°25'E	20,410	1969
Podyji	V	48°51'N/15°57'E	10,300	1978
Poodri	V	?/?	8,150	1991
Slavkovsky les	V	50°05'N/12°42'E	61,896	1974
Strazovske vrchy	V	?/?	30,979	1989
Sumava	V	49°00'N/13°42'E	99,752	1963
Trebonsko	V	49°00'N/14°50'E	70,695	1979
Zdarske vrchy	V	49°40'N/16°01'E	70,881	1970
Zelezne hory	V	?/?	38,000	1991

DENMARK/DANEMARK/DINAMARCA

Summary		
Category I	10	1,073,838
Category II	1	97,200,000
Category III	2	6,290
Category IV	61	1,165,143
Category V	41	193,479
Total	**115**	**99,638,750**

Bird Reserve

Ertholm	I	55°19'N/15°12'E	1,257	?
Hirsholmene	I	57°29'N/10°38'E	380	1948
Ronner (Laeso)	IV	?/?	2,923	1980
Stavns Fjord	IV	55°54'N/10°40'E	16,320	1984
Totten	I	?/?	2,100	?

Major Conservation Area

Aalvand Klithede and Foerby Soe	V	56°57'N/8°25'E	1,200	1977
Agger Tange	IV	56°45'N/8°15'E	6,100	1984
Anholt	V	56°44'N/11°34'E	1,856	1939
Bognaes, Kattinge Vig	V	55°41'N/12°01'E	1,200	1969
Borris Hede	V	55°57'N/8°39'E	1,830	1902
Bulbjerg, Lild Klit and Hjardemaal Klit	V	57°09'N/9°00'E	1,500	1947
Egtved and Vejle River Valleys	V	55°40'N/9°18'E	1,025	1980
Esrum Soe and Surrounding Areas	V	56°00'N/12°25'E	1,900	1952
Fanoe	V	55°24'N/8°25'E	1,400	1964
Flyndersoe and Stubbergaard Soe	V	56°29'N/8°56'E	1,670	1934
Hanstholm Reserve	IV	57°03'N/8°36'E	4,800	1972
Harbooere Tange	V	56°42'N/8°13'E	2,400	1984
Hessel Sea Area	V	56°11'N/11°45'E	5,000	1982
Hoeje Moen	III	54°58'N/12°32'E	2,090	1980
Hulsig Klit	IV	?/?	2,144	1940
Kaergaard Klitplantage-Loevklitterne-Lyngbos	V	55°42'N/8°06'E	1,670	1955
Kongenshus Hede	V	56°24'N/9°08'E	1,300	1953
Ledreborg Gods	V	55°37'N/11°55'E	1,800	1973
Lyngby, Lodbjerg, Flade Soe	V	56°50'N/8°19'E	3,327	1976
Maribo Soerne	V	54°46'N/11°31'E	1,195	1957
Mols Bjerge	V	56°14'N/10°34'E	2,750	1972
Noerre Hvalsoe and Kisserup Area	V	55°37'N/11°53'E	1,132	1980
Nord-Bornholm	V	55°18'N/14°49'E	2,500	1970
North Coast of Vejle Fjord	V	55°42'N/9°44'E	1,004	1949
Raabjerg Mile and Hulsig Hede	III	57°40'N/10°26'E	4,200	1962
Rands Fjord	V	55°37'N/9°44'E	1,047	1968
Roemoe	IV	55°09'N/8°31'E	2,500	1947
Roennerne	V	57°14'N/11°01'E	1,496	1980
Ryegaard Gods, Tempelkrog and Bramsnaes Vig	V	55°40'N/11°51'E	1,515	1940
Saksfjed Inddaemning	IV	?/?	1,100	1989
Saltbaek Vig	IV	?/?	1,185	1992
Salten Langsoe, Vissingkloster, Mossoe	V	56°04'N/9°43'E	3,950	1971
Saltholm	V	55°39'N/12°45'E	1,600	1983

Skagen Klitplantage, Grenen	IV	57°44'N/10°37'E	2,175	1921
Skallingen and Langli	IV	55°30'N/8°17'E	2,400	1939
Soevind, Sondrup, Aakaer and Vorsoe	V	55°53'N/10°01'E	2,200	1974
Stavnsfjord	V	55°54'N/10°40'E	1,525	1984
Stigsnaes Peninsula	V	55°13'N/11°15'E	1,215	1978
Store Vildmose	V	?/?	2,100	1973
Sydlige Fanoe	V	?/?	1,400	1985
Toendermarsken	V	54°56'N/8°38'E	5,650	1988
Tranum Area	V	57°09'N/9°25'E	2,160	1956
Tystrup-Bavelse Soerne	V	55°21'N/11°37'E	3,750	1957
Ulfborg-Vind Area	V	56°15'N/8°22'E	1,300	1949
Ulvedybet og Nibe Breding	V	?/?	20,304	1930
Vadehavet	V	55°17'N/8°31'E	95,000	1985
Valloe Gods	V	55°24'N/12°14'E	1,383	1981
Vestamager	IV	?/?	3,000	1990
Veststadil Fjord and Husby Klit	V	56°11'N/8°08'E	1,465	1969
Vorupoer-Stenbjerg	V	?/?	2,270	1954

National Nature Area

Anholt	IV	?/?	30,300	?
Bornholm-Ertholmene	IV	?/?	6,200	?
Bovbjerg-Blåvands Huk	IV	?/?	50,000	?
Det sydfynske hav	IV	?/?	80,000	?
Grænselandet	IV	?/?	22,500	?
Hindsholm	IV	?/?	12,500	?
Horsens Fjord	IV	?/?	42,500	?
Langeland	IV	?/?	6,500	?
Lillebælt	IV	?/?	42,500	?
Limfjorden	IV	?/?	120,000	?
Læs	IV	?/?	98,300	?
Mariboserne-Sydstlolland	IV	?/?	32,500	?
Midtsjælland	IV	?/?	2,500	?
Mols	IV	?/?	32,500	?
Nakskov Fjord	IV	?/?	12,500	?
Norddjursland	IV	?/?	2,500	?
Nordsams og Stavns Fjord	IV	?/?	25,000	?
Nordsjælland	IV	?/?	2,500	?
Odsherred-Saltbæk Vig	IV	?/?	40,000	?
Ost-og Sydfalster	IV	?/?	2,500	?
Præst Fjord og det sydstlige Sjælland	IV	?/?	12,000	?
Saltsholm	IV	?/?	8,400	?
Skagen-Tolne	V	?/?	2,500	?
Skals Å-Mariager Fjord	IV	?/?	2,500	?
Smålandsfarvandet	IV	?/?	52,500	?
Stevns Klint	IV	?/?	2,500	?
Storstrmmen-Ulvsund-Grnsund	IV	?/?	12,500	?
Sydfyn	IV	?/?	2,500	?
Sydvestsjællands kyst	IV	?/?	32,500	?
Tannis Bugt-Bovbjerg	IV	?/?	10,000	?
Vadehavet	IV	?/?	110,000	?
Vandområdet udfor Mariager Fjord	IV	?/?	37,500	?
Vejle Å-Vejle Fjord	IV	?/?	15,000	?

Nature Reserve

Esrum Soe and Gribskov	IV	56°00'N/12°22'E	7,280	?
Flyndersoe and Stubbergaard Soe	IV	56°29'N/8°56'E	1,670	?
Hansted	IV	?/?	6,500	?
Skagen	IV	?/?	4,300	?
Tipperne and Vaernengene	IV	55°53'N/8°13'E	3,520	1936
Tisvilde, Melby	IV	56°02'N/12°02'E	2,000	?

Protected Region

Selso-Lindholm-Bognaes	V	?/?	1,990	?

Scientific Reserve

Græsholm ved Christians	I	?/?	1,219	?
Hessel	I	56°11'N/11°45'E	10,500	?
Hirsholmene	I	57°29'N/10°38'E	2,095	?
Hirsholmene	IV	57°29'N/10°38'E	2,095	?
Langli	I	?/?	946	?
Tipperne og Klægbanken	I	55°53'N/8°13'E	4,993	?
Vejlerne	IV	57°04'N/9°06'E	5,000	1960
Vors	I	?/?	348	?

Wildlife Reserve

Farum	IV	55°48'N/12°21'E	5,000	?
Fredericia	IV	?/?	1,211	1936
Gudenaens	IV	?/?	6,500	?
Hjarbæk Fjord	IV	56°33'N/9°20'E	2,486	1967
Livo Bredning	IV	?/?	1,000	1978
Nibe og Gjl	IV	?/?	9,500	1989
Nissum Fjord	IV	?/?	6,400	1986
Stavnsfjord	IV	55°54'N/10°40'E	1,564	1926
Ulvshale-Nyord	IV	55°02'N/12°15'E	9,770	1989
Vadehavet	IV	55°17'N/8°31'E	83,000	1979

Faroes/Iles Féroé/Islas Faroes

No Areas Listed

Greenland/Groenland/Groenlandia

National Park

Greenland	II	77°00'N/37°20'W	97,200,000	1974

Nature Reserve

Melville Bay	I	?/?	1,050,000	1977

DJIBOUTI

Summary		
Category I	0	0
Category II	1	10,000
Category III	0	0
Category IV	0	0
Category V	0	0
Total	**1**	**10,000**

National Park

Forêt du Day	II	11°50'N/42°30'E	10,000	1939

DOMINICA/DOMINIQUE

Summary		
Category I	0	0
Category II	1	6,872
Category III	0	0
Category IV	0	0
Category V	0	0
Total	**1**	**6,872**

National Park

Morne Trois Pitons	II	15°18'N/61°18'W	6,872	1975

DOMINICAN REPUBLIC/
REPUBLIQUE DOMINICAINE/
REPUBLICA DOMINICANA

	Summary	
Category I	0	0
Category II	8	563,934
Category III	0	0
Category IV	6	440,140
Category V	3	44,210
Total	**17**	**1,048,284**

Faunal Sanctuary

Banco de la Plata	IV	20°56'N/70°40'W	374,800	1986

National Park

Del Este	II	18°16'N/68°45'W	42,000	1975
Isla Cabritos	II	18°30'N/71°40'W	2,400	1974
Jaragua	II	17°26'N/71°19'W	137,400	1983
Jose Armando Bermúdez	II	19°03'N/71°02'W	76,600	1956
Jose del Carmen Ramírez	II	18°56'N/71°04'W	73,784	1958
Los Haitises	II	19°03'N/69°32'W	20,800	1976
Monte Cristi	II	19°53'N/71°44'W	130,950	1983
Parque Submarino La Caleta	V	18°27'N/69°54'W	1,010	1986
Sierra de Bahoruco	II	18°15'N/71°35'W	80,000	1986

Natural Scientific Reserve

Ebano Verde	IV	19°02'N/70°42'W	2,310	1989
Laguna del Rincón	IV	18°20'N/71°14'W	4,780	1983
Lagunas Redonda y Limón	IV	19°00'N/68°56'W	10,100	1983
Loma Isabel de Torres	V	19°47'N/70°43'W	2,200	1983
Loma Quita Espuela	IV	19°26'N/70°06'W	7,250	1992
Valle Nuevo	IV	18°48'N/70°38'W	40,900	1983

Vía Panorámica

El Aceitillar-Cabo Rojo	V	17°22'N/71°27'W	41,000	1986

ECUADOR/EQUATEUR

	Summary	
Category I	4	658,280
Category II	6	2,428,457
Category III	0	0
Category IV	2	7,994,613
Category V	3	32,543
Total	**15**	**11,113,893**

Biological Reserve

Limoncocha	IV	?/?	4,613	1985

Ecological Reserve

Cayambe-Coca	I	0°01'S/77°49'W	403,103	1970
Cotacachi-Cayapas	I	0°35'N/78°37'W	204,420	1968
El Angel	I	?/?	15,715	1992
Manglares-Churute	I	2°28'S/79°42'W	35,042	1979

Marine Resource Reserve

Galápagos	IV	0°02'N/90°39'W	7,990,000	1986

National Park

Cotopaxi	II	0°38'S/78°25'W	33,393	1975
Galápagos	II	0°36'S/91°04'W	693,700	1959

Machalilla	II	1°33'S/80°40'W	55,059	1979
Podocarpus	II	?/?	146,280	1982
Sangay	II	1°52'S/78°18'W	517,725	1975
Yasuní	II	0°55'S/75°51'W	982,300	1979

National Recreation Area

Cajas	V	3°03'S/79°21'W	28,808	1979
El Boliche	V	0°40'S/78°29'W	1,077	1979

Protection Forest

Bosque Petrificado de Puyango	V	3°52'S/79°37'W	2,658	1987

EGYPT/EGYPTE/EGIPTO

Summary		
Category I	3	37,000
Category II	1	61,500
Category III	0	0
Category IV	8	694,700
Category V	0	0
Total	**12**	**793,200**

Conservation Area

Gebel Elba	IV	22°10'N/36°20'E	480,000	1986
Wadi Allaqi (Aswan)	IV	?/?	27,500	?
Wadi Rayan	IV	?/?	20,000	?

National Park

Ras Mohammed	II	27°44'N/34°15'E	61,500	1983

Natural Area

Ashtoun el Gamil - Tanee Island	IV	31°17'N/32°12'E	1,200	1988
Bardawil Lake	IV	31°10'N/33°15'E	60,000	1985
St. Catherine (Moussa)	IV	28°25'N/34°00'E	45,000	1988
Zaranikh (El Arish)	IV	31°10'N/33°27'E	60,000	1985

Protected Area

Qarun Lake (Quaron)	I	29°28'N/30°37'E	20,000	1989
Saluga and Ghazal Nile Islands	IV	24°05'N/32°13'E	1,000	1986
Wadi el Assuity	I	?/?	10,000	1989

Scientific Reserve

Omayed	I	30°45'N/29°12'E	7,000	1986

EL SALVADOR

Summary		
Category I	0	0
Category II	1	3,222
Category III	0	0
Category IV	1	2,000
Category V	0	0
Total	**2**	**5,222**

National Park

El Imposible	II	13°48'N/89°58'W	3,222	1989
Montecristo	IV	14°25'N/89°23'W	2,000	1987

EQUATORIAL GUINEA/GUINEE EQUATORIALE/GUINEA ECUATORIAL

No Areas Listed

ERITREA/ERYTHREE

No Areas Listed

ESTONIA/ESTONIE

Summary		
Category I	6	68,428
Category II	1	176,922
Category III	0	0
Category IV	28	138,823
Category V	4	55,978
Total	**39**	**440,151**

Landscape Reserve

Ahja	IV	58°08'N/27°01'E	1,040	1957
Islets near Hiiumaa	IV	58°46'N/23°05'E	313	1971
Karula	IV	57°43'N/26°29'E	10,318	1979
Kurtna	IV	59°15'N/27°34'E	2,541	1987
Kôrvemaa	V	59°11'N/25°32'E	21,270	1957
Otepää	V	58°04'N/26°27'E	23,050	1979
Paganamaa	IV	57°35'N/26°47'E	1,107	1979
Rebala	V	59°27'N/25°05'E	2,495	1987
Vooremaa	IV	58°35'N/26°40'E	9,900	1964

National Park

Lahemaa	II	59°32'N/25°53'E	176,922	1971

Nature Park

Haanja	V	57°42'N/27°04'E	9,163	1979

Nature Reserve

Aela-Viirika	IV	59°00'N/25°12'E	2,602	1981
Agusalu	IV	59°05'N/27°36'E	7,657	1981
Avaste	IV	58°39'N/24°11'E	4,188	1981
Emajôe-Suursoo	IV	58°22'N/27°14'E	18,425	1981
Endla	I	58°52'N/26°09'E	8,162	1981
Keava	IV	58°56'N/24°58'E	1,577	1981
Kikerpera	IV	58°24'N/24°58'E	4,700	1981
Kuresoo	IV	58°29'N/25°09'E	11,927	1981
Käina	IV	58°48'N/22°47'E	1,280	1971
Laukesoo	IV	59°02'N/25°19'E	2,141	1981
Läänemaa-Suursoo	IV	59°08'N/23°57'E	9,714	1981
Marimetsa	IV	58°56'N/24°00'E	4,190	1981
Matsalu	I	58°45'N/23°37'E	39,697	1957
Meelva	IV	58°08'N/27°21'E	1,827	1981
Meenikunno	IV	57°56'N/27°18'E	1,757	1981
Muraka	IV	59°09'N/27°04'E	12,274	1957
Nigula	I	58°01'N/24°41'E	2,771	1957
Nätsi-Vôlla	IV	58°26'N/24°07'E	9,772	1957
Parika	IV	58°30'N/25°47'E	1,472	1981
Sirtsi	IV	59°15'N/26°47'E	2,853	1981
Sämi-Kuristiku	IV	59°23'N/26°40'E	1,339	1981
Tuhu	IV	58°35'N/23°50'E	2,771	1981
Valgeraba	IV	58°26'N/25°14'E	2,486	1981
Viidumäe	I	58°18'N/22°05'E	1,194	1957
Vilsandi	I	58°22'N/21°53'E	10,940	1910
Virtsu-Laelatu-Puhtu	IV	58°35'N/23°34'E	3,609	1957
Ördi	IV	58°23'N/25°08'E	5,043	1981
Redenskiy Les	I	?/?	5,664	1976

ETHIOPIA/ETHIOPIE/ETIOPIA

	Summary	
Category I	0	0
Category II	12	3,040,200
Category III	0	0
Category IV	11	2,982,400
Category V	0	0
Total	**23**	**6,022,600**

National Park

Abijatta-Shalla Lakes	II	7°30'N/38°30'E	88,700	1970
Awash	II	8°55'N/40°04'E	75,600	1966
Bale Mountains	II	6°29'N/39°43'E	247,100	1969
Gambella	II	8°00'N/34°15'E	506,100	1974
Mago	II	5°30'N/36°30'E	216,200	1978
Nechisar	II	6°00'N/37°45'E	51,400	1973
Omo	II	6°05'N/35°40'E	406,800	1966
Simen Mountains	II	13°11'N/38°10'E	17,900	1966
Yangudi Rassa	II	8°03'N/40°45'E	473,100	1976

Sanctuary

Babile Elephant	II	9°05'N/42°20'E	698,200	1970
Senkelle Swayne's Hartebeest	II	7°10'N/38°20'E	5,400	1972
Yabello	II	4°55'N/38°25'E	253,700	1985

Wildlife Reserve

Alledeghi	IV	9°12'N/40°27'E	183,200	1973
Awash West	IV	8°54'N/39°46'E	178,100	1973
Bale	IV	6°56'N/39°57'E	176,600	1973
Chew Bahr	IV	4°57'N/36°52'E	421,200	1973
Gash-Setit	IV	15°06'N/36°51'E	70,900	1959
Gewane	IV	10°23'N/40°41'E	243,900	1973
Mille-Sardo	IV	11°52'N/40°56'E	876,600	1973
Nakfa	IV	16°25'N/38°44'E	163,900	1959
Shire	IV	14°05'N/37°44'E	75,300	1973
Tama	IV	5°55'N/36°04'E	326,900	1973
Yob	IV	17°09'N/37°44'E	265,800	1959

FIJI/FIDJI

	Summary	
Category I	5	18,922
Category II	0	0
Category III	0	0
Category IV	0	0
Category V	0	0
Total	**5**	**18,922**

Nature Reserve

Ravilevu	I	?/?	4,020	1959
Tomaniivi	I	?/?	1,322	1958

Reserved Forest

Buretolu	I	?/?	1,198	?
Korotari	I	?/?	1,087	?
Taveuni	I	?/?	11,295	?

FINLAND/FINLANDE/FINLANDIA

	Summary	
Category I	15	150,820
Category II	22	393,990
Category III	0	0
Category IV	45	2,183,835
Category V	0	0
Total	**82**	**2,728,645**

National Park

Helvetinjärvi	II	62°01'N/23°53'E	2,800	1982
Hiidenportti	II	63°56'N/29°06'E	4,400	1982
Isojärvi	II	61°42'N/25°00'E	1,880	1982
Itäinen Suomenlahti	II	60°15'N/27°00'E	520	1981
Kauhanneva-Pohjankangas	II	62°14'N/22°25'E	3,150	1982
Koli	II	63°05'N/29°48'E	1,140	1991
Kolovesi	II	62°15'N/28°50'E	2,300	1990
Lauhanvuori	II	62°08'N/22°11'E	2,600	1982
Lemmenjoki	II	68°35'N/25°38'E	285,500	1956
Linnasaari	II	62°05'N/28°29'E	3,600	1956
Oulanka	II	66°21'N/29°21'E	26,900	1956
Pallas-Ounastunturi	IV	68°10'N/23°50'E	50,600	1938
Patvinsuo	II	63°05'N/30°47'E	9,100	1982
Perämeri	II	65°39'N/27°30'E	15,700	1991
Pyhä-Häkki	II	62°51'N/25°26'E	1,200	1956
Pyhätunturi	II	67°01'N/27°07'E	4,300	1938
Riisitunturi	II	66°14'N/28°27'E	7,700	1982
Saaristomeri	II	59°58'N/21°56'E	2,100	1983
Salamajärvi	II	63°16'N/24°46'E	6,000	1982
Seitseminen	II	61°49'N/23°40'E	4,100	1982
Tammisaaren Saaristo	II	59°44'N/23°30'E	3,900	1990
Tiilikkajärvi	II	63°39'N/28°17'E	2,500	1982
Torronsuo	II	60°43'N/23°39'E	2,600	1990
Urho Kekkonen	IV	68°15'N/28°23'E	255,000	1983

Protected Mire

Ahvenvuoma	IV	?/?	1,382	1988
Haikara-aapa-Vitsikkoaapa	IV	?/?	1,298	1988
Hanhijanka-Pierkivaarjanka	IV	?/?	3,973	1988
Jietanasvuoma	IV	?/?	1,510	1988
Joutenaapa-Kaita-aapa	IV	?/?	10,290	1988
Kaareramia-Kellovuotso	IV	?/?	2,869	1988
Kuortanovuoma-Saivinvuoma	IV	?/?	5,855	1988
Lamsanaapa-Sakkala-aapa	IV	?/?	4,164	1988
Lataseno-Hietajoki	IV	?/?	43,640	1988
Leppavuoma-Mustavuoma	IV	?/?	2,038	1988
Loukisen latvasuot	IV	?/?	4,277	1988
Mustaoja-Nunaravuoma	IV	?/?	1,036	1988
Naatavuoma-Sotkavuoma	IV	?/?	7,180	1988
Naatsukka-aapa	IV	?/?	8,894	1988
Peran-Marinjanka	IV	?/?	2,610	1988
Piessuo-Luomusjoki	IV	?/?	2,593	1988
Pomokaira-Tennioaapa	IV	?/?	43,785	1988
Poyrisvuoma	IV	?/?	4,270	1988
Raakevuoma-Vuossijanka	IV	?/?	6,831	1988
Saaravuoma-Kuoskisvuoma	IV	?/?	15,460	1988
Sammuttijanka-Vaijoenjanka	IV	?/?	51,812	1988
Silmasvuoma	IV	?/?	1,609	1988
Siukatanjarvi	IV	?/?	1,935	1988
Sota-aapa	IV	?/?	2,848	1988

Sotkavuoma	IV	?/?	2,190	1988
Terstojanka	IV	?/?	2,318	1988
Teuravuoma-Kivijarvenvuoma	IV	?/?	4,290	1988
Tollovuoma-Vasanvuoma	IV	?/?	2,365	1988
Uura-aapa	IV	?/?	2,279	1988
Vaaranaapa	IV	?/?	3,460	1988
Viiankivuoma	IV	?/?	4,404	1988

Strict Nature Reserve

Kevo	I	69°40'N/26°40'E	71,170	1956
Koivusuo	I	62°54'N/31°12'E	2,100	1982
Malla	I	69°04'N/20°39'E	2,950	1938
Maltio	I	67°23'N/28°45'E	14,668	1956
Olvassuo	I	65°07'N/27°11'E	5,980	1982
Paljakka	I	64°47'N/28°04'E	2,780	1956
Pelso	I	67°27'N/26°11'E	1,820	1982
Pisavaara	I	66°16'N/25°06'E	4,970	1956
Runkaus	I	66°02'N/25°31'E	7,030	1956
Salama	I	63°13'N/24°51'E	1,270	1956
Sompio	I	68°10'N/27°22'E	17,912	1956
Sukerijärvi	I	66°21'N/28°46'E	2,090	1982
Ulvinsalo	I	63°58'N/30°26'E	2,500	1956
Vaskijärvi	I	60°49'N/22°13'E	1,120	1956
Värriö	I	67°39'N/29°52'E	12,460	1982

Wilderness Area

Hammastunturi	IV	?/?	220,625	1991
Kaldoaivi	IV	?/?	293,643	1991
Kemihaara	IV	?/?	30,597	1991
Käsivarsi	IV	?/?	293,643	1991
Muotkatunturi	IV	?/?	156,772	1991
Paistunturi	IV	?/?	181,878	1991
Pulju	IV	?/?	61,434	1991
Pöyrisjärvi	IV	?/?	127,797	1991
Tarvantovaara	IV	?/?	66,590	1991
Tsarmitunturi	IV	?/?	15,268	1991
Tuntsa	IV	?/?	21,183	1991
Vätsäri	IV	?/?	155,340	1991

FRANCE/FRANCIA

Summary		
Category I	7	43,680
Category II	8	288,797
Category III	0	0
Category IV	58	253,634
Category V	37	5,015,375
Total	**110**	**5,601,486**

Biological Reserve

Bouges	IV	?/?	3,200	1992
Grossmann	IV	?/?	2,218	1993
Hauts de St-Philippe	I	?/?	4,073	1987
Laverq	IV	44°15'N/7°08'E	1,331	1982
Mazerin	I	?/?	1,869	1985

Coastal spaces

Etang de Vic	IV	?/?	1,338	1975
Ile Sainte-Lucie	IV	?/?	227	1975
La Côte Bleue	IV	43°19'N/5°10'E	3,070	1975
Les Agriates	IV	?/?	3,933	1975

Fishing Reserve

Calvi	IV	42°35'N/8°42'E	1,075	1978
Porto-Vecchio	IV	41°59'N/9°22'E	1,615	1978
Saint-Florent	IV	42°40'N/9°20'E	2,440	1977
Tuccia-Sagone-Cargese	IV	42°05'N/8°37'E	1,620	1978
Ventilegne	IV	41°28'N/9°10'E	1,000	1977

Marine Park

Côte Bleue	V	43°19'N/5°10'E	3,070	1982

Marine Reserve

Abers du Léon	IV	?/?	2,020	?
Archipel de Glenon	IV	?/?	3,800	?
Baie de la Seine et marais	IV	?/?	7,800	?
Etang de Bages et Sigean	IV	42°55'N/3°00'E	1,700	?
Fiers d'Ars et Fosse de Loix	IV	?/?	1,300	?

National Park

Cévennes	V	44°05'N/3°50'E	91,279	1970
Ecrins	II	44°50'N/6°20'E	91,800	1973
Mercantour	II	44°12'N/7°03'E	68,500	1979
Port-Cros	II	43°00'N/6°24'E	2,475	1963
Pyrénées occidentales	II	42°45'N/0°19'E	45,705	1967
Vanoise	II	45°22'N/6°57'E	52,839	1963

Nature Reserve

Aiguilles Rouges	IV	45°49'N/6°59'E	3,279	1974
Camargue	I	43°25'N/4°30'E	13,117	1975
Casabianda	IV	?/?	1,760	1978
Contamines-Montjoie	IV	45°54'N/6°53'E	5,500	1979
Forêt de Cerisy	IV	49°10'N/0°55'W	2,124	1976
Gorges de l'Ardèche	IV	44°15'N/4°15'E	1,572	1980
Grande Sassière	IV	45°27'N/6°54'E	2,230	1973
Haute Chaîne du Jura	IV	?/?	10,800	1993
Hauts Plateaux du Vercors	IV	45°00'N/5°30'E	16,662	1985
Hauts de Villaroger	IV	?/?	1,114	1991
Iles Lavezzi	IV	41°38'N/9°15'E	5,172	1982
Lac de Grandlieu	IV	47°05'N/1°40'W	2,695	1980
Mantet	IV	42°30'N/2°00'E	3,028	1984
Marais de Moeze	IV	45°55'N/1°20'W	6,720	1985
Massif du Ventron	IV	?/?	1,647	1988
Néouvielle	IV	42°50'N/0°10'E	2,313	1969
Nohedes	IV	42°30'N/2°00'E	2,137	1986
Passy	IV	45°55'N/6°46'E	2,000	1980
Plan de Tueda	IV	?/?	1,112	1990
Pont d'Arcay	IV	?/?	21,220	1982
Prats de Mollo la Preste	IV	42°25'N/2°30'E	2,186	1986
Py	IV	42°30'N/2°00'E	3,930	1984
Scandola	I	42°21'N/8°38'E	1,731	1975
Sept-Iles	I	48°50'N/3°30'W	320	1976
Sixt fer à cheval	IV	46°04'N/6°47'E	9,200	1977
Val d'Isère	IV	45°27'N/7°00'E	1,491	1964
Vallée d'Eyne	IV	?/?	1,177	1993

Pré-parc

Cévennes	V	44°05'N/3°50'E	229,726	1970
Ecrins	V	44°50'N/6°20'E	178,673	1973
Mercantour	V	?/?	146,500	1979
Pyrénées occidentales	V	?/?	206,352	1967
Vanoise	V	?/?	143,637	1963

Regional Nature Park

Armorique	V	48°20'N/4°00'W	172,000	1969
Ballon des Vosges	V	47°48'N/6°50'E	280,000	1989
Brenne	V	46°30'N/1°00'E	167,200	1989
Brière	V	47°25'N/2°25'W	40,000	1970
Brotonne	V	49°32'N/0°35'E	58,000	1974
Camargue	V	43°28'N/4°33'E	85,000	1970
Corse	V	42°05'N/8°55'E	332,500	1972
Forêt d'Orient	V	48°18'N/4°21'E	70,000	1970
Haut-Languedoc	V	43°30'N/2°43'E	145,000	1973
Haut-Jura	V	46°22'N/5°44'E	75,675	1986
Haute Vallée de Chevreuse	V	48°30'N/2°00'E	25,630	1985
Landes de Gascogne	V	44°23'N/0°50'W	290,000	1970
Livradois-Forez	V	45°50'N/3°33'E	300,000	1986
Lorraine	V	48°50'N/6°00'E	200,000	1974
Lubéron	V	43°45'N/5°29'E	142,000	1977
Marais du Cotentin et du Bessin	V	49°10'N/1°30'W	120,000	1991
Montagne de Reims	V	49°15'N/4°00'E	50,000	1976
Morvan	V	47°09'N/4°07'E	196,120	1970
Nord-Pas-de-Calais	V	50°27'N/3°20'E	146,000	1986
Normandie-Maine	V	48°30'N/0°50'W	224,880	1975
Pilat	V	45°25'N/4°40'E	62,280	1974
Queyras	V	44°45'N/6°47'E	60,000	1977
Vercors	V	45°00'N/5°20'E	172,240	1970
Volcans d'Auvergne	V	45°23'N/2°38'E	393,000	1977
Vosges du Nord	V	48°55'N/7°35'E	119,175	1975

French Guiana/Guyane/Guyana Francés

No Areas Listed

French Polynesia/Polynésie française/ Polinesia Francesa

Nature Reserve

Ile de Eiao	IV	7°59'S/140°42'W	4,000	1971

Other area

Ile de Motane	IV	09°59'S/138°50'W	900	1971

Reserve

Ile de Hatutu	IV	7°55'S/140°34'W	750	1971
Réserve territoriale de Scilly et Bellinghausen	IV	16°32'S/154°41'W	12,540	1992

French Southern Territories/ Terres australes françaises/ Territorios Franceses del Sur

National Park

Antarctique française	IV	44°00'S/64°00'E	36,700	1924

Guadeloupe/Guadalupe

National Park

Guadeloupe	II	16°10'N/61°40'W	17,300	1989

Nature Reserve

Grand Cul de Sac Marin	IV	16°20'N/61°35'W	3,706	1987

Pré-parc

Parc national de la Guadeloupe	V	16°11'N/61°46'W	16,200	1989

Martinique/Martinica

Regional Nature Park

Martinique	V	14°45'N/61°07'W	70,150	1976

Mayotte

No Areas Listed

New Caledonia/Nouvelle-Calédonie/
Nueva Caledonia

Forest Reserve

Mont Mou	IV	22°04'S/166°20'E	5,038	1970

Special Botanical Reserve

Forêt de Sailles	IV	21°04'S/166°14'E	1,100	1983
Mont Humboldt	IV	21°53'S/166°25'E	3,200	1950
Mont Panie	IV	20°36'S/164°46'E	5,000	1950
Pic du Pin	IV	22°15'S/166°48'E	1,482	1972

Special Fauna and Flora Reserve

L'Ilot Maître	V	22°22'S/166°25'E	154	1981

Special Fauna Reserve

Aoupinie	IV	21°10'S/165°18'E	5,400	1975
Haute Yaté	IV	22°08'S/166°40'E	15,900	1960
L'Ile Pam	IV	20°15'S/164°18'E	460	1966
L'Ilot Leprédour	IV	21°58'S/166°00'E	760	1941

Special Marine Reserve

Réserve de la passe Amédée	V	22°31'S/166°26'E	2,780	1991
Yves Merlet	I	22°25'S/167°08'E	16,700	1970

Strict Nature Reserve

Montagne des Sources	I	22°08'S/166°34'E	5,870	1950

Territorial Park

Parc territorial du Lagon Sud: Ilot Amédée	V	22°28'S/166°29'E	154	1981
Rivière Bleue	II	22°06'S/166°38'E	9,045	1980
Thy	II	22°11'S/166°50'E	1,133	1980

Réunion/Isla Reunión

State Biological Reserve

Forêt des Hauts de St-Phillipe	IV	21°17'S/55°45'E	4,073	1987
Mazerin	IV	21°03'S/55°35'E	1,869	1985

Saint-Pierre et Miquelon

No Areas Listed

Wallis and Futuna/
Wallis et Futuna, Iles/
Islas Wallis y Futuna

No Areas Listed

GABON

Summary		
Category I	1	15,000
Category II	0	0
Category III	0	0
Category IV	5	1,030,000
Category V	0	0
Total	**6**	**1,045,000**

Faunal Reserve

Lope	IV	?/?	500,000	1962
Moukalaba-Dougoua	IV	?/?	80,000	1962

Ouanga Plain	IV	?/?	20,000	1966
Petit Loango	IV	?/?	50,000	1966

Presidential Reserve

Wonga-Wongue	IV	0'45'S/9'25'E	380,000	1971

Strict Nature Reserve

Ipassa-Makokou	I	?/?	15,000	1970

GAMBIA/GAMBIE

Summary		
Category I	0	0
Category II	3	18,440
Category III	0	0
Category IV	2	4,500
Category V	0	0
Total	**5**	**22,940**

National Park

Kiang West	II	13'15'N/15'55'W	11,000	1987
Niumi/Sine Saloum	II	13'52'N/16'18'W	4,940	1986
River Gambia	II	13'30'N/15'00'W	2,500	1978

Nature Reserve

Baubolon	IV	13'24'N/15'47'W	3,500	1993

Reserve

Coastal	IV	13'12'N/16'45'W	1,000	?

GEORGIA/GEORGIE

Summary		
Category I	14	167,186
Category II	1	19,700
Category III	0	0
Category IV	0	0
Category V	0	0
Total	**15**	**186,886**

National Park

Tbilisi	II	?/?	19,700	1973

Zapovednik

Adzhametskiy	I	42'09'N/42'50'E	4,848	1957
Akhmetskiy	I	?/?	16,297	1980
Algetskiy	I	41'42'N/44'19'E	6,000	1965
Borzhomskiy	I	41'49'N/43'13'E	18,048	1959
Kazbegskiy	I	42'40'N/44'25'E	8,707	1976
Kintrishskiy	I	41'42'N/42'03'E	13,893	1959
Lagodekhskiy	I	41'52'N/46'19'E	17,818	1912
Liakhvskiy	I	42'15'N/44'00'E	6,385	1977
Mariamdzhvarskiy	I	41'46'N/45'28'E	1,040	1959
Pitsyundo-Myusserskiy	I	43'12'N/40'21'E	3,761	1966
Pskhu-Gumistinskiy	I	43'11'N/41'04'E	40,819	1976
Ritsinskiy	I	43'30'N/40'30'E	16,289	1957
Saguramskiy	I	41'52'N/44'48'E	5,247	1946
Vashlovanskiy	I	41'10'N/46'28'E	8,034	1935

GERMANY/ALLEMAGNE/
ALEMANIA

	Summary	
Category I	0	0
Category II	1	13,100
Category III	0	0
Category IV	88	262,640
Category V	415	8,919,962
Total	**504**	**9,195,702**

Landscape Protected Area

Aga-und Elstertal	V	?/?	2,796	1968
Allgauer Hochalpenkette	V	?/?	19,680	1972
Altmuhltal mit Nebentalern #1	V	?/?	3,322	1961
Altmuhltal mit Nebentalern #2	V	?/?	1,240	1961
Altmuhltal mit Nebentalern #3	V	?/?	25,850	1967
Ammersee mit Ufer- und Moranenlandschaft	V	?/?	9,910	1972
Ammerthal und Hainsberg	V	?/?	1,084	1965
Amperauen	V	?/?	9,750	1968
Amperauen und Mooslandschaft nordostlich	V	?/?	1,801	1983
Amperland sudlich Furstenfeldbruck	V	?/?	3,575	1979
Auerbachtal mit Soinkargebiet	V	?/?	4,815	?
Augustusburg-Sternmuhlental	V	?/?	1,487	1968
Auwald beiderseits der Iller	V	?/?	1,641	1968
Bachmuhlbachtal und Paintner Forst	V	?/?	1,967	1971
Bad Freienwalde	V	52°47'N/14°00'E	4,340	1965
Barlebener-Jerslebener See mit Elbniederung	V	?/?	3,548	1964
Bibert- und Metlachtal	V	?/?	2,047	1967
Bleicheroder Berge	V	51°24'N/10°42'E	4,103	1970
Blumberger Forst	V	?/?	1,960	1965
Bodeniederung	V	?/?	7,200	1975
Boxberg-Reichwalder Wald-und Wiesengebiet	V	51°23'N/14°16'E	1,157	1968
Brandenburger Wald-und Seengebiet	V	52°24'N/12°23'E	16,270	1966
Briesetal und Muhlenbecker See	V	?/?	3,175	1966
Burgrain, Kaltenbrunn und Barmsee	V	?/?	1,434	1976
Burgsteinlandschaft	V	?/?	2,808	1968
Calau-Altdobern-Reddern	V	51°42'N/14°02'E	4,800	1968
Chiemsee, seine Inseln und Ufergebiete #1	V	?/?	2,224	1986
Chiemsee, seine Inseln und Ufergebiete #2	V	?/?	10,466	1986
Choriner Endmoranenbogen	V	?/?	16,500	1957
Colditzer Forest	V	51°08'N/12°46'E	4,600	1963
Colmberg - Sulzbachtal	V	?/?	2,236	1968
Dahlener Heide	V	?/?	16,700	1963
Dammuhlenteich	V	?/?	1,036	1974
Deisenhofener Forst	V	?/?	2,156	1970
Dillberg-Heinrichsberg	V	?/?	1,836	1964
Dippoldiswalder Heide und Wilisch	V	50°55'N/13°40'E	2,420	1974
Dobbertiner Seen u.s.w.	V	53°41'N/12°02'E	12,100	1964
Dobbin-Zietlitzer Feldmark	V	53°38'N/12°17'E	2,000	1938
Dolgener und Hohensprenzer See	V	53°21'N/13°20'E	1,500	1961
Donauauen ostl. Neuburg mit Branst	V	?/?	2,163	1987
Donautal mit Seitentalern	V	?/?	11,850	1986
Dreigleichen	V	?/?	1,698	1960
Dresdener Heide	V	51°06'N/13°47'E	5,876	1971
Dubener Heide	V	?/?	11,380	1961
Duen-Helbetal	V	?/?	5,600	1963
Durnbucher Forst	V	?/?	6,388	?
Ebersberg und Bohlgrund	V	?/?	1,676	1966
Ebersberger Forst	V	?/?	7,548	1984

Egartenlandschaft um Miesbach	V	?/?	10,396	1955
Eisenberger Holzland	V	50°58'N/11°55'E	1,828	1983
Elbaue Martinskirchen-Muhlberg	V	?/?	1,490	1968
Elbhange Dresden-Pirna und Schonfelder Hoch.	V	?/?	3,540	1974
Elbsee bei Aitrang	V	?/?	1,536	1955
Elbtal nordlich von Meissen	V	?/?	2,320	1960
Elsteraue	V	?/?	10,000	1937
Elsteraue und Teichlandschaft u.s.w.	V	51°31'N/13°23'E	1,860	1968
Elsteraue zwischen Herzberg und Ubigau	V	?/?	2,160	1968
Elsterniederung u.s.w.	V	51°31'N/14°00'E	19,650	1968
Endmoranenzug Brohmer u.s.w.	V	?/?	5,000	1962
Fahner Hohe	V	?/?	4,950	1970
Fahrenberg-Zottbachtal	V	?/?	2,300	1965
Faulenbacher Tal, Lechtal und Alpseeraum	V	?/?	1,185	1956
Feldberger Seenlandschaft	V	53°24'N/13°33'E	7,000	1962
Fischland-Darss-Zingst	V	54°26'N/12°32'E	15,000	1966
Flaming	V	?/?	38,670	1961
Flemsdorf	V	53°03'N/14°12'E	1,720	1965
Forggensee und benachbarte Seen	V	?/?	6,050	1956
Forstenrieder Park und Furstenrider Wald	V	?/?	4,921	1963
Frankenalb	V	?/?	17,230	1966
Frankenwald #1	V	?/?	7,381	1986
Frankenwald #2	V	?/?	33,279	1984
Frankenwald #3	V	?/?	3,340	1984
Frankische Schweiz - Flussgebiet der Wiesent	V	?/?	3,509	1955
Freiberger Mulde-Zschopau	V	50°46'N/13°30'E	7,000	1963
Freisinger Moos und Echinger Gfild	V	?/?	4,204	1977
Freudenberg - Wutschdorf - Etsdorf	V	?/?	1,621	1965
Friedewald und Moritzburger Teichgebiet	V	?/?	5,565	1977
Furth	V	?/?	1,629	1976
Gambachtal und Reithenauer Bachtal	V	?/?	2,000	1986
Gamengrund	V	?/?	2,390	1965
Gebiet um Bad Wilsnack	V	52°57'N/11°56'E	2,700	1964
Gebiet um die Wies	V	?/?	3,013	1971
Geichburg, Gugel und Wurgauer Tal	V	?/?	1,770	1953
Gelandestr. langs d. Bundesautobahn Berlin-Munchen	V	?/?	1,500	1954
Gelandestreifen langs der B85	V	?/?	1,000	1970
Geraer Stadtwald	V	?/?	1,575	1972
Glonntal	V	?/?	1,273	1974
Gotzer Berge	V	?/?	2,325	1966
Grabentour	V	?/?	2,864	1968
Grosser See bei Furstenwerder	V	?/?	1,200	1962
Grosser und Kleiner Gleichberg	V	?/?	1,988	1939
Grosssteinberg-Ammelshain	V	?/?	2,440	1963
Grunau-Grunheider Wald-und Seengebiet	V	?/?	21,700	1965
Grunten und Wertacher Hornle	V	?/?	7,650	1972
Gubener Fliesstaler	V	?/?	3,200	1968
Gulitzer Endmorane und Kummerower See	V	?/?	9,000	1962
Haffkuste	V	?/?	12,500	1962
Hainleite	V	?/?	5,976	1970
Hakel	V	?/?	1,425	1939
Harbke-Allertal	V	52°12'N/11°05'E	22,770	1975
Hardtlandschaft und Eberfinger Drumlinfelder	V	?/?	5,814	1985
Harz	V	?/?	154,700	1960
Hauptsmoorwald	V	?/?	2,350	1952
Hausener Tal	V	?/?	1,240	1985
Havelquellseen Kratzeburg	V	53°28'N/12°56'E	2,600	1962
Heiligenstadter Stadtwald	V	51°22'N/10°08'E	3,025	1960
Helmestausee	V	?/?	1,717	1970
Herzogenaurach	V	?/?	1,462	1986

Hesselberg	V	?/?	1,460	1985
Hiddensee	V	54°31'N/13°08'E	1,860	1955
Hienheimer Forst	V	?/?	3,796	1970
Hildburghauser Wald	V	50°26'N/10°46'E	5,250	1978
Hirschbachtal	V	?/?	1,638	1971
Hirschbachtal mit Schwarzem Brand u. Lehenbachtal	V	?/?	1,946	1970
Hirschberg, Kerschlager Forst	V	?/?	1,488	1970
Hofoldinger und Hohenkirchner Forst	V	?/?	4,955	1971
Hogenbachtal	V	?/?	2,282	1970
Hohburger Berge	V	?/?	2,000	1963
Hohes Holz-Saures Holz mit ostlicem Vorland	V	?/?	7,240	1964
Illerdurchbruch	V	?/?	1,517	1976
Ilmtal	V	?/?	19,850	1960
Innerer Bayerischer Wald	V	?/?	32,298	1967
Innerer Bayerischer Wald	V	?/?	22,466	1967
Innerer Bayerischer Wald	V	?/?	4,100	1967
Inntal	V	?/?	6,725	?
Insel Usedom	V	?/?	37,500	1966
Inselsee und Heidberg	V	?/?	1,300	1964
Isarauen	V	?/?	1,547	1964
Isartal	V	?/?	1,840	1969
Isartal und -auen	V	?/?	2,925	?
Jessener Berge	V	?/?	1,025	1968
Kahl a. M. und Alzenau	V	?/?	2,580	1978
Kleinseenplatte Neustrelitz	V	53°22'N/12°57'E	12,000	1962
Klocksiner Seenkette	V	53°38'N/12°32'E	20,000	1962
Knappensee	V	?/?	1,100	1968
Koferinger und Vils-Tal mit Hirschwald	V	?/?	8,736	1965
Kohrener Land	V	?/?	17,000	1959
Konigshainer Berge	V	?/?	4,855	1974
Korbaer Teich und Lebusaer Waldgebiet	V	?/?	2,258	1968
Kothener See	V	?/?	1,790	1966
Krakower Seenlandschaft	V	53°35'N/12°18'E	2,350	1955
Kreuzberg und Semberg	V	?/?	1,332	1954
Kreuzlinger Forst mit Pentenrieder Schlag	V	?/?	2,293	1985
Kuhberg-Steinicht	V	?/?	1,377	1968
Kuhlung	V	54°08'N/11°48'E	14,000	1966
Kyffhauser	V	?/?	7,722	1941
Kyritzer Seenkette	V	?/?	1,600	1958
Landschaftsstreifen beiderseits	V	?/?	1,550	1956
Landschaftsteile um Rothenburg	V	?/?	10,690	1955
Lattengebirge	V	?/?	2,870	?
Lausitzer Grenzwall zwischen u.s.w.	V	51°02'N/14°24'E	14,235	1968
Lauta-Hoyerswerda-Wittichenau	V	?/?	2,920	1968
Lauterachtal	V	?/?	5,215	1962
Lechtal	V	?/?	2,386	?
Lehniner Wald- und Seengebiet	V	?/?	2,525	1966
Leinleitertal mit Nebentalern	V	?/?	1,254	1955
Leipziger Auewald	V	51°19'N/12°20'E	5,700	1959
Leitzachtal	V	?/?	3,304	1955
Leuchtenberg-Luhetal	V	?/?	1,743	1965
Lewitz	V	?/?	12,000	1959
Lindenthaler Forst	V	51°23'N/12°19'E	4,070	1975
Lindhorst-Ramstedter Forst	V	?/?	5,996	1964
Linkselbische Taler zwiscen u.s.w.	V	51°05'N/13°37'E	2,355	1974
Ludwigsluster Schlosspark u.s.w.	V	53°19'N/11°30'E	1,500	1955
Lychen-Boitzenburg	V	53°16'N/13°19'E	7,500	1962
Madlitz-Falenhagener Seengebiet	V	?/?	1,030	1965
Mainhohe	V	?/?	1,042	1968
Malchiner Becken	V	53°42'N/12°33'E	6,000	1962

Markische Schweiz	V	?/?	3,800	1957
Merzdorf-Hirschfelder Waldhohen	V	?/?	2,060	1968
Mittelelbe	V	?/?	48,200	1957
Mittelheide	V	?/?	2,500	1969
Mittlere Frankenalb nordlich Neumarkt	V	?/?	3,598	1964
Mittlere Mulde	V	?/?	9,700	1963
Mittlerer Strelasund	V	54°16'N/13°12'E	2,300	1966
Mittleres Saaletal	V	?/?	19,150	1972
Mittleres Warnowtal	V	?/?	8,500	1964
Mittleres Zschopautal	V	50°45'N/13°04'E	1,487	1968
Mockern-Magdeburgerforth	V	52°14'N/12°12'E	29,140	1975
Muhldorfer Hart	V	?/?	1,100	1979
Muhlhauser Stadtwald	V	51°09'N/10°39'E	3,496	1970
Muldental-Chemnitzal	V	?/?	11,471	1968
Muritz-Seen-Park	V	53°27'N/12°40'E	30,000	1962
Naabtal zwischen Perschen und Wolsendorf	V	?/?	1,364	1962
Naabtal zwischen Wernberg und Pfreimd	V	?/?	1,298	1962
Nauen-Brieselang	V	?/?	3,225	1966
Naunhof-Brandiser Forst	V	?/?	2,750	1963
Neisseaue im Kreis Forst	V	?/?	1,330	1968
Neuendorfer See	V	?/?	1,600	1968
Neuruppin-Rheinsberg u.s.w.	V	53°02'N/12°53'E	80,200	1966
Noitzscher-und Prellheide	V	?/?	1,500	1963
Nordlicher Riesrand	V	?/?	8,000	1973
Nordliches Harzvorland	V	?/?	13,506	1961
Ober-Uecker-See	V	?/?	5,400	1962
Obere Saale	V	?/?	21,240	1965
Oberer Bayerischer Wald	V	?/?	10,214	1969
Oberes Alztal	V	?/?	1,065	1956
Oberes Vogtland	V	?/?	17,100	1968
Oberes Westerzgebirge	V	?/?	17,015	1981
Oberes Zschopautal	V	50°45'N/13°04'E	8,207	1968
Oberlausitzer Bergland	V	?/?	30,730	1963
Oberpfalzer Wald	V	?/?	2,700	1972
Oberpfalzer Wald	V	?/?	16,250	1972
Osterseen	V	?/?	1,266	1955
Osterzgebirge	V	50°46'N/13°46'E	55,025	1968
Ostmarkstrasse - nordlicher Teil	V	?/?	2,000	1967
Ostrand der Arendseer Hochflache	V	?/?	7,210	1964
Ostrugen	V	54°32'N/13°30'E	47,500	1966
Parthenaue-Machern	V	?/?	1,300	1963
Peitzer Teichlandschaft mit Hammergraben	V	51°27'N/14°36'E	2,040	1968
Perlacher und Grunwalder Forst	V	?/?	3,400	1970
Petersberg	V	51°25'N/11°58'E	1,730	1961
Pfreimdtal	V	?/?	2,956	1962
Pfreimdtal-Goldbachtal-Michlbachtal	V	?/?	4,123	1965
Pfuhler-, Finninger- und Bauern-Ried	V	?/?	2,072	1961
Plauer See	V	?/?	3,500	1957
Plothener Teichgebiet	V	50°37'N/11°44'E	1,896	1961
Potsdamer Havelseengebiet	V	52°21'N/13°00'E	16,250	1966
Pressnitztal	V	?/?	2,300	1984
Rabensteiner Wald-Pfaffenberg	V	?/?	1,280	1962
Rambower und Rudower See	V	53°02'N/12°00'E	1,500	1960
Rathenower Wald-und Seengebiet	V	52°37'N/12°20'E	17,325	1966
Regental	V	?/?	2,886	1986
Rennsteigstreifen	V	?/?	3,900	1940
Rinne-Rotenbachtal	V	?/?	6,976	1970
Rippachtal	V	51°13'N/12°03'E	2,880	1968
Roderaue	V	51°20'N/13°21'E	1,720	1960
Rotehofbachtal	V	?/?	2,444	1964
Rotwand	V	?/?	4,412	1987

Saale	V	?/?	28,550	1961
Saaletal	V	?/?	2,534	1982
Sachsische Schweiz	V	50°56'N/14°18'E	36,810	1956
Saidenbachtalsperre	V	50°45'N/13°15'E	4,490	1962
Salzachtal	V	?/?	1,035	1977
Salzwedel-Diesdorf	V	52°21'N/11°10'E	13,310	1975
Schaalsee und Heckenlandschaft Techin	V	?/?	2,500	1958
Schambachtal	V	?/?	1,436	1961
Scharmutzelsee-Storkower u.s.w.	V	52°37'N/12°00'E	10,600	1965
Schellenberg bei Waldkirch	V	?/?	1,002	1965
Schlaubetal	V	52°10'N/13°30'E	6,490	1965
Schleibheimer Forst, Scholbpark	V	?/?	1,578	1970
Schliersee	V	?/?	1,544	1955
Schwarzach- und Auerbachtal	V	?/?	6,100	1962
Schwarzachdurchbruch und Aschabergland	V	?/?	8,100	1972
Schwarzachtal mit Nebentalern	V	?/?	3,597	1970
Schwarze Laber	V	?/?	3,554	1962
Schwarzholzl mit Wurmkanal und Baggersee	V	?/?	1,135	1964
Schweriner Seenlandschaft	V	?/?	4,300	1938
Schwielochsee	V	?/?	4,440	1965
Seendreieck bei Furstensee	V	53°20'N/13°14'E	3,200	1962
Seengebiet Warin-Neukloster	V	?/?	7,500	1938
Seenkette bei Comthurey	V	?/?	1,200	1962
Sempt- und Schwillachtal	V	?/?	1,550	1986
Sewekow	V	53°16'N/12°39'E	2,850	1966
Simssee	V	?/?	2,253	1963
Spitzingsee	V	?/?	1,632	1955
Spree-und Teichgebiet sudlich Uhyst	V	?/?	1,210	1968
Spreeniederung	V	?/?	1,850	1974
Spreewald	V	?/?	28,700	1968
Sprottetal	V	51°29'N/12°43'E	1,100	1984
Stadtwald Berlin	V	?/?	7,548	1972
Staffelsee	V	?/?	2,545	1955
Starnberger See und westliche Uferlandschaft	V	?/?	9,421	1987
Starnberger See-Ost	V	?/?	3,200	1979
Staubeckenlandschaft Brasinchen-Spremberg	V	?/?	2,925	1968
Steigerwald	V	?/?	1,188	1970
Steinachtal mit Nebentalern	V	?/?	1,492	1984
Steinsee - Brucker Moos	V	?/?	2,550	1987
Steinwald	V	?/?	8,500	1974
Stepenitztal	V	53°19'N/12°09'E	1,600	1958
Strausberger und Blumenthaler	V	?/?	6,120	1965
Striegistaler	V	?/?	4,233	1968
Sudlich von Zwickau	V	50°41'N/12°29'E	6,200	1968
Sudlicher Dromling	V	?/?	2,556	1967
Sulzberg-Schneeberg	V	?/?	1,091	1965
Susser See	V	?/?	3,820	1954
Sylvensteinsee bei Fall	V	?/?	5,000	1983
Tal der Frankischen Rezat mit Seitentalern	V	?/?	2,244	1967
Tal der Wassernach	V	?/?	1,166	1966
Tal der Wilden Weisseritz	V	50°54'N/13°33'E	1,415	1960
Talsperre Kriebstein	V	?/?	1,162	1968
Talsperre Pirk	V	?/?	1,432	1940
Talsperre Pohl	V	?/?	2,300	1962
Talsperre Quitzdorf und Kollmer Hohen	V	51°17'N/14°47'E	4,417	1974
Tegernsee mit Sutten und Weissachtal	V	?/?	14,532	?
Templiner Seenkreuz	V	53°07'N/13°30'E	11,500	1962
Teupitz-Koriser Scengebiet	V	52°09'N/13°36'E	23,317	1966
Thanner Grund	V	?/?	2,200	1972
Tharandter Wald	V	50°57'N/13°30'E	5,440	1974
Thummlitzwald	V	?/?	11,500	1984

Thumsee	V	?/?	1,100	1986
Thundorfer Weihergebiet	V	?/?	1,165	1962
Thuringer Wald	V	?/?	151,613	1963
Thuringische Rhon	V	?/?	61,500	1989
Tollense-Becken	V	?/?	10,000	1962
Torgelower See	V	53°37'N/14°00'E	3,000	1962
Triebischtaler	V	?/?	1,940	1974
Uchte-Tangerquellen	V	?/?	6,681	1975
Untere Havel	V	?/?	21,940	1967
Untere Isar	V	?/?	3,336	1973
Unteres Naabtal	V	?/?	4,800	1962
Veldensteiner Forst	V	?/?	4,708	1966
Volkacher Mainschleif	V	?/?	1,132	1969
Volkacher Mainschleife	V	?/?	3,235	1969
Vorderer Bayerischer Wald	V	?/?	33,140	1966
Vorderer Bayerischer Wald	V	?/?	19,611	1964
Waginger-und Tachinger See	V	?/?	2,349	1972
Walchensee	V	?/?	1,640	1955
Wald- und Berglandschaft um Cham	V	?/?	34,214	1967
Wald- und Restseengebiet Dobern	V	?/?	1,850	1968
Wald-u.Seengeb.z.Schwielochsee,Libe.u.Spree.	V	?/?	3,850	1968
Walder u. Forste mit Ossinger und Breitenstein	V	?/?	4,000	1969
Walder um Greiz und Werdau	V	53°45'N/12°21'E	5,525	1961
Waldgebiet bei Crivitz u. Barniner See	V	53°35'N/11°39'E	1,000	1964
Waldgebiet des Fallstein	V	?/?	1,375	1939
Waldgebiet Huy	V	?/?	1,561	1939
Waldmunchen	V	?/?	23,050	1970
Wallensteingraben	V	?/?	2,000	1966
Wandlitz-Biesenthal-Prendener Seegebiet	V	52°47'N/13°33'E	5,600	1965
Webellinsee-Grimnitzsee	V	?/?	3,790	1965
Weidatalsperre	V	?/?	1,680	1961
Weissensee bei Pfronten	V	?/?	1,466	1963
Weissmain	V	?/?	2,973	1954
Wellheimer Donautrockental	V	?/?	2,004	1984
Wermsdorfer Forst	V	51°17'N/12°57'E	13,000	1963
Westlausitz	V	?/?	29,070	1974
Westlicher Teil des Landkreises Starnberg	V	?/?	16,270	1972
Wetterstein mit Vorbergen	V	?/?	12,300	1976
Wiesen-und Teichgebiet Eulo und Jamno	V	?/?	1,440	1968
Wiesen-und Teichlandschaft Kolkwitz-Hanchen	V	?/?	2,020	1968
Wiesent mit Nebentalern	V	?/?	1,570	1955
Wissinger und Bachhaupter Laber	V	?/?	3,638	1961
Wolletzseengebiet	V	?/?	7,000	1965
Wurmtal	V	?/?	3,646	1984
Zeitzgrund	V	51°06'N/12°09'E	1,291	1958
Zichtauer Berge und Klotzer Forst	V	52°32'N/11°10'E	10,800	1964
Zittauer Gebirge	V	50°54'N/14°49'E	6,270	1958
Zuwachs-Kulzauer Forst	V	?/?	5,040	1975

National Park

Bayerischer Wald	II	48°55'N/13°26'E	13,100	1970
Berchtesgaden	V	47°33'N/12°55'E	21,000	1978
Hamburgisches Wattenmeer	V	54°00'N/8°50'E	11,700	1990
Hochharz	V	51°48'N/10°40'E	5,868	1990
Jasmund	V	54°33'N/13°39'E	3,000	1990
Mueritz	V	53°25'N/12°57'E	31,000	1990
Niedersaechsisches Wattenmeer	V	53°45'N/7°38'E	240,000	1986
Saechsische Schweiz	V	50°55'N/14°07'E	9,292	1990
Schleswig-Holsteinisches Wattenmeer	V	54°30'N/8°37'E	285,000	1985
Vorpommersche Boddenlandschaft	V	54°29'N/12°54'E	80,000	1990

Nature Park

Altmuehltal	V	48°58'N/11°17'E	290,800	1969

Arnsberger Wald	V	51°27'N/8°15'E	48,200	1961
Augsburg-Westliche Waelder	V	48°23'N/10°38'E	117,500	1974
Aukrug	V	52°02'N/9°43'E	38,000	1970
Bayerische Rhoen	V	50°22'N/10°03'E	124,000	1967
Bayerischer Spessart	V	50°01'N/9°27'E	171,000	1963
Bayerischer Wald	V	49°02'N/9°32'E	206,800	1967
Bergisches Land	V	51°01'N/7°26'E	191,700	1973
Bergstrase Odenwald	V	49°41'N/8°58'E	162,850	1960
Diemelsee	V	51°24'N/8°44'E	33,436	1965
Drömling	V	52°30'N/11°05E	25,706	1990
Duemmer	V	52°26'N/8°23'E	47,210	1972
Ebbegebirge	V	51°06'N/7°47'E	77,736	1964
Eggegebirge und sudlicher Teutoburger Wald	V	51°47'N/8°57'E	59,300	1965
Elbufer-Drawehn	V	53°08'N/11°00'E	75,000	1968
Elm-Lappwald	V	52°15'N/10°52'E	47,000	1976
Fichtelgebirge	V	50°06'N/11°59'E	102,800	1971
Fraenkische Schweiz-Veldensteiner Forst	V	49°51'N/11°18'E	234,600	1968
Frankenhoehe	V	49°22'N/10°25'E	110,450	1974
Frankenwald	V	50°31'N/11°33'E	97,170	1973
Habichtswald	V	51°20'N/9°16'E	47,106	1962
Harburger Berge	V	53°28'N/9°52'E	3,800	1959
Harz	V	51°47'N/10°25'E	95,000	1960
Hassberge	V	50°10'N/10°37'E	80,400	1974
Hessenreuther und Manteler Wald	V	49°46'N/12°02'E	27,000	1975
Hessische Rhoen	V	50°37'N/9°53'E	70,000	1963
Hessischer Spessart	V	50°12'N/9°20'E	71,000	1962
Hochtaunus	V	50°20'N/8°28'E	120,165	1962
Hohe Mark	V	51°49'N/6°59'E	104,000	1963
Hoher Vogelsberg	V	50°31'N/9°16'E	38,447	1958
Holsteinische Schweiz	V	54°09'N/10°30'E	58,100	1986
Homert	V	51°15'N/6°10'E	55,000	1965
Huettener Berge	V	54°25'N/9°43'E	26,000	1970
Kottenforst-Ville	V	50°46'N/6°50'E	88,122	1959
Lauenburgische Seen	V	53°40'N/10°47'E	44,400	1959
Märkische Schweiz	V	52°34'N/14°06'E	20,500	1990
Meissner-Kaufunger Wald	V	51°16'N/9°45'E	42,058	1962
Muenden	V	51°27'N/9°45'E	37,370	1959
Nassau	V	50°21'N/7°50'E	56,000	1962
Naturschutzpark	V	53°11'N/9°57'E	20,000	1921
Neckartal-Odenwald	V	49°29'N/9°08'E	129,200	1980
Noerdlicher Oberpfaelzer Wald	V	49°41'N/12°21'E	64,380	1971
Noerdlicher Teutoburger Wald-Wiehengebirge	V	52°06'N/8°20'E	121,950	1962
Nordeifel	V	50°20'N/6°30'E	175,116	1960
Obere Donau	V	48°05'N/9°06'E	85,710	1980
Oberer Bayerischer Wald	V	49°10'N/12°41'E	173,800	1965
Oberpfälzer Wald	V	49°27'N/12°25'E	72,385	1971
Pfälzerwald	V	49°09'N/8°07'E	179,800	1958
Rhein-Taunus	V	50°10'N/8°08'E	80,788	1968
Rhein-Westerwald	V	50°33'N/7°26'E	44,600	1962
Rothaargebirge	V	51°05'N/8°17'E	135,500	1963
Saar-Hunsrueck	V	49°30'N/6°50'E	174,650	1980
Schaalsee	V	53°41'N/10°59'E	16,200	1990
Schoenbuch	V	48°34'N/9°00'E	15,564	1974
Schwalm-Nette	V	51°15'N/6°10'E	43,500	1965
Schwäbisch-Fränkischer Wald	V	49°02'N/9°32'E	90,400	1979
Siebengebirge	V	50°38'N/7°19'E	4,800	1959
Solling-Vogler	V	51°46'N/9°32'E	52,750	1966
Steigerwald	V	49°45'N/10°47'E	128,000	1971
Steinhuder Meer	V	52°31'N/9°19'E	31,000	1974
Steinwald	V	49°54'N/12°04'E	23,330	1970
Stromberg-Heuchelberg	V	49°01'N/8°54'E	33,003	1980
Suedeifel	V	49°53'N/6°10'E	43,170	1958
Suedheide	V	52°48'N/10°14'E	50,000	1963

Weserbergland Schaumburg-Hameln	V	52°18'N/8°15'E	111,626	1975
Westensee	V	54°15'N/9°54'E	26,000	1969
Wildeshauser Geest	V	52°56'N/8°30'E	96,500	1984

Nature Reserve

Ahlen-Falkenberger Moor	IV	53°42'N/8°50'E	1,298	1987
Allgäuer Hochalpen	IV	47°24'N/10°20'E	20,724	1992
Alter Stolberg	V	51°30'N/10°50'E	4,520	1970
Altwarper Binnendünen/Neuwarper See & Riether Wehr	IV	53°43'N/14°15'E	1,460	1990
Ammergebirge	IV	47°34'N/10°58'E	28,850	1963
Anklamer Stadtbruch	IV	53°49'N/13°51'E	1,200	1967
Arnimswalde	IV	53°06'N/13°44'E	1,372	1990
Barnbruch	IV	52°20'N/10°46'E	1,200	1986
Bastauniederung	IV	52°19'N/8°46'E	1,844	1988
Beltringharder Koog	IV	54°34'N/8°55'E	3,350	1991
Bruchbach-Otterbachniederung	IV	49°04'N/8°09'E	1,511	1988
Bucher Brack - Bolsdorfer Haken	IV	52°35'N/12°00'E	1,008	1978
Die Lucie	IV	53°03'N/11°07'E	1,800	1951
Dollart	IV	53°17'N/7°13'E	2,140	1980
Düffel-Kellener Altrhein und Flussmarschen	IV	51°49'N/6°02'E	3,800	1987
Eggstaett-Hemhofer Seenplatte	IV	48°55'N/12°19'E	1,000	1982
Elbaue Beuster-Wahrenberg	IV	52°58'N/11°38'E	1,600	1990
Elbdeichvorland	IV	53°11'N/11°01'E	1,412	1990
Eulenberge	IV	53°11'N/13°49'E	1,873	1990
Ewiges Meer	IV	53°33'N/7°26'E	1,180	1949
Federsee	IV	48°05'N/9°38'E	1,401	1939
Fehntjer Tief-Süd	IV	53°23'N/7°29'E	1,280	1992
Feldberg	IV	47°51'N/8°01'E	4,226	1952
Fischteiche in der Lewitz	IV	53°29'N/11°36'E	1,732	1967
Galenbecker See	IV	53°38'N/13°45'E	1,015	1967
Garbe-Aland-Niederung	IV	53°01'N/11°37'E	1,650	1990
Geigelstein	IV	47°40'N/12°17'E	3,135	1991
Granitz	IV	54°23'N/13°39'E	1,130	1990
Grosses Moor	IV	52°30'N/10°40'E	2,720	1984
Grumsiner Forst/Redernswalde	IV	53°00'N/13°51'E	5,718	1990
Grüne Insel mit Eiderwatt	IV	54°17'N/8°54'E	1,000	1989
Hadelner und Belumer Aussendeich	IV	53°50'N/8°59'E	1,283	1984
Hahnheide	IV	53°37'N/10°24'E	1,450	1938
Hasledorfer Binnenelbe mit Elbvorland	IV	53°38'N/9°36'E	2,056	1984
Haunstetter Wald und Stadtwald Augsburg	IV	48°14'N/10°43'E	1,804	1940
Helgolaender Felssockel	IV	54°09'N/7°52'E	5,138	1981
Hinrichshagen	IV	53°25'N/13°31'E	1,124	1967
Hoher Ifen	IV	47°23'N/10°09'E	2,430	1964
Innerer Unterspreewald	IV	52°02'N/13°52'E	1,829	1990
Insel Oie und Kirr	IV	?/?	418	1967
Insel Pulitz	IV	54°25'N/13°30'E	149	1937
Inseln Bohmke und Werder	IV	53°58'N/14°00'E	118	1971
Inseln Oie und Kirr	IV	54°28'N/12°45'E	450	1967
Isarauen zwischen Schaeftlarn und Bad Toelz	IV	47°55'N/11°25'E	1,663	1985
Karwendel und Karwendelvorgebirge	IV	47°33'N/11°28'E	19,100	1959
Kienhorst/Köllnsee/Eichheide	IV	52°56'N/13°39'E	5,030	1961
Krickenbecker Seen	IV	51°20'N/6°18'E	1,240	1990
Kuehkopf-Knoblochsaue	IV	49°48'N/8°28'E	2,369	1952
Laacher See	IV	50°24'N/7°18'E	2,100	1926
Lange Rhoen	IV	50°25'N/10°01'E	2,657	1982
Langeeog	IV	?/?	600	?
Lueneburger Heide	IV	52°59'N/10°07'E	19,720	1920
Melzower Forst	IV	53°10'N/13°55'E	2,760	1990
Moenchgut	IV	54°18'N/13°40'E	2,340	1990
Muendung der Tiroler Achen	IV	47°49'N/12°31'E	1,250	1986
Murnauer Moos	IV	47°40'N/11°13'E	2,355	1980
Noerdlicher Droemling	IV	11°00'N/52°31'E	2,116	1990

Nord-Sylt	IV	55°01'N/8°24'E	1,796	1969
Obere Wuemmeniederung	IV	53°15'N/9°45'E	1,385	1986
Oberharz	IV	51°48'N/10°29'E	7,030	1954
Oestliche Chiemgauer Alpen	IV	47°41'N/12°39'E	9,500	1954
Ostersen	IV	47°42'N/11°17'E	1,086	1981
Peenemunder Haken, Struck und Ruden	IV	54°10'N/13°45'E	1,870	1925
Peenetal-Moor	IV	53°52'N/13°45'E	1,478	1981
Plagefenn	IV	52°50'N/13°57'E	1,047	1907
Poratzer Moraenenlandschaft	IV	53°04'N/13°48'E	3,995	1990
Presseler Heidewald und Moorgebeit	IV	51°34'N/12°45'E	3,804	1990
Rehdener Geestmoor	IV	52°37'N/8°30'E	1,085	1988
Salmorth	IV	51°50'N/6°07'E	1,170	1987
Saupark	IV	52°08'N/9°40'E	2,445	1954
Schachen und Reintal	IV	47°25'N/11°04'E	4,000	1970
Schliffkopf	IV	48°28'N/8°15'E	1,380	1986
Schwarze Berge	IV	50°17'N/9°56'E	3,160	1989
Seegrund Ahlbeck	IV	53°39'N/14°14'E	1,166	1990
Siebengebirge	IV	50°38'N/7°19'E	4,800	1922
Siebertal	IV	51°38'N/10°16'E	1,016	1992
Spiekeroog Ostplate	IV	?/?	885	?
Stechlin	IV	53°08'N/13°00'E	2,134	1938
Steckby-Loedderitzer Forst	IV	52°54'N/12°00'E	3,850	1961
Sudeniederung zw. Boizenburg u. Besitz	IV	53°21'N/10°46'E	1,240	1990
Suedlicher Droemling	IV	11°14'N/52°27'E	1,204	1990
Taubergiessen	IV	48°15'N/7°44'E	1,601	1979
Tinner und Staverner Dose	IV	52°46'N/7°22'E	3,200	1986
Uhlstaedter Heide	IV	50°35'N/11°15'E	1,082	1981
Untere Mulde	IV	51°44'N/12°18'E	1,137	1961
Vessertal	IV	50°35'N/10°50'E	1,649	1939
Vogelinsel Heuwiese und Freesenort	IV	54°26'N/13°05'E	250	1961
Wahner Heide	IV	50°49'N/7°13'E	2,630	1968
Wurzacher Reid	IV	47°55'N/9°53'E	1,387	1981

GHANA

Summary		
Category I	1	38,570
Category II	6	1,058,430
Category III	0	0
Category IV	2	6,620
Category V	0	0
Total	**9**	**1,103,620**

National Park

Bia	II	6°35'N/3°05'W	7,800	1974
Bui	II	8°13'N/2°23'W	182,060	1971
Digya	II	7°25'N/0°17'E	347,830	1971
Kakum National Park	II	5°25'N/1°20'W	20,700	1991
Mole	II	9°37'N/1°51'W	484,040	1971
Nini-Suhien	II	5°19'N/2°38'W	16,000	1976

Strict Nature Reserve

Kogyae	I	7°15'N/1°07'W	38,570	1971

Wildlife Sanctuary

Bomfobiri	IV	6°53'N/1°06'W	5,310	1975
Owabi	IV	5°42'N/1°36'W	1,310	1971

GREECE/GRECE/GRECIA

	Summary	
Category I	0	0
Category II	8	60,392
Category III	2	18,000
Category IV	6	11,483
Category V	8	133,178
Total	**24**	**223,053**

Aesthetic Forest

Kalavrita	V	38°02'N/22°06'E	1,750	1977
Kavala	V	40°58'N/24°22'E	2,816	1979
Skiathos Island	III	39°10'N/23°29'E	3,000	1977
Tembi Valley	V	39°52'N/22°32'E	1,762	1974

Breeding Station

Antimilos Island Game	IV	36°47'N/24°14'E	745	1963

Controlled Hunting Area

Dias Island	IV	35°26'N/25°13'E	1,250	1977
Sapienza Island	IV	36°45'N/21°42'E	850	1977

Game Refuge

Dadia-Lefkimi & Soufli Forest	IV	41°07'N/26°05'E	7,200	1986
Gioura Island	IV	?/?	1,000	1979

Marine Park

Northern Sporades	V	39°20'N/24°10'E	100,000	1992

National Park

Ainos	II	38°08'N/20°38'E	2,862	1962
Mount Oita	II	38°50'N/22°16'E	7,210	1966
Mount Olympos	II	40°05'N/22°22'E	3,998	1938
Parnassos	II	38°32'N/22°30'E	3,513	1938
Parnitha	II	38°10'N/23°41'E	3,812	1961
Pindos	II	39°54'N/21°05'E	6,927	1966
Prespes	II	40°47'N/21°06'E	19,470	1974
Samaria	V	35°16'N/23°56'E	4,850	1962
Sounio	V	37°43'N/24°01'E	3,500	1974
Vikos-Aoos	II	39°58'N/20°45'E	12,600	1973

Natural Monument

Petrified Forest of Lesbos Island	III	39°13'N/25°55'E	15,000	1985
Piperi Island	IV	39°20'N/24°55'E	438	1980

Other area

Mount Athos	V	40°10'N/24°19'E	15,000	1992

Protected Area

Zakynthos sea turtle nesting areas	V	37°47'N/20°54'E	3,500	1986

GRENADA/GRENADE/GRANADA

No Areas Listed

GUATEMALA

	Summary	
Category I	0	0
Category II	6	768,400
Category III	5	10,975
Category IV	5	52,591
Category V	1	1,000
Total	**17**	**832,966**

Biotope

Biotopo Univ. para la Conservación del Quetzal	IV	?/?	1,153	1977
Chocón-Machacas	IV	?/?	6,265	1981
Mario Dary Rivera Quetzal	IV	?/?	1,173	1976
San Miguel - El Zotz	IV	?/?	42,000	1989

Cultural Monument

Aguateca	III	?/?	1,709	1987
Ceibal	III	?/?	2,100	1984
Dos Pilas	III	?/?	3,166	1987
Machaquilla	III	?/?	2,000	1974

National Park

Bahía de Santo Tomás	V	?/?	1,000	1956
El Tigre	II	?/?	350,000	1990
Lacandón	II	?/?	200,000	1990
Laguna Lachua	II	?/?	10,000	1978
Mirador/Dos Lagunas/Río Azul	II	?/?	147,000	1990
Sipacate-Naranjo	IV	?/?	2,000	1969
Tikal	II	17°14'N/89°38'W	57,400	1957
Trifinio National Park	II	?/?	4,000	1987
Volcán de Pacaya	III	14°27'N/90°36'W	2,000	1963

GUINEA/GUINEE

	Summary	
Category I	2	125,300
Category II	1	38,200
Category III	0	0
Category IV	0	0
Category V	0	0
Total	**3**	**163,500**

National Park

Badiar	II	?/?	38,200	1985

Strict Nature Reserve

Massif du Ziama	I	?/?	112,300	1943
Mont Nimba	I	?/?	13,000	1944

GUINEA-BISSAU/GUINEE-BISSAU

No Areas Listed

GUYANA

	Summary	
Category I	0	0
Category II	1	58,559
Category III	0	0
Category IV	0	0
Category V	0	0
Total	**1**	**58,559**

National Park

Kaieteur	II	50°0'N/59°00'W	58,559	1929

HAITI

	Summary	
Category I	0	0
Category II	2	7,500
Category III	0	0
Category IV	0	0
Category V	1	2,200
Total	**3**	**9,700**

Natural National Park

La Citadelle, Sans Souci, Ramiers	V	19°36'N/72°14'W	2,200	1968
La Visite	II	18°20'N/72°20'W	2,000	1983
Pic Macaya	II	18°20'N/74°02'W	5,500	1983

HONDURAS

	Summary	
Category I	0	0
Category II	16	469,453
Category III	0	0
Category IV	28	393,330
Category V	0	0
Total	**44**	**862,783**

Biological Reserve

El Chile	IV	14°20'N/86°50'W	12,000	1987
El Guisayote	IV	14°26'N/89°24'W	7,000	1987
El Pital	IV	14°23'N/89°07'W	3,800	1987
El Uyuca	IV	14°02'N/87°09'W	1,138	1986
Guajiquiro	IV	14°08'N/87°49'W	7,000	1987
Jardín Botánico de Lancetilla	IV	?/?	1,681	1987
Misoco	IV	14°38'N/86°50'W	4,000	1987
Montecillos	IV	14°27'N/88°08'W	12,500	1987
Opalaca	IV	14°31'N/85°23'W	14,500	1987
Río Kruta	IV	15°05'N/85°38'W	50,000	?
Río Negro	IV	15°38'N/85°22'W	60,000	?
Volcán Pacayita	IV	14°25'N/88°50'W	9,700	1987
Yerba Buena	IV	14°08'N/87°27'W	3,600	1987
Yuscarán	IV	13°56'N/86°52'W	2,360	1987

Marine Reserve

Sandy Bay	II	?/?	420	1992

National Park

Capiro-Calentura	II	15°48'N/85°50'W	5,500	1992
Celaque	II	14°30'N/88°44'W	27,000	1987

Cerro Azul de Copán	II	14°22'N/88°22'W	15,500	1987
Cerro Azul Meambar	II	14°39'N/88°06'W	20,000	1987
La Muralla	II	15°07'N/86°42'W	24,850	1987
La Tigra	II	10°12'N/87°07'W	23,821	1980
Montaña de Comayagua	II	14°29'N/87°33'W	18,000	1987
Montaña de Cusuco	II	15°00'N/88°13'W	18,400	1987
Montaña de Yoro	II	15°03'N/87°05'W	30,000	1987
Montecristo-Trifinio	II	15°53'N/85°53'W	5,400	1987
Pico Bonito	II	15°38'N/86°53'W	112,500	1987
Pico Pijol	II	15°12'N/87°34'W	11,400	1987
Punta Sal	II	15°56'N/87°48'W	78,162	1992
Santa Bárbara	II	15°28'N/86°47'W	13,000	1987
Sierra de Agalta	II	15°06'N/85°50'W	65,500	1987

Wildlife Refuge

Cuero y Salado	IV	15°47'N/87°05'W	13,225	1987
El Armado	IV	14°58'N/86°48'W	3,500	1987
Erapuca	IV	14°40'N/89°59'W	6,500	1987
Laguna de Caratasca	IV	15°30'N/84°03'W	120,000	?
Laguna de Guaymoreto	IV	15°59'N/85°53'W	5,000	1992
Las Iguanas	IV	13°16'N/87°14'W	1,426	1992
Mixcure	IV	14°28'N/88°08'W	8,000	1987
Montaña de Corralitos	IV	14°18'N/86°54'W	5,500	1987
Montaña Verde	IV	14°03'N/88°09'W	8,300	1987
Puca	IV	14°31'N/88°24'W	4,900	1987
Punta Condega	IV	13°07'N/87°25'W	3,900	1992
Punta Isopo	IV	15°25'N/87°23'W	11,200	1992
San Bernardo	IV	13°07'N/87°13'W	2,600	?
Texiguat	IV	15°28'N/87°20'W	10,000	1987

HUNGARY/HONGRIE/HUNGRIA

Summary		
Category I	0	0
Category II	5	159,139
Category III	0	0
Category IV	6	13,815
Category V	42	401,060
Total	**53**	**574,014**

Landscape Protected Area

Badacsonyi	V	46°50'N/17°29'E	7,028	1965
Barcsi Osborokas	V	45°59'N/17°33'E	3,417	1974
Beda-Karapancsai	V	45°50'N/18°50'E	6,498	1989
Biharugrai	V	46°55'N/21°15'E	7,899	1990
Borsodi Mezosegi	V	47°45'N/20°48'E	9,168	1989
Borzsonyi	V	47°58'N/18°55'E	17,897	1978
Budai	V	47°33'N/18°54'E	10,234	1978
Devavanyai	V	47°06'N/20°56'E	12,144	1975
Gemenci	V	46°14'N/18°52'E	17,779	1977
Gerecsei	V	47°38'N/18°25'E	8,617	1977
Godolloi Dombvidek	V	47°30'N/19°30'E	11,817	1990
Hajdusagi	V	49°30'N/21°55'E	5,681	1988
Hansagi	V	47°41'N/17°17'E	7,086	1976
Kali-medence	V	46°53'N/17°38'E	9,111	1984
Karancs-Medves	V	48°15'N/19°45'E	6,709	1989
Kecskeri puszta	V	47°20'N/20°45'E	1,226	1990
Kelet-Cserhat	V	48°00'N/19°45'E	6,916	1989
Kelet-Mecsek	V	46°13'N/18°23'E	9,248	1977
Kesznyeteni	V	48°00'N/21°10'E	4,070	1990
Keszthelyi	V	46°48'N/17°20'E	2,711	1984

Kis-Balaton	V	46°39'N/17°13'E	14,745	1986
Koszegi	V	47°22'N/16°29'E	3,987	1980
Kozep-Tiszai	V	47°11'N/20°17'E	7,670	1978
Lazberci	V	48°14'N/20°27'E	3,634	1975
Martelyi	V	46°28'N/20°12'E	2,232	1971
Matrai	V	47°54'N/19°59'E	11,863	1985
Ocsai	V	47°16'N/19°14'E	3,576	1975
Orsegi	V	46°53'N/16°22'E	37,911	1978
Pilisi	V	47°45'N/18°55'E	23,323	1978
Pitvarosi pusztak	V	46°20'N/20°40'E	3,156	1989
Pusztaszeri	V	46°30'N/20°10'E	22,151	1976
Sarreti	V	47°12'N/18°18'E	2,211	1986
Soproni	V	47°40'N/16°31'E	4,905	1977
Szabadkigyosi	V	46°35'N/21°06'E	4,773	1977
Szatmar-Beregi	V	48°08'N/22°35'E	22,246	1982
Szentgyorgyvolgyi	V	46°46'N/16°24'E	1,916	1976
Szigetkozi	V	47°54'N/17°22'E	9,158	1987
Tihanyi	V	46°55'N/17°52'E	1,532	1952
Tokaj-Bodrogzug	V	48°11'N/21°25'E	4,242	1986
Vertesi	V	47°24'N/18°21'E	15,035	1976
Zempleni	V	48°28'N/21°22'E	26,496	1984
Zselicsegi	V	46°14'N/17°46'E	9,042	1976

National Park

Aggteleki	II	48°30'N/20°39'E	19,708	1985
Bukki	II	48°03'N/20°29'E	38,815	1976
Ferto-tavi	II	47°41'N/16°45'E	12,543	1991
Hortobagyi	II	47°35'N/21°07'E	52,213	1973
Kiskunsagi	II	46°55'N/19°34'E	35,860	1975

Nature Conservation Area

Agotapuszta	IV	47°22'N/21°05'E	4,700	1973
Nagybereki Feherviz	IV	46°39'N/17°31'E	1,537	1977
Pusztakocsi mocsarak	IV	47°35'N/20°55'E	2,815	1973
Tiszadobi arter	IV	48°01'N/21°10'E	1,000	1977
Tiszafuredi madarrezervatum	IV	47°40'N/20°43'E	2,500	1973
Tiszatelek-Tiszaberceli arter	IV	48°12'N/21°45'E	1,263	1978

ICELAND/ISLANDE/ISLANDIA

Summary		
Category I	1	270
Category II	3	180,100
Category III	5	38,604
Category IV	5	51,950
Category V	8	645,000
Total	**22**	**915,924**

Conservation Area

Mvatn-Laxá	V	65°23'N/16°44'W	440,000	1974

National Park

Jökulsárgljúfur	II	65°56'N/16°31'W	15,100	1973
Skaftafell	II	64°09'N/17°10'W	160,000	1967
Thingvellir	II	64°16'N/21°05'W	5,000	1928

Natural Monument

Alftaversgígar	III	63°30'N/18°31'W	3,650	1975
Askja i Dyngjufjollum	III	65°03'N/16°47'W	5,000	1978
Lakagígar	III	64°06'N/18°17'W	16,000	1971
Skógafoss	III	63°32'N/19°30'W	2,204	1987

Nature Reserve

Flatey	IV	63°18'N/20°37'W	100	1975
Geitland	III	64°40'N/20°39'W	11,750	1988
Hvannalindir íí Krepputungu	IV	64°51'N/16°22'W	4,300	1973
Kringilsárrani	IV	64°47'N/15°56'W	8,500	1975
Miklavatn	IV	65°42'N/19°34'W	1,550	1977
Thjosárver	IV	64°39'N/18°46'W	37,500	1981

Nature Reserve (Landscape)

Esjufjöll	V	64°13'N/16°32'W	27,000	1978
Fjallabak	V	64°01'N/19°08'W	47,000	1979
Herdubreidarfridland	V	65°15'N/16°15'W	17,000	1974
Herdísarvík	V	63°55'N/21°50'W	4,000	1988
Hornstrandir	V	66°22'N/22°42'W	58,000	1975
Lónsöroefi	V	64°35'N/15°13'W	32,000	1977
Vatnsfjördur	V	65°40'N/23°07'W	20,000	1975

Scientific Reserve

Surtsey	I	63°18'N/20°37'W	270	1965

INDIA/INDE

Summary		
Category I	2	196,043
Category II	64	3,677,580
Category III	0	0
Category IV	307	10,458,515
Category V	1	18,600
Total	**374**	**14,350,738**

Andaman Islands

National Park

Campbell Bay	II	07°09'N/92°50'E	42,623	1992
Galathea	II	07°05'N/93°53'E	11,000	1992
Marine (Wandur)	II	11°29'N/92°35'E	28,150	1983
Mount Harriet Island	II	11°47'N/92°45'E	4,622	1979
Saddle Peak	II	13°10'N/93°01'E	3,255	1979

Sanctuary

Barren Island	IV	12°17'N/94°51'E	810	1977
Battimalve Island	IV	8°49'N/92°50'E	223	1985
Benett Island	IV	12°51'N/92°43'E	346	1987
Bluff Island	IV	12°45'N/92°42'E	114	1987
Bondoville Island	IV	12°53'N/92°45'E	255	1987
Buchaan Island	IV	12°53'N/92°42'E	933	1987
Cinque Island	IV	11°17'N/92°42'E	951	1987
Crocodile (Lohabrrack)	IV	11°38'N/92°37'E	2,221	1983
Defence Island	IV	11°56'N/92°35'E	1,049	1987
East (Inglis) Island	IV	12°07'N/93°06'E	355	1987
East Island	IV	13°37'N/99°04'E	611	1987
Flat Island	IV	12°32'N/93°40'E	936	1987
Interview Island	IV	12°53'N/92°41'E	13,300	1985
James Island	IV	11°57'N/92°43'E	210	1987
Kyd Island	IV	12°56'N/92°45'E	800	1987
Landfall Island	IV	13°39'N/92°58'E	2,948	1987
Narcondum Island	IV	13°24'N/94°15'E	681	1977
North Reef Island	IV	13°04'N/92°42'E	348	1977
Paget Island	IV	13°25'N/92°49'E	736	1987
Pitman Island	IV	11°59'N/92°45'E	137	1987
Point Island	IV	13°24'N/92°48'E	307	1987

Ranger Island	IV	12°50'N/92°41'E	426	1987
Reef Island	IV	13°30'N/92°52'E	174	1987
Roper Island	IV	12°50'N/92°40'E	146	1987
Ross Island	IV	13°18'N/93°04'E	101	1987
Sandy Island	IV	11°47'N/92°31'E	158	1987
Shearme Island	IV	13°24'N/92°51'E	785	1987
Sir Hugh Rose Island	IV	11°47'N/93°05'E	106	1987
South Brother Island	IV	10°55'N/92°36'E	124	1987
South Reef Island	IV	12°46'N/92°39'E	117	1987
South Sentinel Island	IV	10°59'N/92°13'E	161	1977
Spike Island-2	IV	12°15'N/92°43'E	1,170	1987
Swamp Island	IV	12°55'N/92°47'E	409	1987
Table (Delgarno) Island	IV	13°24'N/92°05'E	229	1987
Table (Excelsior) Island	IV	13°25'N/93°06'E	169	1987
Talabaicha Island	IV	12°16'N/92°45'E	321	1987
Temple Island	IV	13°23'N/93°03'E	104	1987
Tillanchang Island	IV	8°29'N/93°37'E	683	1985
West Island	IV	13°35'N/92°54'E	640	1987

Andhra Pradesh

National Park

Shri Venkataswara	II	?/?	35,300	?

Sanctuary

Coringa	IV	16°45'N/82°13'E	23,579	1978
Eturnagaram	IV	18°25'N/80°21'E	80,615	1953
Gundla Brahmeswaram	IV	?/?	119,400	?
Kaundinya	IV	?/?	35,760	?
Kawal	IV	19°10'N/78°59'E	89,300	1965
Kinnerasani	IV	17°53'N/82°34'E	65,541	1977
Kolleru	IV	16°38'N/81°13'E	67,300	1963
Krishna	IV	?/?	19,481	?
Manjira	IV	17°38'N/77°00'E	2,000	1978
Nagarjunasagar Srisailam	IV	16°30'N/79°23'E	356,800	1978
Pakhal	IV	17°30'N/79°30'E	87,930	1952
Papikonda	IV	17°30'N/81°30'E	59,068	1978
Pocharam	IV	18°10'N/78°15'E	13,000	1952
Pranahita	IV	?/?	13,602	1980
Pulicat	IV	13°55'N/80°10'E	50,000	1976
Siwaram	IV	?/?	3,629	1978
Srivenkateswara	IV	?/?	50,694	?

Arunachal Pradesh

National Park

Mouling	II	28°33'N/94°46'E	48,300	1986
Namdapha	II	27°31'N/96°37'E	198,524	1983

Sanctuary

D'Ering Memorial	IV	27°55'N/95°26'E	19,000	1978
Dibang Valley	IV	?/?	414,900	1991
Eagle nest	IV	27°05'N/92°24'E	21,700	1989
Itanagar	IV	27°07'N/93°22'E	14,030	1978
Kamlang	IV	27°44'N/96°39'E	78,300	1989
Kane	IV	27°40'N/94°39'E	5,500	1991
Mehao	IV	28°12'N/95°54'E	28,150	1980
Pakhui	IV	27°06'N/92°48'E	86,195	1977
Sessa Orchid	IV	27°09'N/92°33'E	10,000	1989

Assam

National Park

Kaziranga	II	26°38'N/93°23'E	42,996	1974

Sanctuary

Barnadi	IV	26°45'N/91°40'E	2,622	1980
Dipor Beel	IV	?/?	4,000	1989
Laokhowa	IV	36°15'N/92°30'E	7,014	1979
Manas	IV	26°44'N/90°45'E	39,100	1928
Nameri	IV	?/?	13,707	1985
Orang	IV	26°20'N/92°05'E	7,260	1985
Pabha	IV	?/?	4,900	?
Pobitora	IV	?/?	3,883	1987
Sonai Rupai	IV	26°50'N/92°25'E	17,500	1934

Bihar

National Park

Palamau	II	?/?	21,300	1986

Sanctuary

Bhimbandh	IV	?/?	68,190	1976
Dalma	IV	?/?	19,322	1976
Gautam Budha	IV	?/?	25,948	1976
Hazaribagh	IV	?/?	18,625	1976
Kabar	IV	?/?	20,400	1986
Kaimur S#	IV	?/?	134,222	1978
Koderma	IV	?/?	17,795	1985
Lawalang	IV	?/?	21,103	1978
Mahuadaur	IV	?/?	6,325	1976
Nakti Dam	IV	?/?	20,640	1985
Palamau	IV	23°40'N/84°08'E	76,700	1976
Parasnath	IV	?/?	4,923	1984
Rajgir	IV	?/?	3,584	1978
Valmikinagar	IV	?/?	46,160	1978

Chandigarh

Sanctuary

Sukhna	IV	?/?	2,542	?

Delhi

Sanctuary

Indira Priyadarshini	IV	?/?	1,320	?

Goa, Daman and Diu

National Park

Bhagwan Mahavir	II	15°20'N/74°00'E	10,700	1978

Sanctuary

Bhagwan Mahavir	IV	15°20'N/74°00'E	14,852	1967
Cotigao	IV	15°21'N/74°01'E	10,500	1968

Gujarat

National Park

Bansda	II	?/?	2,399	1979
Gir	II	21°15'N/70°32'E	25,871	1975
Marine (Gulf of Kutch)	II	22°35'N/69°41'E	16,289	1980
Velavadar	II	?/?	3,408	1976

Sanctuary

Balaram-Ambaji	IV	?/?	54,208	1989
Barda	IV	?/?	19,231	1979
Gir	IV	21°15'N/70°32'E	115,342	1965
Jambughoda	IV	?/?	13,038	1990
Jessore	IV	?/?	18,066	1978

Kachchh Desert	IV	?/?	750,622	1986
Marine (Gulf of Kutch) S	IV	22°35'N/69°41'E	29,303	1980
Nal Sarovar	IV	?/?	12,082	1969
Narayan Sarovar	IV	?/?	76,579	1981
Paniya	IV	?/?	3,963	1989
Purna	IV	?/?	16,084	1990
Rampura	IV	?/?	1,501	1988
Ratanmahal	IV	?/?	5,565	1982
Schoolpaneshwar	IV	?/?	60,770	1982
Wild Ass	IV	?/?	495,370	1973

Haryana

Sanctuary

Bir Shikargah	IV	30°30'N/76°30'E	1,093	1975
Chautala	IV	?/?	11,396	1987

Himachal Pradesh

National Park

Great Himalayan	II	31°37'N/77°33'E	60,561	1984
Pin Valley	II	31°58'N/77°56'E	80,736	1987

Sanctuary

Bandli	IV	31°27'N/76°54'E	3,947	1962
Chail	IV	30°58'N/77°12'E	11,004	1976
Churdhar	IV	30°51'N/77°26'E	5,659	1985
Daranghati	IV	31°25'N/77°49'E	2,701	1962
Darlaghat	IV	31°13'N/76°56'E	9,871	1962
Gamgul Siahbehi	IV	32°51'N/75°55'E	10,546	1949
Gobind Sagar	IV	31°20'N/76°38'E	12,067	1962
Kais	IV	32°01'N/77°11'E	1,220	1954
Kalatop & Khajjiar	IV	32°03'N/76°04'E	3,069	1949
Kanawar	IV	31°58'N/77°20'E	6,157	1954
Khokhan	IV	31°52'N/77°05'E	1,760	1954
Kugti	IV	32°30'N/76°49'E	33,000	1962
Lippa Asrang	IV	31°42'N/78°13'E	2,953	1962
Majathal	IV	31°17'N/76°59'E	3,164	1962
Manali	IV	32°14'N/77°08'E	3,127	1954
Naina Devi	IV	31°20'N/76°30'E	3,719	1962
Nargu	IV	31°56'N/76°57'E	24,313	1962
Pong Dam	IV	31°59'N/76°12'E	32,270	1983
Raksham Chitkul	IV	31°30'N/78°23'E	3,827	1962
Rupi Bhabha	IV	31°38'N/77°57'E	85,414	1982
Sechu Tuan Nala	IV	31°08'N/76°40'E	65,532	1962
Shikari Devi	IV	31°29'N/77°09'E	7,119	1962
Simbalbara	IV	30°26'N/77°29'E	1,720	1958
Talra	IV	31°00'N/77°46'E	3,616	1962
Tirthan	IV	31°37'N/77°32'E	6,825	1976
Tundah	IV	32°39'N/76°32'E	41,948	1962

Jammu and Kashmir

National Park

Dachigam	II	34°05'N/74°28'E	14,100	1981
Hemis	II	33°50'N/77°38'E	410,000	1981
Kishtwar	II	33°40'N/75°55'E	31,000	1981

Sanctuary

Baltal	IV	?/?	20,300	1987
Changthang	IV	?/?	400,000	1987
Gulmarg	V	34°05'N/74°25'E	18,600	1987
Hirapora	IV	33°38'N/74°35'E	11,000	1987

Hokarsar	IV	?/?	1,000	?
Kanji	IV	34°11'N/76°40'E	25,000	1988
Karakoram	IV	35°33'N/77°51'E	180,000	?
Lachipora	IV	34°13'N/74°08'E	8,000	1987
Limber	IV	34°09'N/74°09'E	2,600	1987
Nandini	IV	?/?	3,372	1981
Overa	IV	34°05'N/75°14'E	3,237	1981
Overa-Aru	IV	34°05'N/75°14'E	42,500	1987
Ramnagar	IV	?/?	1,290	1981
Surinsar-Mansar	IV	?/?	3,958	1981
Tongri	IV	35°52'N/76°25'E	2,000	?

Karnataka

National Park

Anshi	II	14°45'N/74°16'E	25,000	1987
Bandipur	II	12°03'N/76°07'E	87,420	1974
Bannerghatta	II	12°30'N/77°30'E	10,427	1974
Kudremukh	II	13°00'N/75°05'E	60,032	1987
Nagarahole	II	11°05'N/76°05'E	64,330	1988

Sanctuary

Arabithittu	IV	12°15'N/77°20'E	1,350	1985
Bhadra	IV	13°40'N/75°30'E	49,246	1974
Biligiri Rangaswamy Temple	IV	11°45'N/77°00'E	53,952	1987
Bramhagiri	IV	12°30'N/77°30'E	18,129	1974
Cauvery	IV	11°56'N/77°15'E	51,051	1987
Ghataprabha	IV	10°10'N/74°35'E	2,978	1974
Melkote Temple	IV	12°36'N/77°30'E	4,982	1974
Mookambika	IV	13°35'N/74°35'E	24,700	1974
Nugu	IV	11°50'N/76°30'E	3,032	1974
Pushpagiri	IV	12°29'N/75°37'E	10,259	1987
Ranebennur	IV	14°33'N/75°31'E	11,900	1974
Sharavathi Valley	IV	14°05'N/74°25'E	43,123	1974
Shettihally	IV	13°00'N/75°15'E	39,560	1974
Someswara	IV	13°15'N/74°50'E	8,840	1974
Talacauvery	IV	12°17'N/75°25'E	10,500	1987

Kerala

National Park

Eravikulam	II	10°13'N/76°53'E	9,700	1978
Periyar	II	?/?	30,500	1982
Silent Valley	II	11°09'N/76°26'E	8,952	1980

Sanctuary

Aralam	IV	12°04'N/75°40'E	5,500	1984
Chimony	IV	10°21'N/77°10'E	10,500	1984
Chinnar	IV	10°19'N/77°10'E	9,044	1984
Idukki	IV	9°28'N/77°10'E	7,700	1976
Neyyar	IV	8°34'N/77°11'E	12,800	1958
Parambikulam	IV	10°23'N/76°43'E	28,500	1973
Peechi Vazhani	IV	10°38'N/76°25'E	12,500	1958
Peppara	IV	8°45'N/77°10'E	5,300	1983
Periyar	IV	9°28'N/77°10'E	47,200	1950
Shenduruny	IV	8°54'N/77°08'E	10,032	1984
Thattekkad Bird	IV	10°02'N/76°37'E	2,500	1983
Wynad	IV	11°35'N/76°08'E	34,444	1973

Madhaya Pradesh

National Park

Bandhavgarh	II	23°39'N/81°02'E	44,884	1968

Indravati	II	20°00'N/81°30'E	125,837	1978
Kanger Ghati	II	?/?	20,000	1982
Kanha	II	22°20'N/89°38'E	94,000	1955
Madhav	II	25°45'N/77°40'E	15,615	1959
Panna	II	24°17'N/80°07'E	542,666	1981
Pench	II	?/?	29,286	1977
Sanjay	II	24°00'N/81°38'E	193,801	1981
Satpura	II	?/?	52,437	1981

Sanctuary

Achanakmar	IV	22°29'N/81°45'E	55,155	1975
Badalkhol	IV	22°50'N/23°50'E	10,435	1975
Bagdara	IV	23°50'N/82°10'E	47,890	1978
Barnawapara	IV	21°20'N/82°25'E	24,466	1976
Bhairamgarh	IV	19°10'N/80°40'E	13,895	1983
Bori	IV	22°23'N/78°08'E	51,825	1977
Gandhi Sagar	IV	24°30'N/75°30'E	36,862	1974
Ghatigaon Great Indian Bustard	IV	?/?	51,200	1981
Gomarda	IV	21°30'N/83°15'E	27,782	1972
Karera Great Indian Bustard	IV	?/?	20,221	1981
Ken Gharial	IV	?/?	4,500	1981
Kheoni	IV	22°40'N/76°45'E	12,270	1982
Narsingarh	IV	23°38'N/77°06'E	5,719	1974
National Chambal	IV	20°53'N/77°25'E	42,300	1978
Noradehi	IV	23°20'N/79°13'E	118,696	1975
Pachmarhi	IV	22°30'N/70°25'E	46,086	1977
Palpur (Kuno)	IV	?/?	34,468	1981
Pamed	IV	?/?	26,212	1983
Panpatha	IV	?/?	24,584	1983
Pench	IV	21°40'N/79°15'E	11,847	1977
Phen	IV	?/?	11,024	1983
Ratapani	IV	22°55'N/77°40'E	68,879	1976
Sailana	IV	?/?	1,296	1983
Sanjay (Dubri)	IV	?/?	36,459	1975
Sardarpur	IV	?/?	34,812	1983
Semarsot	IV	23°55'N/82°40'E	43,036	1978
Singhori (Sindhari)	IV	23°20'N/78°25'E	28,791	1976
Sitanadi	IV	20°15'N/81°55'E	55,336	1974
Son Gharial	IV	?/?	4,180	1981
Tamor Pingla	IV	23°50'N/82°10'E	60,852	1978
Udanti	IV	?/?	24,759	1983

Marahashtra

National Park

Gugamal	II	26°52'N/90°58'E	36,180	1987
Navegaon	II	21°10'N/79°41'E	13,388	1975
Pench	II	21°35'N/79°14'E	25,726	1975
Sanjay Gandhi	II	18°56'N/75°51'E	8,696	1983
Tadoba	II	20°20'N/79°20'E	11,655	1955

Sanctuary

Andhari	IV	?/?	50,927	1986
Aner Dam	IV	?/?	8,294	1986
Bhimashankar	IV	?/?	13,078	1985
Bor	IV	?/?	6,110	1970
Chandoli	IV	?/?	30,897	1985
Chaprala	IV	?/?	13,478	1986
Gautala Autramghat	IV	?/?	26,061	1986
Great Indian Bustard	IV	?/?	849,644	1979
Jaikwadi	IV	?/?	34,105	1986
Kalsubai Harishchandra	IV	?/?	36,171	1986

Katepurna	IV	?/?	7,369	1988
Koyana	IV	?/?	42,355	1985
Malvan	IV	?/?	2,912	1987
Melghat	IV	?/?	159,723	1985
Nagzira	IV	21°10'N/17°12'E	15,281	1970
Nandur Madmeshwar	IV	?/?	10,012	1986
Painganga	IV	?/?	32,462	1986
Phansad	IV	?/?	6,979	1986
Radhanagari	IV	17°00'N/73°20'E	37,188	1958
Sagareshwar	IV	?/?	1,087	1985
Tansa	IV	19°14'N/73°02'E	30,481	1970
Yawal	IV	21°15'N/76°05'E	17,752	1969

Manipur

National Park

Keibul Lamjao	II	24°30'N/93°46'E	4,000	1977
Siroi	II	?/?	4,130	1982

Sanctuary

Yagoupokpi Lokchao	IV	?/?	18,480	1989

Meghalaya

National Park

Balphakram	II	25°30'N/90°45'E	22,000	1986
Nokrek	II	25°15'N/90°15'E	4,748	1986

Sanctuary

Nongkhyllem	IV	25°56'N/91°31'E	2,900	1981

Mizoram

National Park

Murlen	II	23°37'N/93°18'E	20,000	1991
Phawngpui	II	22°40'N/93°03'E	5,000	1991

Sanctuary

Dampa	IV	23°40'N/92°22'E	50,000	1985
Khawnglung	IV	23°18'N/92°57'E	4,100	1991
Ngengpui	IV	22°29'N/92°48'E	15,000	1991

Nagaland

Sanctuary

Intanki	IV	25°35'N/93°29'E	20,202	1975

Orissa

National Park

Bhitar Kanika	II	20°15'N/86°26'E	36,700	1988
North Simlipal	II	21°20'N/86°23'E	84,570	1980

Sanctuary

Badrama	IV	21°30'N/84°20'E	30,403	1987
Baisipalli	IV	20°35'N/85°20'E	16,835	1981
Balukhand Konark	IV	19°50'N/85°53'E	7,172	1984
Bhitar Kanika	IV	20°40'N/86°18'E	17,000	1975
Chandaka Dampara	IV	20°23'N/85°44'E	17,579	1982
Chilka (Nalaban)	IV	19°38'N/85°16'E	1,553	1987
Debrigarh	IV	21°34'N/83°38'E	34,691	1985
Hadgarh	IV	21°16'N/82°20'E	19,106	1978
Karlapat	IV	19°40'N/82°30'E	14,766	1992
Khalasuni	IV	21°22'N/84°25'E	11,600	1982
Kotgarh	IV	?/?	39,905	1981
Kuldiha	IV	21°25'N/86°37'E	27,275	1984

Lakhari Valley	IV	19°20'N/84°20'E	18,587	1985
Satkosia Gorge	IV	20°35'N/85°20'E	79,552	1976
Simlipal	IV	21°19'N/86°21'E	220,000	1979
Sunabeda	IV	?/?	60,000	1988

Punjab

Sanctuary

Abohar	IV	?/?	18,824	1975
Harike Lake	IV	?/?	4,300	1982

Rajastan

National Park

Desert	II	26°18'N/71°10'E	316,200	1981
Keoladeo	II	27°10'N/77°31'E	2,873	1981
Ranthambore	II	26°03'N/76°26'E	39,200	1980
Sariska	II	?/?	27,380	1982

Sanctuary

Bandh Baretha	IV	?/?	19,276	1985
Bassi	IV	?/?	15,290	?
Bhensrodgarh	IV	?/?	22,914	1983
Darrah	IV	25°10'N/35°52'E	26,583	1955
Jaisamand	IV	27°42'N/75°33'E	5,200	1956
Jamwa Ramgarh	IV	?/?	30,000	1982
Jawahar Sagar	IV	25°11'N/75°58'E	10,000	1980
Keladevi	IV	?/?	67,600	1983
Kumbhalgarh	IV	25°27'N/73°28'E	57,826	1971
Mount Abu	IV	24°41'N/72°45'E	28,884	1960
Nahargarh	IV	?/?	5,000	1980
National Chambal	IV	?/?	28,000	1983
Phulwari	IV	?/?	51,141	1983
Ramgarh Bundi	IV	?/?	30,700	1982
Sariska	IV	?/?	49,200	1958
Sawai Mansingh	IV	?/?	10,325	1984
Shergarh	IV	?/?	9,871	1983
Sita Mata	IV	?/?	42,294	1979
Sunda Mata	IV	?/?	10,700	?
Todgarh Raoli	IV	?/?	49,527	1983
Van Vihar	IV	?/?	5,993	1955

Sikkim

National Park

Khangchendzonga	II	27°39'N/88°04'E	84,950	1977

Sanctuary

Fambong Lho	IV	?/?	5,176	1984
Maenam	IV	?/?	3,534	1987
Shingba	IV	?/?	3,250	1984

Tamil Nadu

National Park

Indira Gandhi	II	?/?	11,808	1989

Sanctuary

Anamalai	IV	10°00'N/76°00'E	84,935	1976
Kalakad	IV	8°30'N/77°30'E	22,358	1976
Mudumalai	IV	11°38'N/76°34'E	32,155	1940
Mukurthi	IV	?/?	7,846	1982
Mundanthurai	IV	8°53'N/77°20'E	56,738	1962
Point Calimere	IV	10°17'N/79°52'E	1,726	1967
Pulicat	IV	?/?	46,102	1980
Srivilliputhur	IV	?/?	48,520	1988

Tripura

Sanctuary

Gumti	IV	?/?	38,954	1988
Sepahijala	IV	?/?	1,853	1987
Trishna	IV	?/?	17,056	1987

Uttar Pradesh

National Park

Corbett	II	29°32'N/78°56'E	52,082	1936
Dudwa	II	28°31'N/80°43'E	49,029	1977
Gangotri	II	?/?	155,273	1991
Govind	II	?/?	47,208	1991
Nanda Devi	I	30°24'N/79°53'E	63,033	1982
Rajaji	II	30°04'N/78°07'E	83,153	1988
Valley of Flowers	II	30°44'N/79°36'E	8,950	1982

Sanctuary

Binsar	IV	?/?	4,559	1988
Chandra Prabha	IV	?/?	7,800	1957
Govind Pashu Vihar	IV	31°09'N/78°19'E	48,104	1954
Hastinapur	IV	?/?	2,073	1986
Kaimur	IV	?/?	50,075	1982
Katarniaghat	IV	28°14'N/81°13'E	40,009	1976
Kedarnath	IV	30°35'N/79°15'E	97,524	1972
Kishanpur	IV	28°31'N/80°22'E	22,712	1972
National Chambal	IV	26°43'N/78°43'E	63,500	1979
Ranipur	IV	25°27'N/80°53'E	23,031	1977
Sohagabarwa	IV	?/?	42,820	1987
Sonanadi	IV	?/?	30,118	1987

West Bengal

National Park

Neora Valley	II	?/?	8,800	1992
Singalila	II	?/?	7,860	1992
Sunderban	I	21°42'N/88°53'E	133,010	1984

Sanctuary

Buxa	IV	?/?	25,189	1986
Halliday Island	IV	21°38'N/88°37'E	595	1976
Jaldapara	IV	26°40'N/89°30'E	21,651	1990
Lothian Island	IV	21°38'N/88°19'E	3,800	1976
Mahananda	IV	?/?	12,722	1976
Sajnakhali	IV	22°04'N/88°49'E	36,240	1976
Senchal	IV	?/?	3,888	1976

INDONESIA/INDONESIE

Summary		
Category I	73	7,143,310
Category II	28	7,253,936
Category III	0	0
Category IV	46	3,649,132
Category V	28	518,914
Total	**175**	**18,565,292**

Irian Jaya

Game Reserve

Jayawijaya	IV	?/?	800,000	1981

Memberamo Foja	IV	?/?	1,018,000	1982
Pulau Anggrameos	IV	?/?	2,500	1981
Pulau Dolok	IV	8°08'S/138°13'E	600,000	1978
Pulau Sabuda, Pulau Tata Ruga	IV	?/?	5,000	1993
Raja Empat	IV	?/?	60,000	1993

National Park

Marine Teluk Cendrawasih	II	2°33'S/134°38'E	1,453,000	1990
Wasur	II	8°35'S/140°45'E	308,000	1990

Nature Reserve

Batanta Barat	I	0°53'S/130°39'E	10,000	1981
Biak Utara	I	0°45'S/135°52'E	11,000	1982
Enarotali	I	?/?	300,000	1980
Gunung Lorentz	I	4°35'S/137°38'E	2,150,000	1978
Misool Selatan	I	1°56'S/130°15'E	84,000	1982
Peg. Cyclop	I	2°30'S/140°30'E	22,500	1978
Pulau Supriori	I	0°42'S/135°35'E	42,000	1982
Pulau Waigeo	I	0°14'S/130°35'E	153,000	1982
Salawati Utara	I	1°04'S/130°21'E	57,000	1982
Wondi Boy	I	?/?	73,022	1992
Yapen Tengah	I	1°46'S/136°49'E	59,000	1982

Recreation Park

Teluk Yotefa	V	?/?	1,650	1981

Java and Bali

Game Reserve

Banyuwangi	IV	8°43'S/114°29'E	62,000	1919
Bawean	IV	5°50'S/112°45'E	3,832	1979
Cikepuh	IV	7°16'S/106°26'E	8,128	1973
Dataran Tinggi	IV	7°58'S/113°34'E	14,145	1962
Gunung Sawai	IV	?/?	5,400	1979

Grand Forest Park

R. Soeryo	V	?/?	25,000	1992

National Park

Alas Purwo	II	?/?	43,420	1992
Bali Barat (Bali)	II	8°22'S/114°58'E	77,727	1982
Baluran	II	7°50'N/114°35'E	25,000	1980
Bromo Tengger Semeru	II	?/?	58,000	1982
Gunung Gede Pangrango	II	5°46'S/106°58'E	15,000	1980
Gunung Halimun	I	6°45'S/106°30'E	40,000	1992
Marine Kepulauan Karimun Jawa	II	5°49'S/110°24'E	111,625	1986
Marine Kepulauan Seribu	II	5°32'S/106°31'E	110,000	1982
Meru Betiri	II	8°29'S/113°48'E	58,000	1982
Ujung Kulon	II	6°45'S/105°20'E	122,936	1992

Nature Reserve

Batukau I/II/III (Bali)	I	8°20'S/115°05'E	1,763	1974
Gunung Burangrang	I	?/?	2,700	1979
Gunung Celering	I	?/?	1,328	1989
Gunung Simpang	I	?/?	15,000	1979
Gunung Tilu	I	7°13'S/107°25'E	8,000	1978
Gunung Tukung Gede	I	?/?	1,700	1979
Leuwang Sancang	I	7°44'S/107°51'E	2,157	1978
Nusa Barung	I	8°28'S/113°22'E	6,100	1920
P.Sempu	I	?/?	877	1928
Rawa Danau	I	6°11'S/105°59'E	2,500	1921

Recreation Park

Gunung Tampomas	V	?/?	1,250	1979

Prapat Benoa (Bali)	V	?/?	1,374	1992
Pulau Sangiang	V	?/?	1,420	1991
Tangkuban Perahu	V	?/?	1,290	1974

Kalimantan

Game Reserve

Cunung Nyiut Penrisen	IV	?/?	180,000	1982
Pleihari Martapura	IV	3°50'S/114°53'E	36,400	1980
Pleihari Tanah Laut	IV	3°22'S/116°05'E	35,000	1975

Grand Forest Park

Sultan Adam	V	?/?	112,000	1989

Marine Park

Sangalaki	IV	2°09'N/118°20'E	280	1982

National Park

Bukit Baka- Bukit Raya	II	?/?	181,090	1992
Gunung Palung	II	1°19'S/110°24'E	90,000	1990
Kutai	II	0°23'N/117°19'E	198,629	1982
Tanjung Puting	II	2°58'S/112°02'E	355,000	1982

Nature Reserve

Bukit Tangkiling	I	?/?	2,061	1977
Gunung Bentuang	I	?/?	800,000	1992
Gunung Raya Pasi	I	0°50'S/109°02'E	3,700	1978
Kep Karimata	I	?/?	77,000	1985
Mandor	I	0°17'N/109°33'E	2,000	1937
Muara Kaman Sedulang	I	0°16'S/116°43'E	62,500	1976
Padang Luwai	I	?/?	5,000	1967
Pararawen I,II	I	?/?	6,200	1979
Sungai Kayan Sungai Mentarang	I	3°11'N/115°15'E	1,600,000	1980
Teluk Ampan	I	?/?	46,900	1993
Teluk Kelumpang/Selat Laut/Selat Sebuku	I	?/?	66,650	1981

Recreation Park

Bukit Soeharto	V	?/?	61,850	1991
Pleihari	V	?/?	1,500	1991
Tanjung Keluang	V	?/?	2,000	1984

Lesser Sunda Islands

Game Reserve

Harlu	IV	?/?	2,000	1993
Kateri	IV	?/?	4,560	1981
Perhalu	IV	?/?	1,000	1993

Marine Park

Gili Air, Gili Meno, Gili Trawngan	I	?/?	2,954	1993
Keluk Kupang	I	?/?	50,000	1993
P. Moyo	I	?/?	6,000	1986
Teluk Maumere	I	?/?	59,450	1986

National Park

Gunung Rinjani	II	8°30'S/116°30'E	40,000	1990
Kelimutu	II	?/?	5,000	1992
Komodo	II	8°37'S/119°35'E	173,500	1980

Nature Reserve

Gunung Langgaliru	I	?/?	15,639	1992
Maubesi	I	9°33'S/124°59'E	1,830	1981
Tanah Pedauh	I	?/?	544	1975
Tujuh Belas Pulau	I	?/?	11,900	1987

Way Wuul/Mburak	I	?/?	3,000	1985
Welotedo, Ngadowelo	I	?/?	4,017	1992
Wetu Ata	I	?/?	4,899	1992

Recreation Park

Bangko-bangko	V	?/?	2,169	1992
Manipo	V	?/?	2,500	1992
Pulau Besar	V	?/?	3,000	1986
Tuti Adagae	V	?/?	5,000	1981

Moluccas

Game Reserve

Pulau Baun	IV	6°50'S/134°36'E	13,000	1974
Pulau Kassa	IV	3°30'S/128°20'E	900	1978
Pulau Manuk	IV	5°33'S/130°18'E	100	1981

Marine Park

Kep. Aru Tenggara	I	6°50'S/135°06'E	114,000	1991
Laut Banda	I	4°43'S/129°55'E	2,500	1977
P.Kassa	I	3°30'S/128°20'E	1,100	1978
P.Pombo	I	3°31'S/128°22'E	1,000	1973

National Park

Manusela	II	?/?	189,000	1982

Nature Reserve

Pulau Angwarmase	I	7°32'S/131°20'E	800	1978
Pulau Nustaram	I	7°32'S/131°20'E	3,200	1978
Pulau Nuswotar	I	7°32'S/131°20'E	7,500	1978
Pulau Seho	I	?/?	1,250	1972

Recreation Park

Ruteng	V	?/?	30,000	1993

Sulawesi

Game Reserve

Bontobahari	IV	?/?	4,000	1980
Buton Utara	IV	?/?	82,000	1979
Gunung Manembo-Nembo	IV	?/?	6,500	1978
Lampoko Mampie	IV	3°25'S/119°15'E	2,000	1978
Lombuyan I&II	IV	?/?	3,665	1974
Pinjan/Tanjung Matop	IV	?/?	1,613	1981
Sungai Sopu	IV	?/?	67,000	1981
Tanjung Batikolo	IV	?/?	5,500	1980
Tanjung Peropa	IV	4°05'S/122°45'E	38,000	1986

Marine Nature Reserve

Arakan Wowontulap	I	1°22'N/124°30'E	13,800	1986
Kepulauan Togian	I	0°23'S/121°53'E	100,000	1989
Marine Kepuluan Take Bone Rate	I	6°56'S/121°08'E	530,765	1992
Pulau Bunaken	I	1°42'N/124°46'E	75,265	1986

National Park

Bogani Nani Wartabone	II	?/?	287,115	1991
Lore Lindu	II	1°23'S/120°05'E	231,000	1982
Marine Bunaken Menado Tua	II	1°42'N/124°46'E	89,065	1989
Rawa Aopa Watumohai	II	4°00'S/122°00'E	96,804	1989

Nature Reserve

Bantimurung	I	?/?	1,000	1980
Bulu Saraung	I	?/?	5,690	1980
Dua Saudara	I	1°29'N/125°11'E	4,299	1978

Gunung Ambang	I	0°35'N/123°45'E	8,638	1978
Karaenta	I	?/?	1,000	1976
Morowali	I	1°45'S/121°34'E	225,000	1986
Paboya	I	?/?	1,000	1973
Panua	I	0°25'S/121°50'E	45,000	1984
Peg.Feruhumpenai	I	?/?	90,000	1979
Tangkoko Batuangus	I	1°29'N/125°11'E	3,196	1981
Tanjung Api	I	?/?	4,246	1977

Recreation Park

Cani Sirenreng	V	?/?	3,125	1993
Danau Matano	V	?/?	30,000	1979
Danau Towuti	V	?/?	65,000	1979
Malino	V	?/?	3,500	1991
Patunuang	V	?/?	1,500	1987

Research Forest

Sungai Camba	IV	?/?	1,300	?

Sumatra

Game Reserve

Barumun	IV	?/?	40,330	1989
Bentayan	IV	?/?	19,300	1981
Danau Pulau Besar/Danau Bawah	IV	?/?	25,000	1980
Dangku	IV	?/?	29,080	1981
Dolok Surungan	IV	?/?	23,800	1974
Gumai Pasemah	IV	?/?	45,883	1976
Gunung Raya	IV	?/?	39,500	1978
Isau-Isau Pasemah	IV	4°00'S/103°39'E	12,144	1978
Karang Gading	IV	?/?	15,765	1980
Kerumutan	IV	0°20'S/102°32'E	120,000	1979
Padang Sugihan	IV	3°00'S/104°43'E	75,000	1983
Siranggas	IV	?/?	5,657	1934
Tai-tai Batti	IV	?/?	56,500	1976
Terusan Dalam	IV	?/?	74,750	1988

Grand Forest Park

Bukit Barisan	V	?/?	51,600	1988
Dr. Moch. Hatta	V	?/?	70,000	1986
Wan Abdul Rachman	V	?/?	22,244	1992

Marine Park

Pulau Weh	IV	?/?	2,600	1978

National Park

Berbak	II	1°20'S/104°17'E	162,700	1935
Bukit Barisan Selatan	II	5°14'S/103°54'E	365,000	1982
Gunung Leuser	II	3°30'N/97°43'E	792,675	1980
Kerinci Seblat	II	2°05'S/101°25'E	1,484,650	1982
Way Kambas	II	4°52'S/105°36'E	130,000	1989

Nature Reserve

Dolok Sibual Bual	I	?/?	5,000	1982
Dolok Sipirok	I	?/?	6,970	1982
Hutan Pinus/Janthoi	I	?/?	8,000	1984
Kelompok Hutan Bakau Pantai Timur	I	1°05'S/103°49'E	6,500	1981
Pulau Berkch	I	?/?	500	1968
Pulau Burung	I	0°25'N/103°34'E	200	1968

Recreation Park

Batam	V	?/?	2,066	1992
Bukit Kaba	V	?/?	13,490	?

Holiday Resort	V	?/?	1,964	1990
Pulau Weh	V	?/?	1,300	1982
Pungguk Menakar	V	?/?	1,122	1991

IRAN, ISLAMIC REPUBLIC OF/
IRAN, REPUBIQUE ISLAMIQUE D'/
IRAN, REPUBLICA ISLAMICA DEL

Summary		
Category I	18	1,904,503
Category II	7	1,075,300
Category III	2	6,150
Category IV	4	1,144,918
Category V	37	4,168,695
Total	**68**	**8,299,566**

National Nature Monument

Alborz-e-Markazi (Central Alborz)	III	36°15'N/51°30'E	4,750	1977
Dehloran	III	32°41'N/47°18'E	1,400	1976

National Park

Bamou	II	29°45'N/52°45'E	48,075	1962
Golestan (Mohammad Reza Shah)	II	37°25'N/56°00'E	91,895	1957
Kavir	II	34°16'N/53°07'E	420,000	1964
Khogir	II	?/?	11,570	1982
Sorkheh Hesar	II	35°30'N/52°00'E	9,380	1982
Tandoureh	II	37°25'N/58°50'E	30,780	1968
Uromiyeh Lake	II	37°36'N/45°23'E	463,600	1967

Protected Area

Alborz-e-Markazi	V	36°15'N/51°30'E	399,000	1961
Angoran	V	36°40'N/47°45'E	96,130	1971
Arasbaran	V	38°51'N/46°41'E	72,460	1971
Arjan	IV	29°30'N/51°50'E	5 2,800	1972
Bahramgor	IV	29°30'N/55°00'E	385,000	1973
Bahukalat (Gando)	IV	25°42'N/61°28'E	382,430	1971
Bazman	IV	28°05'N/60°00'E	324,688	1968
Bigar	V	35°55'N/47°45'E	25,000	1971
Bisotun	V	34°30'N/47°29'E	50,850	1968
Dez	V	31°40'N/48°51'E	10,633	1960
Faro	V	?/?	2,620	?
Geno	V	27°30'N/56°18'E	27,500	1972
Ghorkhod	V	37°25'N/56°10'E	34,000	1971
Haftadgoleh	V	34°10'N/50°25'E	82,000	1970
Hamoun	V	31°20'N/61°40'E	193,500	1967
Hara	V	26°52'N/55°41'E	85,686	1972
Heleh	V	28°30'N/50°55'E	42,600	1976
Hormoud	V	27°25'N/55°08'E	151,284	1976
Jagrud	V	35°10'N/52°00'E	51,650	?
Jahannoma	V	36°40'N/54°20'E	30,600	1974
Kalmand	V	?/?	300,000	?
Karkheh	V	31°40'N/48°25'E	9,427	1960
Kavir	V	34°40'N/52°20'E	250,000	?
Lar River	V	36°00'N/51°40'E	28,000	1976
Lashkardar	V	?/?	16,000	?
Lisar	V	37°59'N/48°55'E	33,050	1970
Marakan	V	39°10'N/45°17'E	92,715	1966
Mond	V	28°35'N/51°10'E	46,700	1976
Moteh	V	33°58'N/51°14'E	200,000	1964
Nayband	V	27°22'N/53°38'E	195,000	?

Oshtran Kuh	V	33°19'N/49°18'E	93,950	1970
Parvar	V	35°39'N/53°39'E	59,840	1962
Salouk	V	37°20'N/57°15'E	16,000	1973
Sarigol	V	36°15'N/58°20'E	28,000	?
Sekidkuh Khoramabad	V	?/?	69,500	1992
Serany	V	37°45'N/58°03'E	17,800	1971
Siahkesheim	V	37°30'N/49°25'E	4,500	1967
Tandoureh	V	37°25'N/58°50'E	2,300	?
Tang Sayyad	V	32°05'N/51°10'E	27,000	1971
Touran	V	36°15'N/57°05'E	1,295,400	1973
Vargin	V	35°52'N/51°10'E	28,000	?

Wildlife Refuge

Amirkelayeh	I	37°17'N/50°12'E	1,230	1971
Angoran	I	36°40'N/47°45'E	28,600	1971
Bakhtegan	I	29°23'N/53°40'E	327,820	1968
Bisotun (Varmangeh)	I	34°30'N/47°29'E	31,250	?
Dez	I	31°40'N/48°51'E	5,240	1960
Dodangeh	I	35°42'N/53°42'E	6,700	1974
Gamishlo	I	32°59'N/51°18'E	49,250	1971
Karkheh	I	31°40'N/48°25'E	3,600	1960
Khab-o-Rochon	I	28°57'N/56°32'E	173,750	1971
Kharko	I	29°02'N/50°29'E	312	1960
Khoshyeylag	I	36°55'N/55°25'E	154,400	1963
Kiamaky	I	38°57'N/45°40'E	84,400	1974
Kolahghazi	I	32°29'N/52°06'E	48,683	1964
Mehroyeh	I	28°04'N/57°22'E	7,468	1971
Miandasht	I	36°52'N/57°15'E	52,000	1974
Miankaleh	I	36°50'N/53°45'E	68,800	1970
Shadegan	I	30°22'N/48°52'E	296,000	1972
Touran	I	36°15'N/57°05'E	565,000	1973

IRAQ

No Areas Listed

IRELAND/IRLANDE/IRLANDA

Summary		
Category I	0	0
Category II	5	36,798
Category III	0	0
Category IV	7	10,033
Category V	0	0
Total	**12**	**46,831**

National Park

Burren	II	53°00'N/9°55'W	1,511	1991
Connemara	II	53°31'N/9°55'W	2,699	1980
Glenveagh	II	55°01'N/8°00'W	9,737	1984
Killarney	II	52°01'N/9°32'W	10,129	1932
Wicklow Mountains	II	53°00'N/6°22'W	12,722	1991

Nature Reserve

Drumcliffe Bay	IV	?/?	1,545	?
Glenealo Valley / Glendalough	IV	53°01'N/6°23'W	2,115	1988
Knockadoon Head & Capel Island	IV	51°52'N/7°50'W	127	1985
Knockmoyle/Sheskin	IV	52°30'N/7°28'W	1,198	1986
North Bull Island	IV	53°17'N/6°05'W	1,436	1988
Owenduff Catchment	IV	?/?	1,382	1986
Slieve Bloom Mountains	IV	53°05'N/7°45'W	2,230	1985

ISRAEL

	Summary	
Category I	0	0
Category II	1	3,090
Category III	0	0
Category IV	13	296,345
Category V	1	8,400
Total	**15**	**307,835**

National Park

Mount Carmel	V	32°42'N/35°04'E	8,400	?

Nature Reserve

Amasa Mont	IV	31°22'N/35°08'E	1,145	1981
Ashosh	IV	?/?	34,500	1992
En Gedi (Ein Gedi)	IV	31°27'N/35°23'E	1,400	1971
Har Ha-Negev	IV	31°03'N/34°44'E	104,900	1989
Har Meron (Mount Meron)	IV	33°00'N/35°26'E	9,600	1965
Hof Ha-Almogim Be-Elat	IV	?/?	8,450	1964
Holot Mashabim (Mashabim dunes)	IV	31°01'N/34°45'E	1,300	1992
Karmel (Carmel)	II	32°42'N/35°04'E	3,090	1971
Masiv Elat (Eilat Mountains)	IV	29°40'N/34°50'E	39,900	1986
Mazoq Ha-Zinim	IV	?/?	63,200	1989
Nahal Prat	IV	?/?	2,805	1988
Nehalim Gdolim U-Qtura	IV	?/?	24,800	1986
Tel Qraiot	IV	?/?	1,145	1981
Yotveta (Hai Bar Yotvata)	IV	29°53'N/35°03'E	3,200	1970

ITALY/ITALIE/ITALIA

	Summary	
Category I	0	0
Category II	11	471,918
Category III	1	1,500
Category IV	86	221,922
Category V	74	1,579,485
Total	**172**	**2,274,825**

Marine Reserve

Isola di Ustica	IV	?/?	4,280	1986
Isole Tremiti	IV	42°10'N/15°30'E	2,116	1989

National Park

Abruzzo	II	41°45'N/13°53'E	43,950	1923
Arcipelago Toscano	II	?/?	67,500	1989
Aspromonte	II	?/?	50,000	1989
Calabria	II	39°13'N/16°51'E	15,894	1968
Circeo	V	41°17'N/13°00'E	8,622	1934
Delta Padano	II	?/?	30,000	1986
Dolomiti Bellunesi	II	?/?	31,000	1990
Foreste Casentinesi	II	?/?	30,000	1989
Gran Paradiso	II	45°12'N/7°16'E	70,200	1922
Pollino	V	40°00'N/16°14'E	196,437	1990
Sibillini	II	42°56'N/13°10'E	71,374	1990
Stelvio	V	46°28'N/10°38'E	148,271	1935
Val Grande	II	?/?	50,000	1992
Vesuvio	II	?/?	12,000	1991

Nature Monument

Campo Soriano	III	41°22'N/13°15'E	1,500	1985

Regional Nature Park

Adamello	V	46°04'N/10°28'E	48,000	1983
Adamello Brenta	V	45°51'N/10°21'E	61,864	1967
Adda Nord	V	45°37'N/9°29'E	5,580	1983
Adda Sud	V	45°18'N/9°42'E	23,600	1983
Alpe Devero	V	?/?	6,588	1990
Alpe Veglia	V	46°16'N/8°08'E	4,120	1978
Alpi Apuane	V	44°04'N/10°15'E	60,000	1985
Alpi Giulie	V	?/?	11,074	1990
Alta Valle Pesio	V	44°12'N/7°39'E	3,955	1978
Alta Valsesia	V	45°54'N/7°58'E	6,508	1979
Alto Appennino Modenese	V	?/?	14,844	1988
Alto Appennino Reggiano	V	?/?	16,981	1988
Alto Garda Bresciano	V	?/?	38,269	1989
Argentera	V	44°12'N/7°20'E	25,643	1980
Aveto	V	?/?	10,380	1989
Boschi di Carrega	V	44°43'N/10°12'E	1,270	1982
Bosco della Sorti della Partecipanza di Trino	V	?/?	1,068	1991
Bracco-Mesco Cinque Terre Montemarcello	V	44°08'N/9°41'E	15,390	1985
Campo dei Fiori	V	45°53'N/8°47'E	5,400	1984
Capanne di Marcarolo	V	44°34'N/8°49'E	8,211	1979
Colli di Bergamo	V	45°44'N/9°40'E	4,000	1977
Colli Euanei	V	?/?	14,840	1989
Conero	V	?/?	5,820	1987
Corno alle Scale	V	?/?	2,653	1988
Crinale Romagnolo	V	?/?	16,083	1988
Delta del Po	V	44°54'N/12°26'E	59,118	1988
Dolomiti d'Ampezzo	V	?/?	11,192	1990
Dolomiti di Sesto	V	46°30'N/12°19'E	11,635	1981
Etna	V	?/?	58,095	1987
Fanes Sennes Braies	V	46°38'N/12°04'E	25,680	1980
Fiume Stirone	V	?/?	1,769	1988
Fiume Taro	V	?/?	2,567	1988
Gessi Bolognesi e Calanchi Abbadessa	V	?/?	3,804	1988
Groane	V	45°27'N/9°06'E	3,200	1976
Gruppo di Tessa	V	46°47'N/11°01'E	33,430	1976
La Mandria	V	45°10'N/8°35'E	6,534	1978
Lessinia	V	?/?	10,368	1990
Lucretili	V	?/?	18,000	1989
Madonie	V	?/?	39,941	1989
Maremma o Monti dell'Uccelina	V	42°38'N/11°05'E	9,800	1975
Migliarino-San Rossore-Massaciuccoli	V	43°44'N/10°20'E	22,000	1979
Mincio	V	45°13'N/10°53'E	13,708	1984
Mont Avic	V	?/?	3,521	1989
Monte Antola	V	?/?	8,719	1989
Monte Corno	V	46°17'N/11°17'E	6,660	1980
Monte Fenera	V	?/?	3,364	1987
Montevecchia e Valle del Curone	V	45°43'N/9°22'E	1,598	1983
Monti Simbruini	V	41°55'N/13°13'E	29,000	1983
Oglio Nord	V	?/?	14,170	1988
Oglio Sud	V	?/?	12,800	1988
Orobie Bergamasche	V	?/?	63,000	1989
Orobie Valtellinesi	V	?/?	44,000	1989
Orsiera-Rocciavre	V	45°04'N/7°08'E	10,927	1980
Paveneggio-Pale di San Martino	V	46°18'N/11°46'E	19,097	1967
Pineta di Appiano Gentile e Tradate	V	45°44'N/8°56'E	4,597	1983
Po	V	?/?	24,854	1990
Prealpi Carniche	V	?/?	25,874	1990
Puez Odle	V	46°37'N/11°48'E	9,210	1977
Salbertrand	V	?/?	2,028	1980
Sciliar	V	46°30'N/11°35'E	5,850	1974
Serio	V	45°29'N/9°43'E	7,750	1985

Sirente Velino	V	?/?	50,000	1989
Stupinigi	V	?/?	1,622	1992
Val Troncea	V	44°56'N/6°57'E	3,265	1980
Valle del Lambro	V	45°41'N/9°17'E	6,452	1983
Valle del Ticino (Lombardia)	V	45°49'N/8°56'E	90,640	1974
Valle del Ticino (Piemonte)	V	45°32'N/8°44'E	6,136	1978
Vedrette di Ries	V	?/?	20,581	1988

Regional Nature Reserve

Area piu alta del Massiccio del Pollino	IV	?/?	3,000	1985
Baragge	IV	?/?	2,805	1992
Bosco della Favara e Bosco Granza	IV	?/?	2,978	1991
Bosco della Ficuzza, Rocca Busambra, ecc.	IV	?/?	7,397	1991
Bosco di Malabotte	IV	?/?	3,222	1991
Bosco di San Pietro	IV	?/?	6,559	1991
Bosco di Sperlinga ed Alto Salso	IV	?/?	1,300	1991
Bosco e Laghi di Palanfre	V	44°11'N/7°29'E	1,061	1979
Cavagrande del Cassibile	IV	37°00'N/15°28'E	2,696	1990
Faggeta Madonia	IV	37°53'N/14°11'E	2,949	1984
Fiume Sile	V	?/?	3,097	1991
Fiumedinisi e Monte Scuderi	IV	?/?	4,609	1991
Foce del Crati	IV	?/?	1,490	1990
Isola di Lampedusa	IV	?/?	275	1984
Isola di Lipari	IV	?/?	1,585	1991
Isola di Pantelleria	IV	?/?	2,627	1991
Isola di Stromboli e Strombolicchio	IV	?/?	1,053	1991
Isola di Vulcano	IV	?/?	1,362	1991
Isola Marettimo	IV	?/?	1,132	1991
Isole dello Stagnone di Marsala	IV	37°52'N/12°27'E	2,012	1984
Laghi Lungo e Ripasottile	IV	42°28'N/12°50'E	3,000	1985
Lago di Mezzola - Pian di Spagna	IV	46°12'N/9°30'E	1,740	1980
Lago di Vico	V	42°19'N/12°11'E	3,300	1982
Le Montagne delle Felci e dei Porri	IV	?/?	1,521	1984
Maiella Orientale	IV	?/?	1,680	1991
Montagne della Duchessa	IV	?/?	3,900	1990
Monte Cammarata	IV	?/?	2,049	1991
Monte Capodarso e Valle Imera setteutrionale	IV	?/?	1,485	1991
Monte Carcaci	IV	?/?	1,438	1991
Monte Genuardo e Santa Maria del Bosco	IV	?/?	2,553	1991
Monte Navegna e Monte Cervia	IV	?/?	1,350	1988
Monte Pellegrino	IV	?/?	1,021	1991
Monte Quacella	IV	37°49'N/14°13'E	2,010	1984
Monte Rufeno	IV	42°47'N/11°55'E	2,840	1983
Monte San Calogero	IV	?/?	2,819	1991
Monte Soro	IV	?/?	4,396	1985
Monti di Palazzo Adriano e Valle del Sosio	IV	?/?	5,862	1991
Oasi del Simeto	IV	37°28'N/15°20'E	1,859	1984
Oasi Faunistica di Vendicari	IV	36°52'N/15°23'E	1,512	1984
Pantalica., Valle dell'Anapo e Torrente Cava Grand	IV	?/?	3,712	1991
Pantani Sicilia S.O.	IV	?/?	1,385	1991
Pian di Spagna-Lago di Mezzola	IV	?/?	1,586	1985
Pino d'Aleppo	IV	?/?	2,921	1990
Rocche di Alcara Li Fusi	IV	?/?	1,461	1991
Rossomanno-Grottascura	IV	?/?	2,011	1991
Sambuchetti-Campanito	IV	?/?	2,358	1991
Serra del Re, Grappida e Foresta Vecchia	IV	?/?	1,298	1991
Sorgive di Bars-Fortezza Di Osoppo	IV	?/?	1,665	1987
Stretta del Cellina	IV	?/?	1,430	1990
Sughereta ni Niscemi	IV	?/?	2,939	1991
Tarsia	IV	?/?	1,510	1990
Valli del Mincio	IV	45°08'N/10°46'E	1,082	1984

Voltigno e Valle d'Angri	IV	?/?	5,172	1989
Zingaro	IV	38°06'N/12°53'E	1,600	1981
Zompo lo Schioppo	IV	?/?	1,025	1987
Zona tra Monte Mia ed Erbezzo	IV	?/?	1,340	1990

State Nature Reserve

Abbadia di Fiastra	IV	?/?	1,808	1985
Badia Prataglia	IV	43°44'N/11°57'E	1,631	1977
Bosco della Mesola	IV	44°50'N/12°18'E	1,058	1977
Camaldoli	IV	?/?	1,168	1977
Campigna	IV	43°51'N/11°47'E	1,191	1977
Fara S.Martino-Palombaro	IV	42°08'N/14°15'E	4,202	1983
Feudo Ugni	IV	42°08'N/14°10'E	1,563	1981
Foresta Demaniale del Circeo	IV	41°18'N/13°27'E	3,070	1977
Gole del Raganello	IV	?/?	1,600	1987
Grotticelle	IV	40°58'N/15°32'E	21,422	1971
Isola di Caprera	IV	41°13'N/9°27'E	1,575	1980
Lago di Campotosto	IV	?/?	1,600	1984
Lama Bianca di S. Eufemia a Maiella	IV	?/?	1,407	1987
Marchesale	IV	?/?	1,257	1977
Monte Mottac	IV	46°05'N/8°25'E	2,410	1971
Monte Rotondo	IV	42°20'N/13°50'E	1,452	1982
Monte Velino	IV	?/?	3,550	1987
Montecristo	IV	42°20'N/10°18'E	1,039	1971
Monti del Sole	IV	46°12'N/12°04'E	3,035	1972
Piani Eterni - Errera - Val Falcina	IV	46°09'N/11°58'E	5,463	1975
Poverella Villaggio Mancuso	IV	39°04'N/16°28'E	1,086	1977
Salina di Margherita di Savoia	IV	41°24'N/16°05'E	3,871	1977
Schiara Occidentale	IV	46°14'N/12°08'E	3,172	1975
Somadida	IV	46°30'N/12°14'E	1,676	1972
Stornara	IV	40°42'N/17°05'E	1,456	1977
Tirone-Alto Vesuvio	IV	40°51'N/14°29'E	1,019	1972
Valle del Fiume Argentino	IV	39°48'N/15°55'E	3,980	1987
Valle del Fiume Lao	IV	39°52'N/15°55'E	5,200	1987
Valle dell'Orfento	IV	42°09'N/14°00'E	1,920	1971
Vallombrosa	IV	43°39'N/11°30'E	1,300	1977
Vette Feltrine	IV	46°04'N/11°50'E	2,764	1975

JAMAICA/JAMAÏQUE

Summary		
Category I	0	0
Category II	1	1,520
Category III	0	0
Category IV	0	0
Category V	0	0
Total	**1**	**1,520**

Marine Park

Montego Bay	II	18°27'N/77°58'W	1,520	1991

JAPAN/JAPON

Summary		
Category I	22	214,484
Category II	15	1,299,148
Category III	0	0
Category IV	30	492,342
Category V	13	752,252
Total	**80**	**2,758,226**

Forest Ecosystem Reserve

Iriomote Island	I	?/?	11,590	1991
Kakkonda and Tama River Head	I	?/?	9,366	1991
Mount Hakusan	I	?/?	14,826	1991
Mount Hayachine	I	?/?	8,100	1993
Mount Iide	I	?/?	27,251	1992
Mount Ishizuchi	I	?/?	4,245	1991
Mount Saburu	I	?/?	12,792	1993
Mount Somo, Katamuki and Okue	I	?/?	5,978	1991
Mount Tekari of Southern South Alps	I	?/?	4,566	1991
Osugi Valley	I	?/?	1,391	1991
Shirakami mountains	I	?/?	16,971	1991
Shiretoko	I	?/?	35,527	1991
Tone River Head and Mount Hiuchi	I	?/?	22,835	1991
Yaku Island	I	?/?	14,600	1992

National Park

Akan	II	43°30'N/144°10'E	90,481	1934
Ashizuri - Uwakai	V	33°01'N/132°38'E	10,967	1972
Aso - Kuju	V	33°00'N/131°05'E	72,680	1934
Bandai-Asahi	II	38°00'N/140°00'E	187,041	1950
Chichibu-Tama	V	35°50'N/138°50'E	121,600	1950
Chubu-Sangaku	II	36°18'N/137°40'E	174,323	1934
Daisen - Oki	V	35°50'N/133°30'E	31,927	1936
Daisetsuzan	II	43°40'N/142°51'E	230,894	1934
Fuji-Hakone-Izu	V	34°40'N/139°00'E	122,686	1936
Hakusan	II	36°10'N/136°43'E	47,700	1962
Iriomote	II	24°19'N/123°53'E	12,506	1972
Ise - Shima	V	34°25'N/136°53'E	55,549	1946
Joshinetsu Kogen	II	36°43'N/138°30'E	189,062	1949
Kirishima-Yaku	II	31°24'N/130°50'E	54,833	1934
Kushiro Shitsugen	II	43°09'N/144°26'E	26,861	1987
Minami Arupusu (Minami Alps)	II	35°30'N/138°20'E	35,752	1964
Nikko	V	36°56'N/139°37'E	140,164	1934
Ogasawara	II	26°52'N/142°11'E	6,099	1972
Rikuchu - Kaigan	V	39°20'N/142°00'E	12,348	1955
Rishiri-Rebun-Sarobetsu	II	45°26'N/141°43'E	21,222	1974
Saikai	V	33°16'N/129°23'E	24,653	1955
Sanin - Kaigan	V	35°37'N/134°37'E	8,763	1963
Seto-Naikai	V	34°03'N/133°09'E	62,828	1934
Shikotsu - Toya	II	42°40'N/141°00'E	98,332	1949
Shiretoko	II	44°04'N/145°08'E	38,633	1964
Towada-Hachimantai	II	40°20'N/140°50'E	85,409	1936
Unzen - Amakusa	V	32°45'N/130°16'E	28,289	1934
Yoshino - Kumano	V	34°10'N/136°00'E	59,798	1936

National Wildlife Protection Area

Asama	IV	?/?	32,247	1951
Daisen	IV	?/?	6,025	1957
Daisetsuzan	IV	?/?	35,534	1992
Gamo	IV	38°15'N/141°01'E	7,790	?
Hakusan	IV	36°00'N/136°00'E	35,912	1969
Hamatonbetsu-kuccharoko	IV	45°10'N/142°20'E	2,803	1983
Ina	IV	?/?	1,173	1989
Iriomote	IV	?/?	3,841	1992
Ishiduchisankei	IV	?/?	10,858	1977
Izunuma	IV	?/?	1,450	1982
Kiinagashima	IV	?/?	7,452	1969
Kirishima	IV	?/?	1,400	1975
Kitaarupusu	IV	?/?	110,323	1975
Kominato	IV	?/?	4,515	1971
Kushiro Marsh	IV	?/?	29,084	1935

Kushirositsugen	IV	?/?	10,940	1958
Moriyoshiyama	IV	?/?	6,062	1973
Nakaumi	IV	?/?	8,462	1974
Ogasawarashotoh	IV	?/?	5,899	1980
Ohdaisankei	IV	?/?	18,054	1972
Ohtoriasahi	IV	?/?	38,285	1984
Seinan	IV	?/?	1,561	1979
Sendaikaihin	IV	?/?	7,790	1987
Shimokitaseibu	IV	?/?	5,300	1984
Shiretoko	IV	?/?	43,172	1982
Tohutsuko	IV	?/?	2,051	1992
Towada	IV	?/?	39,163	1953
Tsurugiyamasankei	IV	?/?	10,139	1989
Yagachi	IV	?/?	3,680	1976
Yakushidae	IV	?/?	1,377	1979

Nature Conservation Area

Hayachine	I	39°35'N/141°28'E	1,370	1975
Shirakami-sanchi	I	40°27'N/140°07'E	14,043	1992
Tonegawa-genryubu	I	37°02'N/138°07'E	2,318	1977
Wagadake	I	39°34'N/140°46'E	1,451	1981

Wilderness Area

Oigawa-Genryubu	I	35°20'N/138°04'E	1,115	1976
Onnebetsudake	I	44°10'N/145°00'E	1,895	1980
Tokachigawa-genryubu	I	43°28'N/143°56'E	1,035	1977
Yakushima	I	30°20'N/130°30'E	1,219	1975

JORDAN/JORDANIE/JORDANIA

Summary		
Category I	1	1,200
Category II	0	0
Category III	0	0
Category IV	6	79,200
Category V	3	209,900
Total	**10**	**290,300**

National Park

Dibbeen	V	32°15'N/35°50'E	10,200	1968
Petra	V	30°20'N/35°25'E	12,200	1968
Wadi Rum	V	?/?	187,500	1965

Reserve

Azraq Desert	IV	31°49'N/36°48'E	32,000	1987

Wetland Reserve

Azraq	I	31°49'N/36°48'E	1,200	1965

Wildlife Reserve

Dana	IV	30°40'N/35°34'E	15,000	1989
Shaumari	IV	31°48'N/36°47'E	2,200	1975
Wadi Mujib	IV	31°27'N/35°48'E	21,200	1985
Wadi Rum	IV	29°35'N/35°25'E	7,500	1989
Zubiya	IV	32°27'N/35°45'E	1,300	1987

KAZAKHSTAN/KAZAJSTAN

	Summary	
Category I	8	845,972
Category II	1	45,500
Category III	0	0
Category IV	0	0
Category V	0	0
Total	**9**	**891,472**

National Park

Bayanaul'sky	II	?/?	45,500	1985

Zapovednik

Aksu-Dzhabagly	I	42°15'N/70°39'E	75,094	1926
Alma-Atinskiy	I	43°01'N/77°10'E	73,302	1931
Barsakel'messkiy	I	45°39'N/59°54'E	18,300	1939
Kurgal'dzhinskiy	I	50°28'N/69°15'E	237,138	1968
Markakol'skiy	I	49°16'N/86°37'E	75,040	1976
Naurzumskiy	I	51°30'N/64°19'E	87,694	1934
Ustiyurtskiy	I	43°57'N/55°15'E	223,300	1984
Zapadno-Alta	I	50°30'N/83°50'E	56,104	1992

KENYA

	Summary	
Category I	0	0
Category II	32	3,451,383
Category III	0	0
Category IV	4	52,373
Category V	0	0
Total	**36**	**3,503,756**

Marine National Park

Kisite/Mpunguti	II	4°42'S/39°23'E	3,900	1978
Mombasa	II	3°59'S/39°46'E	1,000	1986
Watamu	II	3°23'S/39°59'E	3,200	1968

National Park

Aberdare	II	0°25'S/36°44'E	76,619	1950
Amboseli	II	2°39'S/37°15'E	39,206	1974
Chyulu	II	2°39'S/37°49'E	47,090	1983
Hell's Gate	II	1°25'S/36°05'E	6,800	1984
Kora	II	0°17'S/38°47'E	178,780	1989
Lake Nakuru	II	0°21'S/36°05'E	18,800	1967
Longonot	II	0°55'S/36°26'E	5,200	1983
Malka Mari	II	4°41'N/40°46'E	87,600	1989
Meru	II	0°04'N/38°14'E	87,044	1966
Mount Elgon	II	5°36'N/34°41'E	16,923	1968
Mount Kenya	II	0°10'S/37°20'E	71,759	1949
Nairobi	II	1°21'S/36°51'E	11,721	1946
Ol Donyo Sabuk	II	1°09'S/37°15'E	1,842	1967
Ruma	II	0°40'S/34°17'E	12,000	1983
Sibiloi	II	4°00'N/36°20'E	157,085	1973
South Island	II	2°55'N/37°00'E	3,880	1983
Tsavo East	II	3°04'S/38°41'E	1,174,700	1948
Tsavo West	II	3°00'S/38°30'E	906,500	1948

National Reserve

Buffalo Springs	II	0°35'N/37°36'E	13,100	1985
Kakamega	II	0°47'N/34°45'E	4,468	1985

Lake Bogoria	II	0°17'N/36°07'E	10,705	1970
Marsabit	II	2°23'N/37°59'E	155,400	1949
Masai Mara	II	1°30'S/35°05'E	151,000	1974
Nasolot	II	1°52'N/35°24'E	19,400	1979
Samburu	II	0°37'N/37°32'E	16,500	1985
Shaba	II	0°39'N/37°50'E	23,910	1974
Shimba Hills	II	4°15'S/39°23'E	19,251	1968
South Turkana	II	1°50'N/35°43'E	109,100	1979
Tana River Primate	II	1°50'S/40°08'E	16,900	1976

Nature Reserve

Arabuko Sokoke	IV	3°30'S/39°30'E	4,332	1979
Nandi North	IV	?/?	3,434	1978
South-Western Mau	IV	0°30'S/35°30'E	43,032	1961
Uaso Narok	IV	?/?	1,575	1981

KIRIBATI

Summary		
Category I	2	20,130
Category II	0	0
Category III	0	0
Category IV	1	6,500
Category V	0	0
Total	**3**	**26,630**

Wildlife Sanctuary

Malden Island (Closed Area)	I	4°03'S/155°01'W	3,930	1975
Phoenix Island (Rawaki)	IV	3°42'S/170°43'W	6,500	1975
Starbuck (Closed Area)	I	5°37'S/155°56'W	16,200	1975

KOREA, DEMOCRATIC PEOPLE'S REPUBLIC OF/ REPUBLIQUE POPULAIRE DEMOCRATIQUE DE COREE/ REPUBLICA POPULAR DEMOCRATICA DE COREA

Summary		
Category I	0	0
Category II	1	43,890
Category III	0	0
Category IV	1	14,000
Category V	0	0
Total	**2**	**57,890**

National Park

| Mount Kumgang | II | 38°39'N/128°08'E | 43,890 | ? |

Nature Protection Area

| Mount Paekdu | IV | 42°01'N/128°04'E | 14,000 | 1976 |

KOREA, REPUBLIC OF/
REPUBLIQUE DE COREE/
REPUBLICA DE COREA

	Summary	
Category I	5	19,346
Category II	0	0
Category III	0	0
Category IV	3	27,148
Category V	20	647,304
Total	**28**	**693,798**

Historic National Park

Kyongju	V	35°46'N/129°16'E	13,816	1968

Marine National Park

Hallyo-Haesang Sea	V	34°42'N/128°34'E	51,032	1968
T'ae-an-hae-an Seashore	V	36°38'N/126°12'E	32,899	1978
Tadohae-Haesang Sea	V	34°10'N/126°43'E	234,491	1981

National Park

Ch'iak Mountain	V	37°19'N/128°03'E	18,209	1984
Chiri Mountain	V	35°18'N/127°37'E	44,045	1967
Chuwang Mountain	V	36°23'N/129°13'E	10,558	1976
Halla Mountain	V	33°22'N/126°32'E	14,900	1970
Kaya Mountain	V	35°47'N/128°08'E	8,016	1972
Kyeryong Mountain	V	36°22'N/127°12'E	6,112	1968
Naejang Mountain	V	35°26'N/126°53'E	7,603	1972
Odae Mountain	V	37°45'N/128°37'E	29,850	1975
Puk'an Mountain	V	37°41'N/126°59'E	7,845	1983
Pyonsan Bando Peninsula	V	35°37'N/126°34'E	15,700	1988
Sobaeksan	V	36°57'N/128°32'E	32,050	1987
Songni Mountain	V	36°36'N/127°52'E	28,340	1970
Sorak Mountain	V	38°08'N/128°24'E	37,300	1970
Togyu Mountain	V	35°51'N/127°44'E	21,900	1970
Wolchlul Mountain	V	34°44'N/126°41'E	4,188	1988
Worak Mountain	V	36°50'N/128°11'E	28,450	1984

Natural Ecological System Preservation Area

Chiri Mountain	I	35°18'N/127°33'E	2,020	1989
Myongii-san	I	?/?	2,500	1993
Nakdong River Mouth	I	35°04'N/128°55'E	3,421	1989

Nature Reserve

Daeamsan-Daewoosan	I	38°12'N/128°08'E	3,074	1973
Hallasan	IV	33°21'N/126°32'E	9,187	1966
Hongdo Island	IV	34°42'N/125°13'E	587	1965
Hyangrobong-Kunbongsan	I	38°20'N/128°19'E	8,331	1973
Soraksan	IV	38°07'N/128°28'E	17,374	1965

KUWAIT/KOWEÏT

Summary		
Category I	1	2,000
Category II	0	0
Category III	0	0
Category IV	0	0
Category V	1	25,000
Total	**2**	**27,000**

National Park

Jal Az-Zor	V	29°40'N/47°50'E	25,000	1990

Scientific Reserve

Sulaybia Experimental Station	I	29°10'N/47°40'E	2,000	1979

KYRGYZSTAN/KIRGHIZISTAN/KIRGUISTAN

Summary		
Category I	4	264,668
Category II	1	19,400
Category III	0	0
Category IV	0	0
Category V	0	0
Total	**5**	**284,068**

National Park

Ala-Archa	II	42°20'N/74°45'E	19,400	1976

Zapovednik

Besh-Aral'skiy	I	38°15'N/70°55'E	114,000	1979
Issyk-Kul'skiy	I	41°36'N/77°09'E	40,800	1948
Narynskiy	I	38°09'N/70°25'E	86,000	1983
Sary-Chelekskiy	I	38°09'N/71°56'E	23,868	1959

LAO PEOPLE'S DEMOCRATIC REPUBLIC/ REPUBLIQUE DEMOCRATIQUE LAO/ REPUBLICA DEMOCRATICA POPULAR LAO

No Areas Listed

LATVIA/LETTONIE/LETONIA

Summary		
Category I	4	38,443
Category II	0	0
Category III	1	2,520
Category IV	23	62,177
Category V	17	671,584
Total	**45**	**774,724**

Botanical Reserve

Ziemupe	IV	56°47'N/21°05'E	1,835	1987

Complex Nature Reserve

Abava	IV	57°03'N/22°15'E	6,697	1957
Augstroze	IV	57°32'N/24°57'E	3,540	1987
Cirisa	IV	56°08'N/27°00'E	1,298	1977
Dridzis	III	55°57'N/27°15'E	2,520	1977

Medumi	V	55°43'N/26°20'E	1,375	1977
Rics	IV	55°37'N/26°43'E	3,791	1977
Salaca	IV	57°50'N/24°40'E	5,323	1977
Slocene	IV	57°02'N/23°23'E	1,612	1977
Svente	IV	55°50'N/26°20'E	2,348	1977
Tuja	V	57°25'N/24°25'E	1,322	1957
Venta	V	57°05'N/21°55'E	1,638	1957

Cranberry Resources Reserve

Olla and Pigele	IV	57°52'N/24°54'E	2,949	1977

Mire Reserve

Klesniki	IV	56°37'N/28°01'E	1,736	1977
Kraukli	IV	56°25'N/25°58'E	1,003	1987
Lielais Kemeru tirelis	IV	56°52'N/23°29'E	5,762	1977
Niedraju-Pilkas	IV	57°46'N/24°40'E	1,057	1987
Orlova (Ergli)	IV	57°03'N/27°27'E	2,638	1977
Sarnate	IV	57°07'N/21°26'E	1,413	1987
Soku (Kodu-Kapzemes)	IV	57°53'N/24°48'E	1,925	1977
Stiklu	IV	57°18'N/22°15'E	1,720	1977
Supe	IV	56°14'N/25°32'E	1,185	1987

National Park

Gauja	V	57°15'N/25°08'E	92,048	1973

Nature Park

Daugavas Loki	V	55°52'N/27°00'E	10,500	1990
Gaizinkalns	V	56°52'N/25°57'E	1,500	1957
Piejura	V	57°07'N/24°15'E	1,629	1962
Sauka	V	56°17'N/26°28'E	5,377	1987
Talsi	V	57°16'N/23°40'E	2,827	1987
Tervete	V	56°28'N/23°22'E	1,350	1957

Other area

Northern Vidzeme Reg. Nature Protection Complex	V	57°45'N/25°05'E	400,000	1990

Protected Landscape

Augsdaugava	V	55°52'N/27°00'E	52,000	1990
Augszeme	V	55°47'N/26°20'E	20,419	1977
Ezernieki	V	56°13'N/27°40'E	23,541	1977
Veclaicene	V	57°33'N/26°54'E	20,649	1977
Vecpiebalga	V	57°07'N/23°16'E	9,532	1987
Vestiena	V	56°52'N/25°54'E	25,877	1977

Scientific Reserve

Grini	I	56°47'N/21°06'E	1,457	1936
Krustkalni	I	56°45'N/26°05'E	2,902	1977
Slitere	I	57°38'N/22°27'E	15,037	1921
Teici	I	56°37'N/26°22'E	19,047	1982

Zoological Reserve

Engure	IV	57°15'N/23°08'E	4,278	1957
Kanieris	IV	57°01'N/23°29'E	1,128	1977
Liepaja	IV	56°25'N/21°04'E	3,715	1977
Pape	IV	56°11'N/21°03'E	1,205	1977
Salas I	IV	56°47'N/27°03'E	4,019	1987

LEBANON/LIBAN/LIBANO

Summary		
Category I	0	0
Category II	1	3,500
Category III	0	0
Category IV	0	0
Category V	0	0
Total	**1**	**3,500**

National Park
Mashgara (Machgharah)   II   33°33'N/35°38'E   3,500   1988

LESOTHO

Summary		
Category I	0	0
Category II	0	0
Category III	0	0
Category IV	1	6,805
Category V	0	0
Total	**1**	**6,805**

National Park
Sehlabathebe   IV   29°55'S/29°08'E   6,805   1970

LIBERIA

Summary		
Category I	0	0
Category II	1	129,230
Category III	0	0
Category IV	0	0
Category V	0	0
Total	**1**	**129,230**

National Park
Sapo   II   52°0'N/9°15'W   129,230   1983

LIBYAN ARAB JAMAHIRIYA/ JAMAHIRIYA ARABE LIBYENNE/ JAMAHIRIYA ARABE LIBIA

Summary		
Category I	0	0
Category II	3	51,000
Category III	0	0
Category IV	3	122,000
Category V	0	0
Total	**6**	**173,000**

National Park

Karabolli	II	32°45'N/13°35'E	15,000	1992
Kouf	II	32°40'N/21°40'E	35,000	1979
Sirman	II	?/?	1,000	1992

Nature Reserve

Bier Ayyad	IV	32°10'N/12°30'E	2,000	1976
Zellaf	IV	27°32'N/14°50'E	100,000	1978

Protected Area

Nefhusa	IV	32°00'N/12°50'E	20,000	1978

LIECHTENSTEIN

Summary		
Category I	0	0
Category II	0	0
Category III	0	0
Category IV	0	0
Category V	1	6,000
Total	**1**	**6,000**

Protection Area

Liechtenstein Floral Mountain	V	47°05'N/9°37'E	6,000	1989

LITHUANIA/LITUANIE/LITUANIA

Summary		
Category I	4	20,784
Category II	5	132,950
Category III	0	0
Category IV	37	99,615
Category V	30	381,370
Total	**76**	**634,719**

Botanical / Zoological Reserve

Amalvas	IV	?/?	1,473	1992
Baranava	IV	?/?	3,468	1960
Berstai	IV	?/?	1,010	1992
Kaukine	IV	?/?	1,134	1992
Margininkai	IV	?/?	1,302	1992
Pravirsulio tyrelis	IV	?/?	2,929	1969
Rekyva	IV	?/?	1,638	1992
Svencele	IV	?/?	1,204	1992
Tyruliai	IV	?/?	3,688	1992
Zalioji giria	IV	?/?	9,237	1960

Geomorphological Reserve

Kuosine	IV	?/?	1,514	1992
Lapes	IV	?/?	1,168	1992
Sirvinta	IV	?/?	1,043	1992

Hydrogeological Reserve

Klaipedos kanalas	IV	?/?	3,981	1980

Hydrographical Reserve

Vilnia	IV	?/?	1,221	1992

Hydrological Reserve

Juosta	IV	?/?	11,209	1980
Upita	IV	?/?	5,839	1980

Ichtiological Reserve

Merkys	IV	?/?	1,050	1974
Minija	IV	?/?	1,976	1974

Landscape Reserve

Alionys	IV	?/?	2,096	1992
Baravykine	IV	?/?	2,281	1974
Daugyvene	IV	?/?	3,870	1992
Gomerta	IV	?/?	4,873	1992
Kuliai	IV	?/?	4,054	1960
Levuo	IV	?/?	1,426	1992
Minijos senslenis	IV	?/?	1,575	1992
Musos tyrelis	IV	?/?	1,449	1988
Nevezis	IV	?/?	1,118	1988
Notigale	IV	?/?	1,539	1992
Plinksiai	IV	?/?	1,239	1974
Smalvas-Smalvykstis	IV	?/?	2,813	1960
Strosiunai	IV	?/?	3,138	1992
Suvainiskis	IV	?/?	1,201	1988
Sventoji	IV	?/?	1,211	1974
Ula	IV	?/?	6,756	1960
Veivirzas	IV	?/?	1,632	1992

National Park

Aukstaitija	II	55°27'N/26°00'E	30,300	1974
Dzukija	II	54°10'N/24°17'E	55,450	1991
Kursiu nerija	II	55°30'N/21°07'E	18,800	1991
Trakai	II	54°38'N/24°53'E	8,300	1991
Zemaitija	II	56°05'N/21°57'E	20,100	1991

Nature Reserve

Cepkeliai	I	54°00'N/24°27'E	8,477	1975
Kamanos	I	56°17'N/22°43'E	3,650	1979
Viesvile	I	55°06'N/22°34'E	3,200	1991
Zuvintas	I	54°27'N/23°34'E	5,457	1937

Ornithological Reserve

Kretuonas	IV	?/?	1,260	1974

Regional Park

Anyksciai	V	55°30'N/25°12'E	14,080	1992
Asveja	V	55°03'N/25°30'E	10,970	1992
Aukstadvaris	V	54°34'N/24°35'E	15,350	1992
Birzai	V	56°13'N/24°42'E	14,030	1992
Dieveniskes	V	54°12'N/25°37'E	11,000	1992
Dubysa	V	55°20'N/23°20'E	8,900	1992
Grazute	V	55°38'N/26°07'E	24,230	1992
Kauno marios	V	54°50'N/24°12'E	9,600	1992
Krekenava	V	55°36'N/24°09'E	8,680	1992
Kurtuvenai	V	55°47'N/23°05'E	13,600	1991
Labanoras	V	55°12'N/25°45'E	39,730	1992
Meteliai	V	54°18'N/23°44'E	15,300	1992
Nemuno delta	V	55°23'N/21°21'E	23,950	1992
Nemuno kilpu	V	54°32'N/24°02'E	24,800	1992
Neris	V	54°48'N/24°52'E	9,900	1992
Pagramantis	V	55°18'N/22°12'E	14,420	1992
Pajuris	V	55°45'N/21°08'E	3,000	1992
Panemuniai	V	55°07'N/23°15'E	10,380	1992
Pavilniai	V	54°40'N/25°22'E	1,800	1991
Rambynas	V	55°03'N/22°06'E	4,530	1992
Salantai	V	56°00'N/21°33'E	13,630	1992
Sartai	V	55°48'N/25°50'E	13,650	1992
Sirveta	V	55°13'N/26°15'E	8,650	1992
Tytuvenai	V	55°35'N/23°17'E	11,430	1992
Varniai	V	55°43'N/22°20'E	16,000	1992
Veisiejai	V	54°06'N/23°45'E	12,200	1992

Venta	V	56°12'N/22°42'E	10,630	1992
Verkiai	V	54°48'N/25°18'E	2,300	1992
Vistytis	V	54°25'N/22°47'E	9,700	1992
Zagare	V	56°13'N/23°12'E	4,930	1992

LUXEMBOURG/LUXEMBURGO

	Summary	
Category I	0	0
Category II	0	0
Category III	0	0
Category IV	0	0
Category V	1	36,000
Total	**1**	**36,000**

Nature Park

Parc Germano-Luxembourgcois (Our)	V	49°53'N/6°10'E	36,000	1965

MACEDONIA (FORMER YUGOSLAV REPUBLIC OF)/
MACEDOINE, (EX-REPUBLIQUE YOUGOSLAVE DE)/
MACEDONIA (EX REPUBLICA YUGOSLAVIA DE)

	Summary	
Category I	0	0
Category II	3	108,338
Category III	5	47,515
Category IV	5	46,894
Category V	3	13,771
Total	**16**	**216,518**

Historical Sanctuary

Katlanovski predel	V	41°54'N/21°42'E	5,442	1991
Lopusnik - Memorijalen sapovcdnik na prirodata	V	41°30'N/20°16'E	2,887	1973

Landscape Park

Katlanovski predel	V	?/?	5,442	1991

National Park

Galicica	II	40°59'N/20°52'E	22,750	1958
Mavrovo	II	41°40'N/20°46'E	73,088	1949
Pelister	II	40°57'N/21°14'E	12,500	1948

Natural Monument

Dojransko Ezcro	III	41°13'N/22°45'E	2,730	1970
Markovi Kuli	III	41°24'N/21°33'E	2,320	1967
Ohridsko Ezero	III	41°03'N/20°47'E	23,000	1958
Prespansko Ezero	III	40°57'N/21°03'E	17,680	1977
Suma od Krivulj na Jakupica	III	41°44'N/21°26'E	1,785	1970

Nature Reserve

Jorgov kamen	IV	41°12'N/21°01'E	1,500	1988
Korab	IV	41°40'N/20°34'E	2,601	1988
Ohrid (Ohridsko) jezero	IV	41°03'N/20°47'E	38,000	1958
Planina Vodno	IV	41°58'N/21°24'E	2,840	1970
Senecka planina	IV	41°39'N/20°39'E	1,953	1988

MADAGASCAR

	Summary	
Category I	10	568,802
Category II	6	171,307
Category III	0	0
Category IV	21	375,190
Category V	0	0
Total	**37**	**1,115,299**

National Park

Isalo	II	22°26'S/49°16'E	81,540	1962
Mananara marin	II	16°20'S/49°51'E	1,000	1989
Mananara terrestre	II	16°20'S/49°43'E	23,000	1990
Mantadia	II	17°11'S/49°11'E	10,000	1989
Montagne d'Ambre	II	12°36'S/49°09'E	18,200	1958
Ranomafana	II	21°16'S/47°26'E	37,567	1991

Special Reserve

Ambatovaky	IV	16°55'S/48°35'E	60,050	1958
Ambohijanahary	IV	18°20'S/45°30'E	24,750	1958
Ambohitantely	IV	18°10'S/47°12'E	5,600	1982
Analamerana	IV	12°50'S/49°20'E	34,700	1956
Andranomena	IV	20°15'S/44°30'E	6,420	1958
Anjanaharibe-Sud	IV	14°45'S/49°20'E	32,100	1958
Ankarana	IV	13°05'S/49°20'E	18,220	1956
Bemarivo	IV	17°00'S/44°20'E	11,570	1956
Bora	IV	14°59'S/48°14'E	4,780	1956
Cap Sainte Marie	IV	25°36'S/49°09'E	1,750	1962
Foret d'Ambre	IV	12°30'S/49°10'E	4,810	1958
Kalambatritra	IV	23°30'S/46°20'E	28,250	1959
Kasijy	IV	16°50'S/46°00'E	18,800	1956
Mangerivola	IV	18°26'S/48°54'E	11,900	1958
Maningozo	IV	17°00'S/45°10'E	7,900	1956
Manombo	IV	22°30'S/47°20'E	5,020	1962
Manongarivo	IV	14°10'S/48°00'E	35,250	1956
Marotandrano	IV	17°50'S/47°40'E	42,200	1956
Nosy Mangabé	IV	15°25'S/49°45'E	520	1965
Pic d'Ivohibe	IV	22°32'S/46°59'E	3,450	1964
Tampoketsa d'Analamaitso	IV	16°15'S/48°00'E	17,150	1958

Strict Nature Reserve

Andohahela	I	24°44'S/46°42'E	76,020	1939
Andringitra	I	22°14'S/46°55'E	31,160	1927
Ankarafantsika	I	16°11'S/46°34'E	60,520	1927
Betampona	I	17°53'S/49°14'E	2,228	1927
Marojejy	I	14°29'S/49°43'E	60,150	1952
Tsaratanana	I	13°57'S/48°52'E	48,622	1927
Tsimanampetsotsa	I	24°07'S/43°44'E	43,200	1927
Tsingy de Bemaraha	I	18°40'S/44°46'E	152,000	1927
Tsingy de Namoroka	I	16°25'S/45°21'E	21,742	1927
Zahamena	I	17°35'S/48°58'E	73,160	1927

MALAWI

		Summary		
Category I	0	0		
Category II	5	696,200		
Category III	0	0		
Category IV	4	362,300		
Category V	0	0		
Total	**9**	**1,058,500**		

National Park

Kasungu	II	13°00'S/33°10'E	231,600	1970
Lake Malawi	II	14°02'S/34°53'E	8,700	1980
Lengwe	II	16°15'S/34°45'E	88,700	1970
Liwonde	II	14°50'S/35°20'E	53,800	1973
Nyika	II	10°40'S/33°45'E	313,400	1965

Wildlife Reserve

Majete	IV	16°00'S/34°45'E	70,000	1955
Mwabvi	IV	16°40'S/35°05'E	13,500	1953
Nkhota-Kota	IV	13°00'S/34°00'E	180,200	1954
Vwaza Marsh	IV	11°00'S/33°20'E	98,600	1977

MALAYSIA/MALAISIE/MALASIA

		Summary	
Category I	28	90,070	
Category II	16	814,009	
Category III	0	0	
Category IV	9	579,745	
Category V	1	1,011	
Total	**54**	**1,484,835**	

Peninsular Malaysia/Péninsule Malaise/Malasia Peninsular

National Park

Taman Negara	II	4°40'N/102°30'E	434,351	1939

Park

Templer	V	3°16'N/101°38'E	1,011	1956

Virgin Jungle Reserve

Berembun	I	2°51'N/102°04'E	1,619	1959
Bukit Larut	I	4°50'N/100°48'E	2,747	1962
Gunung Jerai	I	5°48'N/100°27'E	1,569	1960
Gunung Ledang	I	2°21'N/102°35'E	1,134	1969

Wildlife Reserve

Endau-Kluang	IV	?/?	101,174	1933
Endau-Kota Tinggi (East)	IV	?/?	7,413	1933
Endau-Kota Tinggi (West)	IV	?/?	61,959	1933
Krau	IV	3°44'N/102°11'E	53,095	1923
Sungei Dusun	IV	3°39'N/101°22'E	4,330	1964

Wildlife Sanctuary

Cameron Highlands	IV	4°30'N/101°30'E	64,953	1962

Sabah

National Park

Crocker Range	II	5°33'N/116°08'E	139,919	1984

Park

Bukit Tawau	II	4°20'N/117°54'E	27,972	1979
Kinabalu	II	6°00'N/116°30'E	75,370	1964
Pulau Penyu (Turtle Islands)	II	6°10'N/118°05'E	1,740	1977
Pulau Tiga	II	5°44'N/115°40'E	15,864	1978
Tunku Abdul Rahman	II	6°00'N/116°02'E	4,929	1974

Virgin Jungle Reserve

Brantian-Tatulit	I	4°40'N/117°33'E	4,140	1984
Crocker Range	I	5°53'N/116°16'E	3,279	1984
Gomantong,Materis,Bod Tai,Keruak,Pangi	I	5°32'N/118°13'E	1,816	1984
Kabili Sepilok	I	5°49'N/117°57'E	4,294	1931
Kalumpang	I	4°34'N/118°15'E	3,768	1984
Lungmanis	I	5°45'N/117°40'E	6,735	1984
Madai Baturong	I	4°44'N/118°09'E	5,867	1984
Maligan	I	4°34'N/115°38'E	9,240	1984
Mengalong	I	5°00'N/115°29'E	1,008	1984
Milian-Labau	I	5°05'N/116°32'E	2,812	1984
Pin-Supi	I	5°28'N/117°57'E	4,696	1984
Pulau Batik	I	4°43'N/118°27'E	353	1984
Pulau Berhala	I	5°51'N/118°09'E	173	1984
Pulau Sakar	I	4°58'N/118°20'E	760	1984
Sepagaya	I	4°59'N/118°07'E	4,128	1984
Sepilok (Mangrove)	I	5°48'N/117°57'E	1,235	1931
Sungai Imbak	I	5°05'N/117°00'E	18,113	1984
Sungai Kapur	I	5°20'N/118°56'E	1,250	1984
Sungai Lokan	I	5°29'N/117°40'E	1,852	1984
Sungai Siliawan	I	4°45'N/116°33'E	2,136	1992
Sungai Simpang	I	5°22'N/118°25'E	1,149	1984
Tabawan,Bohayan,Maganting,Silumpat Islands	I	4°48'N/118°23'E	1,009	1984

Wildlife Reserve

Tabin	IV	5°15'N/118°45'E	111,971	1984

Sarawak

National Park

Bako	II	1°43'N/110°31'E	2,728	1957
Batang Ai	II	1°19'N/112°07'E	24,040	1990
Gunung Gading	II	1°42'N/109°50'E	4,106	1983
Gunung Mulu	II	4°06'N/114°53'E	52,865	1974
Kubah	II	1°36'N/110°10'E	2,230	1989
Lambir Hills	II	4°13'N/113°59'E	6,952	1975
Loagan Bunut	II	3°48'N/114°13'E	10,736	1991
Niah	II	3°50'N/113°52'E	3,140	1974
Similajau	II	3°26'N/113°15'E	7,067	1979

Wildlife Sanctuary

Lanjak-Entimau	IV	1°35'N/112°09'E	168,758	1983
Samunsam	IV	1°57'N/109°35'E	6,092	1979

MALDIVES/MALDIVAS

No Areas Listed

MALI

	Summary	
Category I	0	0
Category II	1	350,000
Category III	0	0
Category IV	10	3,661,989
Category V	0	0
Total	**11**	**4,011,989**

Faunal Reserve

Badinko	IV	14°04'N/8°54'W	193,000	1951
Bafing Makana	IV	12°38'N/10°20'W	158,989	1990
Banifing-Baoulé	IV	?/?	13,000	1954
Douentza	IV	?/?	1,200,000	1960
Fenié-Baoulé	IV	13°45'N/10°25'W	67,500	1952
Fina	IV	14°04'N/8°54'W	136,000	1954
Kongossambougou	IV	14°04'N/8°54'W	92,000	1955
Sousan	IV	13°30'N/10°20'W	37,600	1954
Talikourou	IV	?/?	13,900	1953

National Park

Boucle du Baoulé	II	14°04'N/8°54'W	350,000	1954

Partial Faunal Reserve

Ansongo-Menaka	IV	?/?	1,750,000	1956

MALTA/MALTE

No Areas Listed

MARSHALL ISLANDS/ ILES MARSHALL/ ISLAS MARSHALL

No Areas Listed

MAURITANIA/MAURITANIE

	Summary	
Category I	1	310,000
Category II	2	1,186,000
Category III	0	0
Category IV	1	250,000
Category V	0	0
Total	**4**	**1,746,000**

Integral Reserve

Baie du Levrier (Cap Blanc)	I	21°00'N/17°00'W	310,000	1986

National Park

Banc d'Arguin	II	20°36'N/16°23'W	1,173,000	1976
Diawling	II	16°26'N/16°21'W	13,000	1990

Partial Faunal Reserve

El Agher	IV	?/?	250,000	1937

MAURITIUS/MAURICE/MAURICIO

	Summary	
Category I	0	0
Category II	0	0
Category III	0	0
Category IV	3	4,023
Category V	0	0
Total	**3**	**4,023**

Nature Reserve

Ile Plate (Flat Island)	IV	19°53'S/57°39'E	253	1972
Ile Ronde (Round Island)	IV	19°51'S/57°47'E	159	1957
Macchabee-Bel Ombre	IV	20°25'S/57°26'E	3,611	1951

MEXICO/MEXIQUE

	Summary	
Category I	6	316,498
Category II	33	1,597,788
Category III	3	9,558
Category IV	12	3,886,725
Category V	11	3,918,163
Total	**65**	**9,728,732**

Aquatic and Wild Flora and Fauna Protection Area

Chan-Kin	IV	16°36'N/90°43'W	12,184	1992
Corredor Biológico Chichinautzin	IV	19°10'N/99°10'W	37,302	1988

Biosphere Reserve

Calakmul	V	18°23'N/89°40'W	723,185	1989
El Triunfo	I	15°40'N/92°53'W	119,177	1972
El Vizcaíno	V	28°14'N/114°44'W	2,546,790	1988
La Michilía	V	23°27'N/104°15'W	35,000	1977
Lacan-Tun	V	16°20'N/90°52'W	6,833	1992
Mapimí	V	26°42'N/103°42'W	20,000	1977
Montes Azules (Selva Lacandona)	II	16°27'N/91°09'W	331,200	1978
Pantanos de Centla	V	18°16'N/92°30'W	302,706	1992
Sian Ka'an	II	19°35'N/87°44'W	528,147	1986
Sierra de Manantlán	V	19°30'N/104°20'W	139,577	1987

Marine National Park

Sistema Arrecifal Veracruzano	II	19°05'N/95°55'W	52,238	1992

Marine Reserve

La Blanquilla	IV	?/?	66,868	1975

Natural and Typical Biotope

La Encrucijada	IV	15°12'N/92°53'W	30,000	1972

Natural Monument

Bonampak	III	16°40'N/91°05'W	4,357	1992
Cerro de la Silla	I	25°30'N/10°01'W	6,045	1991
Yaxchilán	III	16°53'N/90°56'W	2,621	1992

National Park

Benito Juárez	II	17°10'N/96°40'W	2,737	1937
Bosencheve	II	19°29'N/100°11'W	15,000	1940
Cascada de Bassaseachic	II	28°10'N/108°12'W	5,802	1981
Cañón de Río Blanco	II	18°45'N/97°10'W	55,690	1938

Cañón del Sumidero	II	16°50'N/93°06'W	21,789	1980
Cerro de la Estrella	II	19°20'N/99°05'W	1,100	1938
Constitución de 1857	II	32°03'N/115°57'W	5,009	1962
Cumbres de Majalca	II	28°45'N/106°29'W	4,772	1939
Cumbres de Monterrey	II	25°43'N/100°44'W	246,500	1939
El Chico	II	20°11'N/98°44'W	2,739	1982
El Cimatario	II	20°31'N/100°20'W	2,447	1982
El Gogorrón	II	21°45'N/100°45'W	25,000	1936
El Potosí	II	22°01'N/99°58'W	2,000	1936
El Tepozteco	II	19°03'N/98°59'W	24,000	1957
El Veladero	II	16°52'N/99°53'W	3,159	1980
Insurgente José María Morelos y Pavón	II	19°37'N/100°59'W	1,813	1939
Insurgente Miguel Hidalgo y Costilla	II	19°17'N/99°21'W	1,750	1936
Isla Isabela	II	21°55'N/105°55'W	194	1980
Iztaccihuatl-Popocatepetl	II	19°07'N/98°38'W	25,679	1935
La Malinche	II	19°14'N/98°00'W	45,711	1938
Lagunas de Chacahua	II	16°00'N/97°40'W	14,187	1937
Lagunas de Montebello	II	16°08'N/91°45'W	6,022	1959
Lagunas de Zempoala	II	19°04'N/99°19'W	4,669	1936
Los Mármoles	II	20°55'N/99°01'W	23,150	1936
Nevado de Toluca	II	19°06'N/99°44'W	51,000	1936
Palenque	V	17°29'N/92°03'W	1,772	1981
Pico de Orizaba	II	19°01'N/97°16'W	19,750	1937
Pico de Tancitaro	II	19°23'N/102°24'W	29,316	1940
Volcán Nevado de Colima	II	19°32'N/103°37'W	22,200	1936
Zoquiapán y Anexas	II	19°20'N/98°45'W	19,418	1937

Park

Omiltemi	II	17°30'N/99°40'W	3,600	?

Refuge

La Mojonera	IV	?/?	9,201	1981
La Primavera	IV	?/?	30,500	1980
Sierra de Alvarez	IV	?/?	16,900	1981
Sierra del Pinacate	IV	31°51'N/113°32'W	28,660	1979
Valle de los Cirios	IV	?/?	3,500,000	1980

Special Biosphere Reserve

Cascadas de Agua Azul	III	17°15'N/92°03'W	2,580	1980
Isla Contoy	I	21°30'N/86°49'W	176	1961
Isla Guadalupe	I	29°02'N/118°22'W	25,000	1922
Isla Tiburón	V	28°55'N/112°20'W	120,800	1963
Islas del Golfo de California	I	29°15'N/113°30'W	150,000	1978
Mariposa Monarca	I	19°35'N/100°15'W	16,100	1980
Ría Celestún	IV	20°55'N/90°23'W	59,130	1979
Ría Lagartos	IV	21°30'N/87°52'W	47,840	1979
Selva El Ocote	IV	17°05'N/93°40'W	48,140	1982
Sierra de Santa Martha	V	18°21'N/94°50'W	20,000	1980
Volcán de San Martín	V	18°32'N/95°10'W	1,500	1979

MICRONESIA, FEDERATED STATES OF/
MICRONESIE, ETATS FEDERES DE/
MICRONESIA, ESTADOS FEDERADOS DE

No Areas Listed

MOLDOVA, REPUBLIC OF/
REPUBLIQUE DE MOLDOVA/
REPUBLICA DE MOLDOVA

Summary		
Category I	2	6,200
Category II	0	0
Category III	0	0
Category IV	0	0
Category V	0	0
Total	**2**	**6,200**

Zapovednik

Kodry	I	44°42'N/28°01'E	5,200	1971
Yagorlyk	I	39°56'N/28°31'E	1,000	1988

MONACO

No Areas Listed

MONGOLIA/MONGOLIE

Summary		
Category I	12	224,280
Category II	2	5,393,560
Category III	0	0
Category IV	0	0
Category V	1	550,000
Total	**15**	**6,167,840**

National Park

Ar-Toul	II	48°20'N/107°50'E	93,560	1984
Dzungarian Gobi Wildlife Reserve	V	45°00'N/93°00'E	550,000	1976
Transalti Gobi	II	43°25'N/97°20'E	5,300,000	1975

Reserve

Batkhan	I	47°16'N/104°00'E	2,000	1957
Bogdkhan	I	47°57'N/107°00'E	4,080	1978
Bogdo-ula	I	47°54'N/106°21'E	54,100	1778
Bulgan-gol	I	46°21'N/91°21'E	2,700	1965
Bulgan-ula	I	47°36'N/101°46'E	4,800	1965
Khasagt-Khayrkhan	I	46°15'N/96°39'E	33,600	1965
Khorgo	I	48°14'N/99°15'E	20,000	1965
Lkhachinvandan-ula	I	45°57'N/115°20'E	75,000	1965
Nagalkhan	I	47°34'N/106°36'E	2,000	1957
Tulga-togo-Zhallavch-ula	I	48°53'N/101°49'E	3,000	1965
Uran-ula	I	49°05'N/102°05'E	3,000	1965
Yolyn-am	I	43°51'N/104°24'E	20,000	1965

MOROCCO/MAROC/MARRUECOS

Summary		
Category I	5	55,320
Category II	0	0
Category III	0	0
Category IV	3	237,000
Category V	2	69,800
Total	**10**	**362,120**

Biological Reserve

Bokkoyas	I	35°14'N/35°6'W	43,000	1986
Khnifiss/Puerto Cansado	I	27°58'N/12°55'W	6,500	1962
Merja Zerga	IV	34°50'N/6°20'W	7,000	1978

Botanical Reserve

Talassantane	I	35°10'N/5°16'W	2,603	1972

National Park

Souss-Massa	V	30°02'N/9°40'W	33,800	1991
Toubkal	V	31°05'N/7°57'W	36,000	1942

Permanent Hunting Reserve

Bouarfa	IV	32°30'N/1°59'W	220,000	1967
Iriki	IV	29°50'N/5°35'W	10,000	1967
Sidi Chiker (M'Sabih Talaa)	I	31°45'N/8°38'W	1,987	1952
Takherkhort	I	31°08'N/8°00'W	1,230	1967

MOZAMBIQUE

Summary		
Category I	0	0
Category II	0	0
Category III	0	0
Category IV	1	2,000
Category V	0	0
Total	**1**	**2,000**

Faunal Reserve

Ilhas da Inhaca e dos Portugueses	IV	26°03'S/32°57'E	2,000	1965

MYANMAR

Summary		
Category I	0	0
Category II	1	160,580
Category III	0	0
Category IV	0	0
Category V	1	12,691
Total	**2**	**173,271**

National Park

Alaungdaw Kathapa	II	22°25'N/94°26'E	160,580	1984

Park

Popa Mountain Park	V	?/?	12,691	1985

NAMIBIA/NAMIBIE

Summary		
Category I	0	0
Category II	5	8,975,751
Category III	1	24,462
Category IV	4	434,664
Category V	2	782,900
Total	**12**	**10,217,777**

Game Park

Daan Viljoen	IV	22°30'S/16°54'E	3,953	1968
Khaudom	IV	18°50'S/20°48'E	384,162	1989

Mahango	III	18°23'S/21°41'E	24,462	1989
Namib Naukluft	II	24°40'S/15°16'E	4,976,800	1979
Skeleton Coast	II	19°14'S/12°48'E	1,639,000	1971
Waterberg Plateau	IV	20°25'S/17°18'E	40,549	1972

National Park

Etosha	II	18°56'S/15°42'E	2,227,000	1907
Mamili	II	18°23'S/23°38'E	100,959	1990
Mudumu	II	18°04'S/23°34'E	31,992	1990

Nature Reserve

Cape Cross Seal	IV	21°50'S/14°07'E	6,000	1969

Recreation Area

National Diamond Coast	V	26°53'S/15°07'E	2,900	1977
National West Coast Tourist	V	21°53'S/14°14'E	780,000	1973

NAURU

No Areas Listed

NEPAL

Summary		
Category I	0	0
Category II	8	1,014,400
Category III	0	0
Category IV	4	94,100
Category V	0	0
Total	**12**	**1,108,500**

National Park

Khaptad	II	29°22'N/81°07'E	22,500	1986
Langtang	II	28°10'N/85°38'E	171,000	1976
Makalu-Barun	II	27°45'N/87°00'E	150,000	1991
Rara	II	29°34'N/82°05'E	10,600	1977
Royal Bardia	II	28°28'N/81°28'E	96,800	1988
Royal Chitwan	II	27°28'N/84°20'E	93,200	1973
Sagarmatha	II	27°56'N/86°48'E	114,800	1976
Shey-Phoksundo	II	29°26'N/82°56'E	355,500	1984

Wildlife Reserve

Koshi Tappu	IV	26°38'N/87°00'E	17,500	1976
Parsa	IV	27°28'N/84°20'E	49,900	1984
Royal Sukla Phanta	IV	28°53'N/80°11'E	15,500	1976
Shivapuri	IV	27°48'N/85°20'E	11,200	1985

NETHERLANDS/PAYS-BAS/PAISES BAJOS

Summary		
Category I	3	4,211
Category II	6	21,370
Category III	23	226,195
Category IV	47	136,765
Category V	0	0
Total	**79**	**388,541**

National Park

De Biesbosch	IV	51°45'N/4°48'E	7,100	1987
De Groote Peel	IV	51°20'N/5°45'E	1,440	1987
De Hamert	II	51°34'N/6°07'E	1,560	1989

De Meijnweg	IV	51°11'N/6°08'E	1,600	1990
De Weerribben	IV	52°48'N/5°57'E	3,450	1992
Dwingelderveld	IV	52°50'N/6°26'E	3,600	1986
Hoge Veluwe	II	52°05'N/5°46'E	5,400	1935
Kennemerduinen	II	?/?	1,250	1950
Schiermonnikoog	II	53°30'N/6°15'E	5,400	1984
Veluwezoom	IV	52°05'N/6°09'E	4,800	1930
Zuid-Kennemerland	IV	52°25'N/4°35'E	2,090	1990
Natural Monument				
Berkheide	III	?/?	1,000	1990
Boschplaat	III	53°27'N/5°30'E	4,400	1974
Deurnse Peel	III	?/?	1,500	1980
Dollard	III	53°17'N/7°07'E	5,000	1977
Eemmeer	III	?/?	1,200	1976
Engbertsdjiksvenen	III	?/?	1,000	1985
Gras- & Rietgorzen Haringvliet	III	?/?	1,030	1971
Kop van Schouwen	III	?/?	2,200	1988
Krammer-Volkerak	III	51°39'N/4°15'E	3,430	1988
Kwelders Friesland	III	?/?	1,370	1982
Kwelders Groningen	III	?/?	1,230	1982
Mariapeel	III	51°27'N/5°51'E	1,100	1976
Markiezaatsmeer Zuid	III	?/?	1,860	1985
Mispeleindse -/Landschotse Heide	III	?/?	1,135	1983
Oosterschelde	III	51°33'N/4°00'E	24,000	1990
Oostvaardersplassen	III	?/?	5,600	1986
Schorren van de Eendracht	III	?/?	1,000	1982
Ventjagersplaten & Slijkplaat	III	?/?	1,090	1980
Verdronken Land van Saeftinghe	III	?/?	3,500	1976
Waddenzee	III	53°13'N/5°59'E	154,800	1981
Zwarte Meer	III	52°37'N/5°50'E	1,650	1990
Nature Reserve				
Alde Feanen and De Deelen	IV	?/?	1,850	?
Ameland	IV	53°28'N/5°45'E	4,500	?
Amsterdamse Waterleiding Duinen	IV	52°20'N/4°33'E	3,370	?
Ankeveense-Kortenhoefse-Loosdrechtse Plassen	IV	?/?	1,450	1969
Bargerveen	IV	52°41'N/7°02'E	2,100	?
Berkenheuvel	IV	52°49'N/6°15'E	1,000	1956
Bocht van Molkwerum & Steile Bank	IV	?/?	2,500	?
Boswachterij Schoorl	IV	52°35'N/4°37'E	2,000	1894
De Geul en Westerduinen	I	53°00'N/4°45'E	1,681	1926
Deelerwoud	IV	?/?	1,150	?
Diependal	IV	?/?	1,310	?
Duinen Terschelling	IV	53°26'N/5°20'E	9,500	?
Duinen Texel	IV	53°06'N/4°45'E	2,300	?
Duinen Vlieland	IV	53°15'N/4°58'E	5,000	?
Eierlands Gat Zeehondenreservaat	IV	?/?	20,000	1947
Fochteloerveen	IV	53°00'N/6°25'E	1,715	1972
Goois	III	52°15'N/5°11'E	1,500	1987
Haarler & Holterberg	IV	52°21'N/6°25'E	1,600	?
Hardenberg	IV	?/?	1,190	?
Haringvliet Forelands	IV	51°48'N/4°11'E	3,600	?
Jisperveld	IV	52°31'N/4°48'E	1,516	1961
Kampina & Oisterwijkse Vennen	IV	?/?	2,000	?
Kootwijkerzand/Garderen	IV	?/?	1,500	?
Lauwersmeer	IV	53°22'N/6°14'E	2,500	?
Leuvenhorst & Leuvenumse Bos	IV	52°15'N/5°47'E	1,855	?
Loonse & Drunense Duinen	IV	51°39'N/5°06'E	1,730	?
Makkumerwaard, Kooiwaard & Workumerwaard	IV	?/?	1,375	?
Meijendel	IV	52°09'N/4°21'E	2,000	?

Meijnweg	IV	51°11'N/60°8'E	1,015	?
Mokkebank	IV	?/?	2,000	?
Nieuwkoopse Plassen	IV	52°09'N/4°46'E	1,500	1968
Noordhollands	IV	?/?	4,800	?
North Veluwe	IV	?/?	2,850	1954
Oerd en Steile Bank	I	53°17'N/5°00'E	1,200	?
Oostvaardersplassen	III	52°27'N/5°20'E	5,600	?
Planken Wambuis	IV	?/?	1,965	?
Schouwen Duinen	IV	?/?	3,064	1980
Slikken van Flakkee	IV	?/?	3,700	?
Strabrechtse Heide	IV	51°23'N/5°47'E	1,020	1951
Stroomdallandschap Drenthse Aa	IV	53°04'N/6°40'E	1,750	1965
Tjonger- & Lindevallei	IV	52°53'N/5°59'E	1,000	?
Varkensland & Waterland	IV	?/?	1,010	?
Voornes Duin	IV	?/?	1,400	?
Wassenaarse Duinen	I	52°08'N/4°24'E	1,330	?
Wieden	IV	?/?	5,000	?

Aruba

No Areas Listed

Netherlands Antilles/
Antilles néerlandaises/
Antillas Holandesas

National Park

Christoffel (Curacao)	II	12°21'N/69°07'W	1,860	1978
Washington-Slagbaai (Bonaire)	II	12°14'N/68°23'W	5,900	1969

NEW ZEALAND/
NOUVELLE-ZELANDE/
NUEVA ZELANDIA

Summary		
Category I	102	1,693,285
Category II	30	4,214,581
Category III	7	23,545
Category IV	66	216,223
Category V	0	0
Total	**205**	**6,147,634**

Conservation Park (Forest Park)

Catlins	II	46°30'S/169°19'E	60,588	1974
Coromandel	II	37°08'S/175°41'E	74,961	1972
Craigieburn	II	43°07'S/171°40'E	44,165	1967
Haurangi	II	41°27'S/175°19'E	18,382	1974
Kaimai Mamaku	II	37°47'S/175°56'E	39,682	1975
Kaimanawa	II	39°08'S/175°56'E	76,684	1969
Kaweka	II	39°19'S/176°21'E	66,972	1974
Lake Sumner	II	42°42'S/172°12'E	105,771	1974
Mt Richmond	II	41°23'S/173°24'E	188,392	1977
North West Nelson	II	41°02'S/172°31'E	421,200	1970
Pirongia	II	37°59'S/175°02'E	17,141	1971
Pureora	II	38°33'S/175°34'E	80,344	1978
Raukumara	II	37°58'S/177°53'E	115,102	1979
Rimutaka	II	41°16'S/175°04'E	14,771	1972
Ruahine	II	39°54'S/176°07'E	93,260	1976
Tararua	II	40°47'S/175°25'E	117,226	1967
Victoria	II	42°10'S/172°02'E	210,731	1981

Ecological Area

Ajax	I	?/?	9,200	1984

Big River	I	42°17'S/171°52'E	6,733	1980
Blackwater	I	41°56'S/171°45'E	9,150	1980
Card Creek	I	?/?	2,870	1983
Central Maruia	I	?/?	6,646	1983
Coal Creek	I	41°59'S/172°00'E	3,025	1980
Diggers Ridge	I	45°51'S/167°35'E	4,325	1982
Dunsdale	I	?/?	3,217	1984
Flatstaff	I	42°28'S/171°44'E	1,622	1980
Fletchers Creek	I	41°59'S/171°47'E	2,586	1980
Greenstone	I	42°36'S/171°14'E	1,144	1980
Heaphy	I	?/?	26,377	1986
Hokaihaha	I	?/?	1,445	1985
Kaihu	I	?/?	2,425	1984
Kapowai	I	37°01'S/175°47'E	1,477	1982
Kohaihai	I	?/?	1,288	1986
Kopuapounamu	I	?/?	1,148	1985
Lake Christabel	I	42°24'S/172°10'E	10,648	1981
Lake Hochstetter	I	42°24'S/171°37'E	1,803	1981
Lillburn	I	45°56'S/167°25'E	2,670	1982
Manganuiowae	I	35°12'S/173°55'E	1,760	1981
Mangatutu	I	38°20'S/175°29'E	2,533	1980
Mangawaru	I	?/?	2,634	1986
Maramataha	I	?/?	6,772	1985
Mathias	I	?/?	1,538	1984
Moehau	I	36°32'S/175°23'E	3,634	1977
Mount Hobson/Kaitoke Swamp	I	?/?	1,085	1985
Onekura	I	35°12'S/173°45'E	2,351	1981
Opuiaki	I	?/?	3,816	1984
Oriuwaka	I	?/?	1,650	1983
Otupaka	I	?/?	1,880	1985
Papakai	I	36°56'S/175°36'E	3,366	1982
Paraumu	I	?/?	1,590	1986
Pororari	I	42°08'S/171°28'E	6,448	1980
Pukepoto	I	38°59'S/175°32'E	1,906	1980
Puketoetoe	I	?/?	1,925	1986
Pureora Mountain	I	?/?	2,257	1986
Raukokere	I	?/?	3,590	1986
Roaring Meg	I	42°18'S/171°24'E	3,600	1980
Saltwater	I	43°04'S/170°25'E	1,738	1981
Saxton	I	42°12'S/171°31'E	4,120	1980
Tautuku	I	?/?	5,836	1984
Te Kohu	I	?/?	2,180	1983
Tiropahi	I	41°59'S/171°28'E	3,451	1980
Tuwatawata	I	?/?	2,346	1984
Upper Hope	I	?/?	5,980	1986
Waihaha	I	?/?	11,920	1985
Waikoau	I	46°03'S/167°22'E	2,800	1982
Waiomu	I	?/?	1,080	1985
Waipapa	I	38°28'S/175°35'E	1,696	1979
Waipuna	I	42°23'S/171°45'E	1,910	1980
Whanokoa	I	?/?	4,406	1986
Whenuakura	I	?/?	1,764	1985
Marine Park				
Mimiwhangata	IV	?/?	2,000	1984
Sugarloaf Islands	IV	?/?	800	1991
Marine Reserve				
Kapiti Island	I	40°51'S/174°55'E	2,167	1975
Kermadec Islands	I	?/?	748,000	1990
Poor Knights Islands	I	35°28'S/174°44'E	2,410	1981
Tonga Island	I	?/?	1,835	1993
Tuhua	I	?/?	1,060	1992

National Park

Abel Tasman	II	40°34'S/172°56'E	22,543	1942
Arthur's Pass	II	42°53'S/171°40'E	99,195	1929
Egmont	II	39°15'S/174°04'E	33,540	1900
Fiordland	II	45°27'S/167°20'E	1,257,000	1904
Mount Aspiring	II	44°22'S/168°53'E	355,518	1964
Mount Cook	II	43°36'S/170°18'E	69,923	1953
Nelson Lakes	II	41°58'S/172°45'E	101,753	1956
Paparoa	II	?/?	30,560	1987
Tongariro	II	39°11'S/175°35'E	76,504	1894
Urewera	II	38°32'S/177°02'E	212,600	1954
Westland	II	43°29'S/170°05'E	117,547	1960
Whanganui	II	39°25'S/174°55'E	74,231	1986

National Park Special Area

Secretary Island	I	45°14'S/166°59'E	8,980	1973
Sinbad Gully Stream	I	44°47'S/167°50'E	2,160	1974
Solander Island	I	46°34'S/166°54'E	120	1973
Takahe Fiordland	I	45°23'S/167°32'E	177,252	1953
Slip Stream	I	44°35'S/168°19'E	1,722	1973

National Park Wilderness Area

Glaisnock	I	?/?	124,800	1974
Hauhangatahi	I	?/?	8,500	1966
Otebake	I	?/?	12,100	1955
Pembroke	I	?/?	18,000	1974
Te Tatou Pounamu	I	?/?	6,500	1962

National Reserve

Lewis Pass	II	42°26'S/172°20'E	18,295	1907

Nature Reserve

Alderman Islands	I	36°58'S/176°05'E	134	1971
Anglem	I	46°47'S/167°53'E	16,997	1907
Antipodes Islands	I	49°40'S/178°50'E	2,100	1961
Auckland Islands	I	50°45'S/166°00'E	62,564	1934
Bench Island	I	46°55'S/168°15'E	121	1926
Bounty Islands	I	47°42'S/179°03'E	135	1961
Campbell Islands	I	52°33'S/169°09'E	11,331	1954
Chetwode Islands	I	40°53'S/174°05'E	324	1962
Codfish Island	I	?/?	1,396	1915
Cuvier Islands	I	36°26'S/175°47'E	194	1951
Double and Stanley Islands	I	36°38'S/175°54'E	120	1963
Farewell Spit	I	40°33'S/172°56'E	11,423	1938
Hen and Chickens Islands	I	35°55'S/174°45'E	844	1928
Kapiti Island	I	?/?	1,761	1975
Little Barrier Island	I	36°12'S/175°07'E	2,817	1895
Mangere Island	I	44°17'S/176°18'E	113	1967
Mokohinau Islands	I	35°56'S/175°07'E	108	1888
Mount Uwerau	I	42°15'S/173°35'E	1,012	1966
Pegasus	I	47°07'S/167°46'E	67,441	1907
Poor Knights Islands	I	35°28'S/174°44'E	271	1975
Rangatira (South East Island)	I	44°21'S/176°11'E	219	1967
Raoul Island and Kermadec Group Nature Reserve	I	29°32'S/177°18'E	3,280	1934
Snares Islands	I	48°02'S/166°33'E	243	1961
Three Kings	I	34°10'S/172°06'E	685	1956
Tuku	I	?/?	1,238	1987
Waitangiroto	I	43°09'S/171°45'E	1,230	1957

Sanctuary Area

Hihitahi	I	39°33'S/175°44'E	2,170	1973
Ngatukituki	I	37°33'S/176°49'E	1,600	1973
Waipoua	I	35°36'S/173°33'E	9,105	1952

Scenic Reserve

Arapawa Island	IV	41°09'S/174°21'E	1,035	1973
Blumine Island	IV	41°10'S/174°14'E	377	1912
Chance, Penguin and Fairy Bays	IV	41°08'S/173°50'E	1,599	1903
Chaslands	IV	46°35'S/169°13'E	1,334	1937
D'Urville Island	IV	40°51'S/173°52'E	4,072	1912
Glen Allen	IV	45°20'S/168°40'E	1,000	1914
Glenhope	IV	41°42'S/172°36'E	5,936	1907
Glory Cove	IV	47°00'S/168°07'E	1,297	1903
Gordon Park	IV	37°46'S/175°54'E	1,817	1938
Gouland Downs	IV	40°54'S/172°20'E	6,564	1917
Hakarimata	IV	37°38'S/175°08'E	1,795	1905
Isolated Hill	IV	41°55'S/173°59'E	2,160	1924
Jordan Stream	IV	42°14'S/173°43'E	1,151	1916
Karamea Bluff	IV	41°30'S/172°00'E	1,445	1910
Kenepuru Sound	IV	41°10'S/173°56'E	1,687	1895
Lake Ianthe	IV	43°03'S/170°38'E	1,308	1905
Lake Kaniere	III	42°50'S/171°09'E	7,252	1906
Lake Okareka	III	38°11'S/176°21'E	1,143	1930
Lake Okataina	III	38°07'S/176°25'E	4,388	1974
Lake Tarawera	III	38°11'S/176°29'E	5,819	1973
Leithen Bush	IV	45°46'S/169°02'E	1,342	1978
Lower Buller Gorge	IV	41°51'S/171°44'E	5,941	1907
Mangamuka Gorge	IV	35°11'S/173°29'E	2,832	1927
Matahuru	IV	37°23'S/175°14'E	1,336	1905
Maungatautari	III	28°02'S/175°34'E	2,389	1927
Maurihoro	IV	37°42'S/175°52'E	1,797	1936
Meremere Hill	IV	38°04'S/177°28'E	1,368	1982
Mocatoa	IV	38°25'S/174°48'E	1,212	1927
Mokau River	IV	38°43'S/174°46'E	2,273	1920
Mount Stokes	IV	41°05'S/174°06'E	4,396	1977
Mt Courtney	IV	41°50'S/171°58'E	1,772	1912
Mt Hercules	IV	43°11'S/170°27'E	8,024	1911
Mt Te Kinga	IV	42°39'S/171°29'E	3,747	1905
Nydia Bay	IV	41°10'S/173°46'E	1,408	1938
Paradise Bay	IV	41°13'S/173°50'E	2,743	1977
Paterson Inlet Islands	IV	46°55'S/168°03'E	126	1907
Pelorus Bridge	IV	41°19'S/173°33'E	1,010	1906
Pokaka	IV	39°18'S/176°25'E	8,068	1982
Port Pegasus Islands	IV	47°10'S/167°40'E	838	1907
Pryse Peak	IV	46°58'S/168°00'E	3,646	1903
Pukeamaru Range	IV	37°39'S/178°15'E	3,265	1907
Punakaiki	IV	42°00'S/171°20'E	2,037	1914
Rahu	IV	42°17'S/171°34'E	2,132	1936
Rakeahua	IV	46°52'S/167°58'E	6,463	1903
Rangitoto Island	III	36°47'S/174°51'E	2,333	1980
Robertson Range	IV	41°21'S/174°01'E	3,689	1912
Saltwater Lagoon	IV	43°05'S/170°22'E	1,359	1928
Ship Cove	IV	41°06'S/174°14'E	1,093	1896
South Cape	IV	47°12'S/167°37'E	5,077	1903
Tahuakai	IV	41°03'S/174°08'E	1,561	1983
Tangarakau	IV	39°00'S/174°52'E	2,640	1918
Tapuaenuku	IV	42°00'S/173°38'E	2,226	1962
Te Arowhenua	IV	41°44'S/173°22'E	1,705	1981
Te Kopia	IV	38°25'S/176°14'E	1,408	1911
Te Tapui	IV	37°50'S/175°38'E	2,382	1925
Tennyson Inlet	IV	41°06'S/173°46'E	5,596	1896
Toatoa	IV	38°09'S/177°32'E	2,847	1982
Ulva Island	IV	46°56'S/168°07'E	259	1922
Upper Buller Gorge	IV	41°47'S/172°08'E	5,920	1979
Waioeka Gorge	IV	38°14'S/177°21'E	18,645	1933
Waipapa	IV	38°20'S/175°41'E	2,528	1974

Waipori Falls	IV	45°56'S/170°00'E	1,352	1913
Waituhui Kuratau	IV	38°54'S/175°34'E	1,319	1953
Wanganui River	IV	39°22'S/175°09'E	35,858	1915
Warbeck River	IV	42°01'S/172°17'E	1,283	1931
Whangamumu	IV	35°15'S/174°18'E	2,154	1981

Scientific Reserve

Tiritiri Matangi Island	III	?/?	221	1980
Waituna Wetlands	I	46°37'S/168°40'E	3,596	1983

Wilderness Area

Hooker/Landsborough	I	?/?	41,000	1990
Raukaumara (Rankumarn FP)	I	?/?	39,650	1988
Tasman (North-West Nelson FP)	I	?/?	86,946	1988

Wildlife Refuge

Lake Alexandrina WR/McGregor's Lagoon	IV	43°57'S/170°27'E	2,200	1957
Pouto Point	IV	36°21'S/174°05'E	6,789	1957
Wairau River Lagoons	IV	41°32'S/174°06'E	1,040	1959
Whale (Motuhora) Island	IV	37°51'S/176°59'E	140	1953

Wildlife Sanctuary

Stephens Island (Taka Pourewa)	I	40°40'S/174°00'E	150	1966

Cook Islands/Iles Cook/Islas Cook

National Park

Suwarrow Atoll	IV	13°14'S/163°06'W	160	1978

Niue/Nioué/Isla Niue

No Areas Listed

Tokelau

No Areas Listed

NICARAGUA

Summary		
Category I	2	345,000
Category II	3	25,327
Category III	1	18,930
Category IV	53	514,193
Category V	0	0
Total	**59**	**903,450**

Biological Reserve

Cayos Miskitos	I	14°20'N/82°50'W	50,000	1991
Río Indio Maíz	I	?/?	295,000	1990

Genetic Reserve

Yucul	IV	?/?	4,826	1990

National Monument

Archipiélago de Solentiname	III	?/?	18,930	1990

National Park

Archipiélago Zapatera	II	?/?	5,227	1983
Saslaya	II	13°45'N/83°00'W	15,000	1971
Volcán Masaya	II	11°57'N/86°11'W	5,100	1979

Nature Reserve

Alamikamba	IV	?/?	2,100	1991

Apante	IV	?/?	1,230	1991
Cabo Viejo	IV	?/?	5,800	1991
Cerro Bana Cruz	IV	?/?	10,130	1991
Cerro Cola Blanca	IV	?/?	22,200	1991
Cerro Cumaica - Cerro Alegre	IV	?/?	5,000	1991
Cerro Datanli - El Diablo	IV	?/?	2,216	1991
Cerro Kilambe	IV	?/?	10,128	1991
Cerro Kuskawas	IV	?/?	4,760	1991
Cerro Musún	IV	?/?	4,142	1991
Cerro Quiabuc (Las Brisas)	IV	?/?	3,630	1991
Cerro Tisey - Estanzuela	IV	?/?	6,400	1991
Complejo Volcánico Momotombo y Momotombito	IV	?/?	8,500	1983
Complejo Volcánico Pilas - El Hoyo	IV	?/?	7,422	1983
Complejo Volcánico San Cristóbal	IV	?/?	17,950	1983
Complejo Volcánico Telica - Rota	IV	?/?	9,088	1983
Cordillera de Yolaina	IV	?/?	40,000	1991
Cordillera Dipilto y Jalapa	IV	?/?	41,200	1991
Delta del Estero Real	IV	12°53'N/87°15'W	55,000	1983
Estero Padre Ramos	IV	?/?	8,800	1983
Fila Cerro Frío - La Cumplida	IV	?/?	1,761	1991
Fila Masigüe	IV	?/?	4,580	1991
Guabule	IV	?/?	1,100	1991
Isla Juan Venado	IV	?/?	4,600	1983
Kligna	IV	?/?	1,000	1991
Laguna Bismuna-Raya	IV	14°47'N/83°22'W	11,800	1991
Laguna de Apoyo	IV	?/?	3,500	1991
Laguna de Mecatepe	IV	?/?	1,200	1983
Laguna de Pahara	IV	?/?	10,200	1991
Laguna de Tisma	IV	?/?	10,295	1983
Laguna Kukalaya	IV	?/?	3,500	1991
Laguna Layasica	IV	?/?	1,800	1991
Laguna Tala - Sulamas	IV	?/?	31,400	1991
Laguna Yulu Karata	IV	?/?	25,300	1991
Limbaika	IV	?/?	1,800	1991
Llanos de Karawala	IV	?/?	2,000	1991
Macizos de Peñas Blancas	IV	?/?	11,308	1991
Makantaka	IV	?/?	2,000	1991
Mesas de Monopotente	IV	?/?	7,500	1991
Península de Chiltepe	IV	?/?	1,800	1983
Río Manares	IV	?/?	1,100	1983
Sierra Amerrisque	IV	?/?	12,073	1991
Sierra Kiragua	IV	?/?	9,097	1991
Tepesomoto / Pataste	IV	?/?	8,700	1991
Volcán Concepción	IV	?/?	2,200	1983
Volcán Cosigüina	IV	?/?	12,420	1983
Volcán Madera	IV	?/?	4,100	1983
Volcán Mombacho	IV	?/?	2,487	1983
Volcán Yali	IV	?/?	3,500	1991
Yulu	IV	?/?	1,000	1991

Wildlife Refuge

Los Guatusos	IV	?/?	43,750	1990
Río Escalante-Chococente	IV	?/?	4,800	1983

NIGER

	Summary	
Category I	0	0
Category II	1	220,000
Category III	0	0
Category IV	4	8,196,240
Category V	0	0
Total	**5**	**8,416,240**

National Nature Reserve				
Aïr et Ténéré	IV	18°40'N/8°30'E	7,736,000	1988
National Park				
W du Niger	II	12°15'N/2°28'E	220,000	1954
Partial Faunal Reserve				
Dosso	IV	?/?	306,500	1962
Total Faunal Reserve				
Gadabedji	IV	15°10'N/7°10'E	76,000	1955
Tamou	IV	12°43'N/2°20'E	77,740	1962

NIGERIA

	Summary	
Category I	0	0
Category II	6	2,226,400
Category III	0	0
Category IV	13	744,869
Category V	0	0
Total	**19**	**2,971,269**

Game Reserve				
Baturiya Wetlands	IV	12°27'N/10°17'E	29,700	1976
Dagida	IV	9°42'N/5°31'E	29,422	1971
Falgore (Kogin Kano)	IV	11°10'N/8°39'E	92,000	1969
Gilli-Gilli	IV	6°05'N/5°20'E	36,300	1960
Kambari	IV	84°8'N/10°38'E	41,400	1969
Kashimbila	IV	73°0'N/11°40'E	139,600	1977
Kwale	IV	5°43'N/6°27'E	1,340	1960
Lame-Burra	IV	10°27'N/9°15'E	205,767	1972
Margadu-Kabak Wetlands	IV	?/?	10,000	?
Nguru/Adiani Wetlands	IV	?/?	7,500	?
Ologbo	IV	?/?	19,440	1981
Orle River	IV	6°50'N/6°36'E	110,000	1960
Pandam	IV	8°36'N/8°25'E	22,400	1972
National Park				
Chad Basin	II	12°25'N/14°15'E	230,000	1991
Cross River	II	6°05'N/9°02'E	400,000	1991
Gashaka-Gumti	II	7°30'N/11°40'E	586,000	1991
Kainji Lake	II	10°05'N/4°41'E	532,000	1975
Old Oyo	II	8°44'N/3°44'E	253,000	1991
Yankari	II	9°45'N/10°30'E	225,400	1991

NORTHERN MARIANA ISLANDS/
ILES MARIANNES SEPTENTRIONALES/
ISLAS MARIANAS

	Summary	
Category I	4	1,541
Category II	0	0
Category III	0	0
Category IV	0	0
Category V	0	0
Total	**4**	**1,541**

Preserve

Asunción Island	I	19°40'N/143°24'E	722	1985
Guguan Island	I	17°19'N/143°51'E	412	1985
Maug Island	I	20°01'N/145°13'E	205	1985
Uracas Island	I	20°32'N/144°54'E	202	1985

NORWAY/NORVEGE/NORUEGA

	Summary	
Category I	54	2,726,383
Category II	20	2,328,110
Category III	0	0
Category IV	8	17,645
Category V	31	464,374
Total	**113**	**5,536,512**

Landscape Protected Area

Brannsletta	V	69°55'N/29°14'E	1,880	1983
Drivdalen-Kongsvoll-Hjerkinn	V	62°20'N/9°35'E	6,600	1974
Favnvassdalen	V	65°46'N/14°30'E	1,390	1983
Femundsmarka	V	62°20'N/12°02'E	7,040	1971
Fodalen	V	60°52'N/7°55'E	10,100	1992
Froan	V	64°00'N/8°59'E	8,000	1979
Gaasvatnan	V	66°58'N/15°02'E	12,000	1989
Garsjoen	V	69°54'N/28°55'E	2,000	1983
Hodalen	V	62°19'N/11°15'E	1,050	1989
Hovden	V	59°35'N/7°28'E	5,900	1986
Hydalen	V	60°58'N/8°35'E	3,400	1989
Indre Vassfaret	V	60°35'N/9°25'E	4,200	1985
Innerdalen	V	62°42'N/8°55'E	7,300	1967
Jaerstrendene	V	58°38'N/5°35'E	1,608	1977
Lusaheia	V	59°15'N/6°45'E	12,200	1991
Mosvasstangen	V	59°48'N/8°10'E	1,436	1989
Mosvatn-Austfjellet	V	59°58'N/8°13'E	29,900	1981
Osterdalen	V	67°10'N/15°18'E	2,700	1983
Raisduottarhaldi	V	69°20'N/21°20'E	8,000	1986
Saltfjellet	V	66°40'N/15°30'E	50,800	1989
Skaupsjoen/Hardangerjokulen	V	60°30'N/7°40'E	55,100	1981
Skipsfjord	V	70°11'N/19°45'E	4,200	1978
Stolsheimen	V	61°05'N/6°10'E	36,700	1990
Strandaa-Os	V	67°29'N/14°59'E	1,670	1983
Trollheimen	V	62°47'N/9°15'E	116,050	1987
Utladalen	V	61°25'N/7°55'E	31,400	1980
Vaeret	V	63°48'N/9°30'E	2,100	1982
Vassbotndalen	V	69°57'N/22°45'E	7,550	1991
Vassfaret-Vidalen	V	60°32'N/9°40'E	20,000	1985
Veoy	V	62°40'N/7°25'E	100	1970
Vormedalsheia	V	59°15'N/6°30'E	12,000	1991

Managed Nature Reserve

Bjortjonn	IV	59°47'N/8°10'E	1,640	1990
Flottin	IV	59°42'N/8°35'E	1,480	1990
Koltjerndalen	IV	63°32'N/12°08'E	3,800	1984
Kraakvaagsvaet	IV	63°44'N/9°22'E	1,190	1983
Leknesoyene	IV	65°07'N/11°44'E	1,350	1984
Svaet	IV	63°34'N/10°10'E	1,770	1984
Vignesholmane	IV	59°10'N/5°46'E	1,515	1982

National Park

Anderdalen	II	69°15'N/17°17'E	6,900	1970
Borgefjell	II	65°15'N/14°00'E	110,650	1963
Dovrefjell	II	62°20'N/9°27'E	25,580	1974
Femundsmarka	II	69°19'N/12°08'E	39,030	1971
Gressamoen	II	64°16'N/13°05'E	18,150	1970
Gutulia	II	62°01'N/12°11'E	1,900	1968
Hardangervidda	II	60°10'N/7°30'E	342,200	1981
Jostedalsbreen	II	61°30'N/6°50'E	123,000	1991
Jotunheimen	II	61°35'N/18°30'E	114,540	1980
Ovre Anarjakka	II	68°47'N/24°47'E	139,870	1975
Ovre Dividal	II	68°22'N/19°48'E	74,280	1971
Ovre Pasvik	II	69°05'N/28°56'E	6,660	1970
Rago	II	67°24'N/15°58'E	16,720	1971
Reisa	II	69°20'N/21°30'E	80,300	1986
Rondane	II	61°52'N/19°50'E	58,010	1962
Saltfjellet-Svartisen	II	66°40'N/14°30'E	210,500	1989
Stabbursdalen	II	70°06'N/24°31'E	9,820	1970

Nature Reserve

Arvasslia	I	64°04'N/13°46'E	2,850	1992
Atnoset	I	61°44'N/10°50'E	1,080	1989
Bliksvaer	I	67°17'N/13°55'E	4,000	1970
Blodskyttodden-Barvikmyran	I	70°25'N/30°55'E	2,650	1983
Borgann-Frelsoy	I	64°56'N/10°45'E	5,500	1973
Faerdesmyra	I	69°45'N/29°14'E	1,200	1972
Flaamen	I	62°17'N/9°50'E	2,920	1989
Forra	I	63°36'N/11°35'E	10,800	1990
Froan	I	64°02'N/9°08'E	40,400	1979
Gammeldalen	I	62°16'N/10°58'E	2,140	1989
Grandefjaera	I	63°42'N/9°33'E	1,500	1983
Grimsmoen	I	62°07'N/10°12'E	1,440	1989
Grovelsjoen	I	62°11'N/12°12'E	1,360	1989
Grytdalen	I	63°23'N/9°33'E	2,330	1992
Hanestadnea	I	61°50'N/10°35'E	1,760	1989
Havmyran	I	63°35'N/8°45'E	4,000	1982
Hogkjolen-Bakkjolen	I	63°02'N/9°30'E	1,130	1990
Hukkelvatna	I	63°02'N/10°56'E	1,045	1983
Hynna	I	61°12'N/9°55'E	1,546	1990
Javreoaivit	I	69°35'N/21°13'E	3,000	1981
Karlsoyvaer	IV	67°32'N/14°38'E	4,900	1977
Kvaloy-Ranoy	I	65°02'N/11°05'E	3,850	1973
Kvisleflaet	I	61°47'N/12°08'E	3,300	1981
Laksmarkdalen	I	65°32'N/12°45'E	2,460	1992
Lille Solensjoen	I	62°00'N/11°34'E	1,655	1981
Makkaurhalvoya	I	70°35'N/30°00'E	11,350	1983
Moffen	I	80°10'N/14°30'E	1,600	1983
Myldingi	I	61°55'N/10°00'E	1,240	1989
Neiden-Munkefjord	I	69°40'N/29°35'E	1,180	1991
Nekmyrene	I	6205'N/11°11'E	1,858	1981
Nigardsbreen	I	61°40'N/7°15'E	2,800	1985
Nord-Fugloy	I	70°16'N/20°07'E	2,130	1975
Nordre Oyeren	I	59°53'N/11°11'E	6,260	1975

Ora	I	55°10'N/11°00'E	1,560	1979
Osdalen	I	61°37'N/11°41'E	4,800	1969
Ostmarka	I	59°48'N/110°05'E	1,250	1990
Ovdaldasvarri	I	69°59'N/27°00'E	1,430	1983
Ovre Sandoldal	I	64°29'N/131°05'E	1,550	1992
Oyenskavlen	I	64°17'N/11°05'E	5,316	1992
Rangeldalen	I	63°12'N/12°00'E	2,600	1988
Reinoya	I	70°16'N/25°16'E	1,300	1981
Semska-Stoedi	I	66°37'N/15°22'E	1,300	1976
Skjorlaegda	I	65°37'N/13°05'E	7,430	1992
Skogvoll	I	69°10'N/15°45'E	2,800	1983
Smoldalen	I	61°30'N/12°25'E	1,325	1974
Stabbursneset	I	70°11'N/24°54'E	1,620	1983
Storbjorhusdalen	I	64°58'N/13°02'E	1,081	1992
Storlia	I	66°32'N/14°57'E	2,400	1989
Storlonen	I	61°17'N/9°36'E	1,147	1990
Tanamunningen	I	70°30'N/28°23'E	3,360	1991
Varnvassdalen	I	65°47'N/14°15'E	1,970	1992

Other area

Osdalen	I	61°43'N/11°32'E	1,360	1989

Bouvet Island/Ile Bouvet/ Isla Bouvet

Nature Reserve

Bouvetøya	I	54°25'S/3°20'E	5,850	1971

Svalbard and Jan Mayen Islands/ Svalbard et des Îles de Jan Mayen/ Islas Jan Mayen y Svalbard

National Park

Forlandet	II	78°30'N/11°00'E	64,000	1973
North-west Spitzbergen	II	79°40'N/12°00'E	356,000	1973
South Spitzbergen	II	77°10'N/16°00'E	530,000	1973

Nature Reserve

Moffen	I	80°10'N/14°30'E	1,600	1983
North-east Svalbard	I	80°00'N/23°00'E	1,903,000	1973
South-east Svalbard	I	77°50'N/22°00'E	638,000	1973

OMAN

Summary		
Category I	0	0
Category II	1	46,000
Category III	0	0
Category IV	27	3,688,650
Category V	1	1,600
Total	**29**	**3,736,250**

Managed Nature Reserve

Al Hallaniyah	IV	17°30'N/56°00'E	250,000	?
Jiddat al Harasis	IV	20°00'N/57°00'E	2,750,000	?
Quru	IV	23°37'N/58°30'E	1,000	1986
Ra's al Hadd (Turtle Reserve)	IV	22°30'N/59°50'E	8,000	1989
Sadh	IV	17°08'N/55°10'E	3,500	?
Wadi Sarin	IV	?/?	53,000	?

National Nature Reserve

East Sharbithat	IV	17°55'N/56°18'E	1,200	?
Jabal Aswadd	II	23°12'N/58°35'E	46,000	?
Jabal Samhan	IV	17°25'N/55°53'E	346,000	?

Khaur Ghauri	IV	18°37'N/56°40'E	1,250	?
Khawr Rawri	IV	17°02'N/54°25'E	1,100	?
Mazraq	IV	18°31'N/55°20'E	10,650	?
Raha	IV	16°58'N/54°50'E	18,750	?
Shuwagmiyah	IV	17°53'N/55°30'E	47,000	?
Sidah	IV	16°54'N/53°53'E	9,750	?
Wadi A' Shuwaymiyah	IV	17°55'N/55°30'E	12,500	?
Wadi Ayun	IV	17°15'N/53°49'E	3,700	?
Wadi Gubbarah	IV	18°38'N/56°01'E	4,550	?
Wadi Nahiz	IV	17°10'N/54°06'E	3,000	?
Wadi Nhart	IV	16°48'N/53°32'E	9,000	?
Wadi Sayq	IV	16°45'N/53°17'E	6,300	?

National Scenic Reserve

Jabal Qamar	IV	16°45'N/53°20'E	42,000	?
Marbat	IV	17°01'N/54°54'E	18,750	?
South Jazir	IV	18°25'N/56°37'E	18,000	?
Wadi Darbat	IV	17°05'N/54°29'E	4,800	?
Wadi Hinna	IV	17°05'N/54°40'E	24,000	?

Other area

Hanoon	IV	17°22'N/54°08'E	3,350	?
Jabal Haner	V	16°54'N/53°57'E	1,600	?
Wadi Muqshin	IV	19°30'N/54°30'E	37,500	?

PAKISTAN

Summary		
Category I	0	0
Category II	6	882,195
Category III	0	0
Category IV	45	2,716,693
Category V	4	122,051
Total	**55**	**3,720,939**

National Park

Ayubia	V	84°03'N/73°25'E	1,684	1984
Chinji	II	?/?	6,095	1987
Chitral Gol	II	35°50'N/71°47E	7,750	1984
Dhrun	II	25°55'N/65°32'E	167,700	1988
Hazar Ganji-Chiltan	V	30°03'N/66°39'E	15,555	1980
Hingol	II	25°30'N/65°17'E	165,004	1988
Khunjerab	II	36°50'N/75°35'E	226,913	1975
Kirthar	II	25°38'N/67°33'E	308,733	1974
Lal Suhanra	V	29°30'N/71°50'E	87,426	1972
Margalla Hills	V	34°00'N/73°30'E	17,386	1980

Wildlife Sanctuary

Agram Basti	IV	?/?	29,866	1983
Astore	IV	35°38'N/74°40'E	41,472	1975
Bajwat	IV	32°00'N/75°00'E	5,464	1964
Baltistan	IV	35°36'N/75°08'E	41,457	1975
Borraka	IV	33°32'N/71°15'E	2,025	1976
Buzi Makola	IV	25°25'N/64°05'E	145,101	1972
Chashma Lake	IV	32°25'N/71°22'E	33,084	1974
Cholistan	IV	?/?	661,216	1981
Chorani	IV	27°30'N/66°42'E	19,433	1972
Chumbi Surla	IV	32°40'N/72°20'E	55,945	1978
Daphar	IV	32°10'N/73°20'E	2,886	1978
Dhoung Block	IV	28°15'N/68°30'E	2,098	1977
Dureji	IV	25°40'N/67°15'E	178,259	1972
Gut	IV	?/?	165,992	1983

Hab Dam	IV	25°15'N/67°07'E	27,219	1972
Hadero Lake	IV	24°49'N/67°52'E	1,321	1977
Haleji Lake	IV	24°48'N/67°47'E	1,704	1977
Islamabad	IV	33°35'N/72°50'E	7,000	1980
Kachani	IV	25°50'N/66°32'E	21,660	1972
Kargah	IV	35°56'N/74°06'E	44,308	1975
Keb Bunder North	IV	24°15'N/67°45'E	8,948	1977
Keti Bunder South	IV	24°15'N/67°45'E	23,046	1977
Khurkhera	IV	25°32'N/66°34'E	18,345	1972
Kinjhar (Kalri) Lake	IV	24°56'N/68°03'E	18,468	1977
Koh-e-Geish	IV	20°08'N/66°45'E	24,356	1969
Kolwah Kap	IV	25°45'N/64°30'E	33,198	1972
Kotla Isan	IV	?/?	2,179	1990
Mahal Kohistan	IV	25°30'N/67°40'E	70,577	1972
Manshi	IV	34°40'N/73°34'E	2,321	1977
Maslakh	IV	30°05'N/66°35'E	46,550	1968
Naltar	IV	36°07'N/74°14'E	27,206	1975
Nara Desert	IV	26°40'N/69°05'E	223,590	1980
Raghai Rakhshan	IV	27°15'N/65°30'E	125,425	1971
Rakh Ghulaman	IV	?/?	4,338	1989
Rann of Kutch	IV	25°05'N/69°30'E	320,463	1980
Ras Koh	IV	28°20'N/65°05'E	99,498	1962
Rasool Barrage	IV	32°43'N/73°33'E	1,138	1974
Salpara	IV	35°12'N/75°07'E	31,093	1975
Sasnamana	IV	30°22'N/67°52'E	6,607	1971
Shashan	IV	27°15'N/66°27'E	29,555	1972
Sheikh Buddin	IV	32°20'N/70°30'E	19,540	1977
Sodhi	IV	32°05'N/72°20'E	5,415	1983
Takkar	IV	27°15'N/68°55'E	43,513	1968
Taunsa Barrage	IV	30°42'N/70°50'E	6,567	1972
Ziarat Juniper	IV	29°55'N/67°52'E	37,247	1971

PALAU

Summary		
Category I	0	0
Category II	0	0
Category III	1	1,200
Category IV	0	0
Category V	0	0
Total	**1**	**1,200**

Wildlife Reserve

Ngerukewid Islands	III	7°10'N/134°15'E	1,200	1956

PANAMA

Summary		
Category I	0	0
Category II	12	1,318,674
Category III	1	5,400
Category IV	2	2,258
Category V	0	0
Total	**15**	**1,326,332**

National Park

Altos de Campana	II	8°44'N/79°57'W	4,816	1977
Camino de Cruces	II	9°02'N/79°35'W	4,000	1992
Cerro Hoya	II	7°11'N/80°55'W	32,557	1984
Chagres	II	9°21'N/79°28'W	129,000	1984

Coiba	II	7°33'N/81°46'W	270,125	1991
Darién	II	7°52'N/77°47'W	579,000	1980
La Amistad	II	9°10'N/82°38'W	207,000	1988
Marino Isla Bastimentos	II	9°17'N/82°06'W	13,226	1988
Portobelo	II	9°30'N/79°40'W	34,846	1976
Sarigua	II	8°03'N/80°28'W	8,000	1984
Soberanía	II	9°10'N/79°44'W	22,104	1980
Volcán Barú	II	8°48'N/82°32'W	14,000	1976

Nature Monument

| Barro Colorado | III | 9°08'N/79°49'W | 5,400 | 1977 |

Wildlife Refuge

| Islas Taboga y Urabá | IV | 8°48'N/79°33'W | 258 | 1984 |
| Peñón de la Onda | IV | 7°56'N/80°20'W | 2,000 | 1984 |

PAPUA NEW GUINEA/
PAPOUASIE-NOUVELLE-GUINEE/
PAPUA NUEVA GUINEA

Summary		
Category I	0	0
Category II	3	7,323
Category III	0	0
Category IV	2	74,693
Category V	0	0
Total	**5**	**82,016**

National Park

Jimi Valley	II	?/?	4,180	1991
McAdam	II	7°15'S/146°39'E	2,080	1970
Varirata	II	9°28'S/147°22'E	1,063	1978

Wildlife Management Area

| Crown Island (III) | IV | ?/? | 58,969 | 1977 |
| Long Island (III) | IV | ?/? | 15,724 | 1977 |

PARAGUAY

Summary		
Category I	0	0
Category II	12	1,362,811
Category III	1	2,500
Category IV	1	30,000
Category V	5	87,695
Total	**19**	**1,483,006**

Biological Refuge

| Mbaracayú | V | 24°00'S/54°16'W | 1,356 | 1983 |
| Tatí Yupí | V | 25°22'S/54°37'W | 2,536 | 1983 |

Biological Reserve

| Itabó | V | 25°02'S/54°40'W | 11,260 | 1983 |
| Limo'y | V | 24°48'S/54°27'W | 14,828 | 1983 |

National Park

Caaguazú	II	26°05'S/55°45'W	16,000	1976
Cerro Corá	II	22°39'S/56°00'W	11,538	1976
Defensores del Chaco	II	20°14'S/60°09'W	780,000	1975
Lago Ypoá	II	26°03'S/57°33'W	100,000	1992
San Rafael	II	26°25'S/57°40'W	78,000	1992

Serranía San Luis	II	22°35'S/57°24'W	10,273	1991
Teniente Enciso	II	21°05'S/61°38'W	40,000	1980
Tinfunqué	II	24°00'S/60°00'W	280,000	1966
Ybycuí	II	26°06'S/56°49'W	5,000	1973
Ybytyruzú	II	25°45'S/56°30'W	24,000	1990
Ypacaraí	II	26°18'S/57°20'W	16,000	1990
Ñacunday	II	26°03'S/54°32'W	2,000	1993

Nature Monument

Macizo Acahay	III	25°52'S/57°10'W	2,500	1992

Nature Reserve

Bosque Mbaracayú	V	24°08'S/55°25'W	57,715	1991

Wildlife Refuge

Yabebyry	IV	?/?	30,000	1993

Wildlife Refuge

Yabebyry	IV	?/?	30,000	1993

PERU/PEROU

	Summary		
Category I	0	0	
Category II	8	2,413,718	
Category III	7	1,629,908	
Category IV	2	75,347	
Category V	5	57,217	
Total	**22**	**4,176,190**	

Historic Sanctuary

Chacamarca	V	11°12'S/75°58'W	2,500	1974
Machu Picchu	II	12°12'S/72°35'W	32,592	1981

National Park

Cerros de Amotape	II	4°02'S/80°37'W	91,300	1975
Cutervo	II	6°14'S/78°47'W	2,500	1961
Huascarán	II	9°45'S/77°28'W	340,000	1975
Manú	II	12°11'S/71°47'W	1,532,806	1973
Río Abisco	II	?/?	274,520	1983
Tingo María	II	9°16'S/75°59'W	18,000	1965
Yanachaga Chemillén	II	10°23'S/75°28'W	122,000	1986

National Reserve

Calipuy	IV	8°34'S/78°29'W	64,000	1981
Lachay	III	11°22'S/77°22'W	5,070	1977
Titicaca	V	15°31'S/69°51'W	36,180	1978

National Sanctuary

Ampay	V	?/?	3,635	1987
Calipuy	III	8°20'S/78°17'W	4,500	1981
Huayllay	III	10°56'S/76°19'W	6,815	1974
Manglares de Tumbes	III	?/?	2,972	1988
Pampas del Heath	III	?/?	102,109	1983
Tabaconas-Namballe	III	?/?	29,500	1988

Reserved Zone

Laquipampa	IV	?/?	11,347	1982
Racali	V	?/?	6,433	1985
Tambopata-Candamo	III	12°50'S/69°25'W	1,478,942	1977
Udima	V	?/?	8,469	1991

PHILIPPINES/FILIPINAS

	Summary	
Category I	0	0
Category II	10	247,050
Category III	5	19,715
Category IV	8	321,243
Category V	4	17,919
Total	**27**	**605,927**

Marine Park

Tubbataha Reefs	II	8°53'N/119°53'E	33,200	1988

Marine Reserve

Taklong Island	V	10°24'N/122°30'E	1,143	1990

National Park

Basilan	II	6°35'N/122°06'E	3,100	1939
Bataan	IV	14°50'N/120°24'E	23,688	1945
Bulusan Volcano	II	13°15'N/123°41'E	3,673	1935
Lake Dapao	IV	7°16'N/120°32'E	1,500	1967
Mainit Hot Spring	III	7°28'N/126°01'E	1,381	1957
Mayon Volcano	III	13°16'N/123°42'E	5,459	1938
Minalungao	III	?/?	2,018	1967
Mount Apo	II	6°58'N/125°17'E	72,814	1936
Mount Arayat	V	15°12'N/120°45'E	3,715	1933
Mount Canlaon	II	10°25'N/123°01'E	24,558	1934
Mount Data	V	16°53'N/120°54'E	5,512	1940
Mount Isarog	II	14°14'N/123°15'E	10,112	1938
Mount Kitanglad Range	II	8°12'N/128°48'E	31,297	1990
Mount Malindang	II	8°17'N/123°32'E	53,262	1971
Mounts Banahaw-San Cristobal	II	13°10'N/120°35'E	11,133	1941
Mounts Banahaw-San Cristobal Geothermal Res.	V	?/?	7,549	1973
Mounts Iglit-Baco	IV	12°49'N/121°19'E	75,445	1970
Naujan Lake	IV	13°21'N/121°20'E	21,655	1956
Rajaha Sikatuna	IV	9°44'N/124°13'E	9,023	1987
St Paul Subterranean River	II	10°10'N/118°55'E	3,901	1971
Taal Volcano	III	14°02'N/120°59'E	4,537	1967
Tirad Pass	III	16°58'N/120°40'E	6,320	1938

Wildlife Sanctuary

F.B. Harrison	IV	13°10'N/120°10'E	140,000	1920
Liguasan Marsh	IV	7°08'N/124°25'E	43,930	1941
Magapit	IV	?/?	6,002	1932

POLAND/POLOGNE/POLONIA

	Summary	
Category I	1	1,592
Category II	15	148,326
Category III	0	0
Category IV	21	67,967
Category V	74	2,845,668
Total	**111**	**3,063,553**

Landscape Park

Barlinecko-Gorzowski	V	52°53'N/15°19'E	40,302	1991
Biebrzanski	V	53°28'N/22°34'E	87,474	1989
Bolimowski	V	52°02'N/20°10'E	25,900	1986

Brodnicki	V	53°23'N/19°23'E	22,240	1985
Brudzenski	V	52°38'N/19°33'E	7,507	1988
Chelmski	V	51°12'N/23°33'E	23,500	1983
Chelmy	V	51°03'N/16°03'E	28,461	1992
Cisniansko-Wetlinski	V	49°16'N/22°18'E	46,025	1992
Doliny Bobru	V	51°00'N/15°39'E	23,760	1989
Doliny Sanu	V	49°11'N/22°41'E	35,635	1992
Doliny Slupi	V	54°20'N/17°15'E	120,201	1981
Drawski	V	53°38'N/16°10'E	63,642	1979
Gor Opawskich	V	50°17'N/17°27'E	10,070	1988
Gor Opawskich	V	?/?	4,830	1988
Gor Slonnych	V	40°33'N/22°25'E	38,096	1992
Gor Sowich	V	50°52'N/16°45'E	6,890	1991
Gora sw. Anny	V	50°28'N/18°13'E	13,730	1988
Gory Sw. Anny	V	50°27'N/18°09'E	5,780	1988
Gorzniansko-Lidzbarski	V	53°12'N/19°42'E	45,150	1990
Gostyn sko-Wloclawski	V	52°33'N/19°24'E	51,344	1979
Inski	V	53°27'N/15°32'E	51,843	1982
Jasielski	V	49°25'N/21°50'E	19,520	1992
Kaszubski	V	54°15'N/17°55'E	34,544	1983
Kazimierski	V	51°20'N/22°00'E	38,670	1979
Kozienicki	V	51°31'N/21°26'E	45,535	1983
Kozlowiecki	V	51°25'N/22°32'E	13,018	1990
Krasnabrodzki	V	?/?	40,184	1988
Krasnobrodzki	V	50°32'N/23°15'E	40,184	1988
Krzczonowski	V	51°02'N/22°50'E	26,275	1990
Ksiazanski	V	50°54'N/16°18'E	4,500	1981
Lagowski	V	52°20'N/15°20'E	10,070	1985
Lasy Janowskie	V	50°37'N/22°27'E	62,950	1984
Lednicki	V	52°33'N/17°24'E	6,202	1988
Mazowiecki	V	52°04'N/21°26'E	25,510	1986
Mazurski	V	53°44'N/21°35'E	69,219	1977
Miedzyrzecza Warty i Widawki	V	51°28'N/18°55'E	26,636	1989
Mierzeja Wislana	V	54°23'N/19°25'E	22,390	1985
Nadmorski	V	54°45'N/18°25'E	27,610	1978
Nadwieprzanski	V	51°18'N/22°55'E	17,491	1990
Narwianski	V	53°02'N/22°56'E	47,915	1985
Pogorza Przemyskiego	V	49°44'N/22°33'E	61,862	1991
Pojezierze Leczynski	V	51°29'N/23°00'E	19,955	1990
Poleski	V	51°27'N/23°09'E	27,500	1983
Poludnioworoztoczanski	V	50°16'N/23°26'E	20,376	1989
Popradzki	V	?/?	78,000	1987
Przedborski	V	?/?	31,120	1988
Przemecki	V	51°57'N/16°18'E	21,450	1991
Pszczewski	V	52°28'N/15°44'E	57,587	1986
Puszcza Knyszynska	V	53°14'N/23°23'E	123,349	1988
Puszczy Solskiej	V	50°23'N/23°08'E	30,952	1988
Puszczy Solskiej	V	?/?	115,246	1988
Rudawski	V	50°50'N/15°54'E	23,700	1989
Sierakowski	V	52°38'N/16°05'E	30,413	1991
Slezanski	V	?/?	12,200	1988
Snieznicki	V	50°14'N/16°48'E	28,800	1981
Sobiborski	V	51°25'N/23°36'E	19,000	1983
Stolowogorski	V	50°27'N/16°23'E	13,600	1981
Strzelecki	V	51°10'N/23°50'E	10,300	1983
Suwalski	V	54°15'N/22°51'E	14,901	1976
Szczebrzeszynski	V	50°41'N/22°52'E	20,209	1991
Szczecinski	V	53°30'N/14°45'E	22,384	1982
Trojmiejski	V	54°27'N/18°21'E	33,107	1979
Tucholski	V	53°41'N/17°56'E	52,928	1985
Wdzydzki	V	53°59'N/17°54'E	17,650	1983
Wigierski	V	54°03'N/23°04'E	21,301	1976
Wrzelowiecki	V	51°05'N/21°54'E	18,614	1990

Wzniesienie Elblaskie	V	54°16'N/19°34'E	33,292	1985
Zaborski	V	53°53'N/17°33'E	38,815	1990
Zaleczanski	V	51°08'N/18°48'E	14,278	1979
Zespol Jurajskich	V	50°28'N/19°40'E	246,276	1980
Zespol Parkow Ponidzia	V	50°25'N/20°41'E	82,648	1986
Zespol Swietokrzyskie	V	?/?	100,625	1988
Zywiecki	V	49°42'N/19°12'E	57,587	1986

National Park

Babia Gora	II	49°35'N/19°31'E	1,734	1933
Bialowieza	II	52°45'N/23°49'E	5,317	1932
Bieszczady	II	49°05'N/22°45'E	15,337	1973
Drawski	II	53°41'N/16°08'E	8,691	1990
Gorce	II	49°34'N/20°09'E	6,750	1981
Kampinos	II	52°18'N/20°38'E	35,486	1959
Karkonoski	II	50°46'N/15°41'E	5,563	1959
Ojcow	I	50°13'N/19°50'E	1,592	1956
Pieniny	II	49°25'N/20°23'E	2,329	1932
Polskie	II	51°17'N/23°27'E	4,903	1990
Roztocze	II	50°37'N/23°03'E	6,857	1974
Slowinski	II	54°43'N/17°18'E	18,247	1967
Swietokrzyski	II	50°53'N/20°57'E	5,906	1950
Tatra	II	49°16'N/19°56'E	21,164	1955
Wielkopolski	II	52°15'N/16°47'E	5,198	1933
Wigierski	V	54°03'N/23°04'E	14,840	1989
Wolinski	II	53°57'N/14°34'E	4,844	1960

Nature Reserve

Czerwone Bagno (Faunal-Peatbog Reserve)	IV	53°38'N/22°49'E	11,630	1957
Jata (Forest Reserve)	IV	51°58'N/22°11'E	1,117	1952
Jezioro Dobskie (Landscape)	IV	54°04'N/21°37'E	1,833	1976
Jezioro Druzno (Bird Reserve)	IV	54°06'N/19°30'E	3,022	1967
Jezioro Kosno (Landscape)	IV	53°39'N/20°42'E	1,248	1982
Jezioro Nidzkie (Landscape)	IV	53°34'N/21°33'E	2,935	1973
Jezioro Siedmiu Wys (Bird Reserve)	IV	54°17'N/21°36'E	1,007	1956
Kurianskie Bagno	IV	?/?	1,714	1985
Las Warminski	IV	53°39'N/20°31'E	1,816	1982
Las Warminski NR (Forest Reserve)	IV	?/?	1,798	1982
Lasy Janowskie	IV	50°37'N/22°27'E	2,677	1984
Nadgoplanski Park Tysiaclecia NR (Landscape)	IV	52°34'N/18°19'E	12,684	1967
Paslece (Faunal Reserve)	IV	54°13'N/19°58'E	4,116	1970
Puszcza Bialowieska (Landscape)	IV	52°44'N/23°35'E	1,357	1969
Rzeka Drweca (Water Reserve)	IV	53°38'N/19°46'E	1,287	1961
Slonsk	IV	52°34'N/14°43'E	1,248	1977
Slonsk NR (Faunal-Peatbog Reserve)	IV	52°34'N/14°43'E	4,166	1977
Stawy Milickie NR (Bird Reserve)	IV	51°32'N/17°22'E	5,324	1963
Stawy Przemkowskie NR (Bird Reserve)	IV	?/?	1,046	1984
Wielki Bytyn	IV	?/?	1,826	1989
Wielki NR (Faunal Reserve)	IV	?/?	4,116	1970

PORTUGAL

Summary		
Category I	2	13,072
Category II	1	21,100
Category III	1	2,730
Category IV	10	108,616
Category V	11	437,102
Total	**25**	**582,620**

National Park

Peneda-Geres	II	41°57'N/8°15'W	21,100	1971
Peneda-Geres Buffer Zone	V	41°57'N/8°15'W	49,190	1971

Natural Monument

Gruta do Zambujal	III	38°26'N/9°08'W	2,730	1979

Natural Reserve

Berlenga	IV	39°25'N/9°30'W	1,063	1981
Estuario do Sado	IV	38°27'N/8°44'W	23,160	1980
Estuario do Tejo	IV	38°50'N/8°58'W	14,560	1976
Sapal de Castro Marim	IV	37°12'N/7°27'W	2,089	1975
Serra da Malcata	IV	40°15'N/7°02'W	21,760	1981

Nature Park

Alvao	V	41°22'N/7°49'W	7,220	1983
Arrábida	V	38°29'N/9°00'W	10,821	1976
Montesinho	V	41°54'N/6°52'W	74,800	1979
Ria Formosa	V	37°01'N/7°48'W	18,400	1987
Serra de Estrela	V	40°28'N/7°32'W	101,060	1976
Serra de S. Mamede	V	39°18'N/7°18'W	31,750	1989
Serras de Aires e Candeeiros	V	39°32'N/8°48'W	38,900	1979

Protected Landscape

Costa Vicentica e Sudoeste Alentejano	V	37°29'N/8°45'W	74,786	1988

Azores/Açores

Natural Reserve

Caldeira do Faial	IV	38°38'N/28°43'W	1,086	1972
Ilheu de Vila Franca do Campo	IV	37°42'N/25°27'W	101	1983
Ilheus das Formigas	IV	37°15'N/24°45'W	40,000	1988
Lagoa do Fogo	IV	37°46'N/25°29'W	2,413	1974
Montanha da Ilha do Pico	IV	38°28'N/28°24'W	2,384	1972

Protected Landscape

Lagoa das Sete Cidades	V	37°51'N/25°47'W	2,175	1980

Macau/Macao

No Areas Listed

Madeira/Madère

Natural Reserve

Ilhas Desertas	I	32°16'N/16°27'W	9,672	1990
Ilhas Selvagens	I	30°10'N/15°50'W	3,400	1971

Nature Park

Madeira	V	32°45'N/17°00'W	28,000	1979

QATAR

Summary		
Category I	0	0
Category II	0	0
Category III	0	0
Category IV	1	1,619
Category V	0	0
Total	**1**	**1,619**

Protected Area

Ras Asharij Gazelles Conservation Farm	IV	?/?	1,619	1991

ROMANIA/ROUMANIE/RUMANIA

	Summary	
Category I	12	60,741
Category II	11	841,561
Category III	0	0
Category IV	11	22,788
Category V	5	159,815
Total	**39**	**1,084,905**

Biosphere Reserve

Danube Delta	II	44°56'N/28°56'E	591,000	1991

National Park

Apuseni	II	?/?	37,900	1990
Bucegi	II	45°27'N/25°22'E	35,700	1990
Calimani	II	47°13'N/25°16'E	15,300	1971
Ceahliu	II	46°57'N/25°59'E	17,200	1971
Cheile Bicazului-Hasmas	II	46°50'N/25°50'E	11,600	1990
Cheile Carasului	V	?/?	30,400	1990
Cheile Nerei-Beusnita	II	44°54'N/21°53'E	45,561	1982
Cheile-Bicazului	V	46°50'N/25°50'E	11,600	1990
Cozia	II	45°22'N/24°16'E	17,100	1966
Domogled-Valea Cernei	V	?/?	60,100	1982
Gradista de Munte-Cioclovina	II	?/?	1,000	1979
Piatra Craiului	II	45°28'N/25°21'E	14,800	1990
Retezat	II	45°22'N/22°50'E	54,400	1935
Rodna	V	?/?	56,700	1990

Nature Reserve

Bila-Lala	IV	?/?	5,135	1973
Carorman	I	45°04'N/29°24'E	2,250	1990
Chitu-Bratcu forest	IV	?/?	1,319	1982
Ciclova-Simionu-Rolu	I	?/?	1,327	1973
Coronini-Bedina	I	?/?	2,839	1980
Grindul Chituc	I	44°33'N/28°54'E	2,300	1990
Grindul Lupilor	I	44°40'N/28°55'E	2,075	1990
Gropul Sec (Plesu mountain-Patrunsa gorge)	IV	?/?	1,562	1982
Ipotesti	V	?/?	1,015	1975
Letea	I	45°20'N/29°31'E	2,825	1990
Little island of Braila	IV	?/?	5,336	1979
Moldoveanu, Capra-Fagaras mountains	IV	?/?	1,000	1966
Paring mountain	IV	?/?	2,000	1982
Periteasca-Bisericuta-Portita	I	44°44'N/29°02'E	4,125	1990
Postavarul mountain	IV	?/?	1,026	1980
Rachiteaua forest	IV	?/?	1,200	1982
Raducu	I	45°15'N/29°17'E	2,500	1990
Rosca-Buhaiova	I	45°22'N/29°25'E	9,625	1990
Sahalin-Zatoane	I	44°50'N/29°26'E	24,250	1990
Snagov Forest and Snagov Lake	IV	44°41'N/26°09'E	1,010	1952
Snagov Lake	IV	?/?	1,000	1952
Vama Veche- 2 Mai marine aquatorium	I	?/?	5,000	1980
Vatafu-Lungulet	I	45°07'N/29°34'E	1,625	1990
Zerind-Bustard	IV	?/?	2,200	1982

RUSSIAN FEDERATION/
FEDERATION DE RUSSIE/
FEDERACION DE RUSIA

Summary		
Category I	75	37,649,408
Category II	23	4,545,515
Category III	4	8,990
Category IV	95	23,279,636
Category V	2	53,210
Total	**199**	**65,536,759**

National Park

Bashkiriya	II	53°25'N/57°42'E	98,000	1987
Chavash Varmane	II	?/?	25,247	1993
Kenozyerskiy	II	64°48'N/40°44'E	139,200	1991
Kurshskaya Kosa	II	55°00'N/21°00'E	7,000	1987
Losinyy Ostrov	II	56°00'N/37°25'E	10,058	1983
Mariy Chodra	II	56°00'N/48°00'E	36,602	1985
Meshera	II	?/?	118,800	1992
Mesherskiy	II	?/?	103,000	1992
Nizhnaya Kama	II	?/?	26,100	1991
Pereslavsky historic	V	56°45'N/39°00'E	23,210	1990
Pribaikalskiy	II	52°00'N/104°10'E	452,700	1986
Pripyohminskie Borny	II	?/?	49,050	1993
Pryelbrussky	II	43°30'N/42°45'E	100,400	1986
Rouskyi Sevier	II	60°00'N/38°50'E	166,400	1992
Samarskaya Luka	II	52°00'N/48°15'E	134,000	1984
Shorsky	II	52°50'N/88°00'E	338,345	1989
Smolenslkoe Pohohzerye	II	?/?	146,200	1992
Sochynsky	II	43°45'N/39°25'E	189,600	1983
Taganai	II	?/?	56,400	1991
Transbaikal	II	?/?	269,000	1986
Tunkinskiy	II	?/?	1,183,700	1991
Valdaiskiy	II	58°10'N/33°20'E	158,513	1990
Vodlozerskiy	II	63°00'N/39°00'E	470,000	1991
Zabaikalskiy	II	53°40'N/109°00'E	267,200	1986

Natural Monument

Irgizskaya floodplain	III	?/?	3,026	?
Kodar glaciers	III	?/?	1,600	?
Pokhvistnevskie suburb oak forests	III	?/?	2,969	?
Shilanskiegenkovskie polosy	III	?/?	1,395	?

Other area

Solovetsky Historical Cultural and Natural Complex	V	65°11'N/35°44'E	30,000	1986

Zakaznik

Agrakhansky	IV	?/?	39,000	1983
Altacheysky	IV	50°50'N/107°00'E	60,000	1984
Amachtonski	IV	61°00'N/160°00'E	50,000	?
Anadyrskii	IV	64°00'N/173°00'E	300,000	?
Badzhalsky	IV	?/?	275,000	1987
Bairovsky	IV	?/?	64,800	1959
Barsovy	IV	?/?	106,000	1979
Belozersky	IV	?/?	17,900	1979
Birsky	IV	?/?	51,600	?
Bolshoe Tokko	IV	?/?	265,800	?
Burkalsky	IV	?/?	195,700	?
Cape Loptka	IV	51°00'N/156°30'E	500,000	?

Central Priochotie	IV	56°00'N/137°00'E	100,000	?
Chaigurgino	IV	?/?	2,375,000	1983
Dautsky	IV	?/?	74,900	?
Elizarovsky	IV	?/?	76,700	1982
Eloguysky	IV	?/?	747,600	?
Frolikhinsky	IV	?/?	109,200	1976
Golovinsky	IV	?/?	50,000	1968
Iona Island	IV	56°30'N/143°00'E	50,000	?
Kabansky	IV	?/?	12,000	1974
Kanozersky	IV	?/?	65,700	1980
Karaginskii	IV	58°00'N/163°30'E	200,000	?
Kharbinsky	IV	?/?	163,900	?
Khekhtsirsky	IV	?/?	102,000	1959
Khingano-Arkhar	IV	?/?	48,800	1958
Kirzinsky	IV	?/?	119,800	1958
Kizhsky	IV	?/?	50,000	1973
Kletnyansky	IV	?/?	30,000	?
Klyazminsky	IV	?/?	21,000	1978
Kunovatsky	IV	?/?	220,000	1976
Kurgansky	IV	?/?	31,800	1984
Kursky	IV	?/?	172,700	?
Lebediny	IV	?/?	400,000	?
Malye Kurily	IV	?/?	45,000	1983
Malyi Abakan	IV	?/?	119,000	1982
Manytch-Goodilo	IV	?/?	68,500	1975
Mekletinsky	IV	?/?	102,500	?
Middle Kurilskii	IV	48°00'N/153°00'E	1,000,000	?
Mshinskoe Boloto	IV	?/?	60,400	1982
Murmansky Tundra	IV	?/?	295,000	1987
Muromsky	IV	?/?	62,700	1967
Nadymsky	IV	?/?	564,000	?
Nenetsky	IV	?/?	440,000	1967
Nizhne-Obsky	IV	?/?	128,000	?
Norsky	IV	?/?	213,600	1968
North Kurilskii	IV	50°00'N/154°30'E	200,000	?
North Sakchalinskii	IV	53°30'N/142°30'E	100,000	?
Oldzhikansky	IV	?/?	159,700	1987
Olonetsky	IV	?/?	27,000	1980
Olutorskii	IV	60°30'N/168°00'E	90,000	?
Priazovsky	IV	?/?	45,000	1958
Purinsky	I	60°00'N/?	787,500	1990
Ratmanovskii	IV	51°30'N/143°30'E	50,000	?
Remdovsky	IV	?/?	64,900	?
Ryazansky	IV	?/?	36,000	?
Samursky	IV	?/?	11,200	1982
Saratovsky	IV	?/?	44,300	1983
Sarpinskky	IV	?/?	195,900	?
Siysky	IV	?/?	43,000	1963
South Sakchalinskii	IV	46°00'N/141°30'E	200,000	?
Sovietskii	IV	?/?	100,500	1968
Starokulatkinsky	IV	?/?	20,200	1973
Stepnoi	IV	?/?	75,000	1977
Sursky	IV	?/?	22,200	1969
Tchecheno-Ingushsky	IV	?/?	70,000	1971
Tlyaratinsky	IV	?/?	83,500	1957
Tomsky	IV	?/?	46,900	1963
Tophalarsky	IV	?/?	132,700	1971
Tsasucheisky Bor	IV	?/?	57,000	1982
Tseisky	IV	?/?	28,900	1971
Tsymlyansky	IV	?/?	45,000	?
Tulomsky	IV	?/?	33,700	1989

Tumninsky	IV	?/?	143,100	1987
Tungussky	IV	?/?	250,000	?
Tyumensky	IV	?/?	53,600	1958
Udyl	IV	?/?	100,400	1988
Ust-Vilyuisky	IV	?/?	101,600	?
Vaspukholsky	IV	?/?	93,200	?
Verkhne-Kondinsky	IV	?/?	241,600	1968
West Kamtchatskii	IV	57°00'N/157°00'E	100,000	?
Yaroslavsky	IV	?/?	17,000	1971
Yuzhno-Kamchatsky	IV	?/?	225,000	1983

Zapovednik

Altaiskiy	IV	51°06'N/88°42'E	8,812,386	1932
Astrakhanskiy	IV	42°04'N/48°28'E	63,400	1919
Azas	I	52°38'N/96°32'E	337,290	1985
Baikal'skiy	I	54°24'N/107°50'E	200,500	1969
Baikalo-Lenskiy	I	49°44'N/107°34'E	6,599,196	1987
Barguzinskiy	I	54°33'N/109°54'E	374,800	1916
Bashkirskiy	I	50°36'N/57°59'E	79,600	1930
Bassegi	I	58°09'N/58°36'E	19,202	1982
Bol'shekhekhtsizskiy	I	47°47'N/134°53'E	45,123	1963
Bolshaya Kokshaga	I	?/?	21,405	1993
Bolshoi Arkticheski (Great Arctic)	I	75°00'N/110°00'E	4,169,222	1993
Bryanskiy Les	I	54°29'N/33°52'E	12,200	1987
Bureinskiy	I	52°20'N/134°30'E	358,444	1987
Chernye Zemli	I	?/?	125,000	1990
Dagestanskiy	I	44°00'N/47°15'E	18,900	1987
Dal'nevostochnyy Morskoy	I	42°00'N/131°12'E	64,316	1978
Darvinskiy	I	58°22'N/37°38'E	112,630	1945
Daurskiy	I	50°10'N/115°17'E	44,700	1987
Dzhercinski	I	?/?	237,806	1992
Dzhgdzhurskiy	I	56°30'N/138°10'E	806,300	1990
Il'menskiy	I	55°10'N/60°12'E	30,380	1920
Kabardino-Balkarskiy	I	40°59'N/43°16'E	74,099	1976
Kaluzhskie Zaseki	I	?/?	18,533	1992
Kandalakshshkiy	I	66°32'N/27°30'E	70,500	1932
Katunskiy	I	49°20'N/86°15'E	150,079	1991
Kavkazskiy	IV	40°13'N/40°22'E	263,277	1924
Kedrovaya Pad'	I	36°52'N/131°27'E	17,897	1916
Kerzhenski	I	?/?	46,940	1993
Khankaiskiy	I	43°31'N/132°36'E	38,000	1990
Khinganskiy	I	46°58'N/130°36'E	97,836	1963
Khoperskiy	I	48°48'N/41°42'E	16,178	1935
Kivach	IV	57°42'N/33°58'E	10,900	1931
Komandorskyi	I	?/?	3,648,679	1993
Komsomolskiy	I	50°43'N/137°19'E	63,866	1963
Kostomukshskiy	I	64°31'N/30°25'E	47,457	1983
Kronotskiy	I	49°24'N/160°54'E	1,099,000	1967
Kuril'skiy	I	43°30'N/146°00'E	65,400	1984
Kuznetskiy Alatau	I	55°00'N/88°15'E	453,524	1989
Laplandskiy	I	60°10'N/32°16'E	268,400	1930
Lazovskiy	I	36°54'N/134°02'E	120,024	1957
Lena Delta	I	72°58'N/32°33'E	1,433,000	1985
Les na Vorskle	I	50°05'N/35°39'E	1,038	1979
Magadanskiy	I	51°46'N/146°46'E	883,805	1982
Malaya Soz'va	I	62°00'N/64°00'E	92,921	1975
Malyi Abakan	I	?/?	97,829	1993
Mordovskiy	I	53°12'N/43°20'E	32,200	1936
Nizhne-Svirskiy	I	60°18'N/33°04'E	41,436	1980
Okskiy	I	53°15'N/40°49'E	55,700	1935
Olekminskiy	I	55°12'N/122°09'E	847,102	1984
Orenburgsky	IV	51°15'N/57°20'E	21,653	1984

Ostrov Vrangelya	I	68°46'N/?	795,700	1976
Pasvik	I	69°30'N/30°00'E	14,586	1992
Pechoro-Ilychskiy	I	62°13'N/58°42'E	721,322	1930
Pinezhskiy	I	63°24'N/45°23'E	41,344	1974
Poronaiskiy	I	?/?	56,700	1988
Potoransky	I	69°24'N/94°12'E	1,887,300	1988
Prioksko-Terrasnyy	IV	53°06'N/37°39'E	4,945	1945
Pryvolzhskaya Lesostep'	I	53°00'N/46°35'E	8,242	1989
Putoranskiy	I	66°36'N/94°12'E	1,887,300	1988
Sayano-Shushenskiy	I	43°49'N/91°47'E	390,368	1976
Severo-Osetinskiy	I	43°14'N/43°01'E	29,100	1967
Shul'gan Tash	I	53°00'N/56°48'E	22,531	1986
Sikhote-Alinskiy	I	42°43'N/136°12'E	347,052	1935
Sokhondinskiy	I	49°53'N/111°05'E	211,007	1973
Stolby	IV	55°12'N/92°56'E	47,200	1925
Taimyrskiy	I	73°45'N/98°47'E	1,348,308	1979
Tchazy	IV	58°50'N/?	11,825	1991
Tchernye zemly	IV	45°28'N/46°10'E	125,000	1990
Teberdinskiy	IV	42°12'N/43°43'E	84,996	1936
Tsentral'nochernozemnyy	I	44°28'N/36°05'E	4,847	1935
Tsentral'nolesnoy	I	55°28'N/32°56'E	21,380	1931
Tsentralno-Sibirskiy	I	57°31'N/90°18'E	972,017	1985
Ubsunurskaya Kotlovina	I	?/?	39,640	1993
Ussuriyskiy	I	36°24'N/132°24'E	40,432	1932
Ust'Lenskiy	I	71°02'N/123°35'E	1,433,000	1985
Verkhne-Tazovskiy	I	62°59'N/83°38'E	631,308	1986
Visherskiy	IV	?/?	241,200	1991
Visimskiy	I	54°36'N/59°38'E	13,500	1971
Vitimskiy	I	58°00'N/115°00'E	585,021	1982
Volzhsko-Kamskiy	IV	52°06'N/48°48'E	8,054	1960
Voronezhskiy	IV	30°05'N/50°18'E	31,100	1927
Vrangel Island	I	71°10'N/179°02'W	795,650	1976
Yuganskiy	I	60°09'N/74°36'E	622,900	1982
Yuzhno-Uzalskiy	I	54°00'N/59°00'E	254,914	1978
Zavidovskiy	I	56°05'N/36°27'E	125,442	1929
Zeyskiy	I	54°00'N/127°12'E	99,400	1963
Zhygulevskiy	I	52°36'N/48°40'E	23,140	1927

RWANDA

Summary		
Category I	0	0
Category II	2	327,000
Category III	0	0
Category IV	0	0
Category V	0	0
Total	**2**	**327,000**

National Park

Akagera	II	1°32'S/30°38'E	312,000	1934
Volcans	II	1°28'S/29°33'E	15,000	1929

**SAINT KITTS AND NEVIS/
SAINT-KITTS-ET-NEVIS/
SAINT KITTS Y NEVIS**

	Summary	
Category I	0	0
Category II	1	2,610
Category III	0	0
Category IV	0	0
Category V	0	0
Total	**1**	**2,610**

National Park

Southeast Peninsula	II	?/?	2,610	?

**SAINT LUCIA/SAINTE-LUCIE/
SANTA LUCIA**

	Summary	
Category I	0	0
Category II	0	0
Category III	0	0
Category IV	1	1,494
Category V	0	0
Total	**1**	**1,494**

Sanctuary

Parrot Sanctuary	IV	13°52'N/61°00'W	1,494	1980

**SAINT VINCENT AND THE GRENADINES/
SAINT-VINCENT-ET-LES-GRENADINES/
SAN VICENTE Y LAS GRANADINAS**

	Summary	
Category I	0	0
Category II	0	0
Category III	0	0
Category IV	2	8,284
Category V	0	0
Total	**2**	**8,284**

Marine Reserve

Tobago Cays Marine Reserve	IV	12°38'N/61°22'W	3,885	1986

Reserve

St. Vincent Parrot Reserve	IV	13°15'N/61°12'W	4,399	1987

SAN MARINO/SAINT-MARIN

No Areas Listed

**SAO TOME AND PRINCIPE/
SAO TOME-ET-PRINCIPE/
SANTO TOME Y PRINCIPE**

No Areas Listed

SAUDI ARABIA/ARABIE SAOUDITE/
ARABIA SAUDITA

	Summary		
Category I	2	279,000	
Category II	0	0	
Category III	0	0	
Category IV	7	5,472,400	
Category V	1	450,000	
Total	**10**	**6,201,400**	

National Park

Asir	V	18°00'N/42°00'E	450,000	1981

Protected Area

Farasan Islands	I	16°45'N/42°00'E	60,000	1989
Harrat al-Harrah	IV	31°00'N/38°40'E	1,377,500	1987
Hawtat Bani Tamin National Ibex Hima	IV	23°25'N/46°45'E	236,900	1988
Khunfah	IV	28°40'N/38°35'E	2,045,000	1987
Mahazat As Sayd	I	22°52'N/41°00'E	219,000	1988
Majami al-Hadb	IV	?/?	380,000	1989
Raydah Escarpment	IV	?/?	3,000	1989
Tubayq	IV	29°47'N/37°25'E	1,220,000	1989

Reserve

Dawat Ad-Dafl, Dawat Al-Musallamiyah & Coral Island	IV	?/?	210,000	?

SENEGAL

	Summary		
Category I	0	0	
Category II	6	1,012,450	
Category III	0	0	
Category IV	4	1,168,259	
Category V	0	0	
Total	**10**	**2,180,709**	

Faunal Reserve

Ferlo-Nord	IV	15°10'N/13°55'W	487,000	1971
Ferlo-Sud	IV	15°10'N/13°55'W	633,700	1972
Ndiael	IV	?/?	46,550	?
Popenguine Special	IV	14°33'N/17°09'W	1,009	1986

National Park

Basse-Casamance	II	12°25'N/16°35'W	5,000	1970
Delta du Saloum	II	13°45'N/16°38'W	76,000	1976
Djoudj	II	16°30'N/16°10'W	16,000	1971
Iles de la Madeleine	II	14°40'N/17°40'W	450	1949
Langue de Barbarie	II	14°55'N/16°30'W	2,000	1976
Niokolo-Koba	II	12°55'N/16°02'W	913,000	1954

SEYCHELLES

	Summary		
Category I	1	35,000	
Category II	2	2,893	
Category III	0	0	
Category IV	0	0	
Category V	0	0	
Total	**3**	**37,893**	

Marine National Park

Curieuse	II	4°17'S/55°43'E	1,470	1976
St. Anne	II	4°35'S/55°30'E	1,423	1973

Special Nature Reserve

Aldabra	I	9°25'S/46°25'E	35,000	1976

SIERRA LEONE/SIERRA LEONA

	Summary		
Category I	0	0	
Category II	0	0	
Category III	0	0	
Category IV	2	82,013	
Category V	0	0	
Total	**2**	**82,013**	

Game Reserve

Tiwai Island	IV	7°33'N/11°19'W	1,200	1987

National Park

Outamba-Kilimi	IV	9°45'N/12°13'W	80,813	1986

SINGAPORE/SINGAPOUR/SINGAPUR

	Summary		
Category I	0	0	
Category II	0	0	
Category III	0	0	
Category IV	1	2,796	
Category V	0	0	
Total	**1**	**2,796**	

Nature Reserve

Central Catchment and Bukit Timah	IV	1°23'N/103°48'E	2,796	1990

SLOVAKIA/SLOVAQUIE/ESLOVAQUIA

	Summary		
Category I	1	1,193	
Category II	5	199,724	
Category III	1	1,517	
Category IV	15	41,990	
Category V	18	771,085	
Total	**40**	**1,015,509**	

National Nature Reserve

Belianske Tatry	IV	?/?	5,408	1991
Bielovodska dolina	IV	?/?	3,712	1991

Dolina Bielej vody	IV	?/?	1,661	1991
Dumbier	IV	48°57'N/19°39'E	2,043	1973
Janska dolina	IV	49°00'N/19°40'E	1,696	1984
Javorova dolina	IV	?/?	2,251	1991
Koprova dolina	IV	?/?	3,221	1991
Mengusovska dolina	IV	?/?	1,613	1991
Salatin	I	48°59'N/19°22'E	1,193	1982
Skalnata dolina	IV	?/?	1,069	1991
Studene doliny	IV	?/?	2,222	1991
Ticha dolina	IV	?/?	5,967	1991
Tlsta	IV	48°55'N/18°59'E	3,066	1981
Vazecka dolina	IV	?/?	1,186	1991
Velicka dolina	IV	?/?	1,217	1991

National Park

Mala Fatra	II	49°10'N/19°00'E	22,630	1988
Nizke Tatry	II	48°57'N/19°41'E	81,095	1978
Pieninsky	II	49°23'N/20°27'E	2,125	1967
Slovensky raj	II	48°55'N/20°22'E	19,763	1988
Tatransky	II	49°12'N/19°58'E	74,111	1948

Natural Area

Demanovske jaskyne	III	49°00'N/19°33'E	1,517	1972

Protected Landscape Area

Biele Karpaty	V	48°54'N/17°48'E	43,519	1979
Cerova vrchovina	V	?/?	16,280	1989
Ceske stredohori	V	50°40'N/14°15'E	107,113	1976
Horna Orava	V	49°29'N/19°24'E	70,333	1979
Kysuce	V	49°25'N/18°35'E	65,462	1984
Latorica	V	?/?	15,620	1990
Luzicke Hory	V	50°50'N/14°38'E	26,441	1976
Male Karpaty	V	48°24'N/17°16'E	65,504	1976
Muranska planina	V	48°45'N/19°58'E	21,931	1976
Palava	V	48°50'N/16°40'E	8,017	1976
Polana	V	48°40'N/19°28'E	20,079	1981
Ponitrie	V	48°33'N/18°22'E	37,665	1985
Slovensky kras	V	48°35'N/20°40'E	36,166	1973
Stiavnicke vrchy	V	48°25'N/18°52'E	77,630	1979
Velka Fatra	V	48°59'N/19°06'E	60,610	1973
Vihorlat	V	48°54'N/22°13'E	4,383	1973
Vychodne Karpaty	V	49°05'N/22°15'E	66,810	1977
Zahorie	V	?/?	27,522	1988

Protected Locality

Dropie	IV	47°49'N/17°54'E	5,658	1955

SLOVENIA/SLOVENIE/ESLOVENIA

	Summary	
Category I	0	0
Category II	1	84,805
Category III	0	0
Category IV	0	0
Category V	9	23,282
Total	**10**	**108,087**

Landscape Park

Caven-Trnoski gozd	V	45°55'N/13°50'E	4,776	1987
Golte	V	46°22'N/14°54'E	1,148	1987
Jeruzalemske gorice	V	46°30'N/14°54'E	1,370	1992
Logarska dolina	V	46°23'N/14°38'E	2,475	1987

Nanos	V	45°50'N/13°59'E	2,632	1984
Porezen-Davca	V	46°23'N/13°51'E	3,895	1990
Robanov Kot	V	46°22'N/14°40'E	1,423	1987
Topla	V	46°29'N/14°47'E	1,368	1966
Zgornia Idrijca	V	45°59'N/13°57'E	4,195	1993

National Park

Triglavski	II	46°23'N/13°51'E	84,805	1981

SOLOMON ISLANDS/
ILES SALOMON /ISLAS SALOMON

No Areas Listed

SOMALIA/SOMALIE

Summary		
Category I	0	0
Category II	0	0
Category III	0	0
Category IV	1	180,000
Category V	0	0
Total	**1**	**180,000**

Nature Reserve

Alifuuto (Arbowerow)	IV	3°47'N/45°53'E	180,000	?

SOUTH AFRICA/AFRIQUE DU SUD/
SUDAFRICA

Summary		
Category I	1	39,000
Category II	53	4,200,111
Category III	0	0
Category IV	183	2,689,147
Category V	0	0
Total	**237**	**6,928,258**

Bophuthatswana

National Park

Borakalalo	IV	25°10'S/27°55'E	12,500	1970
Pilanesberg	II	25°15'S/27°05'E	55,000	1979

Cape Province

Indigenous Forest

Knysna	IV	33°56'S/22°43'E	44,230	1894
Tsitsikamma	IV	33°56'S/23°55'E	15,651	1890

Marine Reserve

De Hoop	IV	?/?	23,000	1986

Mountain Catchment Area

Cederberg	IV	32°23'S/19°08'E	59,133	1978
Groot Winterhoek	IV	33°00'S/19°05'E	81,188	1913
Hawequas	IV	33°38'S/19°13'E	50,900	1981
Hottentots Holland	IV	34°06'S/19°01'E	23,579	1979
Kammanassie	IV	33°38'S/22°44'E	25,044	1978
Klein Swartberg	IV	33°24'S/21°15'E	29,678	1978
Langeberg East	IV	33°53'S/21°09'E	40,931	1981

Langeberg West	IV	33°48'S/20°11'E	62,408	1979
Matroosberg	IV	33°27'S/19°31'E	79,105	1979
Outeniqua	IV	33°51'S/22°32'E	38,000	1936
Riviersonderend	IV	34°00'S/19°41'E	43,037	1981
Rooiberg	IV	33°39'S/21°30'E	12,417	1978

National Park

Addo Elephant	II	33°30'S/25°46'E	11,718	1931
Augrabies Falls	II	28°37'S/20°19'E	88,218	1966
Bontebok	II	34°02'S/20°25'E	3,189	1931
Kalahari Gemsbok	II	25°40'S/20°20'E	959,103	1931
Karoo	II	32°09'S/24°31'E	32,792	1979
Knysna Lake Area	II	34°07'S/23°05'E	13,000	1985
Langebaan	II	?/?	1,850	1985
Mountain Zebra	II	32°15'S/25°26'E	6,536	1937
Richtersveld Contractual	II	28°29'S/17°07'E	162,445	1991
Tankwa Karoo	II	32°17'S/19°48'E	27,063	1986
Tsitsikamma Coastal	II	34°03'S/23°57'E	25,400	1964
Tsitsikamma Forest	II	34°03'S/23°57'E	3,011	1964
Vaalbos	II	28°36'S/24°18'E	22,696	1986
West Coast	II	33°08'S/18°10'E	23,220	1985
Wilderness	II	34°01'S/22°40'E	10,600	1975
Zuurberg	II	33°20'S/25°29'E	34,683	1985

Nature Area

Langebaan	IV	?/?	10,000	?

Nature Reserve

Akkerendam	IV	31°26'S/19°46'E	2,301	1962
Andries Vosloo Kudu	IV	33°07'S/26°43'E	7,695	1976
Anysberg	IV	?/?	33,977	1978
Attakwaskloof	IV	?/?	9,655	1988
Bosberg	IV	?/?	3,521	1967
Cape of Good Hope	IV	34°17'S/18°26'E	7,675	1939
Ceres Bergfynbos	IV	?/?	6,820	1964
Commandodrift	IV	32°07'S/26°02'E	5,983	1980
De Hoop	IV	34°27'S/20°25'E	35,846	1956
De Mond	IV	?/?	1,227	1975
De Vasselot	IV	33°59'S/23°32'E	2,560	1974
Doornkloof	IV	30°19'S/24°59'E	9,215	1981
Fernkloof	IV	34°24'S/19°16'E	1,446	1957
Gamka Mountain	IV	33°43'S/21°53'E	9,428	1970
Gamkapoort	IV	33°16'S/21°39'E	8,002	1980
Goegap	IV	24°38'S/17°59'E	14,864	1966
Goukamma	IV	34°03'S/22°55'E	2,230	1960
Greyton	IV	34°02'S/19°38'E	2,220	1977
Hawequas	IV	?/?	117,000	1906
Helskloof	IV	?/?	10,984	1987
Hottentots Holland	IV	?/?	67,404	1929
Karoo	IV	32°15'S/24°30'E	16,500	1975
Kogelberg	IV	?/?	14,006	1937
Ladismith-Klein Karoo	IV	33°32'S/21°14'E	2,766	1974
Langkloof	IV	?/?	25,098	?
Leon Taljaard	IV	?/?	2,068	1969
Little Karoo	IV	?/?	35,000	1987
Marloth	IV	?/?	11,269	1935
Molopo	IV	?/?	23,890	1987
Mont Rochelle	IV	33°54'S/19°10'E	1,759	1982
Montagu	IV	33°48'S/20°06'E	1,200	1972
Oorlogskloof	IV	?/?	5,070	1984
Otterford	IV	33°40'S/25°00'E	11,467	1896
Oviston	IV	30°41'S/25°47'E	13,000	1971

Paarl Mountain	IV	33°44'S/18°56'E	2,000	1977
Pauline Bohnen	IV	?/?	1,407	1982
Riverlands	IV	?/?	1,297	1985
Rolfontein	IV	30°02'S/24°45'E	6,938	1970
S. le Roux	IV	?/?	2,575	1983
Sam Knott	IV	?/?	15,000	1988
Sandveld	IV	32°47'S/18°15'E	3,624	1966
Somerset East-Bosberg	IV	32°42'S/25°35'E	3,521	1967
Spitskop	IV	28°22'S/21°10'E	2,740	1967
Storms River	IV	33°55'S/23°59'E	13,700	1925
Suurberg	IV	33°20'S/25°38'E	21,121	1896
Swartberg	IV	33°22'S/22°29'E	121,002	1912
Table Mountain	IV	33°58'S/18°24'E	2,904	1964
Thomas Baines	IV	33°24'S/26°30'E	1,003	1980
Vrolijkheid	IV	33°56'S/19°55'E	1,827	1959
Walker Bay	IV	34°35'S/19°31'E	6,734	1895
Waterval	IV	?/?	16,151	?
Ysterhck	IV	?/?	1,212	1972

Sanctuary

Melkbos-Houtbay Rock Lobster	IV	?/?	83,400	?
Saldanha Bay Rock Lobster	IV	?/?	83,400	?
St. Helena Bay Rock Lobster	IV	?/?	14,000	?

Wilderness Area

Cederberg	IV	?/?	64,400	1973
Doringrivier	IV	?/?	9,395	1988
Groendal	IV	33°43'S/25°18'E	29,916	1976
Groot Winterhoek	IV	?/?	23,615	1985

Ciskei

Game Park

Tsolwana	IV	32°11'S/26°30'E	7,557	1977

Nature Reserve

Cata Forest	IV	32°34'S/27°08'E	1,592	1913
Dontsa Forest	IV	32°35'S/27°13'E	1,209	1913

Protected Area

Cwengcwe Forest	IV	32°42'S/27°18'E	3,276	1926
Izeleni Forest	IV	32°40'S/27°25'E	1,330	1917
Pirie Forest	IV	32°43'S/27°16'E	5,239	1922
Rabula Forest	IV	32°44'S/27°12'E	3,884	1912
Zingcuka Forest	IV	32°40'S/27°00'E	3,731	1913

Natal

Forest Reserve

Kosi Bay	IV	26°51'S/32°51'E	21,772	1950

Game Reserve

Giant's Castle	II	29°11'S/29°24'E	34,638	1903
Hluhluwe	II	28°04'S/32°04'E	23,067	1895
Mahushe Shongwe	IV	?/?	1,100	1986
Mkuzi	II	27°40'S/32°14'E	37,985	1912
Mthethomusha	IV	?/?	7,200	1986
Ndumo	IV	26°52'S/32°15'E	10,117	1924
Songimvelo	IV	?/?	50,000	1983
St. Lucia	II	28°13'S/32°28'E	36,826	1895
Umfolozi	II	28°20'S/31°47'E	47,753	1895

Marine Reserve

Maputaland	II	27°00'S/32°50'E	39,740	1987

St. Lucia	II	28°00'S/32°30'E	44,280	1979
National Park				
Royal Natal	II	28°42'S/28°56'E	8,094	1916
Nature Reserve				
Blouberg	IV	?/?	4,827	1985
Coleford	II	29°56'S/29°26'E	1,272	1975
Corridor	II	28°14'S/31°58'E	25,633	1989
False Bay	II	28°00'S/32°19'E	2,247	1954
Gxalingenwa	IV	30°00'S/29°39'E	1,500	1906
Impofana	IV	?/?	7,626	1989
Itala	II	27°30'S/31°25'E	29,653	1972
Kamberg	II	29°20'S/29°43'E	2,980	1951
Karkloof	IV	29°24'S/30°16'E	1,726	1980
Loteni	II	29°24'S/29°37'E	3,984	1953
Makasa	IV	27°45'S/32°25'E	1,700	1992
Mapelane	II	28°26'S/32°25'E	1,103	1953
Mfifiyela	IV	?/?	2,200	1989
Mt Currie	IV	30°31'S/29°25'E	1,777	1981
Ncandu	IV	?/?	3,520	1989
Oribi Gorge	IV	30°43'S/30°14'E	1,917	1950
Richards Bay	IV	29°50'S/32°01'E	1,200	1935
Umtamvuna	IV	31°00'S/30°10'E	3,257	1971
Vergelegen	II	29°27'S/29°30'E	1,159	1967
Vernon Crookes	IV	30°17'S/30°35'E	2,189	1973
Weenen	IV	28°56'S/30°04'E	4,183	1975
Park				
St. Lucia	II	28°16'S/32°24'E	12,545	1939
Tembe Elephant	IV	26°51'S/32°24'E	29,878	1983
State Forest				
Cape Vidal	II	28°03'S/32°33'E	11,313	1956
Cathedral Peak	II	29°00'S/29°16'E	32,246	1927
Cobham	II	29°42'S/29°25'E	30,498	1927
Drakensberg State Forests	IV	30°18'S/29°20'E	193,443	1930
Dukuduku	II	29°21'S/32°20'E	10,125	?
Eastern Shores	II	28°10'S/32°30'E	12,873	?
Garden Castle	II	29°46'S/29°11'E	30,766	1951
Highmoor	II	29°20'S/29°36'E	28,151	1951
Mhlatuze	IV	?/?	1,103	1956
Mkhomazi	II	29°27'S/29°35'E	49,156	1951
Monks Cowl	II	29°04'S/29°23'E	20,379	1927
Normandien	II	27°58'S/29°43'E	1,875	1925
Nyalazi	II	28°07'S/32°23'E	1,367	?
Sodwana	II	27°41'S/32°32'E	47,127	1956
Wilderness Area				
Mdelelelo	II	29°02'S/29°18'E	27,000	1973
Mkhomazi	II	29°23'S/29°18'E	48,600	1973
Mzimkulu	II	29°40'S/29°17'E	28,340	1973
Mzimkuluwana	II	29°46'S/29°12'E	22,751	1989
Ntendeka	IV	27°50'S/31°24'E	5,230	1905

Orange Free State

National Park				
Golden Gate Highlands	II	28°30'S/28°37'E	11,633	1963
Nature Reserve				
Caledon (Orange Free State)	IV	29°50'S/26°54'E	5,254	1985
Erfenisdam	IV	28°29'S/26°47'E	3,808	1988

Hendrik Verwoerddam	IV	30°40'S/25°45'E	47,201	1979
Kalkfontein	IV	29°32'S/25°16'E	5,263	1988
Koppiesdam	IV	27°15'S/27°45'E	4,325	1976
Rustfonteindam	IV	29°18'S/26°37'E	2,170	1974
Sandveld	IV	27°40'S/25°45'E	37,735	1980
Soetdoring	IV	28°50'S/26°02'E	6,137	1978
Sterkfonteindam	IV	?/?	17,770	1987
Tussen die Riviere	IV	30°30'S/26°15'E	22,000	1972
Willem Pretorius	IV	28°20'S/27°15'E	12,005	1970

Prince Edward Islands

Strict Nature Reserve

Prince Edward Islands	I	46°53'S/37°45'E	39,000	1948

Transkei

National Wildlife Reserve

Cwebe	IV	32°13'S/28°56'E	2,140	1975
Dwesa	II	32°16'S/28°52'E	3,900	1975

Transvaal

Game Reserve

Manyeleti	IV	24°35'S/31°29'E	22,744	1967

Mountain Catchment Area

Sterkspruit	IV	25°07'S/30°26'E	9,850	1978

National Park

Kruger	II	24°01'S/31°23'E	1,948,528	1926

Nature Reserve

Abe Bailey	IV	26°20'S/27°16'E	4,197	1982
AFB Hoedspruit	IV	?/?	4,236	?
Atherstone	IV	24°25'S/26°45'E	13,575	1990
Barberspan	IV	26°35'S/25°35'E	3,086	1954
Barberton	IV	?/?	23,530	1986
Bloemhof Dam	IV	27°36'S/25°35'E	22,211	1975
Blouberg East	IV	23°02'S/29°05'E	9,300	1983
Blouberg West	IV	23°03'S/28°53'E	4,450	1982
Blyderivierspoort	IV	24°35'S/30°50'E	22,664	1965
Boskop Dam	IV	26°32'S/27°06'E	3,160	1975
Bothasvley	IV	25°03'S/28°19'E	1,619	1986
Bronkhorstspruit Dam	IV	25°55'S/28°42'E	1,285	1977
D'Nyala	IV	23°44'S/27°47'E	8,281	1986
Doorndraai Dam	IV	24°20'S/28°45'E	7,229	1973
Fanie Botha (Tzaneen Dam)	IV	23°50'S/30°10'E	2,850	1978
Hans Merensky	IV	23°42'S/30°40'E	5,182	1954
Hans Strydom	IV	24°00'S/27°43'E	3,618	1978
Happy Rest	IV	22°59'S/29°35'E	1,585	1975
Hartebeespoort Dam	IV	25°45'S/27°50'E	2,500	1969
Jericho Dam	IV	26°40'S/30°20'E	2,186	1977
Langjan	IV	22°50'S/29°13'E	4,774	1954
Lebwena	IV	?/?	1,610	1985
Lekgalameetse	IV	24°05'S/30°15'E	18,124	1984
Loskop Dam	IV	25°30'S/29°20'E	17,800	1954
Malmaniesoog	IV	25°50'S/26°03'E	5,880	1992
Mangombe	IV	?/?	3,000	1982
Marievale Bird Sanctuary	IV	26°21'S/28°31'E	1,009	1978
Masebe	IV	?/?	4,541	1985
Messina	IV	22°24'S/30°03'E	5,113	1980
Nooitgedacht Dam	IV	25°58'S/30°04'E	3,420	1980
Nylsvley	IV	24°39'S/28°42'E	3,121	1973

Ohrigstad Dam	IV	24°57'S/30°38'E	2,563	1954
Percy Fyfe	IV	25°02'S/29°10'E	2,985	1954
Pilgrim's Rest	IV	24°35'S/30°50'E	1,899	1980
Pongola	IV	27°20'S/31°58'E	10,485	1979
Potlake	IV	24°15'S/29°56'E	2,786	1985
Roodeplaat Dam	IV	25°40'S/28°20'E	1,667	1977
Rust de Winter Dam	IV	25°12'S/28°30'E	1,654	1954
Rustenburg	IV	25°43'S/27°12'E	4,257	1967
S A Lombard	IV	27°35'S/25°30'E	3,663	1949
Schuinsdraai	IV	?/?	7,900	?
Steilloop	IV	?/?	16,500	?
Sterkspruit	IV	25°09'S/30°33'E	1,600	1969
Suikerbosrand	IV	26°30'S/28°15'E	13,337	1974
Thabina	IV	?/?	1,153	1985
Vaal Dam	IV	26°53'S/28°15'E	1,075	1954
Vaalkop Dam	IV	25°18'S/27°25'E	1,873	1983
Verloren Valei	IV	25°18'S/30°07'E	5,870	1984
Vhembe	IV	22°13'S/29°17'E	2,504	1975
Witvinger	IV	?/?	4,450	1986
Wolkberg Caves	IV	24°06'S/29°53'E	1,488	1969
Wolwespruit	IV	27°25'S/26°15'E	2,333	1975
Wonderkop	IV	?/?	3,500	1992
Zandspruit	IV	?/?	3,035	?

Protected Natural Environment

Magaliesberg	IV	?/?	40,627	1977

State Forest

Ceylon	IV	25°05'S/30°40'E	3,500	1935
Entabeni	IV	23°01'S/30°14'E	1,924	1924
Morgenzon	IV	24°47'S/30°44'E	1,264	1978
Nelshoogte/Berlin	IV	25°43'S/30°48'E	3,500	1923
Uitsoek	IV	25°18'S/30°35'E	2,270	1953
Woodbush/De Hoek	IV	23°49'S/30°32'E	6,626	1916

Wilderness Area

Wolkberg	IV	24°05'S/30°05'E	22,009	1977

Venda

National Park

Nwanedi	IV	22°39'S/30°25'E	3,200	1980

SPAIN/ESPAGNE/ESPAÑA

Summary		
Category I	0	0
Category II	10	132,478
Category III	0	0
Category IV	86	1,736,920
Category V	119	2,376,232
Total	**215**	**4,245,630**

National Biological Reserve

Bosque de Muniellos	V	43°03'N/6°44'W	5,542	1982

National Game Reserve

Alto Pallars-Aran	IV	42°39'N/1°07'E	94,231	1966
Arroyo de la Rocina	IV	37°10'N/6°34'W	1,005	?
Bahia del Santona	IV	43°26'N/3°25'W	2,893	?
Benasque	IV	42°38'N/0°28'E	23,750	1966
Cadi	IV	42°20'N/1°40'E	27,202	1966

Cameros	IV	42°10'N/2°45'W	92,918	1973
Cerdana	IV	42°25'N/1°41'E	19,437	1966
Cijara	IV	39°18'N/4°55'W	24,999	1966
Cortes de la Frontera	IV	36°35'N/5°25'W	12,342	1973
Degana	IV	42°55'N/6°30'W	11,914	1966
Fresser y Setcasas	IV	42°22'N/2°12'E	20,200	1966
Fuentes Carrionas	IV	42°56'N/4°40'W	47,755	1966
Islas d'Espalmador, Espardell y Islotes	IV	?/?	175	?
La Buitrera	IV	?/?	1,200	1982
Las Batuecas	IV	40°29'N/6°08'W	20,976	1973
Los Ancares	IV	42°49'N/6°53'W	7,975	1966
Los Ancares Leoneses	IV	42°48'N/6°44'W	38,300	1973
Los Circos	IV	42°39'N/0°13'E	22,844	1966
Los Valles	IV	42°47'N/0°40'W	28,765	1966
Mampodre	IV	43°00'N/5°16'W	30,858	1966
Montes Universales	IV	40°25'N/1°40'W	59,260	1973
Muela de Cortes	IV	39°12'N/0°50'W	36,009	1973
Picos de Europa	IV	43°13'N/4°50'W	7,630	1970
Puertos de Beceite	IV	40°45'N/0°15'E	30,418	1966
Ria de Villaviciosa	IV	?/?	1,032	?
Ria del Eo	IV	?/?	2,000	?
Riano	IV	43°06'N/4°58'W	71,538	1966
Saja	IV	43°13'N/4°25'W	180,186	1966
Serrania de Cuenca	IV	40°20'N/1°55'W	25,724	1973
Serrania de Ronda	IV	36°40'N/5°00'W	21,982	1970
Sierra de Gredos	IV	40°20'N/5°15'W	22,815	1970
Sierra de la Culebra	IV	41°55'N/6°22'W	65,891	1973
Sierra de la Demanda	IV	42°08'N/3°06'W	73,819	1973
Sierra de Tejeda y Almijara	IV	36°48'N/3°54'W	20,398	1973
Sierra Espuna	IV	39°10'N/0°58'W	13,855	1973
Sierra Nevada	IV	37°05'N/3°20'W	35,430	1966
Somiedo	IV	43°10'N/6°00'W	89,650	1966
Sonsaz	IV	41°07'N/3°25'W	68,106	1973
Sueve	IV	43°35'N/5°14'W	8,300	1966
Urbion	IV	41°57'N/2°46'W	100,023	1973
Villafafila	IV	41°50'N/5°37'W	42,000	1986
Vinamala	IV	4°237'N/0°10'E	49,230	1966

National Park

Aigüestortes y Llac de Sant Maurici	II	42°38'N/0°31'W	10,230	1955
Archipielago de Cabrera	II	39°13'N/2°53'E	9,715	1991
Caldera de Taburiente	II	28°44'N/17°53'W	4,690	1954
Donana	II	37°00'N/6°28'W	50,720	1969
Garajonay	II	28°09'N/17°14'W	3,984	1981
Montana de Covadonga	II	43°14'N/4°59'W	16,925	1918
Ordesa y Monte Perdido	II	42°37'N/0°10'W	15,608	1918
Tablas de Daimiel	II	39°20'N/3°38'W	1,928	1973
Teide	II	28°16'N/16°37'W	13,571	1954
Timanfaya	II	29°01'N/13°47'W	5,107	1974

Natural Area

Ses Salines de Ibiza, Formentera e Islotes	IV	39°00'N/1°30'E	1,180	1985

Natural Area of National Interest

Algendar y Costa Sud de Cuitadella	IV	?/?	1,131	?
Amunts d'Eivissa	IV	?/?	12,337	?
Areas Naturales de la Serra de Tramuntana	IV	?/?	69,947	?
Barrancs de Son Gual y Xorrigo	IV	?/?	4,106	?
Cala de Sant Esteva-Calo den Rafalet	IV	?/?	1,337	?
Cap de Ses Salines	IV	?/?	1,762	?
Cap Llentrisca-Sa Talaiassa	IV	?/?	2,907	?
De Addaida a S'Albufera	IV	?/?	1,038	?
De Binigaus a Cala Mitjana	IV	?/?	1,813	?
De Biniparratx a Llucalari	IV	?/?	3,896	?

Del Alocs a Fornells	IV	?/?	2,736	?
Dunas de Son Real	IV	?/?	1,048	?
El Toro	IV	?/?	1,573	?
Es Fangar	IV	?/?	1,148	?
La Mola	IV	?/?	1,088	?
La Mola de Mao	IV	?/?	1,806	?
La Vall d'Algaiarens	IV	?/?	13,075	?
La Victoria	IV	?/?	1,198	?
La y S'Albufera de Fornells Mola	IV	?/?	1,583	?
Marina de Llucmajor	IV	?/?	3,034	?
Massis de Randa	IV	?/?	3,673	?
Montanas de Arta	IV	?/?	7,295	?
S'Albufera de Mallorca	IV	?/?	2,443	?
Sa Canova	IV	?/?	1,021	?
Salto de las Hiedras	IV	?/?	1,778	?
Sant Salvador-Santueri	IV	?/?	1,682	?
Santa Agueda-S'Esclusa	IV	?/?	3,042	?
Serra de Ses Fontanelles-Serra Grossa	IV	?/?	4,359	?
Ses Salines	IV	?/?	1,076	?
Son Bou y Barranc de Sa Vall Menorca	IV	?/?	1,210	?
Torrent de Na Borges	IV	?/?	3,044	?
Natural Landscape				
Brazo del Este	V	?/?	1,336	1989
Desfiladero de los Gaitanes	V	?/?	2,016	1989
Desierto de Tabernas	V	?/?	11,625	1989
El Hondo	V	?/?	2,387	?
Embalse de Cordobilla	V	?/?	1,460	1989
Karst de Yesos de Sorbas	V	?/?	2,375	1989
Ladera de Vallebron	V	?/?	2,142	1987
Lagunas de la Mata y Torrevieja	V	?/?	3,693	?
Los Ajaches	V	?/?	2,876	1987
Los Reales de Sierra Bermeja	V	?/?	1,236	1989
Macizo de Pedraforca	V	?/?	1,671	1982
Macizo de Tauro	V	?/?	1,179	1987
Marismas de Isla Cristina	V	?/?	2,145	1989
Marismas del Odiel	V	37°20'N/6°58'W	7,185	1984
Marismas del Rio Piedras y Flecha del Rompido	V	?/?	2,530	1989
Punta Entina-Sabinar	V	?/?	1,960	1989
Reales de Sierra Bermeja	V	?/?	1,236	?
Sierra Alhamilla	V	?/?	8,500	1989
Sierra Pelada y Rivera del Asserador	V	?/?	12,980	1989
Torcal de Antequera	V	36°24'N/4°33'W	1,171	1978
Valle del Monasterio de Poblet	V	?/?	2,477	1984
Vertiente sur del Massis de l'Albera	V	?/?	2,413	1986
Natural Reserve				
Caidas de la Negra	IV	42°05'N/1°21'W	1,926	1987
Foz de Arbayun	IV	42°40'N/1°00'W	1,164	1987
Laguna de Fuentepiedra	IV	37°07'N/4°46'W	1,364	1984
Larra	IV	?/?	2,353	1987
Mas de Melons	IV	41°25'N/1°00'E	1,140	1987
Natural Site of National Interest				
Aiguamolls de l'Emporda	IV	42°13'N/3°05'E	4,824	1985
Ajaches	IV	28°54'N/13°46'W	2,876	1984
Albufera des Grau	IV	39°57'N/4°15'E	1,187	1986
Cumbre, Circo y Lagunas de Penalara	IV	40°43'N/3°50'W	1,012	1930
Es Trenc Salobrar de Campos	IV	39°20'N/3°00'E	1,493	1984
Pinar de la Acebeda	IV	?/?	1,000	1930
Salines d'Eivissa i Formentera	IV	38°50'N/1°28'E	1,180	1985
Nature Park				
Acantilado y Pinar de Barbate	V	?/?	2,017	1989

Albufera de Valencia	V	39°26'N/0°21'W	21,000	1986
Anaga	V	28°33'N/16°13'W	14,119	1987
Ayagaures y Pilancones	V	27°53'N/15°37'W	10,166	1987
Bahia de Cadiz	V	?/?	10,000	1989
Bandama	V	28°03'N/15°27'W	1,508	1987
Barranco de la Rajita y Roque de la Fortaleza	V	28°05'N/17°15'W	1,788	1987
Barranco de las Angustias	V	28°43'N/17°55'W	1,508	1987
Barranco Quintero, El Río, La Madera y Dorado	V	28°43'N/17°43'W	1,485	1987
Barrancos de los Hombres y Fagundo y Acantila	V	28°48'N/17°58'W	1,058	1987
Betancuria	V	28°26'N/14°05'W	15,538	1987
Cabaneros	V	?/?	25,615	1988
Cabo de Gata-Nijar	V	?/?	26,000	1987
Cadi Moixero	V	42°20'N/1°55'W	41,342	1983
Canon del Rio Lobos	V	41°46'N/3°28'W	9,580	1985
Carrascal de la Font Roja	V	?/?	2,450	1987
Cornalvo	V	?/?	10,570	1988
Corona Forestal de Tenerife	V	28°20'N/16°33'W	37,173	1987
Cuenca Alta del Rio Manzanares	V	40°44'N/3°55'W	37,500	1978
Cuenca de Tejeda	V	28°00'N/15°40'W	5,968	1987
Cumbre Vieja y Teneguia	V	28°35'N/17°50'W	8,023	1987
Cumbres	V	27°59'N/15°33'W	8,929	1987
Dehesa del Moncayo	V	41°45'N/1°50'W	1,389	1978
Delta del Ebro	V	40°43'N/0°44'E	7,736	1983
Despenaperros	V	?/?	6,000	1989
Dunas de Corralejo e Isla de Lobos	V	28°43'N/13°51'W	2,526	1982
El Hierro	V	27°43'N/18°05'W	11,980	1987
El Montgo	V	?/?	2,700	1987
El Valle	V	?/?	1,900	?
Entorno de Donana	V	?/?	54,250	1989
Garraf	V	?/?	10,638	?
Guara	V	?/?	81,350	?
Guayadeque	V	27°56'N/15°30'W	1,203	1987
Hayedo de Tejera Negra	V	41°14'N/3°27'W	1,641	1978
Hoces del Duraton	V	?/?	2,600	?
Inagua, Ojeda y Pajonales	V	27°56'N/15°43'W	8,448	1987
Islas Cies	V	42°12'N/8°53'W	433	1980
Islas Columbretes	V	?/?	2,500	?
Islotes del Norte de Lanzarote y de los Risco	V	29°24'N/13°31'W	8,929	1986
Jandia	V	28°05'N/14°20'W	11,938	1987
La Geria	V	29°00'N/13°41'W	15,189	1987
La Isleta	V	28°10'N/15°25'W	1,258	1987
Ladera S. Ursula, Los Organos, Altos del Valle	V	28°24'N/16°27'W	12,114	1987
Lago de Sanabria	V	42°09'N/6°45'W	5,027	1978
Lagunas de Ruidera	V	38°57'N/2°52'W	3,772	1979
Los Alcornocales	V	?/?	170,025	1989
Los Alcornocales	V	?/?	170,025	?
Macizo de Adeje y Barranco del Infierno	V	?/?	2,057	1987
Macizo de Pena Cabarga	V	?/?	2,588	1989
Macizo de Suroeste	V	27°55'N/15°47'W	10,538	1987
Majona	V	28°08'N/17°10'W	1,920	1987
Moncayo	V	?/?	1,389	?
Monfrague	V	39°48'N/5°53'W	17,852	1979
Mont negre i el Corredor	V	?/?	15,010	?
Montana de Montserrat	V	41°36'N/1°49'E	3,630	1987
Monte Doramas	V	28°05'N/15°35'W	4,262	1987
Monte el Valle	V	37°55'N/1°06'W	1,900	1979
Monte Lentiscal	V	28°03'N/15°29'W	2,969	1987
Montes de los Sauces y Punta Llana	V	28°46'N/17°48'W	3,173	1987
Montes de Malaga	V	?/?	4,762	1989
Montseny	V	41°43'N/2°23'E	17,370	1928
Oyambre	V	?/?	5,000	?
Pena Cabarga	V	?/?	2,588	?
Pozo Negro	V	28°17'N/13°57'W	9,237	1987

S'Albufera de Mallorca	V	39°47'N/3°06'E	1,700	1988
Saja Besaya	V	43°10'N/4°09'W	24,500	1988
Saninas de Santa Pola	V	?/?	2,496	?
Sant Llorenc de Munt i L'Obal	V	41°40'N/1°59'E	9,638	1987
Senorio de Bertiz	V	42°09'N/1°39'W	2,040	1984
Sierra de Andujar	V	?/?	60,800	?
Sierra de Aracena y Picos de Aroche	V	?/?	184,000	1989
Sierra de Baza	V	?/?	52,337	1989
Sierra de Cardena y Montoro	V	?/?	41,212	1989
Sierra de Castril	V	?/?	12,265	1989
Sierra de Cazorla, Segurla y las Villas	V	38°00'N/2°45'W	214,300	1986
Sierra de Grazalema	V	36°32'N/5°28'W	51,695	1984
Sierra de Hornachuelos	V	?/?	67,202	1989
Sierra de Huetor	V	?/?	12,428	1989
Sierra de las Nieves	V	36°42'N/5°00'W	16,564	1989
Sierra de Maria	V	37°39'N/2°14'W	18,962	1987
Sierra Espuna	V	39°10'N/0°58'W	9,961	1978
Sierra Nevada	V	?/?	140,200	1989
Sierra Norte	V	?/?	164,840	?
Sierras de Andujar	V	?/?	60,800	1989
Sierras Magina	V	?/?	19,900	1989
Sierras Subbeticas de Cordoba	V	?/?	31,568	1988
Somiedo	V	?/?	29,122	1988
Tamadaba	V	28°03'N/15°42'W	8,010	1987
Teno	V	28°20'N/16°56'W	7,647	1987
Tigaiga	V	28°23'N/16°35'W	1,735	1987
Urdaibai	V	43°20'N/2°41'W	22,500	?
Urkiola	V	?/?	5,768	1989
Valle Gran Rey	V	28°07'N/17°19'W	1,960	1987
Volcan de la Corona y el Malpais de la Corona NaP	V	29°11'N/13°27'W	2,690	1987
Zona Volcanica de la Garrotxa	V	42°08'N/2°34'E	12,112	1982

Park

Collserola	V	?/?	7,992	?

SRI LANKA

Summary		
Category I	3	31,575
Category II	22	436,339
Category III	0	0
Category IV	31	328,039
Category V	0	0
Total	**56**	**795,953**

National Heritage Wilderness Area

Sinharaja	IV	6°23'N/80°28'E	11,187	1988

National Park

Flood Plains	II	8°01'N/81°07'E	17,351	1984
Gal Oya Valley	II	7°12'N/81°29'E	25,900	1954
Horton Plains	II	6°49'N/80°48'E	3,160	1988
Lahugala Kitulana	II	6°54'N/81°41'E	1,554	1980
Maduru Oya Block 1	II	7°29'N/81°13'E	51,469	1983
Maduru Oya Block 2	II	7°29'N/81°13'E	7,381	1985
Ruhuna (Yala) Block 1	II	6°29'N/81°28'E	13,679	1938
Ruhuna (Yala) Block 2	II	6°29'N/81°28'E	9,931	1954
Ruhuna (Yala) Block 3	II	6°29'N/81°28'E	40,775	1967
Ruhuna (Yala) Block 4	II	6°29'N/81°28'E	26,418	1969
Ruhuna (Yala) Block 5	II	6°29'N/81°28'E	6,656	1973
Somawathiya Block 1	II	8°12'N/81°06'E	21,057	1986

Somawathiya Block 2	II	8°12'N/81°06'E	16,589	1987
Uda Walawe	II	6°29'N/80°51'E	30,821	1972
Wasgomuwa Lot 1	II	7°46'N/80°58'E	29,036	1984
Wasgomuwa Lot 2	II	7°46'N/80°58'E	4,613	1984
Wilpattu Block 1	II	8°34'N/80°01'E	54,953	1938
Wilpattu Block 2	II	8°34'N/80°01'E	7,021	1967
Wilpattu Block 3	II	8°34'N/80°01'E	22,981	1969
Wilpattu Block 4	II	8°34'N/80°01'E	25,253	1969
Wilpattu Block 5	II	8°34'N/80°01'E	1,878	1938
Yala East Block 1	II	6°36'N/81°10'E	17,863	1969

Nature Reserve

Minneriya-Giritale Block 1	IV	7°55'N/80°55'E	7,529	1988
Tirikonamadu	IV	8°12'N/81°18'E	25,019	1986

Sanctuary

Anuradhapura	IV	8°20'N/80°24'E	3,501	1938
Bar Reef Marine	IV	8°22'N/79°44'E	30,670	1992
Buddhangala	IV	7°11'N/80°54'E	1,841	1974
Bundala	IV	6°11'N/81°12'E	6,216	1969
Chundikulam	IV	9°29'N/80°31'E	11,149	1938
Gal Oya Valley North-East	IV	7°12'N/81°29'E	12,432	1954
Gal Oya Valley South-West	IV	7°12'N/81°29'E	15,281	1954
Giant's Tank	IV	8°52'N/80°02'E	3,941	1954
Kahalla-Pallekele	IV	?/?	21,690	1989
Katagamuwa	IV	6°24'N/81°23'E	1,004	1938
Kokilai Lagoon	IV	8°59'N/80°55'E	2,995	1951
Kudumbigala	IV	6°41'N/81°45'E	4,403	1973
Madhu Road	IV	8°56'N/80°14'E	26,677	1968
Mihintale	IV	8°21'N/80°31'E	1,000	1938
Minneriya-Giritale	IV	8°02'N/80°53'E	6,693	1938
Padaviya Tank	IV	8°48'N/80°45'E	6,475	1963
Peak Wilderness	IV	6°49'N/80°37'E	22,379	1940
Polonnaruwa	IV	7°56'N/81°00'E	1,522	1938
Ravana Ella	IV	8°50'N/81°3'E	1,932	1979
Senanayake Samudra	IV	7°12'N/81°29'E	9,324	1954
Seruwila-Allai	IV	8°23'N/81°22'E	15,540	1970
Sigiriya	IV	7°57'N/80°45'E	5,099	1990
Telwatte	IV	6°11'N/80°06'E	1,425	1938
Trincomalee Naval Headworks	IV	8°31'N/81°03'E	18,130	1963
Vavunikulam	IV	9°04'N/80°21'E	4,856	1963
Victoria-Randenigala-Rantambe	IV	7°14'N/80°51'E	42,087	1987
Wilpattu North	IV	8°34'N/79°59'E	1,878	1938
Wirawila-Tissa	IV	6°17'N/81°17'E	4,164	1938

Strict Natural Reserve

Hakgala	I	6°55'N/80°48'E	1,142	1938
Ritigala	I	8°07'N/80°39'E	1,528	1941
Yala	I	6°29'N/81°28'E	28,905	1938

SUDAN/SOUDAN

Summary		
Category I	0	0
Category II	8	8,499,000
Category III	1	15,000
Category IV	6	752,500
Category V	1	116,000
Total	**16**	**9,382,500**

Game Reserve

Bengangai	IV	5°00'N/27°30'E	17,000	1939

Jebel Gurgei Massif	IV	?/?	10,000	?
Red Sea Hills	III	?/?	15,000	?
Sabaloka	V	?/?	116,000	1946
Tokar	IV	?/?	630,000	1939

Marine National Park

Sanganeb Atoll	II	19°45'N/3725'E	26,000	1990

National Park

Bandingilo	II	5°20'N/32°08'E	1,650,000	1986
Boma	II	6°09'N/33°47'E	2,280,000	1986
Dinder	II	12°17'N/35°29'E	890,000	1935
Nimule	II	3°42'N/31°55'E	41,000	1954
Radom	II	9°50'N/24°45'E	1,250,000	1980
Shambe	II	7°12'N/30°40'E	62,000	1985
Southern	II	6°25'N/28°25'E	2,300,000	1939

Wildlife Sanctuary

Arkawit	IV	?/?	82,000	1939
Arkawit-Sinkat	IV	?/?	12,000	1939
Khartoum Sunt Forest	IV	?/?	1,500	1939

SURINAME

Summary		
Category I	0	0
Category II	2	86,570
Category III	0	0
Category IV	11	649,400
Category V	0	0
Total	**13**	**735,970**

Nature Park

Brownsberg	II	4°51'N/55°11'W	8,400	1969

Nature Reserve

Boven Coesewijne	IV	5°31'N/55°35'W	27,000	1986
Brinckheuvel	IV	5°10'N/55°19'W	6,000	1972
Copi	IV	5°19'N/54°43'W	28,000	1986
Coppename Monding	IV	5°59'N/55°39'W	12,000	1966
Eilerts de Haan	IV	3°20'N/56°30'W	220,000	1966
Galibi	IV	5°46'N/53°59'W	4,000	1969
Peruvia	IV	5°43'N/56°06'W	31,000	1986
Raleighvallen-Voltzberg	II	4°45'N/56°10'W	78,170	1966
Sipaliwini	IV	2°05'N/55°55'W	100,000	1972
Tafelberg	IV	3°50'N/56°01'W	140,000	1966
Wane kreek	IV	5°37'N/54°09'W	45,400	1986
Wia-wia	IV	5°53'N/54°28'W	36,000	1961

SWAZILAND/SWAZILANDIA

Summary		
Category I	0	0
Category II	0	0
Category III	0	0
Category IV	4	45,920
Category V	0	0
Total	**4**	**45,920**

Nature Reserve

Malolotja	IV	26°04'S/31°06'E	18,175	1972

Mkhaya	IV	?/?	6,200	1981
Mlawula/Ndzindza	IV	26°15'S/32°03'E	17,000	1977

Game sanctuary

Mlilwane	IV	26°26'S/31°07'E	4,545	1972

SWEDEN/SUEDE/SUECIA

Summary		
Category I	38	949,101
Category II	15	495,028
Category III	0	0
Category IV	135	1,254,205
Category V	26	290,711
Total	**214**	**2,989,045**

National Park

Abisko	II	68°20'N/18°42'E	7,700	1909
Björnlandet	II	63°30'N/18°29'E	1,130	1991
Bla Jungfrun	II	57°15'N/16°48'E	198	1926
Djurö	II	58°53'N/13°28'E	2,400	1991
Gotska Sandön	II	58°25'N/19°25'E	4,500	1909
Muddus	II	66°53'N/20°11'E	49,340	1942
Padjelanta	II	67°28'N/16°43'E	198,400	1962
Peljekaise	II	66°22'N/16°45'E	15,340	1909
Sarek	II	67°20'N/17°37'E	197,000	1909
Skuleskogen	II	63°01'N/18°36'E	2,950	1984
Sonfjället	II	62°17'N/13°37'E	2,622	1909
Stora Sjofallet	V	67°40'N/18°00'E	127,800	1909
Store Mosse	II	57°18'N/13°57'E	7,850	1982
Tiveden	II	58°47'N/14°32'E	1,353	1983
Töfsingdalen	II	62°07'N/12°30'E	1,615	1930
Vadvetjåkka	II	68°33'N/18°25'E	2,630	1920

Nature Conservation Area

Agön Kråkön	V	?/?	3,030	1990
Brattforsheden	V	?/?	11,400	1984
Bålsön	V	?/?	740	1990
Fegen-A	V	?/?	2,075	1980
Fegen-B	V	?/?	3,117	1980
Gaso islands	V	?/?	202	1988
Gullmarn	V	?/?	40,300	1983
Halle och Hunnebergs plataer-A	V	?/?	4,100	1982
Halle och Hunnebergs plataer-B	V	?/?	2,035	1982
Hallsundsudde - Sonnerbergen	V	?/?	1,920	1978
Hartso	IV	58°41'N/17°29'E	5,630	1981
Häckeberga	V	?/?	4,482	1982
Kallands Skargardar	V	?/?	6,500	1989
Kalvo skargard	V	?/?	2,190	1986
Kinnekulle	V	?/?	6,655	1982
Malingsbo-Kloten-A	V	?/?	14,800	1981
Malingsbo-Kloten-B	V	?/?	8,700	1981
Malingsbo-Kloten-C	V	?/?	25,000	1981
Nordingrå	V	?/?	6,000	1983
Stenningsundskusten	V	?/?	2,136	1988
Stigfjorden	V	58°05'N/11°40'E	7,000	1979
Svenska Bjorn	V	?/?	4,500	1983
Tanumskusten	V	?/?	1,224	1988
Tullgarn	V	?/?	1,755	1984
Öja-Landsort	V	?/?	500	1985

Nature Reserve

Alajaure	I	68°10'N/20°15'E	17,000	1980

Algon	IV	?/?	1,046	1974
Almo	IV	?/?	880	1987
Ämtö	IV	?/?	458	1975
Ängso	IV	59°37'N/18°26'E	6,860	1960
Anjosvarden	IV	?/?	2,600	1992
Arholam-Ido	IV	?/?	1,035	1978
Arshultsmyren	IV	?/?	1,150	1972
Arvesjåkka	I	?/?	8,000	1988
Aspnas	IV	?/?	1,560	1973
Åsvikelandet	IV	?/?	1,567	1971
Axmor	IV	?/?	4,500	1978
Bennbol	IV	60°00'N/18°30'E	9,370	1970
Billuden	IV	?/?	1,930	1979
Biskopso	IV	?/?	4,000	1983
Bjorko	IV	?/?	300	1980
Bjurälven	IV	?/?	2,290	1982
Blaikfjället	I	?/?	11,000	1988
Braviken	IV	?/?	9,160	1968
Brommö	IV	?/?	955	1987
Bullero	IV	59°12'N/18°52'E	4,300	1967
Bårgå	IV	?/?	4,100	1988
Båtfors	IV	?/?	1,550	1991
Daimadalen	I	?/?	28,400	1990
Dellikälven	I	?/?	8,800	1988
Drakon	IV	?/?	1,510	1990
Dundret	IV	67°07'N/20°40'E	5,500	1970
Esterön	IV	?/?	755	1973
Fjärdlång	IV	?/?	2,000	1986
Florarna	I	60°18'N/17°50'E	5,172	1976
Fullfjallet	IV	?/?	38,060	1973
Fulltofta	IV	?/?	1,020	1971
Gitsfjället	I	?/?	40,000	1988
Glaskogen	IV	59°31'N/12°24'E	28,000	1970
Gryt	IV	58°10'N/16°50'E	2,574	1968
Gyllbergen	IV	?/?	1,020	1982
Gysinge	IV	?/?	2,260	1975
Hall-Hangvar	IV	57°53'N/18°43'E	2,161	1967
Haparanda Sandskar	IV	65°34'N/23°45'E	4,256	1961
Harjaro	IV	?/?	1,130	1975
Harmano	IV	?/?	1,550	1967
Harrejaure	I	?/?	26,700	1988
Hastholmen-Ytteron	IV	?/?	1,160	1975
Hedlandet	IV	?/?	1,365	1978
Hemlingson	IV	?/?	1,789	1989
Hermano	IV	58°09'N/11°23'E	610	1967
Hjälmö-Lådna	IV	?/?	1,370	1991
Holmöarna	I	?/?	25,000	1980
Hornavan	I	?/?	12,000	1988
Hovfjället	IV	60°15'N/13°00'E	1,400	1969
Häringe-Hammersta	IV	?/?	2,020	1991
Hökensås	IV	58°07'N/14°06'E	5,500	1969
Innerviksfjärdarna	I	64°42'N/21°07'E	1,530	1974
Jarflotta	IV	?/?	3,225	1968
Kaitum	I	?/?	40,100	1988
Kallovaratjeh	IV	67°05'N/16°54'E	2,235	1970
Kartevare	I	?/?	2,400	1988
Kilsviken	IV	59°03'N/14°04'E	2,220	1971
Klaveron	IV	57°52'N/11°35'E	2,252	1966
Klingavälsån	IV	55°37'N/13°38'E	2,128	1968
Komosse	IV	?/?	1,117	1980
Kosteröarna	IV	?/?	1,155	1984
Kronören	IV	?/?	4,067	1975
Kungshamn	IV	?/?	1,170	1963

Kvado	IV	?/?	1,569	1979
Käringboda	IV	?/?	1,060	1974
Lacka	IV	58°45'N/17°30'E	4,898	1978
Laholmsbukten	IV	56°33'N/12°50'E	7,500	1972
Lake Takern	IV	58°21'N/14°49'E	5,420	1975
Langfjallet	IV	?/?	51,705	1973
Lango	IV	58°45'N/17°30'E	1,590	1980
Langvattnet	IV	?/?	1,020	1974
Langviksskar	IV	?/?	2,300	1983
Licknevarpefjärden	IV	58°04'N/16°45'E	6,020	1970
Likskar	IV	?/?	2,362	1969
Lilla Husarn	IV	?/?	1,000	1981
Lilla Karlsö	IV	57°19'N/18°06'E	164	1955
Lina	IV	?/?	8,600	1988
Listerby	IV	?/?	1,015	1981
Luro Archipelago	IV	?/?	1,500	1967
Långsjön	I	?/?	2,200	1988
Marsfjället	I	?/?	86,000	1988
Millesvik Archipelago	IV	?/?	8,000	1980
Misterhult	IV	57°24'N/16°38'E	8,500	1967
Nalovardo	I	?/?	4,700	1992
Nimtek	I	?/?	4,400	1988
Njupeskar	I	61°35'N/12°37'E	1,447	1970
Norra Vattens	IV	?/?	2,340	1973
Nuortap-Antivaratj	I	?/?	7,600	1988
Nynas	IV	?/?	3,890	1971
Örskär	IV	?/?	471	1969
Östra friluftsreservat	IV	?/?	1,080	1973
Östra Jarvafaltet	IV	?/?	1,200	1979
Östra Kullaberg	IV	56°15'N/12°30'E	1,000	1965
Oxfjället	I	?/?	1,700	1988
Palja	I	?/?	4,300	1988
Parlalven	IV	?/?	56,600	1988
Pater Noster Skargarden	IV	?/?	3,280	1986
Perso	IV	65°46'N/22°08'E	4,000	1981
Pessinki	I	?/?	51,500	1988
Plassa	I	?/?	1,200	1988
Pälkåive	I	?/?	1,400	1988
Påkketanjaure	I	?/?	21,000	1988
Rago	IV	?/?	1,562	1980
Rautusakkara	IV	?/?	1,200	1988
Revskar	IV	?/?	2,400	1973
Ridö-Sundbyholm	IV	?/?	5,756	1984
Ringso	IV	58°45'N/17°30'E	1,825	1980
Rodkallen-Sor-Aspen	IV	?/?	7,004	1970
Rogen	IV	62°17'N/12°27'E	48,700	1976
Roro	IV	?/?	150	1976
Salvorev	IV	?/?	62,000	1987
Sandsjöbacka	V	57°30'N/12°12'E	2,550	1968
Sankt Anna inkl. Vanso	IV	?/?	1,211	1967
Serri	IV	66°34'N/20°15'E	3,687	1970
Sibberon	IV	?/?	1,015	1979
Sjalbottna-O Lagno	IV	?/?	150	1977
Sjaunja	I	67°15'N/19°40'E	285,000	1986
Skarsåsfjällen	I	?/?	1,200	1990
Skokloster	IV	?/?	1,790	1972
Skäckerfjällen	I	?/?	46,700	1988
Slado-Askeskar	IV	57°50'N/16°45'E	2,000	1965
Slaton-Medholma	IV	?/?	1,790	1970
Stadjan	IV	?/?	20,393	1973
Stadsholmen	IV	57°53'N/16°45'E	1,600	1968
Stenungsundskusten	IV	?/?	2,136	1988
Stora Karlso	IV	57°17'N/17°58'E	1,180	1970

Stora Nassa	IV	?/?	3,000	1965
Storasjoomradet	I	?/?	1,058	1985
Stordalen	I	?/?	1,000	1980
Storrebben	IV	?/?	2,737	1969
Storö-Bockö-Lökaö	IV	?/?	5,900	1972
Storön	IV	?/?	302	1970
Strömsholm	IV	?/?	2,584	1979
Stubba	IV	?/?	8,300	1988
Sundby	IV	?/?	5,000	1965
Svenska Hogarna	IV	?/?	2,600	1976
Svenskadalen	I	?/?	18,700	1990
Svensmarö	IV	?/?	315	1978
Sydbillingen	IV	?/?	1,750	1981
Tandövala	I	?/?	3,450	1987
Tinäset	I	?/?	3,350	1983
Tjadnesvare	I	?/?	4,000	1988
Tjeggelvas	I	?/?	32,100	1988
Toro	IV	?/?	1,174	1973
Tromto	IV	?/?	1,242	1982
Tyresta-Åva	IV	?/?	3,400	1986
Tåkern	IV	?/?	5,420	1975
Uto	IV	?/?	4,110	1974
Vaggo	IV	?/?	136	1975
Vallo	IV	?/?	2,663	1973
Verkean	IV	?/?	2,506	1975
Vindelfjallen	IV	66°00'N/15°55'E	550,630	1974
Vittangi-Soppero	I	?/?	18,800	1988
Vrango	IV	?/?	5,310	1979
Värmland	IV	?/?	24,300	1980
Västra Åsnen	IV	?/?	1,228	1986
Vättlefjäll	IV	?/?	1,621	1987
Vålådalen	I	?/?	117,500	1988
Våmhuskölen	I	?/?	2,694	1987

Wildlife Sanctuary

Annsjon-Enadeltat	IV	63°16'N/12°32'E	1,029	1990
Bjarehalvons kust	IV	?/?	4,700	1967
Bjurum-Dagsnäs	IV	58°18'N/13°25'E	3,600	1992
Enskar	IV	?/?	2,670	1984
Kallskaren	IV	?/?	1,400	1978
Klacksten mfl, Gryt, St Anna	IV	?/?	5,000	1987
Klyndrorna-Svartbadorna-Ekbadorna	IV	?/?	1,065	1974
Lessejaure	IV	?/?	1,010	1982
Lillgrund	IV	?/?	1,300	1981
Oro Sankor	IV	?/?	1,095	1978
Tjalmejaure	IV	67°15'N/16°11'E	44,010	1967
Vaderon	IV	?/?	2,105	1967
Vasterbaden-Lagrunden	IV	?/?	1,540	1976

SWITZERLAND/SUISSE/SUIZA

Summary		
Category I	1	16,887
Category II	0	0
Category III	0	0
Category IV	48	241,198
Category V	60	472,622
Total	**109**	**730,707**

Federal Hunting Reserve

Augstmatthorn	IV	?/?	2,116	?
Bernina-Albris	IV	?/?	7,405	?

Campo Tencia	IV	?/?	3,494	?
Combe-Grede	IV	?/?	1,099	?
Creux-du-Van	IV	?/?	1,443	?
Fellital	IV	?/?	4,133	?
Grand Muveran	IV	?/?	5,006	?
Graue Horner	IV	?/?	5,640	?
Greina	IV	?/?	6,013	?
Hahnen	IV	?/?	2,297	?
Haut de Cry/Derborence	IV	?/?	7,244	?
Hochmatt-Motelon	IV	?/?	3,135	?
Hutstock	IV	?/?	5,385	?
Karpf	IV	?/?	10,681	?
Kiental	IV	?/?	8,337	?
Le Noirmont	IV	?/?	2,584	?
Les Bimis-Ciernes Picat	IV	?/?	1,288	?
Leukerbad	IV	?/?	5,395	?
Mont Pleureur	IV	?/?	11,558	?
Pez Vial	IV	?/?	2,203	?
Pierreuse-Gummfluh	IV	?/?	1,029	?
Piz Beverin	IV	?/?	3,309	?
Piz Ela	IV	?/?	3,656	?
Santis	IV	?/?	2,632	?
Schilt	IV	?/?	1,361	?
Schwarzhorn	IV	?/?	7,671	?
Silbern-Jagern-Bodmerenwald	IV	?/?	10,250	?
Tannhorn	IV	?/?	1,187	?
Trescolmen	IV	?/?	1,965	?
Turtmanntal	IV	?/?	3,781	?
Urirotstock	IV	?/?	2,643	?
Val Ferret/Combe de l'A	IV	?/?	6,613	?

Landscape Protected Area

Aarelandschaft Thun-Bern	V	46°55'N/7°32'E	1,061	1983
Albiskette-Reppischtal	V	47°17'N/8°30'E	4,191	1983
Baselbieter Tafeljura mit Eital	V	47°36'N/7°54'E	4,526	1983
Belchen-Passwang-Gebiet	V	47°22'N/7°45'E	6,557	1983
Bergsturzgebiet von Goldau	V	47°05'N/8°33'E	1,320	1983
Berner Hochalpen & Aletsch-Bietschhorn-Gebiet	V	46°30'N/8°00'E	42,866	1983
Binntal	V	46°23'N/8°13'E	5,084	1977
Campolungo-Campo Tencia-Piumogna	V	46°28'N/8°45'E	5,349	1983
Creux du Van et Gorges de l'Areuse	V	46°58'N/6°43'E	2,123	1971
Dent Blanche-Matterhorn-Monte Rosa	V	46°00'N/7°40'E	30,271	1983
Denti della Vecchia	V	46°05'N/9°02'E	2,137	1983
Flyschlandschaft Hagleren-Glaubenberg-Schlieren	V	46°53'N/8°19'E	11,892	1983
Franches Montagnes	V	47°17'N/7°02'E	3,979	1977
Gelten-Iffigen	V	46°23'N/7°23'E	4,687	1977
Gempenplateau	V	47°28'N/7°40'E	4,458	1983
Glaziallandschaft Neerach-Stadel	V	47°31'N/8°29'E	1,413	1977
Glaziallandschaft zwischen Lorenztobel & Sihl	V	47°10'N/8°36'E	10,904	1983
Glaziallandschaft zwischen Thur und Rhein	V	47°37'N/8°48'E	12,192	1977
Hallwilersee	V	47°18'N/8°11'E	1,903	1977
Hohgant	V	46°45'N/7°52'E	2,275	1977
Irchel	V	47°32'N/8°37'E	2,236	1977
Kesch-Ducan-Gebiet	V	46°30'N/9°52'E	13,760	1977
La Côte	V	46°28'N/6°20'E	1,786	1977
La Pierreuse-Gummfluh-Vallée de l'Etivaz	V	46°25'N/7°01'E	6,282	1983
Lac de Tanay	V	46°20'N/6°51'E	1,503	1977
Lag da Toma	V	46°38'N/8°41'E	1,114	1977
Lagerengebiet	V	47°28'N/8°21'E	2,486	1977
Le Chasseral	V	47°08'N/7°00'E	2,159	1977
Maderanertal-Fellital	V	46°47'N/8°45'E	16,176	1977

Monte Generoso	V	45°52'N/9°02'E	6,203	1977
Monte San Giorgio	V	45°55'N/8°52'E	2,360	1977
Murgtal-Murtschental	V	47°04'N/9°12'E	4,210	1977
Napfbergland	V	47°00'N/7°56'E	16,352	1983
Oberengadiner Seenlandschaft und Berninagruppe	V	46°26'N/9°30'E	37,523	1983
Pilatus	V	46°59'N/8°15'E	5,052	1977
Piora-Lucomagno-Dotra	V	46°33'N/8°45'E	9,690	1977
Piz Arina	V	46°51'N/10°22'E	4,991	1983
Quellgebiet des Hinterrheins & San Bernardino	V	46°30'N/9°10'E	5,833	1977
Randen	V	47°45'N/8°35'E	7,513	1977
Reusslandschaft	V	47°19'N/8°21'E	6,465	1977
Rive sud du lac de Neuchâtel	V	46°00'N/6°50'E	4,218	1983
Ruinaulta	V	46°48'N/9°19'E	2,044	1977
Schrattenflue	V	46°51'N/7°59'E	4,230	1983
Silberen	V	46°58'N/8°52'E	8,369	1977
Silvretta-Vereina	V	46°48'N/10°01'E	14,376	1983
Tafeljura nordlich Gelterkinden	V	47°29'N/7°51'E	1,847	1983
Thurgauisch-furstenlandische Kulturlandschaft	V	47°30'N/9°18'E	1,297	1983
Untersee-Hochrhein	V	47°39'N/8°50'E	12,827	1983
Val Bavona	V	46°24'N/8°31'E	11,969	1983
Val de Bagnes	V	46°00'N/7°21'E	16,869	1977
Val di Campo	V	46°24'N/10°07'E	3,023	1977
Val Verzasca	V	46°19'N/8°49'E	19,932	1983
Vallée du Doubs	V	47°14'N/6°58'E	3,998	1977
Vallée de la Brévine	V	46°58'N/6°30'E	4,218	1977
Vallon de Nant	V	46°13'N/7°06'E	1,492	1977
Vanil Noir	V	46°37'N/7°11'E	4,931	1977
Vierwaldstattersee mit Kernwald Burgenstock	V	46°58'N/8°30'E	38,447	1983
Wassermatten in den Talern der Langete der Rot	V	47°10'N/7°49'E	1,063	1983
Weissenstein	V	47°15'N/7°30'E	2,989	1977
Zugersee	V	47°06'N/8°28'E	1,601	1983

National Park

Suisse	I	46°40'N/10°10'E	16,887	1914

Nature Reserve

Binntal	IV	46°23'N/8°13'E	4,650	?
Combe Grede	IV	47°06'N/7°05'E	1,202	?
Creux du Van et Gorges de L'Areuse	IV	46°52'N/6°44'E	1,100	?
Engstlen See - Junigbach - Achtelsass	IV	46°45'N/8°22'E	10,500	?
Grimsel	IV	46°35'N/8°15'E	10,000	?
Hohgant	IV	46°45'N/7°52'E	1,504	?
Holloch Karst	IV	46°58'N/8°55'E	9,240	?
La Pierreuse	IV	46°30'N/7°15'E	3,255	?
Val de Bagnes	IV	46°00'N/7°21'E	20,000	?
Val Languard, dal Fain, & Minor	IV	46°29'N/9°58'E	1,750	?
Vallée de Joux et Haut-Jura vaudois	IV	46°37'N/6°15'E	22,000	?
Vallée du Doubs	IV	47°14'N/6°58'E	3,400	?
Vallon de Nant	IV	46°10'N/6°55'E	1,368	?

Water and Migratory Bird Reserve

Fanel-Chablais de Cudrefin, Pointe de Martin	IV	46°59'N/7°03'E	1,566	1991
Les Grangettes	IV	46°23'N/6°54'E	6,010	1991
Rhône-Verbois	IV	46°11'N/6°05'E	1,100	1991

SYRIAN ARAB REPUBLIC/ REPUBLIQUE ARABE SYRIENNE/ REPUBLICA ARABE SIRIA

No Areas Listed

TAIWAN, PROVINCE OF CHINA/
TAIWAN, PROVINCE CHINOISE DE/
TAIWAN, PROVINCIA DE CHINA

	Summary	
Category I	0	0
Category II	4	303,486
Category III	0	0
Category IV	8	79,024
Category V	2	44,087
Total	**14**	**426,597**

National Park

Kenting	V	21°57'N/120°46'E	32,631	1982
Lanyu	II	22°04'N/121°32'E	29,146	?
Shei-Pa	II	24°37'N/121°21'E	76,850	1992
Taroko	II	24°13'N/121°28'E	92,000	1986
Yangmingshan	V	25°11'N/121°30'E	11,456	1985
Yushan	II	23°25'N/121°02'E	105,490	1985

Nature Reserve

Cha Tian Mountain	IV	24°52'N/121°26'E	7,760	1992
Chu Yun Mountain	IV	22°59'N/120°48'E	6,249	1992
Ta-Wu Mountain	IV	22°38'N/120°45'E	47,000	1987

Protected Area

Bei-Men Coast	IV	23°19'N/120°03'E	2,980	1987
Jian-Shan Coast	IV	22°08'N/120°41'E	1,090	1987
Lan-Yang River Mouth	IV	24°45'N/121°48'E	4,190	1984
Sue-Hua Coast	IV	24°18'N/121°45'E	7,145	1984
Tan-Shui River Mouth	IV	25°09'N/121°26'E	2,610	1984

TAJIKISTAN/TADJIKISTAN/TAYIKISTAN

	Summary	
Category I	3	85,700
Category II	0	0
Category III	0	0
Category IV	0	0
Category V	0	0
Total	**3**	**85,700**

Zapovednik

Dashti-Dzhumskiy	I	34°12'N/70°02'E	19,700	1983
Ramit	I	37°12'N/69°22'E	16,100	1959
Tigrovaya Balka	I	38°40'N/68°23'E	49,900	1938

TANZANIA, UNITED REPUBLIC OF/
REPUBLIQUE-UNIE DE TANZANIE/
REPUBLICA UNIDA DE TANZANIA

	Summary	
Category I	0	0
Category II	12	4,099,975
Category III	0	0
Category IV	18	9,790,000
Category V	0	0
Total	**30**	**13,889,975**

Forest Reserve

Udzungwa	IV	7°50'S/35°55'E	120,000	1959

Game Reserve

Biharamulo	IV	2°30'S/31°30'E	130,000	1959
Burigi	IV	2°05'S/31°20'E	220,000	1980
Ibanda	IV	1°09'S/30°35'E	20,000	1974
Kigosi	IV	3°42'S/31°34'E	700,000	1983
Kilimanjaro	IV	?/?	90,000	1974
Kizigo	IV	6°40'S/34°33'E	400,000	1974
Maswa	IV	3°20'S/34°30'E	220,000	1969
Mkomazi	IV	4°00'S/38°00'E	100,000	1951
Mount Meru	IV	3°13'S/36°43'E	30,000	1974
Moyowosi	IV	4°08'S/31°00'E	600,000	1982
Rumanyika	IV	11°35'S/30°49'E	80,000	?
Rungwa	IV	6°55'S/34°00'E	900,000	1951
Saadani	IV	6°00'S/38°40'E	30,000	1968
Selous	IV	8°46'S/37°25'E	5,000,000	1922
Ugalla River	IV	5°53'S/31°50'E	500,000	1964
Umba	IV	4°20'S/38°50'E	150,000	1974
Uwanda	IV	8°32'S/32°08'E	500,000	1971

National Park

Arusha	II	3°15'S/36°55'E	13,700	1967
Gombe	II	4°40'S/29°35'E	5,200	1968
Katavi	II	6°53'S/31°10'E	225,300	1974
Kilimanjaro	II	3°00'S/37°30'E	75,575	1973
Lake Manyara	II	3°30'S/35°45'E	32,500	1960
Mahale Mountain	II	6°10'S/29°50'E	157,700	1985
Mikumi	II	7°25'S/37°15'E	323,000	1964
Ruaha	II	7°26'S/34°37'E	1,295,000	1964
Rubondo	II	2°25'S/31°50'E	45,700	1977
Serengeti	II	2°25'S/34°38'E	1,476,300	1951
Tarangire	II	3°50'S/36°00'E	260,000	1970
Udzungwa Mountain	II	7°52'S/36°35'E	190,000	1992

THAILAND/THAÏLANDE/TAILANDIA

Summary		
Category I	0	0
Category II	74	4,336,026
Category III	0	0
Category IV	36	2,671,150
Category V	1	13,100
Total	**111**	**7,020,276**

National Park

Ao Phangnga	II	8°17'N/98°36'E	40,000	1989
Chae Son	II	18°42'N/99°20'E	59,200	1988
Chaloem Rattanakosin (Tham Than Lot)	II	14°20'N/99°10'E	5,900	1980
Chat Trakan	II	?/?	54,300	1987
Doi Inthanon	II	18°32'N/98°34'E	48,240	1972
Doi Khuntan	II	18°27'N/99°17'E	25,529	1975
Doi Luang	II	19°22'N/99°35'E	117,000	1990
Doi Suthep-Pui	II	18°47'N/98°55'E	26,106	1981
Erawan	II	14°15'N/99°15'E	55,000	1975
Hat Chao Mai	II	7°22'N/99°20'E	23,086	1981
Hat Nai Yang	II	8°07'N/98°17'E	9,000	1981
Hat Nopharat Thara - Mu Ko Phi Phi	II	7°52'N/98°50'E	38,996	1983
Hat Vanakorn	II	?/?	3,800	1992
Huai Huat	II	16°52'N/104°17'E	82,856	1988
Kaeng Krachan	II	12°52'N/99°22'E	291,500	1981
Kaeng Krung	II	9°30'N/98°50'E	54,100	1991

Kaeng Tana	II	15°45'N/105°32'E	8,000	1981
Khao Chamao-Khao Wong	II	12°56'N/101°45'E	8,368	1975
Khao Khitchakut	II	13°00'N/102°10'E	5,870	1977
Khao Laem	II	14°55'N/98°32'E	149,700	1991
Khao Laem Ya - Mu Ko Samet	V	12°32'N/101°27'E	13,100	1981
Khao Lak-Lamru	II	8°37'N/98°22'E	12,500	1991
Khao Lam Pi - Hat Thai Muang	II	8°27'N/98°15'E	7,200	1986
Khao Luang	II	8°22'N/99°46'E	57,000	1974
Khao Namkang	II	63°0'N/100°35'E	21,200	1991
Khao Pu - Khao Ya	II	7°45'N/99°50'E	69,400	1982
Khao Sam Lan	II	14°30'N/100°39'E	4,457	1981
Khao Sam Roi Yot	II	12°12'N/100°00'E	9,808	1966
Khao Sok	II	8°57'N/98°40'E	64,552	1980
Khao Yai	II	14°20'N/101°31'E	216,863	1962
Khlong Lan	II	16°25'N/99°10'E	30,000	1982
Klong Wang Chao	II	16°20'N/99°07'E	74,700	1990
Laem Son	II	9°30'N/98°25'E	31,500	1983
Lansang	II	16°04'N/98°00'E	10,400	1979
Mae Ping	II	17°37'N/98°45'E	100,300	1981
Mae Wong	II	15°52'N/99°15'E	89,400	1987
Mae Yom	II	18°42'N/100°07'E	45,475	1986
Mu Ko Chang	II	12°00'N/102°15'E	65,000	1982
Mu Ko Lanta	II	7°32'N/99°07'E	13,400	1990
Mu Ko Phetra	II	6°57'N/99°35'E	49,438	1984
Mu Ko Similan	II	8°32'N/97°25'E	12,800	1982
Mu Ko Surin	II	9°10'N/97°47'E	13,500	1981
Mukdahan	II	16°27'N/104°32'E	4,850	1988
Nam Nao	II	16°52'N/101°37'E	96,600	1972
Namtok Chat Trakan	II	17°17'N/100°40'E	54,300	1987
Namtok Mae Surin	II	19°02'N/98°02'E	39,600	1981
Namtok Phlui (Khao Sabup)	II	12°32'N/102°10'E	13,450	1975
Namtok Yong	II	8°17'N/99°45'E	128,125	1991
Ob Luang	II	18°12'N/98°32'E	345,625	1991
Pang Sida	II	14°05'N/102°12'E	84,400	1982
Phatam	II	15°32'N/105°30'E	34,000	1991
Phu Chong - Na Yoi	II	14°25'N/99°15'E	68,600	1987
Phu Hin Rong Kla	II	17°00'N/100°32'E	30,700	1984
Phu Kao - Phu Phan Kham	II	16°57'N/102°32'E	32,200	1985
Phu Kradung	II	17°02'N/101°44'E	34,812	1962
Phu Pha Man	II	16°45'N/101°45'E	35,000	1991
Phu Phan	II	17°00'N/103°56'E	66,470	1972
Phu Rua	II	17°30'N/101°36'E	12,084	1979
Phu Sa Dok Bua	II	16°12'N/104°42'E	23,000	1992
Phu Wiang	II	16°47'N/102°15'E	32,500	1991
Ramkamhaeng	II	16°27'N/99°40'E	34,100	1980
Sai Thong	II	16°20'N/101°32'E	31,900	1992
Sai Yok	II	14°17'N/98°17'E	50,000	1980
Si Laana	II	19°17'N/99°12'E	140,600	1989
Si Nakarin	II	14°22'N/99°22'E	153,200	1981
Si Phangnga	II	09°07'N/98°27'E	24,608	1988
Si Satchanalai	II	17°35'N/99°27'E	21,320	1981
Tai Romyen	II	8°45'N/99°30'E	42,500	1991
Tarutao	II	6°42'N/99°42'E	149,000	1974
Tat Ton	II	15°47'N/101°20'E	21,718	1980
Thaleban	II	6°40'N/100°07'E	19,600	1980
Thap Lan	II	14°22'N/102°15'E	223,580	1981
Thung Salaeng Luang	II	17°00'N/100°22'E	126,240	1972
Ton Krabak Yai (Taksinmaharat)	II	16°50'N/98°52'E	14,900	1981
Wiang Kosai	II	17°52'N/99°10'E	41,000	1981

Wildlife Sanctuary

Doi Chiang Dao	IV	19°24'N/98°55'E	52,100	1978

Doi Luang	IV	18°25'N/100°06'E	9,705	1984
Doi Pha Chang	IV	19°04'N/100°26'E	57,108	1980
Doi Pha Muang	IV	18°20'N/99°14'E	58,311	1980
Huai Kha Khaeng	IV	15°36'N/99°18'E	278,014	1972
Huai Sa La	IV	14°30'N/104°12'E	38,000	1990
Khao Ang Ru Nai	IV	13°16'N/101°47'E	103,000	1977
Khao Banthat	IV	7°34'N/99°51'E	126,695	1977
Khao Khieo-Khao Chomphu	IV	13°12'N/101°05'E	14,470	1974
Khao Pra Bang Kram	IV	7°50'N/99°22'E	18,640	1987
Khao Sanam Phriang	IV	16°35'N/99°18'E	10,100	1985
Khao Soi Dao	IV	12°50'N/102°15'E	74,502	1972
Khlong Nakha	IV	9°24'N/98°33'E	53,033	1972
Khlong Phraya	IV	8°25'N/98°58'E	9,500	1980
Khlong Saeng	IV	9°13'N/98°29'E	115,530	1974
Khlong Yan	IV	12°25'N/87°45'E	47,200	1992
Mae Tuen	IV	17°07'N/98°39'E	117,300	1978
Mae Yuam Fang Khwa	IV	18°24'N/97°54'E	29,200	1986
Maenam Phachi	IV	13°18'N/99°25'E	48,931	1978
Omgoy	IV	17°50'N/98°28'E	122,400	1983
Pa Pru	IV	06°16'N/101°53'E	20,100	1991
Phanom Dong Rak	IV	14°26'N/104°33'E	31,600	1978
Phu Khieo	IV	16°34'N/101°38'E	156,000	1972
Phu Luang	IV	17°19'N/101°30'E	89,695	1974
Phu Miang-Phu Thong	IV	17°16'N/100°40'E	69,951	1977
Phu Santan	IV	?/?	25,000	1990
Phu Wua	IV	18°08'N/104°01'E	18,650	1975
Phu-si-tan	IV	16°35'N/104°09'E	25,000	1990
Prince Chumphon Park	IV	10°53'N/099°07'E	45,400	1988
Salawin	IV	18°18'N/97°49'E	87,500	1978
Sub-lungka	IV	15°35'N/101°21'E	15,500	1986
Thung Yai Naresuan	IV	15°13'N/98°51'E	364,720	1974
Ton Nga Chang	IV	65°7'N/100°14'E	18,195	1978
Umphang	IV	15°54'N/098°46'E	251,565	1989
Utthayan Krom Luangchumpon	IV	?/?	46,000	1988
Yod Dom	IV	14°21'N/105°01'E	22,535	1977

TOGO

Summary		
Category I	0	0
Category II	3	357,290
Category III	0	0
Category IV	8	289,616
Category V	0	0
Total	**11**	**646,906**

Faunal Reserve

Abdoulaye	IV	8°38'N/1°17'E	30,000	1951
Akaba	IV	7°50'N/1°15'E	25,626	?
Djamdè	IV	9°17'N/0°53'E	1,650	1954
Galangashie	IV	10°20'N/0°17'E	7,500	1954
Haho-Yoto	IV	6°50'N/1°28'E	18,000	1955
Kpessi	IV	8°08'N/1°15'E	28,000	?
Oti-Mandouri	IV	10°40'N/0°43'E	147,840	?
Togodo	IV	6°50'N/1°28'E	31,000	1952

National Park

Fazao-Malfakassa	II	8°55'N/0°47'E	192,000	1951
Fosse aux Lions	II	10°47'N/0°10'E	1,650	1954
Kéran	II	10°13'N/0°43'E	163,640	1950

TONGA

No Areas Listed

TRINIDAD AND TOBAGO/
TRINITE-ET-TOBAGO/
TRINIDAD Y TOBAGO

	Summary	
Category I	1	1,800
Category II	0	0
Category III	0	0
Category IV	5	13,928
Category V	0	0
Total	**6**	**15,728**

Game Sanctuary

Bush Bush	IV	10°23'N/61°04'W	1,554	1968
Central Range	IV	10°26'N/61°14'W	2,153	1934
Little Tobago	IV	11°17'N/60°30'W	101	1928
Southern Watershed	IV	10°05'N/61°29'W	1,874	1934
Trinity Hill	IV	10°08'N/61°08'W	8,246	1934

Prohibited Area

Aripo Savannas	I	10°36'N/61°12'W	1,800	1987

TUNISIA/TUNISIE/TUNEZ

	Summary	
Category I	1	450
Category II	6	44,417
Category III	0	0
Category IV	0	0
Category V	0	0
Total	**7**	**44,867**

Marine Reserve

Galiton	I	37°28'N/8°45'E	450	1980

National Park

Bou Kornine	II	36°42'N/10°30'E	1,939	1987
Djebel Bou-Hedma	II	34°25'N/9°38'E	16,488	1980
Djebel Chambi	II	35°13'N/8°43'E	6,723	1980
El Feidja	II	36°30'N/8°20'E	2,637	1990
Ichkeul	II	37°10'N/9°40'E	12,600	1980
Zembra and Zembretta	II	37°06'N/10°48'E	4,030	1973

TURKEY/TURQUIE/TURQUIA

	Summary	
Category I	4	20,903
Category II	19	395,977
Category III	0	0
Category IV	14	300,650
Category V	7	101,911
Total	**44**	**819,441**

National Park

Altindere Vadisi	II	?/?	4,800	1987
Baskomutan	II	?/?	42,183	1981

Beydaglari coastal	II	36°30'N/30°25'E	34,425	1972
Beyschir Golu	II	?/?	88,750	1993
Bogazkoy-Alacahoyuk historical	II	?/?	2,634	1988
Dilek Yarimadisi	II	37°45'N/27°16'E	10,985	1966
Gelibolu Yarimadisi (Galipoli)	V	40°22'N/26°26'E	33,000	1973
Goreme	V	38°42'N/34°54'E	9,572	1986
Ilgaz Dagi	II	41°02'N/33°32'E	1,088	1976
Karatepe-Aslantas	V	37°15'N/36°04'E	7,715	1958
Kazdagi	II	?/?	21,300	1993
Kizildag	II	38°04'N/31°22'E	59,400	1969
Koprulu Kanyon	II	37°15'N/31°15'E	36,614	1973
Kovada Golu	II	37°37'N/30°52'E	6,534	1971
Macka Altindere Vadisi	II	40°50'N/39°43'E	4,800	1987
Munzur Vadisi	II	39°07'N/39°34'E	42,000	1971
Nemrut Dagi	II	?/?	13,850	1988
Soguksu	II	40°28'N/32°37'E	1,050	1959
Spildag	II	38°33'N/27°29'E	5,505	1968
Termessos	II	36°59'N/30°29'E	6,702	1971
Uludag	II	40°12'N/29°14'E	11,338	1961
Yedigoller	II	41°15'N/31°40'E	2,019	1965

Nature Park

Abant Golu	V	?/?	1,150	1988
Golcuk	V	?/?	6,684	1991
Hacer Ormani	V	?/?	42,165	1991
Uzungol	V	40°56'N/38°00'E	1,625	1989

Nature Reserve

Ciglikara	I	36°43'N/29°56'E	15,889	1991
Gala Golu	I	40°40'N/26°15'E	2,369	1991
Kasnak mesesi	I	?/?	1,300	1987
Sakagolu longozu	I	?/?	1,345	1988
Seyfe Golu	IV	39°12'N/34°25'E	10,700	1990
Sultan Sazligi	IV	38°20'N/35°15'E	17,200	1988
Yukarigokdere	IV	37°52'N/30°51'E	1,300	1987

Specially Protected Area

Belek	IV	?/?	13,500	1990
Fethiye-Göcak	IV	?/?	61,300	1988
Foça	IV	?/?	2,750	1990
Gökova	IV	?/?	52,100	1988
Göksu Deltasi	IV	36°22'N/33°57'E	23,600	1990
Gölbasi	IV	?/?	24,500	1990
Ihlara	IV	38°15'N/34°20'E	5,800	1990
Kekova	IV	?/?	26,000	1990
Köycegiz-Dalyan	IV	?/?	38,500	1988
Pamukkale	IV	?/?	4,400	1990
Patara	IV	?/?	19,000	1990

TURKMENISTAN

Summary		
Category I	8	1,111,637
Category II	0	0
Category III	0	0
Category IV	0	0
Category V	0	0
Total	**8**	**1,111,637**

Zapovednik

Amu-Dar'inskiy	I	32°17'N/62°49'E	50,500	1982

Badkhyzskiy	I	32°12'N/61°37'E	87,700	1941
Kaplankyrskiy	I	39°04'N/57°04'E	570,000	1979
Kopetdagskiy	I	34°09'N/58°03'E	49,800	1976
Krasnovodskiy	I	36°22'N/53°21'E	262,037	1968
Kugitangskiy	I	?/?	27,100	1986
Repetekskiy	I	37°23'N/63°15'E	34,600	1928
Syunt-Khasardagskiy	I	33°33'N/55°54'E	29,900	1978

TUVALU

No Areas Listed

UGANDA/OUGANDA

Summary		
Category I	0	0
Category II	7	876,187
Category III	0	0
Category IV	22	1,026,020
Category V	2	6,539
Total	**31**	**1,908,746**

Game Reserve

Ajai	IV	2°55'N/31°25'E	15,600	1965
Bokora Corridor	IV	2°26'N/34°20'E	203,363	1967
Bugungu	IV	1°55'N/31°30'E	74,830	1968
Karuma	IV	1°55'N/31°58'E	71,272	1964
Katonga	IV	0°15'N/30°45'E	20,662	1964
Kibale Forest Corridor	IV	0°20'N/30°20'E	33,918	1964
Kigezi	IV	0°34'S/29°50'E	32,832	1952
Kyambura	IV	0°10'S/30°12'E	15,513	1965
Matheniko	IV	2°54'N/34°30'E	158,656	1964
Pian Upe	IV	1°45'N/34°28'E	228,715	1964
Toro	IV	0°52'N/30°22'E	54,858	1929

National Park

Bwindi Impenetrable Forest	II	1°02'S/29°42'E	32,092	1991
Gorilla (Mgahinga)	II	1°22'S/29°38'E	2,899	1991
Kidepo Valley	II	3°53'N/33°48'E	134,367	1962
Lake Mburo	II	0°35'S/31°00'E	25,594	1982
Murchison Falls	II	2°15'N/31°53'E	383,907	1952
Queen Elizabeth	II	0°04'S/30°00'E	197,752	1952
Rwenzori Mountains	II	0°15'N/29°57'E	99,576	1991

Nature Reserve

Kasagala	IV	?/?	10,000	1964
Kisanju	IV	?/?	2,000	1960
Maruzi Hills	IV	?/?	6,829	1990
Ngogo	IV	?/?	7,200	?
North Mabira	IV	?/?	3,355	?
Waibira	IV	?/?	3,210	1989
Wambabya	IV	?/?	3,429	1989
Zoka	IV	?/?	6,084	1990

Sanctuary

Difule Animal	IV	3°36'N/32°00'E	1,024	1959
Entebbe Animal & Bird	V	0°03'N/32°28'E	5,120	1951
Mount Kei White Rhino	IV	3°42'N/31°10'E	52,242	1938
Otze Forest White Rhino	IV	3°42'N/31°52'E	20,428	1946

Site of Special Scientific Interest

Kifu	V	?/?	1,419	1989

UKRAINE/UCRANIA

	Summary	
Category I	13	179,197
Category II	2	169,803
Category III	0	0
Category IV	4	173,367
Category V	0	0
Total	**19**	**522,367**

State Hunting Management Units

Azovo-Sivashskoye	IV	46°13'N/35°12'E	57,430	1957
Dneprovsko-Teterevskoye	IV	51°04'N/30°17'E	37,891	1967
Krymskoye	IV	44°45'N/34°18'E	42,957	1957
Zalesskoye	IV	50°45'N/30°45'E	35,089	1957

National Park

Karpatskiy	II	48°06'N/24°24'E	50,303	1980
Shatskiy	II	?/?	82,500	1983
Sinevis	II	?/?	37,000	1987

Zapovednik

Askaniya Nova	I	45°32'N/33°57'E	11,100	1921
Chernomorskiy	I	45°43'N/31°54'E	54,307	1927
Dneprovsko-Orel'skiy	I	?/?	3,766	1990
Dunaiskie Plavni	I	42°40'N/29°42'E	14,851	1981
Kanevskiy	I	46°53'N/32°32'E	2,049	1931
Karadagskiy	I	43°05'N/35°08'E	2,876	1979
Karpatskiy	I	47°55'N/24°35'E	12,706	1968
Luganskiy	I	34°47'N/50°18'E	1,600	1968
Medobory	I	?/?	14,455	1990
Mys Mart'yan	I	43°30'N/34°16'E	24,000	1973
Polesskiy	I	48°29'N/28°00'E	20,097	1968
Ukrainskiy Stepnoy	I	40°38'N/38°17'E	2,800	1961
Yaltinskiy	I	43°32'N/34°00'E	14,590	1973

UNITED ARAB EMIRATES/ EMIRATS ARABES UNIS/ EMIRATOS ARABES UNIDOS

No Areas Listed

UNITED KINGDOM OF GREAT BRITAIN AND NORTHERN IRELAND/ ROYAUME-UNI DE GRANDE-BRETAGNE ET D'IRLANDE DU NORD/REINO UNIDO

	Summary	
Category I	8	23,018
Category II	4	20,272
Category III	0	0
Category IV	64	292,186
Category V	115	4,792,490
Total	**191**	**5,127,966**

Area of Outstanding Natural Beauty

Anglesey	V	53°15'N/4°25'W	22,100	1967
Antrim Coast and Glens	V	55°01'N/6°02'W	70,600	1988
Arnside and Silverdale	V	54°10'N/3°10'W	7,500	1972
Blackdown Hills	V	?/?	3,700	1991
Cannock Chase	V	52°40'N/2°00'W	6,800	1958
Causeway Coast	V	55°14'N/6°31'W	4,200	1989

Chichester Harbour	V	50°30'N/1°00'E	7,400	1964
Chilterns	V	51°40'N/0°40'E	83,300	1965
Clwydian Range	V	53°05'N/3°20'W	15,700	1965
Cornwall	V	50°28'N/4°43'W	95,800	1959
Cotswolds	V	51°45'N/2°00'W	203,800	1966
Cranborne Chase and West Wiltshire Downs	V	50°55'N/2°00'W	98,300	1983
Dedham Vale	V	?/?	9,000	1970
Dorset	V	50°40'N/2°30'W	112,900	1959
East Devon	V	50°40'N/3°10'W	26,800	1963
East Hampshire	V	50°55'N/1°00'W	38,300	1962
Forest of Bowland	V	53°55'N/2°30'W	80,200	1964
Gower	V	51°40'N/4°00'W	18,800	1956
High Weald	V	51°00'N/0°25'E	146,000	1983
Howardian Hills	V	54°05'N/1°00'W	20,400	1987
Isle of Wight	V	50°45'N/1°20'E	18,900	1963
Isles of Scilly	V	49°55'N/6°20'W	1,600	1976
Kent Downs	V	51°15'N/0°45'E	87,800	1968
Lagan Valley	V	?/?	2,072	1965
Lecale Coast	V	?/?	3,108	1967
Lincolnshire Wolds	V	53°15'N/0°10'W	55,800	1973
Lleyn	V	52°55'N/4°30'W	16,100	1957
Malvern Hills	V	52°00'N/2°20'W	10,500	1959
Mendip Hills	V	51°10'N/2°40'W	19,800	1972
Mourne	V	54°05'N/6°00'W	57,012	1986
Norfolk Coast	V	52°55'N/1°00'E	45,100	1968
North Derry	V	?/?	12,950	1966
North Devon	V	51°00'N/4°30'W	17,100	1960
North Pennines	V	54°45'N/2°20'W	198,300	1988
North Wessex Downs	V	51°20'N/1°30'W	173,000	1972
Northumberland Coast	V	55°30'N/2°00'W	13,500	1958
Quantock Hills	V	51°05'N/3°15'W	9,900	1957
Ring Of Guillion	V	54°08'N/6°26'W	15,353	1991
Shropshire Hills	V	52°25'N/2°50'W	80,400	1959
Solway Coast	V	54°50'N/3°15'W	11,500	1964
South Devon	V	51°20'N/3°40'W	33,700	1960
South Hampshire Coast	V	50°40'N/1°25'W	7,700	1967
Sperrin	V	?/?	101,006	1968
Strangford Lough	V	?/?	18,647	1972
Suffolk Coast and Heaths	V	52°10'N/1°40'E	40,300	1966
Surrey Hills	V	51°10'N/0°15'E	41,900	1958
Sussex Downs	V	50°50'N/0°30'E	98,300	1966
Wye Valley	V	51°45'N/2°40'W	32,600	1971
Marine Nature Reserve				
Lundy Island	IV	51°10'N/4°40'W	2,200	1986
Skomer	IV	51°50'N/4°50'W	1,500	1990
National Nature Reserve				
Abernethy Forest	IV	57°16'N/3°38'W	2,296	1982
Beinn Eighe	IV	57°35'N/5°24'W	4,758	1951
Ben Lawers	IV	56°25'N/4°05'W	3,974	1962
Ben Lui	IV	56°50'N/5°00'W	2,104	1961
Ben Wyvis	IV	57°40'N/4°35'W	5,673	1984
Blackwater Estuary	IV	51°44'N/0°50'E	1,031	1983
Blar Nam Faoileag	IV	58°23'N/3°24'W	2,126	1985
Bridgwater Bay	IV	51°13'N/3°04'W	2,559	1954
Caenlochan	IV	56°45'N/3°20'W	3,639	1961
Caerlaverock	IV	54°52'N/3°30'W	5,585	1957
Cairngorm Mountains	IV	?/?	67,200	?
Cairngorms	IV	57°04'N/3°45'W	25,949	1954
Cairnsmore of Fleet	IV	54°58'N/4°17'W	1,922	1975
Creag Meagaidh	IV	56°57'N/4°38'W	3,948	1986

Dengie	IV	51°44'N/0°54'E	2,011	1984
Dyfi	IV	52°32'N/4°00'W	2,095	1972
Glen Roy	IV	56°56'N/4°47'W	1,168	1970
Glen Tanar	IV	57°02'N/2°54'W	4,185	1979
Gualin	IV	58°24'N/4°54'W	2,522	1971
Holkham	IV	52°56'N/0°52'E	3,925	1967
Inchnadamph	IV	58°07'N/4°56'W	1,295	1956
Inverpolly	IV	58°04'N/5°15'W	10,857	1961
Lindisfarne	IV	55°40'N/1°50'W	3,278	1964
Loch Druidibeg	IV	57°20'N/7°15'W	1,677	1958
Loch Leven	IV	56°12'N/3°22'W	1,597	1964
Loch Maree Islands	IV	?/?	200	?
Monach Isles	IV	57°30'N/7°30'W	577	1966
Moor House	IV	54°50'N/2°30'W	3,894	1952
Muir of Dinnet	IV	57°05'N/2°55'W	1,415	1977
Newborough Warren/Ynys Llanddwyn	IV	53°10'N/4°20'W	1,405	1955
North Rona and Sula Sgeir	IV	?/?	130	1959
North Strangford Lough	IV	54°34'N/5°40'W	1,015	1987
Noss	IV	60°09'N/1°01'W	313	1955
Rannoch Moor	IV	56°40'N/4°20'W	1,499	1958
Rhum	IV	57°00'N/6°30'W	10,794	1957
Ribble Marshes	IV	53°45'N/3°00'W	2,302	1979
Scolt Head Island	IV	52°57'N/0°43'E	737	?
Skomer Island	IV	51°50'N/4°50'W	307	1959
St. Kilda	IV	57°49'N/8°34'W	853	1957
Stackpole	IV	?/?	199	1981
Strathfarrar	IV	57°25'N/4°45'W	2,189	1977
Upper Teesdale	IV	54°36'N/2°12'W	3,497	1963
Y Wyddfa-Snowdon	IV	53°00'N/4°00'W	1,677	1964

National Park

Brecon Beacons	V	51°53'N/3°27'W	135,100	1957
Dartmoor	V	50°33'N/3°54'W	95,400	1951
Exmoor	V	51°10'N/4°00'W	69,300	1954
Lake District	V	54°30'N/3°00'W	229,200	1951
New Forest	V	50°50'N/1°35'W	37,500	1993
North York Moors	V	54°22'N/0°52'W	143,600	1952
Northumberland	V	55°16'N/2°13'W	104,900	1956
Peak District	V	53°18'N/1°45'E	143,800	1951
Pembrokeshire Coast	V	51°55'N/4°57'W	58,400	1952
Snowdonia	V	52°54'N/3°49'W	214,200	1951
The Broads	V	52°35'N/1°40'E	30,300	1989
Yorkshire Dales	V	54°20'N/1°50'W	176,900	1954

National Scenic Area

Assynt-Coigach	V	58°00'N/5°15'W	90,200	1980
Ben Nevis and Glen Coe	V	56°50'N/4°50'W	91,600	1980
Cuillin Hills	V	57°13'N/6°14'W	21,900	1980
Deeside and Lochnagar	V	57°00'N/3°08'W	40,000	1980
Dornoch Firth	V	57°50'N/4°08'W	7,500	1980
East Stewartry Coast	V	54°56'N/3°47'W	5,200	1980
Eildon and Leaderfoot	V	?/?	3,600	1980
Fleet Valley	V	54°55'N/4°12'W	5,300	1980
Glen Affric	V	57°15'N/5°00'W	19,300	1980
Glen Strathfarrar	V	57°24'N/4°50'W	3,800	1980
Hoy and West Mainland	V	58°53'N/3°17'W	14,800	1980
Jura	V	55°55'N/6°00'W	21,800	1980
Kintail	V	57°16'N/5°25'W	16,300	1980
Knapdale	V	55°54'N/5°32'W	19,800	1980
Knoydart	V	57°04'N/5°33'W	39,500	1980
Kyle of Tongue	V	58°28'N/4°27'W	18,500	1980
Kyles of Bute	V	55°50'N/5°15'W	4,400	1980

Loch Lomond	V	56°05'N/4°36'W	44,200	1980
Loch na Keal	V	56°28'N/6°03'W	12,700	1980
Loch Rannoch and Glenlyon	V	56°38'N/4°21'W	48,400	1980
Loch Sheil	V	56°50'N/5°40'W	13,400	1980
Loch Tummel	V	56°29'N/3°52'W	9,200	1980
Lynn of Lorn	V	56°50'N/5°50'W	4,800	1980
Morar, Moidart and Ardnamurchan	V	56°49'N/5°44'W	15,900	1980
Nith Estuary	V	54°58'N/3°34'W	9,300	1980
North Arran	V	55°40'N/5°15'W	23,800	1980
North West Sutherland	V	58°20'N/4°56'W	20,500	1980
River Earn (Comrie and St Fillans)	V	56°23'N/4°04'W	3,000	1980
River Tay (Dunkeld)	V	56°34'N/3°35'W	5,600	1980
Scarba, Lunga and the Garvellachs	V	56°11'N/5°42'W	1,900	1980
Shetland	V	60°11'N/1°18'W	15,600	1980
South Lewis, Harris and North Uist	V	57°48'N/6°51'W	108,600	1980
South Uist Machair	V	57°14'N/7°25'W	6,100	1980
St. Kilda	V	?/?	900	1980
The Cairngorm Mountains	V	57°08'N/3°42'W	67,200	1980
The Small Isles	V	57°00'N/6°21'W	15,500	1980
The Trossachs	V	56°15'N/4°27'W	4,600	1980
Trotternish	V	57°37'N/6°13'W	5,000	1980
Upper Tweeddale	V	?/?	12,300	1980
Wester Ross	V	57°45'N/5°12'W	145,300	1980

Anguilla

No Areas Listed

Bermuda/Bermudes

Preserve

North Shore Coral Reef	IV	32°26'N/6°447'W	12,000	1966

British Indian Ocean Territory/ Océan Indien, Territoire britannique de l'/ Territorio Británico del Océano Indico

No Areas Listed

British Virgin Islands/ Iles Vierges britanniques/ Islas Vírgenes (Británicas)

Bird Sanctuary

Cooper Island	IV	18°23'N/64°31'W	138	1959
Ginger Island	IV	18°23'N/64°29'W	105	1959
Peter Island	IV	18°21'N/64°35'W	430	1959

Cayman Islands/Iles Caïmanes/ Islas Caimán

Ecological Zone

Little Sound (Grand Cayman)	I	19°20'N/81°17'W	1,731	1986

Replenishment Zone

North Sound (Grand Cayman)	IV	19°20'N/81°18'W	3,310	1986

Channel Islands/Iles anglo-normandes/ Islas de la Mancha

No Areas Listed

Falkland Islands/Falkland, Iles Malouines/ Islas Malvinas

Nature Reserve

Arch Island East	I	52°13'S/60°26'W	200	1978
Bird Island	I	55°10'S/60°55'W	120	1969

Sanctuary

Beauchene Island	IV	52°54'S/59°11'W	179	1965
Bleaker Island	IV	52°18'S/58°51'W	870	1970
Middle Island	IV	51°38'S/60°20'W	155	1966
Stanley Common and Cape Pembroke Peninsula	IV	51°43'S/57°49'W	2,770	1973
Volunteer and Cow Bay	IV	51°29'S/57°50'W	4,340	1969

Gibraltar

No Areas Listed

Hong Kong

Country Park

Lam Tsuen	V	22°28'N/114°05'E	1,520	1979
Lantau North	V	22°16'N/113°55'E	2,200	1978
Lantau South	V	22°14'N/113°55'E	5,640	1978
Ma On Shan	V	22°23'N/114°14'E	2,280	1979
Pat Shin Leng	V	22°29'N/114°12'E	3,125	1978
Plover Cove	V	22°30'N/114°16'E	5,224	1978
Sai Kung East	V	22°24'N/114°20'E	4,477	1978
Sai Kung West	V	22°25'N/114°18'E	3,000	1978
Shing Mun	V	22°23'N/114°09'E	1,400	1977
Tai Lam	V	22°23'N/114°03'E	5,330	1979
Tai Mo Shan	V	22°24'N/114°07'E	1,440	1979
Tai Tam	V	22°15'N/114°12'E	1,585	1977

Site of Special Scientific Interest

Inner Deep Bay	IV	?/?	2,300	1986
Pat Sin Range	IV	22°29'N/114°13'E	1,505	1980
South Lamma Island	IV	?/?	450	1980
Tai Tam Reservoir Catchment Area	IV	22°14'N/114°12'E	1,315	1979

Isle of Man/Ile de Man

No Areas Listed

Montserrat/Ile Monserrat/ Islas Montserrat

No Areas Listed

Pitcairn Islands/Ile Pitcairn/ Islas Pitcairn

No Areas Listed

Saint Helena and Dependencies / Sainte-Hélène/Santa Helena (Ascension and Tristan da Cunha)

Protected Area

Green Mountain (Ascension)	V	?/?	1,000	1988

Wildlife Reserve

Gough Island (Tristan)	I	40°20'S/09°56'E	6,500	1976

South Georgia and South Sandwich Islands/ Géorgie de Sud et Iles Sandwich du Sud

Area of Special Tourist Interest

Bay of Isles	II	54°02'S/37°18'W	14,245	1975

Site of Special Scientific Interest

Annenkov Island	I	54°29'S/37°05'W	2,072	1975
Bird Island	I	54°00'S/38°03'W	1,036	1975

Specially Protected Area

Cooper Island	I	54°49'S/35°47'W	259	1975

Turks and Caicos/Turques et Caïques, Iles/ Islas Turks y Caicos

Area of Historical Interest

Salt Cay	V	21°16'N/71°12'W	176	1987

National Park

Chalk Sound	II	21°40'N/72°18'W	1,460	1987
East Bay Islands	II	21°55'N/71°53'W	3,541	1987
Grand Turk Cays, Land and Sea	IV	21°23'N/71°06'W	156	1987
North West Point Marine	II	21°51'N/72°20'W	1,026	1987
Princess Alexandra Land and Sea	V	21°48'N/72°12'W	2,645	1992

Nature Reserve

Bell Sound	IV	21°32'N/71°31'W	1,142	1975
North, Middle & East Caicos	IV	21°47'N/71°55'W	54,400	1992
Pigeon Pond and Frenchman's Creek	IV	21°40'N/72°20'W	2,393	1992

Sanctuary

Big Sand Cay	IV	21°11'N/71°14'W	151	1987

UNITED STATES OF AMERICA/ ETATS-UNIS D'AMERIQUE/ ESTADOS UNIDOS DE AMERICA

Summary		
Category I	451	14,324,126
Category II	176	22,004,214
Category III	70	8,138,507
Category IV	394	47,263,252
Category V	389	12,442,379
Total	**1,480**	**104,172,478**

Alabama

National Estuarine Research Reserve

Weeks Bay	IV	?/?	1,483	1986

National Marine Sanctuary

Cordell Bank	V	?/?	128,777	1989

National Wildlife Refuge

Bon Secour	IV	30°15'N/87°45'W	1,819	?
Choctaw	IV	31°53'N/87°58'W	1,708	?
Eufaula	IV	32°02'N/85°11'W	3,211	?
Wheeler	IV	34°44'N/86°41'W	13,839	?

Parkway

Natchez Trace	V	?/?	18,300	1938

State Park

Cheaha	V	?/?	1,133	1933
De Soto	V	?/?	2,051	1935
Gulf	V	?/?	2,428	1935
Joe Wheeler	V	?/?	1,032	1949
Lake Guntersville	V	?/?	2,391	1947
Oak Mountain	V	?/?	4,023	1935

Wilderness (Forest Service)

Cheaha	I	33°24'N/85°50'W	3,031	1983
Sipsey	I	34°21'N/87°19'W	5,103	1974

Alaska

National Forest

Chugach	IV	61°15'N/149°20'W	2,404,000	1907
Tongass	IV	57°00'N/134°00'W	6,708,900	1907

National Monument

Admiralty Island	IV	57°30'N/134°20'W	387,530	1980
Aniakchak	III	56°50'N/158°02'W	55,514	1978
Bering Land Bridge	II	65°55'N/165°10'W	1,121,457	1980
Cape Krusenstern	III	67°30'N/163°30'W	267,206	1978
Gates of the Arctic	III	68°00'N/152°00'W	2,939,689	1980
Misty Fjords	IV	55°30'N/130°30'W	928,491	1980

National Natural Landmark

Alaska Maritime	III	?/?	355,000	1980
Aniakchak Crater	III	56°30'N/157°30'W	8,080	?
Arrigetch Peaks	III	?/?	10,342	?
Lake George	III	?/?	25,856	?
Malaspina Glacier	III	?/?	387,840	?
Mount Veniaminof	III	?/?	323,200	?
Unga Island	III	?/?	2,586	?
Walker Lake	III	?/?	73,173	?
Yukon Delta	III	?/?	760,850	1980

National Park

Denali	II	63°20'N/150°30'W	1,911,495	1917
Glacier Bay	II	58°43'N/136°58'W	1,304,550	1925
Katmai	II	58°23'N/154°50'W	1,504,774	1980
Kenai Fjords	II	59°45'N/150°15'W	271,255	1980
Kobuk Valley	II	67°25'N/159°05'W	708,502	1978
Lake Clark	II	60°40'N/153°45'W	1,068,805	1978
Wrangell-St Elias	II	61°13'N/142°10'W	3,382,014	1978

National Preserve

Aniakchak	IV	56°50'N/158°02'W	188,427	1978
Bering Land Bridge	V	66°16'N/164°38'W	1,125,124	1978
Denali	V	63°32'N/149°55'W	529,800	1980
Gates of the Arctic	V	68°00'N/152°00'W	383,246	1980
Glacier Bay	V	?/?	23,385	1978
Katmai	V	?/?	151,096	1980
Lake Clark	V	?/?	568,546	1980
Noatak	II	68°00'N/159°00'W	2,655,870	1978
Wrangell-St. Elias	V	?/?	1,962,115	1980
Yukon Charley Rivers	III	65°00'N/143°00'W	915,000	1978

National Wildlife Refuge

Alaska Maritime	IV	600°0'N/153°00'W	1,390,384	1980
Alaska Peninsula	IV	56°30'N/159°30'W	1,416,430	1980
Arctic	IV	69°00'N/144°00'W	7,804,905	1980
Becharof	IV	58°00'N/156°30'W	485,640	1978
Innoko	IV	65°00'N/158°30'W	1,558,073	1980
Izembek	IV	55°12'N/162°43'W	122,660	1960
Kanuti	IV	66°30'N/151°30'W	578,713	1980
Kenai	IV	60°30'N/150°10'W	770,842	1980
Kenai National Moose Range	IV	?/?	698,920	?
Kodiak	IV	57°00'N/154°00'W	670,320	?
Koyukuk	IV	65°40'N/156°20'W	1,436,665	1980
Nowitna	IV	64°30'N/154°00'W	631,323	1980
Selawik	IV	66°30'N/159°00'W	870,093	1980
Tetlin	IV	62°45'N/142°00'W	283,307	1980
Togiak	IV	59°00'N/160°00'W	1,658,207	1980

Yukon Delta	IV	61°00'N/164°00'W	7,742,470	1980
Yukon Flats	IV	66°30'N/146°00'W	3,492,513	1980

Preserve

Chilkat Bald Eagle	II	?/?	19,960	?

State Marine Park

Canoe Passage	II	?/?	1,107	?
Chilkat Islands	II	?/?	2,655	?
S.Esther Island	II	?/?	1,360	?
Shelter Island	II	?/?	1,441	?
Shoup Bay	II	?/?	1,845	?

State Park

Chilkat	II	?/?	2,446	?
Chugach	II	61°00'N/149°00'W	200,406	?
Denali	II	?/?	131,218	?
Kachemak Wilderness	II	?/?	149,045	1972
Point Bridge	II	?/?	1,133	?
Shuyah Island	II	?/?	4,452	?
Wood-Tikchik	II	?/?	629,380	?

State Recreation Area

Caines head	II	?/?	2,413	?
Captain Cook	II	?/?	1,403	?
Chena River	II	?/?	102,825	?
Nancy Lake	II	?/?	9,180	?
Willow Creek	II	?/?	1,450	?

Wilderness (Fish and Wildlife Service)

Aleutian Islands	I	51°59'N/174°46'W	526,093	1980
Andreafsky	I	62°47'N/162°25'W	526,093	1980
Arctic	I	69°22'N/142°08'W	3,237,498	1980
Becharof	I	57°54'N/155°38'W	161,875	1980
Bering Sea	I	60°20'N/172°29'W	32,917	1970
Forrester Island	I	54°53'N/133°42'W	1,146	1970
Innoko	I	63°11'N/158°15'W	501,812	1980
Izembek	I	55°24'N/162°32'W	121,406	1980
Kenai	I	60°21'N/150°11'W	546,328	1980
Koyukuk	I	65°46'N/157°19'W	161,875	1980
Nunivak	I	59°55'N/166°46'W	242,812	1980
Selawik	I	67°01'N/158°50'W	97,125	1980
Semidi	I	55°42'N/155°31'W	101,172	1980
Simeonof	I	54°54'N/159°18'W	10,463	1976
Togiak	I	59°39'N/160°17'W	918,640	1980
Tuxedni	I	60°15'N/152°28'W	2,252	1970
Unimak	I	54°46'N/164°27'W	368,265	1980

Wilderness (Forest Service)

Admiralty Island National Monument	I	57°45'N/134°09'W	380,376	1980
Chuck River	I	?/?	29,341	1990
Coronation Island	I	56°01'N/134°22'W	7,776	1980
Endicott River	I	58°53'N/135°14'W	40,540	1980
Karta River	I	?/?	15,640	1990
Kuiu	I	?/?	24,514	1990
Maurelle Islands	I	55°47'N/133°38'W	1,790	1980
Misty Fiords National Monument	I	55°40'N/130°35'W	867,510	1980
Petersburg Creek-Duncan Salt Chuck	I	56°56'N/133°03'W	18,994	1980
Pleasant/Lemusurier/Inian Islands	I	?/?	9,364	1990
Russell Fiord	I	59°51'N/138°52'W	141,993	1980
South Baranof NFW	I	56°51'N/134°50'W	153,535	1980
South Etolin	I	?/?	33,849	1990
South Prince of Wales NFW	I	55°03'N/132°25'W	36,612	1980

Stikine-LeConte NFW	I	56°54'N/132°02'W	182,128	1980
Tebenkof Bay NFW	I	56°36'N/134°01'W	26,730	1980
Tracy Arm-Fords Terror NFW	I	57°48'N/132°48'W	264,343	1980
Warren Island NFW	I	56°03'N/133°54'W	4,536	1980
West Chicagof-Yakobi NFW	I	57°54'N/135°48'W	107,244	1980

Wilderness (National Park Service)

Denali	I	63°32'N/149°55'W	859,873	1980
Gates of the Arctic	I	68°06'N/153°04'W	2,900,472	1980
Glacier Bay	I	59°04'N/136°59'W	1,078,427	1980
Katmai	I	58°34'N/154°44'W	1,369,607	1980
Kobuk Valley	I	67°12'N/158°47'W	70,636	1980
Lake Clark	I	60°49'N/153°11'W	1,060,099	1980
Noatak	I	68°21'N/159°35'W	2,333,195	1980
Wrangell-St. Elias	I	61°16'N/141°36'W	3,674,024	1980

Arizona

National Memorial

Coronado	V	31°22'N/110°22'W	1,145	1952

National Monument

Canyon de Chelly	III	36°12'N/109°30'W	33,536	1931
Chiricahua	III	31°57'N/109°23'W	4,853	1924
Marble Canyon	III	?/?	13,197	1969
Organ Pipe Cactus	III	32°00'N/112°50'W	133,925	1937
Saguaro	III	32°11'N/110°37'W	33,836	1933
Sunset Crater	III	35°21'N/111°36'W	1,230	1930
Wupatki	III	35°29'N/111°26'W	14,267	1924

National Natural Landmark

Hualapai Valley Joshua Trees	III	?/?	1,212	?

National Park

Grand Canyon	II	36°14'N/112°46'W	493,441	1919
Petrified Forest	II	34°56'N/109°48'W	37,880	1962

National Recreation Area

Glen Canyon (Arizona)	V	?/?	483,404	1972
Lake Mead (Arizona)	IV	?/?	1,000	1964

National Wildlife Refuge

Buenos Aires	IV	31°41'N/111°32'W	46,110	?
Cabeza Prieta	IV	32°23'N/113°17'W	348,031	?
Cibola	IV	33°24'N/114°41'W	3,483	?
Havasu	IV	34°00'N/114°00'W	14,704	1941
Imperial	IV	32°30'N/114°40'W	7,207	1941
Kofa	IV	33°15'N/114°00'W	269,716	1939
San Bernadino	IV	?/?	1,460	?

Outstanding Natural Area

Vermillion Cliffs	V	?/?	20,255	1969

State Park

Alamo Lake	V	?/?	2,279	?
Catalina	V	?/?	2,226	?
Lake Havasu	V	?/?	5,252	?
Painted Rocks	V	?/?	1,131	?
Pichacho Peaks	V	?/?	1,374	?

Wilderness (Bureau of Land Management)

Aravaipa Canyon	I	32°54'N/110°30'W	7,972	1984
Arrastra Mountain	I	34°22'N/113°26'W	52,528	1990
Aubrey Peak	I	34°24'N/113°49'W	6,232	1990

Beaver Dam Mountains	I	37°00'N/113°47'W	6,070	1984
Big Horn Mountains	I	33°37'N/113°09'W	8,498	1990
Cottonwood Point	I	37°00'N/112°55'W	2,776	1984
Coyote Mountains	I	32°00'N/111°32'W	2,064	1990
Dos Cabezas	I	32°13'N/109°32'W	4,735	1990
Eagletail Mountains	I	33°25'N/113°24'W	40,712	1990
East Cactus Plain	I	34°04'N/113°57'W	5,921	1990
Fishhooks	I	33°13'N/109°59'W	4,249	1990
Gibraltar Mountain	I	34°11'N/114°06'W	7,604	1990
Grand Wash Cliffs	I	36°28'N/113°47'W	14,986	1984
Harcuvar Mountains	I	34°02'N/113°26'W	10,137	1990
Harquahala Mountains	I	33°50'N/113°18'W	9,259	1990
Hassayampa River Canyon	I	34°07'N/112°36'W	4,978	1990
Hells Canyon	I	33°56'N/112°23'W	4,290	1990
Hummingbird Springs	I	33°40'N/113°05'W	12,626	1990
Kanab Creek	I	36°30'N/112°40'W	2,711	1984
Mount Logan	I	36°20'N/113°12'W	5,929	1984
Mount Nutt	I	35°06'N/114°22'W	11,194	1990
Mount Tipton	I	35°33'N/114°12'W	13,258	1990
Mount Trumbull	I	36°25'N/113°08'W	3,189	1984
Mount Wilson	I	35°58'N/114°35'W	9,672	1990
Muggins Mountains	I	32°45'N/114°14'W	3,092	1990
Needle's Eye	I	33°09'N/110°37'W	3,545	1990
New Water Mountains	I	33°35'N/113°58'W	9,955	1990
North Maricopa Mountains	I	33°06'N/112°31'W	25,576	1990
North Santa Teresa	I	32°56'N/110°09'W	2,347	1990
Paiute	I	36°49'N/113°50'W	35,572	1984
Paria Canyon-Vermilion Cliffs	I	36°55'N/111°39'W	36,179	1984
Peloncillo Mountains	I	32°23'N/109°05'W	7,867	1990
Rawhide Mountains	I	34°13'N/113°37'W	15,568	1990
Redfield Canyon	I	32°27'N/110°17'W	4,019	1990
Sierra Estrella	I	33°13'N/112°14'W	5,827	1990
Signal Mountain	I	33°12'N/112°58'W	5,403	1990
South Maricopa Mountains	I	32°56'N/112°24'W	24,322	1990
Swansea	I	34°14'N/113°52'W	6,637	1990
Table Top	I	32°46'N/112°08'W	13,921	1990
Tres Alamos	I	34°14'N/113°12'W	3,359	1990
Trigo Mountains	I	33°11'N/114°37'W	12,262	1990
Upper Burro Creek	I	34°41'N/113°17'W	11,105	1990
Wabayuma Peak	I	34°58'N/114°00'W	16,187	1990
Warm Springs	I	34°55'N/114°17'W	45,487	1990
White Canyon	I	33°10'N/111°06'W	2,343	1990
Woolsey Peak	I	33°08'N/112°55'W	25,900	1990

Wilderness (Fish and Wildlife Service)

Cabeza Prieta	I	32°15'N/113°28'W	325,133	1990
Havasu	I	34°38'N/114°26'W	5,911	1990
Imperial	I	33°06'N/114°41'W	3,731	1990
Kofa	I	33°15'N/113°58'W	208,900	1990

Wilderness (Forest Service)

Apache Creek	I	34°52'N/112°56'W	2,193	1984
Bear Wallow	I	33°37'N/109°28'W	4,484	1984
Castle Creek	I	34°13'N/112°18'W	10,534	1984
Cedar Bench	I	34°24'N/111°53'W	6,050	1984
Chiricahua	I	31°51'N/109°17'W	7,290	1964
Escudilla	I	33°57'N/109°06'W	2,104	1984
Fossil Springs	I	34°26'N/111°35'W	8,963	1984
Four Peaks	I	33°39'N/111°24'W	24,716	1984
Galluro	I	32°36'N/110°20'W	21,343	1964
Granite Mountain	I	34°39'N/112°37'W	3,966	1984
Hellsgate	I	34°13'N/111°08'W	15,151	1984

Juniper Mesa	I	34°56'N/112°56'W	3,076	1984
Kachina Peaks	I	35°19'N/111°43'W	7,534	1984
Kanab Creek	I	36°32'N/112°36'W	25,803	1984
Kendrick Mountain	I	35°25'N/111°53'W	2,635	1984
Mazatzal	I	34°08'N/111°36'W	83,511	1964
Miller Peak	I	31°24'N/110°19'W	8,171	1984
Mount Wrightson	I	31°43'N/110°51'W	10,222	1984
Mt. Baldy	I	33°57'N/109°32'W	2,835	1970
Munds Mountain	I	34°50'N/111°45'W	9,879	1984
Pajarita	I	31°25'N/111°11'W	3,003	1984
Pine Mountain	I	34°17'N/111°51'W	8,140	1972
Pusch Ridge	I	32°23'N/110°51'W	23,044	1978
Red Rock-Secret Mountain	I	34°56'N/111°53'W	19,099	1984
Rincon Mountain	I	32°15'N/110°30'W	15,617	1984
Saddle Mountain	I	36°22'N/112°03'W	16,406	1984
Salome	I	33°51'N/111°07'W	7,499	1984
Salt River Canyon	I	33°40'N/110°50'W	12,991	1984
Santa Teresa	I	32°54'N/110°15'W	10,838	1984
Sierra Ancha	I	33°50'N/110°55'W	8,464	1964
Strawberry Crater	I	35°27'N/11128'W	4,348	1984
Superstition NFW	I	33°29'N/111°17'W	50,260	1964
Sycamore Canyon NFW	I	34°58'N/112°01'W	19,318	1972
West Clear Creek	I	34°34'N/111°34'W	6,167	1984
Wet Beaver	I	34°40'N/111°36'W	2,491	1984
Woodchute	I	34°43'N/112°11'W	2,266	1984

Wilderness (National Park Service)

Chiricahua	I	31°57'N/109°19'W	3,820	1976
Organ Pipe Cactus	I	32°03'N/112°45'W	126,505	1978
Petrified Forest	I	35°07'N/109°54'W	20,340	1970
Saguaro	I	32°10'N/110°28'W	28,895	1976

Arkansas°

National Military Park

Pea Ridge	V	36°22'N/93°59'W	1,729	1961

National Natural Landmark

Big Lake	III	?/?	4,466	?
White River	III	?/?	45,746	?

National Park

Hot Springs	II	34°30'N/93°03'W	2,330	1921

National River

Buffalo	V	37°30'N/96°00'W	38,100	1972

National Wildlife Refuge

Big Lake	IV	35°54'N/89°58'W	4,466	?
Cache River	IV	35°23'N/91°12'W	8,852	?
Felsenthal	IV	33°00'N/92°00'W	26,265	1975
Holla Bend	IV	35°10'N/93°05'W	2,459	1957
Overflow	IV	33°08'N/91°52'W	4,615	?
Wapanocca	IV	35°21'N/90°14'W	2,219	1961
White River	IV	34°18'N/90°58'W	45,823	?

Wilderness (Forest Service)

Black Fork Mountain	I	34°46'N/94°18'W	3,066	1984
Caney Creek	I	34°27'N/94°04'W	5,791	1974
Dry Creek	I	35°03'N/93°44'W	2,554	1984
East Fork	I	35°37'N/92°50'W	4,361	1984
Flatside	I	34°55'N/92°56'W	4,089	1984
Hurricane Creek	I	35°47'N/93°06'W	6,093	1984
Leatherwood	I	36°08'N/92°20'W	6,772	1984
Poteau Mountain	I	35°01'N/94°01'W	4,405	1984

Richland Creek	I	35°51'N/92°56'W	4,782	1984
Upper Buffalo	I	35°54'N/93°26'W	4,131	1974

Wilderness (National Park Service)

Buffalo National River	I	36°09'N/92°16'W	4,261	1978

California

National Marine Sanctuary

Bitter Creek	IV	?/?	5,482	1973
Channel Islands	V	33°56'N/119°52'W	405,506	1980
Gulf of the Farallones	V	?/?	307,044	1981

National Monument

Death Valley	III	36°22'N/117°00'W	837,388	1933
Joshua Tree	III	34°00'N/116°00'W	226,781	1936
Lava Beds	III	41°45'N/121°30'W	18,856	1925
Pinnacles	III	36°26'N/121°09'W	6,587	1908

National Natural Landmark

Amboy Crater	III	?/?	2,327	?
Anza-Borrego Desert	III	33°10'N/116°20'W	211,016	?
Cinder Cone	III	?/?	10,342	?
Sand Hills	III	?/?	9,696	?
Turtle Mountains	III	?/?	38,525	?

National Park

Channel Islands	II	33°46'N/119°44'W	100,987	1980
Kings Canyon	II	36°45'N/118°30'W	187,069	1940
Lassen Volcanic	II	40°30'N/121°25'W	43,293	1916
Redwood	II	41°27'N/124°02'W	42,400	1968
Sequoia	II	36°45'N/118°30'W	163,115	1890
Yosemite	II	37°50'N/119°32'W	308,273	1890

National Recreation Area

Golden Gate	V	?/?	29,611	1972
Santa Monica Mountains	V	34°08'N/118°41'W	60,729	1978
Whiskeytown Shasta Trinity	V	?/?	17,213	1965

National Seashore

Point Reyes	V	38°01'N/122°49'W	28,733	1972

National Wildlife Refuge

Bitter Creek	IV	?/?	5,656	?
Butte Sink	IV	39°16'N/121°47'W	3,708	?
Cibola	IV	?/?	1,476	?
Clear Lake	IV	41°50'N/121°09'W	13,532	?
Coachella Valley	IV	33°54'N/116°13'W	1,244	?
Colusa	IV	39°10'N/122°13'W	1,636	?
Delevan	IV	39°19'N/122°05'W	2,279	?
Grasslands	IV	37°06'N/120°43'W	17,206	?
Havasu	IV	?/?	2,928	?
Hopper Mountain	IV	?/?	1,000	?
Imperial	IV	33°02'N/114°42'W	3,220	?
Kern	IV	35°42'N/119°40'W	4,297	?
Kesterson	IV	37°28'N/120°59'W	4,653	?
Lower Klamath	IV	41°58'N/122°00'W	16,306	?
Merced	IV	37°20'N/120°28'W	1,038	?
Modoc	IV	41°26'N/120°39'W	2,584	?
North Central Valley	IV	?/?	2,884	?
Pixley	IV	35°57'N/119°24'W	2,505	?
Sacramento	IV	39°25'N/32°10'W	4,364	1937
Sacramento River	IV	?/?	2,282	?

Salton Sea	IV	33°19'N/115°39'W	15,208	?
San Francisco Bay	IV	37°30'N/122°00'W	7,511	1972
San Luis	IV	37°19'N/120°54'W	3,291	?
San Pablo Bay	IV	38°08'N/122°29'W	5,337	?
Sutter	IV	39°05'N/121°45'W	1,049	1945
Tule Lake	IV	42°00'N/121°30'W	15,831	1928
Willow Creek-Lurline	IV	39°32'N/121°51'W	1,860	?

Outstanding Natural Area

Amargosa Canyon-Dumont Dunes	V	?/?	9,196	1975

State Historic Park

Fort Ross	II	38°06'N/123°15'W	1,362	1963
Malakoff Diggins	II	39°22'N/120°55'W	1,200	1965

State Park

Ahjumawi Lava Springs	II	41°07'N/121°25'W	2,596	1983
Andrew Molera	II	36°16'N/121°50'W	1,937	1971
Annadel	II	38°27'N/122°38'W	1,991	1974
Anza-Borrego Desert (California)	II	33°15'N/116°20'W	227,573	1963
Big Basin Redwoods	II	37°11'N/122°14'W	7,360	1963
Calaveras Big Trees	II	38°17'N/120°15'W	2,458	1963
Castle Crags	II	41°10'N/122°20'W	1,773	1963
Castle Rock	II	37°13'N/122°10'W	1,454	1968
Chino Hills	II	33°57'N/117°43'W	4,319	1984
Crystal Cove	II	33°33'N/117°49'W	1,595	1980
Cuyamaca Rancho	II	35°55'N/116°33'W	10,033	1963
Del Norte Coast Redwoods	II	41°43'N/124°05'W	2,578	1963
Forest of Nisene Marks	II	?/?	4,024	?
Garrapata	II	36°25'N/121°55'W	1,189	1985
Gaviota	II	34°28'N/120°14'W	1,117	1968
Great Valley Grasslands	II	37°15'N/120°50'W	1,144	1992
Henry Cowell Redwoods	II	37°20'N/122°00'W	1,675	1963
Henry W. Coe	II	37°10'N/121°35'W	27,603	1963
Humbolt Redwoods	II	40°20'N/123°55'W	20,573	1963
Jedediah Smith Redwoods	II	41°47'N/124°05'W	4,002	1963
Julia Pfeiffer Burns	II	?/?	1,431	?
Malibu Creek	II	34°05'N/118°43'W	2,173	1976
Manchester	II	39°00'N/123°42'W	2,132	1991
Montana de Oro	II	35°17'N/120°52'W	3,358	1965
Mount Diablo	II	37°53'N/121°55'W	8,130	1963
Mount San Jacinto	II	33°47'N/116°40'W	5,551	1963
Mount Tamalpais	II	37°54'N/122°36'W	2,527	1963
Plumas-Eureka	II	39°46'N/120°42'W	1,790	1963
Point Mugo	II	34°05'N/119°02'W	5,635	1971
Portola	II	37°16'N/122°13'W	1,015	1963
Prairie Creek Redwoods	II	41°22'N/124°00'W	5,693	1963
Red Rock Canyon	II	35°23'N/118°00'W	4,186	1980
Robert Louis Stevenson	II	38°38'N/122°35'W	1,512	1963
Saddleback Butte	II	34°40'N/117°48'W	1,320	1963
Salt Point	II	38°34'N/123°19'W	2,301	1969
Samuel P. Taylor	II	38°02'N/122°43'W	1,095	1963
Sinkyone Wilderness	II	39°55'N/123°55'W	3,020	1977
Sugarloaf Ridge	II	38°26'N/122°31'W	1,073	1965
The Forest of Nisene Marks	II	37°50'N/121°55'W	4,085	1962
Topanga	II	34°05'N/118°34'W	3,627	1974
Wilder Ranch	II	36°58'N/122°05'W	1,822	1976

State Recreation Area

Auburn	II	38°55'N/121°00'W	16,997	1979
Austin Creek	II	38°35'N/123°00'W	1,883	1963
Castaic Lake	II	34°34'N/118°30'W	1,255	1974

Folsom Lake	II	38°43'N/121°10'W	7,194	1963
Franks Tract	II	38°05'N/121°35'W	1,433	1963
Lake Del Valle	II	37°35'N/121°40'W	1,538	1974
Lake Elsinore	II	33°40'N/117°22'W	1,204	1963
Lake Oroville	II	39°32'N/121°28'W	11,917	1967
Lake Perris	II	33°52'N/117°11'W	2,310	1973
Millerton	II	37°00'N/119°40'W	2,652	1963
Picacho	II	33°01'N/114°36'W	2,735	1963
Providence Mountains	II	34°57'N/115°30'W	2,384	1972
Salton Sea	II	33°30'N/115°55'W	6,757	1963
San Luis Resevoir	II	37°05'N/121°05'W	10,532	1967

State Vehicular Recreation Area

Ocotillo Wells	II	33°10'N/116°07'W	10,983	1976
Pismo Dunes	II	35°03'N/120°37'W	1,075	1974

State Wilderness

Anza-Borrego	II	?/?	120,356	1982
Boney Mountain	II	?/?	1,696	1981
Cuyamaca Mountain	II	?/?	5,346	1982
Henry W Coe	II	?/?	8,175	1985
Mount San Jacinto	II	?/?	3,966	1974
Santa Rosa Mountains	II	?/?	35,208	1973
West Waddell Creek	II	?/?	2,351	1982

Wilderness (Bureau of Land Management)

Trinity Alps	I	40°49'N/123°02'W	1,871	1984

Wilderness (Forest Service)

Agua Tibia	I	33°25'N/117°03'W	6,439	1974
Ansel Adams	I	37°35'N/119°11'W	93,182	1964
Bucks Lake	I	40°01'N/121°12'W	8,498	1984
Caribou	I	40°32'N/121°15'W	7,614	1964
Carson-Iceberg	I	38°29'N/119°45'W	64,195	1984
Castle Crags	I	41°13'N/122°26'W	3,491	1984
Chanchelulla	I	40°32'N/123°03'W	3,318	1984
Cucamonga	I	34°15'N/117°40'W	3,483	1964
Desolation	I	38°58'N/120°14'W	25,717	1969
Dick Smith	I	34°42'N/119°32'W	27,438	1984
Dinkey Lakes	I	37°10'N/119°03'W	12,141	1984
Dome Land	I	35°51'N/118°13'W	25,393	1964
Emigrant	I	38°12'N/119°48'W	42,970	1974
Golden Trout	I	36°19'N/118°15'W	122,836	1978
Granite Chief	I	39°10'N/120°19'W	7,708	1984
Hauser	I	32°39'N/116°35'W	3,054	1984
Hoover	I	38°09'N/119°24'W	19,683	1964
Ishi	I	40°09'N/121°48'W	16,632	1984
Jennie Lakes	I	36°42'N/118°46'W	4,164	1984
John Muir	I	37°13'N/118°38'W	202,378	1964
Kaiser	I	37°18'N/119°13'W	9,193	1976
Machesna Mountain	I	35°17'N/120°16'W	7,997	1984
Marble Mountain	I	41°31'N/123°17'W	86,548	1964
Minarets	I	?/?	43,497	1964
Mokelumne	I	38°37'N/120°01'W	20,047	1964
Monarch	I	36°51'N/118°48'W	18,169	1984
Mount Shasta	I	41°27'N/122°16'W	13,697	1984
North Fork	I	40°11'N/123°25'W	3,237	1984
Pine Creek	I	32°46'N/116°39'W	5,455	1984
Red Buttes	I	42°01'N/123°21'W	6,536	1984
Russian	I	41°19'N/123°02'W	4,856	1984
San Gabriel	I	34°19'N/118°02'W	14,620	1968
San Gorgonio	I	34°07'N/116°51'W	14,256	1964

San Jacinto	I	33°47'N/116°43'W	8,545	1964
San Mateo Canyon	I	33°33'N/117°30'W	15,574	1984
San Rafael	I	34°47'N/119°49'W	60,345	1968
Santa Lucia	I	35°22'N/120°37'W	7,533	1978
Santa Lucia	I	35°15'N/120°35'W	7,559	1978
Santa Rosa	I	33°33'N/116°26'W	5,579	1984
Sheep Mountain	I	34°19'N/117°48'W	16,950	1984
Siskiyou	I	41°42'N/123°46'W	61,788	1984
Snow Mountain	I	39°27'N/122°50'W	14,718	1984
South Sierra	I	36°08'N/118°06'W	33,218	1984
South Warner	I	41°21'N/120°13'W	27,702	1964
Thousand Lakes	I	40°46'N/121°37'W	6,601	1964
Trinity Alps	I	41°01'N/123°10'W	201,591	1984
Ventana	I	36°13'N/121°36'W	64,374	1978
Yolla Bolly-Middle Eel	I	40°08'N/123°07'W	59,366	1964
Yolla Bolly-Middle Eel	I	40°02'N/123°09'W	45,319	1964

Wilderness (National Park Service)

Joshua Tree	I	34°00'N/115°45'W	173,890	1976
Lassen Volcanic	I	40°32'N/121°23'W	31,963	1972
Lava Beds	I	41°42'N/121°29'W	11,517	1972
Philip Burton	I	38°02'N/122°47'W	10,267	1976
Pinnacles	I	36°35'N/121°13'W	5,242	1976
Sequoia-Kings Canyon	I	36°45'N/118°31'W	298,246	1984
Yosemite	I	37°53'N/119°35'W	274,216	1984

Colorado

National Monument

Black Canyon of the Gunnison	III	38°00'N/107°00'W	5,682	1933
Colorado	III	39°06'N/108°44'W	8,274	1911
Dinosaur	III	40°35'N/108°55'W	82,655	1915
Florissant Fossil Beds	III	38°50'N/105°19'W	1,698	1969
Great Sand Dunes	III	37°46'N/105°34'W	14,596	1932

National Park

Mesa Verde	II	37°10'N/108°33'W	20,830	1906
Rocky Mountain	II	40°22'N/105°42'W	107,519	1915

National Recreation Area

Curecanti	V	38°28'N/107°17'W	16,985	1965

National Wildlife Refuge

Alamosa	IV	37°24'N/105°46'W	4,520	1962
Arapaho	IV	40°40'N/106°15'W	7,387	1967
Browns Park	IV	40°50'N/108°46'W	5,445	?
Monte Vista	IV	37°32'N/106°15'W	5,742	?

State Park

Arkansas	V	?/?	2,023	?
Barr Lake	II	?/?	1,056	?
Bonny	V	?/?	2,792	?
Chatfield	V	?/?	2,152	?
Cherry Creek	V	?/?	1,694	?
Eleven Mile	V	?/?	3,027	?
Golden Gate Canyon	II	?/?	5,350	?
Jackson Lake	V	?/?	1,230	?
Lory	V	?/?	1,003	?
Mueller	V	?/?	4,904	?
Navajo	V	?/?	7,394	?
North Sterling	V	?/?	1,592	?
Pueblo	V	?/?	5,541	?
Ridgeway	V	?/?	1,295	?

San Luis	V	?/?	1,191	?
Spinney	V	?/?	2,396	?
State Forest	V	?/?	28,667	?
Steamboat Lake	V	?/?	1,035	?
Trinidad	V	?/?	1,093	?

Wilderness (Fish and Wildlife Service)

Mount Massive	I	39°10'N/106°28'W	1,036	1980

Wilderness (Forest Service)

Big Blue	I	38°03'N/107°29'W	39,568	1980
Cache La Poudre	I	40°38'N/105°25'W	3,807	1980
Collegiate Peaks	I	38°55'N/106°29'W	64,800	1980
Commanche Peak	I	40°33'N/105°42'W	27,256	1980
Eagles Nest	I	39°41'N/106°15'W	54,189	1976
Flat Tops	I	39°56'N/107°17'W	95,215	1975
Holy Cross	I	39°27'N/106°26'W	49,529	1980
Hunter Fryingpan	I	39°10'N/106°38'W	30,091	1978
Indian Peaks	I	40°05'N/105°39'W	28,552	1980
La Garita	I	37°57'N/106°30'W	42,082	1980
Lizard Head	I	37°48'N/108°04'W	16,200	1980
Lost Creek	I	39°14'N/105°27'W	42,930	1980
Maroon Bells-Snowmass	I	39°05'N/107°03'W	70,470	1980
Mount Evans	I	39°35'N/105°39'W	30,109	1980
Mount Massive	I	39°10'N/106°28'W	10,530	1980
Mount Sneffels	I	37°59'N/107°55'W	6,561	1980
Mount Zirkel	I	40°50'N/106°38'W	56,583	1980
Neota	I	40°31'N/105°49'W	4,131	1980
Never Summer	I	40°23'N/105°54'W	5,548	1980
Raggeds	I	38°58'N/107°12'W	27,540	1980
Rawah	I	40°44'N/105°56'W	30,739	1980
South San Juan	I	37°09'N/106°30'W	54,067	1980
Weminuche	I	37°35'N/107°19'W	187,596	1980
West Elk	I	38°42'N/107°17'W	78,730	1980

Wilderness (National Park Service)

Black Canyon of the Gunnison	I	38°28'N/107°39'W	4,524	1976
Great Sand Dunes	I	37°45'N/105°37'W	13,537	1976
Indian Peaks	I	40°12'N/105°40'W	1,180	1975
Mesa Verde	I	37°16'N/108°25'W	3,278	1976

Delaware

National Wildlife Refuge

Bombay Hook	IV	39°19'N/75°28'W	6,119	?
Prime Hook	IV	38°53'N/75°11'W	3,925	?

State Park

Cape Henlopen	V	?/?	1,272	1964

Wildlife Management Area

C & D Canal	IV	?/?	2,095	1946
Cedar Swamp	IV	?/?	1,124	1981
Little Creek	IV	?/?	1,894	1957
Milford Neck	IV	?/?	1,168	1966
N G Wilder	IV	?/?	1,432	1968
Woodland Beach	IV	?/?	1,957	1953

Florida

National Estuarine Research Reserve

Rookery Bay	IV	?/?	8,585	1991

National Marine Sanctuary

Key Largo Coral Reef	V	25°09'N/8°017'W	32,388	1975
Looe Key	V	24°37'N/81°24'W	1,554	1981

National Monument

Fort Jefferson	III	25°23'N/80°55'W	19,083	1935
Fort Matanzas	III	?/?	120	1924

National Park

Biscayne	II	25°33'N/80°16'W	41,967	1980
Everglades	II	25°23'N/80°55'W	592,920	1947

National Preserve

Big Cypress	II	25°53'N/81°13'W	21,198	1974

National Seashore

Canaveral	V	28°46'N/80°46'W	23,321	1975
Gulf Islands (Florida)	V	30°19'N/87°05'W	57,084	1971

National Wildlife Refuge

Arthur R. Mitchell Loxahatchee	IV	26°30'N/80°10'W	58,949	1951
Chassahowitzka	IV	28°47'N/82°35'W	12,317	?
Crocodile Lake	IV	25°19'N/80°15'W	2,654	?
Florida Panther	IV	?/?	9,461	?
Great White Heron	IV	24°49'N/81°25'W	2,998	1938
J.N. "Dong" Darling	IV	25°26'N/82°05'W	2,164	1945
Lake Woodruff	IV	29°00'N/81°22'W	7,910	1964
Lower Suwannee	IV	29°30'N/83°02'W	20,290	?
Merritt Island	IV	28°40'N/80°40'W	55,953	?
National Key Deer	IV	24°35'N/81°25'W	8,109	1954
Okefenokee (Florida)	IV	30°50'N/82°23'W	1,488	1937
Pelican Island	IV	27°47'N/80°21'W	1,791	?
Pine Island	IV	26°40'N/81°17'W	163	1908
Pinellas	IV	27°41'N/82°41'W	159	1956
St. Johns	IV	28°33'N/80°52'W	2,531	?
St. Mark's	IV	30°15'N/83°56'W	26,467	1931
St. Vincent	IV	29°40'N/85°08'W	5,054	1968

State Park

Caladesi Island	V	?/?	116	1966
Cape Romano Aquatic Preserve	IV	?/?	6,700	1991
Charlotte Harbor Aquatic Preserve	IV	?/?	22,918	1982
Collier-Seminole	V	?/?	1,472	1944
Fakahatchee Strand State Preserve	V	?/?	3,610	1974
Indian River Area Aquatic Preserves	IV	?/?	25,890	1986
John Pennekamp Coral Reef	V	?/?	3,359	1959
Long Key	V	?/?	187	1961
Oleta River	V	?/?	162	1980
Paynes Prairie	V	?/?	7,041	?
Pinellas County Aquatic Preserve	IV	?/?	1,926	1982
Seminole Necklace	V	?/?	2,569	?
St. Martin's Marsh Aquatic Preserve	IV	?/?	1,510	1984
Terra Ceia Aquatic Preserve	IV	?/?	1,383	1982

State Reserve

Paynes Prairie	IV	?/?	5,656	1961

Wilderness (Fish and Wildlife Service)

Chassahowitzka	I	28°44'N/82°40'W	9,543	1976
Florida Keys	I	24°41'N/81°29'W	2,508	1975
J.N. "Ding" Darling	I	26°27'N/82°04'W	1,060	1976
St. Marks	I	30°05'N/84°06'W	7,021	1975

Wilderness (Forest Service)

Alexander Springs	I	29°03'N/81°29'W	3,116	1984
Big Gum Swamp	I	30°20'N/82°24'W	5,504	1984
Billies Bay	I	29°02'N/81°33'W	1,263	1984
Bradwell Bay	I	30°08'N/84°41'W	9,477	1974
Juniper Prairie	I	29°11'N/81°40'W	5,366	1984
Little Lake George	I	29°25'N/81°44'W	1,012	1984
Mud Swamp/New River	I	30°05'N/84°52'W	3,157	1984

Wilderness (National Park Service)

Everglades	I	25°29'N/80°57'W	524,677	1978

Georgia

National Battlefield Park

Kennesaw Mountain	V	33°50'N/84°40'W	1,488	1917

National Estuarine Research Reserve

Sapelo Island	IV	?/?	2,892	1976

National Marine Sanctuary

Gray's Reef	IV	31°24'N/80°56'W	5,441	1981

National Military Park

Chickamauga and Chattanooga	V	34°50'N/85°17'W	3,278	1890

National Monument

Fort Pulaski	V	31°58'N/80°59'W	2,229	1924

National Seashore

Cumberland Island	V	30°51'N/81°27'W	14,924	1972

National Wildlife Refuge

Banks Lake	IV	31°00'N/83°11'W	1,639	?
Blackbeard Island	IV	31°30'N/81°12'W	2,273	1940
Bond Swamp	IV	?/?	1,860	?
Eufaula	IV	?/?	1,308	?
Harris Neck	IV	31°38'N/81°16'W	1,117	1962
Okefenokee (Georgia)	IV	30°48'N/82°12'W	158,395	?
Piedmont	IV	33°08'N/83°50'W	14,125	1939
Savannah	IV	32°12'N/81°08'W	11,323	1927
Wassaw Island	IV	31°54'N/81°00'W	4,075	1968
Wolf Island	IV	31°20'N/81°18'W	2,074	1930

Natural Area

Big Lazer Creek	IV	?/?	1,122	1974
Lewis Island	IV	?/?	2,276	1974
Pigeon Mountain	IV	?/?	2,993	1974

State Park

F.D. Roosevelt	V	?/?	2,017	?
Hard Labor Creek	V	?/?	2,345	?

Wilderness (Fish and Wildlife Service)

Blackbeard Island	I	31°27'N/81°14'W	1,214	1975
Okefenokee	I	30°46'N/82°17'W	143,252	1974
Wolf Island	I	31°18'N/81°20'W	2,074	1975

Wilderness (Forest Service)

Blood Mountain	I	?/?	3,157	1991
Brasstown	I	34°52'N/83°50'W	5,000	1986
Cohutta	I	34°57'N/84°32'W	13,081	1974
Mark Trail	I	?/?	6,831	1991
Raven Cliffs	I	34°41'N/83°51'W	3,465	1986
Rich Mountain	I	34°45'N/84°20'W	3,840	1986

Southern Nantahala	I	35°00'N/83°37'W	5,034	1984
Tray Mountain	I	34°49'N/83°41'W	3,926	1986

Wilderness (National Park Service)

Cumberland Island	I	30°52'N/81°27'W	3,577	1982

Hawaii

Biological Reserve

Kamakou Preserve	IV	21°06'N/156°52'W	1,123	1982
Pelekunu Preserve	IV	?/?	2,332	1987
Waikamoi Preserve	IV	20°45'N/156°11'W	2,117	1983

National Estuarine Research Reserve

Waimanu Valley	IV	?/?	1,763	1976

National Historic Park

Kalapapa	II	?/?	4,343	1980
Kalaupapa	V	21°11'N/157°10'W	5,110	1980

National Park

Haleakala	II	20°43'N/156°09'W	11,728	1916
Hawaii Volcanoes	II	19°22'N/155°20'W	91,960	1916

National Wildlife Refuge

Hakalau	IV	?/?	6,265	1985
Hawaiian Islands (8 sites)	IV	25°27'N/168°53'W	102,960	1945

State Natural Area Reserve

Hanawi	IV	?/?	3,036	1986
Hono O Na Pali	IV	?/?	1,275	1983
Kahaualea	IV	?/?	6,772	1986
Kipahoehoe	IV	?/?	2,260	1983
Laupahoehoe	IV	?/?	3,196	1983
Manuka	IV	?/?	10,344	1983
Mauna Kea Ice Age	IV	?/?	1,577	1981
Puu Makaala	IV	?/?	4,901	1981
Puu O Umi	IV	?/?	4,106	1987
West Maui (4 sites)	IV	?/?	2,714	1986

State Park

Kahana Valley	V	?/?	2,116	?
Kokee	V	?/?	1,758	?
Na Pali	V	?/?	2,499	?

Wilderness (National Park Service)

Haleakala	I	20°44'N/156°04'W	7,798	1976
Hawaii Volcanoes	I	19°21'N/155°26'W	49,817	1978

Idaho

National Historic Park

Nez Perce	V	?/?	1,212	1965

National Monument

Craters of the Moon	III	43°40'N/113°30'W	21,669	1924

National Natural Landmark

Cassia Silent City of Rocks	III	?/?	7,474	?
Hagerman Fauna sites	III	?/?	1,566	?

National Scenic River

Salmon River	V	?/?	12,943	1968

National Wildlife Refuge

Bear Lake	IV	42°10'N/111°20'W	7,312	1968

Camas	IV	44°00'N/112°13'W	4,281	?
Deer Flat	IV	43°46'N/116°48'W	4,559	?
Grays Lake	IV	43°02'N/111°24'W	6,709	1965
Kootenai	IV	48°49'N/116°37'W	1,123	?
Minidoka	IV	42°43'N/113°20'W	8,386	?

Outstanding Natural Area

Snake River Birds of Prey	V	?/?	10,629	1971

State Park

Bruneau	V	?/?	1,212	?
Farragut	V	?/?	1,912	?
Harriman (Idaho)	V	?/?	1,899	?
Heyburn	V	?/?	3,161	?
Indian Rocks	V	?/?	1,438	?
McCroskey	V	?/?	1,846	?

Wilderness (Forest Service)

Frank Church-River of No Return	I	45°27'N/115°51'W	946,580	1980
Gospel Hump	I	45°35'N/115°45'W	83,367	1978
Hell's Canyon	I	45°27'N/116°40'W	86,605	1975
Sawtooth	I	44°01'N/115°02'W	87,854	1972

Wilderness (National Park Service)

Craters of the Moon	I	43°23'N/113°33'W	17,500	1970

Illinois

National Wildlife Refuge

Chautauqua	IV	14°23'N/89°59'W	2,608	1974
Crab Orchard	IV	37°44'N/88°56'W	17,669	?
Cypress creek	IV	?/?	2,203	?
Mark Twain (Illinois)	IV	39°46'N/91°09'W	6,709	1958
Mississippi River Caue (Illinois)	V	?/?	8,142	?
Upper Mississippi River	IV	?/?	1,335	?

State Park

Chain O'Lakes	V	?/?	1,106	1945
Giant City	V	?/?	1,496	1927
Goose Lake Prairie	V	?/?	1,022	1969
Hennepin Canal	V	?/?	2,163	1970
Horseshoe Lake	V	?/?	1,186	1971
Illinois Beach	V	?/?	1,205	1943
Jubilee College	V	?/?	1,289	1933
Kankakee River	V	?/?	1,579	1938
Pere Marquette	V	?/?	3,266	1932
Pyramid	V	?/?	1,023	1965
Rock Cut	V	?/?	1,211	1957
Siloam Springs	V	?/?	1,345	1942
Starved Rock	V	?/?	1,062	1911
Stephen A. Forbes	V	?/?	1,256	1959

Wilderness (Fish and Wildlife Service)

Crab Orchard	I	37°35'N/89°06'W	1,639	1976

Wilderness (Forest Service)

Bald Knob	I	?/?	2,373	1990
Bay Creek	I	?/?	1,160	1990
Burden Falls	I	?/?	1,486	1990
Clear Springs	I	?/?	1,914	1990
Garden of the Gods	I	?/?	1,323	1990
Lusk Creek	I	?/?	1,807	1990

Indiana

National Lakeshore

Indiana Dunes	V	37°30'N/87°00'W	5,073	1966

National Wildlife Refuge				
Muscatatuck	IV	?/?	3,157	?
State Park				
Brown Country	V	?/?	6,475	1929
Chain O'Lakes	V	?/?	1,084	?
Harmonie	V	?/?	1,402	1966
Potato Creek	V	?/?	1,554	1969
Shades	V	?/?	1,247	1947
Summit Lake	V	?/?	1,033	1988
Tippecanoe	V	?/?	1,117	1943
Versailles	V	?/?	2,325	?
Wilderness (Forest Service)				
Charles C. Deam	I	39°00'N/86°23'W	5,235	1982

Iowa

National Natural Landmark				
Loess Hills	III	42°05'N/93°37'W	4,217	1985
National Wildlife Refuge				
De Soto (Iowa)	IV	41°32'N/96°00'W	1,417	?
Mark Twain (Iowa)	IV	40°48'N/91°16'W	4,237	?
Mississippi River Cauc (Iowa)	IV	?/?	12,268	?
Union Slough	IV	43°20'N/94°10'W	1,180	1938
Upper Mississippi (Iowa)	IV	43°02'N/91°13'W	8,364	1924
Walnut Creek	IV	?/?	1,665	?

Kansas

National Wildlife Refuge				
Flint Hills	IV	38°15'N/95°50'W	7,472	1966
Kirwin	IV	39°44'N/99°07'W	4,362	?
Marais des Cygnes	IV	?/?	2,064	?
Quivira	IV	38°11'N/98°29'W	8,830	?
State Park				
Cedar Bluff Reservoir	V	?/?	5,848	?
Swan Marshes	V	?/?	5,147	?

Kentucky

National Historic Park				
Cumberland Gap	V	?/?	8,150	1940
National Natural Landmark				
Henderson Sloughs	III	?/?	1,737	?
National Park				
Mammoth Cave	II	37°12'N/86°08'W	20,541	1934
State Park				
Dale Hollow Lake	V	?/?	1,375	1978
Greenbo Lake Resort	V	?/?	1,217	?
Lake Barkley Resort	V	?/?	1,457	1967
Lake Cumberland Resort	V	?/?	1,261	1954
Taylorsville Lake	V	?/?	1,072	1983
Wilderness (Forest Service)				
Beaver Creek	I	36°52'N/84°25'W	1,944	1974
Clifty	I	37°53'N/83°37'W	5,029	1985

Louisiana

National Historic Park				
Jean Lafitte	V	30°00'N/90°00'W	3,480	1978

National Wildlife Refuge

Atchafalaya	IV	?/?	6,174	?
Bayou Cocodrie	IV	?/?	1,996	?
Bayou Sauvage	IV	?/?	7,284	?
Bogue Chitto (Louisiana)	IV	30°42'N/89°54'W	11,602	?
Breton	IV	29°10'N/89°10'W	3,661	1904
Cameron Prairie	IV	?/?	3,893	?
Catahoula	IV	31°42'N/91°58'W	2,152	?
D'Arbonne	IV	32°41'N/92°12'W	7,049	?
Delta	IV	29°10'N/89°10'W	19,748	1935
Grand Cote	IV	?/?	2,459	?
Lacassine	IV	30°00'N/92°46'W	13,203	?
Sabine	IV	30°04'N/93°27'W	56,428	?
Tensas River	IV	32°11'N/91°19'W	23,886	?
Upper Ouachita	IV	32°55'N/95°00'W	8,454	1978

State Park

Chicot	IV	?/?	2,592	?
Fontainebleau	IV	?/?	1,093	?

Wilderness (Fish and Wildlife Service)

Breton	I	29°46'N/88°51'W	2,023	1975
Lacassine	I	29°54'N/92°57'W	1,354	1976

Wilderness (Forest Service)

Kisatchie Hills	I	31°29'N/92°57'W	3,523	1980

Maine

National Monument

Saint Croix Island	III	?/?	100	1949

National Park

Acadia	II	44°20'N/68°17'W	15,590	1919

National Wildlife Refuge

Mooschorn	IV	45°00'N/67°00'W	9,678	1937
Petit Manan	IV	44°32'N/67°44'W	1,349	?
Rachel Carson	IV	43°36'N/70°24'W	1,706	?
Sunkhaze Meadows	IV	?/?	3,779	?

State Park

Baxter	II	?/?	80,800	1940
Camden Hills	V	?/?	2,211	?
Grafton Notch	V	?/?	1,257	?
Mt. Blue	V	?/?	1,995	?

Wilderness (Fish and Wildlife Service)

Mooschorn, Baring Unit	I	45°02'N/67°16'W	1,894	1975
Mooschorn, Edmunds Unit	I	44°47'N/67°14'W	1,095	1970

Wilderness (Forest Service)

Caribou-Speckled Mountain	I	?/?	4,856	1990

Maryland

National Estuarine Research Reserve

Chesapeake Bay (MD)	IV	?/?	2,374	1981

National Historic Park

Chesapeake and Ohio Canal	V	39°11'N/77°53'W	50,161	1971

National Seashore

Assateague Island	V	38°07'N/75°07'W	16,038	1965

National Wildlife Refuge

Blackwater	IV	38°28'N/75°57'W	7,228	?
Martin	IV	38°04'N/75°56'W	1,790	?
Patuxent	IV	39°05'N/76°47'W	4,968	?

Natural Environment Area

Mattawoman	IV	?/?	1,446	?
Morgan Run	IV	?/?	1,815	?
Zekiah Swamp	IV	?/?	2,023	?

Park

Catoctin Mountain	V	?/?	2,334	1936
Piscataway	V	39°40'N/77°00'W	1,701	1961

State Park

Cunningham Falls	V	?/?	2,171	?
Gunpowder Falls (Maryland)	V	?/?	6,389	?
Janes Island	V	?/?	1,275	?
Patapsco Valley	V	?/?	6,509	?
Patuxent River	V	?/?	3,002	?
Rocky Gap	V	?/?	1,347	?
Seneca Creek	V	?/?	2,631	?
South Mountain	V	?/?	4,405	?
St. Mary's River	V	?/?	1,032	?
Susquehanna	V	?/?	1,471	?
Tuckahoe	V	?/?	1,865	?

Wildlife Management Area

Cedar Island	IV	?/?	1,165	?
Dans Mountain	IV	?/?	5,627	?
Deal Islald	IV	?/?	6,070	?
Fairmount	IV	?/?	1,631	?
Fishing Bay	IV	?/?	11,736	?
Idylwild	IV	?/?	3,287	?
Indian Springs	IV	?/?	2,756	?
Islands of the Potomac	IV	?/?	1,430	?
Millington	IV	?/?	1,757	?
South Marsh Island	IV	?/?	1,214	?
Taylor's Island	IV	?/?	1,463	?
Warrior Mountain	IV	?/?	2,146	?

Massachusetts

National Estuarine Research Reserve

Waquoint Bay	IV	?/?	1,077	1988

National Seashore

Cape Cod	V	41°53'N/69°59'W	18,018	1961

National Wildlife Refuge

Great Meadows	IV	42°26'N/71°20'W	1,364	1944
Monomy	IV	41°42'N/69°55'W	1,093	?
Parker River	IV	42°48'N/70°56'W	1,883	?

State Park

Clarksburg	V	?/?	1,315	?
Holyoke Range	V	?/?	1,188	?
Wompatuck	V	?/?	1,416	?

Michigan

National Lakeshore

Pictured Rocks	V	46°34'N/86°18'W	28,661	1966
Sleeping Bear Dunes	V	45°00'N/86°00'W	28,775	1970

National Park

Isle Royale	II	48°02'N/88°47'W	215,740	1940

National Wildlife Refuge

Kirtlands Warbler	IV	44°15'N/84°22'W	2,554	?
Seney	IV	46°05'N/86°12'W	38,629	1935
Shiawassee	IV	43°20'N/84°00'W	3,636	1953

State Park

Hartwick Pines	V	?/?	3,475	?
Porcupine Mountains Wilderness	II	?/?	20,200	1944
Tahquamenon Falls	V	?/?	7,197	?
Wilderness	V	?/?	2,754	?

Wilderness (Fish and Wildlife Service)

Seney	I	46°15'N/86°13'W	10,178	1970

Wilderness (Forest Service)

Big Island Lake	I	46°19'N/86°29'W	2,363	1987
Delirium	I	46°21'N/84°42'W	4,804	1987
Horseshoe Bay	I	46°01'N/84°30'W	1,534	1987
Mackinac	I	46°12'N/84°42'W	4,949	1987
McCormick	I	46°54'N/87°48'W	6,819	1987
Nordhouse Dunes	I	44°17'N/86°14'W	1,396	1987
Rock River Canyon	I	46°27'N/86°47'W	1,878	1987
Sturgeon River Gorge	I	46°40'N/88°52'W	5,868	1987
Sylvania	I	46°18'N/89°29'W	7,417	1987

Wilderness (National Park Service)

Isle Royale	I	47°59'N/88°53'W	53,370	1976

Wilderness Area

Porcupine Mountains	I	?/?	16,486	1944

Minnesota

National Natural Landmark

Lake Agassiz	IV	?/?	8,888	?

National Park

Voyageurs	II	48°30'N/93°00'W	87,772	1971

National Wildlife Refuge

Agassiz	IV	48°30'N/96°00'W	24,888	1937
Big Stone	IV	45°20'N/96°14'W	4,562	?
Mid-Continent WMP	IV	?/?	2,054	?
Minnesota Valley	IV	44°54'N/93°13'W	3,216	?
Mississippi River Caue (Minnesota)	IV	?/?	6,240	?
Rice Lake	IV	46°42'N/93°28'W	6,625	?
Sherburne	IV	45°30'N/93°40'W	11,981	1965
Tamarac	IV	47°00'N/95°35'W	14,232	1938
Upper Mississippi (Minnesota)	IV	?/?	7,318	?

State Park

Banning	V	?/?	2,524	?
Bear Head Lake	V	?/?	1,774	?
Cascade River	V	?/?	1,138	?
Forestville and Mystery Caves	V	?/?	1,089	?
Fort Snelling	V	?/?	1,335	?
Geo. Crosby Manitou	V	?/?	1,376	?
Hayes Lake	V	?/?	1,194	?
Itasca	IV	?/?	12,950	1938
Jay Cooke	V	?/?	3,567	?
Judge Magney	V	?/?	1,827	?

Lake Bronson	V	?/?	1,207	?
Maplewood	V	?/?	3,743	?
McCarthy Beach	V	?/?	1,038	?
Mille Lacs-Kathio	V	?/?	4,284	?
Minnesota Valley	V	?/?	3,237	?
O.L. Kipp	V	?/?	1,147	?
Savanna Portage	V	?/?	6,401	?
Scenic	V	?/?	1,182	?
Sibley	V	?/?	1,184	?
St. Croix	V	?/?	13,774	?
Tettegouche	V	?/?	1,898	?
Whitewater	V	?/?	1,158	?
Wild River	V	?/?	2,833	?
Zippel Bay	V	?/?	1,192	?

Wilderness (Fish and Wildlife Service)

Agassiz	I	48°24'N/95°54'W	1,619	1976

Wilderness (Forest Service)

Boundary Waters Canoe Area	III	47°58'N/91°27'W	321,165	1978

Mississipppi

National Wildlife Refuge

Bogue Chitto (Mississippi)	IV	30°41'N/89°45'W	2,755	?
Dahomey	IV	?/?	1,962	?
Grand Bay	IV	?/?	1,072	?
Hillside	IV	33°05'N/90°10'W	6,234	1975
Mississippi Sandhill Crane	IV	30°28'N/88°45'W	7,812	1974
Morgan Brake	IV	33°22'N/90°03'W	1,968	?
Noxubee	IV	33°10'N/88°40'W	18,888	1940
Panther Swamp	IV	32°57'N/90°24'W	11,574	?
St. Catherine Creek	IV	?/?	5,275	?
Tallahatchie	IV	?/?	1,577	?
Yazoo	IV	33°11'N/90°54'W	5,237	?

State Park

Natchez	V	31°36'N/91°13'W	1,391	1979
Trace	V	88°54'N/34°15'W	1,030	1986

Wilderness (Forest Service)

Black Creek	I	30°53'N/88°56'W	2,028	1984

Missouri

National Scenic River

Ozark	V	37°00'N/91°00'W	32,209	1972

National Wildlife Refuge

Clarence Cannon	IV	39°30'N/91°30'W	1,517	1964
Mingo	IV	37°00'N/90°05'W	8,800	?
Squaw Creek	IV	40°05'N/95°15'W	2,932	1935
Swan Lake	IV	39°39'N/93°00'W	4,592	1937

State Park

Bennett Spring	V	37°30'N/92°51'W	1,254	1924
Big Spring	V	?/?	2,334	?
Cuivre River	V	39°02'N/90°56'W	2,538	1946
Ha Ha Tonka	V	37°58'N/92°45'W	1,140	1978
Hawn	V	37°49'N/90°13'W	1,858	1955
Johnson's Shut-Ins	V	37°32'N/90°51'W	1,145	1935
Lake of the Ozarc	V	38°07'N/92°35'W	6,966	1946
Meramec	V	38°13'N/91°03'W	2,746	1927
Pershing	V	39°46'N/93°13'W	1,087	1937

Prairie	V	37°31'N/94°35'W	1,339	1980
Roaring River	V	36°35'N/93°48'W	3,403	1928
Sam A. Baker	III	37°15'N/90°32'W	2,090	1928
Taum Sauk Mountain	V	37°32'N/90°44'W	2,519	1991
Trail of Tears	V	37°28'N/89°28'W	1,382	1957
Wappapello	V	?/?	17,038	?

Wilderness (Fish and Wildlife Service)

Mingo	I	36°58'N/90°13'W	3,128	1976

Wilderness (Forest Service)

Bell Mountain	I	37°37'N/90°54'W	3,321	1980
Devil's Backbone	I	36°47'N/92°08'W	2,754	1980
Hercules-Glade	I	36°44'N/92°54'W	49,815	1976
Irish	I	36°47'N/91°11'W	6,522	1984
Paddy Creek	I	37°36'N/92°06'W	2,841	1983
Piney Creek	I	36°43'N/93°36'W	3,402	1980
Rockpile Mountain	I	37°29'N/90°25'W	1,579	1980

Montana

National Park

Glacier	II	48°38'N/113°53'W	410,058	1910

National Recreation Area

Bighorn Canyon (Montana)	V	47°30'N/108°00'W	48,644	1966

National Wildlife Refuge

Benton Lake	IV	47°41'N/111°22'W	5,040	?
Bowdoin	IV	?/?	6,293	?
Charles M. Russell	IV	47°40'N/107°10'W	365,567	1936
Creedman Coulee	IV	48°43'N/109°54'W	1,072	?
Halfbreed Lake	IV	45°55'N/109°03'W	1,747	?
Lake Mason	IV	46°41'N/108°43'W	6,742	?
Lake Thibadeau	IV	48°41'N/109°43'W	1,558	?
Lee Metcalf	IV	46°34'N/114°05'W	1,130	1964
Medicine Lake	IV	48°41'N/104°18'W	12,741	?
National Bison Range	IV	47°22'N/114°13'W	7,486	?
Pablo	IV	47°39'N/114°09'W	1,028	?
Red Rock Lakes	IV	44°51'N/111°42'W	17,870	?
Ul Bend	IV	47°39'N/107°32'W	22,682	?
War Horse	IV	46°59'N/108°28'W	1,292	?

Wilderness (Bureau of Land Management)

Lee Metcalf	I	45°31'N/111°33'W	2,428	1983

Wilderness (Fish and Wildlife Service)

Medicine Lake	I	48°27'N/104°21'W	4,600	1976
Red Rock Lakes	I	44°37'N/111°44'W	13,092	1976
UL Bend	I	47°32'N/107°52'W	8,425	1976

Wilderness (Forest Service)

Absaroka-Beartooth	I	44°40'N/109°59'W	372,445	1978
Anaconda-Pintler	I	45°57'N/113°28'W	63,891	1964
Bob Marshall	I	47°42'N/113°08'W	408,481	1978
Cabinet Mountains	I	48°15'N/116°00'W	38,151	1964
Gates of the Mountain	I	46°53'N/111°58'W	11,559	1964
Great Bear	I	48°07'N/113°25'W	116,026	1978
Lee Metcalf	I	45°08'N/111°27'W	100,744	1983
Mission Mountains	I	47°28'N/113°50'W	29,898	1974
Rattlesnake	I	47°03'N/113°50'W	13,292	1980
Scapegoat	I	47°15'N/112°46'W	96,842	1972
Selway-Bitterroot	I	?/?	541,352	1964
Welcome Creek NFW	I	46°36'N/113°41'W	11,380	1978

Nebraska

National Monument

Agate Fossil Beds	III	42°20'N/103°40'W	1,236	1965
Lehman Caves	III	?/?	3,098	1922
Scotts Bluff	V	41°47'N/103°42'W	1,209	1919

National Wildlife Refuge

Crescent Lake	IV	41°47'N/102°17'W	18,555	?
De Soto (Nebraska)	IV	41°32'N/95°55'W	1,750	?
Fort Niobrara	IV	42°53'N/100°28'W	7,742	1912
North Platte	IV	41°55'N/103°34'W	2,042	?
Valentine	IV	42°30'N/100°32'W	28,942	1935

State Park

Fort Robinson	V	?/?	4,485	?
Indian Cave	V	?/?	1,212	?

Wilderness (Fish and Wildlife Service)

Fort Niobrara	I	42°51'N/100°23'W	1,876	1976

Wilderness (Forest Service)

Soldier Creek	I	42°41'N/103°03'W	3,154	1986

Nevada

National Park

Great Basin	II	40°30'N/115°30'W	31,080	1986

National Recreation Area

Lake Mead	V	?/?	606,123	1964

National Wildlife Refuge

Ash Meadows	IV	36°25'N/116°20'W	5,354	1984
Desert	IV	36°55'N/115°31'W	642,974	?
Fallon	IV	39°42'N/118°16'W	7,244	?
Paharanagat	IV	37°19'N/115°18'W	2,178	?
Ruby Lake	IV	40°18'N/115°17'W	15,229	?
Sheldon	IV	41°52'N/119°15'W	230,858	1931
Stillwater	IV	39°32'N/118°10'W	31,600	?

Outstanding Natural Area

Desert View Natural Environment Area	V	?/?	7,531	1970
Goshute Canyon	V	?/?	3,042	1967
Highland Range Crucial Bighorn	V	?/?	10,213	1970
Lahontan-Cutthroat Trout	V	?/?	4,976	1974
Mt. Grafton Scenic Area	V	?/?	5,898	1967
Sunrise Mountain	V	?/?	4,137	1970
Swamp Cedar	V	?/?	1,293	1967

State Park

Lake Tahoe Nevada	V	391°2'N/119°55'W	5,764	1958
Valley of Fire	II	36°30'N/114°23'W	14,115	1935

Wilderness (Bureau of Land Management)

Mount Moriah	I	39°22'N/114°11'W	2,604	1989

Wilderness (Forest Service)

Alta Toquima	I	38°43'N/116°57'W	15,378	1989
Arc Dome	I	?/?	46,539	1989
Boundary Peak	I	37°51'N/118°19'W	4,047	1989
Currant Mountain	I	38°54'N/115°25'W	14,569	1989
East Humboldt	I	40°52'N/115°05'W	14,933	1989
Grant Range	I	38°20'N/115°30'W	20,234	1989
Jarbridge	I	41°48'N/115°20'W	26,203	1964

Mount Charleston	I	36°17'N/115°46'W	17,402	1989
Mount Moriah	I	39°17'N/114°12'W	33,184	1989
Mount Rose	I	39°22'N/119°54'W	11,331	1989
Quinn Canyon	I	38°01'N/115°47'W	10,927	1989
Ruby Mountains	I	40°29'N/115°27'W	36,422	1989
Santa Rosa - Paradise Peak	I	41°38'N/117°30'W	12,545	1989
Table Mountain	I	?/?	39,659	1989

New Hampshire

National Estuarine Research Reserve

Great Bay	IV	?/?	3,002	1989

State Park

Bear Brook	V	?/?	3,894	?
Crawford Notch	V	?/?	2,404	?
Franconia Notch	V	?/?	2,606	?
Monadnock	V	?/?	2,023	1987
Pawtuckaway	V	?/?	2,222	?
Pillsbury	V	?/?	2,121	?
Pisgah Wilderness	I	?/?	5,331	?
Sunapee, Mount	V	?/?	1,102	?

Wilderness (Forest Service)

Great Gulf	I	44°17'N/71°20'W	2,268	1964
Pemigewasset	I	44°08'N/71°34'W	18,211	1984
Presidential Ridge-Dry River	I	44°11'N/71°21'W	8,262	1974
Sandwich Range	I	43°56'N/71°28'W	10,117	1984

New Jersey

National Recreation Area

Delaware Water Gap (New Jersey)	V	41°05'N/75°00'W	28,340	1965

National Reserve

Pinelands	V	39°45'N/74°45'W	438,210	1978

National Wildlife Refuge

Cape May	IV	?/?	2,301	?
Edwin B. Forsythe	IV	39°50'N/74°12'W	15,969	?
Great Swamp	IV	40°49'N/74°16'W	2,929	1964
Supawna Meadows	IV	?/?	1,156	?

State Park

Allaire	V	?/?	1,199	?
Allamuchy Mt.	V	?/?	2,329	?
Delaware Canal	V	?/?	1,255	?
High Point	V	?/?	5,413	?
Island Beach	V	?/?	1,212	?
Ringwood	V	?/?	1,721	?
Wawayanda	V	?/?	4,265	?

Wilderness (Fish and Wildlife Service)

Brigantine	I	39°31'N/74°16'W	2,704	1975
Great Swamp	I	40°45'N/74°24'W	1,481	1968

New Mexico

National Historic Park

Chaco Culture	V	36°02'N/107°55'W	13,760	1907

National Monument

Bandelier	III	35°45'N/106°20'W	14,904	1916
Chaco Canyon	III	36°01'N/107°56'W	8,708	1907
White Sands	III	32°52'N/106°19'W	58,614	1933

National Natural Landmark

Grants Lava Flow	III	?/?	21,719	?
Kilbourne Hole	III	?/?	2,327	?

National Park

Carlsbad Caverns	II	32°11'N/104°17'W	18,921	1930

National Scenic River

Rio Grande	V	?/?	6,820	1970

National Wildlife Refuge

Bitter Lake	III	33°35'N/104°27'W	9,925	?
Bosque del Apache	IV	33°50'N/106°55'W	23,144	1939
Grulla	III	34°05'N/103°05'W	1,307	1969
Las Vegas	IV	35°35'N/105°11'W	3,509	?
Maxwell	IV	36°36'N/104°39'W	1,497	?
San Andrés	IV	32°44'N/106°35'W	23,154	?
Sevilleta	IV	34°20'N/106°50'W	92,946	1973

Outstanding Natural Area

El Malpais	V	?/?	33,936	1970
Guadalupe Canyon	V	?/?	1,462	1968

State Park

Caballo Lake	V	?/?	2,152	?
Cimarron Canyon	V	?/?	13,332	?
Elephant Butte Lake	V	?/?	8,287	?
Heron Lake	V	?/?	1,659	?
Navajo Lake (Pine)	V	?/?	7,255	?
Santa Rosa Lake	V	?/?	5,072	?
Sumner Lake	V	?/?	2,693	?

Wilderness (Bureau of Land Management)

Bisti	I	36°15'N/108°12'W	1,597	1984
Cebolla	I	34°41'N/108°00'W	25,414	1987
De-na-zin	I	36°19'N/108°02'W	9,087	1984
West Malpais	I	34°48'N/108°13'W	16,066	1987

Wilderness (Fish and Wildlife Service)

Bosque del Apache, Chupadera Unit	I	33°48'N/106°55'W	2,140	1975
Bosque del Apache, Indian Well Unit	I	33°45'N/106°49'W	2,080	1975
Bosque del Apache, Little San Pasqual	I	33°50'N/106°45'W	8,037	1975
Salt Creek	I	33°32'N/104°26'W	3,893	1970

Wilderness (Forest Service)

Aldo Leopold	I	33°10'N/107°51'W	85,576	1980
Apache Kid	I	33°37'N/107°25'W	18,225	1980
Blue Range	I	33°33'N/108°59'W	12,150	1980
Capitan Mountains	I	33°34'N/105°17'W	13,770	1980
Chama River Canyon	I	36°19'N/106°39'W	20,371	1978
Cruces Basin	I	36°56'N/106°19'W	7,290	1980
Dome	I	35°43'N/106°22'W	2,106	1980
Gila	I	33°13'N/108°20'W	230,688	1980
Latir Peak	I	36°45'N/105°29'W	8,100	1980
Manzano Mountain	I	34°39'N/106°26'W	14,944	1978
Pecos	I	35°54'N/105°38'W	90,436	1980
San Pedro Parks	I	36°04'N/106°50'W	16,645	1980
Sandia Mountain	I	35°08'N/106°25'W	12,433	1980
Wheeler	I	36°33'N/105°25'W	7,978	1980
White Mountain	I	33°26'N/105°48'W	19,480	1980
Withington	I	33°52'N/107°27'W	7,695	1980

Wilderness (National Park Service)

Bandelier	I	35°48'N/106°16'W	9,416	1976
Carlsbad Caverns	I	32°08'N/104°33'W	13,405	1978

New York

National Estuarine Research Reserve

Hudson River	IV	?/?	2,023	1982

National Historic Park

Saratoga	V	?/?	2,222	1938

National Seashore

Fire Island	V	40°37'N/72°52'W	7,834	1964

National Wildlife Refuge

Iroquois	IV	43°00'N/78°00'W	4,379	1958
Montezuma	IV	43°04'N/76°46'W	2,609	?
Oyster Bay	IV	40°56'N/73°34'W	1,297	?

State Park

Adirondack	V	44°47'N/74°28'W	2,426,200	1971
Allegany	V	?/?	24,599	?
Bear Mountain	V	?/?	2,050	?
Catskill	V	?/?	99,788	?
Clarence Fahnstock Memorial	V	?/?	2,650	?
Connetquot	V	?/?	1,405	?
Harriman (New York)	V	?/?	18,780	?
Highland Lakes	V	?/?	1,249	?
Hudson Highlands	V	?/?	1,562	?
Letchworth	V	?/?	5,803	?
Minnewaska	V	?/?	4,730	?
Taconic-Rudd Pond-Copake Falls	V	?/?	1,479	?
Wellesley Island	V	?/?	1,067	?

North Carolina

National Estuarine Research Reserve

North Carolina	IV	?/?	4,743	1982

National Seashore

Cape Hatteras	V	35°28'N/75°47'W	12,270	1937
Cape Lookout National Seashore	V	34°43'N/76°26'W	11,493	1966

National Wildlife Refuge

Alligator River	IV	35°54'N/75°51'W	57,302	?
Cedar Island	IV	35°04'N/76°13'W	5,861	?
Great Dismal Swamp	IV	?/?	20,082	?
Mackay Island	IV	36°32'N/75°51'W	2,831	?
Mattamuskeet	IV	35°35'N/75°57'W	20,307	?
Pea Island	IV	35°43'N/75°25'W	2,361	?
Pee Dee	IV	35°10'N/79°56'W	3,415	?
Pocosin Lakes	IV	?/?	43,592	?
Pungo	IV	35°44'N/76°28'W	5,002	?
Roanoke River	IV	?/?	2,452	?
Swanquarter	IV	35°25'N/76°10'W	6,641	?

Natural Area

Chowan Swamp	V	?/?	2,455	?
Dismal Swamp	V	?/?	5,805	?

State Park

Crowders Mountain	V	?/?	1,047	?
Dismal Swamp	V	?/?	5,805	?
Hanging Rock	V	?/?	2,486	?
Lake Phelps	V	?/?	6,475	?
Merchants Millpond	V	?/?	1,335	?
Morrow Mountain	V	?/?	1,899	?

Pilot Mountain	V	?/?	1,004	?
Raven Rock	V	?/?	1,152	?
South Mountain	V	?/?	2,924	?
Stone Mountain	V	?/?	5,437	?
Umstead	V	?/?	2,160	?
Waccamaw River	V	?/?	3,617	?

State Recreation Area

Falls Lake	V	?/?	2,240	?
Kerr Lake	V	?/?	1,214	?

Wilderness (Fish and Wildlife Service)

Swanquarter	I	35°22'N/76°10'W	3,555	1976

Wilderness (Forest Service)

Birkhead Mountains	I	35°35'N/79°54'W	1,938	1984
Catfish Lake South	I	34°56'N/77°10'W	3,076	1984
Ellicott Rock (North Carolina)	I	?/?	1,134	1974
Joyce Kilmer-Slickrock	I	?/?	4,131	1974
Linville Gorge	I	35°58'N/81°53'W	3,078	1964
Middle Prong	I	35°24'N/82°53'W	3,197	1984
Pocosin	I	34°49'N/77°00'W	4,452	1984
Sheep Ridge	I	34°56'N/77°04'W	3,861	1984
Shining Rock	I	35°29'N/82°45'W	5,427	1964
Southern Nantahala	I	35°00'N/83°37'W	4,895	1984

North Dakota

National Park

Theodore Roosevelt	II	46°57'N/103°27'W	28,150	1978

National Wildlife Refuge

Ardoch	IV	48°10'N/97°27'W	1,091	?
Arrowwood	IV	47°16'N/98°50'W	6,448	1935
Audubon	IV	47°39'N/101°09'W	5,965	1956
Chase Lake	IV	47°01'N/99°27'W	1,774	1908
Dakota Lake	IV	?/?	1,133	?
Des Lacs	IV	48°56'N/102°12'W	7,910	?
J. Clark Salyer	IV	48°31'N/100°39'W	24,032	?
Lake Alice	IV	48°18'N/99°03'W	4,595	?
Lake George	IV	46°45'N/99°40'W	1,262	?
Lake Ilo	IV	47°26'N/102°43'W	1,633	?
Lake Nettie	IV	47°36'N/101°03'W	1,236	?
Lake Zahl	IV	48°32'N/103°36'W	1,547	?
Long Lake	IV	46°42'N/100°10'W	9,105	1932
Lostwood	IV	48°42'N/102°33'W	10,887	?
Rock Lake	IV	?/?	2,228	?
Silver Lake	IV	?/?	1,354	?
Slade	IV	46°50'N/99°43'W	1,214	1941
Tewaukon	IV	46°01'N/97°21'W	3,384	1935
Upper Souris	IV	48°41'N/101°33'W	13,072	?
Willow Lake	IV	48°53'N/100°06'W	1,060	?

Wilderness (Fish and Wildlife Service)

Chase Lake	I	46°35'N/99°33'W	1,681	1975
Lostwood	I	48°29'N/102°14'W	2,257	1975

Wilderness (National Park Service)

Theodore Roosevelt	I	47°34'N/103°28'W	12,108	1978

Ohio

National Recreation Area

Cuyahoga Valley	V	?/?	12,950	1975

National Wildlife Refuge

Ottawa	IV	41°42'N/83°10'W	2,344	?

State Park

Alum Creek	V	?/?	2,110	?
Beaver Creek	V	?/?	1,229	?
Burr Oak	V	?/?	1,049	?
Caesar Creek	V	?/?	3,214	?
Deer Creek	V	?/?	2,569	?
Dillon	V	?/?	2,440	?
East Fork	V	?/?	3,407	?
Lake Hope	V	?/?	1,256	?
Mosquito Lake	V	?/?	1,603	?
Paint Creek	V	?/?	3,642	?
Pymatuning	V	?/?	1,416	?
Salt Fork	V	?/?	6,972	?
Strouds Run	V	?/?	1,055	?
West Branch	V	?/?	2,166	?

Oklahoma

National Natural Landmark

McCurtain County Wilderness Area	III	?/?	5,691	?
Salt Plains	II	?/?	12,948	1930

National Recreation Area

Arbuckle	V	?/?	3,576	1965

National Wildlife Refuge

Optima	IV	36°42'N/101°06'W	1,753	?
Salt Plains	IV	36°50'N/98°10'W	12,973	1930
Sequoyah	IV	35°27'N/95°00'W	8,417	1971
Tishomingo	IV	34°12'N/96°37'W	6,663	1943
Washita	IV	35°40'N/99°04'W	3,268	?
Wichita Mountains	IV	34°48'N/98°29'W	23,884	?

State Park

Beavers Bend	V	?/?	1,422	?
Fort Cobb	V	?/?	1,816	?
Foss	V	?/?	2,816	?
Fountainhead	V	?/?	1,374	?
Lake Murray	V	?/?	7,362	?
Little River	IV	?/?	4,868	?
Quartz Mountain	V	?/?	4,465	?
Robbers Cave	V	?/?	3,408	?
Sequoyah	V	?/?	1,161	?
Wister	V	?/?	1,228	?

Wilderness (Fish and Wildlife Service)

Wichita Mountains, Charons Garden Unit	I	34°43'N/98°35'W	2,316	1970
Wichita Mountains, North Mountain Unit	I	34°47'N/98°32'W	1,152	1970

Wilderness (Forest Service)

Blackfork Mountain	I	34°46'N/94°18'W	1,855	1988
Upper Kiamichi	I	34°39'N/94°31'W	3,922	1988

Wilderness Area

McCurtain County	I	?/?	5,691	?

Oregon

National Estuarine Research Reserve

South Slough	IV	?/?	2,502	1974

National Monument

John Day Fossil Beds	III	44°30'N/119°30'W	5,671	1974

National Park

Crater Lake	II	43°00'N/122°10'W	74,150	1902

National Wildlife Refuge

Ankeny	IV	44°45'N/123°05'W	1,132	1965
Baskett Slough	IV	44°59'N/123°15'W	1,008	1965
Bear Valley	IV	42°13'N/122°02'W	1,691	?
Cold Springs	IV	45°55'N/119°11'W	1,261	1909
Hart Mountain	IV	42°39'N/119°45'W	101,696	?
Klamath Forest	IV	?/?	15,251	?
Lewis & Clark	IV	46°09'N/123°33'W	15,448	?
Lower Klamath	IV	42°04'N/121°58'W	2,678	?
Malheur	IV	43°10'N/118°59'W	75,033	?
Oregon Islands	IV	?/?	233	?
Umatilla (Oregon)	IV	45°50'N/119°45'W	3,593	1969
Upper Klamath	IV	42°30'N/122°00'W	6,057	1928
William L. Finley	IV	44°24'N/123°30'W	2,158	?

Refuge

Hart Mountain National Antelope Refuge	IV	?/?	110,231	1935

Research Natural Area

Jordan Craters	I	?/?	12,166	1975
Lost Forest	I	?/?	3,620	1973

State Park

Oswald West	V	?/?	1,000	?
Saddle Mountains	V	?/?	1,164	?
Silver Falls	V	?/?	3,435	?
The Cove Palisades	V	?/?	1,664	?

Wilderness (Bureau of Land Management)

Table Rock	I	45°01'N/122°21'W	2,327	1984

Wilderness (Forest Service)

Badger Creek	I	45°20'N/121°28'W	9,712	1984
Black Canyon	I	44°22'N/119°41'W	5,423	1984
Boulder Creek	I	43°23'N/122°30'W	7,730	1984
Bridge Creek	I	44°30'N/120°14'W	2,185	1984
Bull of the Woods	I	44°53'N/122°06'W	14,124	1984
Columbia	I	45°36'N/121°51'W	15,783	1984
Cummins Creek	I	44°16'N/124°03'W	3,712	1984
Diamond Peak	I	43°33'N/122°05'W	14,580	1964
Drift Creek	I	44°28'N/123°56'W	2,346	1984
Eagle Cap	I	45°13'N/117°25'W	118,867	1964
Gearhart Mountain	I	42°32'N/120°50'W	7,573	1965
Grassy Knob	I	42°45'N/124°21'W	6,961	1984
Kalmiopsis	I	42°18'N/123°57'W	68,404	1978
Menagerie	I	44°26'N/122°19'W	1,942	1984
Middle Santiam	I	44°32'N/122°13'W	3,035	1984
Mill Creek	I	44°30'N/120°32'W	7,042	1984
Monument Rock	I	44°20'N/118°19'W	7,952	1984
Mount Thielsen	I	43°14'N/122°00'W	22,298	1984
Mountain Lakes	I	42°22'N/122°06'W	9,355	1964
Mt. Hood	I	45°23'N/121°45'W	18,832	1978
Mt. Jefferson	I	44°36'N/121°50'W	40,581	1968
Mt. Washington	I	44°19'N/121°53'W	18,670	1964
North Fork John Day	I	44°54'N/118°34'W	49,110	1984
North Fork Umatilla	I	45°44'N/118°10'W	8,270	1984
Red Buttes	I	42°01'N/123°21'W	1,518	1984

Rock Creek	I	44°12'N/124°03'W	3,024	1984
Rogue-Umpqua Divide	I	43°06'N/122°28'W	13,436	1984
Salmon-Huckleberry	I	45°17'N/121°57'W	18,033	1984
Sky Lakes	I	42°38'N/122°13'W	47,065	1984
Strawberry Mountain	I	44°20'N/118°48'W	13,365	1964
Three Sisters	I	44°00'N/121°50'W	115,418	1978
Waldo Lake	I	43°48'N/122°05'W	15,864	1984
Wensha-Tucannon	I	?/?	26,892	?
Wild Rogue	I	42°43'N/123°57'W	10,383	1978
Wild Rogue	I	42°50'N/123°51'W	10,408	1978

Pennsylvania

National Estuarine Research Reserve

Narragonsett Bay	IV	?/?	1,286	1980

National Historic Park

Gettysburg	V	?/?	1,377	1895

National Recreation Area

Delaware Water Gap (Pennsylvania)	V	?/?	11,478	1965

National Scenic River

Middle Delaware	V	?/?	1,113	1978

National Wildlife Refuge

Erie	IV	41°47'N/80°00'W	3,541	?

State Park

Alleghany River	V	?/?	1,257	?
Bald Eagle	II	?/?	2,388	1971
Beltzville	II	?/?	1,203	1971
Black Moshannon	II	?/?	1,409	1937
Blue Knob	II	?/?	2,272	1945
Bucktail	II	?/?	9,308	1933
Codorus	II	?/?	1,344	1970
Cook Forest	II	?/?	2,630	1927
Elk	II	?/?	1,292	1964
Evansburg	II	?/?	1,355	1979
French Creek	II	?/?	2,970	1946
Gouldsboro	II	?/?	1,234	1958
Hickory Run	II	?/?	6,273	1945
Hillman	II	?/?	1,479	1969
Laurel Hill	II	?/?	1,592	1945
Laurel Ridge	II	?/?	5,514	1974
Lehigh Gorge	II	?/?	1,526	1969
M.K.Goddard	II	?/?	1,156	1972
McConnells Mill	II	?/?	1,025	1957
Moraine	II	?/?	6,414	1970
Nescopeck	II	?/?	1,206	1971
Nockamixon	II	?/?	2,138	1961
Ohiopyle	II	?/?	7,575	1970
Oil Creek	II	?/?	2,836	1968
Presque Isle	II	?/?	1,295	1921
Prince Gallitzin	II	?/?	2,529	1965
Promised Land	II	?/?	2,350	1905
Pymatuning	II	?/?	8,548	1921
Raccoon Creek	II	?/?	3,064	1945
Ricketts Glen	II	?/?	5,281	1942
Ridley Creek	II	?/?	1,055	1965
Shawnee	II	?/?	1,612	1947
Swatara	II	?/?	1,397	1970
Tobyhanna	II	?/?	2,202	1949
Yellow Creek	II	?/?	1,206	1971

Wilderness (Forest Service)

Hickory Creek	I	41°40'N/79°16'W	3,468	1984

South Carolina

National Monument

Congaree Swamp	III	33°45'N/80°47'W	6,125	1976

National Wildlife Refuge

Cape Romain	IV	33°00'N/79°30'W	26,396	1932
Carolina Sandhills	IV	34°33'N/80°12'W	18,448	?
Pinckney Island	IV	32°16'N/80°46'W	1,640	1975
Santee	IV	33°30'N/80°27'W	17,659	1941
Savannah	IV	32°16'N/81°01'W	5,781	?

State Park

Caesars Head	V	?/?	3,025	?
Cheraw	V	?/?	2,979	?
Croft	V	?/?	2,855	?
Hunting Island	V	?/?	2,023	?
Huntington Beach	V	?/?	1,012	?
Jones Gap	V	?/?	1,354	?
Kings Mountain	V	?/?	2,485	?
Lee	V	?/?	1,149	?
Santee	V	?/?	1,010	?
Table Rock	II	?/?	1,248	1935

Wilderness (Fish and Wildlife Service)

Cape Romain	I	33°00'N/79°32'W	11,736	1975

Wilderness (Forest Service)

Ellicott Rock (South Carolina)	I	?/?	1,137	1974
Little Wambaw Swamp	I	33°04'N/79°37'W	2,025	1980
Wambaw Swamp	I	33°06'N/79°40'W	2,065	1980

Wilderness (National Park Service)

Congaree Swamp	I	33°52'N/80°31'W	6,074	1988

South Dakota

National Park

Badlands	II	43°45'N/102°00'W	98,463	1978
Wind Cave	II	43°32'N/103°32'W	11,223	1903

National Wildlife Refuge

Lacreek	IV	43°19'N/101°29'W	6,821	?
Pocasse	IV	45°50'N/100°16'W	1,046	?
Sand Lake	IV	45°47'N/98°15'W	8,829	1935
Waubay	IV	?/?	1,918	?

State Park

Custer	V	?/?	29,542	1913

Wilderness (Forest Service)

Black Elk	I	43°52'N/103°33'W	4,333	1980

Wilderness (National Park Service)

Badlands	I	43°31'N/102°19'W	26,001	1976

Tennessee

National Park

Great Smoky Mountains	II	35°37'N/83°53'W	209,160	1934

National Scenic River

Obed	V	36°06'N/84°49'W	2,125	1976

National Wildlife Refuge

Chickasaw	IV	35°48'N/89°24'W	8,878	?
Cross Creeks	IV	36°29'N/87°34'W	3,586	?
Hatchie	IV	35°34'N/89°03'W	5,281	1965
Lower Hatchie	IV	35°36'N/89°47'W	1,757	?
Reelfoot	IV	?/?	3,403	?
Tennessee	IV	36°00'N/87°48'W	20,784	?

State Park

Big Ridge	V	?/?	1,360	?
Montgomery Bell	V	?/?	2,000	?
Natchez Trace	V	?/?	18,400	?

Wilderness (Forest Service)

Bald River Gorge	I	35°18'N/84°10'W	1,506	1984
Big Frog	I	35°01'N/84°40'W	3,232	1984
Big Laurel Branch	I	36°24'N/82°03'W	2,530	1986
Citico Creek	I	35°22'N/84°07'W	6,566	1984
Gee Creek	I	35°18'N/84°27'W	1,012	1974
Joyce Kilmer-Slickrock	I	?/?	1,539	?
Little Frog Mountain	I	35°06'N/84°24'W	1,896	1986
Pond Mountain	I	36°17'N/82°04'W	2,681	1986
Sampson Mountain	I	36°07'N/82°39'W	3,367	1986
Unaka Mountain	I	36°10'N/82°16'W	1,902	1986

Texas

National Natural Landmark

Attwater's Prairie Chicken	III	?/?	3,234	1972
Muleshoe	III	?/?	2,352	?

National Park

Big Bend	II	29°30'N/102°30'W	286,572	1944
Guadalupe Mountains	II	31°57'N/104°49'W	31,364	1972

National Preserve

Big Thicket	V	30°31'N/94°19'W	34,712	1974

National Recreation Area

Amistad	V	?/?	26,260	1965
Sanford	V	?/?	16,603	1965
Shadow Mountain	V	?/?	7,369	1952

National Scenic River

Rio Grande (Texas)	V	29°44'N/102°40'W	3,885	1978

National Seashore

Padre Island	V	26°53'N/97°20'W	54,196	1968

National Wildlife Refuge

Anahuac	IV	29°35'N/94°31'W	11,558	1963
Aransas	IV	28°15'N/96°50'W	45,496	1937
Attwater's Prairie Chicken	IV	29°42'N/96°17'W	3,231	1972
Balcones Canyonlands	IV	?/?	1,431	?
Big Boggy	IV	28°42'N/95°42'W	1,832	?
Brazoria	IV	29°00'N/95°12'W	17,134	?
Buffalo Lake (Texas)	IV	34°58'N/102°00'W	3,102	?
Hagerman	IV	33°43'N/96°45'W	4,914	1945
Laguna Atascosa	IV	26°17'N/97°17'W	18,287	?
Little Sandy	IV	?/?	1,539	?
Lower Rio Grande Valley	IV	26°12'N/98°02'W	24,568	?
McFaddin	IV	29°39'N/94°25'W	17,384	?
Moody	IV	29°35'N/94°40'W	1,423	?

Muleshoe	IV	33°57'N/102°37'W	2,351	?
San Bernard	IV	28°52'N/95°33'W	9,896	1967
Texas Point	IV	?/?	3,623	?

State Natural Area Reserve

Hill Country	I	?/?	1,099	?

State Park

Bastrop	V	?/?	1,418	?
Caprock Canyon	I	?/?	5,526	?
Galveston Island	I	?/?	786	?
Hale Ranch	I	?/?	1,982	?
Lake Mineral Wells	V	?/?	1,155	?
Monahans Sand Hills	V	?/?	1,554	?
Mustang Island	V	?/?	1,499	1964
Palo Duro Canyon	V	?/?	6,638	?
Pedernales Falls	V	?/?	1,967	?
Sea Rim	V	?/?	6,115	?
South Llano River	V	?/?	1,065	?

Wilderness (Forest Service)

Big Slough	I	31°30'N/95°06'W	1,450	1984
Indian Mounds	I	31°20'N/93°44'W	4,418	1984
Little Lake Creek	I	30°31'N/95°34'W	1,542	1984
Turkey Hill	I	31°23'N/94°08'W	2,139	1984
Upland Island	I	31°06'N/94°16'W	5,027	1984

Wilderness (National Park Service)

Guadalupe Mountains	I	31°57'N/104°52'W	18,960	1978

Utah

National Monument

Cedar Breaks	III	37°35'N/112°48'W	2,469	1933
Natural Bridges	III	37°30'N/110°07'W	3,040	1908

National Natural Landmark

Henry Mountains	III	37°55'N/110°45'W	13,187	?

National Park

Arches	II	38°36'N/109°40'W	29,260	1971
Bryce Canyon	II	37°36'N/112°16'W	14,405	1924
Canyonlands	II	38°14'N/109°53'W	136,542	1964
Capitol Reef	II	38°10'N/111°10'W	97,870	1971
Zion	II	37°15'N/113°00'W	59,308	1909

National Recreation Area

Glen Canyon (Utah)	V	?/?	580,558	1927

National Wildlife Refuge

Bear River	IV	41°41'N/112°20'W	26,371	?
Fish Springs	IV	39°50'N/113°23'W	7,281	1959
Ouray	IV	40°13'N/109°35'W	4,912	?

Outstanding Natural Area

Escalente Canyons	V	?/?	52,116	1970
North Escalante Canyon	V	?/?	2,343	1970
Phipps-Death Hollow	V	?/?	13,857	1970
The Gulch	V	?/?	1,386	1970

State Park

Coral Pink Sand Dunes	V	?/?	1,507	?
Dead Horse Point	V	?/?	1,869	?
Deer Creek Lake	V	?/?	1,061	?

Goblin Valley	V	?/?	1,315	?
Great Salt Lake	V	?/?	10,722	?
Snow Canyon	V	?/?	2,298	?
Starvation Lake	V	?/?	1,337	?
Wasatch Mountain	V	?/?	8,869	?
Willard Bay	V	?/?	1,080	?

Wilderness (Bureau of Land Management)

Beaver Dam Mountains	I	37°00'N/113°47'W	1,469	1984
Paria Canyon-Vermilion Cliffs	I	36°55'N/111°39'W	9,308	1984

Wilderness (Forest Service)

Ashdown Gorge	I	37°36'N/112°51'W	2,833	1984
Box-Death Hollow	I	37°53'N/111°37'W	10,421	1984
Dark Canyon	I	37°48'N/109°53'W	18,211	1984
Deseret Peak	I	40°28'N/112°44'W	10,320	1984
High Uintas	I	40°45'N/110°32'W	184,823	1984
Lone Peak	I	40°32'N/111°41'W	12,190	1978
Mount Naomi	I	41°54'N/111°43'W	17,948	1984
Mount Nebo	I	39°51'N/111°46'W	11,331	1984
Mount Olympus	I	40°41'N/111°42'W	6,475	1984
Mount Timpanogos	I	40°25'N/111°35'W	4,350	1984
Pine Valley Mountain	I	37°22'N/113°27'W	20,234	1984
Twin Peaks	I	40°36'N/111°42'W	4,587	1984
Wellsville Mountain	I	41°40'N/111°59'W	9,652	1984

Vermont

National Wildlife Refuge

Missisquoi	IV	44°56'N/73°00'W	2,363	?

State Natural Area Reserve

Camel's Hump	IV	?/?	2,146	?
Mt. Mansfield	IV	?/?	1,558	?

State Park

Bomoseen	V	?/?	1,107	?
Coolidge	V	?/?	6,531	?
Little River (Vermont)	V	?/?	4,848	?

Wilderness (Forest Service)

Big Branch	I	43°19'N/73°01'W	2,719	1984
Breadloaf	I	44°00'N/72°58'W	8,693	1984
Bristol Cliffs	I	44°06'N/73°04'W	1,498	1976
George D. Aiken	I	42°51'N/73°05'W	2,048	1984
Lye Brook	I	43°06'N/73°05'W	5,427	1974
Peru Peak	I	43°18'N/72°56'W	2,800	1984

Virginia

Forest Park

Prince William	III	38°30'N/77°20'W	7,048	1936

National Battlefield

Manassas	V	38°48'N/77°38'W	1,101	1940
Petersburg	V	37°10'N/77°22'W	1,103	1926

National Historic Park

Colonial	V	?/?	3,810	1930

National Memorial

Fredericksburg and Spotsylvania Co. Battle	V	38°13'N/77°29'W	1,483	?

National Park

Shenandoah	II	38°30'N/78°30'W	84,921	1926

National Wildlife Refuge

Back Bay	IV	36°40'N/75°55'W	2,253	1938
Chincoteague	IV	38°00'N/75°15'W	5,444	?
Fishermen Island	IV	37°05'N/75°57'W	415	1969
Great Dismal Swamp	IV	36°32'N/76°26'W	33,245	1973
James River	IV	?/?	1,678	?
Plum Tree Island	IV	37°07'N/76°16'W	1,326	?
Wallops Island	IV	37°55'N/75°23'W	1,365	?

State Park

Douthat	V	?/?	1,815	?
Fairy Stone	V	?/?	1,846	?
False Cape	V	?/?	1,745	?
Grayson Highlands	V	?/?	1,921	?
Occoneechee	V	?/?	1,087	?
Seashore	V	?/?	1,039	?
York River	V	?/?	1,012	?

Wilderness (Forest Service)

Barbours	I	37°33'N/79°55'W	2,266	1988
Beartown	I	37°02'N/81°27'W	2,446	1984
James River Farce	I	37°32'N/79°25'W	3,523	1974
Kimberling Creek	I	37°09'N/81°09'W	2,258	1984
Lewis Fork	I	36°39'N/81°36'W	2,348	1984
Little Dry Run	I	36°46'N/81°18'W	1,376	1984
Little Wilson Creek	I	36°39'N/81°29'W	1,560	1984
Mountain Lake	I	37°22'N/80°28'W	3,340	1984
Peters Mountain	I	37°22'N/80°38'W	1,346	1984
Ramseys Draft	I	37°53'N/79°07'W	2,722	1984
Rich Hole	I	38°01'N/79°05'W	2,610	1988
Rough Mountain	I	37°59'N/79°25'W	3,764	1988
Saint Marys	I	38°21'N/79°14'W	4,083	1984
Shavers Run	I	37°33'N/80°05'W	1,459	1988

Wilderness (National Park Service)

Shenandoah	I	38°46'N/78°13'W	32,205	1976

Washington

Estuarine Sanctuary

Padilla Bay	IV	?/?	12,570	1980

National Historic Park

San Juan Island	III	?/?	100	1966

National Park

Mount Rainier	II	47°45'N/121°55'W	95,268	1899
North Cascades	II	48°40'N/121°20'W	204,284	1968
Olympic	II	47°50'N/123°55'W	371,225	1938

National Recreation Area

Coulee Dam	V	48°00'N/119°00'W	40,424	1946
Lake Chelan	V	?/?	25,044	1968
Ross Lake	V	?/?	47,582	1968

National Wildlife Refuge

Columbia	IV	46°55'N/119°15'W	11,977	1944
Conboy Lake	IV	45°58'N/121°19'W	2,352	1965
Julia Butler Hansen	IV	?/?	1,123	?
Little Pend Oreille	IV	48°24'N/117°47'W	16,187	?
McNary	IV	46°11'N/118°57'W	1,469	1955
Nisqually	IV	47°07'N/122°53'W	1,152	?
Quillayute	IV	?/?	121	?

Ridgefield	IV	45°56'N/122°45'W	2,084	?
Saddle Mountain	IV	46°42'N/119°37'W	12,468	1971
San Juan Islands	IV	48°35'N/122°47'W	182	1914
Turnbull	IV	47°00'N/118°00'W	7,213	1937
Umatilla (Washington)	IV	45°55'N/119°47'W	5,939	?
Willapa	IV	46°29'N/124°00'W	5,825	?

State Park

Beacon Rock	V	?/?	1,717	?
Deception Pass	V	?/?	1,000	?
Gingko Petrified Forest	V	?/?	2,833	1948
Moran	V	?/?	1,860	?
Mount Spokane	V	?/?	6,538	?
Riverside	V	?/?	2,346	?
Steamboat Rock	V	?/?	1,626	?
Sun Lakes	V	?/?	1,626	?

Wilderness (Bureau of Land Management)

Juniper Dunes	I	46°22'N/118°49'W	2,792	1984

Wilderness (Forest Service)

Alpine Lakes	I	47°35'N/121°08'W	123,687	1976
Boulder River	I	48°11'N/121°40'W	19,698	1984
Buckhorn	I	47°50'N/123°05'W	17,911	1984
Clearwater	I	47°03'N/121°49'W	5,908	1984
Colonel Bob	I	47°29'N/123°40'W	4,840	1984
Glacier Peak	I	48°11'N/120°58'W	188,041	1964
Glacier View	I	46°48'N/121°55'W	1,264	1984
Goat Rocks	I	46°34'N/121°27'W	33,453	1964
Henry M. Jackson	I	47°57'N/121°10'W	41,550	1984
Indian Heaven	I	46°01'N/121°46'W	8,482	1984
Lake Chelan-Sawtooth	I	48°19'N/120°28'W	61,284	1984
Mount Adams	I	46°13'N/121°31'W	13,122	1964
Mount Baker	I	48°49'N/121°46'W	47,562	1984
Mount Skokomish	I	47°33'N/123°14'W	5,267	1984
Noisy-Diobsud	I	48°40'N/121°31'W	5,719	1984
Pasayten	I	48°53'N/120°31'W	204,727	1968
Salmo-Priest	I	48°56'N/117°05'W	16,728	1984
Tatoosh	I	46°42'N/121°39'W	6,374	1984
The Brothers	I	47°42'N/123°04'W	6,751	1984
Trapper Creek	I	45°55'N/122°00'W	2,416	1984
Wenaha-Tucannon	I	?/?	44,955	1978
William O. Douglas	I	46°47'N/121°19'W	68,104	1984

Wilderness (National Park Service)

Mount Ranier	I	46°50'N/121°51'W	87,758	1988
Olympic	I	47°51'N/123°46'W	334,542	1988
Stephen Mather	I	48°49'N/121°14'W	256,820	1988

West Virginia

National Natural Landmark

Canaan Valley	III	?/?	6,222	?

National River

New River Gorge	V	81°03'N/37°51'W	25,101	1978

State Park

Babcock	V	?/?	1,670	?
Beech Fork	V	?/?	1,611	?
Cacapon	V	?/?	2,475	?
Canaan Valley	V	?/?	2,475	1968
Chief Logan	V	?/?	1,337	?
Holly River	V	?/?	3,356	?

Lost River	V	?/?	1,502	?
Pipestem	V	?/?	1,628	?
Stonewall Jackson Lake	V	?/?	1,072	?
Twin Falls	V	?/?	1,528	?
Watoga	V	?/?	4,087	?

Wilderness (Forest Service)

Cranberry	I	38°17'N/80°19'W	14,514	1983
Dolly Sods	I	39°00'N/79°24'W	4,131	1974
Laurel Fork North	I	38°51'N/79°38'W	2,450	1983
Laurel Fork South	I	38°47'N/79°43'W	2,427	1983
Mountain Lake	I	37°35'N/80°26'W	1,012	1988
Otter Creek	I	38°59'N/79°40'W	8,100	1974

Wisconsin

National Lakeshore

Apostle Island	V	47°00'N/90°44'W	17,084	1970

National Scenic River

Lower St. Croix (Wisconsin)	V	?/?	3,512	1972
St. Croix	V	46°15'N/91°55'W	25,373	1969
Wolf River	V	?/?	2,228	1968

National Scientific Reserve

Ice Age	I	?/?	13,153	1964

National Wildlife Refuge

Horicon	IV	43°30'N/88°30'W	8,570	1941
Mississippi River Caue (Wisconsin)	IV	?/?	16,325	?
Necedah	IV	44°14'N/90°06'W	17,667	?
Trempealeau	IV	44°10'N/91°14'W	2,273	?
Upper Mississippi (Wisconsin)	IV	44°12'N/91°38'W	19,508	?

State Park

Buckhorn	V	?/?	1,003	?
Devils Lake	V	?/?	3,642	?
Governor Dodge	V	?/?	2,035	?
Penninsula	V	?/?	1,523	?
Wildcat Mountain	V	?/?	1,404	?
Willow River	V	?/?	1,133	?
Wyalusing	V	?/?	1,080	?

Wilderness (Forest Service)

Blackjack Springs	I	45°57'N/89°04'W	2,389	1978
Headwaters	I	45°48'N/88°56'W	7,328	1984
Porcupine Lake	I	46°16'N/91°08'W	1,720	1984
Rainbow Lake	I	46°26'N/91°20'W	2,754	1974
Whisker Lake	I	45°56'N/88°28'W	2,956	1978

Wyoming

National Monument

Devil's Tower	V	44°32'N/104°47'W	1,346	1906
Fossil Butte	III	41°40'N/110°45'W	3,280	1972
J.D. Rockefeller, Jr.	III	44°05'N/110°40'W	9,672	1977

National Natural Landmark

Como Bluff	III	?/?	1,487	?
Lance Creek Fossil Area	III	?/?	4,008	?

National Park

Grand Teton	II	44°50'N/110°45'W	124,140	1929
Yellowstone	II	44°38'N/110°10'W	899,139	1872

National Wildlife Refuge

National Elk	IV	43°43'N/110°47'W	10,026	?

Pathfinder	IV	42°34'N/106°58'W	6,801	?
Seedskadee	IV	41°56'N/109°43'W	6,363	1965

Parkway

John D. Rockefeller, Jr., Memorial	V	?/?	9,700	1972

State Park

Alcova	V	?/?	2,488	?
Big Sandy	V	?/?	3,072	?
Boysen	V	?/?	24,825	?
Buffalo Bill	V	?/?	5,086	?
Glendo	V	?/?	9,614	?
Guernsey	V	?/?	4,633	?
Keyhole	V	?/?	5,730	?
Seminole	V	?/?	23,198	?

Wilderness (Forest Service)

Bridger	I	41°11'N/107°12'W	173,241	1964
Cloud Peak	I	44°24'N/107°08'W	76,502	1984
Encampment River	I	41°05'N/106°44'W	4,097	1984
Fitzpatrick	I	43°16'N/109°31'W	77,800	1976
Gros Ventre	I	43°27'N/110°24'W	116,145	1984
Huston Park	I	41°06'N/106°56'W	12,379	1984
Jedediah Smith	I	43°49'N/110°53'W	49,959	1984
North Absaroka	I	47°00'N/121°23'W	142,114	1964
North Absaroka	I	44°36'N/109°49'W	141,838	1964
Platte River	I	41°05'N/106°21'W	9,206	1984
Popo Agie	I	42°45'N/109°02'W	41,225	1984
Savage Run	I	41°11'N/106°22'W	6,196	1978
Teton	I	44°03'N/110°06'W	225,706	1964
Washakie	I	44°05'N/109°35'W	278,073	1964
Winegar Hole	I	44°07'N/111°00'W	4,336	1984

American Samoa/Samoa américaines/ Samoa Americana

National Park

American Samoa National Park	II	14°15'S/170°28'W	3,725	1988

National Wildlife Refuge

Rose Atoll	I	14°33'S/168°08'W	653	1973

Guam

No Areas Listed

Minor Outlying Islands/Iles mineures / Islas Menores de los Estados Unidos

National Wildlife Refuge

Baker Island	I	0°13'N/176°29'W	12,843	1974
Howland Island	I	0°48'S/176°38'W	13,173	1974
Jarvis Island	I	0°22'S/160°01'W	15,183	1974

Puerto Rico

Wildlife Refuge

Humacao	IV	18°09'N/65°50'W	1,026	1984

National Wildlife Refuge

Culebra	IV	18°20'N/65°20'W	633	1909
Desecheo	IV	18°23'N/67°28'W	146	1968

Nature Reserve

Estuarina Nacional Bahía Jobos	IV	17°50'N/66°14'W	1,133	1981
Isla Caja de Muerto	IV	17°23'N/66°32'W	188	1988

Isla de Mona	IV	18°06'N/67°54'W	5,554	1986
La Parguera	IV	17°51'N/67°05'W	4,973	1979
Laguna Tortuguero	IV	18°28'N/66°25'W	1,000	1979

Virgin Islands/Iles Vierges américaines/ Islas Vírgenes

National Park

Virgin Islands	II	18°21'N/64°44'W	5,308	1956

URUGUAY

Summary		
Category I	0	0
Category II	0	0
Category III	2	15,250
Category IV	1	8,000
Category V	5	8,836
Total	**8**	**32,086**

Fauna Reserve

Laguna de Castillos	IV	34°23'S/53°57'W	8,000	1966

National Park

Anchorena	V	34°16'S/57°59'W	1,450	1978
Arequita	V	34°12'S/55°13'W	1,000	1964
Franklin Delano Roosevelt	V	34°48'S/55°52'W	1,500	1915
San Miguel	V	33°39'S/53°34'W	1,598	1937
Santa Teresa	V	33°57'S/53°32'W	3,288	1927

Nature Monument

Costa Atlántica	III	34°22'S/53°46'W	14,250	1966
Dunas de Cabo Polonio	III	34°22'S/53°48'W	1,000	1966

UZBEKISTAN/OUZBEKISTAN

Summary		
Category I	9	212,686
Category II	1	31,503
Category III	0	0
Category IV	0	0
Category V	0	0
Total	**10**	**244,189**

National Park

Uzbekistan People's Park	II	?/?	31,503	1978

Zapovednik

Baday-Tugay	I	37°55'N/60°28'E	5,900	1971
Chatkal'skiy	I	38°41'N/70°18'E	35,686	1947
Gissarskiy (Kyzylsuyskiy & Mirakinskiy)	I	33°03'N/67°28'E	87,500	1983
Kitabskii	I	32°35'N/67°16'E	5,400	1979
Kyzylkumskiy	I	39°19'N/62°23'E	10,100	1971
Nuratinskiy	I	39°23'N/66°33'E	22,100	1973
Suzkhanskiy	I	?/?	28,000	1986
Zaaminskiy	I	32°13'N/68°18'E	15,600	1959
Zeravshanskiy	I	36°24'N/67°11'E	2,400	1975

VANUATU

No Areas Listed

VATICAN CITY STATE (HOLY SEE)/
SAINT-SIEGE/SANTA SEDE

No Areas Listed

VENEZUELA

	Summary	
Category I	0	0
Category II	42	13,093,019
Category III	11	1,121,753
Category IV	5	96,448
Category V	42	12,011,086
Total	**100**	**26,322,306**

National Park

Aguaro-Guariquito	II	8°20'N/66°40'W	585,750	1974
Archipiélago Los Roques	II	11°50'N/66°45'W	221,120	1972
Canaima	II	5°30'N/61°46'W	3,000,000	1962
Cerro El Copey	II	11°00'N/63°55'W	7,130	1974
Cerro Saroche	II	10°00'N/69°40'W	32,294	1989
Chorro el Indio	II	7°46'N/72°09'W	10,800	1989
Cinaruco-Capanaparo	II	6°50'N/67°45'W	584,368	1988
Ciénagas del Catatumbo	II	9°20'N/72°10'W	269,400	1991
Cueva de la Quebrada del Toro	II	10°51'N/69°07'W	8,500	1969
Delta del Orinoco	II	9°25'N/61°30'W	331,000	1992
Dinira	II	9°35'N/70°00'W	42,000	1988
Duida-Marahuaca	II	3°30'N/65°30'W	210,000	1978
El Avila	II	10°32'N/66°40'W	85,192	1958
El Guache	II	?/?	12,200	1992
El Guácharo	II	10°12'N/63°36'W	62,700	1975
El Tamá	II	7°20'N/72°10'W	139,000	1978
Guaramacal	II	9°12'N/70°10'W	21,000	1988
Guatopo	II	10°05'N/66°29'W	122,464	1958
Henri Pittier	II	10°28'N/67°51'W	107,000	1937
Jaua Sarisariñama	II	4°25'N/64°20'W	330,000	1978
Laguna de la Restinga	II	10°59'N/64°05'W	18,862	1974
Laguna de Tacarigua	II	10°16'N/65°49'W	39,100	1974
Macarao	II	10°20'N/67°10'W	15,000	1973
Mariusa	II	9°25'N/61°30'W	331,000	1991
Mochima	II	10°20'N/64°30'W	94,935	1973
Morrocoy	II	10°53'N/68°15'W	32,090	1974
Médanos de Coro	II	11°40'N/69°45'W	91,280	1974
Parima-Tapirapecó	II	2°30'N/64°30'W	3,420,000	1991
Península de Paria	II	10°40'N/62°15'W	37,500	1978
Perijá	II	9°45'N/73°00'W	295,288	1978
Páramos del Batallón y La Negra	II	8°00'N/71°50'W	95,200	1989
San Esteban	II	10°23'N/68°00'W	43,500	1987
Serranía de la Neblina	II	1°14'N/65°52'W	1,360,000	1978
Sierra de la Culata	II	8°43'N/71°20'W	200,400	1989
Sierra de San Luis	II	11°30'N/69°35'W	20,000	1987
Sierra Nevada	II	8°30'N/70°50'W	276,446	1952
Terepaima	II	9°53'N/69°16'W	18,650	1976
Tirgua	II	?/?	91,000	1992
Turuépano	II	10°20'N/63°35'W	72,600	1991
Yacambú	II	9°43'N/69°33'W	14,580	1962
Yapacana	II	3°45'N/66°50'W	320,000	1978
Yurubí	II	10°25'N/68°44'W	23,670	1960

Nature Monument

Cerro Platillón	III	9°53'N/67°32'W	8,000	1987

Cerro Santa Ana	III	11°49'N/69°56'W	1,900	1972
Cerros Matasiete y Guayamurí	III	11°04'N/63°50'W	1,672	1974
Formaciones de Tepuyes	III	?/?	1,069,820	1990
Laguna de las Marites	III	10°55'N/63°58'W	3,674	1974
Las Tetas de María Guevara	III	10°55'N/64°07'W	1,670	1974
Loma de León	III	10°00'N/69°25'W	7,275	1989
María Lionza	III	9°57'N/67°26'W	11,712	1960
Morros de San Juan (Arístides Rojas)	III	9°56'N/67°27'W	2,755	1949
Pico Codazzi	III	10°25'N/67°19'W	11,850	1991
Piedra Pintada	III	5°33'N/67°33'W	1,425	1992

Protective Zone

Area Metropolitana de Caracas	V	10°20'N/66°55'W	84,300	1972
Barquisimeto	V	10°03'N/69°21'W	46,273	1987
Cabos, Puntas y Lagunas de Isla de Margarita	V	11°00'N/64°05'W	1,549	1988
Cuenca Alta de los Ríos Maticora y Cocuiza	V	10°30'N/70°47'W	241,500	1974
Cuenca Alta del Río Cojedes	V	10°11'N/68°30'W	276,000	1974
Cuenca Alta del Río Tocuyo	V	9°40'N/69°55'W	141,600	1974
Cuenca Alta y Media del Río Machango	V	10°10'N/70°50'W	113,000	1990
Cuenca Alta y Media del Río Orituco	V	9°50'N/66°24'W	43,000	1991
Cuenca del Río Guárico	V	9°50'N/67°30'W	40,207	1974
Cuencas Alta y Media del Río Pao	V	10°00'N/68°10'W	68,000	1974
de la Ciudad de Coro	V	11°18'N/69°37'W	19,720	1987
El Cigarrón	V	9°25'N/65°38'W	45,230	1989
Escalante-Onia-Mucujepe	V	8°50'N/71°19'W	101,125	1975
La Marichí	V	?/?	2,000	1973
La Mariposa	V	10°23'N/66°55'W	2,810	1988
La Tortuga Arrau	V	6°23'N/67°12'W	9,856	1989
Laguna de la Danta	V	8°38'N/69°33'W	2,203	1974
Las González	V	8°37'N/71°15'W	11,220	1980
Litoral Central	V	10°28'N/66°15'W	35,723	1974
Macizo Montañoso del Turimiquire	V	10°05'N/64°00'W	540,000	1974
Maracaibo	V	10°35'N/71°42'W	20,800	1986
Margen Izquierdo del Río Masparro	V	8°27'N/69°46'W	5,000	1974
Mucujún	V	3°36'N/71°04'W	19,450	1985
Piedemonte Norte de la Cordillera Andina	V	9°35'N/71°00'W	431,727	1974
Región Lago de Maracaibo, Sierra de Perijá	V	9°45'N/72°23'W	244,125	1974
Rubio	V	7°41'N/72°21'W	23,760	1978
Río Albarregas	V	9°38'N/71°10'W	11,233	1973
Río Capaz	V	8°42'N/71°21'W	45,700	1989
Río Chuspita	V	10°25'N/66°26'W	5,642	1976
Río Torbes y sus Alrededores	V	7°55'N/72°07'W	12,000	1974
Río Yacambú	V	9°40'N/69°37'W	46,900	1974
Ríos Guanare, Boconó, Tucupido, La Yuca y Masparro	V	8°52'N/70°10'W	400,000	1991
San Antonio - Ureña	V	7°46'N/72°24'W	6,223	1982
San Cristóbal	V	7°54'N/72°11'W	10,000	1978
San Rafael de Guasare	V	10°45'N/72°27'W	302,000	1973
Serranía de San Luis	V	11°10'N/69°40'W	86,000	1987
Sierra de Aroa	V	10°20'N/68°50'W	113,000	1991
Sierra de Bobare	V	10°30'N/68°50'W	140,000	1974
Sierra de Nirgua	V	10°14'N/68°30'W	146,590	1974
Sur del Estado Bolívar	V	5°00'N/63°00'W	7,262,358	1974
Sureste del Lago de Maracaibo Sto. Domingo-Motatán	V	8°48'N/7°28'W	406,662	1974
Sureste del Lago de Maracaibo-Uribante-Caparo	V	8°02'N/71°30'W	446,600	1974

Wildlife Refuge

Caño Guaritico	IV	7°50'N/69°23'W	9,300	1989
Ciénaga Los Olivitos	IV	10°52'N/71°23'W	25,723	1986
Cuare	IV	11°55'N/68°15'W	11,825	1972
De la Tortuga Arrau	IV	6°23'N/67°13'W	17,431	1989
Estero de Chiriguare	IV	8°32'N/68°45'W	32,169	1974

VIET NAM

	Summary	
Category I	0	0
Category II	9	202,427
Category III	0	0
Category IV	50	1,127,361
Category V	0	0
Total	**59**	**1,329,788**

National Park

Ba Be	II	22°24'N/105°37'E	7,600	1977
Ba Vi	II	21°25'N/105°30'E	7,200	1977
Bach Ma	II	16°12'N/107°58'E	22,500	1986
Ben En	II	19°36'N/105°30'E	16,634	1986
Cat Ba	II	20°48'N/107°02'E	15,200	1986
Con Dao	II	8°42'N/106°38'E	15,043	1982
Cuc Phuong	II	20°19'N/105°22'E	22,500	1962
Nam Bai Cat Tien	II	10°56'N/107°20'E	37,550	1978
Yok Don	II	12°46'N/107°40'E	58,200	1988

Nature Reserve

Anh Son	IV	18°50'N/105°05'E	1,500	1986
Ba Mun	IV	21°04'N/107°32'E	1,800	1977
Bac Son	IV	21°53'N/106°25'E	4,000	1977
Ban dao Son Tra	IV	16°09'N/108°16'E	4,439	1977
Bana-Nui Chua	IV	16°00'N/108°00'E	5,217	1986
Bien Lac-Nui Ong (Tanh Linh)	IV	11°10'N/107°30'E	35,400	1986
Binh Chan Phuoc Buu	IV	10°30'N/107°30'E	11,293	1986
Bu Gia Map	IV	12°08'N/107°10'E	22,300	1986
Bu Huong	IV	19°42'N/104°45'E	5,000	1986
Chiem Hoa Nahang	IV	22°20'N/105°23'E	20,000	1986
Chu Yang Sinh	IV	12°25'N/108°25'E	20,000	1986
Cu Lao Cham	IV	15°58'N/108°30'E	1,535	1986
Dao Phu Quoc	IV	10°20'N/104°00'E	14,500	1986
Dat Mui (Nam Can)	IV	08°35'S/104°46'E	4,460	1986
Deo Ngoan Muc	IV	11°50'N/107°45'E	2,000	1986
Dong Phong Nha	IV	17°50'N/105°52'E	41,232	1986
Huu Lien	IV	21°40'N/106°20'E	3,000	1986
Kalon Song Mao	IV	11°26'N/108°28'E	2,000	1986
Khu Dao Thac Ba	IV	21°53'N/104°30'E	5,000	1986
Kon Kai Kinh	IV	14°19'N/108°22'E	28,000	1986
Kong Cha Rang	IV	14°33'N/108°35'E	16,000	1986
Lo Go-Sa Mat	IV	11°42'N/106°00'E	10,000	1986
Mom Ray	IV	14°25'N/107°35'E	45,000	1986
Mount Lang Bian (Nui Ba)	IV	12°05'N/108°25'E	6,000	1986
Muong Cha	IV	22°16'N/102°28'E	390,000	1986
Nam Ca	IV	12°25'N/108°00'E	24,550	1986
Nam Don	IV	21°40'N/103°45'E	18,000	1986
Nam Lung	IV	12°16'N/107°45'E	24,550	1986
Ngoc Linh	IV	15°06'N/107°57'E	20,000	1986
Nui Cam	IV	10°30'N/105°00'E	1,500	1986
Nui Dai Binh	IV	11°25'N/107°47'E	5,000	1986
Nui Hoang Lien	IV	22°15'N/103°48'E	40,000	1986
Nui Pia Oac	IV	22°36'N/105°52'E	10,000	1986
Nui Tam Dao	IV	21°35'N/105°39'E	40,000	1977
Nui Yen Tu	IV	21°10'N/106°40'E	5,000	1986
Pa Co Hang kia	IV	20°42'N/104°56'E	1,000	1986
Phong Quang	IV	22°50'N/104°55'E	20,000	1986
Quang Xuyen	IV	12°25'N/108°00'E	15,000	1986
Rung Kho Phan Rang	IV	11°46'N/108°57'E	1,000	1986

Sop Cop	IV	20°42'N/103°42'E	5,000	1986
Suoi Trai	IV	13°05'N/108°50'E	28,000	1986
Tay Bai Cat Tien	IV	11°32'N/107°12'E	10,000	1986
Thanh Thuy	IV	18°40'N/105°15'E	7,000	1986
Thuong Da Nhim (Bi Doup)	IV	11°52'N/108°37'E	25,000	1986
Thuong Tien	IV	20°40'N/105°26'E	1,500	1986
Trung Khanh	IV	27°36'N/106°30'E	3,000	1986
U Minh	IV	9°33'N/105°00'E	2,000	1986
Vu Quang	IV	18°15'N/105°22'E	56,000	1986
Xuan Nha	IV	20°41'N/104°43'E	60,000	1986
Xuan Son	IV	21°00'N/105°06'E	4,585	1986

WESTERN SAMOA/SAMOA

Summary		
Category I	0	0
Category II	1	2,857
Category III	0	0
Category IV	2	7,215
Category V	0	0
Total	**3**	**10,072**

National Park

O Le Pupu Pu'e	II	13°59'S/171°44'W	2,857	1978

Other area

Falealupo Rainforest Reserve	IV	13°30'S/172°45'W	1,215	1989
Tafua Rainforest Reserve	IV	13°46'S/172°15'W	6,000	1990

YEMEN

No Areas Listed

YUGOSLAVIA/YOUGOSLAVIE

Summary		
Category I	1	1,124
Category II	7	148,775
Category III	1	1,600
Category IV	1	16,133
Category V	11	179,334
Total	**21**	**346,966**

National Park

Biogradska Gora (Montenegro)	II	42°52'N/19°37'E	3,400	1952
Djerdap (Serbia)	V	44°34'N/22°15'E	63,500	1983
Durmitor (Montenegro)	II	43°08'N/19°03'E	33,000	1952
Fruska Gora (Serbia)	V	45°11'N/19°43'E	25,398	1960
Kopaonik (Serbia)	II	43°17'N/20°37'E	11,800	1981
Lovcen (Montenegro)	II	42°22'N/18°52'E	2,400	1952
Sara (Serbia)	II	43°45'N/18°36'E	39,000	1986
Skadarske jezero (Montenegro)	II	42°10'N/19°20'E	40,000	1983
Tara (Serbia)	II	43°55'N/19°31'E	19,175	1981

Natural Monument

Djalovica Klisura (Montenegro)	III	?/?	1,600	1968

Nature Reserve

Deliblatska Pescara (Vojvodina)	V	?/?	29,352	1965
Kotorsko Risanski Zaliv (Montenegro)	V	42°29'N/18°38'E	12,000	1979
Obedska Bara (Vojvodina)	V	44°43'N/20°04'E	17,501	1968
Obedska bara Kod Kupinova (Vojvodina)	IV	?/?	16,133	1968

Veliki i Mali Strbac ra Trajonovum tablom (Serbia)	I	?/?	1,124	1975
Zvijezda (Serbia)	V	43°56'N/19°31'E	2,007	1950

Regional Nature Park

Gornje Podunavlje (Serbia)	V	45°43'N/19°04'E	9,996	1982
Palic-Ludas (Serbia)	V	?/?	6,360	1982
Resava (Serbia)	V	?/?	10,000	1957
Stari Begej (Serbia)	V	?/?	1,327	1986
Zvijezda na Planini Tara (Serbia)	V	43°54'N/19°31'E	1,893	1971

ZAIRE

Summary		
Category I	0	0
Category II	8	9,916,625
Category III	0	0
Category IV	0	0
Category V	0	0
Total	**8**	**9,916,625**

Faunal Reserve

Okapi Faunal Reserve	II	1°45'N/28°30'E	1,372,625	1992

National Park

Garamba	II	4°13'N/29°24'E	492,000	1938
Kahuzi-Biega	II	2°31'S/28°45'E	600,000	1975
Kundelungu	II	10°35'S/28°56'E	760,000	1970
Maiko	II	0°30'S/27°45'E	1,083,000	1970
Salonga	II	2°10'S/21°15'E	3,656,000	1970
Upemba	II	9°10'S/26°40'E	1,173,000	1939
Virunga	II	0°20'S/29°35'E	780,000	1925

ZAMBIA/ZAMBIE

Summary		
Category I	0	0
Category II	19	6,358,500
Category III	2	5,138
Category IV	0	0
Category V	0	0
Total	**21**	**6,363,638**

National Park

Blue Lagoon	II	15°32'S/27°23'E	45,000	1973
Isangano	II	11°13'S/30°32'E	84,000	1972
Kafue	II	15°20'S/26°00'E	2,240,000	1951
Kasanka	II	12°30'S/30°14'E	39,000	1972
Lavushi Manda	II	12°20'S/30°53'E	150,000	1972
Liuwa Plain	II	14°29'S/22°34'E	366,000	1972
Lochinvar	II	15°52'S/27°15'E	41,000	1972
Lower Zambezi	II	15°23'S/29°43'E	409,200	1983
Luambe	II	12°30'S/32°18'E	25,400	1972
Lukusuzi	II	12°49'S/32°38'E	272,000	1972
Lusenga Plain	II	9°23'S/29°13'E	88,000	1972
Mosi-Oa-Tunya	II	17°52'S/25°48'E	6,600	1972
Mweru-Wantipa	II	8°44'S/29°38'E	313,400	1972
North Luangwa	II	11°45'S/32°10'E	463,600	1972
Nsumbu	II	8°47'S/30°30'E	206,300	1985
Nyika (Zambia)	II	10°38'S/33°39'E	8,000	1972

Sioma Ngwezi	II	17°18'S/23°26'E	527,600	1972
South Luangwa	II	12°51'S/31°33'E	905,000	1972
West Lunga	II	12°49'S/24°47'E	168,400	1972

Natural Monument

Bell Point-Lunsemfwa Wonder Gorge	III	14°39'S/29°07'E	3,238	1964
Victoria Falls	III	17°59'S/25°59'E	1,900	1948

ZIMBABWE

Summary		
Category I	0	0
Category II	10	2,701,900
Category III	1	2,000
Category IV	4	18,280
Category V	10	345,643
Total	**25**	**3,067,823**

National Park

Chimanimani	II	19°43'S/33°00'E	17,100	1950
Chizarira	II	17°47'S/27°55'E	191,000	1975
Gonarezhou	II	21°39'S/31°53'E	505,300	1975
Hwange (Wankie)	II	19°11'S/26°38'E	1,465,100	1949
Kazuma Pan	II	18°25'S/25°35'E	31,300	1975
Mana Pools	II	16°02'S/29°43'E	219,600	1975
Matobo (Matopos)	II	20°40'S/28°30'E	42,500	1926
Matusadona	II	17°00'S/28°25'E	140,700	1975
Nyanga	II	18°20'S/32°50'E	33,000	1950
Victoria Falls	III	17°59'S/25°59'E	2,000	1952
Zambezi	II	17°19'S/25°57'E	56,300	1979

Recreation Park

Bangala	V	19°14'S/28°18'E	2,700	1975
Kariba	V	17°15'S/28°02'E	283,000	1979
Kyle	V	16°02'S/29°43'E	16,910	1975
Lake Robertson (Darwendale)	V	21°57'S/29°05'E	11,200	?
Manjirenji	V	20°37'S/31°40'E	3,400	?
McIlwaine	V	17°55'S/30°50'E	6,100	1975
Mufuli	V	18°27'S/28°56'E	12,700	?
Muzingwane	V	20°14'S/28°35'E	1,233	1975
Ngezi	V	18°30'S/30°20'E	5,800	1975
Sebakwe	V	19°00'S/30°10'E	2,600	1975

Sanctuary

Chimanimani Eland	IV	19°45'S/32°55'E	1,800	1975
Mushandike	IV	17°50'S/30°30'E	12,900	1975
Nyamaneche	IV	?/?	2,480	?
Tshabalala	IV	?/?	1,100	?

Analysis of Information

Analyse de l'information

Análisis de la información

Analysis of Information

All of the information provided in this *UN List* is stored within a computer database, and a wide range of other information is held about each site (and about many other sites not covered here). Some of this information will be analysed in publications by WCMC and IUCN staff. As an indication of this analytic capability, two graphs and two tables have been included within the *UN List*.

Growth of the world coverage of protected areas

Two graphs are provided, one illustrating growth in the number and area of protected areas with time (Figure 1), and the other illustrating growth in the number and area within each five year period (Figure 2). It should be noted that establishment of the Northeast Greenland National Park in 1974 (97 million hectares), the Great Barrier Reef Marine Park in 1979 (35 million hectares) and Jiang Tang Nature Reserve in 1990 (24 million hectares) have a very significant effect on the graphs, as these sites are at least an order of magnitude larger than most others on the *UN List*.

Biogeography

As in the previous four editions of the list each of the areas has been located within one of the biogeographical provinces defined by Udvardy (1975), although the province concerned is not actually identified within this list. Of the 9,832* protected areas qualifying for inclusion in the *UN List*, the Udvardy province is known for 8,562. The remaining 1,270 sites include a number of marine areas which cannot be classified within the Udvardy system. The system of biogeographical provinces of the world defined by Udvardy for IUCN divides the world into eight realms, subdivided into 193 provinces, with each province being characterised by one of 14 biome types. This information is used to provide a crude analysis of coverage both by province, and by biome type.

Table 1 provides a summary of protected area coverage (number of sites and total area) of each of the realms and provinces recognised by Udvardy. Approximately 25% of biogeographical provinces appear to have more than 10% of their area within protected areas. However, when analysing this data various limitations of the system must be considered, resulting both from its relative crudity, and, for example, differences in size between provinces. A 5,000 hectare protected area in the relatively small Malagasy Thorn Forest province, for example, would protect a much larger section of that province than an equivalent sized reserve in the huge Somalian province. A number of provinces appear to have 100% or more protection; this is usually due to marine protected areas being included, whilst the extent of the provinces is based on terrestrial area alone. While the results are sufficient to illustrate patchy coverage, more detailed analysis is necessary to determine real needs and priorities.

Table 2 provides a summary of protected area coverage (number of sites and total area) by biome type, indicating the proportion of each biome type protected within each realm. This ranges from as low as 0.69% in temperate grasslands, to a little under 10% in mixed island systems.

Summarisation of coverage by biome gives a first approximation of how well the major ecological formations are protected, although there is, of course, considerable variation of protection within biomes. It is important to appreciate that biome type does not mean the same as habitat type; a protected area within a tropical humid forest biome may not necessarily contain tropical humid forest, and an area containing tropical humid forest could occur in another biome altogether (such as mixed island systems). Note in this regard that Udvardy identifies all of Indonesia, Sabah and Sarawak and the Philippines as mixed island systems rather than tropical humid forest. Also, as was noted above for provinces, it is important to realise that there are significant differences between the areas covered by different biome types. For example, in the Neotropics there are extensive areas covered by the tropical humid forest biome (about a quarter of the continent), but only a small area covered by the lake systems biome (Lake Titicaca on the Peru/Bolivia border).

Summary		
Category I	1,460	86,473,325
Category II	2,041	376,784,187
Category III	250	13,686,191
Category IV	3,808	308,314,011
Category V	2,273	141,091,932
Total	**9,832**	**926,349,646**

*In a number of cases, a protected area may be located within another. In these instances, the summary totals may be inflated. In the case of the USA, wilderness areas in National Park Service and in Fish and Wildlife Service properties have been excluded from the summary data and analyses, due to their very large size.

Analyse de l'information

Toute l'information donnée dans la *Liste des Nations Unies* est stockée dans la base de données informatisée du WCMC qui détient beaucoup d'autres informations sur chaque site (et sur beaucoup d'autres sites ne figurant pas dans la Liste). Une partie de cette information sera analysée dans des publications, par le personnel du CMSC, entre autres. Deux graphiques et deux tableaux présentant cette capacité analytique ont été inclus dans la *Liste des Nations Unies*.

Expansion de la superficie mondiale des aires protégées

Les deux graphiques illustrent, respectivement l'augmentation du nombre et de la superficie des aires protégées dans le temps (Figure 1) et l'augmentation du nombre et de la superficie par période de cinq ans (Figure 2). Il convient de noter que la création du Parc national du Nord-Est du Groenland, en 1974 (97 millions d'hectares), du Parc marin du Récif de la Grande-Barrière en 1979 (35 millions d'hectares) et de la Réserve naturelle de Jiang Tang en 1990 (24 millions d'hectares) a eu un effet très marqué sur les graphiques, car l'ordre de grandeur de ces sites est pour le moins supérieur à celui de la plupart des autres sites de la *Liste des Nations Unies*.

Biogéographie

Comme dans les quatre éditions précédentes de la Liste, chacune des aires a été replacée dans une des provinces biogéographiques définies par Udvardy (1975), même si la province en question n'est pas réellement identifiée dans cette Liste. Sur les 9832* aires protégées répondant aux critères d'inscription sur la Liste des Nations Unies, 8562 correspondent à des provinces reconnues par Udvardy. Les 1270 sites restants comprennent un certain nombre d'aires marines qui ne rentrent pas dans le réseau défini par Udvardy. Le système mondial de provinces biogéographiques défini par Udvardy pour l'UICN divise le monde en huit domaines, subdivisés en 193 provinces, chacune étant caractérisée par un des 14 types de biomes. Cette information est utilisée pour donner une analyse brute de la couverture par province et par type de biome.

Le Tableau 1 propose un résumé de la couverture des aires protégées (nombre de sites et superficie totale) de chacun des domaines et provinces reconnus par Udvardy. Environ 25% des provinces biogéographiques ont plus de 10% de leur superficie incluse dans des aires protégées. Toutefois, dans l'analyse de ces données, il convient de prendre en considération diverses limites du système, venant à la fois de sa simplicité relative et, par exemple, de dimensions différentes entre les provinces. Une aire protégée de 5000 hectares dans la province relativement petite de la forêt épineuse malgache, par exemple, protège une plus grande proportion de cette province qu'une réserve de taille équivalente dans l'immense province somalienne. Plusieurs provinces semblent bénéficier d'un degré de protection de 100%, voire davantage; cela est généralement dû au fait que les aires protégées marines sont incluses, cependant que l'étendue des provinces est exclusivement fondée sur les terres émergées. Alors que les résultats sont suffisants pour illustrer une couverture en "patchwork", une analyse plus précise est nécessaire pour déterminer les besoins et les priorités réels.

Le Tableau 2 propose un résumé de la couverture des aires protégées (nombre de sites et superficie totale) par type de biome, et indique quelle proportion de chaque type de biome est protégée dans chaque domaine. Celle-ci s'échelonne entre 0,69%, dans les prairies tempérées, et un peu plus de 10%, dans les systèmes insulaires mixtes.

Le résumé de la couverture par biome donne un premier aperçu de la protection réelle des principales formations écologiques bien qu'il y ait, naturellement, des variations considérables dans le degré de protection à l'intérieur de chaque biome. Il importe de retenir que "type de biome" n'a pas le même sens que "type d'habitat"; une aire protégée se trouvant dans un biome de forêt humide tropicale ne contient pas nécessairement de forêt humide tropicale et une aire contenant une forêt humide tropicale peut se trouver dans un biome tout à fait différent (par exemple, un système insulaire mixte). A cet égard, il convient de noter qu'Udvardy identifie l'ensemble de l'Indonésie, du Sabah, du Sarawak et des Philippines à des systèmes insulaires mixtes et non pas à des biomes de forêts humides tropicales. De plus, comme nous l'avons déjà mentionné pour les provinces, il importe de savoir qu'il y a des différences marquées entre les aires couvertes par différents types de biomes. Par exemple, dans la région néotropicale, de vastes zones sont couvertes par le biome de forêt tropicale humide (environ un quart du continent) alors qu'une seule région, de faibles dimensions, est incluse dans le biome des systèmes lacustres (le lac Titicaca, à la frontière du Pérou et de la Bolivie).

	Résumé	
Catégorie I	1,460	86,473,325
Catégorie II	2,041	376,784,187
Catégorie III	250	13,686,191
Catégorie IV	3,808	308,314,011
Catégorie V	2,273	141,091,932
Total	**9,832**	**926,349,646**

*Il arrive qu'une aire protégée en englobe une autre, ce qui peut donner lieu à un total cumulé excessif. Aux Etats-Unis, par exemple, les aires de nature sauvage qui sont la propriété du *National Park Service* et du *Fish and Wildlife Service* ont été délibérément exclues des données et analyses récapitulatives, en raison de l'importance de leur superficie.

Análisis de la información

Toda la información suministrada en esta lista de las Naciones Unidas es almacenada en una base de datos computarizada, la cual incluye además una amplia gama de información adicional sobre cada sitio, así como sobre muchos otros sitios no cubiertos aquí. Parte de ésta información será analizada en publicaciones elaboradas por el personal del WCMC y de la UICN. Como indicación de esta capacidad analítica, se han incluido dos gráficos y dos tablas en la lista de las Naciones Unidas.

Expansión de la superficie mundial de áreas protegidas

Se suministran dos gráficos, uno ilustrando el crecimiento en el número y el área de las áreas protegidas a través de los años (Figura 1) y el otro ilustrando el crecimiento del número y del área en períodos de cinco años (Figura 2). Se debe resaltar que el establecimiento del Parque Nacional Northeast Greenland (Northeast Greenland National Park) en 1974 (97 millones de hectáreas), el Parque Marino Great Barrier Reef (the Great Barrier Reef Marine Park) en 1979 (35 millones de hectáreas) y la Reserva Natural Jiang Tang (Jiang Tang Nature Reserve) en 1990 (24 millones de hectáreas) tienen un efecto significativo en los gráficos, ya que estos sitios son más grandes, al menos en un orden de magnitud, que la mayoría de los otros en la lista de las Naciones Unidas.

Biogeografía

Así como en los cuatro ediciones previas de la lista, cada una de las áreas ha sido ubicada dentro de una de las provincias biogeográficas definas por Udvardy (1975), a pesar de que la provincia concerniente no se encuentre identificada en esta lista. De las 9.832* áreas protegidas que califican para ser incluidas en la Lista de las Naciones Unidas, se conoce la provincia de Udvardy en 8.562 de ellas. Los 1.270 sitios restantes corresponden a una cantidad de áreas marinas que no pueden ser clasificadas dentro del sistema de Udvardy. El sistema mundial de provincias biogeográficas definido por Udvardy para la UICN divide el mundo en ocho reinos, subdivididos en 193 provincias, siendo cada provincia caracterizada por uno de los catorce tipos de bioma. Esta información es utilizada para proveer un anális bruto de la cantidad de áreas protegidas en términos de provincia y tipo de bioma.

La Tabla 1 presenta un resumen de la cobertura de áreas protegidas (número de sitios y área total) en cada uno de los reinos y provincias reconocidos por Udvardy. Aproximadamente 25% de las provincias biogeográficas parecen tener mas del 10% de su área dentro de áreas protegidas. Sin embargo, al analizar estos datos se deben tener en cuenta una serie de limitaciones presentes en este sistema, las cuales surgen por la naturaleza bruta de los datos y por diferencias en tamaño entre las provincias. Por ejemplo, un área protegida de 5.000 hectáreas en la relativamente pequeña provincia de bosque espinoso de Madagascar (Malagasy Thorn Forest province) protegerá una sección mayor de dicha provincia que una reserva equivalente en tamaño en la enorme provincia Somalí (Somalian province). Varias provincias parecen tener una protección del 100% o más. Usualmente esto se debe a que están siendo incluidas áreas protegidas marinas, si bien la extensión de las provincias está basada en áreas terrestres solamente. Si bien los resultados son suficiente para ilustrar la cobertura por parches de las áreas protegidas, hace falta un análisis más detallado para determinar las necesidades reales y las prioridades.

La Tabla 2 presenta un resumen de la cobertura en áreas protegidas (número de sitios y área total) por tipo de bioma, indicando la proporción de cada tipo de bioma protegido dentro de cada reino. Esto fluctua desde porcentajes tan bajos como 0.69% en praderas templadas, hasta un poco menos de 10% en sistemas insulares mixtos.

Un resumen de la cobertura de áreas protegidas por bioma permite una primera aproximación de cuan adecuada es la protección dedicada a las mayores formaciones ecológicas, aunque por su puesto existe una variación considerable de protección dentro de los diferentes biomas. Es importante tener en cuenta que tipo de bioma no significa lo mismo que tipo de habitat. Un área protegida en un bosque húmedo tropical puede no contener bosque húmedo tropical, y un área que contenga bosque humedo tropical puede presentarse en otro tipo de bioma completamente diferente, tal como un sistema insular mixto. Nótese en este sentido que Udvardy identifica toda Indonesia, Malasia Insular y las Filipinas como sistemas insulares mixtos, en lugar de como bosque húmedo tropical. Asi mismo, tal como fue indicado en el caso de las provincias, es importante comprender que hay diferencias significativas entre las áreas cubiertas por biomas diferentes. Por ejemplo, en el Neotrópico hay áreas extensas cubiertas por bioma de bosque húmedo tropical (aproximadamente un cuarto del continente), pero sólo una pequeña área cubierta por el bioma de sistemas de lagos (El Lago Titicaca en la frontera Perú/Bolivia).

	Resumen	
Categoría I	1.460	86'473.325
Categoría II	2.041	376'784.187
Categoría III	250	13'686.191
Categoría IV	3.808	308'314.011
Categoría V	2.273	141'091.932
Total	**9.832**	**926'349.646**

*En algunos casos, puede que un área protegida esté ubicada dentro de otra. En estas circunstancias, los totales pueden resultar exagerados. En el caso de los Estados Unidos, las áreas virgenes de propiedad del Servicio de Parques Nacionales (National Park Service) y del Servicio de Peces y Vida Silvestre (Fish and Wildlife Service) han sido excluidos de los datos y del análisis debido a su gran tamaño.

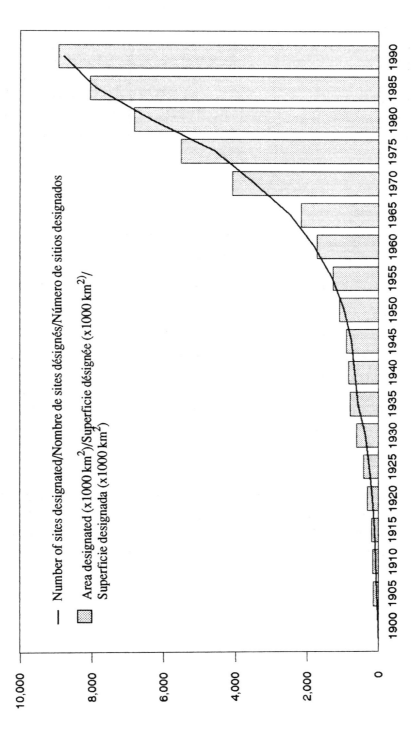

Figure 1: Growth of the World Coverage of Protected Areas
Figure 1: Expansion de la superficie mondiale des aires protégées
Figura 1: Expansión de la superficie mundial de áreas protegidas

— Number of sites designated/Nombre de sites désignés/Número de sitios designados

Area designated (x1000 km²)/Superficie désignée (x1000 km²)/ Superficie designada (x1000 km²)

Five year period beginning...
Période de cinq ans commençant en...
Periodo de cinco años comenzando...

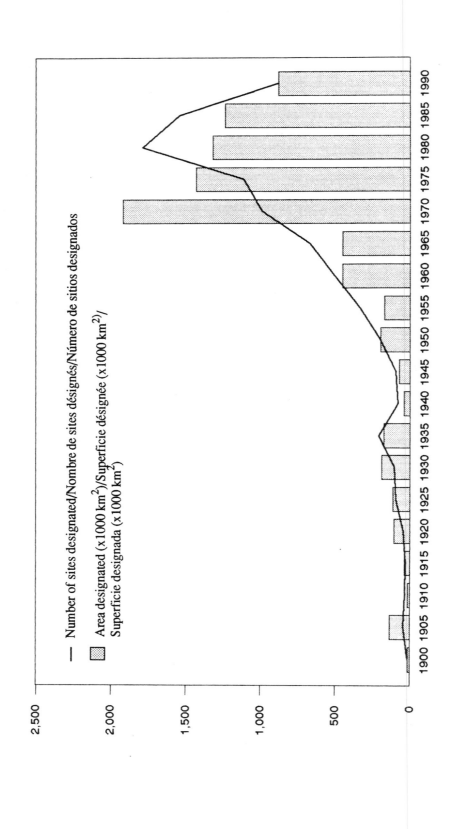

Figure 2: Growth of the World Coverage of Protected Areas: Number of sites designated in each five year period
Figure 2: Expansion de la superficie mondiale des aires protégées: Nombre de sites désignés par période de cinq ans
Figura 2: Expansión de la superficie mundial de áreas protegidas: Número de sitios designados cada periodo de cinco años

— Number of sites designated/Nombre de sites désignés/Número de sitios designados

▨ Area designated (x1000 km²)/Superficie désignée (x1000 km²)/Superficie designada (x1000 km²)

Five year period beginning...
Période de cinq ans commençant en...
Periodo de cinco años comenzando...

Table 1/Tableau 1/Tabla 1. Analysis of protected areas coverage of the world by biogeographical province (after Udvardy, 1975)/Analyse de la couverture des aires protégées du globe par province biogéographique/Análisis de la expansión de la superficie mundial de áreas protegidas por provincias biogeográficas

Name of Province Nom de la province Nombre de la Provincia	Area (km^2) Superficie (km^2) Superficie (km^2)	Protected Areas/Aires protégées/Areas protegidas		
		No. of areas Nombre d'aires Número de áreas	Area (ha) Superficie (ha) Superficie (ha)	% % %
Nearctic Realm				
Sitkan	349,903	75	16,998,219	48.58
Oregonian	124,604	52	1,280,699	10.28
Yukon Taiga	1,019,584	30	21,029,795	20.63
Canadian Taiga	5,127,155	386	45,954,320	8.96
Eastern Forest	2,222,997	375	5,230,027	2.35
Austroriparian	596,892	139	1,842,724	3.09
Californian	526,507	51	1,164,885	2.21
Sonoran	507,770	108	11,170,992	22.00
Chihuahuan	577,181	22	646,803	1.12
Tamaulipan	210,371	3	50,232	0.24
Great Basin	660,356	59	2,053,507	3.11
Aleutian Islands	124,511	9	7,765,585	62.37
Alaskan Tundra	958,491	26	30,924,255	32.26
Canadian Tundra	1,733,377	15	16,721,130	9.65
Arctic Archipelago	689,965	1	14,200	0.02
Greenland Tundra	498,731	0	0	0.00
Arctic Desert and Icecap	2,120,078	4	103,287,810	48.72
Grasslands	2,442,342	126	1,240,185	0.51
Rocky Mountains	1,578,491	205	14,528,041	9.20
Sierra-Cascade	228,720	125	3,602,318	15.75
Madrean-Cordilleran	763,250	98	2,490,852	3.26
Great Lakes	254,499	11	338,817	1.33
Palaearctic Realm				
Chinese Subtropical Forest	862,946	81	1,926,440	2.23
Japanese Evergreen Forest	266,882	34	1,390,067	5.21
West Eurasian Taiga	4,000,000	204	10,910,953	2.73
East Siberian Taiga	5,536,078	17	12,865,468	2.32
Icelandian	101,591	22	915,924	9.02
Subarctic Birchwoods	100,000	17	284,596	2.85
Kamchatkan	283,311	5	2,624,000	9.26
British Islands	266,599	113	4,223,528	15.84
Atlantic	715,955	201	7,044,782	9.84
Boreonemoral	1,285,235	281	3,537,919	2.75
Middle European Forest	1,467,342	450	8,543,150	5.82
Pannonian	102,530	35	375,060	3.66
West Anatolian	37,610	5	70,091	1.86
Manchu-Japanese Mixed Forest	1,252,284	45	3,221,383	2.57
Oriental Deciduous Forest	2,751,446	196	6,681,169	2.43
Iberian Highlands	316,084	115	3,041,453	9.62
Mediterranean Sclerophyll	1,194,658	255	4,456,971	3.73
Sahara	6,960,804	20	20,887,545	3.00
Arabian Desert	2,996,082	49	9,718,950	3.24
Anatolian-Iranian Desert	2,203,749	62	5,274,306	2.39
Turanian	2,116,829	17	1,538,117	0.73
Takla-Makan-Gobi Desert	2,184,554	28	12,837,722	5.88
Tibetan	1,268,119	4	24,024,367	18.94
Iranian Desert	403,527	9	980,732	2.43
Arctic Desert	195,915	6	3,492,600	17.83

Table 1/Tableau 1/Tabla 1 (cont'd)

Name of Province Nom de la province Nombre de la Provincia	Area (km^2) Superficie (km^2) Superficie (km^2)	Protected Areas/Aires protégées/Areas protegidas		
		No. of areas Nombre d'aires Número de áreas	Area (ha) Superficie (ha) Superficie (ha)	% % %
Higharctic Tundra	859,865	3	6,397,872	7.44
Lowarctic Tundra	2,158,146	4	1,993,308	0.92
Atlas Steppe	421,541	6	91,498	0.22
Pontian Steppe	1,945,402	27	1,313,837	0.68
Mongolian-Manchurian Steppe	2,605,123	19	2,302,980	0.88
Scottish Highlands	46,791	44	778,828	16.64
Central European Highlands	369,903	447	7,547,096	20.40
Balkan Highlands	221,241	106	1,145,148	5.18
Caucaso-Iranian Highlands	936,015	70	5,496,803	5.87
Altai Highlands	1,048,263	11	11,211,336	10.70
Pamir-Tian-Shan Highlands	643,207	29	6,155,949	9.57
Hindu Kush Highlands	217,105	6	218,438	1.01
Himalayan Highlands	860,070	86	8,343,702	9.70
Szechwan Highlands	578,558	58	2,771,588	4.79
Macaronesian Islands	14,032	13	132,165	9.42
Ryukyu Islands	2,479	0	0	0.00
Lake Ladoga	17,606	1	41,436	2.35
Aral Sea	67,548	1	18,300	0.27
Lake Baikal	32,260	0	0	0.00

Afrotropical realm

Guinean Rain Forest	607,048	23	1,345,863	2.22
Congo Rain Forest	1,921,970	24	7,017,294	3.65
Malagasy Rain Forest	200,573	16	455,575	2.27
West African Woodland/Savanna	3,247,618	88	18,754,963	5.77
East African Woodland/Savanna	1,510,608	71	14,443,773	9.56
Congo Woodland/Savanna	1,356,749	6	3,774,200	2.78
Miombo Woodland/Savanna	2,432,142	42	15,735,038	6.47
South African Woodland/Savanna	1,694,787	119	8,749,646	5.16
Malagasy Woodland/Savanna	324,074	19	614,774	1.90
Malagasy Thorn Forest	70,676	2	44,950	0.64
Cape Sclerophyll	129,683	50	1,383,542	10.67
Western Sahel	2,814,709	12	14,121,240	5.02
Eastern Sahel	1,169,711	7	5,781,800	4.94
Somalian	2,166,783	31	6,079,269	2.81
Namib	364,602	7	9,635,653	26.43
Kalahari	504,861	12	9,966,826	19.74
Karroo	377,735	16	431,115	1.14
Ethiopian Highlands	505,387	13	2,534,000	5.01
Guinean Highlands	80,030	4	1,321,625	16.51
Central African Highlands	269,463	8	4,435,825	16.46
East African Highlands	65,457	11	267,700	4.09
South African Highlands	198,957	48	523,890	2.63
Ascension and St Helena Islands	187	1	1,000	5.35
Comores Islands and Aldabra	1,860	1	35,000	18.82
Mascarene Islands	4,494	5	9,965	2.22
Lake Rudolf	7,331	0	0	0.00
Lake Ukerewe (Victoria)	69,504	1	45,700	0.66
Lake Tanganyika	32,753	0	0	0.00
Lake Malawi (Nyasa)	28,949	1	8,700	0.30

Indomalayan Realm

Malabar Rainforest	223,556	44	1,029,838	4.61
Ceylonese Rainforest	31,104	5	68,320	2.20

Table 1/Tableau 1/Tabla 1 (cont'd)

Name of Province Nom de la province Nombre de la Provincia	Area (km²) Superficie (km²) Superficie (km²)	Protected Areas/Aires protégées/Areas protegidas		
		No. of areas Nombre d'aires Número de áreas	Area (ha) Superficie (ha) Superficie (ha)	% % %
Bengalian Rainforest	179,943	20	477,099	2.65
Burman Rainforest	257,585	2	20,455	0.08
Indochinese Rainforest	452,508	71	3,862,453	8.54
South Chinese Rainforest	188,979	72	487,472	2.58
Malayan Rainforest	179,164	27	1,325,103	7.40
Indus-Ganges Monsoon Forest	1,412,232	128	5,671,096	4.02
Burma Monsoon Forest	297,201	31	1,012,147	3.41
Thailandian Monsoon Forest	959,750	77	3,903,347	4.07
Mahanadian	219,436	26	1,368,769	6.24
Coromandel	88,401	5	183,822	2.08
Ceylonese Monsoon Forest	34,912	50	696,963	19.96
Deccan Thorn Forest	338,415	9	215,473	0.64
Thar Desert	711,809	38	3,923,444	5.51
Seychelles and Amirantes Islands	204	2	2,893	14.18
Laccadives Islands	32	0	0	0.00
Maldives and Chagos Islands	36	0	0	0.00
Cocos-Keeling and Christmas Islands	149	2	17,652	100.00
Andaman and Nicobar Islands	6,225	44	123,944	19.91
Sumatra	461,939	33	3,641,290	7.88
Java	137,874	31	897,672	6.51
Lesser Sunda Islands	86,613	21	398,962	4.61
Sulawesi (Celebes)	197,144	34	2,127,586	10.79
Borneo	740,970	72	4,768,694	6.44
Philippines	292,156	27	605,927	2.07
Taiwan	36,558	17	454,534	12.43

Oceania Realm

Papuan	960,158	39	7,674,529	7.99
Micronesian	2,170	6	8,741	4.03
Hawaiian	16,715	23	276,255	16.53
Southeastern Polynesian	4,162	10	69,438	16.68
Central Polynesian	4,171	7	40,966	9.82
New Caledonian	16,723	20	87,327	5.22
East Melanesian	32,655	2	5,342	0.16

Australian Realm

Queensland Coastal	300,248	122	5,909,556	19.68
Tasmanian	67,979	46	1,125,128	16.55
Northern Coastal	350,382	8	553,257	1.58
Western Sclerophyll	410,814	57	1,661,340	4.04
Southern Sclerophyll	246,678	73	2,946,645	11.94
Eastern Sclerophyll	643,808	179	3,930,856	6.11
Brigalow	231,581	14	358,790	1.55
Western Mulga	778,120	10	2,697,267	3.47
Central Desert	1,777,073	19	5,821,907	3.28
Southern Mulga/Saltbush	837,032	17	7,008,399	8.37
Northern Savanna	580,938	13	4,212,244	7.25
Northern Grasslands	966,966	9	1,300,590	1.35
Eastern Grasslands and Savannas	527,831	58	1,059,030	2.01

Antarctic Realm

Neozealandia	270,000	205	6,147,634	22.77
Maudlandia	10,465,150	9	216,195	0.02
Marielandia	2,193,955	4	1,330	0.00
Insulantarctica	19,206	24	1,327,426	69.12

Table 1/Tableau 1/Tabla 1 (cont'd)

Name of Province Nom de la province Nombre de la Provincia	Area (km²) Superficie (km²) Superficie (km²)	Protected Areas/Aires protégées/Areas protegidas		
		No. of areas Nombre d'aires Número de áreas	Area (ha) Superficie (ha) Superficie (ha)	% % %
Neotropical Realm				
Campechean	259,164	27	1,648,207	6.36
Panamanian	40,065	10	1,111,924	27.75
Colombian Coastal	237,201	13	1,743,845	7.35
Guyanan	1,009,104	30	3,252,583	3.22
Amazonian	2,509,392	43	26,083,065	10.39
Madeiran	1,671,819	16	2,898,149	1.73
Serro Do Mar	243,787	73	4,328,032	17.75
Brazilian Rain Forest	1,533,869	81	1,977,872	1.29
Brazilian Planalto	219,152	9	23,372	0.11
Valdivian Forest	111,933	12	4,016,359	35.88
Chilean Nothofagus	123,711	8	3,948,382	31.92
Everglades	6,827	26	830,363	100.00
Sinaloan	192,114	4	295,994	1.54
Guerreran	158,439	4	125,827	0.79
Yucatecan	39,959	3	107,146	2.68
Central American	309,974	106	2,134,606	6.89
Venezuelan Dry Forest	270,319	39	3,681,071	13.62
Venezuelan Deciduous Forest	58,928	22	1,148,910	19.50
Equadorian Dry Forest	50,343	5	187,031	3.72
Caatinga	899,739	11	380,461	0.42
Gran Chaco	988,513	15	1,329,675	1.35
Chilean Araucaria Forest	32,867	2	45,414	1.38
Chilean Sclerophyll	57,331	8	147,008	2.56
Pacific Desert	290,390	2	48,824	0.17
Monte	1,234,810	21	648,288	0.53
Patagonian	413,118	15	371,112	0.90
Llanos	437,988	8	1,198,487	2.74
Campos Limpos	207,269	7	11,933,692	57.58
Babacu	293,021	7	963,205	3.29
Campos Cerrados	1,778,650	31	7,484,877	4.21
Argentinian Pampas	512,152	10	42,235	0.08
Uruguayan Pampas	522,200	18	118,970	0.23
Northern Andean	256,507	18	3,708,406	14.46
Colombian Montane	154,776	25	3,992,784	25.80
Yungas	483,142	17	5,409,751	11.20
Puna	464,873	18	2,185,740	4.70
Southern Andean	662,939	50	8,530,608	12.87
Bahamas-Bermudean	12,821	12	151,364	11.81
Cuban	109,758	54	882,798	8.04
Greater Antillean	95,752	29	1,074,157	11.22
Lesser Antillean	6,604	25	205,815	31.17
Revilla Gigedo Island	196	0	0	0.00
Cocos Island	24	1	2,400	100.00
Galapagos Islands	7,665	2	8,683,700	100.00
Fernando De Noronja Island	26	2	37,941	100.00
South Trinidade Island	11	0	0	0.00
Lake Titicaca	7,245	1	36,180	4.99
Classification Unknown **(including marine sites)**		**1,270**	**92,785,970**	

Table 2/Tableau 2/Tabla 2. Analysis of protected areas coverage of the world by biome type/Analyse de la couverture des aires protégées du globe par type de biome/Análisis de la expansión de la superficie mundial de áreas protegidas por tipo de bioma

| Biome Type
Type de biome
Tipo de bioma | Protected Areas/Aires protégées/Areas protegidas | | | |
	Area (km²) Superficie (km²) Superficie (km²)	No. of areas Nombre d'aires Número de áreas	Area (ha) Superficie (ha) Superficie (ha)	% % %
Temperate grasslands	8,976,591	264	6,168,735	0.69
Lake systems	517,695	16	489,133	0.94
Cold-winter deserts	9,250,252	194	47,079,863	5.09
Temperate broad-leaf forests	11,216,659	1,939	44,919,325	4.00
Warm deserts/semi-deserts	24,279,843	400	108,648,152	4.47
Tropical dry forests/woodlands	17,312,538	918	85,946,882	4.96
Evergreen sclerophyllous forests	3,757,144	798	19,089,392	5.08
Temperate needle-leaf forests/woodlands	15,682,817	637	90,760,536	5.79
Tropical grasslands/savannas	4,264,832	75	27,093,095	6.35
Tundra communities	22,017,390	105	172,141,711	7.82
Tropical humid forests	10,513,210	636	87,048,623	8.28
Mixed mountain systems	10,633,145	1,497	97,200,428	9.14
Subtropical/temperate rainforests/woodlands	3,930,979	603	38,834,720	9.88
Mixed island systems	3,252,563	535	32,418,057	9.97
Classification Unknown		**1,215**	**68,510,994**	

World Heritage Sites

Natural sites inscribed by the Committee of the Convention
concerning the protection of the world cultural and natural heritage

Biens du patrimoine mondial

Biens naturels inscrits par le Comité de la Convention concernant
la protection du patrimoine mondial, culturel et naturel

Sitios de Patrimonio Mundial

Sitios Naturales inscritos por el Comité de la Convención
concerniente a la protección del patrimonio cultural y natural

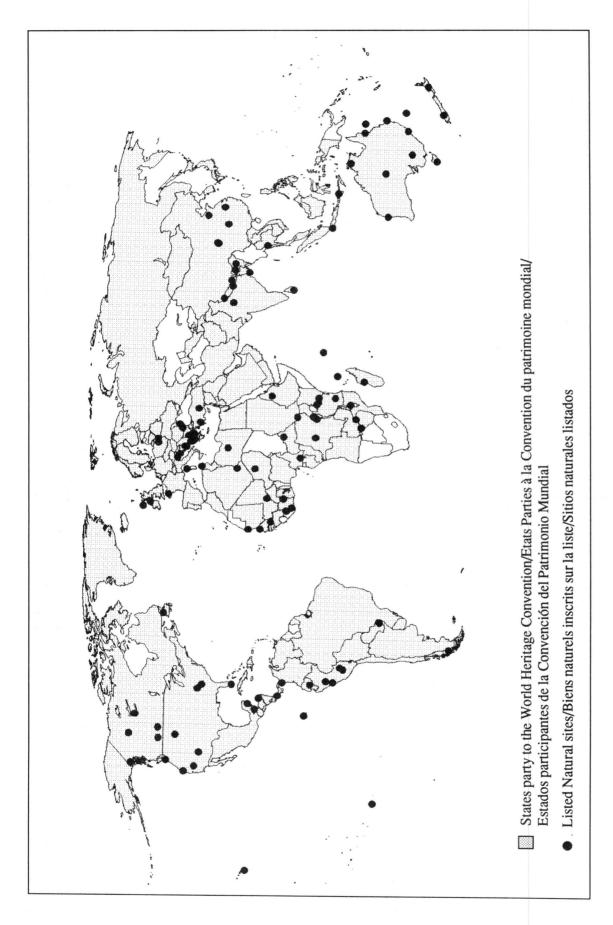

Map 1. States party to the **World Heritage Convention** and the location of inscribed natural sites
Carte 1. Etats Parties à la Convention du patrimoine mondial et emplacement des biens naturels inscrits
Mapa 1. Estados Participantes en la Convención del Patrimonio Mundial y ubicación de sitios natureles registrados

☒ States party to the **World Heritage Convention**/Etats Parties à la Convention du patrimoine mondial/
Estados participantes de la Convención del Patrimonio Mundial

● Listed Natural sites/Biens naturels inscrits sur la liste/Sitios naturales listados

World Heritage Sites

The *Convention Concerning the Protection of the World Cultural and Natural Heritage* was adopted in Paris in 1972, and came into force in December 1975. The Convention provides for the designation of areas of "outstanding universal value" as world heritage sites, with the principal aim of fostering international cooperation in safeguarding these important areas. Sites, which must be nominated by the signatory nation responsible, are evaluated for their world heritage quality before being declared by the World Heritage Committee. Only natural sites are considered here.

Article 2 of the World Heritage Convention considers as natural heritage: natural features consisting of physical and biological formations or groups of such formations, which are of outstanding universal value from the aesthetic or scientific point of view; geological or physiographical formations and precisely delineated areas which constitute the habitat of threatened species of animals and plants of outstanding universal value from the point of view of science or conservation; and natural sites or precisely delineated areas of outstanding universal value from the point of view of science, conservation or natural beauty. Criteria for inclusion in the List are published by Unesco.

Biens du patrimoine mondial

La *Convention concernant la protection du patrimoine mondial, culturel et naturel* a été adoptée à Paris en 1972 et est entrée en vigueur en décembre 1975. La Convention prévoit la désignation de régions de "valeur universelle exceptionnelle" en tant que biens du patrimoine mondial, dans le but premier d'encourager la coopération internationale pour la sauvegarde de ces régions importantes. Les sites, qui doivent être désignés par l'Etat signataire responsable, sont évalués en fonction de leur valeur pour le patrimoine mondial avant d'être acceptés par le Comité du patrimoine mondial. Nous ne tenons compte ici que des biens naturels.

L'article 2 de la Convention du patrimoine mondial considère comme patrimoine naturel: les monuments naturels constitués par des formations physiques et biologiques ou par des groupes de telles formations, qui ont une valeur universelle exceptionnelle du point de vue esthétique ou scientifique; les formations géologiques et physiographiques et les zones strictement délimitées constituant l'habitat d'espèces animales et végétales menacées, qui ont une valeur universelle exceptionnelle du point de vue de la science ou de la conservation; les sites naturels ou les zones naturelles strictement délimitées, qui ont une valeur universelle exceptionnelle pour la science, pour la conservation ou pour leur beauté naturelle. Les critères déterminant l'inscription sur la Liste sont publiés par l'UNESCO.

Sitios de Patrimonio Mundial

La *Convención sobre la Protección del Patrimonio Mundial, Cultural y Natural* fué adoptada en París en al año 1974, y entró en vigor en Diciembre de 1975. Esta convención estipula la designación de áreas de 'valor universal excepcional' como sitios de patrimonio mundial con el objetivo principal de fomentar la cooperación internacional para salvaguardar estas áreas. Estos sitios, los cuales deben ser nominados por los Estados signatarios responsables, son evaluados con relación a su valor como patrimonio mundial y declarados por el Comité de Patrimonio Mundial. Aquí sólo se considera sitios naturales.

El artículo 2 de la Convención de Patrimonio Mundial considera como patrimonio natural: áreas naturales que consisten de formaciones o grupos de formaciones biológicas y físicas, con un valor universal excepcional desde el punto de vista estético o científico; formaciones geológicas o fisiográficas que constituyen el hábitat de especies amenazadas de animales y de plantas de valor universal excepcional desde el punto de vista de la conservación o de la ciencia; y áreas naturales de valor universal excepcional desde el punto de vista de la ciencia, de la conservación o como bellezas naturales. Los criterios para inclusión en la Lista son publicados por la Unesco.

List of World Heritage Sites
Liste du patrimoine mondial
Lista del Patrimonio Mundial

Name of Area/Nom de l'aire/Nombre de Unidad	Latitude/longitude Latitude/longitude Latitud/longitud	Area (ha) Superficie (ha) Superficie(ha)	Year Année Año
AFGHANISTAN/AFGANISTAN			
(No natural sites inscribed/Pas de biens naturels inscrits sur la liste/ No hay sitios naturales registrados)			
ALBANIA/ALBANIE			
(No natural sites inscribed/Pas de biens naturels inscrits sur la liste/ No hay sitios naturales registrados)			
ALGERIA/ALGERIE/ARGELIA			
Tassili N'Ajjer	24°55'N/8°40'E	300,000	1982
ANGOLA			
(No natural sites inscribed/Pas de biens naturels inscrits sur la liste/ No hay sitios naturales registrados)			
ANTIGUA AND BARBUDA/ANTIGUA-ET-BARBUDA/ ANTIGUA Y BARBUDA			
(No natural sites inscribed/Pas de biens naturels inscrits sur la liste/ No hay sitios naturales registrados)			
ARGENTINA/ARGENTINE			
Iguazú National Park	25°36'S/54°34'W	55,000	1984
Los Glaciares National Park	49°58'S/73°08'W	600,000	1981
ARMENIA/ARMENIE			
(No natural sites inscribed/Pas de biens naturels inscrits sur la liste/ No hay sitios naturales registrados)			
AUSTRALIA/AUSTRALIE			
Australian East Coast Rain Forest Parks	32°30'S/152°00'E	203,564	1986
Fraser Island	25°00'S/153°00'E	181,000	1992
Great Barrier Reef	17°35'S/149°30'E	34,870,000	1981
Kakadu National Park	12°47'S/132°26'E	1,980,400	1981
Lord Howe Island Group	31°40'S/159°08'E	1,540	1982
Shark Bay	26°00'S/113°30'E	2,197,300	1991
Uluru (Ayers Rock) National Park	24°55'S/131°01'E	132,566	1977
Western Tasmania Wilderness National Parks	42°43'S/146°07'E	1,081,348	1982
Wet Tropics of Queensland	17°28'S/145°43'E	920,000	1988
Willandra Lakes Region of Western NSW	34°00'S/143°00'E	600,000	1981

AUSTRIA/AUTRICHE

(No natural sites inscribed/Pas de biens naturels inscrits sur la liste/
No hay sitios naturales registrados)

BAHRAIN/BAHREÏN/BAHREIN

(No natural sites inscribed/Pas de biens naturels inscrits sur la liste/
No hay sitios naturales registrados)

BANGLADESH

(No natural sites inscribed/Pas de biens naturels inscrits sur la liste/
No hay sitios naturales registrados)

BELARUS

Belovezhskaya Puscha State National Park	52°42'N/21°36'E	87,600	1992

BELIZE/BELICE

(No natural sites inscribed/Pas de biens naturels inscrits sur la liste/
No hay sitios naturales registrados)

BENIN

(No natural sites inscribed/Pas de biens naturels inscrits sur la liste/
No hay sitios naturales registrados)

BOLIVIA/BOLIVIE

(No natural sites inscribed/Pas de biens naturels inscrits sur la liste/
No hay sitios naturales registrados)

BOSNIA AND HERZEGOVINA/BOSNIE-HERZEGOVINE/ BOSNIA Y HERZEGOVINA

(No natural sites inscribed/Pas de biens naturels inscrits sur la liste/
No hay sitios naturales registrados)

BRAZIL/BRESIL/BRASIL

Iguaçu National Park	25°23'S/54°07'W	170,000	1986

BULGARIA/BULGARIE

Pirin National Park	41°40'N/22°50'E	40,060	1983
Srebarna Nature Reserve	44°05'N/27°07'E	600	1983

BURKINA FASO

(No natural sites inscribed/Pas de biens naturels inscrits sur la liste/
No hay sitios naturales registrados)

BURUNDI

(No natural sites inscribed/Pas de biens naturels inscrits sur la liste/
No hay sitios naturales registrados)

CAMBODIA/CAMBODGE/CAMBOYA

(No natural sites inscribed/Pas de biens naturels inscrits sur la liste/
No hay sitios naturales registrados)

CAMEROON/CAMEROUN/CAMERUN

Réserve faunique du Dja	3°06'N/13°00'E	526,000	1987

CANADA

Canadian Rockies	50°39'N/116°11'W	2,304,114	1984
Dinosaur Provincial Park	50°49'N/111°36'W	6,622	1979
Gros Morne National Park	49°38'N/57°48'W	180,500	1987
Kluane-Wrangell/St Elias (Canada section)	60°40'N/139°00'W	7,545,629	1979
Nahanni National Park	61°32'N/125°33'W	476,560	1978
Wood Buffalo National Park	59°20'N/113°15'W	4,480,000	1983

CAPE VERDE/CAP-VERT/CABO VERDE

(No natural sites inscribed/Pas de biens naturels inscrits sur la liste/
   No hay sitios naturales registrados)

CENTRAL AFRICAN REPUBLIC/
REPUBLIQUE CENTRAFRICAINE/
REPUBLICA CENTROAFRICANA

Parc National de Manovo-Gounda-St Floris	8°55'N/21°25'E	1,740,000	1988

CHILE/CHILI

(No natural sites inscribed/Pas de biens naturels inscrits sur la liste/
   No hay sitios naturales registrados)

CHINA/CHINE

Huanglong Scenic & Historic Interest Area	32°40'N/103°30'E	60,000	1992
Jiuzhaigou Valley Scenic & Historic Interest Area	33°06'N/104°00'E	132,000	1992
Mount Huangshan	30°40'N/118°09'E	29,600	1990
Mount Taishan	36°21'N/117°01'E	?	1987
Wulingyuan Scenic & Historic Interest Area	29°20'N/110°32'E	26,400	1992

COLOMBIA/COLOMBIE

(No natural sites inscribed/Pas de biens naturels inscrits sur la liste/
   No hay sitios naturales registrados)

CONGO

(No natural sites inscribed/Pas de biens naturels inscrits sur la liste/
   No hay sitios naturales registrados)

COSTA RICA

Talamanca Range-La Amistad Reserves	9°23'N/83°14'W	584,592	1983

CÔTE D'IVOIRE

Parc national de la Comoé	8°35'N/3°33'W	1,150,000	1983
Réserves du Mont Nimba (secteur ivoirien)	7°18'N/8°18'W	5,000	1982
Parc national de Taï	5°41'N/7°40'W	330,000	1982

CROATIA/CROATIE/CROACIA

Plitvice Lakes National Park	44°52'N/15°36'E	19,200	1979

CUBA

(No natural sites inscribed/Pas de biens naturels inscrits sur la liste/
   No hay sitios naturales registrados)

CYPRUS/CHYPRE/CHIPRE

(No natural sites inscribed/Pas de biens naturels inscrits sur la liste/
   No hay sitios naturales registrados)

CZECH REPUBLIC/REPUBLIQUE TCHEQUE/ REPUBLICA CHECA

(No natural sites inscribed/Pas de biens naturels inscrits sur la liste/
No hay sitios naturales registrados)

DENMARK/DANEMARK/DINAMARCA

(No natural sites inscribed/Pas de biens naturels inscrits sur la liste/
No hay sitios naturales registrados)

DOMINICAN REPUBLIC/REPUBLIQUE DOMINICAINE/ REPUBLICA DOMINICANA

(No natural sites inscribed/Pas de biens naturels inscrits sur la liste/
No hay sitios naturales registrados)

ECUADOR/EQUATEUR

Galapagos Islands	0°02'N/90°39'W	766,514	1978
Sangay National Park	1°52'S/78°18'W	271,925	1983

EGYPT/EGYPTE/EGIPTO

(No natural sites inscribed/Pas de biens naturels inscrits sur la liste/
No hay sitios naturales registrados)

EL SALVADOR

(No natural sites inscribed/Pas de biens naturels inscrits sur la liste/
No hay sitios naturales registrados)

ETHIOPIA/ETHIOPIE/ETIOPIA

Simen National Park	13°11'N/38°04'E	22,000	1978

FIJI/FIDJI

(No natural sites inscribed/Pas de biens naturels inscrits sur la liste/
No hay sitios naturales registrados)

FINLAND/FINLANDE/FINLANDIA

(No natural sites inscribed/Pas de biens naturels inscrits sur la liste/
No hay sitios naturales registrados)

FRANCE/FRANCIA

Cap Girolata, Cap Porto & Scandola RN	42°20'N/8°37'E	12,000	1983
Mont-Saint-Michel et sa baie	48°42'N/2°29'W	?	1979

GABON

(No natural sites inscribed/Pas de biens naturels inscrits sur la liste/
No hay sitios naturales registrados)

GAMBIA/GAMBIE

(No natural sites inscribed/Pas de biens naturels inscrits sur la liste/
No hay sitios naturales registrados)

GEORGIA/GEORGIE

(No natural sites inscribed/Pas de biens naturels inscrits sur la liste/
No hay sitios naturales registrados)

GERMANY/ALLEMAGNE/ALEMANIA

(No natural sites inscribed/Pas de biens naturels inscrits sur la liste/
No hay sitios naturales registrados)

GHANA

(No natural sites inscribed/Pas de biens naturels inscrits sur la liste/
   No hay sitios naturales registrados)

GREECE/GRECE/GRECIA

Meteora Group of Monasteries	39°45'N/21°37'E	375	1988
Mount Athos	40°10'N/24°19'E	?	1988

GUATEMALA

Tikal National Park	17°14'N/89°38'W	57,600	1979

GUINEA/GUINEE

Réserves du Mont Nimba (secteur guinéen)	7°18'N/10°35'W	13,000	1981

GUYANA

(No natural sites inscribed/Pas de biens naturels inscrits sur la liste/
   No hay sitios naturales registrados)

HAITI

(No natural sites inscribed/Pas de biens naturels inscrits sur la liste/
   No hay sitios naturales registrados)

HONDURAS

Río Platano WHS	15°50'N/85°00'W	500,000	1982

HUNGARY/HONGRIE/HUNGRIA

(No natural sites inscribed/Pas de biens naturels inscrits sur la liste/
   No hay sitios naturales registrados)

INDIA/INDE

Kaziranga National Park	26°38'N/93°23'E	42,996	1985
Keoladeo National Park	27°10'N/77°31'E	2,873	1985
Manas Wildlife Sanctuary	26°44'N/90°45'E	39,100	1985
Nanda Devi National Park	30°24'N/79°53'E	63,033	1988
Sundarbans National Park	21°42'N/88°53'E	133,010	1987

INDONESIA/INDONESIE

Komodo National Park	8°37'S/119°36'E	219,322	1991
Ujung Kulon National Park	6°45'S/105°40'E	78,359	1991

IRAN, ISLAMIC REPUBLIC OF/IRAN, REPUBIQUE ISLAMIQUE D'/IRAN, REPUBLICA ISLAMICA DEL

(No natural sites inscribed/Pas de biens naturels inscrits sur la liste/
   No hay sitios naturales registrados)

IRAQ

(No natural sites inscribed/Pas de biens naturels inscrits sur la liste/
   No hay sitios naturales registrados)

IRELAND/IRLANDE/IRLANDA

(No natural sites inscribed/Pas de biens naturels inscrits sur la liste/
   No hay sitios naturales registrados)

ITALY/ITALIE/ITALIA

(No natural sites inscribed/Pas de biens naturels inscrits sur la liste/
   No hay sitios naturales registrados)

JAMAICA/JAMAÏQUE
(No natural sites inscribed/Pas de biens naturels inscrits sur la liste/
No hay sitios naturales registrados)

JAPAN/JAPON
(No natural sites inscribed/Pas de biens naturels inscrits sur la liste/
No hay sitios naturales registrados)

JORDAN/JORDANIE/JORDANIA
(No natural sites inscribed/Pas de biens naturels inscrits sur la liste/
No hay sitios naturales registrados)

KENYA/KENIA
(No natural sites inscribed/Pas de biens naturels inscrits sur la liste/
No hay sitios naturales registrados)

KOREA, REPUBLIC OF/REPUBLIQUE DE COREE/
REPUBLICA DE COREA
(No natural sites inscribed/Pas de biens naturels inscrits sur la liste/
No hay sitios naturales registrados)

LAO PEOPLE'S DEMOCRATIC REPUBLIC/REPUBLIQUE
DEMOCRATIQUE POPULAIRE LAO/REPUBLICA
DEMOCRATICA POPULAR LAO
(No natural sites inscribed/Pas de biens naturels inscrits sur la liste/
No hay sitios naturales registrados)

LEBANON/LIBAN/LIBANO
(No natural sites inscribed/Pas de biens naturels inscrits sur la liste/
No hay sitios naturales registrados)

LIBYAN ARAB JAMAHIRIYA/JAMAHIRIYA ARABE LIBYENNE/
JAMAHIRIYA ARABE LIBIA
(No natural sites inscribed/Pas de biens naturels inscrits sur la liste/
No hay sitios naturales registrados)

LITHUANIA/LITUANIE/LITUANIA
(No natural sites inscribed/Pas de biens naturels inscrits sur la liste/
No hay sitios naturales registrados)

LUXEMBOURG/LUXEMBURGO
(No natural sites inscribed/Pas de biens naturels inscrits sur la liste/
No hay sitios naturales registrados)

MACEDONIA (FORMER YUGOSLAV REPUBLIC)/
MACEDOINE (EX-REPUBLIQUE YOUGOSLAVE DE)/
MACEDONIA (EX-REPUBLICA DE YUGOSLAVIA)

Ohrid	41°06'N/20°44'E	38,000	1979

MADAGASCAR

Réserve naturelle intégrale de Bemaraha	18°40'S/44°46'E	152,000	1990

MALAWI

Lake Malawi National Park	14°02'S/34°53'E	9,400	1984

MALAYSIA/MALAISIE/MALASIA

(No natural sites inscribed/Pas de biens naturels inscrits sur la liste/
No hay sitios naturales registrados)

MALDIVES/MALDIVAS

(No natural sites inscribed/Pas de biens naturels inscrits sur la liste/
No hay sitios naturales registrados)

MALI

Falaise de Bandiagara	14°23'N/3°25'W	400,000	1989

MALTA/MALTE

(No natural sites inscribed/Pas de biens naturels inscrits sur la liste/
No hay sitios naturales registrados)

MAURITANIA/MAURITANIE

Parc national du Banc d'Arguin	20°36'N/16°23'W	1,200,000	1989

MEXICO/MEXIQUE

Sian Ka'an Biosphere Reserve	19°35'N/87°44'W	528,000	1987

MONACO

(No natural sites inscribed/Pas de biens naturels inscrits sur la liste/
No hay sitios naturales registrados)

MONGOLIA/MONGOLIE

(No natural sites inscribed/Pas de biens naturels inscrits sur la liste/
No hay sitios naturales registrados)

MOROCCO/MAROC/MARRUECOS

(No natural sites inscribed/Pas de biens naturels inscrits sur la liste/
No hay sitios naturales registrados)

MOZAMBIQUE

(No natural sites inscribed/Pas de biens naturels inscrits sur la liste/
No hay sitios naturales registrados)

NEPAL

Royal Chitwan National Park	27°28'N/84°20'E	93,200	1984
Sagarmatha National Park	27°56'N/86°48'E	114,800	1979

NETHERLANDS/PAYS-BAS/PAISES BAJOS

(No natural sites inscribed/Pas de biens naturels inscrits sur la liste/
No hay sitios naturales registrados)

NEW ZEALAND/NOUVELLE-ZELANDE/ NUEVA ZELANDIA

South West New Zealand (Te Wahipounamu)	44°45'S/168°33'E	2,600,000	1990
Tongariro National Park	39°11'S/175°35'E	76,504	1990

NICARAGUA

(No natural sites inscribed/Pas de biens naturels inscrits sur la liste/
No hay sitios naturales registrados)

NIGER

Réserve de l'Aïr et Ténéré	18°40'N/8°30'E	7,736,000	1991

NIGERIA

(No natural sites inscribed/Pas de biens naturels inscrits sur la liste/
No hay sitios naturales registrados)

NORWAY/NORVEGE/NORUEGA

(No natural sites inscribed/Pas de biens naturels inscrits sur la liste/
No hay sitios naturales registrados)

OMAN

(No natural sites inscribed/Pas de biens naturels inscrits sur la liste/
No hay sitios naturales registrados)

PAKISTAN

(No natural sites inscribed/Pas de biens naturels inscrits sur la liste/
No hay sitios naturales registrados)

PANAMA

Darién National Park	7°52'N/77°47'W	597,000	1981
La Amistad International Park	9°23'N/83°14'W	207,000	1990

PARAGUAY

(No natural sites inscribed/Pas de biens naturels inscrits sur la liste/
No hay sitios naturales registrados)

PERU/PEROU

Huascarán National Park	9°45'S/77°28'W	340,000	1985
Manu National Park	12°11'S/71°47'W	1,532,806	1987
Río Abiseo National Park	7°23'S/77°02'W	274,520	1990
Santuario Histórico de Machu Picchu	13°12'S/72°35'W	32,592	1983

PHILIPPINES/FILIPINAS

(No natural sites inscribed/Pas de biens naturels inscrits sur la liste/
No hay sitios naturales registrados)

POLAND/POLOGNE/POLONIA

Bialowieza National Park	52°46'N/23°52'E	5,316	1979

PORTUGAL

(No natural sites inscribed/Pas de biens naturels inscrits sur la liste/
No hay sitios naturales registrados)

QATAR

(No natural sites inscribed/Pas de biens naturels inscrits sur la liste/
No hay sitios naturales registrados)

ROMANIA/ROUMANIE/RUMANIA

Danube Delta Biosphere Reserve	45°00'N/28°50'E	547,000	1991

RUSSIAN FEDERATION/FEDERATION DE RUSSIE/ FEDERACION DE RUSIA

(No natural sites inscribed/Pas de biens naturels inscrits sur la liste/
No hay sitios naturales registrados)

SAINT KITTS AND NEVIS/SAINT-KITTS-ET-NEVIS/ SAINT KITTS Y NEVIS

(No natural sites inscribed/Pas de biens naturels inscrits sur la liste/
No hay sitios naturales registrados)

SAINT LUCIA/SAINTE-LUCIE/SANTA LUCIA

(No natural sites inscribed/Pas de biens naturels inscrits sur la liste/
No hay sitios naturales registrados)

SAN MARINO/SAINT-MARIN

(No natural sites inscribed/Pas de biens naturels inscrits sur la liste/
No hay sitios naturales registrados)

SAUDI ARABIA/ARABIE SAOUDITE/ARABIA SAUDITA

(No natural sites inscribed/Pas de biens naturels inscrits sur la liste/
No hay sitios naturales registrados)

SENEGAL

Sanctuaire national d'oiseaux du Djoudj	16°30'N/16°10'W	16,000	1981
Niokolo-Koba National Park	12°55'N/12°58'W	913,000	1981

SEYCHELLES

Aldabra Atoll	9°25'S/46°25'E	35,000	1982
Vallée de Mai Nature Reserve	4°19'S/55°44'E	18	1983

SLOVAKIA/SLOVAQUIE/ESLOVAQUIA

(No natural sites inscribed/Pas de biens naturels inscrits sur la liste/
No hay sitios naturales registrados)

SLOVENIA/SLOVENIE/ESLOVENIA

Skocjan Caves	45°40'N/14°00'E	200	1986

SOLOMON ISLANDS/ILES SALOMON/ISLAS SALOMON

(No natural sites inscribed/Pas de biens naturels inscrits sur la liste/
No hay sitios naturales registrados)

SPAIN/ESPAGNE/ESPAÑA

Garajonay National Park	28°08'N/17°14'W	3,984	1986

SRI LANKA

Sinharaja National Heritage Wilderness Area	6°23'N/80°28'E	8,864	1988

SUDAN/SOUDAN

(No natural sites inscribed/Pas de biens naturels inscrits sur la liste/
No hay sitios naturales registrados)

SWEDEN/SUEDE/SUECIA

(No natural sites inscribed/Pas de biens naturels inscrits sur la liste/
No hay sitios naturales registrados)

SWITZERLAND/SUISSE/SUIZA

(No natural sites inscribed/Pas de biens naturels inscrits sur la liste/
No hay sitios naturales registrados)

SYRIAN ARAB REPUBLIC/REPUBLIQUE ARABE SYRIENNE/REPUBLICA ARABE SIRIA

(No natural sites inscribed/Pas de biens naturels inscrits sur la liste/
No hay sitios naturales registrados)

TAJIKISTAN/TADJIKISTAN/TAYIKISTAN

(No natural sites inscribed/Pas de biens naturels inscrits sur la liste/
   No hay sitios naturales registrados)

TANZANIA, UNITED REPUBLIC OF/REPUBLIQUE-UNIE DE TANZANIE/REPUBLICA UNIDA DE TANZANIA

Mt Kilimanjaro National Park	3°05'S/37°17'E	75,575	1987
Ngorongoro Conservation Area	3°00'S/35°23'E	828,800	1979
Selous Game Reserve	8°46'S/37°25'E	5,000,000	1982
Serengeti National Park	2°25'S/34°38'E	1,476,300	1981

THAILAND/THAÏLANDE/TAILANDIA

Thung Yai - Huai Kha Kaeng Wildlife Sanctuary	15°40'N/99°05'E	622,200	1991

TUNISIA/TUNISIE/TUNEZ

Parc national de l'Ichkeul	37°10'N/9°40'E	12,600	1980

TURKEY/TURQUIE/TURQUIA

Göreme National Park	38°26'N/34°54'E	9,576	1985
Hierapolis-Pamukkale	37°57'N/28°50'E	?	1988

UGANDA/OUGANDA

(No natural sites inscribed/Pas de biens naturels inscrits sur la liste/
   No hay sitios naturales registrados)

UKRAINE/UCRANIA

(No natural sites inscribed/Pas de biens naturels inscrits sur la liste/
   No hay sitios naturales registrados)

UNITED KINGDOM/ROYAUME-UNI/REINO UNIDO

Giant's Causeway	55°15'N/6°31'W	70	1986
Henderson Island	24°22'S/128°20'W	3,700	1988
St. Kilda	57°49'N/8°34'W	853	1986

UNITED STATES/ETATS-UNIS D'AMERIQUE/ ESTADOS UNIDOS DE AMERICA

Everglades National Park	25°23'N/80°55'W	592,920	1979
Grand Canyon National Park	36°14'N/112°46'W	493,270	1979
Great Smoky Mountain National Park	35°37'N/83°53'W	209,000	1983
Hawaii Volcanoes National Park	19°22'N/155°20'W	92,934	1987
Kluane-Wrangell/St Elias (U.S. section)	60°40'N/139°00'W	8,881,121	1979
Mammoth Cave National Park	37°12'N/86°08'W	21,191	1981
Olympic National Park	47°50'N/123°55'W	362,848	1981
Redwood National Park	41°27'N/124°02'W	42,400	1980
Yellowstone National Park	44°38'N/110°10'W	898,349	1978
Yosemite National Park	37°50'N/119°32'W	308,283	1984

URUGUAY

(No natural sites inscribed/Pas de biens naturels inscrits sur la liste/
   No hay sitios naturales registrados)

UZBEKISTAN/OUZBEKISTAN

(No natural sites inscribed/Pas de biens naturels inscrits sur la liste/
   No hay sitios naturales registrados)

VATICAN CITY STATE (HOLY SEE)/
SAINT-SIEGE/SANTA SEDE

(No natural sites inscribed/Pas de biens naturels inscrits sur la liste/
No hay sitios naturales registrados)

VENEZUELA

(No natural sites inscribed/Pas de biens naturels inscrits sur la liste/
No hay sitios naturales registrados)

VIET NAM

(No natural sites inscribed/Pas de biens naturels inscrits sur la liste/
No hay sitios naturales registrados)

YEMEN/YEMEN

(No natural sites inscribed/Pas de biens naturels inscrits sur la liste/
No hay sitios naturales registrados)

YUGOSLAVIA/YOUGOSLAVIE

Durmitor National Park	43°08'N/18°52'E	32,000	1980
Kotor	42°27'N/18°37'E	?	1979

ZAIRE/ZAÏRE

Parc national de la Garamba	4°13'N/29°24'E	492,000	1980
Parc national de Kahuzi-Biega	2°31'S/28°45'E	600,000	1980
Parc national de Salonga	2°10'S/21°15'E	3,600,000	1984
Parc national des Virunga	0°20'S/29°35'E	790,000	1979

ZAMBIA/ZAMBIE

Victoria Falls/Mosi-oa-Tunya (Zambia section)	17°48'S/25°55'E	3,779	1989

ZIMBABWE

Mana Pools NP, Sapi and Chewore Safari Areas	16°02'S/29°43'E	1,092,300	1984
Victoria Falls/Mosi-oa-Tunya (Zimbabwe section)	17°56'S/25°55'E	3,081	1989

Biosphere Reserves

Réserves de la Biosphère

Reservas de la Biosfera

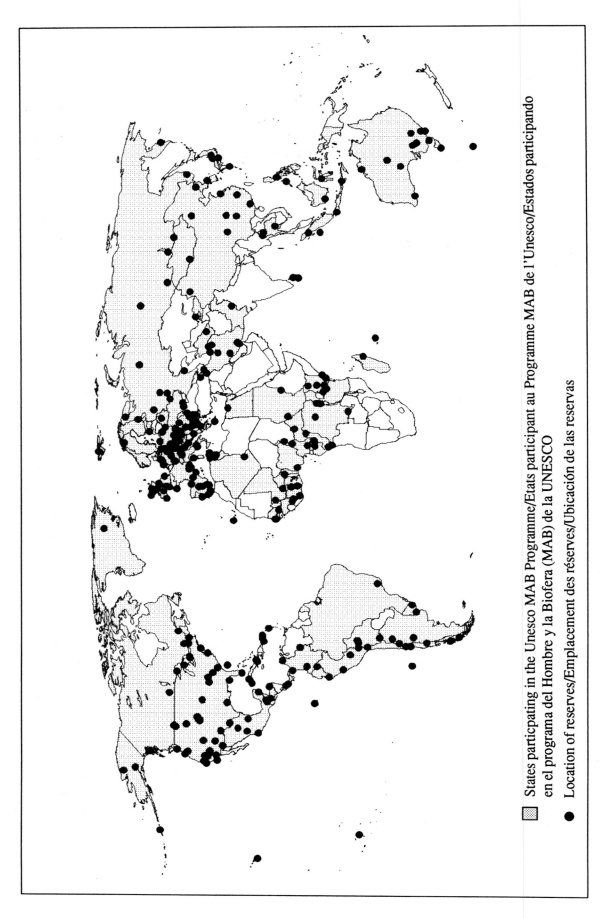

Map 2. States with Biosphere Reserves
Carte 2. Etats possédant des réserves de la biosphère
Mapa 2. Estados con Reservas de la Biosfera

☐ States particpating in the Unesco MAB Programme/Etats participant au Programme MAB de l'Unesco/Estados participando en el programa del Hombre y la Biofera (MAB) de la UNESCO

● Location of reserves/Emplacement des réserves/Ubicación de las reservas

Biosphere Reserves

The establishment of biosphere reserves is not covered by a specific convention, but is part of an international scientific programme, the Unesco Man and the Biosphere (MAB) Programme. The objectives of the network of biosphere reserves, and the characteristics which biosphere reserves might display, are identified in various Unesco-MAB documents, including the Action Plan for Biosphere Reserves published in 1984.

Biosphere Reserves differ from the preceding types of site in that they are not exclusively designated to protect unique areas or important wetlands, but for a range of objectives which include research, monitoring, training and demonstration, as well as conservation roles. In most cases the human component is vital to the functioning of the biosphere reserve which does not necessarily hold for either World Heritage or Ramsar sites. A further fundamental difference is the stated aim of developing a biosphere reserve network representative of the world's ecosystems.

Réserves de la Biosphère

La création de réserves de la biosphère ne relève d'aucune convention mais entre dans le cadre d'un programme scientifique international, le Programme de l'UNESCO sur l'homme et la biosphère (Programme MAB). Les objectifs du réseau de réserves de la biosphère et les caractéristiques qui doivent être celle des réserves de la biosphère sont définis dans divers documents UNESCO-MAB, notamment le Plan d'action pour les réserves de la biosphère, publié en 1984.

Les réserves de la biosphère diffèrent des sites décrits précédemment en ce qu'elles ne sont pas exclusivement désignées afin de protéger des régions uniques ou des zones humides importantes mais pour toutes sortes d'autres raisons, notamment la recherche, la surveillance continue, la formation et la démonstration, sans oublier la conservation. Dans la plupart des cas, l'élément humain est vital pour le fonctionnement des réserves de la biosphère ce qui n'est pas nécessairement le cas pour les biens du patrimoine mondial ou les sites Ramsar. Autre différence fondamentale: un des objectifs fixés consiste à mettre sur pied un réseau de réserves de la biosphère représentatif des écosystèmes de la planète.

Reservas de la Biosfera

El establecimiento de reservas de la biosfera no está cubierto por ninguna convención específica, pero es parte de un programa científico internacional: el Programa de la UNESCO del Hombre y la Biosfera (MAB). Los objetivos de la red de reservas de la biosfera, y las características de las cuales que puede tener una reserva, se encuentran en varios documentos de la Unesco-MAB, entre los cuales se incluye el Plan de Acción para Reservas de la Biosfera publicado en 1984.

La diferencia fundamental entre las reservas de la biosfera y los tipos de sitios antes expuestos está en que estas no son designadas exclusivamente para proteger áreas únicas o humedales importantes, sino por una gama de objetivos, desde investigación, monitoreo, entrenamiento y demostración hasta conservación. En la mayoría de los casos el componente humano es vital para el funcionamiento de las reservas de la biosfera, lo cual no se aplica necesariamente ni en el caso de los sitios del Patrimonio Mundial o en los sitios Ramsar. Otra diferencia fundamental está en el objetivo manifiesto de desarrollar una red de reservas de la biosfera representativa de los ecosistemas del mundo.

List of Biosphere Reserves
Liste des Réserves de la Biosphère
Lista de Reservas de la Biosfera

Name of Area/Nom de l'aire/Nombre de Unidad	Latitude/longitude Latitude/longitude Latitud/longitud	Area (ha) Superficie (ha) Superficie(ha)	Year Année Año
ALGERIA/ALGERIE/ARGELIA			
Réserve de la biosphère El Kala	36°54'N/8°27'E	76,438	1990
Parc national du Tassili	24°55'N/8°40'E	7,200,000	1986
ARGENTINA/ARGENTINE			
Parque Costero del Sur	35°00'S/57°15'W	30,000	1984
Reserva de la Biosfera "San Guillermo"	29°10'S/69°20'W	981,460	1980
Reserva de la Biosfera de Pozuelos	22°21'S/65°59'W	400,000	1990
Reserva Ecológica de Ñacuñán	34°03'S/67°58'W	11,900	1986
Reserva Natural de Vida Silvestre "Laguna Blanca"	26°45'S/67°05'W	981,620	1982
AUSTRALIA/AUSTRALIE			
Croajingolong	37°37'S/149°29'E	101,000	1977
Danggali Conservation Park	33°17'S/140°46'E	253,230	1977
Fitzgerald River National Park	34°04'S/119°35'E	242,727	1978
Hattah-Kulkyne NP & Murray-Kulkyne Park	34°35'S/142°32'E	49,500	1981
Kosciusko National Park	36°10'S/148°28'E	625,525	1977
Macquarie Island Nature Reserve	54°38'S/158°53'E	12,785	1977
Prince Regent River Nature Reserve	15°30'S/125°15'E	633,825	1977
Southwest National Park	43°09'S/146°11'E	403,240	1977
Uluru (Ayers Rock-Mount Olga) National Park	24°26'S/131°00'E	132,550	1977
Unnamed Conservation Park of South Australia	29°08'S/130°00'E	2,132,600	1977
Wilson's Promontory National Park	39°00'S/146°25'E	49,000	1981
Yathong Nature Reserve	32°40'S/145°30'E	107,241	1977
AUSTRIA/AUTRICHE			
Gossenkollesee	47°14'N/1°01'E	100	1977
Gurgler Kamm	46°51'N/11°04'E	1,500	1977
Lobau Reserve	48°10'N/16°32'E	1,000	1977
Neusiedler See-Österreichischer Teil	47°48'N/16°46'E	25,000	1977
BELARUS			
Berezinskiy Zapovednik	54°07'N/28°15'E	76,201	1978
BENIN			
Reserve de la biosphère de la Pendjari	11°00'N/1°30'E	880,000	1986
BOLIVIA/BOLIVIE			
Estación Biológica Beni	14°38'S/66°18'W	135,000	1986
Parque Nacional Pilón-Lajas	15°00'S/67°20'W	100,000	1977
Reserva Nacional de Fauna "Ulla Ulla"	15°02'S/69°10'W	200,000	1977

BRAZIL/BRESIL/BRASIL

Reserva da Biósfera da Mata Atlântica	?/?	4,936,825	1992

BULGARIA/BULGARIE

Parc national Steneto	42°48'N/24°40'E	2,889	1977
Réserve Alibotouche	41°25'N/23°32'E	1,628	1977
Réserve Bistrichko Branichté	42°35'N/23°15'E	1,177	1977
Réserve Boatione	42°52'N/24°20'E	1,281	1977
Réserve Djendema	42°47'N/24°45'E	1,775	1977
Réserve Doupkata	41°50'N/24°15'E	1,210	1977
Réserve Doupki-Djindjiritza	44°48'N/23°25'E	2,873	1977
Réserve Kamtchia	43°02'N/27°50'E	842	1977
Réserve Koupéna	42°05'N/24°20'E	1,084	1977
Réserve Mantaritza	41°58'N/24°02'E	576	1977
Réserve Maritchini ezera	42°14'N/23°35'E	1,510	1977
Réserve Ouzounboudjak	42°00'N/27°45'E	2,575	1977
Réserve Parangalitsa	42°15'N/23°15'E	1,509	1977
Réserve Srébarna	44°05'N/27°07'E	600	1977
Réserve Tchervenata sténa	41°52'N/24°45'E	812	1977
Réserve Tchoupréné	43°43'N/22°30'E	1,440	1977
Réserve Tsaritchina	42°50'N/24°30'E	1,420	1977

BURKINA FASO

Forêt classée de la mare aux Hippopotames	11°38'N/4°08'W	19,200	1986

CAMEROON/CAMEROUN/CAMERUN

Parc national de la Benoué	8°25'N/13°48'E	180,000	1981
Parc national de Waza	11°15'N/14°44'E	170,000	1979
Réserve forestière et de faune du Dja	3°06'N/13°00'E	500,000	1981

CANADA

Long Point Biosphere Reserve	43°35'N/80°20'W	27,000	1986
Mont St. Hilaire	45°33'N/75°10'W	5,550	1978
Niagara Escarpment Biosphere Reserve	43°37'N/79°56'W	207,240	1990
Riding Mountain Biosphere Reserve	50°46'N/100°18'W	297,591	1986
Réserve de la biosphère de Charlevoix	47°40'N/70°33'W	460,000	1988
Waterton Lakes National Park	49°06'N/113°55'W	52,597	1979

CENTRAL AFRICAN REPUBLIC/REPUBLIQUE CENTRAFRICAINE/REPUBLICA CENTROAFRICANA

Aire de conservation de Bamingui-Bangoran	7°35'N/19°38'E	1,622,000	1979
Forêt de Basse-Lobaye	3°40'N/17°50'E	18,200	1977

CHILE/CHILI

Parque Nacional Fray Jorge	31°30'S/71°06'W	14,074	1977
Parque Nacional Juan Fernández	33°41'S/79°47'W	9,290	1977
Parque Nacional Laguna San Rafael	47°08'S/74°08'W	1,742,448	1979
Parque Nacional Lauca	18°11'S/69°13'W	358,312	1981
Parque Nacional Torres del Paine	50°14'S/74°00'W	184,414	1978
Reserva de la Biósfera Araucarias	38°40'S/71°42'W	81,000	1983
Reserva de la Biósfera La Campana-Peñuelas	33°10'S/71°32'W	17,095	1984

CHINA/CHINE

Bogdhad Mountain Biosphere Reserve	44°00'N/83°00'E	217,000	1990
Changbai Mountain Nature Reserve	42°04'N/127°58'E	217,235	1979
Dinghu Nature Reserve	23°10'N/112°34'E	1,200	1979
Fanjingshan Mountain Biosphere Reserve	27°55'N/108°47'E	41,533	1986
Fujian Wuyishan Nature Reserve	27°45'N/117°38'E	56,527	1987

Shennongjia	31°29'N/110°19'E	147,467	1990
Wolong Nature Reserve	31°05'N/103°08'E	207,210	1979
Xilin Gol Natural Steppe Protected Area	43°34'N/116°22'E	1,078,600	1987
Yancheng	?/?	280,000	1992

COLOMBIA/COLOMBIE

Cinturón Andino Cluster Biosphere Reserve	2°48'N/75°57'W	855,000	1979
El Tuparro Nature Reserve	5°17'N/68°31'W	928,125	1979
Sierra Nevada de Santa Marta (incl. Tayrona NP)	11°18'N/74°10'W	731,250	1979

CONGO

Parc national d'Odzala	0°50'N/14°53'E	110,000	1977
Réserve de la biosphère de Dimonika	4°10'S/12°25'E	62,000	1988

COSTA RICA

Cordillera Volcánica Central	10°03'N/84°00'W	144,363	1988
Reserva de la Biósfera de la Amistad	9°23'N/83°22'W	584,592	1982

CROATIA/CROATIE/CROACIA

Velebit Mountain	44°30'N/15°23'E	150,000	1977

CUBA

Baconao	20°00'N/75°31'W	84,600	1987
Cuchillas del Toa	20°26'N/74°49'W	127,500	1987
Península de Guanahacabibes	21°52'N/84°34'W	101,500	1987
Sierra del Rosario	22°50'N/82°56'W	10,000	1984

CZECH REPUBLIC/REPUBLIQUE TCHEQUE/ REPUBLICA CHECA

Krivoklátsko Protected Landscape Area	50°02'N/13°55'E	62,792	1977
Krkonose Biosphere Reserve	?/?	54,787	1992
Palava Protected Landscape Area	48°50'N/16°45'E	8,017	1986
Sumava Biosphere Reserve	49°00'N/13°50'E	167,117	1990
Trebon Basin Protected Landscape Area	49°00'N/14°50'E	70,000	1977

CÔTE D'IVOIRE

Parc national de la Comoé	8°35'N/3°33'W	1,150,000	1983
Parc national de Taï	5°41'N/7°40'W	330,000	1977

DENMARK/DANEMARK/DINAMARCA

North-east Greenland National Park	77°00'N/11°39'W	70,000,000	1977

ECUADOR/EQUATEUR

Archipiélago de Colón (Galápagos)	0°02'N/90°39'W	766,514	1984
Reserva de la Biósfera de Yasuni	0°43'S/76°02'W	679,730	1989

EGYPT/EGYPTE/EGIPTO

Omayed Experimental Research Area	30°45'N/29°12'E	1,000	1981

ESTONIA/ESTONIE

West Estonia Archipelago Biosphere Reserve	58°30'N/22°50'E	1,560,000	1990

FINLAND/FINLANDE/FINLANDIA

Northern Karelian	?/?	350,000	1992

FRANCE/FRANCIA

Atoll de Taiaro	15°42'S/144°34'W	2,000	1977

Archipel de la Guadeloupe	?/?	69,000	1992
Mont Ventoux	44°09'N/5°16'E	72,956	1990
Réserve de la biosphère d'Iroise	48°24'N/4°58'W	21,400	1988
Réserve de la biosphère de la Vallée du Fango	42°34'N/8°46'E	25,110	1977
Réserve de la biosphère des Cévennes	44.°083/1°40'E	323,000	1984
Réserve de la biosphère des Vosges du Nord	48°58'N/7°36'E	120,000	1988
Réserve nationale de la biosphère de Camargue	43°30'N/4°30'E	13,117	1977

GABON

Réserve naturelle intégrale d'Ipassa-Makokou	0°31'N/12°48'E	15,000	1983

GERMANY/ALLEMAGNE/ALEMANIA

Bayerischer Wald National Park	48°55'N/13°23'E	13,100	1981
Berchtesgaden Alps	47°38'N/13°00'E	46,800	1990
Middle Elbe Biosphere Reserve	51°53'N/11°59'E	43,000	1979
Pfälzerwald	?/?	179,800	1992
Rhön	50°35'N/10°05'E	130,488	1991
Rügen	54°20'N/13°39'E	22,800	1991
Schorfheide-Chorin	53°00'N/13°40'E	125,891	1990
Spreewald	51°57'N/13°54'E	47,600	1991
Vessertal - Thüringen Forest Biosphere Reserve	50°36'N/10°48'E	12,670	1979
Waddensea of Hamburg	?/?	11,700	1992
Waddensea of Lower Saxony	?/?	240,000	1992
Waddensea of Schleswig-Holstein	54°28'N/8°37'E	285,000	1990

GHANA

Bia National Park	6°35'N/3°05'W	7,770	1983

GREECE/GRECE/GRECIA

Gorge of Samaria National Park	35°16'N/23°56'E	4,840	1981
Mount Olympus National Park	40°05'N/22°22'E	4,000	1981

GUATEMALA

Maya	17°00'N/90°30'W	1,000,000	1990
Sierra de las Minas	?/?	236,300	1992

GUINEA/GUINEE

Réserve de la biosphère des Monts Nimba	7°18'N/10°35'W	17,130	1980
Réserve de la biosphère du Massif du Ziama	8°20'N/9°20'W	116,170	1980

HONDURAS

Río Plátano Biosphere Reserve	15°50'N/85°00'W	500,000	1980

HUNGARY/HONGRIE/HUNGRIA

Aggtelek Biosphere Reserve	48°30'N/20°39'E	19,247	1979
Hortobágy National Park	47°20'N/21°08'E	52,000	1979
Kiskunság Biosphere Reserve	46°54'N/19°22'E	22,095	1979
Lake Fertö Biosphere Reserve	47°00'N/16°43'E	12,542	1979
Pilis Biosphere Reserve	47°45'N/18°49'E	23,000	1980

INDONESIA/INDONESIE

Cibodas Biosphere Reserve (Gunung Gede-Pangrango)	7°00'S/106°58'E	14,000	1977
Gunung Leuser National Park	2°53'N/9823'E	946,400	1981
Komodo National Park	8°37'S/119°35'E	30,000	1977
Lore Lindu National Park	1°40'S/120°10'E	231,000	1977
Siberut Nature Reserve	1°22'S/98°56'E	56,000	1981
Tanjung Puting National Park	2°58'S/112°02'E	205,000	1977

IRAN, ISLAMIC REPUBLIC OF/
IRAN, REPUBIQUE ISLAMIQUE D'/
IRAN, REPUBLICA ISLAMICA DEL

Arasbaran Protected Area	39°07'N/47°01'E	52,000	1976
Arjan Protected Area	30°00'N/52°12'E	65,750	1976
Geno Protected Area	27°30'N/56°21'E	49,000	1976
Golestan National Park	37°31'N/56°35'E	125,895	1976
Hara Protected Area	26°45'N/55°40'E	85,686	1976
Kavir National Park	34°16'N/53°07'E	700,000	1976
Lake Oromeeh National Park	38°06'N/45°15'E	462,600	1976
Miankaleh Protected Area	36°57'N/54°01'E	68,800	1976
Touran Protected Area	36°25'N/57°05'E	1,000,000	1976

IRELAND/IRLANDE/IRLANDA

Killarney National Park	52°01'N/9°35'W	8,308	1982
North Bull Island	53°17'N/6°05'W	500	1981

ITALY/ITALIE/ITALIA

Collemeluccio-Montedimezzo	41°40'N/14°15'E	478	1977
Forêt Domaniale du Circeo	41°20'N/13°35'E	3,260	1977
Parc marin Miramare	45°42'N/13°42'E	60	1979

JAPAN/JAPON

Mount Hakusan	36°10'N/136°50'E	48,000	1980
Mount Odaigahara & Mount Omine	34°10'N/136°00'E	36,000	1980
Shiga Highland	36°43'N/138°30'E	13,000	1980
Yakushima Island	30°20'N/130°30'E	19,000	1980

KENYA/KENIA

Amboseli National Park	2°40'S/37°15'E	483,200	1990
Kiunga Marine National Reserve	1°59'S/41°23'E	60,000	1980
Malindi-Watamu Biosphere Reserve	3°20'S/40°04'E	19,600	1979
Mount Kenya Biosphere Reserve	0°10'S/37°20'E	71,759	1978
Mount Kulal Biosphere Reserve	2°55'N/37°00'E	700,000	1978

KOREA, DEMOCRATIC PEOPLE'S REPUBLIC OF/
REP. POPULAIRE DÉMOCRATIQUE DE COREE/
REPUBLICA POPULAR DEMOCRATICA DE COREA

Mount Paekdu Biosphere Reserve	41°56'N/128°10'E	132,000	1989

KOREA, REPUBLIC OF/REPUBLIQUE DE COREE/
REPUBLICA DE COREA

Mount Sorak Biosphere Reserve	28°09'N/128°24'E	37,430	1982

KYRGYZSTAN/KIRGHIZISTAN/KIRGUISTAN

Chatkal Mountains Biosphere Reserve	42°00'N/71°00'E	71,400	1978

MADAGASCAR

Réserve de la biosphère du Mananara Nord	16°10'S/49°30'E	140,000	1990

MALI/MALI

Parc national de la Boucle du Baoulé	14°04'N/8°54'W	771,000	1982

MAURITIUS/MAURICE/MAURICIO

Macchabee-Bel Ombre Nature Reserve	20°25'S/57°26'E	3,594	1977

MEXICO/MEXIQUE

Montes Azules	16°31'N/91°08'W	331,200	1979
Reserva de la Biósfera "El Cielo"	23°10'N/99°16'W	144,530	1986
Reserva de la Biósfera de Sian Ka'an	19°35'N/87°44'W	528,147	1986
Reserva de la Biósfera Sierra de Manantlán	19°35'N/104°09'W	139,577	1988
Reserva de la Michilía	23°27'N/104°15'W	42,000	1977
Reserva de Mapimí	26°41'N/103°48'W	103,000	1977

MONGOLIA/MONGOLIE

Great Gobi National Park	44°05'N/97°20'E	5,300,000	1990

NETHERLANDS/PAYS-BAS/PAISES BAJOS

Waddensea Area	53°13'N/5°59'E	260,000	1986

NIGERIA/NIGERIA

Omo Strict Natural Reserve	6°30'N/4°15'E	460	1977

NORWAY/NORVEGE/NORUEGA

North-east Svalbard Nature Reserve	79°45'N/16°35'E	1,555,000	1976

PAKISTAN

Lal Suhanra National Park	29°30'N/71°50'E	31,355	1977

PANAMA

Parque Nacional Fronterizo Darién	7°52'N/77°47'W	597,000	1983

PERU/PEROU

Reserva de Huascarán	9°45'S/77°28'W	399,239	1977
Reserva del Manu	12°11'S/71°47'W	1,881,200	1977
Reserva del Noroeste	4°53'S/80°15'W	226,300	1977

PHILIPPINES/FILIPINAS

Palawan Biosphere Reserve	10°38'N/119°38'E	1,150,800	1990
Puerto Galera Biosphere Reserve	14°00'N/121°49'E	23,545	1977

POLAND/POLOGNE/POLONIA

Babia Gora National Park	49°34'N/19°32'E	1,741	1976
Bialowieza National Park	52°46'N/23°52'E	5,316	1976
East Carpathian/East Beskid	?/?	108,924	1992
Karkonosze Biosphere Reserve	?/?	11,128	1992
Lukajno Lake Reserve	53°49'N/21°38'E	710	1976
Slowinski National Park	54°41'N/17°17'E	18,069	1976
Tatra Biosphere Reserve	?/?	17,906	1992

PORTUGAL

Paul do Boquilobo Biosphere Reserve	39°24'N/9°28'W	395	1981

ROMANIA/ROUMANIE/RUMANIA

Danube Delta Biosphere Reserve	?/?	591,200	1992
Pietrosul Mare Nature Reserve	47°40'N/25°00'E	3,068	1979
Retezat National Park	45°25'N/22°45'E	20,000	1979

RUSSIAN FEDERATION/FEDERATION DE RUSSIE/ FEDERACION DE RUSIA

Astrakhanskiy Zapovednik	45°56'N/48°20'E	63,400	1984
Kavkazskiy Zapovednik	40°15'N/43°47'E	263,477	1978

Kronotskiy Zapovednik	54°38'N/160°53'E	1,099,000	1984
Lake Baikal Region Biosphere Reserve	51°50'N/105°50'E	559,100	1986
Laplandskiy Zapovednik	68°00'N/33°00'E	278,400	1984
Oka River Valley Biosphere Reserve	54°43'N/40°50'W	45,845	1978
Pechoro-Ilychskiy Zapovednik	62°29'N/58°14'E	721,322	1984
Sayano-Shushenskiy Zapovednik	52°04'N/91°51'E	389,570	1984
Sikhote-Alin Zapovednik	45°16'N/136°11'E	340,200	1978
Sokhondinskiy Zapovednik	49°44'N/110°58'E	211,000	1984
Tsentral'nochernozem Zapovednik	51°00'N/36°40'E	4,795	1978
Tsentral'nolesnoy Zapovednik	57°00'N/33°00'E	21,348	1985
Tzentralnosibirskii Biosphere Reserve	62°05'N/88°23'E	5,000,000	1986
Voronezhskiy Zapovednik	52°00'N/39°41'E	31,053	1984

RWANDA

Parc national des Volcans	1°28'S/29°33'E	15,065	1983

SENEGAL

Delta du Saloum	13°45'N/16°38'W	180,000	1980
Forêt classée de Samba Dia	14°08'N/16°45'W	756	1979
Parc national du Niokolo-Koba	12°55'N/12°58'W	913,000	1981

SLOVAKIA/SLOVAQUIE/ESLOVAQUIA

East Carpathian Biosphere Reserve	?/?	40,601	1992
Polana Biosphere Reserve	48°39'N/19°29'E	20,079	1990
Slovensky Kras Protected Landscape Area	48°35'N/20°40'E	36,165	1977
Tatra Biosphere Reserve	?/?	105,660	1992

SPAIN/ESPAGNE/ESPAÑA

Cuenca Alta del Río Manzanares	?/?	101,300	1992
Las Sierras de Cazorla y Segura Biosphere Reserve	37°55'N/3°00'W	190,000	1983
Parque Natural del Montseny	41°47'N/6°03'E	17,372	1978
Reserva de Grazalema	36°35'N/5°26'W	32,210	1977
Reserva de la Biósfera de Doñana	37°00'N/6°30'W	77,260	1980
Reserva de la Biósfera de la Mancha Húmeda	39°16'N/3°24'E	25,000	1980
Reserva de la Biósfera de las Marismas del Odiel	37°20'N/6°58'W	8,728	1983
Reserva de la Biósfera de Urdaibai	43°20'N/2°41'W	22,500	1984
Reserva de la Biósfera del Canal y los Tiles	28°40'N/17°40'W	511	1983
Reserva de la Biósfera Sierra Nevada	37°05'N/3°08'W	190,000	1986
Reserva de Ordesa-Vinamala	42°45'N/0°10'E	51,396	1977

SRI LANKA

Hurulu Forest Reserve	8°13'N/80°51'E	512	1977
Sinharaja Forest Reserve	6°23'N/80°28'E	8,864	1978

SUDAN/SOUDAN

Dinder National Park	12°17'N/35°29'E	650,000	1979
Radom National Park	9°50'N/24°45'E	1,250,970	1979

SWEDEN/SUEDE/SUECIA

Lake Torne Area	68°25'N/19°00'E	96,000	1986

SWITZERLAND/SUISSE/SUIZA

Parc national suisse	46°40'N/10°10'E	16,870	1979

TANZANIA, UNITED REPUBLIC OF/REPUBLIQUE-UNIE DE TANZANIE/REPUBLICA UNIDA DE TANZANIA

Lake Manyara National Park	3°30'S/35°45'E	32,500	1981
Serengeti-Ngorongoro Biosphere Reserve	2°25'S/34°38'E	2,305,100	1981

THAÏLAND/THAÏLANDE/TAILANDIA

Hauy Tak Teak Reserve	18°30'N/100°00'E	4,700	1977
Mae Sa-Kog Ma Reserve	18°53'N/98°53'E	14,200	1977
Sakaerat Environmental Research Station	14°30'N/101°55'E	7,200	1976

TUNISIA/TUNISIE/TUNEZ

Parc national de Djebel Bou-Hedma	34°40'N/9°38'E	11,625	1977
Parc national de Djebel Chambi	35°13'N/8°43'E	6,000	1977
Parc national de l'Ichkeul	37°10'N/9°40'E	10,770	1977
Parc national des Iles Zembra et Zembretta	37°06'N/10°48'E	4,030	1977

TURKMENISTAN

Repetek Zapovednik	38°16'N/63°13'E	34,600	1978

UGANDA/OUGANDA

Queen Elizabeth (Rwenzori) National Park	00°2'S/29°55'E	220,000	1979

UKRAINE/UCRANIA

Askaniya-Nova Zapovednik	46°27'N/33°53'E	33,307	1985
Carpathian	?/?	38,930	1992
Chernomorskiy Zapovednik	46°12'N/32°00'E	87,348	1984

UNITED KINGDOM/ROYAUME-UNI/REINO UNIDO

Beinn Eighe National Nature Reserve	57°35'N/5°24'W	4,800	1976
Braunton Burrows National Nature Reserve	51°06'N/4°12'W	596	1976
Caerlaverock National Nature Reserve	54°52'N/3°30'W	5,501	1976
Cairnsmore of Fleet National Nature Reserve	54°58'N/4°17'W	1,922	1976
Claish Moss National Nature Reserve	56°00'N/5°45'W	480	1977
Dyfi National Nature Reserve	52°32'N/4°00'W	1,589	1976
Isle of Rhum National Nature Reserve	57°00'N/6°30'W	10,560	1976
Loch Druidibeg National Nature Reserve	57°20'N/7°15'W	1,658	1976
Moor House-Upper Teesdale Biosphere Reserve	54°56'N/2°45'W	7,399	1976
North Norfolk Coast Biosphere Reserve	52°57'N/0°43'E	5,497	1976
Silver Flowe-Merrick Kells Biosphere Reserve	55°06'N/4°30'W	3,088	1976
St. Kilda National Nature Reserve	57°49'N/8°34'W	842	1976
Taynish National Nature Reserve	56°00'N/5°38'W	326	1977

UNITED STATES//ETATS-UNIS D'AMERIQUE/ ESTADOS UNIDOS DE AMERICA

Aleutian Islands National Wildlife Refuge	53°53'N/167°53'W	1,100,943	1976
Beaver Creek Experimental Watershed	34°32'N/111°59'W	111,300	1976
Big Bend National Park	29°30'N/102°30'W	283,247	1976
Big Thicket National Preserve	30°31'N/94°19'W	34,217	1981
California Coast Ranges Biosphere Reserve	38°30'N/122°30'W	62,098	1983
Carolinian-South Atlantic Biosphere Reserve	30°30'N/78°47'W	125,545	1986
Cascade Head Expt. Forest & Scenic Research Area	45°02'N/123°52'W	7,051	1976
Central California Coast Biosphere Reserve	37°30'N/123°00'	543,385	1988
Central Gulf Coastal Plain Biosphere Reserve	29°44'N/84°58'W	72,964	1983
Central Plains Experimental Range	40°50'N/104°45'W	6,210	1976
Champlain-Adirondak Biosphere Reserve	44°00'N/74°23'W	3,990,000	1989
Channel Islands Biosphere Reserve	33°46'N/119°44'W	479,652	1976
Coram Experimental Forest	48°24'N/113°59'W	3,019	1976
Denali National Park and Biosphere Reserve	63°20'N/150°30'W	2,441,295	1976
Desert Experimental Range	38°40'N/113°45'W	22,513	1976
Everglades National Park (with Fort Jefferson NM)	25°23'N/80°55'W	585,867	1976
Fraser Experimental Forest	39°54'N/105°53'W	9,328	1976
Glacier Bay-Admiralty Island Biosphere Reserve	58°00'N/135°00'E	1,515,015	1986
Glacier National Park	48°38'N/113°53'W	410,202	1976

Guanica Commonwealth Forest Reserve	17°55'N/67°05'W	4,006	1981
H.J. Andrews Experimental Forest	44°15'N/122°10'W	6,100	1976
Hawaii Islands Biosphere Reserve	22°12'N/159°28'W	99,545	1980
Hubbard Brook Experimental Forest	43°56'N/71°45'W	3,076	1976
Isle Royale National Park	48°02'N/88°47'W	215,740	1980
Jornada Experimental Range	32°37'N/106°45'W	78,297	1976
Konza Prairie Research Natural Area	39°05'N/96°34'W	3,487	1979
Land between the lakes	36°47'N/88°03'W	1,560,000	1991
Luquillo Experimental Forest (Caribbean NF)	18°21'N/65°45'W	11,340	1976
Mammoth Cave Area	37°11'N/86°06'W	83,337	1990
Mojave and Colorado Deserts Biosphere Reserve	36°22'N/117°00'W	1,297,264	1984
New Jersey Pinelands Biosphere Reserve	39°45'N/74°45'W	445,300	1988
Niwot Ridge Biosphere Reserve	40°00'N/105°30'W	1,200	1979
Noatak National Preserve	68°00'N/160°00'W	3,035,200	1976
Olympic National Park	47°50'N/123°55'W	363,379	1976
Organ Pipe Cactus National Monument	32°00'N/112°50'W	133,278	1976
Rocky Mountain National Park	40°22'N/105°42'W	106,710	1976
San Dimas Experimental Forest	34°12'N/117°46'W	6,947	1976
San Joaquin Experimental Range	37°05'N/119°43'W	1,832	1976
Sequoia-Kings Canyon National Parks	36°45'N/118°30'W	343,000	1976
South Atlantic Coastal Plain Biosphere Reserve	33°45'N/80°47'W	6,125	1983
Southern Appalachian Biosphere Reserve	36°30'N/84°30'W	6,416,545	1988
Stanislaus-Tuolumne Experimental Forest	38°03'N/119°57'W	607	1976
The University of Michigan Biological Station	45°34'N/84°40'W	4,048	1979
The Virginia Coast Reserve	37°20'N/75°47'W	13,511	1979
Three Sisters Wilderness	44°00'N/121°50'W	80,900	1976
Virgin Islands National Park and Biosphere Reserve	18°21'N/64°44'W	6,127	1976
Yellowstone National Park	44°38'N/110°10'W	898,349	1976

URUGUAY

Bañados del Este	33°30'S/54°00'W	200,000	1976

YUGOSLAVIA/YOUGOSLAVIE

Réserve écologique du Bassin de la Rivière Tara	42°32'N/19°17'E	200,000	1976

ZAIRE/ZAÏRE

Réserve floristique de Yangambi	0°20'N/24°30'E	250,000	1976
Réserve forestière de Luki	5°35'S/13°10'E	33,000	1979
Vallée de la Lufira	10°58'S/26°55'E	14,700	1982

Wetlands of International Importance

Designated by the Contracting parties—Convention on Wetlands of International Importance especially as Waterfowl Habitat

Zones Humides d'importance internationale

Désignées par les Parties contractantes—Convention relative aux zones humides d'importance internationale, particulièrement comme habitats des oiseaux d'eau

Humedales de Importancia Internacional

Designada por las partes contratantes—Convención Relativa a los Humedales de Importancia Internacional Especialmente como Hábitat de Aves Acuáticas.

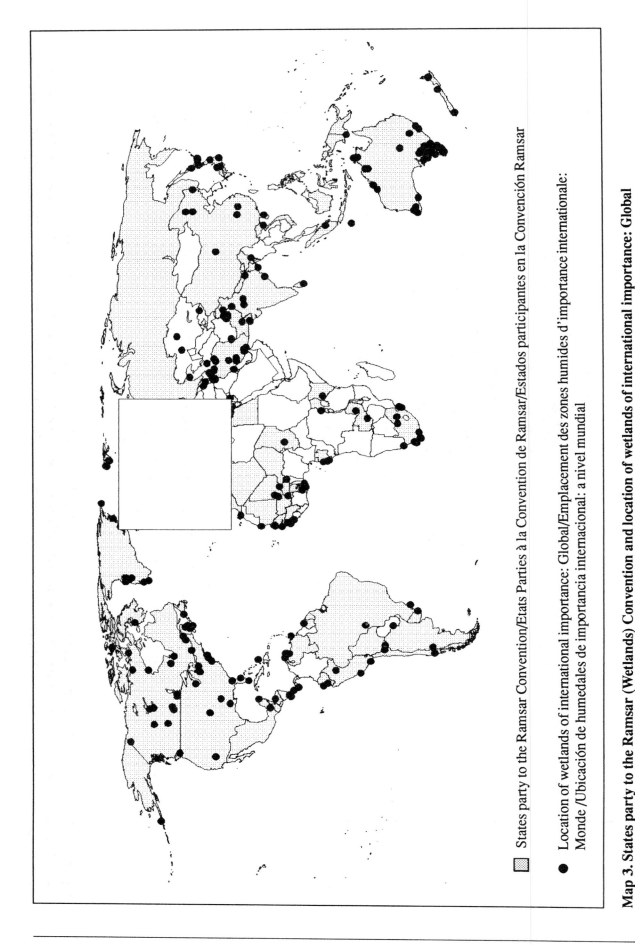

Map 3. **States party to the Ramsar (Wetlands) Convention and location of wetlands of international importance: Global**
Carte 3. **Etats Parties à la Convention de Ramsar (zones humides) et emplacement des zones humides d'importance internationale: Monde**
Mapa 3. **Estados participantes en la Convención Ramsar (de Humedales) y ubicación de humedales de importancia internacional: a nivel mundial**

⬚ States party to the Ramsar Convention/Etats Parties à la Convention de Ramsar/Estados participantes en la Convención Ramsar

● Location of wetlands of international importance: Global/Emplacement des zones humides d'importance internationale:
Monde /Ubicación de humedales de importancia internacional: a nivel mundial

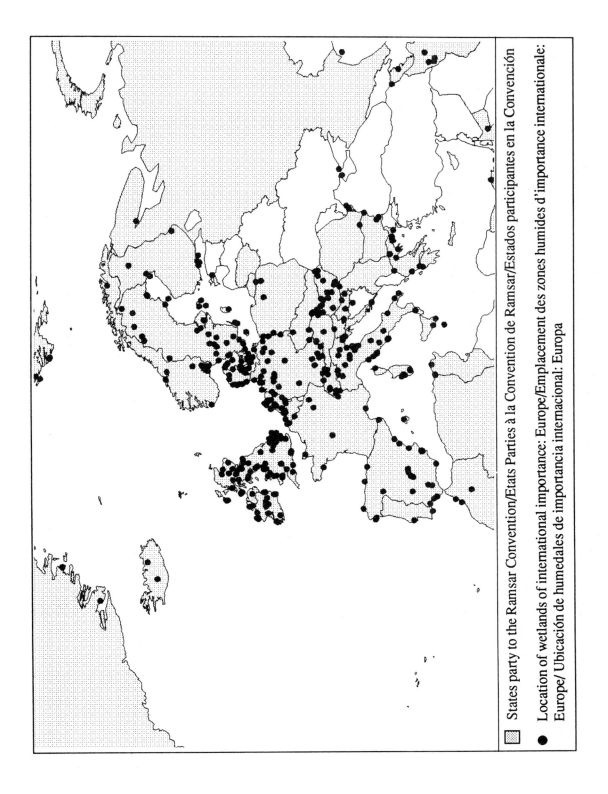

☐ States party to the Ramsar Convention/Etats Parties à la Convention de Ramsar/Estados participantes en la Convención

● Location of wetlands of international importance: Europe/Emplacement des zones humides d'importance internationale: Europe/ Ubicación de humedales de importancia internacional: Europa

Map 4. States party to the Ramsar (Wetlands) Convention and location of wetlands of international importance: Europe
Carte 4. Etats Parties à la Convention de Ramsar (zones humides) et emplacement des zones humides d'importance internationale: Europe
Mapa 4. Estados participantes en la Convención Ramsar (de Humedales) y ubicación de humedales de importancia internacional: Europa

Wetlands of International Importance (Ramsar Sites)

The *Convention on Wetlands of International Importance Especially as Waterfowl Habitat* was signed in Ramsar (Iran) in 1971, and came into force in December 1975. This Convention provides a framework for international cooperation for the conservation of wetland habitats. It places general obligations on contracting party states relating to the conservation of wetlands throughout their territories, with special obligations pertaining to those wetlands which have been designated to the List of Wetlands of International Importance.

Each State Party is obliged to list at least one site. Wetlands are defined by the convention as: areas of marsh, fen, peatland or water, whether natural or artificial, permanent or temporary, with water that is static or flowing, fresh, brackish or salt, including areas of marine waters, the depth of which at low tide does not exceed six metres.

Zones humides d'importance internationale (sites Ramsar)

La *Convention relative aux zones humides d'importance internationale, particulièrement comme habitats des oiseaux d'eau* a été signée à Ramsar (Iran), en 1971 et est entrée en vigueur en décembre 1975. Elle fournit un cadre à la coopération internationale pour la conservation des habitats contenus dans les zones humides. Les Parties contractantes à la Convention ont l'obligation générale de conserver les zones humides se trouvant sur leur territoire et, plus particulièrement, celles qui ont été inscrites sur la Liste des zones humides d'importance internationale.

Chaque Etat Partie a l'obligation d'inscrire au moins un site. La Convention définit les zones humides comme étant des étendues de marais, de fagnes, de tourbières ou d'eaux naturelles ou artificielles, permanentes ou temporaires, où l'eau est stagnante ou courante, douce, saumâtre ou salée, y compris des étendues d'eau marine dont la profondeur à marée basse n'excède pas six mètres.

Humedales de Importancia Internacional (sitios Ramsar)

La *Convención Relativa a los Humedales de Importancia Internacional Especialmente como Hábitat de Aves Acuáticas* fue firmada en Ramsar (Irán) en 1971 y se hizo vigente en Diciembre de 1975. Esta convención provee lineamentos de cooperación internacional para la conservación de humedales. Asigna obligaciones generales a los Estados contratantes con relación a la conservación de humedales a lo largo de sus territorios, con obligaciones especiales hacia aquellos humedales que han sido designados en la Lista de Humedales de Importancia Internacional.

Cada Estado está en la obligación de listar por lo menos un sitio. Los humedales están definidos por la convención como: extensiones de marismas, pantanos, turberas o aguas de régimen natural o artificial, permanentes o temporales, estancadas o corrientes, dulces, salobres o saladas, incluyendo las extensiones de agua marina cuya profundidad en marea baja no exceda de seis metros.

List of Wetlands of International Importance (Ramsar Sites)
Liste des Zones Humides d'importance internationale (sites Ramsar)
Lista de Humedales de Importancia Internacional (sitios Ramsar)

Name of Area/Nom de l'aire/ Nombre deUnidad	Latitude/longitude Latitude/longitude Latitud/longitud	Area (ha) Superficie (ha) Superficie (ha)	Year Année Año
ALGERIA/ALGERIE/ARGELIA			
Lac Oubeïra	36°50'N/008°23'E	2,200	1983
Lac Tonga	36°51'N/008°30'E	2,700	1983
ARGENTINA/ARGENTINE			
Laguna Blanca	39°02'S/070°21'W	11,250	1992
Laguna de los Pozuelos	22°20'S/066°00'W	16,224	1992
Rio Pilcomayo	25°07'S/058°02'W	55,000	1992
ARMENIA/ARMENIE			
Lake Arpi	41°03'N/043°37'E	3,139	1993
Lake Sevan	40°24'N/045°17'E	489,100	1993
AUSTRALIA/AUSTRALIE			
Apsley Marshes	41°56'S/148°12'E	940	1982
Barmah Forest	35°55'S/145°08'E	28,500	1982
Bool and Hacks Lagoons	37°08'S/140°41'E	3,200	1985
Cape Barren Island, east coast lagoons	40°22'S/148°23'E	4,230	1982
Cobourg Peninsula	11°15'S/132°15'E	220,700	1974
Coongie Lakes	27°20'S/140°00'E	1,980,000	1987
Corner Inlet	38°45'S/146°32'E	51,500	1982
Eighty-mile Beach	19°31'S/120°48'E	125,000	1990
Forrestdale and Thomsons Lakes	32°09'S/115°52'E	754	1990
Gippsland Lakes	38°00'S/147°36'E	43,046	1982
Gunbower Forest	35°49'S/144°19'E	19,450	1982
Hattah-Kulkyne Lakes	34°41'S/142°26'E	1,018	1982
Hosnie's Spring	10°28'S/105°41'E	1	1990
Jocks Lagoon	41°21'S/148°18'E	70	1982
Kakadu (Stage I)	12°40'S/132°45'E	667,000	1980
Kakadu National Park (Stage II)	12°30'S/132°30'E	692,940	1989
Kerang Wetlands	35°40'S/143°56'E	9,172	1982
Kooragang	32°51'S/151°47'E	2,206	1984
Lake Albacutya	35°46'S/141°58'E	10,700	1982
Lake Crescent	42°09'S/147°10'E	470	1982
Lake Toolibin	32°55'S/117°36'E	437	1990
Lake Warden system	33°48'S/121°56'E	2,300	1990
Lakes Argyle and Kununurra	16°20'S/128°42'E	150,000	1990
Little Waterhouse Lake	40°52'S/147°37'E	90	1982
Logan Lagoon	40°10'S/148°17'E	2,320	1982
Lower Ringarooma River	41°54'S/147°56'E	4,160	1982
Macquarie Marshes	30°45'S/147°33'E	18,143	1986
Moulting Lagoon	42°05'S/148°10'E	4,760	1982
Ord River floodplain	15°15'S/128°22'E	130,000	1990
Peel-Yalgorup system	32°49'S/115°42'E	21,000	1990

Pittwater-Orielton Lagoon	42°47'S/147°30'E	2,920	1982
Port Phillip Bay & Bellarine Peninsula	38°04'S/144°36'E	7,000	1982
Riverland	34°02'S/140°51'E	30,600	1987
Roebuck Bay	18°07'S/122°16'E	50,000	1990
Sea Elephant Conservation Area	39°45'S/144°05'E	1,730	1982
The Coorong, Lake Alexandrina & Lake Albert	35°40'S/139°00'E	140,500	1985
Towra Point	34°00'S/151°10'E	364	1984
Vasse-Wonnerup system	33°37'S/115°25'E	740	1990
Western District Lakes	38°10'S/143°31'E	30,182	1982
Western Port	38°22'S/145°17'E	52,325	1982

AUSTRIA/AUTRICHE

Donau-March-Auen	48°11'N/016°56'E	38,500	1982
Neusiedlersee, Seewinkel & Hanság	47°51'N/016°46'E	60,000	1982
Pürgschachen Moor	47°35'N/014°21'E	62	1991
Rheindelta Bodensee	47°30'N/009°37'E	1,970	1982
Sablatnigmoor	46°34'N/014°36'E	100	1992
Stauseen am Unteren Inn	48°18'N/013°16'E	870	1982
Untere Lobau	48°10'N/016°30'E	1,039	1982

AZERBAIJAN/AZERBAIDJAN/AZERBAIYAN

Kirov Bays	39°05'N/048°57'E	132,500	1976

BANGLADESH

The Sundarbans	22°03'N/089°25'E	59,600	1992

BELGIUM/BELGIQUE/BELGICA

De Ijzerbroeken te Diksmuide en Lo-Reninge	50°59'N/002°51'E	2,360	1986
Kalmthoutse Heide	51°23'N/004°28'E	2,200	1986
Marais d'Harchies	50°28'N/003°41'E	535	1986
Schorren van de Beneden Schelde	51°20'N/004°15'E	420	1986
Vlaamse Banken	51°10'N/002°44'E	1,900	1986
Zwin	51°21'N/003°22'E	530	1986

BOLIVIA/BOLIVIE

Laguna Colorada	22°11'S/067°47'W	5,240	1990

BRAZIL/BRESIL/BRASIL

Lagoa do Peixe	31°09'S/050°07'W	33,400	1993
Pantanal	15°30'S/057°00'W	135,000	1993

BULGARIA/BULGARIE

Arkoutino	42°18'N/027°45'E	97	1975
Lac Atanassovo	42°30'N/027°29'E	1,050	1984
Lac Durankulak	43°42'N/028°30'E	350	1984
Srébarna	44°08'N/027°06'E	600	1975

BURKINA FASO

La Mare aux Hippopotames	11°37'N/004°08'W	19,200	1990
La Mare d'Oursi	14°30'N/000°30'W	45,000	1990
Parc National du W	12°00'N/002°30'E	235,000	1990

CANADA

Alaksen	49°05'N/123°15'W	586	1982
Baie de l'Isle-Verte	48°01'N/069°20'W	2,028	1987
Beaverhill Lake	53°30'N/113°30'W	18,050	1987
Cap Tourmente	47°04'N/070°48'W	2,398	1981
Chignecto	45°48'N/064°16'W	1,020	1985
Delta Marsh	50°05'N/098°00'W	23,000	1982
Dewey Soper Migratory Bird Sanctuary	66°10'N/074°00'W	815,900	1982

Grand Codroy Estuary	47°50'N/059°18'W	925	1987
Hay-Zama Lakes	58°30'N/119°00'W	50,000	1982
Lac Saint-François	45°02'N/074°29'W	2,214	1987
Last Mountain Lake	51°20'N/105°15'W	15,602	1982
Long Point	42°35'N/080°15'W	13,730	1982
Malpeque Bay	46°32'N/063°48'W	24,440	1988
Mary's Point	45°44'N/064°45'W	1,200	1982
McConnell River	60°50'N/094°20'W	32,800	1982
Musquodoboit Harbour	44°42'N/063°06'W	1,925	1987
Oak Hammock Marsh	50°10'N/097°06'W	3,600	1987
Old Crow Flats	67°34'N/139°50'W	617,000	1982
Peace-Athabasca Delta	58°42'N/111°08'W	321,300	1982
Point Pelee	41°59'N/082°30'W	1,564	1987
Polar Bear Pass	75°43'N/098°40'W	262,400	1982
Polar Bear Provincial Park	52°30'N/084°30'W	2,408,700	1987
Queen Maud Gulf	67°00'N/100°30'W	6,278,200	1982
Quill Lakes	51°55'N/104°20'W	63,500	1987
Rasmussen Lowlands	68°40'N/093°00'W	300,000	1982
Shepody Bay	45°47'N/064°35'W	12,200	1987
Southern Bight-Minas Basin	45°13'N/064°16'W	26,800	1987
Southern James Bay (Moose River & Hannah Bay)	51°20'N/080°25'W	25,290	1987
St. Clair	42°22'N/082°22'W	244	1985
Tabusintac Lake and Estuary	47°20'N/064°56'W	4,087	1993
Whooping Crane Summer Range	60°15'N/113°15'W	1,689,500	1982

CHAD/TCHAD

Lac Fitri	12°50'N/017°30'E	195,000	1990

CHILE/CHILI

Carlos Anwandter Sanctuary	39°41'S/073°11'W	4,877	1981

CHINA/CHINE

Dongdongtinghu	29°20'N/112°55'E	190,000	1992
Dongzhaigang	20°00'N/110°35'E	5,400	1992
Niaodao	36°50'N/100°10'E	53,600	1992
Poyanghu	29°06'N/116°16'E	22,400	1992
Xianghai	44°52'N/122°30'E	105,470	1992
Zhalong	47°15'N/124°15'E	210,000	1992

COSTA RICA

Caño Negro	10°52'N/084°45'W	9,969	1991
Palo Verde	10°20'N/085°20'W	19,800	1991
Tamarindo	10°18'N/085°25'W	500	1993

CROATIA/CROATIE/CROACIA

Crna Mlaka	45°37'N/015°44'E	625	1993
Delta Neretve	42°57'N/017°34'E	11,500	1993
Kopacki Rit	45°35'N/018°51'E	17,770	1993
Lonjsko Polje & Mokro Polje (incl. Krapje Djol)	45°30'N/017°00'E	50,560	1993

CZECH REPUBLIC/REPUBLIQUE TCHEQUE/
REPUBLICA CHECA

Lednické rybníky (Lednice fishponds)	48°46'N/016°46'E	650	1990
Novozámecky a Brehynsky rybník (Novozámecky/Brehynsky ponds)	50°37'N/014°34'E	923	1990
Sumavská raselinisté (Sumava peatlands)	49°00'N/013°27'E	6,371	1990
Trebonské rybníky (Trebon fishponds)	49°03'N/014°43'E	10,165	1990

DENMARK/DANEMARK/DINAMARCA

Anholt Island (waters north of)	56°42'N/011°34'E	12,720	1977

Aqajarua-Sullorsuaq	69°40'N/052°00'W	30,000	1988
Eqalummiut Nunaat-Nassuttuup Nunaa	67°25'N/050°30'W	500,000	1988
Ertholmene Islands (east of Bornholm)	55°19'N/015°11'E	1,257	1977
Fejo and Femo Isles (waters south-east of)	54°54'N/011°30'E	32,640	1977
Fiil-So	55°42'N/008°15'E	4,320	1977
Heden (Jameson Land)	71°00'N/024°00'W	125,000	1988
Hirsholmene	57°29'N/010°38'E	480	1977
Hochstetter Forland	75°30'N/020°00'W	140,000	1988
Horsens Fjord & Endelave	55°51'N/010°10'E	43,200	1977
Ikkattoq	62°40'N/050°15'W	35,000	1988
Karrebæk, Dybso and Avno Fjords	55°10'N/011°45'E	19,200	1977
Kilen	81°15'N/012°00'W	30,000	1988
Kitsissunnguit	68°50'N/051°50'W	16,000	1988
Kitsissut Avalliit (Ouder Kitsissut)	60°45'N/048°30'W	8,000	1988
Kuannersuit Kuussuat	69°40'N/053°17'W	4,500	1988
Lillebælt	55°21'N/009°43'E	37,330	1977
Læso	57°12'N/011°10'E	67,840	1977
Maribo Lakes	54°46'N/011°31'E	4,400	1977
Nakskov Fjord and Inner Fjord	54°50'N/011°02'E	8,960	1977
Naternaq	68°20'N/052°00'W	150,000	1988
Nissum Bredning with Harboore & Agger Peninsulas	56°38'N/008°15'E	13,280	1977
Nissum Fjord	56°21'N/008°14'E	11,600	1977
Nordre Ronner	57°22'N/010°56'E	2,923	1977
Nærå Coast and Æbelo area	55°36'N/010°13'E	13,800	1977
Præsto Fjord, Jungshoved Nor, Ulvshale & Nyord	55°05'N/012°15'E	25,960	1977
Qínnguata Marraa-Kuussuaq	69°56'N/054°17'W	60,000	1988
Randers and Mariager Fjords and adjacent coastal waters	56°39'N/010°20'E	41,440	1977
Ringkobing Fjord	56°00'N/008°15'E	27,520	1977
Sejero Bugt, Nekeselo Bugt & Saltbæk Vig	55°47'N/011°18'E	42,560	1977
Skælskor Nor and Glæno (waters south of)	55°10'N/011°30'E	17,120	1977
South Funen Archipelago	55°00'N/010°20'E	39,200	1977
Stadil and Veststadil Fjords	56°11'N/008°09'E	7,184	1977
Stavns Fjord and adjacent waters	55°54'N/010°40'E	16,320	1977
Ulvedybet and Nibe Bredning	57°02'N/009°35'E	20,304	1977
Vadehavet (Wadden Sea)	55°16'N/008°32'E	140,830	1987
Vejlerne and Logstor Bredning	57°01'N/009°00'E	45,280	1977
Waters between Lolland & Falster (incl. Rodsand etc.)	54°38'N/011°45'E	36,800	1977

ECUADOR/EQUATEUR

Machalilla	01°00'S/080°45'W	55,095	1990
Manglares Churute	02°28'S/079°42'W	35,042	1990

EGYPT/EGYPTE/EGIPTO

Lake Bardawil	31°05'N/033°05'E	59,500	1988
Lake Burullus	31°30'N/030°50'E	46,200	1988

ESTONIA/ESTONIE

Matsalu Bay	58°48'N/023°22'E	48,634	1976

FINLAND/FINLANDE/FINLANDIA

Aspskär	60°16'N/026°25'E	369	1974
Björkör and Lågskär	59°56'N/020°10'E	5,760	1974
Koitilaiskaira	67°45'N/027°00'E	34,400	1974
Krunnit	65°23'N/024°47'E	4,600	1974
Martimoaapa - Lumiaapa	65°49'N/025°15'E	7,400	1974
Ruskis	60°22'N/025°40'E	235	1974
Signilskär	60°09'N/019°22'E	11,600	1974
Suomujärvi - Patvinsuo	63°05'N/030°35'E	9,400	1974
Söderskär and Långören	60°07'N/025°25'E	9,632	1974
Valassaaret and Björkögrunden	63°25'N/021°05'E	17,700	1974
Viikki	60°13'N/025°00'E	247	1974

FRANCE/FRANCIA

Camargue	43°30'N/004°30'E	85,000	1986
Etang de Biguglia	42°36'N/009°29'E	1,450	1991
Etangs de la Champagne humide	48°35'N/004°45'E	135,000	1991
Etangs de la Petite Woëvre	49°02'N/005°48'E	5,300	1991
Golfe du Morbihan	47°35'N/002°47'W	23,000	1991
La Brenne	46°44'N/001°15'E	140,000	1991
Marais du Cotentin et du Bessin, Baie des Veys	49°23'N/001°10'W	32,500	1991
Rives du Lac Léman	46°23'N/006°28'E	3,335	1991

GABON

Petit Loango	02°15'S/009°45'E	480,000	1986
Setté Cama	02°40'S/010°05'E	220,000	1986
Wongha-Wonghé	00°45'S/009°25'E	380,000	1986

GERMANY/ALLEMAGNE/ALEMANIA

Ammersee	48°01'N/011°08'E	6,517	1976
Bodensee: Wollmatinger Ried & Mindelsee	47°41'N/009°07'E	1,286	1976
Chiemsee	47°53'N/012°29'E	8,660	1976
Diepholzer Moorniederung	52°34'N/008°48'E	15,060	1976
Donauauen & Donaumoos	48°28'N/010°13'E	8,000	1976
Dümmersee	52°32'N/008°23'E	3,600	1976
Elbaue, Schnackenburg - Lauenburg	53°08'N/011°05'E	7,560	1976
Galenbecker See	53°38'N/013°44'E	1,015	1978
Hamburgisches Wattenmeer	53°53'N/008°17'E	11,700	1990
Ismaninger Speichersee & Fischteichen	48°13'N/011°41'E	955	1976
Krakower Obersee	53°37'N/012°18'E	870	1978
Lech - Donau - Winkel	48°44'N/011°00'E	239	1976
Lower Elbe, Barnkrug - Otterndorf	53°47'N/009°07'E	11,760	1976
Mühlenberger Loch	53°32'N/009°48'E	675	1992
Müritz See	53°27'N/012°49'E	4,830	1978
Odertal, Schwedt	53°04'N/014°20'E	5,400	1978
Ostfriesisches Wattenmeer & Dollart	53°42'N/007°21'E	121,620	1976
Peitz Teichgebiete	51°51'N/014°25'E	1,060	1978
Rhein, Eltville - Bingen	50°00'N/008°00'E	475	1976
Rieselfelder Münster	52°02'N/007°39'E	233	1983
Rügen/Hiddensee/Zingst	54°30'N/012°45'E	25,800	1978
Schleswig-Holsteinisches Wattenmeer	54°28'N/008°42'E	299,000	1991
Starnberger See	47°45'N/011°18'E	5,720	1976
Stausee Berga-Kelbra	51°26'N/011°00'E	2,790	1978
Steinhuder Meer	52°28'N/009°20'E	5,730	1976
Untere Havel/Gülper See/Schollener See	52°45'N/012°11'E	5,792	1978
Unterer Inn, Haiming - Neuhaus	48°20'N/013°09'E	1,955	1976
Unterer Niederrhein	51°43'N/006°14'E	25,000	1983
Wattenmeer, Elbe - Weser - Dreieck	53°50'N/008°24'E	38,460	1976
Wattenmeer, Jadebusen & westliche Wesermündung	53°40'N/008°19'E	49,490	1976
Weserstaustufe Schlüsselburg	52°27'N/008°59'E	1,600	1983

GHANA

Anlo-Keta lagoon complex	05°55'N/000°50'E	127,780	1992
Densu delta	05°33'N/000°18'W	4,620	1992
Muni Lagoon	05°22'N/000°40'W	8,670	1992
Owabi	06°44'N/001°41'W	7,260	1988
Sakumo lagoon	05°40'N/000°10'W	1,340	1992
Songor lagoon	05°45'N/000°30'E	28,740	1992

GREECE/GRECE/GRECIA

Amvrakikos Gulf	39°05'N/020°50'E	25,000	1975
Axios, Loudias and Aliakmon Delta	40°34'N/022°39'E	11,000	1975

Evros Delta	40°52'N/026°00'E	10,000	1975
Kerkini reservoir	41°12'N/023°09'E	9,000	1975
Kotychi Lagoon	38°01'N/021°18'E	3,700	1975
Lake Mikri Prespa	40°45'N/021°06'E	8,000	1975
Lake Mitrikou & adjoining lagoons	41°00'N/025°15'E	3,800	1975
Lake Vistonis and Porto Lagos Lagoons	41°00'N/025°00'E	10,000	1975
Lakes Volvi and Langada (Koronia)	40°25'N/023°40'E	2,400	1975
Messolonghi Lagoons	38°20'N/021°26'E	13,900	1975
Nestos Delta and Gumburnou Lagoon	40°57'N/024°44'E	10,600	1975

GUATEMALA

Laguna del Tigre	17°27'N/090°52'W	48,372	1990

GUINEA/GUINEE

Ile Alcatraz	10°38'N/015°23'W	1	1992
Ile Blanche	09°26'N/013°46'W	10	1993
Iles Tristao	10°55'N/015°00'W	85,000	1992
Konkouré	09°45'N/013°41'W	90,000	1992
Rio Kapatchez	10°25'N/014°33'W	20,000	1992
Rio Pongo	10°08'N/014°08'W	30,000	1992

GUINEA-BISSAU/GUINEE-BISSAU

Lagoa de Cufada	11°43'N/015°02'W	39,098	1990

HONDURAS

Barras de Cuero y Salado	15°45'N/087°02'W	8,500	1993

HUNGARY/HONGRIE/HUNGRIA

Bodrogzug	48°11'N/021°24'E	3,782	1989
Hortobagy	47°39'N/020°45'E	19,473	1979
Kardoskút	46°30'N/020°28'E	488	1979
Kisbalaton	46°40'N/017°15'E	14,745	1979
Kiskunság	46°49'N/019°12'E	3,903	1979
Lake Balaton	46°42'N/017°15'E	59,800	1989
Lake Fertö	47°40'N/016°47'E	2,870	1989
Mártély	46°25'N/020°13'E	2,232	1979
Ocsa	47°18'N/019°14'E	1,078	1989
Pusztaszer	46°36'N/020°05'E	5,000	1979
Szaporca	45°50'N/018°06'E	257	1979
Tata, Old Lake	47°39'N/018°18'E	269	1989
Velence - Dinnyés	47°10'N/018°32'E	965	1979

ICELAND/ISLANDE/ISLANDIA

Myvatn-Laxá region (part)	65°40'N/017°00'W	20,000	1977
Thjórsárver	64°35'N/019°15'W	37,500	1990

INDIA/INDE

Chilka Lake	19°42'N/085°21'E	116,500	1981
Harike Lake	31°13'N/075°12'E	4,100	1990
Keoladeo National Park	27°13'N/077°32'E	2,873	1981
Loktak Lake	24°26'N/093°49'E	26,600	1990
Sambhar Lake	27°00'N/075°00'E	24,000	1990
Wular Lake	34°16'N/074°33'E	18,900	1990

INDONESIA/INDONESIE

Berbak	01°24'S/104°16'E	162,700	1992

IRAN, ISLAMIC REPUBLIC OF/
IRAN, REPUBIQUE ISLAMIQUE D'/
IRAN, REPUBLICA ISLAMICA DEL

Alagol, Ulmagol and Ajigol Lakes	37°23'N/054°35'E	1,400	1975
Amirkelayeh Lake	37°17'N/050°12'E	1,230	1975
Anzali Mordab (Talab) complex	37°25'N/049°25'E	15,000	1975
Bandar Kiashahr Lagoon and mouth of Sefid Rud	37°25'N/049°29'E	500	1975
Deltas of Rud-e-Gaz and Rud-e-Hara	26°15'N/057°10'E	15,000	1975
Deltas of Rud-e-Shur, Rud-e-Shirin and Rud-e-Minab	27°00'N/056°45'E	20,000	1975
Gavkhouni Lake and marshes of the lower Zaindch Rud	32°15'N/052°45'E	43,000	1975
Hamoun-e-Puzak, south end	31°20'N/061°45'E	10,000	1975
Hamoun-e-Saberi & Hamoun-e-Helmand	31°20'N/061°20'E	50,000	1975
Khuran Straits	26°45'N/055°40'E	100,000	1975
Lake Gori	37°55'N/046°42'E	120	1975
Lake Kobi	36°57'N/045°52'E	1,200	1975
Lake Oroomiyeh	37°30'N/045°30'E	483,000	1975
Lake Parishan and Dasht-e-Arjan	29°30'N/052°00'E	6,600	1975
Miankaleh Peninsula, Gorgan Bay and Lapoo-Zaghmarz Ab-bandan	36°50'N/053°17'E	100,000	1975
Neiriz Lakes & Kamjan Marshes	29°40'N/053°30'E	108,000	1975
Shadegan Marshes & mudflats of Khor-al Amaya & Khor Musa	30°30'N/048°45'E	400,000	1975
Shurgol, Yadegarlu & Dorgeh Sangi Lakes	37°00'N/045°30'E	2,500	1975

IRELAND/IRLANDE/IRLANDA

Baldoyle Bay	53°24'N/006°08'W	203	1988
Castlemaine Harbour	52°07'N/009°55'W	923	1990
Clara Bog	53°19'N/007°37'W	460	1988
Coole Lough & Garryland Wood	53°05'N/008°51'W	364	1990
Easky Bog	54°11'N/008°49'W	607	1990
Knockmoyle/Sheskin	54°12'N/009°33'W	1,198	1987
Lough Barra Bog	54°57'N/008°07'W	176	1987
Meenachullion Bog	54°54'N/008°07'W	194	1990
Mongan Bog	53°19'N/007°58'W	127	1988
North Bull Island	53°22'N/006°08'W	1,436	1988
Owenboy	54°06'N/009°28'W	397	1987
Owenduff catchment	54°03'N/009°40'W	1,382	1986
Pettigo Plateau	54°37'N/007°57'W	900	1986
Pollardstown Fen	53°11'N/006°51'W	130	1990
Raheenmore Bog	53°20'N/007°21'W	162	1988
Rogerstown Estuary	53°30'N/006°08'W	195	1988
Slieve Bloom Mountains	53°03'N/007°38'W	2,230	1986
The Gearagh	51°52'N/009°01'W	307	1990
The Raven	52°20'N/006°19'W	589	1986
Tralee Bay	52°16'N/009°48'W	861	1989
Wexford Wildfowl Reserve	52°30'N/006°20'W	194	1984

ITALY/ITALIE/ITALIA

Bacino dell'Angitola	38°44'N/016°14'E	875	1989
Biviere di Gela	37°01'N/014°20'E	256	1988
Isola Boscone	45°03'N/011°14'E	201	1989
Lago dei Monaci	41°23'N/012°56'E	94	1976
Lago di Barrea	41°47'N/013°58'E	303	1976
Lago di Burano	42°24'N/011°23'E	410	1976
Lago di Caprolace	41°21'N/012°59'E	229	1976
Lago di Fogliano	41°24'N/012°54'E	395	1976
Lago di Nazzano	42°13'N/012°36'E	265	1976
Lago di Sabaudia	41°17'N/013°02'E	1,474	1976
Lago di Tovel	46°10'N/011°17'E	37	1980
Laguna di Marano: Foci dello Stella	45°45'N/013°08'E	1,400	1979

Laguna di Orbetello	42°27'N/011°13'E	887	1976
Laguna di Venezia: Valle Averto	45°21'N/012°09'E	200	1989
Le Cesine	40°20'N/018°23'E	620	1977
Ortazzo e Ortazzino	44°21'N/012°19'E	440	1981
Palude Brabbia	45°44'N/008°40'E	459	1984
Palude della Diaccia Botrona	42°46'N/010°55'E	2,500	1991
Palude di Bolgheri	43°14'N/010°33'E	562	1976
Palude di Colfiorito	43°01'N/012°53'E	157	1976
Palude di Ostiglia	45°04'N/011°06'E	123	1984
Piallassa della Baiona e Risega	44°30'N/012°15'E	1,630	1981
Pian di Spagna - Lago di Mezzola	46°13'N/009°26'E	1,740	1976
Punte Alberete	44°32'N/012°09'E	480	1976
Sacca di Belócchio	44°37'N/012°16'E	223	1976
Saline di Cervia	44°15'N/012°20'E	785	1981
Saline di Margherita di Savoia	41°24'N/016°05'E	3,871	1979
Stagno di Cagliari	39°13'N/009°03'E	3,466	1976
Stagno di Corru S'Ittiri, Stagni di San Giovanni e Marceddì	39°44'N/008°30'E	2,610	1979
Stagno di Cábras	39°57'N/008°29'E	3,575	1979
Stagno di Mistras	39°54'N/008°28'E	680	1982
Stagno di Molentargius	39°14'N/009°09'E	1,401	1976
Stagno di Pauli Maiori	39°52'N/008°37'E	287	1979
Stagno di S'Ena Arrubia	39°50'N/008°34'E	300	1976
Stagno di Sale Porcus	40°01'N/008°21'E	324	1982
Torbiere d'Iseo	45°30'N/010°02'E	324	1984
Torre Guaceto	40°43'N/017°48'E	940	1981
Valle Bertuzzi	44°47'N/012°14'E	3,100	1981
Valle Campotto e Bassarone	44°35'N/011°49'E	1,363	1979
Valle Cavanata	45°45'N/013°29'E	243	1978
Valle di Gorino	44°49'N/012°21'E	1,330	1981
Valle Santa	44°34'N/011°50'E	261	1976
Valli del Mincio	45°03'N/010°46'E	1,081	1984
Valli residue del comprensorio di Comacchio	44°30'N/012°07'E	13,500	1981
Vendicari	36°48'N/015°07'E	1,450	1989
Vincheto di Cellarda	46°01'N/011°58'E	99	1976

JAPAN/JAPON

Akkeshi-ko and Bekambeushi-shitsugen	43°03'N/144°54'E	4,896	1993
Biwa-ko	35°15'N/136°05'E	65,602	1993
Izu-numa and Uchi-numa	38°43'N/141°06'E	559	1985
Katano-kamoike	36°19'N/136°17'E	10	1993
Kiritappu-shitsugen	43°05'N/145°05'E	2,504	1993
Kushiro-shitsugen	43°09'N/144°26'E	7,726	1980
Kutcharo-ko	45°09'N/142°20'E	1,607	1989
Utonai-ko	42°42'N/141°43'E	510	1991
Yatsu-higata	35°41'N/140°00'E	40	1993

JORDAN/JORDANIE/JORDANIA

Azraq Oasis	31°49'N/036°48'E	7,372	1977

KAZAKHSTAN/KAZAJSTAN

Kourgaldzhin and Tengiz Lakes	50°27'N/069°10'E	260,500	1976
Lakes of the lower Turgay and Irgiz	48°42'N/062°11'E	348,000	1976

KENYA/KENIA

Lake Nakuru	00°24'S/036°05'E	18,800	1990

KYRGYZSTAN/KIRGHIZISTAN/KIRGUISTAN

Issyk-kul Lake	42°27'N/077°16'E	629,800	1976

LIECHTENSTEIN

Ruggeller Riet	47°15'N/009°33'E	101	1991

LITHUANIA/LITUANIE/LITUANIA
(No natural sites inscribed)

MALI

Lac Horo	16°13'N/003°55'W	18,900	1987
Séri	14°50'N/004°40'W	40,000	1987
Walado Debo/Lac Debo	15°15'N/004°15'W	103,100	1987

MALTA/MALTE

Ghadira	35°58'N/014°21'E	11	1988

MAURITANIA/MAURITANIE

Banc d'Arguin	20°50'N/016°45'W	1,173,000	1982

MEXICO/MEXIQUE

Ría Lagartos	21°30'N/088°00'W	47,840	1986

MOROCCO/MAROC/MARRUECOS

Baie de Khnifiss	28°00'N/012°25'W	6,500	1980
Lac d'Afennourir	33°20'N/005°10'W	380	1980
Merja Sidi Boughaba	34°15'N/006°40'W	200	1980
Merja Zerga	34°50'N/006°20'W	3,500	1980

NEPAL

Koshi Tappu	26°37'N/087°00'E	17,500	1987

NETHERLANDS/PAYS-BAS/PAISES BAJOS

Alde Feanen	53°02'N/005°55'E	2,500	1993
Bargerveen	52°41'N/007°02'E	2,100	1993
Boschplaat	53°27'N/005°30'E	4,400	1980
De Biesbosch (southern part)	51°45'N/004°48'E	1,700	1980
De Deelen	53°07'N/005°55'E	520	1993
De Slagbaai	12°16'N/068°25'W	90	1980
Deurnese Peelgebieden	51°25'N/005°51'E	1,450	1993
Engbertsdijksvenen	52°29'N/006°40'E	975	1989
Griend	53°15'N/005°15'E	23	1980
Groote Peel	51°20'N/005°25'E	900	1980
Het Gotomeer	12°14'N/068°22'W	150	1980
Het Lac	12°06'N/068°14'W	700	1980
Het Pekelmeer	12°02'N/068°19'W	400	1980
Het Spaans Lagoen	12°30'N/070°00'W	70	1980
Klein Bonaire Island and adjacent sea	12°10'N/068°19'W	600	1980
Naardermeer	52°17'N/005°07'E	752	1980
Oosterschelde & Markiezaatmeer	51°30'N/004°10'E	38,000	1987
Oostvaardersplassen	52°27'N/005°20'E	5,600	1989
Waddenzee (Wadden Sea)	53°15'N/005°15'E	249,998	1984
Weerribben	52°46'N/005°59'E	3,400	1980
Zwanenwater	52°49'N/004°42'E	600	1988

NEW ZEALAND/NOUVELLE-ZELANDE/ NUEVA ZELANDIA

Farewell Spit	40°32'S/172°50'E	11,388	1976
Firth of Thames	37°13'S/175°23'E	7,800	1990
Kopuatai Peat Dome	37°26'S/175°33'E	9,665	1989
Waituna Lagoon	46°34'S/168°36'E	3,556	1976
Whangamarino	37°18'S/175°07'E	5,690	1989

NIGER

Parc national du "W"	12°15'N/002°25'E	220,000	1987

NORWAY/NORVEGE/NORUEGA

Dunoyane	77°04'N/015°00'E	120	1985
Forlandsoyane	78°20'N/011°36'E	60	1985
Gåsoyane	78°20'N/011°36'E	100	1985
Ilene and Presterodkilen	59°15'N/010°20'E	177	1985
Isoyane	77°08'N/014°48'E	30	1985
Jaeren	58°50'N/005°34'E	400	1985
Kongsfjorden	78°55'N/012°10'E	140	1985
Kurefjorden	59°30'N/011°00'E	400	1985
Nordre Oyeren	59°53'N/011°09'E	6,260	1985
Ora	59°10'N/011°00'E	1,560	1985
Orlandet	63°42'N/009°35'E	2,920	1985
Stabbursneset	70°10'N/024°40'E	1,620	1985
Tautra & Svaet	63°35'N/010°37'E	2,054	1985
Åkersvika	60°50'N/011°08'E	415	1974

PAKISTAN

Drigh Lake	27°34'N/068°06'E	164	1976
Haleji Lake	24°47'N/067°46'E	1,704	1976
Kandar Dam	33°36'N/071°29'E	251	1976
Khabbaki Lake	32°37'N/072°00'E	283	1976
Kheshki Reservoir	34°02'N/072°01'E	263	1976
Kinjhar (Kalri) Lake	24°56'N/068°03'E	13,468	1976
Malugul Dhand	33°00'N/070°36'E	405	1976
Tanda Dam	33°35'N/071°22'E	405	1976
Thanedar Wala	32°37'N/071°05'E	4,047	1976

PANAMA

Golfo de Montijo	07°40'N/081°30'W	80,765	1990
San San - Pond Sak	09°24'N/082°57'W	16,414	1993

PAPUA NEW GUINEA/PAPOUASIE-NOUVELLE-GUINEE/PAPUA NUEVA GUINEA

Tonda Wildlife Management Area	08°45'S/141°23'E	590,000	1993

PERU/PEROU/PERU

Lagunas de Mejía	17°19'S/071°51'W	691	1992
Pacaya Samiria	05°15'S/074°40'W	2,080,000	1992
Paracas	13°55'S/076°15'W	335,000	1992

POLAND/POLOGNE/POLONIA

Jezioro Karas	53°33'N/019°29'E	815	1984
Jezioro Luknajno	53°49'N/021°38'E	710	1977
Jezioro Siedmiu Wysp	54°20'N/021°36'E	999	1984
Jezioro Swidwie	53°34'N/014°22'E	382	1984
Slonsk Reserve	52°33'N/014°43'E	4,235	1984

PORTUGAL

Estuário do Tejo	38°50'N/008°57'W	14,563	1980
Ria Formosa	37°03'N/007°47'W	16,000	1980

ROMANIA/ROUMANIE/RUMANIA

Danube Delta	45°10'N/029°15'E	647,000	1991

RUSSIAN FEDERATION/FEDERATION DE RUSSIE/FEDERACION DE RUSIA

Kandalaksha Bay	66°57'N/033°18'E	208,000	1976
Lake Khanka	44°53'N/132°26'E	310,000	1976
Volga Delta	45°54'N/048°47'E	650,000	1976

SENEGAL

Bassin du Ndiael	16°10'N/016°05'W	10,000	1977
Delta du Saloum	13°37'N/016°42'W	73,000	1984
Djoudj	16°20'N/016°12'W	16,000	1977
Gueumbeul	15°57'N/016°28'W	720	1986

SLOVAKIA/SLOVAQUIE/ESLOVAQUIA

Cicovské mrtve rameno (Cicov oxbow)	47°45'N/017°44'E	135	1990
Dunajské luhy (Danube flood plains)	47°56'N/017°35'E	14,335	1993
Latorica	48°28'N/022°00'E	4,358	1993
Moravské luhy (Morava flood plains)	48°41'N/016°55'E	4,971	1993
Parízské mociare (Pariz marshes)	47°51'N/018°31'E	141	1990
Senné-rybníky (Senné fishponds)	48°11'N/022°04'E	442	1990
Súr	48°15'N/017°13'E	1,137	1990

SLOVENIA/SLOVENIE/ESLOVENIA

Secoveljske soline (Secovlje salt pans)	45°29'N/013°36'E	650	1993

SOUTH AFRICA/AFRIQUE DU SUD/SUDAFRICA

Barberspan	26°33'S/025°37'E	3,118	1975
Blesbokspruit	26°17'S/028°30'E	1,858	1986
De Hoop Vlei	34°27'S/020°20'E	750	1975
De Mond (Heuningnes Estuary)	34°43'S/020°07'E	1,318	1986
Kosi Bay	27°01'S/032°48'E	8,000	1991
Lake Sibaya	27°20'S/032°38'E	7,750	1991
Langebaan	33°06'S/018°01'E	6,000	1988
Orange River Mouth	28°40'S/016°30'E	2,000	1991
St. Lucia System	28°00'S/032°28'E	155,500	1986
Turtle Beaches/Coral Reefs of Tongaland	27°30'S/032°40'E	39,500	1986
Verlorenvlei	32°24'S/018°26'E	1,700	1991
Wilderness Lakes	33°59'S/022°39'E	850	1991

SPAIN/ESPAGNE/ESPAÑA

Aiguamolls de l'Emporda	42°14'N/003°06'E	4,784	1993
Albufera de Valencia	39°20'N/000°21'W	21,000	1989
Complejo de Corrubedo	42°33'N/009°02'W	550	1993
Complejo intermareal Umia-Grove	42°28'N/008°50'W	2,561	1989
Delta del'Ebro	40°43'N/000°44'E	7,736	1993
Doñana	36°57'N/006°19'W	50,720	1982
Embalse de Orellana	38°59'N/005°32'W	5,500	1993
Laguna de Fuente de Piedra	37°07'N/004°46'W	1,364	1983
Laguna de la Vega (o del Pueblo)	39°25'N/002°56'W	34	1989
Laguna de Manjavacas	39°25'N/002°50'W	231	1993
Laguna de Villafáfila	41°49'N/005°37'W	2,854	1989
Laguna del Prado	38°55'N/003°49'W	52	1993
Laguna y arenal de Valdoviño	43°36'N/004°28'W	255	1993
Lagunas de Alcazar de San Juan	39°24'N/003°15'W	160	1993
Lagunas de Cádiz (Laguna de Medina y Laguna Salada)	36°37'N/006°03'W	158	1989
Lagunas de la Mata y Torrevieja	38°00'N/000°42'W	3,700	1989
Lagunas del sur de Córdoba (Zóñar, Rincón y Amarga)	37°29'N/004°41'W	86	1989
Las Tablas de Daimiel	39°09'N/003°40'W	1,928	1982
Marismas del Odiel	37°17'N/006°55'W	7,185	1989
Pantano de El Hondo	38°10'N/000°42'W	2,387	1989
Prat de Cabanes - Torreblanca	40°14'N/000°12'E	812	1989
Ria de Mundaka-Guernika	43°22'N/002°40'W	945	1993
Rias de Ortigueira y Ladrido	43°42'N/007°47'W	2,920	1989
S'Albufera de Mallorca	39°49'N/003°07'E	1,700	1989
Salinas de Santa Pola	38°08'N/000°37'W	2,496	1989
Salinas del Cabo de Gata	36°44'N/002°12'W	300	1989

SRI LANKA

Bundala	06°10'N/081°12'E	6,216	1990

SURINAME

Coppenamemonding	05°56'N/055°43'W	12,000	1985

SWEDEN/SUEDE/SUECIA

Dättern	58°23'N/012°37'E	3,920	1989
Falsterbo - Foteviken	55°25'N/012°55'E	7,530	1974
Gammelstadsviken	65°38'N/022°00'E	430	1974
Getterön	57°08'N/012°14'E	340	1974
Gotland, east coast	57°07'N/018°28'E	4,220	1974
Helgeån	56°00'N/014°13'E	5,480	1974
Hjälstaviken	59°40'N/017°23'E	770	1974
Hornborgasjön	58°19'N/013°33'E	6,370	1974
Hovran area	60°20'N/016°03'E	4,750	1989
Kilsviken	59°03'N/014°04'E	8,910	1989
Klingavälsån - Krankesjön	55°37'N/013°38'E	3,970	1974
Kvismaren	59°10'N/015°23'E	780	1974
Laidaure	67°07'N/017°45'E	4,150	1974
Ottenby	56°12'N/016°24'E	1,610	1974
Persöfjärden	65°46'N/022°08'E	3,320	1974
Sjaunja	67°17'N/019°49'E	188,600	1974
Stigfjorden	58°07'N/011°40'E	5,180	1989
Stockholm, outer archipelago	59°26'N/019°22'E	15,000	1989
Store Mosse and Kävsjön	57°18'N/013°57'E	7,580	1974
Svartån	59°57'N/016°20'E	1,990	1989
Tavvavuoma	68°30'N/020°45'E	28,700	1974
Tjålmejaure - Laisdalen	66°15'N/016°11'E	21,400	1974
Träslövsläge - Morups Tånge	56°59'N/012°20'E	1,990	1989
Tärnasjön	66°00'N/015°29'E	11,800	1974
Tåkern	58°21'N/014°49'E	5,650	1974
Umeälv delta	63°45'N/020°20'E	1,040	1989
Ånnsjön	63°16'N/012°33'E	11,000	1974
Åsnen	56°37'N/014°43'E	16,800	1989
Öland, eastern coastal areas	56°27'N/016°36'E	8,460	1974
Östen	58°35'N/013°57'E	1,010	1989

SWITZERLAND/SUISSE/SUIZA

Baie de Fanel et le Chablais	46°59'N/007°03'E	1,155	1976
Bolle di Magadino	46°09'N/008°52'E	661	1982
Kaltbrunner Riet	47°12'N/008°59'E	150	1990
Lac artificiel de Klingnau	47°35'N/008°14'E	355	1990
Lac artificiel de Niederried	46°59'N/007°15'E	303	1990
Les Grangettes	46°23'N/006°54'E	330	1990
Rade de Genève et Rhône en aval de Genève	46°11'N/006°05'E	1,032	1990
Rive sud du lac de Neuchâtel	46°00'N/006°50'E	3,063	1990

TRINIDAD AND TOBAGO/TRINITE-ET-TOBAGO/ TRINIDAD Y TABAGO

Nariva Swamp	10°23'N/061°04'W	6,234	1992

TUNISIA/TUNISIE/TUNEZ

Ichkeul	37°10'N/009°40'E	12,600	1980

TURKMENISTAN

Krasnovodsk and North-Cheleken Bays	39°49'N/053°10'E	188,700	1976

UGANDA/OUGANDA
Lake George   00°07'N/030°02'E   15,000   1988

UKRAINE/UCRANIA
Dounai and Yagorlits & Tendrov Bays   45°25'N/029°40'E   128,051   1976
Karkinitski Bay   45°51'N/033°33'E   37,300   1976
Sivash Bay   46°09'N/034°21'E   45,700   1976

UNITED KINGDOM/ROYAUME-UNI/REINO UNIDO
Abberton Reservoir   51°49'N/000°52'E   716   1981
Alt Estuary   53°30'N/003°10'W   1,160   1985
Bridgend Flats   55°45'N/006°15'W   331   1988
Bridgwater Bay   51°13'N/003°04'W   2,703   1976
Bure Marshes   52°41'N/001°29'E   412   1976
Burry Inlet   51°39'N/004°10'W   6,654   1992
Cairngorm Lochs   57°04'N/003°47'W   179   1981
Chesil Beach and The Fleet   50°36'N/002°32'W   763   1985
Chichester and Langstone Harbours   50°50'N/001°00'W   5,749   1987
Chippenham Fen   52°18'N/000°25'E   115   1992
Claish Moss   56°45'N/005°44'W   563   1981
Cors Caron   52°15'N/003°55'W   872   1992
Cors Fochno and Dyfi   52°31'N/004°00'W   2,497   1976
Crymlyn Bog   51°38'N/003°53'W   267   1993
Dee Estuary   53°17'N/003°05'W   13,055   1985
Din Moss - Hoselaw Loch   55°35'N/002°18'W   46   1988
Eilean Na Muice Duibhe (Duich Moss)   55°42'N/006°15'W   574   1988
Esthwaite Water   54°21'N/002°59'W   134   1991
Exe Estuary   50°37'N/003°25'W   2,389   1992
Fala Flow   55°49'N/002°54'W   323   1990
Feur Lochain   55°50'N/006°21'W   384   1990
Glac-na-Criche   55°51'N/006°27'W   265   1990
Gladhouse Reservoir   55°44'N/003°07'W   186   1988
Gruinart Flats   55°50'N/006°20'W   3,170   1988
Hamford Water   51°53'N/001°14'E   2,179   1993
Hickling Broad and Horsey Mere   52°45'N/001°39'E   892   1976
Holburn Lake and Moss   55°37'N/001°57'W   22   1985
Irtinghead Mires   55°04'N/002°22'W   608   1985
Leighton Moss   54°10'N/002°47'W   125   1985
Lindisfarne   55°41'N/001°48'W   3,625   1976
Llyn Idwal   53°06'N/004°01'W   14   1991
Llyn Tegid   52°53'N/003°38'W   484   1991
Loch Eye   57°48'N/003°56'W   195   1986
Loch Ken & River Dee Marshes   55°04'N/004°07'W   773   1992
Loch Leven   56°13'N/003°23'W   1,597   1976
Loch Lomond   56°04'N/004°35'W   253   1976
Loch of Lintrathen   56°41'N/003°11'W   218   1981
Loch of Skene   57°09'N/002°20'W   125   1986
Loch Spynie   57°41'N/003°17'W   93   1992
Loch-an-Duin   57°10'N/007°24'W   3,606   1990
Lochs Druidibeg, a'Machair and Stilligarry   57°21'N/007°24'W   1,780   1976
Lough Neagh and Lough Beg   54°40'N/006°25'W   39,500   1976
Lower Derwent Valley (including Derwent Ings)   53°50'N/000°54'W   1,089   1985
Martin Mere   53°35'N/002°49'W   119   1985
Minsmere - Walberswick   52°17'N/001°37'E   2,004   1976
Nene Washes   52°35'N/000°03'W   1,310   1993
North Norfolk Coast   52°58'N/000°53'E   7,700   1976
North, Middle & East Caicos Islands   21°45'N/071°45'W   54,400   1990
Old Hall Marshes   51°44'N/000°53'E   627   1992
Ouse Washes   52°30'N/000°13'E   2,403   1976

Pagham Harbour	50°46'N/000°46'W	616	1988
Rannoch Moor	56°39'N/004°40'W	1,499	1976
Redgrave and South Lopham Fens	52°23'N/001°00'E	125	1991
Rostherne Mere	53°21'N/002°23'W	79	1981
Roydon Common	52°46'N/000°30'E	194	1993
Rutland Water	52°39'N/000°39'W	1,339	1991
Silver Flowe	55°07'N/004°23'W	608	1981
South Tayside Goose Roosts	56°21'N/003°51'W	409	1993
The Swale	51°21'N/000°51'E	5,790	1985
The Wash (including Gibraltar Point)	52°55'N/000°20'E	63,538	1988
Upper Severn Estuary	51°46'N/002°23'W	1,437	1988
Upper Solway Flats & Marshes (including Rockcliffe Marsh)	54°52'N/003°30'W	29,950	1986
Walmore Common	51°50'N/002°23'W	51	1991

UNITED STATES/ETATS-UNIS D'AMERIQUE/ ESTADOS UNIDOS DE AMERICA

Ash Meadows	36°25'N/116°20'W	9,509	1986
Cache-Lower White Rivers	34°40'N/091°11'W	145,690	1989
Catahoula Lake	31°30'N/092°06'W	12,150	1991
Chesapeake Bay	38°00'N/076°20'W	45,000	1987
Cheyenne Bottoms	38°29'N/098°40'W	8,036	1988
Delaware Bay	39°11'N/075°14'W	51,252	1992
Edwin B Forsythe NWR	39°36'N/074°17'W	13,080	1986
Everglades	25°00'N/080°55'W	566,143	1987
Horicon Marsh	43°30'N/088°38'W	12,911	1990
Izembek	55°45'N/162°41'W	168,433	1986
Okefenokee	30°49'N/082°20'W	159,889	1986
Pelican Island	27°48'N/080°25'W	1,908	1993

URUGUAY

Bañados del Este y Franja Costera	33°40'S/05°320'W	435,000	1984

VENEZUELA

Cuare	10°55'N/068°20'W	9,968	1988

VIET NAM

Red River Estuary	20°10'N/106°20'E	12,000	1988

YUGOSLAVIA/YOUGOSLAVIE

Ludasko Lake	46°04'N/019°48'E	593	1977
Obedska Bara	44°47'N/017°40'E	17,501	1977

ZAMBIA/ZAMBIE

Bangweulu Swamps: Chikuni	12°00'S/030°15'E	250,000	1991
Kafue Flats: Lochinvar & Blue Lagoon	16°00'S/027°15'E	83,000	1991

Annex

Annexe

Anexo

Annex. 1994 Protected areas management categories[1]

CATEGORY I   **Strict Nature Reserve / Wilderness Area: protected area[2] managed mainly for science or wilderness protection**

CATEGORY Ia   **Strict Nature Reserve: protected area managed mainly for science**

Definition   Area of land and/or sea possessing some outstanding or representative ecosystems, geological or physiological features and/or species, available primarily for scientific research and/or environmental monitoring.

CATEGORY Ib   **Wilderness Area: protected area managed mainly for wilderness protection**

Definition   Large area of unmodified or slightly modified land, and/or sea, retaining its natural character and influence, without permanent or significant habitation, which is protected and managed so as to preserve its natural condition.

CATEGORY II   **National Park: protected area managed mainly for ecosystem protection and recreation**

Definition   Natural area of land and/or sea, designated to (a) protect the ecological integrity of one or more ecosystems for present and future generations, (b) exclude exploitation or occupation inimical to the purposes of designation of the area and (c) provide a foundation for spiritual, scientific, educational, recreational and visitor opportunities, all of which must be environmentally and culturally compatible.

CATEGORY III   **Natural Monument: protected area managed mainly for conservation of specific natural features**

Definition   Area containing one, or more, specific natural or natural/cultural feature which is of outstanding or unique value because of its inherent rarity, representative or aesthetic qualities or cultural significance.

CATEGORY IV   **Habitat/Species Management Area: protected area managed mainly for conservation through management intervention**

Definition   Area of land and/or sea subject to active intervention for management purposes so as to ensure the maintenance of habitats and/or to meet the requirements of specific species.

CATEGORY V   **Protected Landscape/Seascape: protected area managed mainly for landscape/ seascape conservation and recreation**

Definition   Area of land, with coast and sea as appropriate, where the interaction of people and nature over time has produced an area of distinct character with significant aesthetic, ecological and/or cultural value, and often with high biological diversity. Safeguarding the integrity of this traditional interaction is vital to the protection, maintenance and evolution of such an area.

CATEGORY VI   **Managed Resource Protected Area: protected area managed mainly for the sustainable use of natural ecosystems**

Definition   Area containing predominantly unmodified natural systems, managed to ensure long term protection and maintenance of biological diversity, while providing at the same time a sustainable flow of natural products and services to meet community needs.

---

[1] For further information on the new management categories, readers should consult the *Guidelines for Protected Area Management Categories* (IUCN, 1994).

[2] A protected area is defined in the new *Guidelines for Protected Area Management Categories* as: *An area of land and/or sea especially dedicated to the protection and maintenance of biological diversity, and of natural and associated cultural resources, and managed through legal or other effective means.*

Annexe. Catégories de gestion des aires protégées (1994)[1]

CATEGORIE I   **Réserve naturelle intégrale /zone de nature sauvage: aire protégée[2] gérée principalement à des fins scientifiques ou de protection des ressources sauvages**

CATEGORIE Ia   **Réserve naturelle intégrale: aire protégée gérée principalement à des fins scientifiques**

Définition   Espace terrestre et/ou marin comportant des écosystèmes, des caractéristiques géologiques ou physiologiques et/ou des espèces remarquables ou représentatives, géré principalement à des fins de recherche scientifique et/ou de surveillance continue de l'environnement.

CATEGORIE 1b   **Zone de nature sauvage: aire protégée gérée principalement à des fins de protection des ressources sauvages**

Définition   Vaste espace terrestre et/ou marin, intact ou peu modifié, ayant conservé son caractère et son influence naturels, dépourvu d'établissements permanents ou importants, protégé et géré aux fins de préserver son état naturel.

CATEGORIE II   **Parc national: aire protégée gérée principalement dans le but de protéger les écosystèmes et à des fins récréatives**

Définition   Zone naturelle, terrestre et/ou marine, désignée (a) pour protéger l'intégrité écologique dans un ou plusieurs écosystèmes dans l'intérêt des générations actuelles et futures, (b) pour exclure toute exploitation ou occupation incompatible avec les objectifs de la désignation et (c) à des fins spirituelles, scientifiques, éducatives, récréatives et touristiques, dans le respect du milieu naturel et de la culture des communautés locales.

CATEGORIE III   **Monument naturel: aire protégée gérée principalement dans le but de préserver des éléments naturels spécifiques**

Définition   Aire contenant un ou plusieurs éléments naturels ou naturels/culturels particuliers, d'importance exceptionnelle ou unique, méritant d'être protégée du fait de sa rareté, de sa représentativité, de ses qualités esthétiques ou de son importance culturelle intrinsèque.

CATEGORIE IV   **Aire de gestion des habitats ou des espèces: aire protégée gérée principalement à des fins de conservation, avec intervention au niveau de la gestion**

Définition   Aire terrestre et/ou marine faisant l'objet d'une intervention active au niveau de la gestion, de façon à garantir le maintien des habitats et/ou à satisfaire aux exigences d'espèces particulières.

CATEGORIE V   **Paysage terrestre ou marin protégé: aire protégée gérée principalement dans le but d'assurer la conservation de paysages terrestres ou marins et à des fins récréatives**

Définition   Zone terrestre, comprenant parfois le littoral et les eaux adjacentes, où l'interaction entre l'homme et la nature a, au fil du temps, modelé le paysage aux qualités esthétiques, écologiques et/ou culturelles particulières et exceptionelles, et présentant souvent une grande diversité biologique. Préserver l'intégrité de cette interaction traditionelle est essentiel à la protection, au maintien et à l'évolution d'une telle aire.

CATEGORIE VI   **Aire protégée de ressources naturelles gérée: aire protégée gérée principalement à des fins d'utilisation durable des écosystèmes naturels**

Définition   Aire contenant des systèmes naturels, en grande partie non modifiés, gérée aux fins d'assurer la protection et le maintien à long terme de la diversité biologique, tout en garantissant la durabilité des fonctions et produits naturels nécessaires au bien-être de la communauté.

---

[1] Pour tout renseignement complémentaire concernant les nouvelles catégories de gestion, le lecteur consultera les *Lignes directrices pour les catégories de gestion des aires protégées* (UICN, 1994).

[2] Les nouvelles *Lignes directrices pour les catégories de gestion des aires protégées* définissent une aire protégée comme étant: *Une portion de terre et/ou de mer vouée spécialement à la protection et au maintien de la diversité biologique, ainsi que des ressources naturelles et culturelles associées, et gérée par des moyens efficaces, juridiques ou autres.*

Anexo. Categorías de manejo de áreas protegidas[1] de 1994

CATEGORIA I   **Reserva Natural Estricta /Area Natural Silvestre: área protegida[2] manejada principalmente con fines científicos o con fines de protección de la naturaleza.**

CATEGORIA Ia   **Reserva Natural Estricta: área protegida manejada principalmente con fines científicos.**

Definición   Area terrestre y/o marina que posee ecosistemas, rasgos geológicos o fisiológicos y/o especies, destacados o representativos, destinada principalmente a actividades de investigación científica y/o monitoreo ambiental.

CATEGORIA Ib   **Area Natural Silvestre: área protegida manejada principalmente con fines de protección de la naturaleza**

Definición   Vasta superficie de tierra y/o mar no alterada o ligeramente alterada, que conserva su carácter e influencia natural, que no esté habitada de forma permanente o significativa, y la cual se protege y maneja para preservar su condición natural.

CATEGORIA II   **Parque Nacional: área protegida manejada principalmente para la conservación de ecosistemas y con fines de recreación**

Definición   Area terrestre y/o marina natural designada para a) proteger la integridad ecológica de uno o más ecosistemas para las generaciones actuales y futuras, b) excluir los tipos de explotación u ocupación que sean contrarios a los propósitos por los cuales fue designada el área, y c) proporcionar un marco para actividades espirituales, científicas, educativas, recreativas y turísticas, las cuales deben ser compatibles desde el punto de vista ecológico y cultural.

CATEGORIA III   **Monumento Natural: área protegida manejada principalmente para la conservación de características naturales específicas**

Definición   Area que contiene una o más características naturales o naturales/culturales específicas de valor destacado o excepcional por su rareza implícita, sus calidades representativas o estéticas o por su importancia cultural.

CATEGORIA IV   **Area de Manejo de Hábitat/Especies: área protegida manejada principalmente para la conservación, con intervención a nivel de gestión**

Definición   Area terrestre y/o marina sujeta a intervención activa con fines de manejo, para garantizar el mantenimiento de los hábitat y/o satisfacer las necesidades de determinadas especies.

CATEGORIA V   **Paisaje Terrestre/Marino Protegido: área protegida manejada principalmente para la conservación de paisajes terrestres y marinos, con fines recreativos**

Definición   Superficie de tierra, con costas y mares según sea el caso, en la cual las interacciones del ser humano con la naturaleza a lo largo de los años ha producido una zona de carácter propio con importantes valores estéticos, ecológicos y/o culturales, y que a menudo alberga una rica diversidad biológica. Salvaguardar la integridad de esta interacción tradicional es esencial para la protección, el mantenimiento y la evolución del área.

CATEGORIA VI   **Area Protegida con Recursos Manejados: área protegida manejada principalmente para la utilización sustentable de los ecosistemas naturales**

Definición   Area que contiene predominantemente sistemas naturales no modificados, que es objeto de actividades de manejo para garantizar la protección y el mantenimiento de la diversidad biológica a largo plazo, a la vez que proporciona un flujo sostenible de productos naturales y servicios para satisfacer las necesidades de las comunidades.

---

[1] Para mayor información de las nuevas categorías de manejo, los lectores deben consultar *las Directrices para las Categorías de Manejo de Areas Protegidas* (UICN, 1994)

[2] La definición de área protegida en *las Directrices para las Categorías de Manejo de Areas Protegidas* es: una superficie de tierra y/o mar especialmente consagrada a la protección y al mantenimiento de la diversidad biológica, así como a la protección de los recursos naturales y de los recursos culturales asociados, y que sea manejada a través de medios jurídicos u otros medios eficaces.